JAINISM

A Concise Encyclopaedia

JAINISM

A Concise Encyclopaedia

N.N. BHATTACHARYYA

MANOHAR
2009

First published 2009

ISBN 81-7304-312-4

Published by
Ajay Kumar Jain for
Manohar Publishers & Distributors
4753/23 Ansari Road, Daryaganj
New Delhi 110002

Typeset by
A J Software Publishing Co. Pvt. Ltd.
New Delhi 110005

Printed at
Salasar Imaging Systems
Delhi 110035

For
Phattelalji

Contents

Preface

The publication of a multi-volume encyclopaedia of Jainism with contributions from eminent scholars and edited by a board of experts is long overdue. The present work is by no means a substitute for such a comprehensive encyclopaedia, but it may be regarded as a curtain-raiser. The entries in this volume cover a wide range of topics and could be elaborated in a bigger project. At the same time it should also be noted that since Jainism is taught in different universities and there are people who want to know more about this system, a venture such as this *Concise Encyclopaedia* will serve its own academic purpose as the entries are complete in themselves, and in required cases are authenticated by references from the original sources. A separate glossary of technical terms appears at the end of the volume and two bibliographies are supplied, one for the original sources and the other for secondary works.

My Sincere thanks to Sri Kamala Kanta Das, my research assistant, whose earnest cooperation and indefatigable labour have been responsible for the timely completion of this project. I am also grateful to Sri Ramesh Jain and Sri Ajay Jain for the interest they have taken in publishing this work.

Joraghat, Chinsurah
West Bengal

N.N. BHATTACHARYYA

From the Publisher

I first met Narendra Nath Bhattacharyya as a young fledgling publisher in 1974 in the Kolkata office of Firma KLM who were Narendra da's Bengali Publishers. It was that chance meeting which led me to publish *Ancient Indian Rituals and their Social Contents* and was the start of an extremely affectionate friendship which enriched my life in many ways. A man of prodigious intellect and output yet humble to the core.

Narendra da in his immaculately crisp white Dhoti-Kurta was to me the epitome of the old school scholar to whom their work was everything.Nothing else mattered.

Just before his death in 2001 Narendra da gave me the completed manuscript of the present volume, a long cherished project of ours. At every stage of production of this volume I have sorely missed his counsel and guidance and his uncanny ability to spot an error. Even though this volume has been bereft of the close attention that Narendra da brought to his volumes while seeing them through to the press, it gives me great joy to finally bring it out in print and thus redeem my promise to him.

RAMESH JAIN
Publisher

Introduction

In Edward Moor's *The Hindu Pantheon* (1810) the Jains were described as a sect of Buddhists or as Vaiṣṇavas, and an imperfect account of their tenets, temples, icons, armorial and forehead marks were provided. Western scholars long failed to recognize the distinction between Jainism and Buddhism. Colebrooke, Prinsep and J. Stevenson regarded Mahāvīra as the teacher of the Buddha while Wilson and Weber held Jainism to be an offshoot of Buddhism. Similarities in some names as well as in religious and philosophical concepts occurring in the Buddhist and Jain scriptures contributed to this misconception. It was Hermann Jacobi (1850-1937) who was the first to demonstrate the independence of Buddhism and Jainism. In a broad sense, however, the doctrines of the Buddha, Mahāvīra and their contemporaries were aspects of a single body of teaching. Specifically their views may be different but generically they belong to the same category. This was due to the fact that they belonged to the same age and the same region and they responded and reacted, in their own ways, which were more or less similar, to the same stimuli arising out of the socio-political and religio-philosophical transformations that were taking place in their time.

Jainism and Buddhism belonged to the same civilization and intellectual sphere, and share a religio-philosophical terminology. Though both these systems were different from Vedism or Brahmanism and its sectarian offshoots, from the viewpoint of religio-philosophical terms and concepts they shared a basic similarity. Consider, for instance, such concepts as *jīva*, *ajīva*, *pudgala*, *ākāśa*, *duḥkha*, *nirvāṇa*, *mokṣa*, *karma*, *bandha*, *dravya*, *guṇa*, *paryāya*, *bhāva*, *abhāva*, etc. The logical, epistemological and metaphysical terms and concepts, as also those pertaining to the functional aspects of religious life, originated from one primary source and these were subsequently adapted in all the religio-philosophical systems of India with necessary modification. An in-depth study of religious terminology is therefore expected to demonstrate sufficiently that studies on Indian religion have so far overemphasized the differences and ignored the basic unity.

The problem of the early Brahmanical speculations was to define the relation between the *ātman* and the external world. A painful world, full of hunger and thirst, when equated with the all-perfect, all-pervading, and all-beautiful *ātman* would give birth to pessimism and the concept of metempsychosis—cycles of birth and death, and *karma* as the power predetermining the course of the migration of the soul from one state of being to another. Even the result of good action is impermanent. It arises out of some kind of desire, and hence the doctrine of deliverance gradually came to believe in the conquest of all desire through the right knowledge. And this is what is actually taught by the Buddha and Mahāvīra. One should not fail to recall in this connection that the contemporaries of Buddha and Mahāvīra—Gośāla, Ajita, Sañjaya, Puraṇa and Pakudha—based their doctrines on the same premises though their conclusions were different.

The ideas of the Vedic tradition by which certain fundamentals of Jainism and Buddhism are said to be inspired were the doctrine of transmigration of the soul and rebirth and liberation. In the Upaniṣads the doctrine of *karma* is presented in two forms—simple and sophisticated. The simple form is that just as good seeds produce a good harvest and bad seeds bad, so also a man becomes good by good deeds and bad by bad deeds. At the sophisticated level, however, *karma* is a blind unconscious principle governing the whole universe. It appears that the Jain doctrine of *karma* had derived its main impulses from the sophisticated interpretation. It is conceived in Jainism, unlike other systems, as being material, permeating the *jīvas* and weighing them down to the mundane level. The passions of a man act like a viscous substance that attract *karma*, which pours into the soul and sticks to it, gradually ripening and exhausting itself in accordance with the suffering and enjoyment of the individual. The *karmaśarīra* encircles the soul as its passes from birth to birth.

In the Ṛgvedic eschatology there is no direct reference to transmigration or to the doctrine of rebirth in any form. In the Brāhmaṇas we come across the idea of repeated births and deaths, but this idea is not established in a theoretical framework. It is only in the Upaniṣads that we come across a clear development of the theory of transmigration. This is in three distinct stages. In the first stage the earlier Vedic idea of heaven or the abode of Yama has been replaced by the concept of *yāna* or way, of the fathers (*pitṛ*) or gods (*deva*). In the second stage the doctrine of transmigration is presented without any reference to the idea of *karma* or reaping the fruits of deeds.

In the final stage, however, we have a complete presentation of the transmigration in terms of the doctrine of *karma*. Both Jainism and Buddhism drew much from all the three stages of the Upaniṣadic conception. It deserves special notice that the transmigrating soul of the Jains are thought to have various shapes and sizes. This conception has Upaniṣadic parallels and bears the stamp of animistic beliefs. Like the transmigration and *karma* theories, the Jain and Buddhist conception of liberation has something to do with the Upaniṣadic ideas. In the spirit of the Upaniṣads, the Jains and the Buddhists hold that man holds within himself the constituents of the gross body, the vital functions of life, will and desire, thoughts, and actions. So long as man keeps himself in these spheres and passes through a series of experiences in the present life and in lives to come, he suffers pleasure and pain, disease and death. But if he retires from these into his true unchangeable being, his true self manifests itself. This is a state of pure intelligence, pure being, and pure blessedness.

The basic theoretical difference between Jainism and Buddhism was on the question of momentariness. The Buddhists regarded all changes as being due to the assemblage of momentary conditions and went so far as to deny the existence of any permanent soul. The Jains too believed that changes were produced by an assemblage of conditions, but held that since no ultimate or absolute view of things could logically be taken, the reality of the permanence of the world must be acknowledged side by side with the question of change. According to the Jains those who hold that there is nothing really permanent in the universe and that everything changes from moment to moment, are one-sided because change and permanence are both real. Reality consists of three factors: permanence, origin, and decay—*utpāda-vyaya-dravyayuktaṃ sat.* So far as epistemology is concerned, the Jains do not subscribe to the Buddhist view that knowledge by perception of external objects is indefinite and indeterminate.

The Jains reject the Buddhist view that reality consists in causal efficiency, i.e. an object is real if it is capable of causing an effect. The Jains reject this approach because according to them even an illusory snake is real as it can cause fear. Jainism rejects the Buddhist Śūnyavāda and Vijñānavāda because they do not accept the competence of the sense-organs. The Jains are in agreement with the Vijñānavāda School on the point of the self-revelatory character of cognition, but while the latter holds that there exists no objects apart from cognition, and a particular piece of cognition is possessed of a particular form, the Jains posit the existence of external objects and treat cognition as a general phenomenon. The Buddhist theory of dependent origination conceives a series of qualities and attributes that originate or perish, but it posits no permanent atomic substance in the form of the substratum of those qualities and attributes, while Jainism posits over and above the perceptible world an infinite number of two utterly distinct types of subtle elements, one physical and the other conscious. The gross world is, according to Jainism, only the effect (*kārya*) or modification (*pariṇāma*) of subtle physical elements. The Buddhist viewpoint leads to unfounded nihilism. If we go by experience we can neither reject the self nor the external world.

Jainism, notwithstanding its idealistic tone and colour, has been able to retain its basic materialistic kernel. The Jain criticism of the materialists was directed mainly against their theory of knowledge. Cārvāka theory, for instance, seeks to explain the world as a mechanical or fortuitous combination of elements. Jains agree with the Cārvākas on the point that perception reveals the reality of material substances composed of the four elements. But they add that for the establishment of the concepts of space and time, and of motion and rest, inferential knowledge is necessary. They point out that in some cases even the Cārvākas have to depend on inferential knowledge, e.g. when they say that consciousness is due to the combination of material substances. The Jains do not subscribe to the materialist view that there is no soul apart from the body or that consciousness is the effect of matter, resulting out of the combination of material elements that constitute the body, but support the Cārvāka view that neither perception nor inference can prove god. The diversities of the world are due to cooperative conditions inherent in the nature of things. If things can function only in obedience to the will of god, there is no reason why they should be endowed with distinct attributes.

Jain atheism seems to have been complementary to that of the Sāṅkhya, according to which God as an eternal and immutable self cannot be the cause of the world. To create the world or to control Prakṛti cannot be the end of God's own because a perfect being cannot have any unfulfilled desires or unattained ends. Perception and inference do not prove god. Though the existing Sāṅkhya texts are of late origin, an early form of Sāṅkhya is probable and there are reasons to hold that early Buddhism and Jainism formulated some of their doctrinal standpoints on the basis of Sāṅkhya. The Sāṅkhya theory of knowledge in its basic principles has been shared by Jainism which accepts all three independent sources of valid knowledge (*pramāṇa*): perception, inference, and testimony. Jainism also shares with Sāṅkhya two kinds of perception, namely the *nirvikalpa* or indeterminate arising at the first moment of contact between a sense and its object, and the *svavikalpa* or determinate which is the result of analysis, synthesis, and interpretation of sense-data. A distinction between empirical and transcendental perception is maintained both in the Sāṅkhya and in Jainism. According to Sāṅkhya, the material cause of sense-organs is *abhimāna*, a kind of subtle substance (*sūkṣma dravya*) born of Prakṛti. Jainism likewise maintains that the material cause of sense-organs is a kind of *pudgala*, or physical substance (*jaḍadravyaviśeṣa*). The Jains, however, criticise the Sāṅkhya view that just as a mirror reflects the light of a lamp and thereby reflects other things, so the material principle of intellect, being transparent and bright, reflects the consciousness of the self and illuminates or cognizes the object of knowledge. The Jain conception of *mokṣa*, the Buddhist conception of *nirvāṇa*, and the Sāṅkhya conception of *mukti* have a common source which holds that all pleasures and pains belong to the mind-body complex that acts or causes action and that the attainment of liberation means the clear recognition of the self as a reality beyond time and space, essentially free, eternal, and immortal.

Apparently the Mīmāṃsā philosophy is the antithesis of Jainism, but both have the same cosmological conception. Jains and the Mīmāṃsakas hold that the universe has neither beginning nor end. It is composed of substances of different kinds. There is no creation or destruction of the world. Jainism subscribes to the Mīmāṃsā view that sense-perception does not reveal god and that the conception of god is ontologically irrelevant and logically repulsive. As for theories of knowledge, the Jains do not recognize the validity of such Mīmāṃsaka sources as comparison (*upamāna*), postulation (*arthāpatti*), or non-perception (*anupalabdhi*). Their sole insistence upon pure empirical perception and their denial of transcendental perception have been criticised by the Jain logicians Akalaṅka, Abhayadeva, and Hemacandra. Conceptually the Mīmāṃsaka ideas of *karma*, duty, rebirth, and liberation are not basically different from those of the Jains. Both schools hold that the soul survives death to be able to reap the consequences of its *karma*. Repeated births are caused by *karma*. It is only by disinterested performance of duties and through knowledge of the self that the *karmas* accumulated in the past are gradually worn out. Liberation is achieved, when one is freed of the ties of *karma*.

Except for ideas of bondage and liberation, Jainism has practically nothing in common with the Vedānta. In fact, Jainism and Vedānta stand in virtual opposition to each other. Philosophically Jainism may be designated as pluralistic realism and Vedānta as monistic idealism. Jainism does not subscribe to the Vedāntic view that the cause alone is real and what appears as effect is an illusion. The gross world according to Jainism is an effect (*kārya*) or modification (*pariṇāma*) of subtle physical elements. There is a plurality of conscious elements and a plurality of conscious souls. The Vedāntists on the other hand believe in a supreme soul. To them, *brahman* or the self is the only reality, and its modification in the form of the world is illusory. But to the Jains the world is eternal, without beginning or end and cannot be the modification of any imaginary principle.

The theistic standpoint of the Nyāya-Vaiśeṣikas was the main target of Jain attack. Even so, where logic was concerned the Jains drew heavily from the Nyāya-Vaiśeṣikas. Again, the Nyāya-Vaiśeṣika conception of atomism appears to have been influenced by early Jain thinkers. Later Jain logicians like Yaśovijaya have even employed the refined Navya-Nyāya technique in their analysis of Jain descriptions and definitions. The first five *bhūtas* or elements of the nine Nyāya-Vaiśeṣika substances correspond to Jain *pudgala* which is of the nature of the compounds of atoms. Yet while the former holds that atoms are heterogeneous in quality, the Jains conceive all atoms to be homogeneous. *Guṇa* or quality is recognized in the Nyāya-Vaiśeṣika as a distinct and real category and conceived as inhered in substance and dependent on substance. At the same time they are also conceived as distinct from substance because they can by themselves be known and are thus independent realities. This duality is to be a certain extent maintained in Jainism which treats *guṇa* as the essential character of the substance is possessed of some unchanging qualities as well as changing modes. They, admitting that different qualities are perceived by different sense-organs, argue that since a quality is non-distinct from the substance of which it is a quality, all the sense-organs are competent to perceive qualities as well as substances. Mental qualities such as desire, aversion, pleasure, and pain, and the experience of these qualities, are traced in both the systems to the soul or self. The soul or self, the *ātman*, is associated with the atoms in the Nyāya Vaiśeṣika and with *karmic*-atoms (*karmaṇu*) in Jainism.

We are now in a position to evaluate the Jain standpoint in terms of a subjectwise comparative analysis. The Advaita Vadāntins believe in the doctrine of absolute permanence (*kevala-nityatva*) because, according to them, all changes are mere appearance with no reality of their own. The Buddhists on the other hand believe in the doctrine of absolute change (*kevala-anityatva*) because, according to them, everything has a momentary existence. The Jains speak against both these doctrines and try to show that a real entity is a substance as well as its modes, something existent as well as non-existent, something permanent as well as transient. The idea of a self or soul that may be ubiquitous or non-ubiquitous, momentary or eternal, material or immaterial, is found in most of the systems and there is no dispute with regard to its connection with the causal factor *ajñāna*, *avidyā*, or *karma* that is responsible for transmigration. The self of the Jains is inherently perfect. The obstacles are constituted by matter-particles which infect the self and overpower its natural qualities. Regarding the means of valid knowledge, the Jains take a moderate stand, advocating together with Sāṅkhya-Yoga, Nyāya-Vaiśeṣika, Mīmāṃsā and the Vaibhāṣika and Sautrāntika schools of Buddhism the equal competence of sense-organs and non-sensuous organs. Regarding cause-effect relations, the Jain tendency is towards *pariṇāmavāda,* in which an intimate relation between cause and effect is emphasized. So far as the theory of knowledge is concerned the Jains are advocates of the self-revelatory character of cognition. From their non-absolutist viewpoint they treat a *pramāṇa* and its effect as partly distinct and partly non-distinct. They consider memory to be a *pramāṇa* and classify it in the non-perceptual category. Recognition on the other hand is regarded as a variety of sense-perception. Most of the Indian philosophical schools, including Jainism, divide perception into two kinds, empirical and transcendental. According to Jainism the two types of truth—one revealed through sense-perception and the other through transcendental intuition—may differ as to their quantity but not as to their quality or nature. Jainism posits over and above the perceptible world an infinite number of two utterly distinct types of subtle elements, one physical and the other conscious. The gross world is only an effect (*kārya*) or modification (*pariṇāma*) of the subtle physical elements which are atomic in nature. Atoms are conceived as constantly undergoing change and the gross world is but a transformation (*rūpāntara*) or modification of these very atoms.

II

In the beginning of the twentieth century the French Orientalist A. Guerinot undertook the first systematic survey of all the available publications on Jainism in Europen languages in his *Essai de Bibliographie Jaina* (1906) and *Repertoire d'Epigraphie Jaina* (1908). He found that as early as 1807 three descriptive reports on the Jains based on personal observations had been collected and published by Major Colin Mackenzie in the ninth volume of the *Asiatic Researches*. This also contained a well-researched paper by H.T. Colebrooke under the title 'Observations on the Sect of the Jains'. Colebrooke's paper was based on Hemacandra's *Abhidhāna-cintāmaṇi* and Bhadrabāhu's *Kalpasūtra.* He made use of both in a selective manner and was far from editing or translating them completely, and twenty years had to be pass until the first edited Jain text was published. H.H. Wilson's *Sketches of the Religious Sects of the Hindus*, which originally appeared in the sixteenth and seventeenth volumes of the *Asiatic Researches* (1814-15), presented the most important treatment of the subject at that time. The first book which had 'the Jains' in its title was W. Francklin's *Researches on the Tenets of the Jaynes and Boodhists* (1827). Wilson's *Descriptive Catalogue of the Mackenzie Collection* (1828) dealt with 49 south Indian Jain manuscripts.

J. Stevenson who had translated the *Kalpasūtra* into English in 1848 was the first European scholar to deal with the canonical Prakrit. Weber's edition of Dhaneśvara's *Satruñjaya-māhātmya* came out in 1858 with a detailed preface which was followed by Lassen's *Sketch of Jainism* (1861) in the fourth volume of his famous *Indische Alterthumskunde*. It was Weber, however, who placed the study of Jainism on a solid platform. His *Über ein Fragment der Bhagavatī* came out in 1866-7. This was followed by his treatise *Über die heiligen Schriften der Jaina* (1883-5) based on Jain manuscripts acquired by the Royal Library of Berlin (1873-88) and his descriptive catalogue of the same published in two big volumes (1888-92) contained elaborate analyses of philology, literature, history, and religion. The manuscripts thus described by Weber came to Berlin owing to an agreement between Georg Bühler and the Department of Public Instruction at Bombay which had commissioned him and other scholars in their service to examine private collections and the purchase manuscripts at government cost. Bühler was allowed to acquire manuscripts for foreign libraries provided they existed in duplicate. The manuscripts thus collected were catalogued in the *Reports* of Bhandarkar, Paterson, Jacobi, Klatt and Leumann, Pulle, and others.

The first collection of the canonical *Āgama Saṃgraha* was printed between 1875 and 1885 in Calcutta, Bombay, Benares, and Allahabad. These went to Europe through the efforts of Ray Dhanapati Siṃha Bahādur of Ajimganj (Murshidabad, West Bengal). The work of Bühler and Weber inspired some German scholars to work on Jain texts. Hermann Jacobi, under the shadow of Bühler's influence, edited the *Kalpasūtra* of Bhadrabāhu (1879) and later made a translation of it (*SBE* XXII.1884) that was qualitatively different from the earlier translation by J. Stevenson. He also edited the *Ācārāṅga Sūtra* (1883) and the *Pariśiṣṭaparvan* of Hemacandra (1883). Warren's edition of the *Nirayāvaliāo* was published (1879) with an introduction, analysis, and glossary. Leumann, a pupil of Weber, edited the *Uvavaiya* (*Aupapātika Sūtra*) in 1883 with glossary and notes. It was Leumann who brought to our notice the importance of the Prakrit commentarial literature, the *Nijjutis* and *Cunnis* which, according to him, was 'indispensable for the exploration of the Jain literature of several centuries'. He began to work on these texts since 1892, reading the manuscripts collected by him. His *Āvaśyaka-Erzählungens* (1897) was not, however, continued after the publication of the first series. By 1900, he prepared *Übersicht über die Āvaśyaka-Literatur* for publication on the basis of manuscript materials for the purpose of laying bare the different layers of an extensive scholastic literature. With this great work he was much ahead of his time. Unfortunately, printing of this work was stopped when the fourteenth form had been composed. It was not until 1934 that this great work came to light thanks to the endeavour of W. Schubring.

Another unpublished work on bio-bibliographical materials of Jainism was J. Klatt's *Onomasticon.* Eight volumes in his own hand in alphabetical order contained what was within his reach concerning Jain authors and works. His unfortunate demise prevented the publication of this work, estimated to fill some 1100 pages in print. After his death Weber and Leumann published (1892) its 55 pages under the title 'Specimen of a literary-biographical *Onomasticon* by Dr. Klatt'.

The canonical texts and their commentaries were written in Prakrit dialects and it was not until a later period that the Jains—the Śvetāmbaras from the eighth century and the Digambaras somewhat earlier—used Sanskrit for commentaries and other learned works. From the tenth century onwards there was a transition to the Apabhraṃśa dialect. Jacobi's *Kalpasūtra* and *Ācārāṅga* apart, the *Uvāsagadasāo* in the original Prakrit with the Sanskrit commentary of Abhayadeva and an English translation with notes was edited by A.F.R. Hoernle (1885-8). The edition of the canonical texts did not, however, proceed methodically. R. Pischel hoped that continued Jain research in Europe would lead to the origin of a Jain or Prakrit Text Society as a counterpart of the well-known Pali Text Society. (It is interesting that Jacobi's edition of the *Ācārāṅga* was published by the Pali Text Society.) But Pischel's idea materialized only half a century later, in 1953. The Agamodaya Samiti, founded at Mehsana in 1915, came forward to publish most works of the Śvetāmbara canon and many more non-canonical texts. Other Jain organizations followed suit. Learned societies such as the Jaina Dharma Prakāśa Sabhā in Bhavnagar, the Jaina Vidyā Prasāraka Varga in Palitana, the Jaina Jñāna Prasāraka Varga in Bombay, the Jaina Vidyāsālā at Ahmedabad, the Jaina Sūtra Battīsī at Hyderabad, Śrī-Sūtrāgama Prakāśaka Samiti, Gurgaon, etc., contributed to the publication of Jain texts. Jain saints like Vijaya Dharma Suri and wealthy persons as Devchand Lalbhai Jhavery, Bhagavan Mansukkhai and others associated themselves with the publication of Jain texts. The ground for preparing a well-documented history of Jain literature was prepared by Bühler, Jacobi, and Hoernle. Barodia's pioneering work (1909) in this field was not up to the mark. The most authoritative treatment was to be found in Maurice Winternitz's *Geschichte der Indischen Literatur* (vol. II, pt. II, Leipzig 1920; Eng. trans. vol. II, Calcutta 1933, 424-595) in which all the then known Jain texts were arranged in historical sequence and assessed in analytical and critical perspective. Its adaptation, *The Jainas in the History of Indian Literature*, was edited by Jinavijaya in 1946. The canonical texts were also exhaustively dealt with by W. Schubring (1935) and H.R. Kapadia (1942).

The *Āgama Saṃgraha* published all the Aṅga texts during the 1880s and the *Āgamodaya* did the same between 1916 and 1920. In the 1930s certain Aṅga texts published in *Āgamodaya* were re-edited by P.L. Vaidya. Also published were edited texts of the Uvaṅga and Paiṇṇa categories. The Bambhaceraim section (Rules for the Holy Life) of the *Ācārāṅga Sūtra* was re-edited by W. Schubring, who had translated into German in 1926 selected chapters from the Aṅga texts under the title *Worte Mahāvīras*. The *Viyāhapannati* (*Vyākhyāprajñapti* or *Bhagavatīsūtra*) was first studied by Weber in 1865-6. Portions of this text were translated into German by W. Schubring in *Die Jainas* (1927). A Gujarati rendering was made by Bechardes of this texts in 1927. Two important research works were made on the *Nāyādhammakahāo* in German respectively by Paul Steinthal (1881) and W. Huttemann (1907). An English translation of the *Uvāsagadasāo* was made by A.F.R. Hoernle (1888) and of *Antagaḍadasāo* and *Anuttarovavāiyadasāo* by L.D. Barnett (1907). The *Panhāvāgaraṇaim* was specially studied by A.C. Sen (1936). *Uvavāiya* (*Aupapātika Sūtra*) and *Rāyapasenaijja* were edited with extensive summary of contents, text and glossary by E. Leumann (1883). The contents of the *Surapannatti* were dealt with by Weber, Thibaut, and Shamasastry while the *Jambuddīvapannatti* was extensively used by Wilibald Kirfel in his *Kosmographie der Inder* (1920). The *Nirayāvaliāo* was edited by S. Warren (1879) and *Vivaraṇa* by P.L. Vaidya (1932) with introduction, glossary, notes and appendices. The *Causaraṇa*, *Bhattaparinnā*, *Samthāra*, *Āurapaccakkhāna* and *Mahāpaccakkhāna* were specially studied by Kurt Von Kamptz (1929). The *Kalpasūtra* of Bhadrabāhu was studied (1879) and translated (1882) by Jacobi while the *Kappa*, also known as *Bṛhat-Kalpasūtra* was edited with text, interpretation, summary of contents and glossary in 1905 by Schubring who had also edited the *Vavahāra*, *Nisīha* and *Mahānisīha* (1918). The *Jiyakappa* of Jinabhadra was edited with extracts from Siddhasena's *Cūrṇi* by Leumann in 1892. The *Uttarājjhāyā* or *Uttarādhyayana Sūtra* was edited by Jarl Charpentier (1922) and translated into English by Jacobi (1895). The *Dasaveyāliya* was edited and translated into German by Leumann along with the *Nijjuttis* in 1892. The *Piṇḍa-Nijjutti* and *Ogha-Nijjuttis* were published by Indian concerns, also the *Nandī* and *Annogadārā*. The *Isibhāsiyam* was edited by Schubring (1942) and the *Aṅgavijjā* by Puṇyavijaya (1957).

Leumann in his study of the *Nijjuttis* suggested that these were the earliest commentaries and were closely interwoven with the Sūtras or even supplanted the latter. At a later date, these *Nijjuttis* were extended to form exclusive commentaries in Prakrit (*Bhāṣyas* and *Cūrṇis*). These in their turn formed the foundation for the Sanskrit commentaries (*Ṭīkās, Vṛttis, Avacūrṇis*) complied between the eleventh and twelfth centuries. Jacobi held that an older form of Jain Mahārāṣtrī appeared in the *Cūrṇis*, *Kathānakas* and *Āvaśyaka* narratives, and that the language of the verses differed from that of prose. The legend of the Jina Pārśva was edited and translated by Jarl Charpentier from Devendragaṇin's commentary. The Prakrit epic, *Paumacariya*, which served as a model for later adaptations of the Rāma legend among the Jains, was edited by Jacobi in 1914. Jinasena's *Harivaṃśa Purāṇa*, based on *Mahābhārata*, was edited by Darbari Lal. The *Triṣaṣṭilakṣaṇa Mahāpurāṇa* by Jinasena and Guṇabhadra was studied by Glasenapp on the edition of the text and its Hindi translation by Lalaram Jain. The *Śatruñjayamāhātmya* which was studies as early as in 1858 by Weber, was subsequently translated in 1901 with appendices by J. Burgess. The first canto of Hemacandra's *Triṣaṣṭiśalākāpuruṣa-carita* (1906-13) was translated by Amulyacharan Vidyabhushan with notes and introduction by B.D. Jain (1925). Extracts of Hemacandra's *Pariśiṣṭaparvan*, edited by Jacobi (1891), were translated into German by J. Hertel (1908). The *Caritras* describing the lives of the individual Jinas were edited and a few were translated into European and modern Indian languages. Many works belonging to this category were also composed in Apabhraṃśa. An analysis of the *Pārśvanātha Caritra* of Bhavadeva Suri was given by Bloomfield (1918) who saw numerous parallels in Indian and world literature. Among the works of the semi-historical Prabandha category, Merutuṅga's *Prabandhacintāmaṇi* was edited by R.C. Dinanatha (1888), Prabhācandra's *Prabhāvakacaritra* by H.M. Sharma (1904) and Jinaprabha's *Tīrthakalpa* by D.R. Bhandarkar and K.N. Sahityabhushan (1923). Among religious novels, the *Taraṅgalolā* was translated into German by E. Leumann (1921), Haribhadra's *Samaraiccakahā* was edited (1908, 1926) by H. Jacobi with the text, and an introduction containing a summary of the work.

Siddharṣi's *Upmitibhavaprapañcakathā* was edited by Paterson and Jacobi (1899-1914). The latter also edited Dhanavāla's Apabhraṃśa work *Bhavisatta-kahā* (1918). It was also edited by C.D. Dalal which was completed with introduction, notes, glossary, etc., by P.D. Gune (1923). The Malayasundarī legends were specially studied by Hertel (1919), the *Kālakācārya-Kathānaka* was edited and translated by Jacobi (1880), the *Uttamakumāra-carita* by Weber (1884), the *Pāpabuddhi-Dharmabuddhi* with Italian translation by E. Loarini (1884), the *Campakaśreṣṭhī* (analysis) by Weber (1883) and by (ed. and Eng. tr.) Hertel (1800), the *Aghaṭa Kumāra* (German tr.) by Charlotte Krause (1922), *Ratnacūḍa* (German tr.) by Hertel, etc. Among other Jain narrative works, the *Samyakvakaumudī* was edited by Weber (1889), *Kathākosa* translated (1888) was edited (1887-8) by F.L. Pulle, *Ārādhana-Kathākośa* by C.H. Tawney (1895), *Antarakathāsaṃgraha*, partly translated into Italian by Hertel (1920) deserve special mention. The vast *stotra* literature and collections of didactic poems were published in India by various organizations like the *Kāvyamālā* series (1890 ff.), Yaśovijaya Granthamālā (1905 ff.), etc. Among these the *Bhaktāmara*, *Mandira* and *Śobhana* stotras were edited and translated into German by Jacobi (1878) and the *Ṛṣabhapañcāsikā* by Klatt (1879). The *Uvaesamālā* of Dharmadāsa, a didactic poem in 540 Prakrit stanzas, was edited by P. Tessitori in 1912. The *Subhāṣitaratnasaṃdoha* was edited and translated by R. Schmidt and J. Hertel (1905, 1907). Amitagati's *Dharmaparīkṣā* was edited by N. Mirnov (1903).

Hemacandra's *Yogaśāstra* was originally edited and translated in parts into German by Windisch (1874) and into Italian by F. Belloni Filippi (1908). Somaprabha's *Kumārapālapratibodha* was edited and translated by L. Alsdorf (1929). The latter's *Apabhraṃśa Studien* (Leipzig 1937) is fundamental for the study of the later Jain literature. Among the Apabhraṃśa Jain works the following may be noted: *Sanatkumāracaritam* (ed. Jacobi 1921), *Kālasvarūpakulakam* (ed. L.B. Gandhi 1927), *Vairāgyasāra* (Velankar, *ABORI* 1928, 272-80), *Jasahara-Cariu* (P.L. Vaidya 1931), *Sañjama Mañjarī* (P.D. Gune, *ABORI*, I, 157-66), *Pāhuḍadohā* (H.L. Jain 1933), *Nāyakumāra-cariu* (H.L. Jain 1933), *Karakanda-cariu* (H.L. Jain 1934, *Paramappayāsu* (A.N. Upadhye 1937), *Yogasāra* (A.N. Upadhye 1937), *Mahāpurāṇa* of Puṣpadanta (P.L. Vaidya 1937-41), *Paumacariu* of Svayambhū (H.C. Bhayani 1953), etc.

Among the doctrinal and philosophical works, there were 83 treatises by Kundakunda, of which only seven are known. His *Pañcatthiyasāre* (*Pañcāstikāyasāra* or the five cosmic constituents) was edited in 1920 by A. Chakravartinayanar with philosophical and historical introduction, translation, notes and an original commentary in English (also ed. Pavolini 1901). This work, together with *Pavayanasāra* (*Pravacanāra*, a text composed in Prakrit *Gāthās* on dogmatics, psychology and ethics) and *Samayasāra* (kernel or essence of the doctrine in 414 Prakrit stanzas) forms a trilogy. Umāsvāmin's or Umāsvāti's *Tattvārthādhigama-sūtra* (manual for the understanding of the true nature of things) which is recognized as one of the most authoritative works on logic, psychology, cosmography, ontology and ethics by both Śvetāmbaras and Digambaras, was first edited with the commentary (together with some of Umāsvāmin's minor works in the appendices) by Vakil Keshavlal Premchand Mody in 1903-5, translated into German by Jacobi (1906) and English by J.L. Jaini (1920). Siddhasena Divākara's *Nyāyāvatāra,* a fundamental work on Jain logic, was edited in 1909 with a commentary and English translation by Satish Chandra Vidyabhushan. The introduction of Samantabhadra's *Āptamī-māṃsā* (ed. in Sanātana Jaina Granthamālā 1905, 1910) was treated in Vidyabhushan's *History of Indian Logic*. His second work *Yuktyānusāsana* was also published in the Sanātana Jaina Granthamālā in which were also published Akalaṅka's *Tattvārtharājavārttika*, *Nyāyaviniścaya* and *Svarūpasambodhana*. Jain literary organizations in India published a good number of Jain philosophical texts and commentaries, the more important among them being *Aṣṭasāhasrī* (by Vidyananda which is a com. of Akalaṅka's *Aṣṭaśatī*), *Āptaparīkṣā*, *Pātraparīkṣā*, *Pramāṇanirṇaya*, and *Pramāṇaparīkṣā* (all published between 1914 and 1918), Māṇikyanandin's *Parīkṣāmukhasūtra* (1905) Subhacandra's *Jñānārṇava* (1905), Haribhadra's *Yogabindu*, *Yogadṛṣṭisamuccaya*, *Dharmabindu*, etc. (1908-12), Nemicandra's *Dravyasaṃgraha* and so forth. Śānti Suri's *Jīvavicāra* was edited and translated into French by Guerinot as early as in 1902. The *Jaina Granthāvalī* published by the Śvetāmbara Jaina Conference in 1908 served the purpose of a descriptive bibliography of the Jain texts.

Jain literary researches received further impetus from the compilations in the catalogues of the private libraries, collection of *Paṭṭāvalis*, *Praśastis*, biographies, etc. Of those who worked specially in the field of manuscript collection and making their descriptive lists mention should be made of S.D. Gupta (1919), C.D. Dalal and L.B. Gandhi (1923), Hira Lal (1926), H.D. Velankar (1930), H.R. Kapadia (1935), etc. H.D. Velankar's *Jinaratnakośa* (1944) and C.L. Jain's *Jaina Bibliography* (1949) present valuable information on texts and studies. A new horizon in the field of Jain studies was opened with the publication of *Abhidhānarājendra* (1913-25)—a Sanskrit encyclopaedia in seven volumes whose Prakrit catchwords were taken from the canonical and scholastic literature of the Śvetāmbaras—by Virarajendra Suri. Among other lexical works, a glossary of the canon in three languages were prepared by Muni Ratnacandra in five volumes (1923-32) under the title *Illustrated Ardha-Māgadhī Dictionary*. Pandit Haragovind Das Sheth's *Pāia Sadda Mahārṇava*: *A Complete Prakrit-Hindi Dictionary* (1928) deals with all forms of Prakrit. The Asiatic Society of Calcutta published critical editions of a few important Jain texts in the Bibliothica Indica Series. The Granthamālā series rendered yeoman' service in bringing out editions of canonical and non-canonical texts with translations, commentaries, notes, glossaries, etc. The Āgama Saṃgraha series (1875-85) seems to be the earliest of such publication efforts which was followed by the Yaśovijaya Jaina Granthamālā (1904), Ātmānanda Grantharatnamālā (1911), Āgamodaya Samiti (1915), Devachand Lalbhai Jaina Pustakoddhāra, Māṇikacandra Jaina Granthamālā (1915), Śrī Rāyacandra Jaina Śāstra Granthamālā (1916), Sanātana Jaina Granthamālā (1917), etc. The Digambara enthusiasts started the 'Sacred Books of the Jains' Series (1917) in Arrah in Bihar. Among subsequent enterprises mention may be made of the Singhi Jaina Granthamālā (1933), which started publishing Śvetāmbara works under the editorship of Muni Jinavijaya and the Jñānapīṭha Mūrtidevi Jaina Granthamālā.

For works on Jainism in European and Indian languages by individual scholars, an updated Bibliography has been supplied at the end of this volume.

III

Both the Śvetāmbaras and the Digambaras hold that the original canon of the Jains consisted of twelve Aṅgas, but the Digambaras regard the Śvetāmbara canon as wholly spurious. According to tradition, during the reign of Candragupta (late fourth century BC) there was a great famine in Magadha as a result of which a large number of young monks migrated towards the south under the leadership of Bhadrabāhu while the more elderly ones remained in Magadha under the leadership of Sthūlabhadra. The latter compiled the twelve Aṅgas in a special assembly summoned at Pāṭaliputra. Mahāvīra's teachings were first compiled in fourteen Pūrvas or 'earlier books', now lost. But the Śvetāmbaras believe that the Pūrvas were incorporated in the now lost *Dṛṣtivāda*, the twelfth Aṅga. It is not unlikely that these Pūrvas consisted of traditions handed down orally from teacher to pupil, that some part of this oral tradition was compiled by Sthūlabhadra in the Pāṭaliputra council, and that the council of Valabhi under Devardhi which took place sometime between the sixth and fifth centuries made use of the current oral traditions as well as such texts as might have been reduced to writing. The compiled Śvetāmbara texts, written in Ardha-Māgadhī, are generally known as *Āgama* or *Siddhānta* and are divided into groups such as the Aṅgas, Uvaṅgas, Paiṇṇas, Cheyasuttas, and Mūlasuttas. There are two special texts known as *Nandi* and *Anuogadārā*.

The first Aṅga, *Ācāra* or *Āyāra*, deals with the rules of ascetic life. It is divided into two parts, the second being of later origin. The subjects are *ahiṃsā*, the avoidance of weakness and relapse and endurance in hardship. The last chapter offers a vivid sketch of Mahāvīra's early career. The *Sūyagaḍa*, the second Aṅga which seems to be wrongly Sanskritized as *Sūtrakṛta*, deals with heretical views, hell and the tortures therein, descriptions of forms of life and of their origin as 'told in older ages', discussion of guilts, accumulated either consciously or unconsciously, etc. The third Aṅga *Ṭhāna* or *Sthāna* is a list of dogmatic topics, cases or possibilities, each grouped under ten items. The *Samavāya* or the fourth Aṅga is a supplement and continuation of *Ṭhāna*. One of its appendices deals with the nature of the twelve Aṅgas, another with the qualities of being, while a third with the dates of the spiritual and temporal heroes. The *Viyāhapannatti* (*Vyākhyāprajñapti*, also known as *Bhagavatī*) contains a picture of Mahāvīra's character and activities. It is a proclamation of explanations given by Mahāvīra or answers to individual questions asked by disciples and by far in most cases directed to Goyāma (Gautama). The *Nāyādhammakahāo* (*Jñātādharmakathā*) consists of didactic tales, 19 in number. The second part of this work deals with a nun who was reborn as the goddess Kālī. The *Uvāsagadasāo* (*Upāsakadaśā*) is concerned with pious laymen in Mahāvīra's time. Here an interesting account of Mahāvīra's rivalry with Gośāla is also given. The *Antagaḍadasāo* (*Antaḥkṛddaśā*) contains legends dating from the time of Ariṣṭanemi and deals with individuals who put an end to existence. Likewise the *Anuttarovavāiyadasāo* (*Anuttarupapādikadaśā*) deals with the legends of persons who were reborn in the uppermost heavens. The *Panhavāgaraṇaim* (*Praśnavyākaraṇāni*) describes the good and bad effects respectively of the observation and non-observation of vows. The eleventh Aṅga *Vivāgasuya* (*Vipākaśruta*) describes the consequences of *karma*, generally evil. The last or twelfth Aṅga *Dittihivāya* (*Dṛṣṭivāda*) is now entirely lost.

Of the twelve Uvaṅgas, the *Uvavāiya* is divided into two parts, the first of which describes the preparations made for the approach of Mahāvīra and the sermon he was to deliver before King Kuṇiya, while the second deals with reincarnation and salvation as the reward for certain actions. The *Rāyapasenaijja* is concerned with questions about the soul put by a king named Paesi to the monk Kesin. The *Jīvajīvābhīgama* consists of the classification of various kinds of animate and inanimate objects. The *Pannavanā* also deals with the classification of living beings. The *Sūrpannatti* which may called a scientific treatise, is chiefly concerned with the activities and effects of the sun. Likewise the *Jambuddīvapannatti* is a cosmographic work in which we have a description of Jambūdvīpa, the centre of the universe. The *Candapannatti*, identical in all available manuscripts with *Sūrapannatti*, is an astronomical work. In the *Nirayāveliyāo* we come across the Jain version of the Kuṇiya or Ajātaśatru legends. The *Kappāvadaṃsiyāo* is a story of conversion of Pauma and his liberation. The *Pupphiyāo* describes four stories showing the results of good or bad actions. The *Pupphaeuliāo* and the *Vanhidasāo* also deal with similar subjects.

The Paiṇṇas or Prakīrṇas consist of ten works. Among these the *Cauśaraṇa* contain hymns in honour of the *arhats*, *siddhas*, *sādhus*, and *dharma*. It is said to have been composed by one Vīrabhadra. The *Bhattaparinnā* deals with ritual for the renunciation of food. The *Saṃthāra* is concerned with rituals for the dead. The *Āurapaccakkhāna* is meant for renunciation of all that is evil by persons who are going to die. The *Mahāpaccakkhāna* or the Greater Renunciation is another text of confession. The *Candavijjhaya* is a text of monastic discipline. The *Gaṇivijjā* deals with the ascertaining auspicious and inauspicious days and times. The *Taṇḍulaveyāliya* deals with food and drink, embryology, the stages of human life, the duration of life, and measures of capacity and time. The *Devindatthaya* deals with the Bhavanavāsī, Vyantara, Joisiya and Vimanika kings and gods as to their seats, and the duration of their lives and faculties. The tenth text *Vīratthaya* is a *stotra* of Mahāvīra. Two other texts *Titthogali* and the *Ārāhaṇāpaḍāga* are also said to belong to the Paiṇṇa group. These two deal with the general teachings of Jainism.

The *Cheyasuttas* are six in number. Of them the *Āyāradasāo* deals with monastic life in general, offences against vows, stages of laymanship, stages of monkhood, etc. The *Vavahāra* contains a collection of what is permitted and proper for monks and what is not. The subject-matter of the *Nisīha* and the *Mahānisīha* is prescription of penances for the breach of rules of daily life, the confession of the transgression of rules of conduct, expiation, evil consequences of sinful deeds, etc. The *Paṃcakappa*, now lost and replaced by *Jiyakappa*, attributed to Jinabhadra also deals with the rules of monastic life. The *Kappa* attributed to Bhadrabāhu is the oldest *Cheyasutta*. But what is now regarded as *Bhadrabāhu Kalpasūtra* is a combination of three different works—the *Jinacarita* dealing with the lives of the Tīrthaṃkaras, the *Sthaviravalī* (*Theravali*) dealing with the schools, sub-schools and teachers, and the *Sāmācāri* (*Sāmāyāri*) dealing with the rules observed by ascetics during the monsoon retreat—composed at the different times. Two other texts, *Piṇḍaniryukti* and the *Oghaniryukti* are sometimes included in the *Cheyasutta* group.

The *Mūlasūtras* are four in number. Among these the *Uttarajjhāyā* (*Uttarādhyayana-sūtra*) consists of 36 chapters, composed at different times, and is said to have been spoken by Mahāvīra himself. It appears that the work derived its name from a group of apparently recent chapters following (*uttara*) older ones. The *Dasaveyaliya*, said to have been composed by Sejjaṃbhava, deals with monastic life in general, the six forms of living being and their non-violation, the five vows, the pure and impure aims, allowed and forbidden kinds of speech, devotion to right conduct, etc. The *Avassayanijutti* is a *gāthā* work taking its name from the six *āvassaya* or formulae to be recited daily. It is combined with the *niryukti* of Bhadrabāhu and deals with instructions on religious rules. The *Piṇḍanijjutti*, attributed to Bhadrabāhu, is a treatise on food. It also deals with the mistakes made by the almsgiver and those made by receiver.

Of individual and ungrouped works, the *Nandī* and *Anuogadārā*, are elaborate encyclopaedias of all matters concerning Jain dogmatics. The authorship of the former is attributed to Devardhi. Besides, there are some supplementary texts like the *Isibhāsiyam* dealing with sentences of certain Ṛṣis concerning moral subjects, the *Aṅgaculiyā* and *Viyāhaculiyā* dealing with praises of moral values under the garb of legends, and the *Angavijjā* dealing with various subjects of material importance. The commentarial literature of the Śvetāmbaras are also vast and the oldest among them are the *Niryuktis* written in Prakrit and were further developed into the *bhāṣyas* and *cūrṇis* which again gave rise to *ṭīkās*, *vivaraṇas*, *vṛttis*, and *avacūrṇis* in Sanskrit. Of the important writers of the *bhāṣyas* may be mentioned Saṃghadāsa, Jinadāsa and Siddhasena. It is said that Bhadrabāhu had written *niryuktis* on ten texts. Of other important commentators on the Śvetāmbara canon mention should be made of Haribhadra, Śīlāṅka, Śānti Sūri, Devendra Gaṇin, Abhayadeva, Hemacandra, and Malayagiri.

The Digambaras have authoritative scriptures of their own, described as the four Vedas and divided into four classes, Prathamānuyoga, Karaṇānuyoga, Dravyānuyoga, and Caraṇānuyoga. The *Pavayaṇasāra* (*Pravancanasāra*) *Paṃcatthikāya* (*Pañcāstikāya*), etc., of Kundakunda (first century), the *Tattvārthādhigama* of Umāsvāti, the *Mūlācāra* and *Trivarṇācāra* of Vaṭṭakera (first-third centuries), the *Padmapurāṇa* of Ravisena (seventh century), the *Āptamīmāṃsā* and *Ratnakaraṇḍa-Śrāvakācāra* of Samantabhadra (eighth century), *Harivaṃśapurāṇa* of Jinasena (eighth century), etc., are also regarded by the Digambaras as sacred texts. Of other Digambara writers we may refer to Svāmī Kārttikeya, author of the *Dvādaśānuprekṣā*, Yativṛṣabha, author of the *Tiloyapannatti*, as also to Puṣpadanta, Bhūtabali and Guṇadhara (to whom we owe the Siddānta Granthas) and the Sanskrit writers Samantabhadra, Pūjyapāda, Akalaṅka, Mānatuṅga and others.

In his *Ṣaḍdarśanasamuccaya* Haribhadra has given a brilliant exposition of the different systems of philosophy. He *Samarāicchakahā* is also an important contribution to Jain doctrines. Of other Jain writers of the eighth century, besides Haribhadra, mention may be made of Bappabhaṭṭi, Śobhana, Dhanapāla and Devabhadra. Śobhana's *Tīrtheśastuti* or *Caturviṃśajinastuti* and Dhanapāla's, *Pāiyalacchi* are indeed significant works. Akalaṅka was a great logician whose famous works are *Rājavārttika* and *Aṣṭaśatī*. Jain logic was further enriched by Vidyānanda, Māṇikyanandī and Prabhācandra. The Rāṣṭrakūṭa king Amoghavarṣa I was a devout Jain who composed a *Praśnottaramālikā* (catechism) on Jain ethics. Of the Jain works of the ninth and tenth centuries reference must be made to the famous commentaries *Dhavalā* and *Jayadhavalā*, composed by Vīrasena and Jinasena, the *Tattvārthasāra* and

Puruṣārthasiddhyupāya of Amṛtacandra, the celebrated commentator on Kundakunda's works, and the philosophical compendia of Nemicandra.

From the eighth century onwards the Jain writers adopted Apabhraṃśa as their languages of religious expression. The first Jain writer to use Apabhraṃśa in *dohā* metre was Joindu of the sixth century whose *Paramappapayāsu* and *Jogasāru* deserve special mention. The *Pāhuḍadohā* of Rāmasiṃha Muni, *Sāvayadhammadohā* of Devasena and *Vairāgyasāra* of Suprabhācārya are some of the best example of *dohā* works in Jain literature. These are, however, late works. Jain writers also used Apabhraṃśa in epic poems dealing with the lives of 63 supermen or *śalākāpuruṣa*. The earliest of these are the *Harivaṃśapurāṇa* and *Paumacariu* of Svayambhū. Puṣpadanta's *Mahāpurāṇa*, *Jasaharacariu*, and *Nayakumāracariu* are classics in this field of Apabhraṃśa literature. Of other Apabhraṃśa works, reference may be made to Kaṇakamāra's *Karakaṇḍucariu*, Haribhadra's *Nemināthacariu*, Dhāhila's *Paumaśiricariu*, Padmakīrti's *Pāsanāthacariu*, etc.

Some other important Jain works in Prakrit and Sanskrit composed before the tenth century are Asaga's *Vardhamānacarita*, Dhanañjaya's *Rāghava-Pāṇḍavīya*, or *Dvisandhāna*, Dharmadāsa's *Uvaesamālā*, Jinasena's *Pārśvābhyudaya*, Kaṇakasena's *Yośodhara-caritra*, Maheśvara Suri's *Jñānapañcamīkathā*, Māntuṅga's *Bhaktāmara-stotra*, Nandisena's *Ajitaśāntistava*, etc.

From the tenth century onwards the Jains adopted the epic style for saints and heroes. In Sanskrit the Śvetāmbara version of Kaṇakasena's *Yaśodhara-caritra* was made by Māṇikya Suri (eleventh century). The best work of this type is Hemacandra's *Triṣaṣṭiśalākāpuruṣacarita* describing in ten cantos the lives of 63 Jain saints. His *Pariśiṣṭaparvan* which deals with the lives of the oldest teachers is a supplement to the above work. He also wrote four lexical works, of which the *Abhidhānacintāmaṇi* is widely celebrated. The *Neminirvāṇa* of Vāgbhaṭa, dealing with the life of Neminātha, also belongs to this period. Jain contributions to Sanskrit Kāvya literature are Odeyadeva Vādibhasiṃha's *Kṣatracūḍāmaṇi*, Abhayadeva's *Jayantavijaya*, Devaprabha Suri's *Pāṇḍavacaritra*, Amaracandra's *Bālabhārata*, Abhayacandra's *Padmānanda*, and Udayaprabha Suri's *Dharmābhyudaya*. Jain writers also contributed to the historical Kāvya literature.

Of the Prakrit works composed between the tenth and thirteenth centuries AD, the *Mahāvīracarita* of Guṇacandra, composed about 1082, is unique. Another work of the same name was written by Devendra Gaṇin in 1085. Amitagati's compendium of Jain philosophy called *Pañcasaṃgraha* and Kaṇakasena Vādirāja's work on logic (e.g. *Pramāṇasaṃgraha*, and *Nyāyaviniścayavivaraṇa*) as well as the dramas of Ramacandra and Hastimalla show the extent of Jain contribution to different branches of literary activities. The life of Ṛṣabha is described by Vardhamāna in his *Ādināthacarita* composed about 1103. Of other Carita works, Devacandra's *Śāntināthacarita* (1103), Śānti Suri's *Pṛthivīcandracarita* (1108), Devabhadra's *Pārśvanāthacarita* (1150), Somaprabha's *Sumatināthacarita* (1150), Maladhārī Hemacandra's *Nemināthacarita* (*c.*1106), Śrīcandra's *Munisuvratasvāmīcarita* (1135), another Śrīcandra's *Sanatakumāracarita* (1157), and Haribhadra's *Mallināthacarita* (twelfth century), deserve special mention. Somaprabha's *Kumārapālapratibodha* contains a dialogue between the Caulukya king Kumārapāla and his teacher Hemacandra on Jain precepts. The *Ullāsikkamathaya* of Jinavallabha and *Ajitaśāntithaya* of Vīra Gaṇin are *stotras* in Prakrit in glorification of Ajitanātha and Śāntinātha. The *Saḍbhāṣānirmita-Pārśvajinastavana* by Dharmavardhana, written about AD 1200 is in six languages, Sanskrit, Mahārāṣṭrī, Māgadhī, Saurasenī, Paiśācī, and Apabhraṃśa which also belong to the same category. Of the didactic poems in Prakrit with a pronounced Jain bias reference may be made to Jayakīrti's *Śilovaesamālā* and Municandra's *Gāthākośa* (twelfth century). Important contributions to Jain doctrines in Prakrit are Jinacandra Gaṇin's *Navapaya* (1015), with a Sanskrit commentary and *Navatattvaprakaraṇa*, treatise on nine fundamental truths. Another significant work of the eleventh century is the *Jivaviyāra* by Śānti Suri which deals with the nature of beings grouped in various classes. Abhayadeva (AD 1064) wrote commentaries on the nine Aṅgas while Śānti Suri and Devendragaṇin (eleventh century) wrote exhaustive commentaries on the *Uttarādhyayana*. In AD 1113 Maladhārī Hemacandra Suri wrote *Bhavabhāvanā* in 531 *gāthās*. Devendra Suri wrote in thirteenth century the first five *Karmagranthas* which describes in detail the entire doctrine of *karma*.

Among other works, Mahāsena's *Pradyumnacaritra*, Sūrācārya and Maladhārī Hemacandra's *Nemināthacaritras*, Vādirāja, Bhavadeva and Māṇikyacandra's *Pārśvanāthacaritras*, Vikrama's *Nemidūta*, Maladhārī Devaprabha's *Mṛgāvaticaritra*, Jineśvara's *Kathākośa*, Śrīcandra's *Purāṇasāra*, Āśādhara's *Sāgāradharmāmṛta* and *Anāgāradharmāmṛta*, Guṇacandra's *Mahāvīracarita*, Dhaneśvara's *Surasundarīcarita*, etc., are important. These were all composed between the tenth and thirteenth centuries. Hemacandra's *Kumārapālacarita* was written to illustrate the rules of Prakrit grammar. Of the Apabhraṃśa works on Jainism during this period reference may be made to the *Pajjunnakahā* of Siṃha narrating in fifteen cantos the life of Pradyumna Kumāra, the *Kathākośa* of Śrīcandra (there are many works under this title) containing 53 religious tales, the *Pārśvapurāṇa* of Padmakīrti describing in 18 *sandhis* the life of Pārśva, the *Sukumāracariu* of Śrīdhara describing the story of Sukumāra who became a Jain monk, the *Sudarśanacarita* of Nayanandin, the didactic poem *Kālasvarūpakulakam*, of Jinadatta Suri, the *Neminathacarius* of Haribhadra and Laksmaṇadeva, the *Yogasāra* of Yogicandra Muni, the *Vairāgyasāra* of Suprabhācārya, the *Chakkammovaesa* of Amarakīrtigaṇi, the *Aṇuvayarayaṇapaiu* of Lakṣmaṇa, the *Sañjamamañjarī* of Mahesara Suri, etc.

From the fourteenth century onwards the Jain writers adopted regional languages instead of Prakrit and Apabhraṃśa, but the use of Sanskrit continued. Kīrtirāja's *Neminātha Mahākāvya*, which narrates the life of Neminātha in 12 cantos, is one of the best specimens of Sanskrit epic literature of the fifteenth century. Nayacandra's *Hammīrakāvya* belongs to the category of historical *kāvyas*. Somacaritragaṇi's *Guruguṇaratnākara* (1485), describing the life of Lakṣmīsaragaṇi of Tapāgaccha, is a work of considerable importance for Gujarat history. Sarvānanda's *Gagaḍucarita* is likewise a historical *kāvya* in praise of a Jain layman who served famine-stricken people. Among the devotional poems of the fifteenth and sixteenth century mention may be made of Jinaprabha Suri's *Caturviṃśati Jinastuti* and several other hymns and Munisundara Suri's *Jinastotraratnakośa*. Merutuṅga's *Meghadūta* is an example of Jain *dūtakāvya* literature which describes the life of Neminātha in four cantos. The *Campakaśreṣṭhīkathānaka*, *Pālagopālakathānaka*, *Saṃyaktvakaumudī*, etc., are Jain collections of didactic stories. The first two works were composed by Jinakīrti. Somacandra, a pupil of Ratnaśekhara of Tapāgaccha, composed in 1448 the *Kathāmahodadhi* which is a collection of 126 Jain tales. Merutuṅga's *Mahāpuruṣacarita* is a prose romance on a Jain theme. The Jain writers also employed *campūs* and *prabandhas* for religious propaganda.

The emphasis on Prakrit and Apabhraṃśa shows that Jain writers wanted to make their views accessible to the common people. This again accounts for the immense Jain contribution to the regional languages. In Tamil the earliest Jain works are Tiruthakkathevar's *Jīvakacintāmaṇi* and Konguvelir's *Perunkathai*. The works of Tamil poet Vāmanācaryar may also be referred to in this connection. Like other religions, Jainism also claims the writers of *Tolkappiyam* and *Kural* as its adherents. The *Śilappadikaram*, *Nīlakeci*, and *Yaśodharākāvya* also have a bearing on Jainism. Jain influence has contributed a glorious chapter to Kannaḍa literature. The earliest *Voddha-ārādhana* (eighth century) has a professedly Jain background and its author Sivakotyācārya was a devout Jain, Nṛpatuṅga's *Kavirājamārga* mentions a number of Jain writers. Guṇavarma's *Nemināthapurāṇa* is an important Kannaḍa work of the ninth century. Pasupa's *Ādipurāṇa* (AD 941) described in beautiful language the life of Ṛṣabha. Ponna's *Śāntipurāṇa* contains the life-story of the sixteenth Tīrthaṃkara. Ranna's *Ajitapurāṇa* (AD 993) deals with the second Tīrthaṃkara. Cāvuṇḍa Rāya composed a *Purāṇa* after his name, in which he gives a comprehensive history of the 24 Tīrthaṃkaras. Nāgacandra or Pampa II of the twelfth century wrote *Mallinātha-purāṇa* in Kannaḍa and a Jain version of the *Rāmāyaṇa* with the title *Rāmacandracaritapurāṇa*. Janna was another Kannaḍa poet on the life of Anantanātha, Guṇavarma who wrote the *Puṣpadantapurāṇa*, Karṇapārya who was the author of *Nemināthapurāṇa* and Acanna and Kamalabhava who wrote respectively on Śāntinātha and Mahāvīra, flourished between the twelfth and fourteenth centuries. Among subsequent Kannaḍa writers mention should be made of Madhura, Mangrāsa, Śāntikīrti, Bhāskara, Bommarasa, and Koṭeśvara.

The earliest available specimens of old Gujarati, namely the *Bharateśvara-Bāhubali-ghora* (AD 1170) of Vajrasena and its expanded version *Bharateśvara Bāhubalirāsa* (AD 1185) of Śālibhadra describe the valour and renunciation of Bāhubali. The *Candanabālārasa* (AD 1201) of Asiga, the *Jambusvāmīcariya* (AD 1210) of Dharma and the *Gayasukumālarāsa* (AD 1250) of Delhana deal with Jain mythology, while other *rāsas* like the *Revantagiri* (AD 1232) of Vijayasena, *Ābu* (AD 1233) of Pālhana and *Pethaḍa* (AD 1300) of a writer of the same name eulogize holy places. Works like *Buddhirāsa* (AD 1200), *Jīvadayārāsa* (AD 1201), and *Saptkṣetrirāsa* (AD 1271) composed by Śālibhadra, Āsiga and others, are purely religious and didactic in character. Beside the *rāsa* literature, old Gujarati contains compositions known as *barahamāsā* (cf. *bāramāsyā* of Bengal literature), *mātṛka* and *vivāhala* and most of these writings are of Jain origin. During the second half of the fourteenth century Nemicandra Bhāṇḍārī composed 160 *gāthās* on the Jain faith, upon which two prose commentaries in early Gujarati dating between 1550 and 1560 have been found. The Jain writers have a very great place in the development of Gujarati literature in its different aspects. The Great Hemacandra was a Gujarati and collected over 100 couplets in the Apabhraṃśa of his time (twelfth century), which are claimed by Hindi and Marwari, and also by Gujarati, as specimens of their earliest poems.

IV

According to the Jain belief it was Ṛṣabhadeva, the first of the twenty-four Tīrthaṃkaras, who taught men 72 arts and women 64 and initiated them into the Jain way of life. His mission of elevating the ethical and spiritual standard of mankind was continued and put into practice by successive Tīrthaṃkaras. In the hands of the last two Tīrthaṃkaras, Pārśva and Mahāvīra, the traditional knowledge derived from their spiritual ancestors assumed new form and colour. None of them claimed to be the founder of any system. They were great reformers who modified the essentials of the existing religion evidently to meet the demand of their ages.

After the demise of Mahāvīra the leadership of the four orders of the Jains—monks, nuns, laymen, and laywomen—fell on his disciple Indrabhūti Gautama who was the head of the church for a period of twelve years. He was succeeded by Sudharman who also held office for another twelve years. The latter was succeeded by Jambusvāmin who led the community for twenty-four years. Subsequent leaders were Prabhava, Sayambhava, Yaśobhadra, Sambhūtavijaya, and Bhadrabāhu. Tradition makes Bhadrabāhu a contemporary of Candragupta Maurya during whose leadership a great famine took place, as a result of which a part of the community went with him to south India. The other part remained in Magadha under the leadership of Sthūlabhadra. The latter, interested in preserving the canonical literature, convened a council at Pāṭaliputra to collect the Aṅga texts. The famine over, Bhadrabāhu returned, but refused to accept the proceedings of the Pāṭaliputra council as valid. He also disapproved the use of clothing by those who had stayed behind.

After Sthūlabhadra the Jain church was led respectively by Mahāgiri, Suhastin, Susthita, Supratibuddha, Indradinna, Dinnasuri, Siṃhagiri,Vajrasvāmin and Vajrasena. It was during the patriarchy of Vajrasena that the great schism resulting in the official separation of the Śvetāmbaras and the Digambaras took place. Jain tradition records eight schisms, the first of which took place as early as the days of Mahāvīra under the leadership of his own son-in-law Jamāli. The second was caused by Gośāla (actually he did not belong to the creed), the third by Āsāḍha Ācārya, the fourth by Aśvamitra, the fifth by Gaṅga, the sixth by Rohagupta and the seventh by Goṣṭha, but these were of minor importance in the history of the Jain church. But the last schism which was based on the seven main tenets in which the Digambaras were opposed to the Śvetāmbaras resulted in a sharp division of the church. The points on which emphasis is laid by the Digambaras are that the Tīrthaṃkaras must be represented as nude and with downcast eyes, that women cannot attain *mokṣa*, that the *kevalajñānins* require no food, that Mahāvīra was never married, that the compiled canonical texts are not valid since they are man-made, that ascetics must be entirely nude and that the Ācāryas after Jambusvāmin do not represent the entire community. After Vajrasena the church was led by the following patriarchs: Puṣyagiri, Phalgumitra, Dhanagiri Śivabhūti, Bhadra, Nakṣatra, Rakṣa, Nāga, Jehila, Viṣṇu, Kālaka, Sampalita Bhadra (J), Vṛddha, Saṅghapālita, Hastin, Dharma (J), and Śāṇḍilya.

In the earlier phases of its development, the geographical boundary of Jainism comprised Anga-Magadha, Kauśāmbī, Sthunā and Kunālā according to the *Kalpasūtra*. In the first century BC, Orissa was an important province of Jainism as attested by the Hathigumpha inscription of Khāravela and the Jain caves of Udayagiri and Khaṇḍegiri. Mathura also had become a very important centre of early Jainism where a large number of small dedicatory inscriptions, engraved on the images of the Jins, votive tablets and arches dating from the first century of the Christian era have been found. The country around Ujjayinī was also a stronghold of early Jainism. According to tradition the conversion of Aśoka's grandson Samprati by Suhastin took place in this region. The story of Kālakācārya also implies the spread of Jainism in Malwa in the first century BC. The Junagarh inscription of the grandson of Śaka Jayadāman of the second century AD has Jain affiliation indicating its extension in western India. In the south the spread of Jainism is associated with the legends of Bhadrabāhu and Candragupta. The latter is said to be a devout Jain who breathed his last at Śravaṇabelgola in Karnataka.

By the end of the third century AD Jainism had taken firm root throughout India. But along with its spread and a shift in its centre of gravity, there also occurred changes in organization. The major sects, Śvetāmbaras and Digambaras, were further subdivided. The paucity of epigraphic records about Jainism in the Gupta period and lack of literary evidence from the side of the Jain writers, clearly indicate that Jainism was not very prosperous in those days. And this is partly confirmed by the absence of any reference to it in the description of the Chinese pilgrim Fa-hien. However, there are two inscriptions belonging to the reign of Kumāragupta, one at Mathura (AD 430) speaking of the dedication of a Jain image by a lady and the other at Udayagiri in Malwa (AD 426) recording the erection of a statue of Pārśva by a private individual. The Kahaum inscription of the time of Skandagupta (AD 461) also refers to the setting up of five images of Jain prophets in that village. In North Bengal, the Paharpur copper plates of AD 478 record the donation of some land by a private individual and his wife, for the maintenance of worship at a Jain vihāra at Vaṭa-Gohali, which was presided over by the pupils of the Nirgrantha teacher Guhanandin of the Pañcastūpanikāya of Banaras. This vihāra of the fourth or fifth century, probably occupied the site of the great temple unearthed at Paharpur in the Rajshahi district of Bengal. Hiuen Tsang observed that the monks of the both Śvetāmbara and Digambara sects were to be found near Taxila to the west and Vipula to the east and the Digambara Nirgranthas were very numerous in Puṇḍravardhana and Samataṭa in the east. Uddyotana, author of the *Kuvalayamālā* (AD 779) refers to the Hūṇa King Toramāna's attraction to Jainism; his preceptor was one Harigupta. One of the pupils of the latter was Devagupta, a royal scion of the Gupta family whose pupils carried the torch of Jainism to Rajasthan and Gujarat. In the seventh century, two Gurjara kings, Jayabhaṭa I and Dadda II, were given the epithets *vītarāga* and *praśāntarāga* in their grants which indicate that they were patrons of Jainism. In northern Gujarat, Vanarāja, the founder of the Cāpotkaṭa dynasty at Anahillapura is regarded by Jain tradition as a follower and patron of the faith.

Various ruling dynasties of the Deccan and their ministers, and feudal chieftains from the fifth century onwards extended their patronage to Jainism. The Gaṅgas of Karnataka were intimately associated with Jainism. A later tradition makes the founder of the Gaṅga family a disciple of a Jain teacher named Siṃhanandin. A later ruler, Avinīta, is said to have been brought up by a Jain sage called Vijayakīrti, and the famous Digambara author Pūjyapāda is associated with another king of this family called Durvinīta. The Kadamba rulers of Vijjayantī or Baravasi showed unusual favour towards Jainism. We have many records of kings giving donations to Jain monks, erecting Jain temples, and giving other help to the different sections of the Jain community. There is no reliable evidence that the Cālukyas of Badami showed any particular leaning towards Jainism, but Ravikīrti, the author of the famous Aihole Praśasti, was a devout Jain who had constructed the Jinendra shrine on the Meguti Hill. A Jain cave at Badami and another of Aihole, containing figures of Tīrthaṃkaras, belong to the early Cālukya period. It is difficult to know precisely the condition of Jainism in south India in the early centuries of the Christian era, but the early Tamil literature shows a Jain presence, as do the Tamil Brahmi inscriptions found in the caves of the Ramnad and Tinnevelly districts. A *Mahāvaṃsa* passage says that there were Nirgranthas in Sri Lanka during the time of Paṇḍukabhaya. The famous Jain author Samantabhadra was associated with the town of Kanchi and a Pallava ruler is said to have been the patron of Kundakunda. The Jains of the south formed what is known as the Mūla Saṅgha or the original group of which four *gaṇas* were formed namely, Nandi, Sena, Siṃha, and Deva. Hiuen Tsang speaks of a large number of Nirgranthas in the country of Pāṇḍyas.

Vanarāja Cāvāḍa, founder of a branch of the Cāpa dynasty who established the supremacy of his family at Anahilapāṭaka in AD 745, was installed on the throne according to the Jain Prabandhas, by the Jain Guru Śīlaguṇasuri. Most of the influential persons in the realm were Jains and occupied high positions in the state. Vanarāja's prime minister Campa was the founder of the city of Champaner. Ninnaya, a merchant prince whom the king held in high esteem, built a temple of Ṛṣabha at Anahilavāḍa. Vanrāja himself built a temple known as Pañcasāracaitya in which the idol of Pārśvanātha was installed. The Gurjara-Pratihāra kings of the eighth-ninth centuries were patrons of Jainism. Vatsarāja is said to have built at Kanauj a temple 100 cubits high and consecrated there a golden image of Mahāvīra. At Gwalior he established an image of Mahāvīra 23 cubits high. He is said to have built Jain temples at Mathura, Modhera, and Anahilavāḍa. His son Nāgabhaṭa II is said to have been converted to Jainism and the latter's grandson Bhoja was also a great patron of Jainism. The Paramāra kings patronized Jain authors like Dhaneśvara, Dhanapāla, Śāntisuri, etc.

In the Deccan, the Rāṣṭrakūṭa king Amoghavarṣa's (AD 814-78) chief preceptor was Jinasena and he had appointed Guṇabhadra as the preceptor of his son Kṛṣṇa II. Amoghavarṣa was a great admirer of Jainism. The Rāṣṭrakūṭa Tailapa II had a strong attachment to Jainism and he patronized Ranna, Kaviratna and other Jain authors. Tailapa's son Satyāśraya constructed a monument in honour of his Jain teacher. One of his successor Jayasiṃha III caused a *basadi* to be constructed at Balipura. The Gaṅga ruler Mārasiṃha III (AD 960-74) was a disciple of Ajitasena. He actively supported renowned Jain scholars, maintained the Jain doctrine, caused *hbasadis* and *mānastambhas* to be erected, and after abdication ended his life by *sallekhanā*. His minister Cāmuṇḍa Rāya's contribution to the cause of Jainism has become a legend. Three records of Ammarāja II speak of Jainism as popular religion in the Andhra region in the tenth century. An inscription at Ramatirtham near Vizianagaram indicates that Jainism continued to flourish there till the beginning of the eleventh century and that the Ramatirtham Hill was regarded as a place of Jain pilgrimage. A Kannaḍa inscription of the reign of King Vimalāditya states that Trikālalyogin Siddhāntadevamuni, Ācārya of Deśī-gaṇa, who was the preceptor of the king, paid respect to the Ramatirtham Hill. The Kadamba rulers were also patrons of Jainism. Feudatories and high officials of various ruling dynasties were in many instances patrons of Jainism. So also were some royal women, Jakkiabbe, who was appointed *nāl-gāvunda* in her husband's place in Rāṣṭrakūṭa Kṛṣṇa III's reign, performed the vow of *sallekhanā*. Attimabbe, daughter of Tailapa's commander Mallappa got prepared one thousand manuscripts of Ponna's *Śānti-purāṇa* in Kannaḍa and had them circulated all over the country. Jakkisundari caused a *basadi* to be built in AD 968. Another great Jain devotee was Pembabbe, elder sister of Gaṅga Butaga.

Between the eleventh and the thirteenth centuries, Jainism found a firm footing in Gujarat under the Caulukyas. A Jain temple known as Mūlabasatika is said to have been constructed by Mūlarāja at his capital Anahilapāṭaka or Anahilavāḍa. During the reign of Bhīma I, his minister Vimala of the Prāgvaṭa family constructed the celebrated Ādinātha temple on Mount Abu. The temple was completed in AD 1031, i.e. within seven years after the demolition of Somanātha temple by Mahmud of Ghazni. During the reign of Siddharāja and his successor Kumārapāla Jainism continued to flourish in Gujarat. The latter was converted to Jainism under the influence of the great Hemacandra (AD 1088-1172). The continuity and prosperity of Jainism are attested by the temple of Neminātha built in the vicinity of the Ādinātha temple at Ābu by Tejaḥpāla, a minister of the Caulukya king Somasiṃhadeva. It was completed in AD 1230. To these were added numerous Jain shrines and other structures during the twelfth and thirteenth centuries, the fame of which gave the place its new name, Dilwara. Beside Ābu, Śatruñjaya and Girnar in Kathiawar received the particular attention of the rulers and merchants whose bounty is reflected in the construction of temples.

Satyāśraya (AD 997-1008) the western Cālukya king of the Deccan, was a disciple of the Jain teacher Vimalacandra of the Draviḍa-Saṅgha. Other kings of this dynasty such as Jayasiṃha II (AD 1015-43), Someśvara I (AD 1043-68), Someśvara II (AD 1068-76) and Vikramāditya VI (AD 1076-1126) showed favour to Jainism. A Jain saint Vardhamānadeva was the spiritual guide of the early Hoysala rulers who made grants to Jain temples and settlements. The celebrated Hoysala King Viṣṇuvardhana was a Vaiṣṇava, but did not cease to become a great patron of Jainism. In AD 1125 he built a Jain abode at Chalya and made grants for the repairs of Jain temples. According to a stone inscription at Belur (AD 1128) he made a gift at a Malli Jinālaya. In AD 1133 he granted a village to the Pārśvanātha temple at Dvārasamudra and renamed it Vijaya Pārśvanātha. His queen Śāntaladevī was a staunch Jain who gave up her life by performing the *sallekhanā* rite. Among his ministers and feudatories, Gaṅgarāja built several Jain temples. Other officers of Viṣṇuvardhana like Boppa, Punisa, Maniyane, and Bharateśvara also subscribed to the Jain faith. Viṣṇuvardhana's successor Narasiṃha I paid a visit to Śravaṇabelgola and endowed the *Caturviṃśati-basadi* built by his illustrious general Hulla by the grant of a village. Many feudatory chiefs ruling in different parts of Karnataka between the eleventh and the thirteenth centuries, e.g. the Santara chiefs Bhujabala, Vīra, the minister Nagularasa, the Kāngalva chiefs, the Cāngalva chiefs, etc., were devout Jains who were great builders as well. We possess numerous records ranging between AD 1000 and 1300 of solitary rulers and nobles who built temples or installed images, performed worship, made endowments and ended their lives following the Jain system of renunciation.

After AD 1300 almost the whole of northern India came under Turkish rule. They were iconoclasts and demolished numerous Brahmanical, Buddhist, and Jain temples. The Jains in order to save their religion and culture had taken a defensive attitude. In Gujarat, after the fall of the Vāghelas, the lack of royal patronage was to a certain extent compensated by the merchants, most prominent among them being Samarasiṃha or Samara Shah of the fourteenth century. The name of Jesala Shah may also be mentioned in this connection. The monks of Kharatara-gaccha worked for the propagation of Jainism in Rajasthan and Gujarat under the leadership of Ācārya Jinacandra III in the fourteenth century. He was succeeded by Jinakusalasuri and the latter by Somasundara. In the fifteenth century almost all the standing Hindu and Jain temples of Gujarat were destroyed by Taj-ul-Mulk, the general of Ahmad Shah who was one of the greatest iconoclasts among the Muslim rulers of Gujarat. Somasundara, the Jain patriarch, by virtue of his tactful efforts was able to change the attitude of this king towards Jainism. Somasundara's disciple Munisundara won the admiration of the Muslim Naik of Cambay. Some broken Jain temples were repaired in the fifteenth century, during which period a good number of manuscripts were prepared and copied. In the first half of the sixteenth century Karma Shah, originally a cloth merchant, successfully worked for the propagation of Jainism. The greatest Jain preacher of the sixteenth century was Hīravijaya who came in contact with Emperor Akbar which took place for the first time in AD 1582. It was through his endeavour that Akbar made many concessions to the Jains and conferred on him the title Jagatguru.

As in Gujarat Jainism continued to exist in Rajasthan in the period between AD 1300 and 1600. Bikaner in Rajasthan has yielded more than 2,500 Jain inscriptions written mostly on metal icons. The earliest Jain temple of Bikaner dedicated to Ādīnatha, was founded during the reign of Bikaji in AD 1503. Inscriptions from this temple mention celebrated Jain teachers. Those from other temples of Bikaner refer to Emperor Akbar and king Lūnakaraṇa. Jain epigraphs have also been found from other places of Bikaner district such as Napasar, Rajaldesar, Ratangarh, Sardarsahar, Rini, etc. Several Jain centres like Sanchor, Jalor, Jaisalmer, and Abu were associated with Jainism even before AD 1306. This association continued in subsequent centuries. The Pārśva temple of Jaisalmer was repaired in the fifteenth century during the rule of Lakṣmaṇa. During the reign of his son Vairasiṃha the temple of Sambhavanātha was built at Jaisalmer (AD 1437). The next king, Cācigadeva, was also a great patron of Jainism. Subsequent kings Devakarṇa, Jaitrasiṃha II and Bhīmasena had Jain leanings and associations with Kharatara monks. Fifteenth-century inscription from Mount Abu refer to Ācārya Lakṣmīsāgara of Tapā-gaccha and Duṅgarasiṃha, king of Dungarpur. The latter city continued to be a Jain centre in subsequent periods and contains temples and other Jain antiquities. It was also famous for manuscript-copying.

Mokal or Maukala of Mewar is known to have built a Jina temple through his minister Guṇarāja in AD 1428. His son Kumbhakarṇa was a great patron of Jainism whose name occurs in a Mount Abu inscription. His Jain affiliation is attested by an inscription of AD 1434. A few more inscriptions of Kumbha also point to the same. His son Rāyamalla had also an inclination towards Jainism which is proved by an epigraph from Nadlai. Bairat in eastern Rajasthan was a flourishing centre of Jainism in the sixteenth century as is amply testified by epigraphic evidence. Gwalior too was a stronghold of Jainism. Its rulers Virāmadeva, Duṅgarasiṃha, and Kīrtisiṃha are mentioned in inscriptions and manuscripts. Deogarh in the Lalitpur district of Uttar Pradesh was a Jain centre since the early medieval period.

In the south, like their Hoysala predecessors, the Vijayanagara rulers not only offered protection but also gave unstinted patronage to Jainism and its institutions. Under the influence of king Bukkarāya the Vaiṣṇavas of that region agreed that they should regard the 'loss or advancement' of the Jains as their own and 'as long as the sun and the moon endure, the Vaiṣṇavas will continue to protect the Jain Darśana'. The example of Bukkarāya was followed by his successors who also helped the cause of Jainism. When there was a dispute over land between the Jains and the Śaivas it was settled in favour of the Jains during the time of Devarāya. The latter ordered the building of a Caityālaya dedicated to Pārśvanātha in the capital itself in AD 1426. Bhīmā Devī, queen of Devarāya I, was a follower of the Jain teacher Paṇḍitācārya and installed an image of Śāntinātha in the Mangayi-basti. It was during the reign of Devarāya II that the temple of Pārśvanātha at Kunrai or Kunrattur came into existence. Sāḷuva Narasiṃha revived worship in Jain temples at Paṇappaḍi and Poṇparappa which had suffered during the Orissan invasions. Kṛṣṇadevarāya remitted taxes on the lands belonging to the Buddhist and Jain temples in Padaiviḍu and Candragiri, made land grant to a temple at Jina Kāñcī and ordered in AD 1515 that the lands belonging to the Neminātha-basti at Varāṅga which had been granted by Devarāya should be cleared of forest and restored to the same basti.

Ministers and generals of the Vijayanagara empire such as Baica Daṇḍeśa and his sons Irugappa, Maṅgappa, and Bukkana were devout Jains who erected temples and caityālayas, made charities and public works. Another distinguished general whose contribution to the spread of Jainism was immense was Mallappa who flourished in the reign of Harihara II. Mangarasa Voḍeya, a provincial governor, made a gift of land to the Jain Gurugala-basti at Bidire. Wealthy merchants and even poor citizens donated for the construction of Caityālayas and Basadis among which the Pārśvanātha-basadi in Camarājanagara, Ādi Parameśvara Caityālaya in Harave, Vijayanātha and Candraprabha basadis of Maleyur, Padmavati-basadi in Hunsur, Candraprabha Caityālaya in Avalinad, Śāntinātha-basadi in Tavanidhi, Sankala-basadi at Huligere, Anantatirtha Caityālaya at Gerasoppe, Candra Jina Mandira and Hosa-basti at Mudabidre, Candranātha-basadi of Basarūru, and Caturmukha-basadi at Karkala, deserve mention. The Padmāvatī-basti record of Humaca refers to distinguished Jain teachers such as Viśālakīrti who attained fame in the court of the Vijayanagara King Virūpākṣa and Vādi Vidyānanda of the sixteenth century who defeated the Śaiva teacher Nandamalli Bhaṭṭa in debate who graced the court of Sāḷuva Devarāya.

V

In this introductory section we have made an attempt to present facts about Jainism and Jain studies. In the beginning we have tried to establish the philosophical standpoint of the Jains by following a comparative method of analysis. But Jainism is not a religion in the Western or Semitic sense of the term, but in the Indian or Eastern sense, which is no more than a way of life that insists on cessation from violence, theft, lies, having possessions, or indulgence in sensual pleasures. It is one of the six daily duties of Jain laymen to show compassion to all living beings and to help the needy. Four kinds of gifts are to be offered to the distressed—food (*āhāra*), protection (*abhaya*), medicine (*auṣadha*), and learning (*śāstra*)—irrespective of faith, caste, or creed. Jain inscriptions refer to the fact that medicine, along with food and learning, was given in the *maṭhas*. In order to serve these purposes the Jains have built numerous *dharmaśālās* and *piñjrāpols*, established hospitals, and built educational institutions and libraries or *granthabhaṇḍāras* in different parts of the country.

Like Buddhism, Jainism does not believe in the authority of the Vedas, but this does not mean that it was anti Vedic. In fact, the Jains apply the term Veda to their sacred texts. They were opposed to the animal-slaughter associated with the Vedic *yajñas*, but used the term *yajña* to denote their own rituals. The concept of Vedic *yajña* changed from time to time. The Buddhist and Jain concept of *yajña* is not basically different from that of Manu who also interpreted the purpose of *yajña* in terms of pious activities. Manu's insistence on *ahiṃsā* or non-violence is expressed in far better and forceful language than that found in the Jain and Buddhist texts. Though Manu criticised Buddhism and Jainism as *nāstiko vedamindakaḥ*, he did not hesitate to assert, in accordance with what has been stated by Pārśvanātha in his own way, *ahiṃsā-satyamasteyaṃ śaucamindriya vigraham, etat samasikam dharmaṃ caturvarṇaih avravinmanuḥ* (X-63). So far as the basic way of life and the basic moral values are concerned, there is not much difference among the Hindus, Buddhists and Jains, as there is no difference between them with regard to religio-philosophical terms and concepts such as those of suffering, liberation, transmigration, and rebirth, metempsychosis, the doctrine of *karman*, and so forth. Jainism received patronage from non-Jain kings and feudatories, ministers and officials. This does not however mean that there were no conflict among different communities. Jains often had conflicts with the Vaiṣṇavas and Śaivas, the cause of which was in most cases was the possession of granted lands.

It is often said that Jainism made its way into the religious life of India having overcome the tremendous pressure of its rival creed Buddhism. But before making such a generalization it should be stressed that early Buddhism, unlike Jainism, was meant for monks and not laymen. It was not until the advent of Mahayanism that Buddhism tried to reach out to the masses. Moreover, in India Buddhism was by nature more philosophical than religious (though outside India it assumed the form of institutionalized religion) and like its own theory of momentariness it was always in a state of flux. Jainism from the beginning was concerned with lay devotees and unlike Buddhism never failed to provide personal law, a civil and criminal code, for its adherents. The royal patronage which Jainism received, even from non-Jain rulers during the ancient and medieval periods, in different parts of the country, especially in Karnataka, Gujarat, and Rajasthan, has undoubtedly helped the Jain community in its survival. Second, since the Jains mostly belong to the commercial class, their economic influence in society could not be ignored, even by rulers hostile to their creed. Third, after the Muslim conquest, the Jains earned the goodwill of the Hindus, and the latter that of the former, and this evidently added new strength to the community. And last, thanks to the rigid conservatism of the Jains, their important religious doctrines have remained unaltered to this day and the excellent organization of the community and the strict disciplinary measures have become the strongest safeguard of the Jains. The lay part of the community was not regarded as outsiders as had been the case in early Buddhism. Their position was, from the very beginning, well defined by religious duties and privileges. The close union between laymen and monks brought about by the similarity of their religious duties, differing not in kind but in degree, has enabled Jainism to avoid fundamental change within.

A

Abalwadi: Findspot of Jain inscription of AD 1131 in Mandya taluk of the Mandya district, Karnataka, which records the construction of a Jina temple by one Mallinātha belonging to Mūla-saṅgha, Deśīya-gaṇa and Pustake-gacca. *Epigraphia Carnatica*, III, Mandya 50; *Jaina Śilālekha Saṃgraha*, II. 297.

Ābhānagarī: Modern Abaneri in the Jaipur district of Rajasthan, situated near Bandiquin railway station which contains temples of Ṛṣabhanātha and Mahāvīra.

Abhayadeva: Jain poet who was the author of *Jayantavijaya* in nineteen cantos, composed in VS 1278 (AD 1221). He received the title Vādisiṃha from the king of Kāśī. *Jayantavijaya*, ed. Bhavadatta and K. Parab, Bombay, 1902.

Abhayadeva Suri: Jain author, a pupil of Jineśvara, famous for his commentaries on the nine Aṅgas (q.v.), flourished in the eleventh century. He was also a great logician and has been described as the lion that roared at ease in the wild forest of work on logic. His *Vedamahārṇava* is not, however, extant. His commentary on Siddhasena Divākara's (q.v) *Sammatitarkasūtra* is known as *Tattvabodhinī*. Among his other works mention may be made of *Jayati-huyana-stotra* and a commentary on *Navatattvaprakaraṇa* of Jinacandra. *Tattvabodhinī* was published in Yasovijaya Series No. 13. *Jayati-huyana-stotra* edited with a Sanskrit commentary was published in Ahmedabad in 1890.

***Abhidhānacintāmaṇi*:** See Hemacandra.

Abhijāti: Ājīvika conception of the six classes of mankind, which has evidently some bearing on the Jain classification of beings and the Jain conception of *leśyā* (q.v.). The grouping is made on a supposed attribution of colour to different classes of beings. The highest or milkwhite group contains the followers of Gośāla and his two predecessors. Below this is the category of white, which contains other groups of the Ājīvikas. Below this is green to which belong the Acelakas (q.v.). Below this is red consisting of the Nirgranthas (q.v.) wearing a single garment. Then comes blue in which category belong the Bhikṣus (q.v.) who live as thieves and also believers in *karma* (q.v.). The lowest class is black and contains thieves, hunters, and others who live by violence.

Abhinandana: The fourth Tīrthaṃkara whose parents were Sambara and Siddhārthā of Vinitā. His height was 350 bow-lengths and span of life 5,000 thousand years. Vijranābha and Ajitā were his chief disciples. His emblem is an ape and tree connected with his attainment of supreme knowledge *piyāla* or *veśāli*. His Yakṣa is named Īśvara and Yakṣiṇī Kālī. Not many sculptures of Abhinandana have been found. An inscribed image has been found at Khajuraho. Names of his attendant Yakṣas and Yakṣiṇīs have Śaivite affiliations. According to the *Abhidhāna-cintāmaṇi* he acquired the name Abhinandana because he was honoured by Indra and others.

Abhinava Pampa: See Nāgacandra.

Abhyākhyāna: See Pāpa.

Abhyantara Tapa: Internal austerities meant for *nirjarā* (q.v.) or purging of the *karmas*. They consist of *prāyaścitta*, expiation; *vinaya*, reverence; *vaiyāvṛtya*, service of the saints or worthy persons; *svādhyāya*, study; *vyutsanga*, giving up attachment to the body, etc.; and *dhyāna*, concentration of mind.

Ablūr: Jain temple site in the Dharwar district of Karnataka. An inscription dated *c.* AD 1200 refers to the destruction of this temple by Ekāntada Rāmāyya. *Epigraphia Indica*, V.237ff.

Abu Inscriptions: A good number of Jain epigraphs of the medieval period from the Abu area of Rajasthan are known. The five temples here, the Vimala-vasati, the Lūṇa-vasati, Pittal-hara temple, Caturmukha or Kharatara-vasati, and the Mahāvīra-svāmin temple contain numerous inscriptions which give detailed and dated information pertaining to the founding of these temples, renovations, additional structures, and images. One of them, belonging to AD 1322 (during the time of Tejasiṃha and Tihaṇa of the Cāhamāna dynasty), records the repair of the Ṛṣabha temple by Lalla and Vijaḍa and consecrated by Muni Jinacandra of the spiritual lineage of Dharmaghoṣa who is mentioned in numerous epigraphs from Abu. Two other inscriptions belonging to AD 1468 mention the famous saint Lakṣmīsāgara of Tapā-gaccha in connection with Duṅgarasiṃha or Duṅgarapura. Several other inscriptions from Abu of the fifteenth century mention the monks of Tapā-gaccha. The Kharatara Ācārya Jinaharṣa is mentioned in an inscription dated vs 1523. An earlier inscription incised on a brass image of Ādinātha, dated vs 1518, refers to the celebrated King Kumbha. The saint Lakṣmīsāgara and the Duṅgarapura chief Somadāsa are mentioned in a Śāntinātha image inscription from Abu. *Epigraphia Indica*, II, Nos. 132ff.

***Ābu-Rāsa*:** Composed in Gujarati in AD 1233 by Palhana it commemorates the erection of a temple of Neminātha on Mount Abu by Tejahpala, the famous minister of Viradhavala.

Abu Temple Complex: Better known as Dilwara (q.v.) group, the majority of the temples on Mount Abu were erected before AD 1300. Among these, the Vimala-vasahī and Lūṇa-vasahī, established respectively in AD 1021 and 1230, are acclaimed as fine examples of Jain workmanship. The artistic norms set by the Dilwara group of temples were more or less active throughout the medieval age in western Indian Jain temples. Among other important temples of Dilwara group, the Pittalhara (q.v.) temples constructed by Bhīma Shah in the fourteenth century and dedicated to Ṛṣabhanātha deserves special mention. Besides there are the Caturmukha or Kharatara-vasati and Mahāvīra-svāmin temple. These temples contain informative inscriptions as well. See Dilwara images, Dilwara Temples.

Acalagaḍh: Place of pilgrimage on Mount Arbuda, which contains temples of Ṛṣabhanātha, Kunthunātha, and Śāntinātha.

Ācāra Dinakara: See Vardhamāna Sūri.

***Ācārāṅga Sūtra*:** The first text of the Aṅga (q.v.) category. Original Prakrit name *Āyāraṅga-sutta*. In two lengthy sections (*śruta-skandhas*) it describes the way of life of a monk. The names of the nine chapters (*adhyayana*) of the first *śrutakandha* are as follows—Śāstraparijñā, Lokavijaya, Sitoṣṇīya, Samvyaktva, Lokasāra, Dhūta, Mahāparijñā (now extinct), Vimokṣa, and Upadhāna. The second section contains five *cūlās* (*cūlikās*), the first two of which contain seven chapters each and the third and fourth, one each. The fifth called *Niśītha* is now a separate treatise. While in the first section there is a distinct emphasis on *ahiṃsā*, treated in a variety of contexts, the second section is of the nature of appendices. The first two *cūlās* deal with the rules for begging and wandering and the daily life of monks and nuns. The third contains materials for a biography of Mahāvīra, which have been utilized in Bhadrabāhu's *Kalpasūtra*. On the *Ācārāṅga* there is a *Niryukti* by Bhadrabāhu, a *Cūrṇi* by Jinadāsagaṇi (Ratlam 1944) and a *Vṛtti* or *Ṭīkā* by Śīlāṅka (Āgamodaya Samiti, 1935). Ed. H. Jacobi, Pali Text Society, London, 1882 and trans. by the same in Sacred Books of the East Series, XXII, Oxford, 1884; Part I, ed. W. Schubring, Leipzig, 1910; German trans. by the same in *Worte Mahāvīras*, Gottingen, 1926; ed. Jain Sāhitya Saṃśodhaka Samiti, Poona, 1924; ed. Muni Jinavijaya, Bombay, 1977.

***Ācāravṛtti*:** See Mūlasūtra, Vaṭṭakera.

Ācārya: Teacher or *guru* who is the head of *gaṇa*, vastly learned, well disciplined and master of *ācāra*, *darśana*, *cāritra*, *tapa*, *jñāna*, and *vīrya*. He has the privilege of initiating pupils. There are various kinds of Ācāryas, all with heavy responsibility to guide monks and nuns in their daily duties. They should at least have eight years experience of monkhood.

Ācārya Parameṣṭhins: Objects of Jain worship who, though belong to the group of the *parameṣṭhins* (q.v.), do not represent the stage of complete liberation. They must be free from attachment to external things; must show sympathy and love to all living beings; must be actuated by the three jewels; must illustrate by their conduct the significance of the five great vows; must be able to exercise authority of initiating; must possess knowledge as to the nature of reality; and must whole-heartedly devote themselves to the propagation of religion.

Acetana Dravyas: The *dravyas* (q.v.), which belong to the non-living or *ajīva* (q.v.) category and comprise *pudgala*, *dharma*, *adharma*, *ākāśa*, and *kāla* (q.v.). These are insentient.

Achalgarh: A site on Mount Abu (24° 45' N, 72° 42' E) at the height of 4,668 feet. It contains a decorated Jain temple made of white marble. It is *caturmukha* shrine erected in AD 1509 and contains a large bronze image of Ādīnatha. It was made by *sūtradhara* Haridāsa, son of *sūtradhara* Arbuda.

Acyutā: Śāsanadevatā (q.v.) of Padmaprabha (q.v) who is also known as Śyāmā and, according to the Digambaras, Manovegā. Acyutā is represented riding a man and holding her hands in *varada* and *abhaya* poses, and holding a flute and a bow. Manovegā has a horse as her vehicle and holds a sword, lance, fruit and *varada* pose. Acyutā is also the name of Balā, the Śāsanadevatā of Kunthunātha (q.v.). Acyutā is also a Vidyādevī and in this conception she rides a horse and holds a bow, a sword, a shield, and an arrow.

Āḍaki: A Jain centre in Gulbarga district, which has yielded a few Digambara epigraphs of the twelfth century. The Koppa Jinālaya of this place is dedicated to Pārśvanātha. The eminent Jain philosophers Guṇavīra Siddhāntadeva and Nemicandra Siddhāntadeva flourished in Āḍaki.

Adattadāna: See Pāpa.

Adbhudji: Jain temple at Nagda in Rajasthan which is reduced now to its *garbhagṛha* and attached *antarāla* with tall faceted pillars. It contains a colossal image of Śāntinātha set up in AD 1437 during the reign of Kumbha by a merchant named Sāraṅga. Two other Tīrthaṃkara images are also found here, supposed to be of Kunthunātha and Abhinandana.

Ādhāna: See Garbhādhāna.

Adharma: The necessary counterpart of *dharma* (q.v.) and one of the five constituents of Ajīva (q.v.). It pervades the whole universe and serves as a medium of rest, 'like the shade of a tree helping the wayfarer to stop for rest'. Like *dharma*, it is a non-physical inactive condition of rest conceived as a real substance. Without the complementary principles of *dharma* and *adharma*, there would be no definite structure of the world. The cosmos disintigrates into primordial atoms, which might spread throughout infinite space. Like *dharma*, *adharma* has three divisions—*skandha* (whole), *deśa* (part) and *pradeśa* (portion of a part) and as a condition of rest it is passive. *Adharma*, here, should not be confused with unrighteousness. *Tattvārtha*, V.17-18.

***Adhyagnikṛta*:** A form of *strīdhana* (q.v.) or women's property according to which is given in the presence of the sacred fire to the bride at the time of her marriage.

***Adhyātmaparīkṣā*:** See Yaśovijaya.

***Adhyātmāṣṭaka*:** Philosophical hymn composed by Vādiraja II, pub. in Manikacandra Digambara Jaina Granthamala Series, No.13.

***Adhyātmataraṅgiṇī*:** Composed by Somadeva in the tenth century, it is also known as *Yogamārga*. It deals with methods of spiritual attainment. A commentary on it was written in the first half of the twelfth century by Gaṇadharakīrti. The text of this work is included in *Tattvānuśāsanādisaṃgraha* published in the Manikacandra Digambara Jaina Granthamala Series, No.13, Bombay, 1917.

Adhyāhavanika: A form of *strīdhana* (q.v.) or women's property denoting what the bride brings from her father's house.

Ādinātha: See Ṛṣabhanātha.

Ādinātha-basti: A small shrine dedicated to Ādinātha, which is situated at Basti-halli in Hasan district, Karnataka. Lakshneswar in western Karnataka which was a very important centre of southern Jainism has also an Ādinātha-basti. It is a degenerate version of the Later Cālukya type and is placed in the middle of the late twelfth century. The interior shows an axial layout of the *garbhagṛha* carrying a standing figure of Ādinātha, with side chambers in *trikūṭa* form carrying two Jina images.

***Ādinātha Carita*:** See Vardhamāna Suri.

Ādinātha Temples: There is no dearth of Ādinātha temples in India. The one at Khajuraho is important from a historical point of view: here only the *garbhagṛha* and *antarāla* survive with their roofs while the *maṇḍapa* and *ardhamaṇḍapa* are completely lost and are replaced by a modern entrance chamber. The temple is *saptaratha* on plan as well as in elevation, and each of its *bhadras* shows an additional *nāsikā* or projection. The *jaṅghā* shows three rows of sculptures. The two lower rows contain figures of gods and goddesses alternating with Apsaras on projections and *vyālas* in recesses, while the top row has figures of Vidyādharas on projections and Vidyādhara-mithunas in recesses. The temple enshrines a modern image of Ādinātha in place of the old one, of which only the pedestal survives. The old temple of Ādinātha at Śatruñjaya was replaced by a new one at Śatruñjaya in AD 1155-7. In the beginning of the thirteenth century Vastupāla, minister of the Vāghelas, erected an Ādinātha temple at Dholaka. His brother Tejaḥpāla also had built an Ādinātha temple at Prabhāsa. The Ādinātha temple of Nadlai may also be referred to in this connection. Within the Jaisalmer fort, a temple of Ādinātha was erected in AD 1480. During the reign of Kumbha and his immediate successors a number of Jain temples were constructed at Chittor and among them was the Ādinātha temple standing near the *Kīrti-stambha*. An excellent example of the *caumukha* type may be seen in the Ādinātha or Ādīśvara or Yugādīśvara temple at Ranakpur in Mewar. An inscription records that in 1439 an architect named Depaka constructed this temple, which covers an area of 3,716 metres and consists of 29 halls with as many as 420 pillars.

Ādi Pampa: Also known as Pampa I, he is the most celebrated poet in Kannaḍa who in AD 941 composed the *Ādi Purāṇa* and the *Vikramārjuna-vijaya*, more popularly called *Pampa-Bhārata*. The former of these is a history of the first Tīrthaṃkara, 'the first of the brave heroic souls who have crossed the disturbed and muddy sea of human frailty and misery, and reached the shores of unending indefinable peace'. It tells the story of Ṛṣabha, whose son Bharata gave his name to this country. It is a highly esteemed work not only in the Kannaḍa literature but in the Jain tradition as well.

***Ādi Purāṇa*:** See Ādi Pampa.

***Ādi Purāṇa*:** Composed by Jinasena II (q.v.) in the ninth century in 47 chapters of which the last 5 were written by his disciple Guṇabhadra (q.v.), the *Ādi Purāṇa* contains the story of Ṛṣabha, the first Tīrthaṃkara. In the Brahmanical manner this Purāṇa is at the same time an epic poem and an encyclopaedia. Apart from the facts of the Master's life who is described as the source and spring of all human arts, the arts themselves, such as town-planning, warfare and governance, the characteristics of six seasons, sacraments, consecration, interpretation of dreams, etc., are dealt with in detail. Bhāratīya Jñānapīṭha, 3 vols., Varanasi, 1951-4.

Ādīśvata Temples: See Caturmukha Temples, Rānakpur.

Adoni: Situated in Bellary district, Karnataka, this area has several old Jain settlements. An inscription at Hālaharavi refers to a Jina temple at Nandavara. It is of 933 and mentions a Jain teacher named Padmanandin. It belongs to the time of Rāṣṭrakūṭa Govinda IV. The temple was built by queen Chandiyabbe, wife of Kannara, governor of Sindavadi 1000. *Jaina Śilālekha Saṃgraha*, IV, No. 79; *Annual Report of South Indian Epigraphy*, 1916, App. B.

Adur: An undated stone inscription of the Cālukya King Kīrtivarman I of the second half of the sixth century AD found at this place in Dharwar district, Karnataka, records the grant of a field for the *dānaśālā* of a Jinālaya. It begins with an adoration to Vardhamāna and refers to a line of Jain monks, the earliest of whom was Vinayanandin (here compared to Indrabhūti (q.v.)). The grant was received on behalf of the Jina temple by Prabhācandra. *Indian Antiquary*, XI.68-71.

Āghāṭa: Modern Ahar (q.v.) near the city of Udaipur in Rajasthan which contains a Pārśvanātha temple, constructed in AD 972 and a temple of Mahāvīra.

***Aghaṭakumāra Kathā*:** An important constituent of Jain story literature, extant in three recensions, a longer and a shorter one in verse, and a prose version. The prose version was translated into German by Charlotte Krause, Leipzig, 1922. The shorter metrical version was published by the Nirnaya Sagar Press, Bombay, 1917.

Aghātin Karma: One of the two groups of obstructive *karmas*, which is subdivided into four categories, *vedanīya*, *āyu*, *nāma*, and *gotra* (qq.v.).

Agni: Vedic god regarded as the guardian of south-eastern regions. He is described as riding a ram, holding a spear and bearing seven flames. The Śvetāmbara tradition gives him a bow and arrow, the Digambara a sacrificial pot and rosary as his armlet. His wife is Svāhā.

Agnitā: Name of the goddess Ambikā (q.v.) in her human birth according to the Digambara version of the story of her origin. The wall paintings of the Vardhamāna temple at Tiruparuttikunram or Jaina-Kāñcī illustrate the story of Agnitā and her sons, Śubhaṅkara and Prabhaṅkara.

Agra: Site of Jain shrines which contain collections of medieval images including some in precious stones. Structurally these are ordinary in character and in most cases have retained only a few original features owing to heavy repairs and additions.

Agralapura: Modern Agra which contained as many as 48 Jina temples as is stated in a poem *Agralapura Jinavandana*.

Agranirvṛtti: A stage in the career of the Tīrthaṃkara when he achieves his first deliverance.

Agravāla: Important Jain caste of Uttar Pradesh, Punjab, Rajasthan, and Malwa. It is supposed that the Agravālas are the descendants of King Agrasena of Campāvatī in north India. His 18 sons had founded the city called Agroha in Punjab and established the following *gotras*: Garga, Goila, Gavāla, Batsila, Kasila, Siṃghala, Maṅgala, Bhaddala, Tingala, Airaṇa, Tairaṇa, Thingala, Tittala, Mittala, Tundala, Tayala, Gobhula, and Goina. They have the division of Daśā and Viśā, the 'tens' and the 'twenties' and the new-fangled pañca or 'fives'. The Agarvālas form a mercantile class which is said to have been converted to Jainism by Śrī Lohācārya. The Jain Agravālas maintain matrimonial and social relations with their Hindu Vaiṣṇava counterparts.

Ahar (1): Situated in Tikamgarh in central India, it was a Jain centre patronized by the Candella rulers who constructed here several buildings and ponds. The extant temples were built in the eleventh and succeeding centuries. Apart from the temples of Śāntinātha and other Jinas and Bāhubali, there are several *māna-stambhas*. Inscriptions on the pedestals of images give an account of several branches of the Jains.

Ahar (2): A damaged fragmentary inscription of the time of the Guhila King Allaṭa of the tenth century AD which has been discovered at this place near

Udaipur in Rajasthan, has a Jain character which also pertains to two other undated inscriptions of the Guhila prince Śaktikumāra found here. The Sanskritized name of Ahar is Āghāṭapura. It seems to have been a centre of Jain art during the early medieval period. A bronze image of the same period, now in the Ahar Museum, is more than life-size in height and shows a seated Tīrthaṃkara in a meditative pose.

Ahicchatra: A Kuṣāṇa inscription from Ahicchatra, ancient capital of North Pañcāla, found engraved on a pedestal of the image of Neminātha bearing the date 50 (AD 128) refers to a shrine of Pārśvanātha. Cunningham discovered an inscribed pillar of the Gupta period which mentions Ācārya Indranandin and also refers to the temple of Pārśva. The Jain Kuṣāṇa inscriptions from Ahicchatra refer to such devotees as Gahapalā, Jinadāsī, Rudradeva, Dāttāgālā, Rudra, Grahamitra, Kumārasirī, Vamadāsī, Hastisenā, Grahasiri, Rudradatā, Jayadāsī, Mitrasiri, Dharavalā and Aryadāsī and monks such as Tarika, Pusila and others belonging to *gaṇas* like Koliya, and Vāraṇa, *Kulas* like Sthānīya, Pativāmika, etc., and *śākhās* like Vairā, and Vajanāgarī. Ahicchatra is identified with present-day Ramnagar in the Bareilly district of Uttar Pradesh. Jinaprabha, author of *Vividhatīrthakalpa*, has connected this place with Pārśvanātha and refers to the Jina temples which added glory to this place. *Epigraphia Indica*, X.109ff.

Ahiṃsā: Non-violence, non-injury to living beings, the basic creed of Jainism. *Ahiṃsā* is regarded as the principal vow and the other four vows are considered to be merely details of the first vow. Hiṃsā or violence is defined as injury to beings through passioned activity of mind, speech, and body and *anṛta* or falsehood, *parigraha* or possession, *steya* or theft, and *abrahma* or sexual impurity are expressions of *hiṃsā*, because all indirectly cause injury to others. The giving up of violence may be either complete or partial. The former, accomplished in nine ways, is known as *autsargīkī-nivṛtti* and the latter as *apavādikī-nivṛtti*, meant mainly for householders or lay persons. *Hiṃsā* is of four kinds—*gṛhārambhī* or accidental, that which is unavoidably committed during domestic duties like cooking or washing: *udyamī* or occupational, that which is committed during warfare, agricultural operations, or manufacturing of articles; *virodhī* or protective, that which is unavoidably committed for defending life and property against assailants and enemies; and *saṅkalpī*, that which is committed intentionally, for example, hunting, killing for food, making garments, and so forth. It is enjoined upon the householder to abstain from *saṅkalpi hiṃsā* or intentional violence and not from accidental, occupational protective violence. But ascetics are required to abstain from all four kinds of violence. In their case complete renunciation or *autsargī nivṛtti* is needed and is accomplished in nine ways—by self, through agent or approbation, and in each case through mind, body, and speech.

Aihole Cave: This two-storeyed cave temple of the seventh century in Bijapur district has a pillared quadrangular hall with a cella cut at its far end and chapels on either side. It resembles its sister cave at Badami, which is also of Jain inspiration. It comprises two superposed structural verandahs, each with a façade of four pillars, and two pilasters of square sections and plain curved corbels. In relief, on the upper verandah-ceiling, is a small seated Jina with a triple umbrella over his head. At one end of the same verandah is a long room with three partially rock-cut shrines. The door-frame, leading to the cella behind, of the lower storey is profusely carved with human, animal, and floral designs. The Kannaḍa inscriptions on the pillars and rock outside name persons. The site exhibits other items of interest, some of which are Jain.

Ahmedpur: Situated in the Vidisha district, this place has yielded a Pārśvanātha image standing in *Kāyotsarga* under a serpent canopy.

Aivarmalai: Nine miles from Palni in Madurai district, Tamil Nadu and 1,402 feet above sea-level. On the north-east side of a natural shelter of the hill, which is 160 feet long, we have sixteen Jina images. A number of inscriptions have also been discovered. One of these inscriptions, belonging to the reign of Pāṇḍya Varaguṇa II, dated Śaka 792 (AD 870), registers a gift of 500 *kānam* of gold by Sāntivirakkuravar of Kāḷan for offering in the temple of Pārśvanātha. The donor was a disciple of Guṇavirakkuravaḍigal. *Epigraphia Indica*, XXXII, 337 ff; *South Indian Inscriptions*, XIV, No. 22.

Ajāharā: Place of Jain pilgrimage associated with Pārśvanātha in Jinaprabha's *Vividhatīrthakalpa* which is situated in the Junagarh district near Una railway station. It is also mentioned in the Ranakpur inscription of Kumbha, dated VS 1496.

Ajaigarh: Jain site in the Panna district, Madhya Pradesh, where a remarkable image of Śāntinātha was enshrined in AD 1279 during the reign of the Candella King Vīravarman.

Ajayameru: Modern Ajmer which was closely

associated with the activities of the monks of the Kharatara-gaccha. It is a place of Jain pilgrimage with temples of Ṛṣabha, Pārśva, and Mahāvīra.

Ajayapāla: Caulukya king of Gujarat (AD 1173-5) who was the son of Kumārapāla's (q.v.) brother Mahīpāla and described by Merutuṅga in his *Prabandhacintāmaṇi* as a great enemy of Jainism who destroyed a large number of Jain shrines, which view has also been attested by Rājaśekhara in his *Prabandhakośa.* He did not also hesitate to kill the great Jain scholar Rāmacandra, who was a direct disciple of Hemacandra (q.v.). The fact was that after the death of Kumārapāla, there was a struggle for throne between Kumārapāla's brother's son Ajayapāla and his sister's son Pratāpamalla, and the latter was backed by the Jains. Jain authors such as Yaśaḥpāla and Māṇikyacandra, however, had taken a lenient view of him. Ajayapāla lost his life at the hands of the Pratihāra Vayajaladeva in *circa* AD 1176.

Ajayarāja: Śākambharī Cāhamāna ruler of Rajasthan, a devout Śaiva, had deep respect for Jainism. From the *Kharataragacchapaṭṭāvali* of Jinapāla it is learnt that he had permitted the Jains to build temples in the newly founded city of Ajayameru or Ajmer and that he had presented a golden *kalaśa* to the temple of Pārśvanātha. He acted as a judge in the religious discussion between the Śvetāmbara saint Dharmaghoṣasuri and his Digambara opponent Guṇacandra.

Ajitā: Also known as Rohiṇī, she is the Śāsanadevatā (q.v.) of Ajitanātha (q.v.). Her seat is of iron (*lohāsana*). The *Ācāradinakara* makes her vehicle a bull. In the Śvetāmbara tradition she holds *varada* pose, and a noose, citron and goad. The Digambara tradition retains the first and substitutes others with *abhaya* pose, conch, and disc.

Ajita Keśakambalin: Materialist philosopher who was a contemporary of Mahāvīra. His views were a combination of the Sāyavādins or sensualists, the Samucchedavādins or annihilationists, and the Na-santi-Paralokavādins or disbelievers in existence (discussed in the *Sūyagaḍa*, *Uttarādhyayana* and other Jain texts). These doctrines and their Buddhist counterparts, the Ucchedavāda or Diṭṭhadhammanibbānavāda, speculate on what remains after the extermination of the mortal body. According to Ajita, perfection is wisdom and conduct, claimed by certain recluses and philosophers of his times appeared to him only stupid self-deception. 'It is a doctrine of fools, this talks of gifts. It is an empty lie, mere idle talk, when men say there is profit therein'. For everything led to death and beyond death there was nothing. Ajita, like the later Cārvākas or Lokāyatas, believed that the human body was made of four elements. When one dies the earthly element goes to the earth, the fluid to water, the heat to the fire, the wind to the air, and the faculties to space. According to him, there are in the world no recluses or wise men who have reached the highest point, who walk perfectly and who having understood and realized by themselves alone, both this world and the next, make their wisdom known to others. His views have been summarized in *Sāmannaphala Sutta* of the Buddhist *Dīgha Nikāya*.

Ajitanātha: The second Tīrthaṃkara (q.v.) who hailed from Kosala, a son of Jitaśatru of Ayodhya. His mother's name was Vijayā. His height was 50 bow-lengths and he lived for 7,200 thousand years. Sihasena and Phaggu were his first disciples. His demise was on the summit of the Sammeya or Pareshnath Hill. The Jain texts give him the elephant and *saptaparṇa* tree as symbols. His attendant Yakṣa and Yakṣiṇī are Mahāyakṣa and Ajitabalā. He stands in *Khaḍgāsana*, his two arms hanging on the sides. His *chowri*-bearer is Sāgaracakrī. According to the Jain Purāṇas, his elephant symbol is due to the fact that when he was in his mother's womb, she had several dreams of an elephant. After his birth all his father's enemies were conquered (*jita*), hence his name 'the invincible one'. The *Uttara-Purāṇa* explains the word 'Ajita' as 'not conquered by sin or heresies'. In Nandisena's *Ajiyasāntithaya*, Ajita and Śāntinātha are glorified together, because, according to the legend, both of them spent a rainy season in the caverns of the Śatruñjaya mountain. Ajita is also glorified in the works of Jinavallabha, Vīragaṇin, and Jayaśekhara. A noteworthy figure of Ajita in the Deogarh Fort (q.v.) shows him standing in *Khaḍgāsana* and attended by two *chowrie*-bearers and two devotees. The elephant emblem is shown under his seat. The Yakṣa and Yakṣiṇī occupy the two corners of the pedestal. The Ajitanātha temple at Taranga, the largest construction of Kumārapāla, was built in AD 1165.

***Ajitaprabha*:** Pupil of Vīraprabha, he wrote an epic under the title *Śāntinātha-caritra*, ed. Muni Indravijaya, Bib. Ind., Calcutta, 1909.

***Ajita-Śanti-Stava*:** Hymns dedicated to the second Tīrthaṃkara Ajitanātha and the sixteenth Śāntinātha. Among them, Nandisena's Prakrit poem *Ajiyaśātithaya*, composed before the ninth century, stands unique. The two Tīrthaṃkaras are also glorified by the very erudite Jinavallabha, who died in 1110, in the *Ullāsikkamathaya* (also called *Ajita-Śānti-Laghustavana*), by Vīra Gaṇin in *Ajiyaśāntithaya* (in Prakrit), and by Jayaśekhara in *Ajita-Śānti-Stava* (in Sanskrit). As late as the sixteenth century Śānticandra Gaṇin imitated Nandiṣena in his *Ṛṣabha-Stava* and *Ajita-Śānti-Stava*.

Ajita Yakṣa: Attendant Yakṣa of Suvidhinātha or Puṣpadanta (qq.v.) whose vehicle is the tortoise. The Śvetāmbara image holds in his hands the citron, rosary, mongoose, and spear and the Digambara the spear, *varada-mudrā*, fruit, and rosary.

Ajīva: Non-living entities, objects responding to the sense-organs. They are classified into *rūpa* (those with form, as *pudgala* or matter and *arūpa* (those without form as a *dharma*, *adharma*, *ākāśa*, and *kāla*). These five categories constitute the world of *loka*; beyond lies the immeasurable infinite, *aloka*. Space or *ākāśa* (q.v.) is divided into *lokākāśa* (part occupied by world of things) and *alokākāśa* (space beyond it which is absolutely void and empty). But for motion and rest, things hanging in space would lead to chaos, as space by itself is not a condition of movement. Motion and rest are conceived of in terms of *dharma* and *adharma* (qq.v.), the laws by which things are found to produce a cosmos. Both are devoid of sense-qualities, non-corporeal and co-extensive with *lokākāśa*. The successive movements of the world are strung on time or *kāla*. A distinction is made between eternal time and relative time, the latter being determined by change and motion in things. Matter or *pudgala* (q.v.), are figured objects existing in six different forms and different degrees of fineness and visibility and assimilating the qualities of touch, smell, colour, and sound. Everything in the world except the *ākāśa* is produced from matter. Physical objects apprehended by the senses consist of atoms or *paramāṇus*. This reminds us of the Nyāya-Vaiśeṣika theory, but while the latter holds that there are as many kinds of atoms as there are elements, the Jains think that the homogeneous atoms produce different elements by varying combinations.

Ājīvikas: A religious community that arose at about the time when Mahāvīra and Buddha began to preach their messages. This order, established possibly by Nanda Vaccha and headed by Kisa Samkiccha after him, acquired dynamic energy under the third pontiff Gośāla Maṅkhaliputta (q.v.). Two other contemporaries of Buddha and Mahāvīra, namely Puraṇa Kassapa (q.v.) and Pakudha Kaccāyana (q.v.), seem to have belonged to the Ājīvika creed. The first Ājīvika whom Buddha met immediately after his enlightenment was Upaka. The Pali texts also mention one Pāṇḍuputta as an exponent of Ājīvikism, which seems to have existed as a religio-philosophical system long before the days of Mahāvīra and Buddha. The *Bhagavatī Sūtra* refers to Gośāla as the eighth Ājīvika teacher and his predecessors were Udai Kuṇḍiyāna, Enejja, Mallarāma, Maṇḍiya, Roha, Bhāradvāja, and Ajjuna Goyāmaputta. Udai was associated with Rājagṛha, Enjja with the town of Uddaṇḍapura, Mallarama with Campā, Maṇḍiya with Vārāṇasī, Roha with Alabhiya, Bhāradvāja and Ajjuna with Śrāvastī. The association of Purana and Pakudha with Ajivikism is attested to by the Tamil text *Nīlakeci*. In several places of the Jain canon we find references to Ājīvika devotees and doctrines. In the *Upāsakadaśā* we have one Saddalaputta who was a lay devotee of Gośāla. Another lay devotee called Ayampula is mentioned in the *Bhagavatī*. The cult spread at one time from Avantī to Aṅga. The Ājīvikas enjoyed the patronage of Aśoka and his grandson Daśaratha, both of whom dedicated caves to them. The sect is referred to by Patañjali (*c*.150 BC), in the *Milindapañho* and in the *Arthaśāstra* of Kauṭilya. The *Mahāvaṃsa* informs us that the Ājīvikas could be seen in Sri Lanka during the reign of Pāṇḍukābhaya. There are references to the Ājīvikas in Tamil Saṅgam literature. In a fifth-century inscription from Nellore of the reign of Siṃhavarman Pallava, there is a reference to the Ājīvikas. Varāhamihira and his commentator Utpala knew them. They are also mentioned in Bāṇa's *Harṣacarita* and Kumāradāsa's *Jānakīharaṇa*. In the south Indian epigraphical records they are often confused with the Buddhists and Jains. The sect became extinct in the fourteenth century AD.

Ājīvikism: Although the association of Gośāla and Mahāvīra was not permanent, it is clear from the Buddhist and Jain texts that early Jainism owed something to the doctrines preached by Gośāla (q.v.). The frequent confusion of the terms *nirgrantha* and *ājīvika* in the Buddhist texts points in the same direction. The general outcome of Ājīvikism is the doctrine of *niyati* or fate, which has nothing to do with Jainism. But so far as the particulars are concerned, Jainism and Ājīvikism have many points in common. For example, the Ājīvika conception of *abhijāti* (q.v.)

or six classes of mankind, has evidently some bearing on the Jain classification and conception *laśyā* (q.v.). The expression *sabbe sattā sabbe panā sabbe bhūtā sabbe jīvā* is common to both Gośāla and the Jains. In the *Sāmaññaphala-sutta* of the Buddhist *Dīgha Nikāya* and Buddhaghoṣa's *Sumaṅgalavilāsinī* (a commentary), in the *Aṅguttara Nikāya* and in the Jain *Bhagavatī Sūtra*, we come across Ājīvika concepts such as *yoni-pamukha*, womb or birth; *karma*, their number and classification; *patipadā*, paths; *antarakappa*, ages of the world; *abhijāti*, classes of men; *puriṣabhūmi*, stages of human existence; *manda*, stupid stage; *khiddā*, pleasure; *vīmaṃsā*, investigation; *ujjugata*, upright walking; *sekha*, learning; *samana*, monkhood; *jina*, enlightenment; *pañña*, the stage of highest cognition; *ajīva*, non-sentient; *paribbājaka*, wandering ascetics; *nāgavāsa*, the region of serpents; *indriya*, senses, 2,000 in number; *niraya*, purgatories, *rajo-dhātu*, cf. *rajas* of the Sāṅkhya; *sanni-gabbha*, types of unconscious birth as camel, ox, etc., *asanni-gabba*, types of unconscious birth, such as rice, barley, etc.; *nigaṇṭhi-gabbha*, types of birth from knots (sugar cane, bamboo, reed); *deva*, gods of seven classes; *mānuṣa*, human being or souls; *pesāca*, goblins; *sara*, lakes, *patuvā*, expertise; *papāta*, precipices; *supina* dream; and *mahākappa*, great aeons. A few other Ājīvika categories are found in the *Bhagavatī*, including the four *pāṇagāim* and four *apāṇagāim* rules of conduct of the ascetic in his last penance, eight *carimaim* or finalities and six *anaikkamaṇijjāim* or inevitables (*lābha* gain, *abhāva* loss, *suhka* joy, *dukkha* sorrow, *jiviya* life and *maraṇa* death). The Ājīvikas believed in the existence of seven elemental categories—earth, water, fire, air, joy, sorrow, and life (cf. Pakudha Kaccāyana, q.v.). These are unmanufactured and barren, neither moving nor developing, nor affecting one another. The southern Ājīvikas developed a theory of atomism which is indicated by the *Maṇimekalai*, *Nīlakaci* and *Civaññāṇa-cittiyar*. The atoms move and combine and may come together densely or loosely to form things of different kinds. The combination of atoms occurs in fixed ratios. The soul, pleasure, and pain are conceived in terms of atomic combinations. The conception of the soul's size and colour, which characterizes Ājīvikism, has also something to do with the Jain conception of soul. From the Jain sources it is also learnt that the Ājīvikas have their own epistemology and logic which had much in common with those pertaining to Jainism.

Ajjanandi: A notable Jain preacher in south India whose name is mentioned in short inscriptions found at Villimalai in Chitoor district of Andhra Pradesh and at Anaimalai, Alagarmalai, Karungalakkuḍi, and Uttamapaliyam in Madurai district. His name is also found in a cavern at Eruvāḍi in Tinnevelly district and near Chitaral in Kerala. Ajjanandi has been placed around AD 800. In an epigraph found in Pechcchi Pallam in Madurai taluk of Madurai district his mother Gunamatiyār is mentioned. His image is also found in one of the epigraphs of Kongar Puliyagulam. Ajjanandi was a native of Madura and his preceptor was Bālacandra according to the said Vallimalai inscription. *South Indian Inscriptions*, XIV, Nos. 107ff.

Ajmer: A Jain centre during the time of the Cāhamānas of Śākambharī. Ajmer is a corruption of Ajayameru, named after Ajayarāja, son of Pṛthvīrāja I Cāhamāna, who not only decked this city with Jain temples but also donated a golden pitcher to the Pārśvanātha shrine there. Subsequent rulers Arṇorāja and Vigraharāja IV were devout Jains. The latter not only raised a Jain *maṭha* in his capital but also prohibited the slaughter of animals on certain days. Pṛthvīrāja II and III were patrons of Jainism. But after the Turkish conquest the excellent Cāhamāna temples of Ajmer were lost.

Ajmer Museum Inscription: See Vidagdha.

Ajñānavāda: One of the four major philosophical schools current in the days of Mahāvīra according to Jain texts which refer to its 67 varieties. The Ajñānavādins of the Jain texts were sceptics or agnostics who refused to give categorical answers to questions. Mahāvīra's expression Annaniya or Ajñānika evidently refers to Sañjaya Balaṭṭhiputta (q.v.) and his school, *Sūyagaḍa*, I.6.27; II.2.79; XII.1.2; *Uttarādhyayana*, XVIII.3. This school corresponds to the Amarāvikkhepikas or evasive disputants of the Buddhist texts: according to Mahāvīra, the Ajñānavādins pretend to be intelligent, but in reality do not know the truth. As teachers they mislead their pupils, because they are unfamiliar with it and have not got rid of perplexity and contradictions: *annāniyā le kusalāvi saṃtā, asaṃthnyā no vitigicchatiṇṇā; akoviyā āhu akoviyehim, ananuvi-ittu musam vayaṃti—Sūyagaḍa*, I.12.2.

Akalaṅka: Great logician of the eighth century. Prabhācandra (q.v.) in his *Kathākośa* says that he was the son of the minister of the king Śubhatuṅga. Later writers refer to his debating skills and victory over the Buddhists. He was known to both Haribhadra (q.v.) and Jinasena I (q.v.). His *Tattvārtharājavārttika* is a commentary on the *Tattvārthādhigama* (q.v.) of Umāsvāmin (q.v.) and *Aṣṭaśatī* or the *Āptamīmāṃsā* (q.v.) of Samantabhadra (q.v.). The logical treatises composed by Akalaṅka are *Nyāyaviniścaya*, *Laghiyastraya*, and *Svarūpasambodhana*. His views were opposed by Kumārila belonging to the Bhāṭṭa school of the Mīmāṃsakas and defended by Vidyānanda (q.v.) and Prabhācandra. A treatise on expiatory rites, *Prāyaścittagrantha* or *Prāyaścittavidhi* is attributed to Akalaṅka, but his authorship of this work is doubtful. The *Pramāṇasaṃgraha*, a work on logic in 87 *kārikās* and another work called *Siddhiviniścaya* are also attributed to him. The *Tattvārtharājavārttika* was published in Sanātana Jaina Granthamālā, Varanasi, 1915 and *Aṣṭaśatī* with *Āptamīmāṃsā* itself an Sanātana Jaina Granthamālā 1914; *Laghīyastraya* and *Svarūpasambodhana*, ed. in Manikcandra Digambara Granthamala Series No.1. For *Nayāyaviniścaya* see *Jinarathnakośa*, 221; *Prāyaścitta* together with other three treatises on the same subject are edited in *Prāyaścittasaṃgraha*, Manikcandra Series No. 18; *Prmāṇasaṃgraha* is published in Sanātana Jaina Granthamālā, Ahmedabad, 1939. For *Siddhiviniścaya* see *Jinarathnakośa*, 441.

Ākāśa: That which gives space and makes room for the existence of all extended substance. It is one of the five constituents of Ajīva (q.v.), nonmaterial and infinite. If a lamp is lit it is the space of *ākāśa* that makes room for its beams to shine. Likewise a wall may be the *ākāśa* for a nail to be knocked in, water may be the *ākāśa* for sugar to melt, and so on. *Ākāśa* is divided into *skandha* (whole), *deśa* (part) and *pradeśa* (portion of a part) and is of two kinds—*lokākāśa* or space containing the world where the *jīvas* and other substances live, and *alokākāśa* which is the space beyond. Although imperceptible, the existence of *ākāśa* is inferred on the grounds that without space substances cannot be extended. Since substances are those that occupy and pervade (Guṇaratna on *Ṣaḍdarśanasamuccya* 49) they require space as a necessary condition. It is the nature of space to give room to any amount of atoms, but this applies only to the *lokākāśa*, the other part of the space being void. It is also to be observed that space is definitely singular while Jīvas (q.v.) and matter are of infinite variety. See cosmography.

***Ākhyānamaṇikośa*:** See Nemicandrasūri.

Akkaṇṇa-Basti: The only temple in true Hoysala style at Sravanabelgola (q.v.). It has the full complement of *garbhagṛha*, *ardha-maṇḍapa*, *navaraṅga* and front-porch with side parapets and *kakṣāsana*. The sanctum has a Pārśvanātha image 1.5 metre high. The *ardha-maṇḍapa* carries the images of his Yakṣa and Yakṣiṇī. The outer wall is plain. So is the tower which is of the *arpita* class of storeyed divisions with square *śikhara* and *stūpi*. The temple was erected in AD 1181 by a Jain woman, Aeiyakka, wife of Candramauli, a minister of Ballāla II.

Akota Hoard: Sixty-eight Jain bronzes found at Akota near Baroda which are datable from the late fifth to the eleventh century. They represent figures of the Jinas. Particular interest attaches to the wonderfully executed bronze image of Ṛṣabhanātha, assigned *c.* AD 450, and the images of Ajitanātha, Pārśvanātha, Jīvantasvāmin, Sarasvatī, and Acchuptā, there are *yakṣas* and *yakṣis*, including Ambikā. The Jina figures are depicted either standing or seated, flanked by Sarvānubhūti Yakṣa and Ambikā Yakṣī. Thirty of the sixty-eight bronzes are inscribed and two of them provide definite dates, Śaka year 691 and vs 1006. Not less than twenty-eight images are assignable to AD 700.

Akriyāvāda: One of the four major philosophical schools current in the days of Mahāvīra according to the Jain texts, which refer to its 84 varieties. Akriyāvāda is the doctrine of non-action, which is virtually opposed to Kriyāvāda (q.v.). As Sudharman, the chief disciple of Mahāvīra, expounds his master's view, the Akriyāvādins teach the annihilation of good actions by denying *karma* its potential in future existence. *Suyagaḍa* I.12.4. Mahāvīra has mentioned Akriyāvādins who are Ekkavādins or monists, theists and monotheists; Anikkavādins or pluralists; Samucchedavādins or annihilationists corresponding to the Buddhist Ucchedavādins; Niyavādins or eternalists corresponding to the Buddhist Śāśvatavādins; Na-śantiparalokavādins or disbelievers in existence of the other world like the Cārvākas or Lokāyatas; and Sāyavādins or sensualists. *Ṭhāṇāṅga* IV.4. Śīlāṅka in his *Ācārāṅgaṭīkā*, ed. Dhanapati 14, mentions six types of Akriyāvādins: the upholders of the doctrines of *kāla*, *īśvara*, *ātman*, *niyati*, *svabhāva* and *yadṛcchā* as the First Principles. This list is based on one described in the *Śvetāśvatara Upaniṣad*, I.2; VI.1ff; cf. *Maitrāyaṇī* VI.14ff; VII.8ff. *Māṇḍūkyakārika*, I.7-9; II.30-8. The philosophical doctrines of a good number of contemporaries of Mahāvīra—such as those of Purana Kassapa, Pakudha Kaccāyana, Ajita Keśakambalin and Gośāla

Maṅkhaliputta (qq.v.) are in close agreement with the views upheld by the Akriyāvādins.

Akṣayatṛtīyā: Festival held in common with the Hindus. It is held on the third day of the bright half of the month of Vaiśākha. It is held that on this day Ṛṣabhadeva broke his fast of six months with sugar cane juice from the hands of Śreyāṃśa, king of Hastināpura. On this day Ṛṣabha is worshipped and his idol is bathed in sugar cane juice. People gifts in order to secure indestructible merit.

Ālabhiyā: Ancient city to the east of Ayodhyā visited by Mahāvīra.

Alagarmalai: Early Jain centre of second-first century BC in Melur taluk, Madurai district, Tamil Nadu. It is a cave site where Brahmi inscription are found. It is the Irunkunram of early Tamil literature. One of the eighth-ninth century Jain sculptures from Alagarmalai represents the Jain teacher Ajjanandi (q.v.).

Ālahaḷḷi: Situated in the Shimoga district and in the sub-division of the same name, it is the findspot of an inscription bearing the Vikrama Cālukya year 37 which records the construction of a Jina temple by Bācaladevi dedicated to Pārśvanātha and meant for the monks of the Deśi-gaṇa and Mūla-saṅgha. It was entrusted to Subhacandra, disciple of Maladharideva of the Deśi-gaṇa. The builder was the queen of Gaṅga-Permāḍidevas, a feudatory of the Western Cālukya Vikramāditya VI. *Epigraphia Carnatica*, VII. Shim. No. 97.

Ālambhika: A place frequented by Mahāvīra between Śrāvastī and Rājagṛha.

Alaṅkāramahodadhi: Written by Narendraprabhasūri at the request of Vastupāla in the thirteenth century it is a work of poetics in eight chapters containing also a commentary of the author himself.

Ālapapaddhati: See Devasena.

Ālavi: See Ālambhika.

Alesandra: Findspot of a Jain inscription of AD 1183 in Nagamangala taluk, Karnataka, which records the erection of a Pārśva temple at Sindaghaṭṭa by Sāntaladevī. It also refers to a grant for two other Jain temples situated respectively at Aṇuvasamudra, modern Alesandra, and Cākeyanahalli which was given to Devacandra Paṇḍila, disciple of Gaṇḍavimukta Siddhāntadeva, grand-disciple of Māghanandi Siddhāntadeva belonging to Kollapura and Pustaka-gaccha and Iṅgaleśvara-bali. *Epigraphia Carnatica*, IV, Naga 32.

Aleśī: See Leśyā.

Alirajpur: Site of huge Jain statues and temples in Jhabua district, Madhya Pradesh.

Alladurgam: Findspot of an eleventh-century epigraph in the Medak district of Andhra Pradesh, which refers to the existence of a Jain temple called Kīrtivilāsa, dedicated to Śāntinātha. *Andhra Pradesh Archaeological Series*, III.45.

Alokākāśa: See Ākāśa.

Aluara Bronzes: A good number of Jain images have been found at Aluara in Manbhum, which are now preserved in the Patna Museum. Among these are eight bronzes images of Ṛṣabhanātha. All of them are standing in *Kāyotsarga* posture, except one, seated on a lotus pedestal. In one case Ṛṣabha is shown standing by the side of Pārśvanātha on the same pedestal. There is a single bronze image of Ajitanātha standing on a lotus pedestal with his elephant emblem. Two bronze images of Candraprabha are in Aluara collection. In both, the Jina stands on a lotus pedestal in *Kāyotsarga* posture with his emblem, the crescent moon. The hoard contains six bronze images of Kunthunātha with usual emblems. Two of these figures have eight attendants and one ninth. An image of Vimalanātha is also in this hoard as also one of Neminātha standing on a lotus pedestal. There are two bronze images of Pārśvanātha: one, with a seven-hooded serpent, seated in *padmāsana* on a four-pillared lotus-throne and nine attendants also seated on a pedestal, and the other, standing on a lotus pedestal with two serpent devotees. Among the six bronze images of Mahāvīra, three are inscribed. They stand on a lotus pedestal with a *chatra* in some cases, and in one case with nine seated attendants on pedestal. A solitary Ambikā image is also in this hoard, which is represented as standing on a lotus pedestal with two attendants on lion.

Āma: Ruler of Kanauj and Gwalior in the ninth century, a patron of Jainism according to the Jain *Prabandhas*. He built a temple at Kanauj 100 cubits high and erected a golden image of Mahāvīra. He also set up an image of Mahāvīra at Gwalior 23 cubits high, and is further said to have built Jain temples at Mathura, Anahilavāḍa, Modera, etc. King Āma of the Jain tradition is likely to be Pratihāra Nāgabhaṭa II of the ninth century who is known to have had Jain leanings.

Amarabhaṭṭa: A minister of King Kumārapāla (q.v.) and brother of Vāgbhaṭṭa who replaced the old Śakunikā-vihāra by a splendid new shrine in AD 1166.

Amaracandra: Poet patronized by Vastupāla (q.v.) whose *Bāla-bhārata* is a summary of the *Mahābhārata* in 6,000 verses. His *Padmānanda Mahākāvya*, also called *Jinendracarita*, is in two recensions. The former (the longer one) is exclusively devoted to Ṛṣabhanātha while the shorter one concerns all the Tīrthaṃkaras. Amaracandra flourished in the thirteenth century. *Bālabhārata*, Kavyamala edn., Bombay, 1926; *Padmānanda Mahākāvya*, ed. H.R. Kapadia, Gaikward's Oriental Series, Baroda, 1932.

Amarakīrtigaṇi: Author of the Apabhraṃśa *Chakkammovaesa* (Sanskrit form *Ṣaṭkarmopadeśa*) in fourteen cantos which deals with the sixfold duties of the householders: worship of god, attendance on the teacher, study of the sacred texts, self-restraint, austerity, and charity, with illustrative stories. It was composed in AD 1190. Amarakīrti names seven other works composed by him, *Nemināha-cariu*, *Mahāvīra-cariu*, *Jasahara-cariu*, *Dhammacariyaṭippaṇa*, *Suhāsiyarayanaṇihi*, *Dhammovaesacūḍāmaṇi* and *Jhānapaīn.* He was fifth in succession from the scholar Amitagati (q.v.).

Amarapura: Findspot of a Jain inscription of AD 1278 in Sira taluk, Tumkar district, Karnataka which mentions a Jina temple called Brahma-Jinālaya and two monks of Pustaka-gacca and Ingaḷeśvara-bali. *Epigraphia Carnatica* XI. Sira, No. 32.

Amarapuram: Site of a Pārśvanātha temple in the Anantapur district in Andhra Pradesh which, according to an inscription of AD 1278, was under the control of the monks of the Deśi-gaṇa, *Jaina Śilālekha Saṃgraha*, IV, No. 347.

Amara Suri: See *Ambaḍa-Caritra.*

***Ambaḍa-Caritra*:** An important work in Jain narrative literature written by Amara Suri. Ambaḍa or Ammada was a magician who succeeded in carrying out the seven difficult tasks assigned to him by the witch Gorakha and won 32 beautiful wives, untold wealth, and a kingdom. But eventually he gave up his Śaiva faith, became a Jain monk, faced death by starvation, and reached heaven. Ed. Hiralal Hamsaraj, Jamnagar, 1910; German trans. Charlotte Krause, Leipzig, 1922.

Amījharā: Place of Jain pilgrimage, modern Amjhara in Dhar district, Madhya Pradesh.

Ambikā: Also known as Āmrā and Kusmāṇḍinī, she is the Sāsana-devatā (q.v.) of Neminātha and the consort of Gomeda. Her iconographic features leave little doubt that she is a Jain adaptation of the Hindu goddess of the same name. But the Jains developed a mythology of their own which had very little in common with the stories connected with the Hindu original. She is one of the Jain goddesses whose images have been found all over India and her two-, four-, eight- and even twenty-armed varieties of the early and late medieval periods are known. Her symbol is a bunch of mangoes; and a child (sometimes two children) near her with her lion mount are her characteristic cognizances. Sometimes she is shown accompanied by seven dancing female figures by her side, and at other times she is seated or standing by Gomedha. Several medieval relief of the Varendra Research Society's Museum, Rajshahi, show a couple seated underneath the spreading branches of a tree with children in their laps. These sculptures may be taken as the eastern mode of representing Gomedha and Ambikā, and there is little doubt that they are adaptations of the figures of Pañcika and Hārītī associated with Mahāyāna Buddhism. Another name of Ambikā is Āmrā. The state Archaeological Gallery, West Bengal, preserves a bronze image of Ambikā, found in Nalgora, 24-Parganas. The goddess stands on a lotus pedestal beneath the bough of a mango tree clasping a child at her waist with her left hand and holding in her right another nude child. Just near the bottom of the tree, which is bent with fruits, is the miniature figure of a lion. Another bronze image of Ambikā found at Aluara in Manbhum is now in the Patna Museum. The goddess is represented as standing on a lotus pedestal with two attendants and a lion. There is an Ambikā image in the temple of Pattani Devī at Pithora near Bharhut. Here she has other Yakṣīs on her three sides. An image of Ambikā found at Mayurbhanj in Orissa is now in the British Museum. The popularity of this goddess, owing to her being the protector of children, crossed the limits of religious sectarianism, and she was venerated by the non-Jains as well. Some place names are also associated with this goddess.

Ambikanagar: Jain site in Bankura district, West Bengal, named after goddess Ambikā. Among the Jain finds of this place mention must be made of an eleventh-century Ṛṣabhanātha image, now enshrined in a Śiva temple. Its height is about 3 feet 6 inches. Wearing a carved *jaṭāmukuṭa*, it stands against a throne in usual *kāyotsarga* on a double-petalled lotus. The canopy is of a succession of gradually diminishing *chatras* over the head. Two pairs of celestial hands are seen playing on instruments over the *chatra.* The back slab shows in high relief the figures of the twenty-four Tīrthaṃkaras in two rows. In the collection of the State Archaeological Gallery of West Bengal there are two Ajitanātha or Suvidhinātha images from Ambikanagar. These are small images, standing in *kāyotsarga* under a canopy on a lotus on a *triratha* pedestal, flanked by *chowrie*-bearers. There is an indistinct emblem below the Jina's feet which seems to be an elephant or a *makara.* There are two Ambikā images from this place, one enshrined in a modern temple and the other preserved in the State Archaeological Gallery, West Bengal. The first is about four feet and six inches in height, lavishly ornamented, one hand broken, another touching the head of a small figure; attendants are on either side, one on the right pot-bellied. There is the mount lion below the deity. The top corner shows a portion of mango branches. The figure is crowned by group of musicians and dancers. Pendant mangoes are also seen. A broken portion of the slab is kept outside the temple. The other image is in *dvibhaṅga* pose flanked by attendant figures. Mount lion is carved on the pedestal. Two hands of the goddess carry the *tridaṇḍī* and *kamaṇḍalu*; the third is in *varada mudra* while the fourth is mutilated. Ambikanagar is situated on the confluence of the Kaṃsāvatī and the Kumārī rivers.

Amer: Jain site in Rajasthan during the period of Cāhamānas of Śākambharī. Three Jain temples of this place were later converted into Śiva temples. Among these the oldest appears to be Lāl-Shāh-kā-Mandir, which consists of three contiguous shrines with a *gūḍha-maṇḍapa.* The lintels and doors frames of the shrine and *maṇḍapa* contain sculptured figures of Jinas.

Amitagati: Author of the didactic poem *Subhāṣita-ratnasaṃdoha*, a collection of beautiful aphorisms who flourished in the tenth-eleventh century and belonged to the Digambara tradition. Each of the 32 chapters deals with a special subject of the Jain ethics like the wickedness of women, the sin of eating flesh or drinking intoxicants and so forth. Twenty years after the *Subhāṣitaratnasaṃdoha* in 1014, was written his second work, *Dharmaparīkṣā.* It is a dogmatic-polemic work, but so closely interwoven with narratives that it may be included in narrative literature as well. Amitagati's third work, *Yogasāra*, is a didactic poem in nine chapters giving moral instruction in simple *ślokas.* His *Dvātriṃśatikā*, poem in 32 stanzas, is of high ethical value. *Subhāṣitaratnasaṃdoha*, edited in Kavyamala Series No. 82; ed. with German trans. by R. Schmidt and J. Hertel in ZDMG, LIX, 1905; LXI, 1907; *Darmaparīkṣā*, N. Mironov, *Die-Dharmaparīkṣā des Amitagati*, Leipzig, 1903, Jain Siddhanta Prakasini, Calcutta, 1908; Hindi trans. Bombay, 1908; *Yogasāra*, ed. with Hindi explanation, Sanatana Jaina Granthamala, No. 16, 1918; *Dvātriṃśatikā*, in Manikacandra Digambara Series, No. 13, 132ff; under the title *Sāmayika Pāṭha* with Eng. trans. By Ajit Prasad in Jaina Scripture Gif Series No. 2; among other works of Amitagati, *Pañcasaṃgraha* pub. in Manika Candra Digambara Series, No. 25; *Upāsakācāra*, Anantakirti Granthamala, Bombay, 1921.

Aṃkaleśvara: Place of Jain pilgrimage near Broach in Gujarat, where stands a shrine of Cintāmaṇi Pārśvanātha erected in the sixteenth century.

Aṃkuśā: Śāsanadevatā of Anantanātha (q.v.) according to the Śvetāmbara tradition. She is conceived of as seated on a lotus and holding a sword, a noose, a spear, and a goad in her four hands. Her Digambara variant Anantamatī is described as being carried by a swan and holding in her hands a bow, an arrow, fruit and the *varada mudra.* See Vajrāṅkuśā.

Ammacharram: Also known as Aluruttimalai, it is a hill in the Tiruchirapalli district, north of Sittannavasal, which contain later Jain images of the seventh to ninth centuries on the overhanging rock of the cavern.

Ammasattiram: Site of a Jain temple in the Tiruchirapalli district of Tamil Nadu to which a grant was made according to an inscription of Māravarman Sundara Pāṇḍya I in the first quarter of the thirteenth century. *South India Inscriptions*, XVII, No. 397.

Amoghavarṣa: Rāṣṭrakūṭa king of the ninth century who, notwithstanding his association with the traditional religion of India, was a patron of Jainism. His other name was Sarva and he took the titles Nṛpatuṅga, Mahārājaṣaṇḍa, Vīra-nārāyaṇa, and Atiśayadhavala. His court was adorned by a number of Jain writers such as Jinasena (q.v.) author of the *Ādipurāṇa* (q.v.), Mahāvīrācarya (q.v.), the author of *Gaṇita-sārasaṃgraha* and Śākaṭāyana (q.v.), the author of *Amoghavṛtti.* He was himself the author of *Kavirājamārga*, the earliest Kannaḍa work on poetics. The early period of Kannaḍa literature, extending from the fifth to the ninth century, is well reflected in the *Kavirājamārga.* Among the earlier Jain writers the *Kavirājamārga* especially mentions Samantabhadra and Pūjyapāda (qq.v.), besides Kaviparameṣṭhin, Udaya, Vimala, Jayabandha, Durvīnita and Śrīvijaya.

Āmrā: See Ambikā.

Amradeva Sūri: Commentator on Nemicandrasūri's (q.v.) *Ākhyānamaṇikośa* written about AD 1134 at Dhavalakkapura, modern Dholkā. He was a pupil of Jinacandra.

Amraśālavana: Site of the Pūrṇanabhadra Caitya on

the north-east of Campā (q.v.) according to the *Aupapātika Sūtra* 2-5.

Amrol: Situated some distance south-east of Gwalior and known for its early medieval Mahāvīra temple, this site has yielded sculptures of Pārśvanātha end Ādinātha. That of the latter is sensitively modelled and surrounded by small figures of yakṣas seated in *sukhānana* on lotus seats linked with exquisitely carved lotus scrolls.

Amṛtacandra: Philosopher of the early tenth century who in about AD 904 composed the *Puruṣārthasiddhayupāya* or *Jinapravacana-rahasyakośa* in 226 Sanskrit verses. *Tattavārthasāra Tattvadīpikā* and commentaries on Kundakunda's works. The *Tattavārthasāra* has 618 verses and is divided into nine chapters. The seven *padārthas* are discussed in this work. The *Ātmakhyāti* is the author's commentary on the *Samayasāra* of Kundakunda. *Puruṣārthasiddhyupāya*, ed. in Rayacandra Jaina Śāstramālā, Bombay, 1905, *Tattvārthasāra*, edited in Digambara Jaina Granthabhāṇḍāra, Benares, 1924 in which we also find a philosophical poem by Amṛtacandra under the title *Nāṭakasamayasārakalaśāḥ*.

Anahilapāṭaka: Ancient city, situated on the Sarasvatī, 105 km to the west of Ahmedabad. Its present name is Patan. It is a Jain centre adorned with medieval temples. See Anahilavāḍa.

Anahilavāḍa: Also known as Anahillapura, Anahilapāṭaka and Abhilvad-patan. It is modern Patan (23° 52' N 72° 10' E) in Gujarat. It was established by the Cāpa King Vanarāja in AD 745 as his capital. It was the capital of Gujarat even in the thirteenth century during the reign of the Vāghela kings. It was a Jain centre containing many temples. King Āma, identified with Nāgabhaṭa II, is said to have built here a magnificent temple. The Caulukya Mūlarāja I (AD 942-95) built Mūla-*vasatika* for the Digambaras and a temple of Mūlanātha Jinadeva for the Śvetāmbara sect at this place.

Anaimalai: Situated not far from the Vaigai River this hill village in Madurai taluk and Madurai district, Tamil Nadu, has a natural cavern with one Brahmi inscription. On the huge overhanging rock are sculptures of Tīrthaṃkaras and the Yakṣī Siddhāyikā. The name of Ajjanandi (q.v.) is found in an inscription. Anaimalai provides also an example of the conversion of a Jain centre into a Brahmanical one. Anaimalai is also known as 'Elephant Hill'.

Anamakonda: Findspot of Vikramāditya VI's pillar inscription near Warangal dated Cālukya Vikrama year 42 (AD 1137), which mentions the king's Kākatīya feudatory Polarasa's erection of a Jain temple. *Epigraphia Indica* IX.25ff.

Anandamangalam: Findspot of an inscription of Kulottuṅga III (AD 1178-1218) in Chengalpattu district, Tamil Nadu, which records a grant for a Śrāvaka at a village called Jinagiripalli. *Jaina Śilālekha Saṃgraha* IV, No. 324.

Anantagumpha: See Bhuvaneśvara Caves, Khaṇḍagiri Caves.

Anantamatī: See Aṃkuśā.

Anantanātha: The fourteenth Tīrthaṃkara who was the son of Siṃhasena and Sujasā or Jayasyāmā of Ayodhya. He had a height of 50 bow-lengths and a life-span of three million years. His sacred tree is *aśvattha*. His first disciples were Yaśa and Padmā. He attained liberation on mount Sammeya. The symbolic mark which distinguishes Anantanātha from other the Tīrthaṃkaras is the hawk according to the Śvetāmbaras and the bear according to the Digambaras. He was named Ananta because his mother has seen an endless necklace of pearls. His attendants are Pāṭalā and Anantamatī/Aṃkuśā respectively. The *chowrie*-waver was King Puruṣottama Vāsudeva.

Anantānubandhi: See Kaṣāya, Pāpa.

Anarthadaṇḍa Vrata: Taking a vow not to commit purposeless sins.

Anastikāya: Substance which has no extension or body by which term *kāla* or time is indicated. Other substances, apart from time, belong to the Astikāya (q.v.) group.

Andar-Madam: A natural cavern on the eastern part of the Tenimalai Hill in the Tiruchchirapalli district, Tamil Nadu, which was a place of Jain penance in ancient times. By the side of the cavern there are some seventh-ninth centuries images.

Andimalai: A group of boulders with sculptures of Jain deities in Solavandipuram, South Arcot district, Tamil Nadu.

Anegondi: Situated on the northern bank of the Tungabhadra just opposite Hampi, the site contains a very early group of Jain sculptures found carved on the rock-surface. They belong to the fourteenth century. The standing figures in the *kāyotsarga* posture with the usual triple umbrella above their heads are beautifully proportioned. The workmanship of one group is obviously different from that of the other. The attendant seated figures are also well proportioned. It is the findspot of a Jain inscription, which records the construction of a Jina temple at the time of the Vijayanagara Emperor Harihara II by an official named Irugapa.

Jaina Śilālekha Saṃgraha, V, No. 192.

Anekāntajayapatākā: See Haribhadra.

Anekāntavāda: According to the Jains, reality is so complex in structure that it baffles all attempts to describe it directly and once for all. Hence the limitation of a particular judgement and the possibility of alternative judgements from other points of view must always be borne in mind. For example, on perceiving a black earthen jar in a room at particular times it should not be unconditionally asserted that 'the jar exists'. It should rather be said that 'perhaps the jar exists', which should remind us that the judgement is true only with regard to the condition of space, time, quality, etc., under which the jar exists. It prevents the possibility of the misapprehension that the pot exists at all times or in every place. Again an object may be described affirmatively by a judgement which predicates of it any of the characters it possesses; or it may be described negatively, which denies of its characters belonging to other objects but absent in this. Jain logicians insist on the conditional or relative character of both affirmative and negative judgements. Thus when we say, 'may be this is a jar' it is only in the sense of its existence at a particular place and time and with a particular description. Again, when we say 'may be, the jar is red', its redness or blackness depends on perception conditioned by factors like light and darkness. May be the jar observed during the daytime is red, not red when observed at night. Thus every object *is* in one sense and *is not* in another sense. While the opposition between the predicates *is* and *is not* is reconciled, when they are thought of as characterizing an object successively, the nature of the object becomes indescribable (*avaktavya*). A jar is black when raw and red when it is baked. But if one asks, what is the real colour of the jar always and under all conditions, the only reply would be that the colour of the jar is indescribable. Three other forms of judgement can also be obtained by combining successfully each of the first three standpoints with the fourth. From the viewpoints of space, time, colour, shape, ingredients and so on, an indescribable existence may be affirmed or denied, and also affirmed and denied simultaneously. Thus what is emphasized in Jain logic is the relative and conditional character of the judgements. An object cannot be described at all if no distinction of standpoints and aspects in made. This does not, however, mean that the different judgements about an object are mere subjective ideas. They are meant to reveal the different real aspects of the object, not dependent upon the mood of the judging mind but upon the relational characters of the many sided reality itself.

***Anekārthasaṃgraha*:** See Hemacandra.

Ānesejjeya-Basadi: One of the most prominent Jain temples at Lakshmeswar in Dharwar district of Karnataka which is mentioned in the Ablur epigraph mentioning it in connection with eight hundred Jain temples. It was originally built by Kumkumadevī, the younger sister of Cālukaya Vijayāditya. *Indian Antiquary* XVIII. 37-8.

Ānevālu: Findspot of a Jain inscription of AD 1430 in Honsur taluk, Mysore district, which refers to a temple of the Jain goddess Padmāvatī. *Epigraphia Carnatica* IV, Honsur 62.

***Aṅga*:** A class of Śvetāmbara canonical literature. It comprises twelve texts, supposedly complied in a special assembly summoned at Pāṭaliputra (fourth century BC) and finished at the council of Valabhi (fifth-sixth century AD). The texts are *Ācāra* (Āyāra), *Sūtrakṛta* (Sūyagaḍa), *Sthāna* (*Ṭhāṇa*), *Samavāya*, *Vyākhyāprajñapti* (Viyahāpannatti or Bhagavatī), *Jñātādharmakathā* (Nāyādhammakahāo), *Upāsakadaśā* (Uvāsagadasāo), *Antaḥkṛd-daśā* (Antagaḍadasāo), *Anuttarapapādikadaśā* (Anuttarovavaiyadasāo), *Praśnavyākaraṇa* (Panhavāgaraṇaim), *Vipākaśruta* (Vivāgasūya) and *Dṛṣṭivāda* (Ditthivāya) (qq.v.). The Digambaras consider the existing versions of the Aṅga texts to be spurious, but recognize the existence of the twelve Aṅgas. They, too, include in the twelfth *Aṅga* the fourteen Pūrvas. They call those texts, which do not belong to the Aṅgas, *Aṅgabāhya* (q.v.) or *Prakīrṇa* (q.v.) and declare them to be intended for simple lay persons.

***Aṅga*:** Requirements. These are eight in number, which are conducive to the development of *samyag-darśana* (q.v.) or right belief in individuals. These are *niḥśaṅkita*, freedom from doubt; *niṣkāṅkṣita*, freedom from desire of worldly comforts; *nirvicikitsita*, freedom from aversion to or regard for the body; *amūḍhadṛṣṭi*, freedom from inclination for the wrong path; *upaguhana*, redeeming the defects of false believers; *sthitikaraṇa*, sustaining souls in right convictions; *vātsalya*, loving regard for pious persons; *prabhāvana*, publishing the greatness of Jain doctrine. There are eight other *aṅgas*, which are conducive to the development of *samyag-jñāna* (q.v.) or right knowledge. These are *grantha*, correct use of the words; *artha*, full understanding of their meanings; *ubhaya*, combination of the both preceding; *kāla*, observance regularity and property of time; *vinaya*, reverent attitude; *sopādhāna*, propriety of behaviour, *bahumāna*, zeal; and *aninhava* without of knowledge or of its sources.

***Aṅgabāhira, Aṅgabāhya*:** Those texts which do not belong to the *Aṅgas* according to the Digambara tradition. They are also called *Prakīrṇa* (q.v.) or miscellanea, standing outside the *Aṅgas*, and meant for simple-minded lay-persons. The first four Aṅgabāhyas—*Sāmāyika*, *Caturviṃśatistava*, *Vandana*, and *Pratikarmaṇa*—correspond to sections of the second Mūlasūtra (q.v.). Besides these, other texts of this category which occur in the canon of the Śvetāmbaras are the *Dasavaikālika*, *Uttarādhyayana* and *Kalpa-Vyavahāra*, the last probably corresponding to the *Dasakappa-Vavahāra*. These texts may remotely be related to the now-extinct *Pūrva* (q.v.) texts and also to the lost *Dṛṣṭivāda*. Texts like the *Nandī* (q.v.) and the *Anuyogadvāra* divide the substance of the Jain teaching into *aṅgapavittha* and *anaṅgapavittha* or *aṅgabāhira* (not belonging to the *Aṅgas*). The traditional scheme places all the Pūrvas in the twelfth *Aṅga*, and another old tradition tells that the immediate disciples of Mahāvīra composed the *Aṅgas* after receiving the ideas from the Master himself. Moreover, all the later works which are said to be derived from the Pūrvas form part of the *aṅgabāhira* group. From the name *pavāya* applied to most of them, we may conclude that they contained matter of controversial nature, probably stating the views of the opponents and their refutations. Some of the schismatic views are said to be drawn from them. Their place in the *Dṛṣṭivāda* (q.v.) suggests similar contents.

***Aṅgacūliyā*:** See Prakīrṇa.

Angadi: Findspot of many Jain inscriptions in the Mudigire taluk of the Chikmagalur district, Karnataka. The earliest, assigned to *c.* AD 990, records the death of Vimalacandra Paṇḍita belonging to Drāviḍa-saṅgha, Kondakunda-anvaya and Pustaka-gaccha. The next one records the death of Vajrapāṇi of the same saṅgha and gaṇa, *guru* of the King Rajamalla of Gaṅgavadi. Another memorial tablet of AD 1054 refers to him as belonging to Surastha-gaṇa and also to temple called Sosavura-basadi and grant to it by Jakiyabbe, a woman disciple of the said Vajrapāṇi. The fourth inscription from Angadi dated Śaka 984 (AD 1062) mentions one Śāntideva as the *guru* of Hoysala Vinayāditya while the fifth mentions the erection of a Jain temple in AD 1063 by the son of the architect Māṇika Poysalacāri and the appointment of Guṇasena Paṇḍita as its caretaker. The next inscription of AD 1164 mentions a gift by Vijaya Narasiṃha, the Hoysala king, for a basadi while another of AD 1172 refers to the name of a Jain temple called Honnangi-basadi. *Epigraphia Carnatica*, VI, Mudi. Nos. 9, 11-13, 15, 17.

***Aṅgavidyā*:** Prakrit *Aṅgavijjā*, often considered to belong to the Prakīrṇa (q.v.) category. It is basically encyclopaedic in nature and a veritable storehouse of information relating to various horizons material aspects of human life. In sixty chapters it throws light on administration, social and cultural life, professions, ornaments, food grains, conveyances, textiles, eatables, coinage, deities, seats, boats, arts and crafts, types of women, list of *gotras*, science of erotics, birds and beasts, towns and settlements and so forth. It deals with the science of divination, not through the movement of stars or constellations or reading the horoscope, but through physical signs and symbols (*aṅga*). The eighth chapter deals with magical incantations and the ninth records 270 items of interest, some of which have been mentioned above. The eleventh chapter gives a list of architectural terms. The twenty-sixth is devoted to stars and planets and the twenty-seventh to royal officers. The thirty-sixth chapter is devoted to pregnancy, thirty-seventh to *lakṣaṇas* or signs, the forty-second to dreams, the forty-seventh to military expeditions, and so on. The present form of this text seems to be a production of the early centuries of the Christian era. It was edited by Muni Puṇyavijaya with introductions of Motichand and V.S. Agrawala (Hindi) and published in 1957 by Prakrit Text Society.

Animal Tales: In Jain tradition, each Tīrthaṃkara is associated with a holy tree, and each one is supposed to have an emblem of an animal. In Jain narrative literature the hero is supposed to be efficient in the language of the birds. The *Āvaśyaka Cūrṇi* records the story of a parrot who entertained its owner by narrating 500 fascinating stories. In a fable animals appear as characters talking and behaving like human beings as we find in the *Pañcatantra*. There had been a number of Jain editions of the *Pañcatantra*, one such edition being the *Pañcākhyāna* of Pūrṇabhadra composed in AD 1199. Then we have *Pañcākhyānoddāra* by Meghavijaya. The *Vinoda-*

kathāsaṃgraha (also known as *Kathākośa*) by Maladhārī Rājaśekhara, composed about the middle of the fourteenth century, is an important collection of animal tales. The *Kathāratnākara* of Hemavijaya is another work comprising 258 stories composed in the style of *Pañcatantra*. The *Pañcaśatiprabodha* by Śubhaśīlagaṇi contains 500 such stories. The *Vasudevahiṇḍi* which is often described as an authentic Jain version of the *Bṛhatkathā* also contains a good number of animal stories. These stories have been recorded by Jain writers with the idea of propagating their religion. Many are based on folk tales and many seem to be taken from the *Pañcatantra* and *Hitopadeśa*. Jain authors were always in search of interesting popular tales to incorporate in their teachings. Animal tales are divided into two categories, realistic and imaginary. The former is based on a narrative which is either seen, heard or personally experienced, either pertaining to righteousness (*dharma*), attainment of wealth (*artha*) or desire for sensual-enjoyment (*kāma*); the latter is a product of imagination. A good number of them, however, reflect a very primitive heritage.

Aniyatibādra: The ninth *guṇasthāna* (q.v.) in which stage deceit disappears while greed persists.

Anjanagiri: Findspot of a Jain inscription of AD 1514 in the Coorg area of Karnataka which mentions a temple, images of Śāntinātha and Anantanātha, and the teacher Abhinava Cārukīrtipaṇḍita of the Mūla-saṅgha, Deśī-gaṇa, Pustaka-gaccha and Inguleśvara-bali. *Jaina Śilālekha Saṃgraha*, III, No. 673.

Anjaneri: Situated on a hill, 21 km from Nasik in Maharashtra, it is a site of Jain temples which came into existence under the patronage of the Yādavas of Saunadeśa and Devagiri. The temples are in the local style. They are built in the northern *śikhara* style of a particular variety which went by the popular name of Hemāḍpanthī style.

Aṅkai-Taṅkai: Jain site in the Nasik district, Maharashtra, which has yielded a number of sculptures, a few of which are now in the Prince of Wales Museum, Bombay. One belonging to the ninth-tenth centuries shows a triad of Jinas, all standing in *Kāyotsarga,* their hair falling on their shoulders. The *Mūla-nāyaka* or the central figure which appears to be Ṛṣabhanātha is flanked by a *chowrie*-bearer on either side. On the top of the *parikara* are represented the *pratihāryas*. It belongs to the *tri-tirthika* type. The second one is of *pañcatirthika* type. The Jina standing in *kāyotsarga* is flanked on either side by a seated Jina in a niche at the top and a standing Jina in *Kāyotsarga* below. The style is elaborate, with architectural pilasters supporting the attendant Jinas and the miniature shrines above.

Aṅkeśvara Temple Inscriptions: Belong to the Raṭṭas of Saundatti who flourished in the ninth-tenth centuries. Here it is stated that in the year śaka 797 (AD 865) King Pṛthvīrāma, who was a vassal of the Rāṣṭrakūṭa Kṛṣṇa II, made a land grant for a Jinendrabhavana or Jain temple at Sugandhavarti (Saundatti). He was a lay disciple of Indrakīrti, whose spiritual predecessors were Guṇakīrti and Mūlabhaṭṭāraka of Kāreya-gaṇa hailing from Mallapatirtha. The next inscription of the Raṭṭas, dated in śaka 902 (AD 980), found in the same temple, belongs to Mahāsāmanta Śāntivarman, grandson of Pṛthvīrāma, refers to Raṭṭara-paṭṭa Jinālaya, their family shrine. It refers to a donation made by Śāntivarman's mother to the preceptor Bāhubali Bhaṭṭāraka. The line of this preceptor comprised Ravicandra, Arhanandin, Śubhacandra, Munideva, and Prabhācandra of the Kandura-gaṇa, a branch of the Yāpanīya Saṅgha. *Journal of the Bombay Branch of the Royal Asiatic Society*, X, 194ff; *Jaina Śilālekha Saṃgraha*, II, No. 130.

Aṇṇalvāyil: Mentioned in an inscription from the rock-cut Jain temple at Sittannavasal. Arivarkovil of Aṇṇalvāyil denotes the temple of the Arhat at Annavāśal.

Annamas: Also known as Anuvratins, they represent an upgraded stage of priesthood in southern Jainism. The priestly class of the lower grade is known as that of the Arcakas (q.v.). By effort an Arcaka may reach the next higher stage of Annama. At this stage he can marry and have a family life, but he has to observe certain vows and practices. He can then again rise to the highest of the three classes and become a Muni or monk. The two classes of Anuvratins (Annamas) and Munis are open to all Digambara Jains according to their scriptures irrespective of the fact whether they stay in the north or in the south.

Annaprāśana: Sacrament. It is the ritual feeding of the child after worship in its eighth month or so. The Śvetāmbaras do it during the sixth month in the case of a male child and fifth month in the case of female child.

Annigeri: A Jain place of pilgrimage, in Navalgund taluk of the Dharwar district. An inscription discovered at this place belongs to the sixth year of the western Cālukya King Kīrtivarman II corresponding to AD 751 and records the construction of a Jain temple by Kaliyamma who was the headman of Jebulagiri. *Epigraphia Indica*, XXI, 204ff.

Anṛta: Falsehood, to tell lies, abstinence from which is the second vow for the monks and householders. The monk's vow is to renounce all vices arising from anger, greed, fear, or mirth. He shall neither himself tell lies, nor cause others to tell lies, nor consent to the speaking of lies by others. To the householder falsehood means forgery, falsely accusing a person, passing wrong judgements, speaking hurtful words, spreading false doctrines, backbiting, breach of trust, etc. These are all forms of falsehood.

***Antagaḍadasāo*:** See *Antakṛtadaśā*.

Antakarma: Ritual on the death-bed comprising repentence, prayer, charity, fast and contemplation of *pañcaparameṣthins*.

***Antakṛtadaśā*:** Prakrit *Antagaḍadasāo*, the eighth text of the Aṅga (q.v) series. It originally consisted of ten chapters, but is now divided into eight sections. These deal with the legends of pious ascetics. Apart from its typical Jain content, the text deals as well with the Vṛṣṇis and Vāsudeva, different Janapadas, seventy-two arts, Yakṣa cult, and so forth. Edited with Abhayadeva's com. in Agamodaya, Bombay, 1920; Eng. trans. by L.D. Barnett, London, 1907.

***Antara-Kathāsaṃgraha*:** Collection of stories, mostly from earlier works, especially from the commentaries, made by Rājaśekhara Maladhārin of the fourteenth century. It is also known as *Vinodakathāsaṃgraha*, Bombay, 1918, Gujarati trans. Bombay, 1920.

Antarāla: One of the four constituents of the *ghātin karma* (q.v.), which refers to individual differences.

Antarikṣa Pārśvanātha: Aerial form of Pārśvanātha to which a Jain temple at Sirpur, 19 km north-west of Basim in Berar is dedicated.

Antakṛtakevalin: See Arhanta.

Anuloma Marriage: See Inter-caste marriage.

Anumāna: Knowledge derived from inference. In the *Sthānāṅga* the word *hetu* (q.v.) is used in the sense of *anumāna*, but in later works both the terms have received their distinctive significance. Umasvati was the first to use the term anumāna to denote logical inference. According to Siddhasena Divākara, inference or anumāna is the correct knowledge of the major term (*sādhya*) derived through the middle term (*hetu* or *liṅga*), which is inseparably connected with it. Inference is of two kinds, *svārtha* and *parārtha*. The first is deduced in one's own mind after repeated observation (cf. the concomitance of fire and smoke observed in kitchen extended to that of fire-in-general and smoke-in-general) while the second is its communication to others through words. Without inseparable connection or invariable concomittance (*vyāpti*) the constant accompaniment of the middle term by the major term inference is impossible. This has been maintained by Māṇikya Nandi, Deva Sūri and all other Jain logicians. See Fallacies, Hetu, Syllogism.

***Anumatityāga Pratimā*:** Increasing the rigour in the direction of asceticism and refraining even from giving advice on matters relating to family honour, business, and the like.

Anuprekṣā: Twelve meditations or reflections required for *saṃvara* (q.v.) or stoppage of the influx of Karmic matter into the soul. These are *anitya-anuprekṣā*, the transitoriness of everything; *asaraṇa-anuprekṣā*, unprotectiveness or helplessness; *saṃsāra*, mundaneness; *ekatva-anuprekṣā*, the transitoriness of everything; *aśaraṇa-anuprekṣā*, unprotectiveness or helplessness; *saṃsāra*, mundaneness; *ekatva-anuprekṣā*, feeling of loneliness; *anyatva-anuprekṣā*, alienation; *aśuci-anuprekṣā*, impurity; *āsrava-anuprekṣā*, influx of Karmic matter into the soul; *saṃvara-anuprekṣā*, stoppage of influx of Karmic matter into the soul; *nirjarā-anuprekṣā*, shedding of Karmic matter; *loka-anuprekṣā* universe, its nature and constituent elements; *bodhidurlabha-anuprekṣā*, rarity of religious knowledge; and *dharma-anuprekṣā*, nature of the threefold path of liberation. Sometimes *anuprekṣās* are also termed *bhāvanās*.

***Anuttarapapātikadaśā*:** Prakrit *Anuttarovavāiyadasāo*, the ninth text of Aṅga (q.v.) series. It denotes 'ten chapters on the pious ascetics who have attained the highest heaven'. There are only two original pieces in this text, and they contain legends of persons who were reborn in the uppermost regions. The text is divided into three sections with thirty-three lessons instead of the original ten. Āgamodaya edition with Abhayadeva's com. Bombay, 1920; Eng. trans, by L.D. Barnett, London, 1907.

***Anuttarovavāiyadasāo*:** See *Anuttarapapātikadaśā*.

***Aṇuvaya-Rayaṇa-Paīu*:** Sanskrit *Anuvrata-ratna-pradīpa*, an Apabhraṃśa text dealing with the religious vows of Jain house-holders written by Lakkhaṇa, i.e. Lakṣmaṇa, son of Sāhula and Jaitā of the Jaisa family of Rāyavaḍḍiya on the Yamuna (modern Raibha in the Agra district). It was written in eight cantos in AD 1256.

***Anuvrata*:** Lesser vows, meant for the householders. These are the *mahāvratas* (q.v.) simplified. It is not expected that the most rigid *mahāvratas* meant for the ascetics, complete abstinence from violence, worldly things, sensuality and attachment in speech, thought, behaviour, and action can be followed by common persons (householders), which is why they are tutored to accept these five vows in theory. So far as practice is concerned the great vows are reduced for laymen to abstaining from (1) gross offences against living beings, (2) gross untruthfulness, (3) gross appropriation, (4) adultery, and (5) greed. These have been specified in the *Uvāsagadasāo* in which the restrictions concern mainly agricultural and commercial activities. Gross offence against living beings is understood as fettering, beating, wounding, overloading, and cruelty, especially with reference to domestic animals used in agriculture and trade. Likewise gross untruthfulness is understood as falsely accusing a person, passing wrong judgements, forgery, etc. Gross appropriation consists in receiving stolen goods, theft and other illegal economic transactions, using false weights and measures, the adulteration of goods, etc. Gross sensuality consists in offences against matrimonial faith, adultery, harlotism, incest, etc. Gross greed, the abstinence of which is demanded in the fifth vow, is understood in terms of attachment to gold, cattle, land, cart, carriages, jewellery, etc. *Uvāsagadasāo*, 13ff, 45ff., *Thāṇa* 290, *Samavāya* 10. See Cāritra.

Anuvratin: See Annama.

***Anuyogadvāra*:** Independent treatise, not strictly a canonical work, but regarded as a sacred text from very early times. It is ascribed to Āryarakṣita and has a *cūrṇi* by Jinadāsagaṇi and a *Ṭīkā* by Haribhadra. Like another text of this category, *Nandi* (q.v.), it does not deal exclusively with themes pertaining to religion, but treats also of profane branches of knowledge. It contains an interesting enumeration of false tradition and worldly sciences. *Cūrṇi* by Jinadasagani Mahattara, Ratlam, 1928; *Ṭīkā* by Haribhadra Ratlam, 1928; *Ṭīkā* by Maladhari Hemacandra, Bhavnagar, 1935; ed. Punyavijaya, Bombay, 1968; critical study by T. Hanaki, Vaishali, 1970.

Anvādheya: A form of *strīdhana* (q.v.) or women's property which comprises things received from the women of the bride's own or groom's household at the wedding.

Anvaya: Linkage of a branch, an intermediate classificatory stage with no fixed definition. Among the *anvayas* mentioned in the inscriptions, Kundakunda with variant readings, Kuṇḍakunda or Koṇḍakunda, is most frequent and widely distributed. The Siddhara-basti pillar inscription of AD 1398 records the tradition that Arhadbali split the Mūla-*saṅgha* and Kundakunda-*anvaya* into four branches, Sena, Nandī, Deva, and Siṃha. The earliest mention of the Kundakunda-*anvaya* is met with in the copper-plate grants of the fifth century. The Karnataka inscriptions refer to Mūla-*saṅgha*, Rāṣṭrakūṭa, Sena and Saṅgha *anvayas*. Inscriptions from Gujarat refer to Lakṣmaṇasūri-*anvaya*. Besides we have the names of other *anvayas*, Arungala, Mailāpa, Malanura, Virannaya, etc. The *anvayas* are connected with saṅghas and *gaṇas* (qq.v.). For example, the Ingalgi inscription of AD 1094 from Chitapur in Gulbarga district mentions Malanura-*anvaya* as belonging to the Drāviḍa-*saṅgha* and the Sena-*gaṇa*. The Arungala-*anvaya* is mentioned in the Karnataka inscriptions as belonging to the Drāviḍa-*saṅgha* and Nandī-*saṅgha* and Nandī-*gaṇa*. According to an eleventh-century inscription from Belgaum district, a teacher named Guṇakīrtideva belonged to Mailāpa-*anvaya*, Kareya-*gaṇa* and Yāpanīya-*saṅgha*. The most celebrated Kundakunda-*anvaya* was designated after an individual which holds good also in the case of Laksmaṇa-sūri-*anvaya*. Rāṣṭrakūṭa-*anvaya* is named after a lineage. See Saṅgha, Gaṇa, Śākhā, Gaccha, Kula, Bali.

Apabhraṃśa: An important stage in the development of Middle Indo-Aryan language. Historically it represented the colloquial speech which emerged when Prakrit had become archaic and stereotyped. Apabhraṃśa had attained literary form before the time of Hemacandra (q.v.) as is proved by the illustrations in the Prakrit grammar, and by the literature available so far and known to be of an earlier date. Glimpses of Apabhraṃśa are found in early Sanskrit drama. From the eighth to the thirteenth century the Western Apabhraṃśa or Saurasenī Apabhraṃśa became a source of expression of the Jains of northern and western India. The poets Yogindra, Devasena, Rāmasiṃha, Dhanapāla, Harisena, Nayanandi, Jinadatta, Laksmaṇagani, Haribhadra, Hemacandra, Somapāla (qq.v.) and others were representatives of the Western school. Ācārya Hemacandra was the pioneer of this school. While describing the character of this dialect he has provided illustration in forms of verses. See also Amarakīrtigaṇi, Dhāhila, Dhanapāla, Hariṣena, Jinadattasūri, Kaṇakamāra, Mahāsenasūri, Nayanandi, Padmakīrti, Puṣpadanta, Śrīdhara, Suprabhācārya, Svayambhūdeva.

Apadhyāna: see Caritra.

Apāpā: Earlier name of Pāvā, the place of Lord Mahāvīra's demise.

Aparajitā: Śāsanadevatā (q.v.) of Mallinātha (q.v.) according to the Digambara tradition. She is conceived of as riding a lion, holding a citron, a sword and a shield, and showing *varada mudrā*.

Aparigraha: Non-possession, which is the fifth vow. The Jain monk is required to renounce all attachments, small and great, living and lifeless, not to cause such attachment for himself or for others. To the householder the fault of *parigraha* or worldly attachment consists in desiring more than what one needs. Accumulating even necessary articles in large numbers, expressing wonder at the prosperity of another, excessive greed, attachment to gold, cattle, estate, carts, carriages, jewellery, etc. This vow prevents the undue accumulation of wealth in the hands of a few.

***Apkāya*:** Water-bodied; characteristics of immobile or one-sensed Jīva (q.v.).

***Apramatta*:** The seventh *guṇasthāna* (q.v.) in which anger is practically controlled, but pride, deceit and greed remain in a slight degree.

Apraticakrā: Vidyā-devī (q.v.) who in Śvetāmbara tradition rides Garuḍa and all her four hands are armed with discs which accounts for her name. She is called Jambunadā by the Digambaras, who represent her as riding a peacock and bearing a sword and a spear. Apraticakrā by name and symbols bears equality with the Yakṣinī of Ṛṣabhanātha.

Apratyakhyana: See Kaṣāya, Pāpa.

***Āptamīmāṃsā*:** Also known as *Devāgamastotra* it is the introduction of Samantabhadra's (q.v.) commentary on the *Tattvārthādhigama* (q.v.) in which the Jain doctrine of Syādvāda (q.v.) has been explained. It is in 114 verses replete with discussions on logical principles, besides a review of contemporary schools of philosophy including the Advaita Vedānta. The work was known to the philosophers Kumārila Bhaṭṭa and Vācaspati Miśra. The latter cited it in explaining Śaṅkara's criticism of the Syādvāda. The earliest commentator on the *Āptamīmāṃsā* was Akalaṅka (q.v.) who was followed by Vidyānanda and others. Several commentaries on it exist in southern languages, which testify to the philosophical importance of this work. Edition in Jaina Grantha Ratnākara and in Sanātana Jaina Granthmālā, Bombay, 1905, 1910, ed. Pannalal Chaudhari in Digambara Jaina Granthamālā, Benares, 1924-5.

Āptaparīkṣā: See Vidyānanda.

Apūrvakaraṇa: The eighth *guṇasthāna* (q.v.) in which pride is controlled and the fetters of *karma* (q.v.) tend to become loose.

***Ārādhanā-Kathākośa*:** Collection of narratives written by Nemidatta in about AD 1530.

***Ārādhanāsāra*:** See Devasena.

***Ārāhaṇāpadāga*:** See Prakīrṇa.

***Ārambhatyāga Pratimā*:** Abandonment of worldly engagements and occupations.

Aranātha: The eighteenth Tīrthaṃkara who was the son of Sudarśana and Devī of Hastinapura. His height was 30 bow-lengths and his sacred tree was the mango. Kumbha and Rakkhiyā were his chief disciples. He attained liberation on Mount Sammeya at the age of 84,000 years. He is referred to in the well-known Mathura inscription of the year vs 79 (AD 157). His cognizance is either the *nandyā-varta* (a king of *svastika*) or a fish. His attendants are Yakṣendra and Dhāraṇī. Govinda holds his fly-whisk. Images of Aranātha belonging to the Kuṣāṇa period have been discovered in Mathura.

Arang: Jain centre in the Raipur district, Chhattisgarh, which has yielded images of eleventh-twelfth centuries, besides a dilapidated shrine known as Bhāṇḍ-Dewal (q.v.). The temple is the most easterly example of a Bhumija mode of architecture in the regional Kalacuri style. It belongs to the eleventh century.

Ārāsāṇa: A celebrated place of Jain pilgrimage in Gujarat. It is modern Kumbhariya (q.v.) well known for the temples of Śāntinātha, Neminātha, Pārśvanātha and Mahāvīra. Valuable medieval inscriptions have also been obtained from the temple sites.

Ārāsaṇā: A place in the Sirohi district, Rajasthan, whence an inscription of the time of Paramara Dhārāvarṣa mentions the setting up of an image of Sumatinātha.

Arasara-basadi: Jina temple at Hungund in Bijapur district mentioned in an inscription of AD 1074 belonging to the time of Cālukya Someśvara II. *South Indian Inscriptions*, XI.111; *Jaina Śilālekha Saṃgraha*, IV, No. 158.

Arasibidi: Findspot of a Jain epigraph in the Bijapur district dated śaka 969 (AD 1047) of the time of the Western Cālukya Someśvara I. It refers to a Jain temple called Goṇada Beḍangi Jinālaya, named Akkādevī, sister of Someśvara. She made a grant for this temple, which was entrusted to Nāgasena Paṇḍita of the Mūla-*saṅgha*, Sena-*gaṇa* and Hogeri-gaccha. The earlier name of this place was Vikramapura. Two more inscriptions from Arasibidi are known in which the aforesaid temple is mentioned. *Epigraphia Indica*, XVII.121ff; *South Indian Inscriptions*, XI.239. *Report on South Indian Epigraphy*, 1928-29, 44 *Jaina Śilālekha Saṃgraha* IV, Nos. 166, 261.

Arbuda: Same as Mount Abu celebrated for the Ṛṣabha temple established by Vimala and Neminātha temple erected by Tejaḥpāla. See Dilwara temples.

Arcakas: A class of priests among the southern Jains. They worship in temples and belong to the category of the Indras (q.v.). An ordinary person cannot become an Arcaka or have any marital relationship with him though there is no restriction in interdining. An Arcaka can, however, rise to the next higher stages of the priestly class up to the level of Muni.

Architecture: Jain architecture belonging to different types and ages is scattered all over the country. The early Jain monks being mostly forest recluses and wandering ascetics favouring natural caves on the sides or tops of hills as temporary refuges. This seems to have been the beginning of the conception of cave temples (q.v.) and cave architecture. The Jain caves at Udayagiri and Khaṇḍagiri near Bhubaneswar in Orissa, going back to the time of Khāravela (q.v.) of the first century BC, are not laid out on definite and regular plan, but located at convenient places according to the physical configuration of the rock. Many of the caves contain a number of sculptured friezes and panels. The Manchapuri cave relief on Udayagiri and Anantagumpha reliefs in Khaṇḍagiri are marked by poor workmanship. The long friezes of Ranigumpha and Gaṇeśagumpha came out much later. The reliefs follow mythological narratives with Jain affiliation. To the first century BC may also be assigned the Pabhosa caves (q.v.), near Allahabad, dedicated for the use of the Kāśyapīya monks, i.e. the followers of Mahāvīra. The Tamil country comes up with an interesting series of natural caverns on hills, with early Brahmi inscriptions found at several spots, suitably altered by the cutting of beds and drip-ledges to render them habitable for ascetics. The most notable among these early Jain foundations and one which was in continuous occupation of the Jains from about the second century BC to the ninth century AD is that at Sittannavasal (q.v.) in Tirumayam taluk of Tiruchchirapalli district. Among the four cave temples excavated on the northern scarp of the Badami (q.v.) cliff, the topmost and the most ornamented one belongs to the Jains. The Mena-basti (q.v.) on the south-east face of the Meguti Hill at Aihole is also a nice illustration of a seventh-century Jain cave temple. The Jain caves at Elapura or Ellora (q.v.) contain a specimen of a monolithic cut out *vimāna*, the Chotā Kailāsa (q.v.) and the still smaller one, the Indra-sabhā (q.v.) occupying the northern horn of the ridge. These are not earlier than AD 800. In the courtyard of the Indra-sabhā there is on the right a figure of an elephant and on the left a monolithic column surmounted by a quadruple image of a Tīrthaṃkara. In the centre of the court there is a square *maṇḍapa* and beyond it the passage leading to the lower hall of the temple. At the left end of the passage there are two big images of Śāntinātha, and on the right a stairway leading to the upper hall of the temple.

The Jain temple of Meguti at Aihole, erected in śaka 556 (AD 634) by Ravikīrti during the reign of the Cālukyan King Pulakeśin II is especially important from structural point of view. Two small Jain shrines at Than in Saurashtra belonging to the post-Gupta period also deserve special mention, the structural style of which had been imitated by a number of later temples like the one of Paṭṭaini Devī at Pithora near Bharhut. The Mahāvīra temple at Osia in Rajasthan, originally constructed in the reign of Vatsyarāja of the Pratihāra dynasty, has an open porch, a closed hall and a sanctum. The courtyard of the temple contains a row of subsidiary shrines erected at a later time. The Makrabai temple near Mahoba in Uttar Pradesh constructed evidently before AD 1000 contains three cells, one at the back of the *maṇḍapa* and two respectively on the north and south of it, and figures of the Jinas on the lintel.

The much mutilated Ghaṇṭai temple at Khajuraho (q.v.) is also a unique specimen of Jain architecture. Of other Jain temples at Khajuraho, that of Pārśvanātha probably belonging to the period between AD 950 and 1050, is about 62 feet in length and half of that in breadth, the outside walls of which are adorned with numerous bands of mouldings and with three horizontal rows of sculptured statues.

At Sravanabelgola (q.v.) in Karnataka numerous Jain shrines were constructed in medieval and later times. The ordinary temples which contain only the image of a Jina is known as basti, while a specially arranged kind consisting of cloisters around an open courtyard with a colossal statue is called betta. Some of the Jain temples at Deogarh (q.v.) fort, Jhansi district, which date from the tenth century, contain, besides the image of the Jinas, well-known figures of Jain mythology.

Most famous of all are the temples of Mount Abu (q.v.), the Dilwara (q.v.) group of which consists of four large temples. Of them the two most important ones are in certain respects unrivalled anywhere in India, the older of which was built in AD 1031 by Vimala Sāha and the other, completed in AD 1230 by Tejaḥapala and Vastupāla. Both of the temples, constructed entirely of white marble, are similar in plan, relatively plain on the exterior but amazingly rich in interior decoration, each standing in a rectangular walled area, surrounded by recesses with numerous statues. The central cell contains a statue of a Jina, with a pyramidal roof, and connected with this is a closed hall. In front of the hall is an extensive open portico adorned with free standing columns.

Of other interesting Jain temples of the medieval period mention is to be made of the shrines at Kumbharia in north Gujarat belonging to the twelfth and thirteenth centuries; the Digambara Kīrtistambha at Chittor built in AD 1100 and repaired in 1430; the temples near Indore which were mostly built by later Paramāras of Malwa in the eleventh and twelfth centuries; the Kumārapāla temples on the Taranga Hill, north Gujarat and at Jalor, about 80 miles south of Jodhpur; the temple at Sarotra in north Gujarat which contains 52 cells in the courtyard; the Varavan shrine in the Thar district of Sindh; the beautifully carved fana at Mirpur between Abu and Sirohi, and the Caumukha temple at Ranakpur (qq.v.). Other interesting Jain towers and temples are to be found at Pareshnath, Chitorgarh and Gwalior, Jaipur and Bikaner in Rajasthan possess some Digambara remains while Jaisalmer has a group of Śvetāmbara temples. Digambara temples exist in Miri and Ghotan in the Ahmednagar district. The temple city of Śatruñjaya in Saurashtra is considered especially sacred to Ṛṣabha. The temples are numerous, grouped in separate enclosures, generally containing one principal temple with other smaller ones. Some of the temples are believed to be as old as the eleventh century, while the majority range from around AD 1500 to the present time. The hill of Girnar, not far from Junagarh, contains a group of Jain temples, some sixteen in number. Of these the largest and perhaps also the oldest is the Neminātha temple. An inscription upon it records that it was repaired in AD 1278 and the original construction must have been considerably earlier than this date.

The temple is called *āyatana* or *caitya* (*caityavihāra*, *caityagṛha* or *caityālaya*) and in the Jain concept it serves the purpose of *samavasaraṇa* or the auditorium of the Tīrthaṃkara who is enshrined there as *mūla-nāyaka*, the chief hero. According to the canons of Jain architecture, the residential buildings or places comprising *paṭṭa-sāla* or main hall, *kakṣa-śālās* or smaller rooms, *alinda* or the outer corridor and *maṇḍapa* or pavilion do not differ much from the temple in the basic principles of construction. The moulded basement of a temple is known as *adhiṣṭhāna* or *vedi-bandha*. The *sanctum sanctorum* is the *garbha-gṛha*, the middle portion above the basement and below the *śikhara* is *jaṅghā* and the superstructure or roof is *śikhara*. A north Indian *śikhara* is normally curvilinear while a southern *śikhara* is domical, octagonal or four-sided. The *gopura* is the main gateway, a structure over the entrance. *Maṇḍapa* is the generic term for a hall which has many variations. *Mahāmaṇḍapa* or *navaraṅga* is central pillared hall with openings on the lateral sides; *agramaṇḍapa* is same as *mukhamaṇḍapa* or entrance porch and *nṛtyamaṇḍapa* is same as *raṅgamṇḍapa* pillared hall open on all sides. *Antarāla* is the intermediate compartment between shrine and *maṇḍapa*. Besides there are *toraṇa* or ornamental entrance of numerous varieties and designs, *pradaksiṇā-patha* or circumambulatory passage and *mānastambha* or free-standing pillar-standard crowned by Jina images.

Temples are of various types: *caturmukha* or *sarvatobhadra* with openings on all the four sides; *devakulika*, a small shrine; *hāra*, a string of miniature shrines; *pañcāyatana*, a temple surrounded by four minor shrines; *pañcaratha*, a temple with five projections; *sahasrakūṭa*, a pyramidal shrine model with numerous figure of the Jinas; *sāndhāra-prāsāda*, a temple with ambulatory; *triratha*, a temple with three projections; and so forth.

Ardha-Māgadhī: Why the word *ardha* (half) was prefixed to Māgadhī is a problem with which earlier writers were confronted. Authorities like Jinadāsagaṇi Mahattara, Abhayadevasūri, Nemisādhu, Hemacandra and others have their own views, none of them satisfactory. Hemacandra while dealing with six major dialects, ignored Ardha-Māgadhī, the language of the Jain canon. This may be due to the fact that the Jain canonical literature was so confused on account of different versions that he did not feel comfortable in laying down the rules of the Ardha-Māgadhī dialect, which was never uniform. It changed from region to region as the Jain monks travelled from one place to another, which explains the development of the regional colouring on it and why the commentators like Śīlāṅka. Abhayadeva, Malayagiri and others found it difficult to interpret the Āgamic texts faithfully and why notwithstanding its voluminous literature Ardha-Māgadhī could not find a place in ancient grammars. Vararuci did not consider Ardha-Māgadhī an independent dialect. Kramadīśvara considered it a mixture of Mahārāṣṭrī and Māgadhī and not an independent dialect.

Arhaddāśa: Author of the *Munisuvratacarita*, composed in the thirteenth century, which deals with the idealized biography of Munisuvrata. It has 10 cantos and 408 verses. His other work, *Purudevacampū*, deals with Ṛṣabha's life in 10 chapters. *Munisvaratacarita*, Arrah, 1929; *Purudevacampū*, Manikacandra Digambara Jaina Granthamala, No. 27, Bombay, 1927.

Arhants: An advanced stage of spiritual life in which anger, pride, deceit, greed, attachment, hatred and ignorance are absent. A person attains all-round perfection and his mere presence is considered to have the potential to convert hundreds of people to the path of spirituality. Among the seven categories of Arhants, namely the Pañcakalyāṇadhārī, the Tinakalāyaṇadhārī, the Dokalyāṇadhārī, the Samanyakevalin, the Upasargakevalin and the Antakṛtakevalin, the first three are only of the Tīrthaṃkara (q.v.) type. The remaining four, though they have the same spiritual experience as the first three, are not capable of preaching and professing religious doctrines. Tīrthaṃkara and Arhant need to be an emancipated and omniscient, but the former has the special right to form the communities (*tīrtha*) of monks, nuns, lay-men, and lay-women. Those belonging to the non-Tīrthaṃkara group can attain the next higher stage of the Siddha (q.v.) by dint of spiritual attainment, which can be had only through pure meditation and contemplation. The latter is described as an ideal saint, a *paramātman* or god whom the Jains assign an enormous list of attributes.

Ārhantya: A stage in the career of the Tīrthaṃkara when he attains the status of an Arhat.

Arhat Parameṣṭhins: Also known as *tīrthaṃkara-parameṣṭhins*, they are the objects of Jain worship. It is through these *arhat-parameṣṭhins* that the scriptures embodying the knowledge of ultimate reality are periodically revealed for the benefit of mankind. Born with the privilege of becoming the lord of religion after destroying the most powerful *karmic* bondages, the Tīrthaṃkaras (q.v.) attain omniscience. Uncontaminated by the limitation of bodily covering, they symbolize universal love and mercy for all living beings, which is why they are worshipped by the lords of the three worlds. They wandered over the country, propounding the religion and defining the path of salvation. According to tradition Indra had constructed for each Tīrthaṃkara an elaborate moving audience hall which served as a vehicle for him and accommodation for his devout followers. Each Tīrthaṃkara is worshipped with one thousand and eight names. They appear in the world in different cosmic periods and are twenty-four in number. A Tīrthaṃkara is associated with five kinds of festivals, known as *pañcakalyāṇa*, in which the gods take part. These are *svargāvataraṇa*, descent of a god to become a Tīrthaṃkara; *maṇḍābhiṣeka* or *janmābhiṣeka*, rejoicing in birth by performing an *abhiṣeka* or consecration; *dīkṣā*, initiation renouncing kingdom and worldly pleasure; *kevalotpatti*, appearance or omniscience; and *parinirvāṇa*, attainment of salvation.

Arisiṃha: A Jain lay-devotee and follower of Jinadatta of the Vāyaḍa-gaccha, whose *Sukṛtasaṅkīrtana* has Vastupala (q.v.) as its hero. It has eleven *sargas* and 553 verses. Five verses, at the end of each canto, are by his friend Amaracandra. Ātmānanda Sathe Series, Bhavnagar, 1917; ed. Punyavijaya, Singha Jainaśāstra Śikṣāpīṭha, Bombay, 1961.

Ariṣṭanemi: See Neminātha.

Armamalai: Jain site in North Arcot district, which contains fragments of sculptures and evidence of structural additions inside a cave. The cave was converted into a triple-celled Jain temple of the *trikūṭa* type with brickwork. The sculptural remains are those of two *dvārapālas* in rather low relief on slabs of stone. The central cell of the *trikūṭa* is larger than two flanking ones. It was for the principal Tīrthaṃkara. There are interesting remains of mural paintings on the walls and plastered ceiling. The complex probably belongs to the tenth century.

Arṇorāja: Śākambharī Cāhamāna ruler of Ajmer. Although he followed his ancestral religion of Śaivism, he was generous to the Jains. The Kharatara Ācārya Jinadatta was honoured by him.

He gave the followers of this *gaccha* an extensive plot of land for the construction of a temple at Ajmer. A Jain manuscript was copied during his reign in the year VS 1198 (AD 1140).

Ārṣa: One of the eight forms of Jain marriage adopted from Brahmanical legal texts with some modification. Here the father gives his daughter in marriage to the bridegroom after accepting from him a small gift in accordance with the requirements of *dharma*, and the marriage ceremony is performed according to the prescribed mode. *Trivarṇikācāra* XI.73; *Nītivākyāmṛta* XXXI.6.

Arsikere: Findspot of a Jain inscription of AD 1219 in the Hassan district, Karnataka, which records the construction of the Sahasrakūṭa Jinālaya by Recarasa during the reign of Ballāla II. A grant for this temple was given to Sāgaranandi Siddhāntadeva, disciple of Subhacandra Traividya and grand-disciple of Māghanandi Siddhāntadeva, belonging to the Pustaka-gaccha and the Ingaleśvara-bali. *Jaina Śilālekha Saṃgraha* III, No. 465; *Epigraphia Carnatica* V, Arsi 77.

Arthakathā: Tales of adventure and the acquisition of wealth. As merchant Jains laid stress on acquiring wealth without which one was not able to lead a virtuous life. In Jain narrative literature like *Kuvalayamālā* we have the story of a Sthānu who made a trip outside the country to earn wealth. The same text says that just as a woman who goes to meet her lover rests on his chest, similarly the goddess of wealth rests on the chest of one who, even in a difficult situation, does not give up endeavour. This refers to ambitious young sons of merchants who in spite of their forefathers having plenty of money wished to travel abroad in order to make their own fortune. Similar ideals are found in works like *Kumārapālapatiboha*. The stories of Sāgaradatta, Lobhadeva, etc., found in the narrative literature are instructive in this respect. The *Vasudevahiṇḍi* refers to Cārudatta who lost all his wealth in the company of the prostitutes. But he set out on commercial journey to rebuild his fortune. He met with a terrible shipwreck, travelled through inaccessible mountains, was attacked by a band of robbers, reached Ratnadvīpa being picked up and carried through the air by a big bird (cf. the Sindbad story of the *Arabian Nights*), and endured terrible hardship in order to get rich. Even the canonical texts like the *Nāyādhammakahāo* refer to such *arthakathās*. The *Bṛhatkathā* was a storehouse of such tales but unfortunately has been lost to us. The stories are also important as they contain useful information on inland and foreign trade, export and import, trade routes, traders' associations, dialects spoken by traders of different regions, various customs, nautical knowledge and many other details which are rarely noticed in non-Jain literature.

Arthūna: Twenty-eight miles to the west of Banswara in Rajasthan. A Jain temple inscription from this place dated VS 1159 (AD 1101) belongs to the Paramāras of Banswara (Vāgaḍa). Another inscription records the installation of an image of Ṛṣabha in the reign of Vijayarāja (VS 1165 = AD 1108) as also a temple at Uthaṅka (Arthūna) by one Bhūṣaṇa, a pious Jain layman. *Epigraphia Indica* XXI.50.

Arugar Temples: Two Jain temples at Venkunram and Biruder in North Arcot district. The main temple at Venkunram is two-storeyed with a circular *śikhara* and a simple wall-section and *mañca-bandha* plinth. The Birudur temple has an earlier stone image of Vardhamāna, now broken, in a front *maṇḍapa* and a later image within the sanctum. This shrine is also two-storyed with a circular *śikhara*. Both shrines have associated Devī shrines and belong to early Vijayanagara period.

Āryadinna: See Dinnasūri.

***Āryanandin*:** See *Dhavalā*.

Āryāṅganai: Sisterhood of nuns among the southern Jains. They are sometimes maidens and sometimes women who have left their husbands but must in either case take a vow of chastity. They are maintained by the community.

Āryarakṣita: See Digambara-Śvetāmbara split.

Āśādhara: Poet and scholar of the first half of the thirteenth century who wrote a number of *stotras*, a narrative work, and several scholarly texts. He was a friend of King Arjunadeva of Malwa. He was the son of Sallakṣaṇa of the Vyāghraravāla family and held important offices as well. His admirers compared him with Kālidāsa and described him as the son of Sarasvatī. The principal work of Āśādhara is *Dharmāmṛta*, nectar of the faith, which in two part—*sāgāra* and *anāgāra*—treats of the duties of laymen as well as those of homeless ascetics. He himself wrote a commentary on this work in AD 1243. His *Jinayajñakalpa* is dated AD 1228. Āśādhara was a contemporary of no less than five successive kings of Malwa, from Vindhyavarman to Jaitugi. *Dharmāmṛta* edited with Āśādhara's own com. in Manikacandra Digambara Jaina Granthamālā, VS 1972.

Asaga: Jain poet, author of *Vardhamānacarita* or *Mahāvīracarita* or *Sanmaticarita*, an epic in

18 cantos composed in AD 853. Author of eight works, Asaga was an inhabitant of Dharalā in the Cola country.

Asapalli: A Jain centre of repute, modern Ashawul in Ahmedabad, Gujarat. The importance of this place is attested to in Merutuṅga's *Prabandha-cintāmaṇi*.

Āsarāja Vihāra: Jain establishment at Patan and Junagarh built by Tejaḥpāla.

Asavarṇa Marriage: See Inter-caste marriage.

Asceticism: Notwithstanding the influence of Brahmanical asceticism, Jain asceticism has a distinctiveness of its own. Its theoretical basis was undoubtedly supplied by the Brahmanical *āśrama* theory in which the third stage of the (*vānaprastha*) is the period of retirement from worldly activities and the fourth stage (*sannyāsa*) is the time of absolute renunciation. In Jain asceticism there is renunciation no doubt. There is absolute giving up of the worldly comforts, but a Jain ascetic, unlike his Brahmanical counterpart who aspires for his own *mokṣa* in individual capacity, has a good number of social and religious commitments. His asceticism is directly or indirectly concerned with evangelism, and it is for this that the Jain monks endure all forms of hardship. A close study of the Chedasūtras with their extensive commentaries reflects the extreme conditions through which the earlier Jain monks had to pass in order to propagate their religion. They had to occupy deserted places, often infested with women, eunuchs, wild beasts, snakes, mosquitos, ants, dogs and robbers. Cf. *Bṛhatkalpa Bhāṣya* I.2493-9; *Niśīthabhāṣya Cūrṇi* V. 1914; *Ogha Niryukti* 218. During political disturbances often the monks were held as spies and prosecuted. If the ruler was a non-Jain, Jain ascetics had to undergo a lot of trouble. As a general rule under unbearable conditions, they were supposed even to commit suicide rather than violate their vows. But at times under unavoidable calamities, they were advised to allow an exception to the rule. Monks were exhorted to guard themselves even at the risk of violating their self-restraint (*sañjamāo appāṇameva rakkhanto*). If a monk came out safe from calamity, he could purify himself by the act of atonement and could practice more righteousness. *Niśīthacūrṇi-pīṭhikā* 451; *Bṛhatkalpa Bhāṣya* I.2900; *Bhagavatī Ārādhanā* 625. The rules of conduct, however, are exactly the same for both laymen and ascetics with the only obvious difference that while the former observed them partially, the latter has to observe them strictly. The ascetic life is thus a continuation of the householder's life and this has fostered an intimate relationship between the two main divisions of the Jain community. This is basically different from the Brahmanical attitude in which an ascetic in his *sannyāsa* stage has to sever all previous relations with others, even with his own past life, which is declared as officially dead. His ascetic stage is considered a new life, a new birth, and worldly rules and customs are not meant for him. A Brahmanical ascetic is above all identity; he is above kinship, caste, laws, religion, and all that which go on in the name of human relations. But as the Jain ascetics are taken from the *śrāvakas* or householders, a feeling of oneness exists between both sections. This oneness was absent even in the case of the Buddhists. Notwithstanding the commonness with the Jains in regard to monastic life, the Buddhist monks remained aloof and lay devotees had no special religious rights apart from chanting the *triśaraṇa*, lighting candles around *stūpas*, and giving alms to the *saṅgha*. Until the advent of Mahāyānism Buddhism was meant only for monks. The close union between Jain monks and laity brought about by the similarity of their religious duty, differing not in kind but in degree, has enabled Jainism to avoid fundamental changes within. The same rules of conduct observed by laymen are to be followed by ascetics, with the only difference that while laymen practice them partially, the ascetics observe them fully and more rigorously which is why the five vows of householders are known as *anuvratas* or lesser vows compared with the *mahāvratas* or great vows practised by ascetics. A laymen on attainment of the eleven *pratimās* (q.v.) or stages in householder's life is qualified to become an ascetic having undergone an impressive *dīkṣā* or initiation ceremony. Ascetics who observe the rules of conduct in their strictest form and called Jinakalpī Sādhus while those who observe them in a milder form are known as Sthavirakalpī Sādhus. Further, the heads of groups of saints are called Ācāryas, those who are in charge of instruction are known as Upādhyāyas and the other ascetics are known as mere Sādhus. There are also different grades of ascetics. Among the Digambaras these in ascending order are Kṣullaka, Aillaka, and Nirgrantha and among the Śvetāmbaras Yatis, Sādhus, and Ācāryas. The Jain texts are burdened with rules about the lives of the monks. The rules are severe and rigid. The Jain monks are to this day forbidden to have anything to call their own. This is the vow of *aparigraha* originally enunciated by Pārśva. According to Mahāvīra this should include not only non-attachment to all sorts of property but also the non-attachment to everything connected with the five organs of sense, *Ācārāṅga* II.15.5. Even those things which the Jain monk always carries about himself as clothes, alms-bowl, broom, etc., are not his property, but *dharmaprakaraṇa*, things necessary for the exercise of religious duties. The Digambaras regard the abandonment of all clothing as the *sine qua non* of the monastic order. The ascetic disciplines his body and mind by practising 22 *parisahas* (q.v.). For the observances of his vows, he should cultivate the *samitis* (q.v.) or certain forms of carefulness. He must so train himself as not to be moved by the object of senses. A beautiful or ugly sight, a charming note or a jarring sound, a fragrant or foul smell, a flavourful or tasteless dish, a tender or rough touch, should arouse in him no feelings of joy or hatred, attraction or repulsion. He should devote himself to deep meditation, confession of sins unwittingly committed and fresh determination to be more cautious and careful, and detachment of thought from the body. All these came under the twenty-eight *mūlaguṇas* or fundamental qualities of an ascetic. Forgiveness to all creatures, complete absence of self-conceit, deceitfulness and greed, honesty, self-control and chastity should characterize all his thought and action. He should be friendly towards all, pleased with the learned, compassionate to the suffering, and indifferent to those who are uncharitably inclined towards him.

Āsiga: See *Candanabālā Rāsa*, *Jivadayā-Rāsa*.

Aśokā: The Śāsanadevatā (q.v.) of Śītalanātha (q.v.) according to the Śvetāmbara tradition. She is described as seated on a lotus and bearing in her hands *varada*, noose, fruit, and goad.

Aśokan Inscriptions: The earliest epigraphic references to the Jains under the name Nigantha is found in the Seventh Pillar Edict which Aśoka issued in the 29th year of his reign. 'My Censors of the Law of Piety, too, are occupied with various objects of the (royal) favour, affecting both ascetics and householders, and are likewise occupied with all denominations. I have arranged, also, that they should be occupied with the affairs of the Buddhist clergy, as well as among the Brāhmaṇas and the Ājīvikas, the Niganthas and, in fact various denominations.' *Epigraphia Indica* II.274.

***Āsrava*:** The influx of *karma* particles into the soul. Just as water flows into a boat through a hole in it, so also the *āsravas* represent the channels or modes through which the *karmas* enter the soul. *Āsrava* is broadly divided into *bhāvāsrava* (q.v.) and *karmāsrava* (q.v.), the former denoting thought-activities through which the *karma* particles enter the soul, and the latter, their actual entrance. The *bhāvāsravas* are generally of five kinds, delusion (*mithyātva*), want of control (*avirati*), inadvertence (*pramāda*), activities of body, mind, and speech (*yoga*) and passions (*kaṣāya*). *Dravyāsravas* (q.v.) are concerned with the externals. Both forms of *āsravas* make room for *karmāsrava* (q.v.), i.e. actual entrance of the *karma* particles into the Jīva. The actual influx of *karma* affects the soul in eight ways in accordance with which it is divided into eight kinds, viz., *jñānāvaraṇīya*, *darśanāvaraṇīya*, *vedanīya*, *mohanīya*, *āyu*, *nāma*, *gotra*, and *antarāya*. Influx takes place only as a result of the *bhāvāsrava* or reprehensible thought, or changes (*pariṇāma*) of the Jīva. There are 42 ways through which the said process works out. Of these 17 are major including five *indriyas*, four *kaṣāyas*, five *avratas*, and three *yogas*. The easiest way for *karma* to enter is through the five senses. Then come the activities of the four *kaṣāyas*, anger, conceit, deceit, and avarice. There are 25 minor ways also by which *karma* is acquired.

***Aṣṭakāni*:** Poems of eight verses each, 32 such poems on the Jina, cult, knowledge, renunciation, etc., have been written by Haribhadra (q.v.). Published in Surat in 1918.

***Aṣṭamaṅgala*:** Eight auspicious signs associated with the Jain image-complex. These are (1) a *svastika*, (2) a mirror, (3) an urn, (4) a cane-seat shaped like an hour glass, (5-6) two fish, (7) *yugmamīna*, a flower-garland, and (8) a manuscript, which are sometimes carved on the pedestal or other parts of the back slab. The signs do not seem to have stereotyped in earlier relief. The *āyāgapaṭa* Sihanādika shows the eight symbols in the following order from the top left (1) two fish, (2) cane-seat (3) *śrīvatsa* (4) offering *naivedya*, (5) *nandyāvarta*, i.e. 'a *svastika* with nine corners', a sort of geometrical pattern, (6) garland in a leaf-cup, (7) manuscript on ornate stand, (8) pitcher, *bhadraghaṭa*. In other *āyāgapaṭas*, the number, variety, and order seem to differ. It should be noted in this connection that these iconographic features came to be developed gradually and some of the principal distinctive traits are often absent in the earliest extant Jina images. The Digambara tradition gives the following set of *aṣṭamaṅgalas*: *bhṛṅgāra*, a type of vessel; *kalaśa*, a full vase; *darpaṇa*, a mirror; *cāmara*, a fly-wisk; *dhvaja*, a banner; *vyajana*, a fan; *chatra*, a parasol; and *supratiṣṭha*, an auspicious seat. Small metal platters of *aṣṭa-maṅgalas* are often dedicated to Jain temples. Hemacandra has referred to *bali-paṭṭas* with *aṣṭamaṅgala* symbols.

***Aṣṭāhnika*:** A fast of the Digambaras performed thrice a year during the week beginning from lunar eighth in the months of Āṣāḍha, Kārttika and Phālguna. It is observed with varying strictness.

Aṣṭāpada Prāsāda: Jain edifice built by Vastupāla (q.v.) at Prabhāsa. There was another in Jalor where Udyotana Sūri completed his *Kuvalaya-mālā*.

***Aṣṭa Pratihārya*:** Eight marks which are occasionally carved on the *Prabhāvalī* or aureole against the background of which the Jina images characterized by their long hanging arms, the *śrīvatsa* symbol, the suavity of form, the youthful body and nudity are represented. The eight *pratihāryas* are the (1) celestial tree, (2) celestial flowers, (3) drum, (4) throne-seat, (5) heavenly music, (6) yak-tail, (7) trilinear umbrella, and (8) the dazzling aura.

Aṣṭa-Pravacana Mātā: Three Guptis (q.v.) and five Samitis (q.v.) required for Saṃvara (q.v.) or stoppage of the influx of Karmic matter into the soul are grouped together under this name meaning 'eight mothers of the creed'.

***Aṣṭasāhasrī*:** See Vidyānanda.

***Aṣṭaśatī*:** See Akalaṅka.

***Aṣṭā Vasus*:** eight identical figures of two-armed bull-headed seated gods carrying *abhaya* and water vessel carved for the purpose of Jain temple decoration.

Asteya: Non-stealing, the third vow, an ascetic is required to renounce anything that is not given, either in village, or a town or a wood, either small or great, of living or lifeless things. He shall neither take himself what is not given, nor cause others to take it, nor consent to their taking it. To a householder theft means receiving of, or dealing in, stolen goods, telling someone how to steal illegal economic transactions, receiving stolen property, using false weights and measures, adulteration, etc.

Asthikagrāma: A place frequented by Mahāvīra, which was on the road from Vaiśālī to Pāvā.

***Astikāya*:** Literally 'mass of all that is'. Every substance of this kind exists (*asti*) like a body (*kāya*) possessing extension. According to the Jains, the entire cosmos is composed of substances (q.v.) of different kinds possessing some unchanging essential characters (*guṇas*, q.v.) and changing modes (*paryāyas*, q.v.). These are broadly classified into two groups, extended (*astikāya*) and non-extended (*anastikāya*). There is only one substance, time (*kāla*), which is devoid of extension and hence falls into *anastikāya* group. *Astikāya* substances are again divided into—living (Jīva, q.v.) and non-living (Ajīva, q.v.). Jīva is of two kinds, emancipated (*mukta*) and fettered (*baddha*). The latter is also of two kinds, moving (*trasa*) and non-moving (*sthāvara*). The moving Jīvas are again classified on the basis of the number of sense-organs. In the same way Ajīva is divided into four categories—*ākāśa* (space), *dharma* (conditions of movements), *adharma* (conditions of rest) and *pudgala* (matter). *Pudgala* is of two kinds—the atoms (*aṇu*) of earth, water, fire, air, etc., and the compounds (*saṃghāta*).

Astronomy: Jain studies in astronomy and astral physics are recorded mainly in the *Sūrapannatti* and *Jambuddīvapannatti*. The *Candapannatti* is completely identical in all the available manuscripts with the *Sūrapannatti*, which deals with the orbits which the sun traverses during the year, with the rising and sitting the sun, with the speed of the course of the sun through each of its 184 circuits, with the measure of the shadow at various seasons, the connection of the moon with the steller bodies, with the waxing and waning of the moon, with the velocity of different kinds of heavenly bodies and so forth. The *Sūrapannatti* is divided into 20 *pāhuḍas*, beginning with the *maṇḍalas*, i.e. the narrower and wider circles formed by the two suns around Mount Meru (q.v.) according to the seasons. Then it goes on to describe the horizontal path of the suns through the quarters of the compass, their transition from one circle over to the next, the distance covered by one sun in a moment, the range illumined by the suns and the moons, the figures formed by their light, the atoms of the Mandara which are impervious to the light of the sun, the time in which the power of the sun's rays remains constant, the course of sun in relation to day, night and other earthly time measures, process of the earth's temperature effected by the sun, and the length of the shadow depending on the height and light of the sun. All these have been the subject matter from the first to the ninth *pāhuḍa*. In the tenth and in most of the following *pāhuḍas*, the moons and stars dominate. This portion was probably the original *Candapannatti* which contains the list of 28 stars, the duration of their conjunction with the moon, the moments and positions of day and night when the conjunction starts, the relationship of the stars with the months, the new-moon and full-moon days, the numbers and shapes of individual stars, the stars as the guides of the months and as the measures of the shadow cast on them by the sun, the position of the stars in the course of the moon, the orbit of the moon, the division of time, the conception of *yuga*, the kind of the years, the waxing and waning of the moon, the bright and dark halves of the month, the velocity of the moon, stars, and planets, the tendency of the stars, the innermost, outermost, topmost, and lowest stars relative to Jambūdvīpa, the velocity of the stars, their power, their mutual distance, their duration and relative number, the fixed stars beyond the human world and so on. In the *Jambuddīva-Pannatti* we have an astronomical section, the contents of which to some extent correspond with those of the *Sūrapannatti*. Besides, the work deals with the visibility, presence, and temperature of the sun, the circles of the stars and their mutual distances, calculations of year, months and dates, etc. From the modern viewpoint, Jain astronomy is inadequate, and full of speculative and imaginative concepts without a scientific basis, and saturated with *a priori* doctrinal principles obscuring the limited scope of scientific postulations. Yet it should also be held that the Jain thinkers at least tried to explain in their own way the facts relating to the waxing and waning of the moon, the equinoxes, the relative existence of the stars and planets, the known stars, the points of the zodiac, and other kindred subjects. They came to the conclusions that astronomical events take place at regular intervals of time, that in the beginning of the ages the planets were in the same line, that the stars and planets have a uniform linear motion, and that the uneven distances are responsible for the varying rates of their angular motion. Schubring, *DJ*, 101-3.

Āśuka: Minister of the Cālukya King Jayasiṃha Siddharāja (AD 1092-1142) of Gujarat, who built, with the permission of the king, a magnificent temple of Nābheya (Ṛṣabha), which was consecrated by four saints including Śrīdeva or Devasūri (qq.v.) in AD 1125. *Prabhāvakacarita* 181.

***Āsura*:** One of the eight forms of Jain marriage adopted from Brahmanical legal texts with some modification. Here the bride is obtained by paying an adequate sum of money to her father. This form of marriage is regarded as unethical and sinful: *Trivarṇikācāra* XI.75; *Nītivākyāmṛta* XXXI.8.

Asuras: Sworn enemies of the gods in Brahmanical tradition, though both groups have a common ancestor and a kinship bond. The Asuras in Jain conception have no difference with the gods. It is due to the fact that both the gods and the Asuras have an inferior position compared to Tīrthaṃkaras and other enlightened beings and that mortals can easily excel them in merit. Moreover, neither the state of a god or that of an Asura is permanent. Whether they would continue as god or Asura depends on their *karma*. The good gods are described as Daivī and Āsuī while the evil ones are known as Kudeva. In some texts the Asuras are described as former gods. Often the term Asurakumāra has been used. The Asuras may be good or bad, but there are fifteen extremely wicked Asuras such as Ambarīṣa and others who administer tortures in the three uppermost hills. The *Bhagavatī* 169, 180 describes them as gods of the lower world. But they may go down into the deep beyond the Ratnaprabha and reach both the central world and the upper world. The Asuras are described in the Jain texts as belonging to the Bhavanavāsin group of gods. The stories of the conflict between the gods and Asuras which has characterized the Brahmanical epic-Puranic tradition are absent in Jain narrative literature. A Jain version of the Bali (q.v.) legend is, however, found. It is interesting to note that in the lists of goddesses, as found in the *Aṅgavijjā*, occur Asurakanyā and Asurāgramahiṣī. In the *Kuvalayamālā* the cave of the Asuras is mentioned in which connection the hand of an Asura maid is fervently sought.

Aśvāvabodha: A Jain *tīrtha*, in Bhṛgukaccha or Broach, dedicated to Munisuvrata mentioned in the tenth chapter of the *Vividha-tīrthakalpa*.

Atarañjiya: Same as Atranjikhera where remains of a pre-Muslim Jain shrine have been discovered.

Atheism: Since the Jains hold that the universe has neither a beginning nor an end, they do not believe in the existence of God as the creator of the world. They have, however, a host of gods and goddesses who are embodied souls, just like men or animals, differing from them in degree, not in kind, and regarded as inferior to the Jinas. Jain atheism was principally directed against the theism of the Nyāya-Vaiśeṣikas. The Jains have strenuously combated and denounced the fallacies by which the Nyāya-Vaiśeṣikas tried to prove the existence of an eternal and omniscient god as the creator and ruler of all things. The essence of the Nyāya-Vaiśeṣika argument is that all things, being products, presuppose a maker who has an intimate knowledge of their material cause. The world has the atoms for its material cause and God for its efficient. They argue that just as a potter produces a pot by combining prefabricated parts, so god produces the world by combining atoms. All composite objects, formed by the combination of atoms, must have a cause, because they are of the nature of a pot, being made up of parts and possessed of limited dimensions. Hence there must be an intelligent cause or agent (*kartā*) without whose guidance these objects cannot be what they are, cannot attain just that order, direction and coordination which would enable them to be produced as definite effects. This intelligent cause must have a *direct knowledge* of the material causes, i.e. the atoms, *desire* to combine and reproduce them in different forms and also the *power* to accomplish the task. So he requires to be *sarvajña* or omniscient because only an omniscient being can have direct knowledge of all these. In the *Tarkarahasyadīpikā* of Guṇaratna, which is a commentary on Haribhadra's *Ṣaḍdarśanasamuccaya*, the arguments are as follows. If it be said that the world is created by an intelligent being just like a potter making a pot, this cannot be an argument. An ordinary agent like a potter can produce something since he possesses a *body*, has the *will* to produce and further he puts forth the specific *effort* required for the production. None of these, however, is possible in the case of god. When it is said that atoms perform the work of creation, being guided by the will of god, the inference is clearly wrong, because the atoms are devoid of intelligence and it is impossible on their part to follow, even to understand the will of god. The Nyāya-Vaiśeṣikas argue that the existence of god can definitely be proved by inference, an instrument of valid knowledge. The inference is as follows: *Earth, etc., are caused by an intelligent agent, because these are of the nature of being effects, as for instance the jar.* This inference is based on the universal concomitance between 'being effect' and 'having an intelligent cause'. Guṇaratna asks: what is exactly meant by the term 'being effect' by which earth, etc., have been characterized? If 'being effect' means 'being composed of parts' and is understood in the sense of 'the presence of the effect in the component parts', there results, according to Guṇaratna, the fallacy of the 'irregular' (*savyabhicāra*) because here the relation between the probans 'being effect' and the probandum 'having an intelligent cause' had not been established, the former being present in spite of the absence of the latter. According to Guṇaratna when god is conceived as the cause of the world, the latter is viewed as his effect. An effect is something which sometimes exists and sometimes does not. The world does not satisfy this condition of being an effect because it is ever existing. The world exists because nobody had any experience to the contrary. Event for the sake of argument, admitting that the world is an effect, it is not possible to prove that the world presupposes an intelligent cause or god. If the world is viewed as an effect in the general sense of the term it presupposes a cause, but not specifically an intelligent cause or god, because there is no universal concomitance between 'being a bare effect' and 'having an intelligent cause'. Even admitting the world to be an effect in the special sense in which the jar is an effect, we cannot infer any disembodied intelligent cause thereof. According to Guṇaratna, the very logic of the Nyāya-Vaiśeṣikas inevitably leads us to the theory that the knowledge, and will of god are also to be considered effects. But are they prepared to admit that these qualities being effects, presuppose an intelligent cause in the sense in which a jar does? To suggest that god himself is the intelligent cause of his knowledge virtually amounts to a surrender to the Nyāya-Vaiśeṣika position. If it is argued that knowledge of god presupposes an intelligent cause other than god himself, such an assumption would require infinite intelligent causes of god's knowledge will, etc. Again, what would be the cases of such things as trees, plants, etc., which, inspite of being effects, are devoid of intelligent cause. Guṇaratna says that there is no conceivable explanation of how actually god can cause the world. If it is said that god causes the world by virtue of his mere being in existence, there is nothing to prevent the idea of anyone creating the world, since existence is fixed as the only criterion. If it is said that god causes the world by virtue of his knowledge, the wise men may also be viewed as causing the world. To say that god causes the world by virtue of his being characterized by knowledge, will and effect is quite illogical because without a body he cannot be the substratum of knowledge, etc. It is said that god causes the world by virtue of the 'functional intermediacy of knowledge, here also the vexed question of god's body will arise. Then again we are confronted with another question regarding the motive that leads god to create the world. If it is out of purely personal whim, it leads to the possibility of creation being at least occasionally imperceptible, because something done to satisfy a purely personal whim is not necessarily meant for public exhibition. If god creates the world under the guidance of destiny of the individual soul, he loses his independence. If he creates the world out of compassion, everything of the world would then be pleasant. If god creates the world for sport, and for rewarding and punishing, he is characterized by attachment and hatred. According to Guṇaratna any probans that may be cited to prove god as the cause of the world must necessarily be contradictory, because the corroborative instance will always indicate an embodied and non-omniscient cause. Any probans to infer god as the cause of the world must also suffer from the fallacy of the 'counteracted', the fallacy of allowing scope for a counter inference to prove the opposite of the desired thesis. God cannot be eternal, because only by virtue of some transformation of his own nature can he be conceived as the cause of the world. His knowledge also cannot be eternal, because this is contradicted by perception and inference. God cannot be omniscient because there is no concomitance between the varieties of worldly objects and omniscience. If by god is understood a supreme being responsible for the creation of the world, Jainism must be declared to be atheistic since it deliberately rejects the notion of divinity as self-discrepant. If god needs to create the world, it means that he feels a want which is inconsistent with his necessary perfection as the supreme. So there is no god and the world was never created.

Aticāras: Five shortcomings of faith which laymen should avoid. These are *śaṅkā*, doubt or scepticism; *kāṅkṣā*, desire of sense-pleasure; *vicikitsā*, disgust at anything; *anyadṛṣṭipraśaṃsā*, thinking admirably of wrong believers, and *anyadṛṣṭisaṃstava* or praising wrong believers.

***Atithi-Samvibhāga*:** Taking a vow to eat only after feeding ascetics or, in their absence, pious householders.

Atiśayakṣetras: Those holy places where the Tīrthaṃkaras are born such as Kuṇḍalapura, birthplace of Mahāvīra, Rājagṛha, birthplace of Munisuvrata, Varanasi, birth place of Supārśvanātha and Pārśvanātha, etc., the places where the Tīrthaṃkaras first renounced the world, for example, Kampil in Uttar Pradesh where Vimalanātha was initiated into religious life; the places where the Tīrthaṃkaras practised austerities, for example, Prayaga there Ṛṣabhanātha made such efforts; the places where they attained omniscience, for example, Hastināpura where Śāntinātha, Kunthunātha, and Aranātha achieved *kevalajñāna*; and places famous for temples, sculpture, and legends (Mount Abu, Sravanabelgola, etc.).

Atithisaṃvibhagāvrata: See Caritra.

***Ātmakhyāti*:** See Amṛtacandra.

Ātmānuśāsana: See Guṇabhadra.

Atomism: The Jains were probably the earliest thinkers in India to formulate the atomic theory. This theory was formulated in ancient Greece by Demokritos, Empedocles, and others. The Nyāya-Vaiśeṣikas also advanced an atomic theory according to which all composite objects are formed by the combination of atoms. There are nine substances of which only earth, water, fire, and air can be reduced to material atoms. These are eternal and indivisible. They can be neither produced nor destroyed. But the compounds made of them are non-eternal. The Jain doctrine of atomism may be summarized as follows: matter or *pudgala* has certain features, but in spite of this, the transmutation of the elements of earth, water, fire, and air is possible. Each of these elements has a structure, and each is divisible into atoms. The atoms are all of the same kind but can give rise to an infinite variety of things. Matter produced by a combination or compound of atoms is called *skanda* to which category all perceivable objects belong. Our bodies and objects of nature are such compounds. Mind, speech, and breath are also products of matter and hence constituted by atoms. In the *Tattvārthādhigama* V.4ff., it is stated that the atom is eternal as is the substance of which it is the ultimate particle. There are two grades of atoms, smooth (*snigdha*) and rough (*rukṣa*). One smooth atom cannot combine with another of the same grade, but it can be combined with a rough one. This, however, does not hold good in the case of rough atoms. The number of the atoms is infinite. Their combination is revealed in the *pariṇāma* or transformation into the being of an object. Aggregates come about through different processes of amalgamation. The aggregates belong to the categories of geometrical and non-geometrical formations. Atoms are arranged in two or three-dimensional order, in circular, orbicular, triangular, and square formations, except in the case of linear formations. The formation of aggregates results in the substance of a second order, the material masses called *dravya*.

There are eight kinds of combination through which substances are shaped. The qualities of touch, smell, taste, or colour, which characterize a material substance, are possessed by atoms and their compounds. Sound, along with light, heat, shadow, darkness, union, disunion, fineness, grossness, shape, etc., is produced by accidental modification of matter and hence is constituted by atoms. Since matter is qualitatively infinite and quantitatively undetermined it may increase or decrease in volume without addition or loss. When it is in a subtle state, any number of its particles may occupy the space of one gross atom. The difference between the Jain and the Nyāya-Vaiśeṣika viewpoints regarding atomism may be summarized as follows. According to the Jains, the atoms are all of the same kind while the Nyāya-Vaiśeṣikas hold that they are different in kind. The atomic theory of the Nyāya-Vaiśeṣikas seeks to explain that part of the world which is supposed to be non-eternal. The five substances of ether, time, space, mind, and soul do not come within the purview of the Nyāya-Vaiśeṣika atomic theory, but the Jain scheme is more comprehensive and includes many other categories. The Jains also differ from the Nyāya-Vaiśeṣikas on the point that all composite objects of the world formed by the combination of atoms must have an intelligent maker.

***Āturapratyākhyāna*:** Prakrit *Aura-Pacckkhāna*, the fourth text in the Prakīrṇa (q.v.) series which deals with the 'sick' man's refusal of the pleasures of life, the need for confession, voluntary fasting, penances, and so forth. Bhavanagar edn., 1908; Agamodaya, Bombay edn., 1925.

***Audārika Śarīra*:** The gross organic body, which is born of the parents, nourished by food, and subject to decease, decay and death—the body which is given birth to and cast away by the Jīva associated with it at the time of death.

***Audāyika*:** Also known as Saudāyika, it is a form of *strīdhana* (q.v.) or women's property. Whatever is received by the bride from her parents or husband is denoted by this term.

***Aupapātika*:** Prakrit *Uvavāiya* or *Ovavāiya,* the first text of the Upāṅga (q.v.) category. Its first part describes Mahāvīra's visit to the Pūrṇabhadra-Yakṣa temple at Campa and King Kuṇika Ājataśatru's pilgrimage to the same place with his wife Dhariṇī in order to hear the Master's sermon. The second part deals with the questions of Indrabhūti Gautama to the Master on rebirth and various worlds. As early as in 1883 this text was worked in parts by E. Leumann. The Sanskritized form, *Aupapātika*, given by the commentaries seems to be erroneous. *Uvavāiya* means 'the attainment of an existence'. Agamodaya edition with Abhayadeva's commentary, Bombay, 1916.

***Āura-Paccakkāhana*:** See Āturapratyākhyāna.

Auspicious Dreams: Those experienced by the mothers of the Tīrthaṃkaras, Cakravartins, Śalākāpuruṣas, etc., during pregnancy. According to the Śvetāmbara tradition Mahāvīra's mother saw a white elephant, a white bull, a sportive lion, the goddess Śrī, garland of flowers, full moon, the sun, a banner, a full vase, a lake, an ocean of milk, a jewel-heap and a smokeless fire in her dreams. Some available manuscripts of the *Kalpasūtra* show these dreams in paintings. According to Digambara tradition the Jina's mother had sixteen dreams. The elephant is specified as Airāvata and the two extras are a pair of fish and an agitated ocean. These are often carved on the door-lintels of shrines, an early specimen being available on the door-frame of the Śāntinātha temple at Khajuraho.

***Avacūrṇis*:** See Ṭīkās.

Avadhi: One of the five kinds of knowledge. It corresponds to what is known as clairvoyance. It is a kind of extra-sensory perception, not ordinarily evident in all persons, but latent in everyone. Through the instrument of extra-sensory perception, one may actually see events taking place in a distant land or at a distant time. It belongs to the category of *akevalajñāna* and *pratyakṣa-jñāna* or direct knowledge. *Tattvārtta* I.9ff. See Epistemology.

Avanti Kumāra: Avanti the Delicate. His story is still remembered as a warning against rash entrance into the Order. Avanti Kumāra was the son of a rich man who had been brought up in comfort and luxury. In his zeal to recruit new disciples, the patriarch Suhastin readily admitted him into the Order. The hard life of an ascetic did not, however, suit Avanti Kumāra. He put an end to his intolerable position by starving himself to death.

***Āvaśyaka*:** Prakrit *Āvassaya* or *Āvassaga*, the second Mūlasūtra (q.v.) which consists of six sections.

These sections deal with six *āvassayas*, or essential daily duties of a Jain monk. These are: desisting from all evil, glorification of the Tīrthaṃkaras, veneration of the teacher, confession, asceticism, and renunciation of sensual pleasures. *Niryukti* by Bhadrabāhu, *Bhāṣya*, i.e. *Vaiśeṣāvaśyaka Mahābhāṣya* by Jinabhadragaṇi-kṣamāśramaṇa; *Cūrṇi* by Jinadāsgaṇi Mahattara, Ratlam, 1928; *Śiṣyahitā Ṭīkā* by Haribhadra together with the *Niryukti*, Āgamodaya, Bombay, 1916-17; Ṭīkā by Malayagiri together with the *Niryukti*, Āgamedaya, Bombay, 1928, 1932, 1936; *Pradeśa-Vyākhyā* by Maladhārī Hemacandra, Devchand Lalbhai Jaina Pustokoddhāra, 1920; *Niryukti-dīpikā* by Māṇikyaśekharasūri, Surat, 1939; Ernst Leumann, *Übersicht über Āvaśyaka Literature*, ed. W. Schubring, Hamburg, 1934; ed. Muni Puṇyavijaya, Bombay, 1977; Klaus-Bruhn, *Āvaśyaka Studies* I, published in *Studien Zum Jainismus uns Buddhismus—Gedenkschrift für Ludwig Alsdorf*, Wiesbaden, 1918; Index by Ānandasāgara Suri, Bombay, 1928.

***Āvaśyakas*:** Six daily duties of a layman. There is a difference of opinion among Jain authors regarding the *āvaśyakas*. According to one tradition these comprise *deva-pūjā*, worship of god; *guru-pūjā*, worship of the preceptor; *svādhyāya*, study of scriptures; *saṃyama*, practice of self-control; *tapa*, practice of austerities; and *dāna*, bestowing gifts. According to another tradition the *āvaśyakas* are *sāmāyika*, meditation; *caturviṃśati-jina-stuti*, praise of the 24 Jinas; *vandanā*, the ceremonial by greeting spiritual teachers; *pratikramaṇa*, repentance of all transgressions; *kāyotsarga*, austerity performed by standing motionless in a specific posture; and *pratyākhyāna*, a formal vow taken in the presence of a teacher with reference to any kind of restriction or renunciation to be performed.

***Āvassaya, Āvassaga*:** See *Āvaśyaka*.

Avatāra: Descent from heaven to earth to become a Tīrthaṃkara.

Avirati: Want of control. It is of five kinds—*hiṃsā* or violence, *anṛta* or falsehood, *caurya* or stealing, *abrahma* or incontinence and *parigrahākāṅkṣā* or desire to possess things of other persons.

Aviratisamyagdṛṣṭi: The fourth *Guṇasthāna* (q.v.) ascending on which the Jīva feels the urge within himself to control anger, pride, and greed, but cannot become completely free of their influence.

Āyāgapaṭa: Votive slabs erected in Jain shrines for the adoration of the Arhats. These votive slabs are traditional in conception and treatment, the figures and other features of the composition following the indigenous art movement in all details. Particularly interesting is the Āmohini relief which exhibits all the mass and volume of early Indian art. This was dedicated by a lady named Āmohini about the beginning of the Christian era. A nice *āyāgapaṭa* was dedicated, the inscription on it informs us, by a courtesan named Loṇaśobhikā. One *āyāgapaṭa* from Kankali Tila showing the seated figure of a Jina in the centre is a pleasing study of auspicious symbols and motifs, and is composed in a remarkable sense of harmony. Not all the *āyāgapaṭas* have the same auspicious symbols. The tablet set up by Acalā shows four symbols in the upper panel and eight more in the lower one. The lower panel comprises a *śrīvatsa*, *svastika*, half-open lotus-bud, pair of fish, water-jar, heap of jewels, cross-stand, and defaced *triratna*. A better-preserved set of eight symbols is obtained on the *āyāgapaṭa* set up by Sihanādika. It is now in the Lucknow Museum and shows in the central square four composite *triratnas*. In the uppermost central rectangular panel are a pair of fish, a heavenly car, a *śrīvatsa* mark, and a powder-box. In the corresponding part of the lowermost panel are a *triratna* symbol, a full blown lotus, and an object difficult to identify. Among other *āyāgapaṭas* of the Lucknow Museum, one has in the centre a sixteen-spoked wheel, the *dharmacakra*. Another, set up by the wife of Śivaghoṣaka, has four composite *triratnas*. A third, set up by an unknown donor, has an ornamental *svastika* enclosing other symbols. The central smaller circle has composite *triratnas* with an inset Jina figure. The lowermost panel of the tablet has some defaced symbols where a water-jar, a half-open lotus, a *triratna*, and a *svastika* can be recognized. The fragmentary *āyāgapaṭa* of Śivamitra is also interesting. These votive slabs are special features of Mathura sculpture. V.N. Smith, *Jain Stūpa and other Antiquities from Mathura*, Allahabad, 1901, pls. VII, IX; A.K. Coomaraswamy, *History of Indian and Indonesian Art*, London, 1927, 37, fig. 71; *Archaeological Survey of India: Annual Report*, 1922-3, 90, pl. V. 2; U.P. Shah, *Studies in Jaina Art*, Benares, 1955, 77ff.

Āyāra: See Ācārāṅga Sūtra.

Āyāradasāo: See Daśaśrutaskandha.

Ayodhyā: Birthplace of Ādīnātha. The earlier Jain

shrines of Ayodhya are lost. One at Katra, not earlier than the eighteenth-century, houses a few medieval icons. An Ādīnātha image has been found at Fyzabad. An interesting seated image of Śāntinātha is in the collection of the Fyzabad Museum, which shows the dancing Navagrahas in the lowermost section of the pedestal, the Upāsaka, Śāsanadevatā, an antelope on either side of a wheel on the *siṃhāsana* above it, two *chowrie*-bearers, one on each side of the central figure, two elephants with pitchers carrying riders on lotuses parallel to the head of the Jina, and lastly on the topmost section of the rectangular *prabhāvalī* two garland-bearing Vidyādhara couples of the right and left and one single garland-bearer over the triple umbrella above the Jina's head, all three being depicted in the flying posture. Ayodhya is the birthplace of five Tīrthaṃkaras, viz., Ṛṣabha, Ajita, Abhinandana, Sumati, and Ananta. The temple of Munisuvrata in this town is mentioned in the *Paumacariya*.

***Ayogikevalin*:** The fourteenth and last *guṇasthāna* (q.v.), the highest step of the ladder, ascending on which the Jīva becomes absolutely free from the fetters of *karma*.

***Āyu*:** One of the four constituents of the *aghātin karma* (q.v.), which determines the length of time, which a Jīva (q.v.) must spend in the form with which his *karma* had endowed him. It is subdivided into Deva, Manuṣya, Tiryak, and Naraka, each concerned with gods, human beings, animals, and demons respectively.

Ayyavale: Aihole in the Bijapur district of Karnataka which was a Jain centre. An inscription of the seventh century refers to the existence of a Jinendra temple in this place which was reconstructed at a later date according to the evidence provided by an inscription dated AD 1116.

B

Babanagar: Situated in the Bijapur district this place has yielded an inscription of AD 1161, of the time of King Bijjala, which mentions a monk called Māṇkya Bhaṭṭāraka belonging to the Mūla-saṅgha and Deśī-gaṇa and records a grant to a local Jain shrine. *Jaina Śilālekha Saṃgraha* IV, No. 256.

Badali Stone Inscription: Discovered by G.H. Ojha in 1912 at Badali in Ajmer district, Rajasthan, who had attributed it to 400 BC on the assumption that it referred to the year 84 of the Vīra Nirvāṇa era. D.C. Sircar for his part assigned this inscription to the close of the second century BC. *Journal of the Bihar and Orissa Research Society* XVI.67-8; D.C. Sircar, *Select Inscriptions* I.89.

Badami Cave: A Jain cave at Badami which appears to date from about the middle of the seventh century AD. It is essentially similar in plan and other arrangements to its sister cave at Aihole. It is the last and topmost of the series of four such cave temples excavated on the northern scarp of the Badami cliff. With a pillared quadrangular hall and a cella cut out at its far end and chapels on either side, it is essentially of the same plan as the other three Brahmanical caves on the cliff, but the smallest and most lavishly embellished. The facade of the *mukha-maṇḍapa* has four pillars and two pilasters, one at either extreme, the central pair of pillars with greater inter-columnation as the characteristic of the Cālukyan style and its derivatives. The pillars have well-formed capitals with the *kalaśa*, *taḍi*, and *kumbha*. A second set of four pillars and two pilasters separate the outer and the inner *maṇḍapas*. The ceiling of the front *maṇḍapa* is divided into five bays by cross-rafters. The shrine cell shows Mahāvīra seated on a throne. Carved in the end-walls of the two *maṇḍapas* are reliefs of Gommaṭeśvara and of Pārśvanātha and Ṛṣabhanātha, surrounded by a *prabhāvalī* containing reliefs of twenty-four Tīrthaṃkaras.

Badanāvara: Site of the Ādīśvara temple in the Dhar district of Madhya Pradesh.

Baddha Jīva: See Saṃsārin Jīva.

Badli: Site of Brahma Jinālaya built by Narasiṃha in the Belgaum district of Karnataka.

Badnawar: Find spot of a beautiful fragmentary image of Cakreśvarī now preserved in the Jaisinghapura Jaina Archaeological Museum, Ujjain.

Badoh: Situated in the Vidisha district of Madhya Pradesh it is reputed for its medieval Pratihāra art and architecture. The site has a fairly large Jain temple showing a quadrangular arrangement of *devakulikas*, each with a towered square sanctum. Remains show that the *devakulikas*, numbered twenty-four, enshrining all the Jinas and the central one with the tallest *śikhara* was probably dedicated to Ṛṣabhanātha.

Badwani: Known as Siddhanagara, this site in Madhya Pradesh has several Jain temples. An image of Ādinātha carved in the rock is 26 m high. On a hillock called Culagiri there are twenty-two Jain temples.

Bagh-Gumpha: Cave 12 of the Udayagiri Hill, Bhuvaneswar, which has Jain affiliation.

Baghelkhand: Region in Madhya Pradesh, a few Jain images from which representing the Kalacuri art tradition are preserved in the Dhubela State Museum.

Bāhaḍameru: Modern Barmer, a Jain centre, associated with a Ṛṣabha temples and Jineśvara II of the Kharatara Gaccha who visited this place in AD 1225. A Mahāvīra temple was erected here in AD 1269.

Bahiryāna: Sacrament. It is taking the child, out of the house two to four months after its birth, on an auspicious day.

Bāhubali: See Gommaṭeśvara.

Bahulārā: Find spot of an eleventh-century Pārśvanātha image in Bankura district, now in the back wall of the *garbhagṛha* of Siddeśvara temple. The image is about 5 ft in height, standing in *kāyotsarga* on lotus pedestal. Snake coils seem to go up forming seven hoods and over the Jina's head is the prominent *uṣṇīṣa*. A Nāga couple and *chowrie*-bearers are on both sides. There are *navagrahas* at the level of the Jina's waist and flying Gandharvas on the upper corners of the black slab.

Bahuriband Inscription: Incised on a colossal statue of Śāntinātha found at Bahuriband in Jabalpur district, this epigraph records that during the reign of Kalacuri Gayākarṇadeva in the middle of the twelfth century, one Mahābhoja, son of Sādhu

Sarvadhara, favoured by the illustrious Jain logician Māghanandin erected the temple of Śāntinātha, the image installed therein being consecrated by Ācārya Subhadra belonging to the line of Deśī-gaṇa in the *āmnāya* of Candrakara Ācārya. *Corpus Inscriptionum Indicarum*, IV (1), No. 59.

Bahurūpiṇī: See Naradattā.

Bāhya Tapa: External austerities meant for *nirjarā* (q.v.) or purging off the *karmas* consisting of *anaśana*, fasting; *avamodarya*, eating a mouthful less everyday; *vṛtti-parisaṅkhyāna*, restrictions with regard to food; *rasa-parityāga*, abstinence from tasty food; *vivikta-śayyāsana*, sitting and sleeping in a lonely place; and *kāyakleśa*, mortification of the body so long as the mind is not disturbed.

Bairampalli: Findspot of a fifteenth-century Gommaṭeśvara figure in Andhra Pradesh.

Bairat: Jain site in Rajasthan, ancient Virāṭanagara of *Mahābhārata* fame. An image of Supārśvanātha, now in the Cintāmaṇi temple of Bikaner, contains an inscription which shows that in AD 1511 it was set up at Virāṭanagara. In the Vimalanātha temple of this place there is an inscription of AD 1587 which records its erection by Indrarāja, a local chief. It was inaugurated by Kalyāṇavijaya, disciple of Hiravijaya. Another temple, dedicated to Pārśva, was in existence in Bairat in the sixteenth century. Jinavijaya, *Prācīna Jaina Lekhasaṃgraha* II, 379.

Balā: Śāsanadevatā of Kunthunātha (q.v.) who is conceived of as riding a peacock and with a citron, spear, musaṇḍi and lotus in his four hands.

***Bālabhārata*:** See Amaracandra.

Bālacandra: See Mahendrasūri.

Bālacandra: See Karuṇā-Vajrāyudha.

Bālacandrasūri: Thirteenth-century author of an historical poem *Vasantavilāsa* dealing with various episodes in the career of Vastupāla, the minister of the Vāghelas of Gujarat. Edited with intro. by G. Bühler, Bombay, 1875.

Balātkāra-Gaṇa: See Gaṇa.

Bali: The celebrated righteous demon. According to the Puranic version, the gods being afraid of the valour and greatness of Bali, king of the demons, requested Viṣṇu to destroy him, so that they might not be dislodged from heaven. While Bali was performing a grand sacrifice, Viṣṇu descended on the earth in the form of a dwarf, and, disguised as a mendicant, went to the place of Bali's sacrifice. He asked of him as much earth as could cover in his three steps. When his request was granted, Viṣṇu assumed a mighty form and covered the entire earth with his first step, all the heavens with the second, and sought a place to set his third step. Bali thereupon offered his own head, on which Viṣṇu put his third foot and pushed him down to the underworld. There is a Jain version of the Bali-legend. Budhasvāmin in his *Bṛhatka-thāślokasaṃgraha* narrates the following: In ancient times Viṣṇu, the holder of the disc, took the form of a dwarf in order to humble the demon Bali and overpowered heaven with three steps. The earliest form of this story is found in the *Vasudevahiṇḍi* in which it is said that Namuci, the minister of King Mahāpadma of Hastinapura, was hostile to Jain monks and started giving them trouble. Thereupon the sage Viṣṇu was called to rescue the monks. He asked his minister to grant him space for three steps so that the Jain monks could live peacefully. The minister reluctantly agreed. Viṣṇu inflated his body. He placed his right foot on the peak of Mount Mandara and the whole earth began to tremble. This is a very crude adaptation of the Puranic Bali legends. Jinasena in his *Harivaṃśa-purāṇa* names Bali as one of the four ministers of the king. The sage Viṣṇukumāra asked Bali to permit him three steps on the earth. He took one step on Mount Meru, the other on Mount Mānasottara, and as there was no space left for the third, he moved it round and round in heaven. According to Guṇabhadra's *Uttara-purāṇa*, Viṣṇukumāra assumed the form of the dwarf Brāhmaṇa and asked Bali for three steps on the earth. Nemicandra in his commentary on *Uttarapurāṇa* and Hemacandra in his *Triṣaṣṭhi* went closer to the Puranic version and addressed Viṣṇu as *trivikrama* in his dwarf incarnation.

Bali: A branch or subdivision of the nature of the *gacchas*. The major Jain sects themselves are subdivided into smaller groups like the *saṅghas* and *gaṇas* in the south and into *kulas* and *śākhās* (and later *gacchas*) in the north. Epigraphical records show that the *saṅghas*, *gaṇas*, *gacchas*, *balis*, and *śākhās* had grown to a very large number by AD 1000. Among the *balis* Iṅguleśvara and Panasoge are important and mentioned frequently in inscriptions.

Baligrāma: Also known as Balgamba and Baḷḷigava, it is in Shimoga district, Karnataka, wherefrom a good number of eleventh-century Jain inscriptions have been found. The earliest of them was issued in AD 1040 during the reign of Cālukya Someśvara I whose feudatory Cāmuṇḍarāja Rāyarasa made a grant for the local Aṣṭopāvasi Bhaṭṭāraka-basadi. The second inscription is of AD 1048 and refers to the contribution of the feudatory Lakṣma to the shrine of Śānti Tīrtheśa.

The shrine formerly of wood, was converted to stone at the request of Lakṣma's general Śāntinātha. The latter is described as a royal swan of the lotus of Jain religion. The epigraph mentions the recipient of the grant as Māghanandi Bhaṭṭāraka, disciple of Munichandra, granddisciple of Vardhamāna Munīndra, belonging to the Mūla-saṅgha, Deśī-gaṇa and Kondakunda-anvaya. A short inscription of about AD 1075 mentions the monk Anantakīrti, disciple of Municandra belonging to Balātkāra-gaṇa. Another inscription of AD 1077 refers to a gift to the Jain monk Rāmasena, disciple of Guṇabhadra of the Mūla-saṅgha, Sena-gaṇa and Pogari-gaccha. The gift was meant for the Cālukya-Gaṅga Permānaḍi Jinālaya. An important epigraph of AD 1319, of the time of Hoysala Ballāla III, mentions the Mallikamoda Jina temple, dedicated to Śāntinātha. It further mentions a gift to a sage called Padmanandin for the maintenance of temple. *Epigraphia Carnatica* VII. Shik 120, 124, 134, 136; *Jaina Śilālekha Saṃgraha* II, Nos. 181, 204, 208, 217; IV. 391.

Bāmaṇi Inscription of Vijayāditya: Dated in Saka 1073 (AD 1151) of the time of the Kolhapur Śilāhāra chief Vijayāditya (AD 1138-75), this inscription, found at Bamani, 25 miles south-west of Kagal in Kolhapur district, Maharashtra, refers to a Pārśvanātha temple, situated probably at Madur, for which a grant was made by the king at the request of his maternal uncle Sāmanta Lakṣmaṇa. It also refers to Arhanandi-Siddhāntadeva, disciple of Meghanandi (q.v.) *Corpus Inscriptionum Indicarum* VI, No. 54.

Baṃbhī: Disciple of Ṛṣabhanātha (q.v.) who led in collaboration with Sundarī the order of nuns comprising 300,000 members established by Ṛṣabha himself, according to the *Samavāya.*

Banavasi Grants of Mṛgeśavarman: Two grants of the Kadamba King Mṛgeśa who ruled in the late fifth century, issued from the capital city Banavasi in favour of Jain monks. By the first grant, three equal portions of the donated village Kālavaṅga are given respectively to the temple of Jinendra, the Saṅgha of the Śvetapaṭa-mahāśramaṇa and the Nrgranthamahāśramaṇa. The second inscription records a grant of black soil in a village called Bṛhat-Paralura for the maintenance of a Jain shrine. *Indian Antiquary*, VII, 35-8.

Bandha: Bondage. It is what binds the soul to the body. It is caused by the union of the soul with *pudgala*. There are four ways in which such bondage takes place, classified according to their nature (*prakṛti*), duration (*sthiti*), intensity (*anubhāga*), and mass (*pradeśa*). The states of thought which condition the accumulation of *karma* are called *bhāvabandha* (q.v.) and the actual bondage of the soul is technically called *dravyabandha*. It is of the account of the former that the actual connection between *karma* and Jīva takes place. The connection is like the sticking of dust on oily cloth. The cloth represents the Jīva, the oil the passions, transgressions, and activities, and the dust, the *pudgala* or matter. Thus *bandha* is caused by wrong belief (*mithyādarśana*), non-renunciation (*avirati*), carelessness (*pramāda*) body, and speech (*yoga*). *Dravyasaṃgraha*, vṛtti 30ff, *Vardhamāna Purāṇa*, XVI.44.

Bāndhavapura: Sanskrit name of the well-known Bandalika in the Shikarpur taluk of Shimoga district in Karnataka. An inscription of AD 1074 mentions Cālukya feudatory Permāḍi Udayāditya and his grant to Śāntinatha temple. The recipient was Kulacandradeva, disciple of Paramānanta Siddhāntadeva belonging to the Mūla-saṅgha, Kāṇūra-gaṇa. A good description of the temple complex of Śāntinātha, at this place, is also found in an epigraph of AD 1203 which mentions the erection of a *maṇḍapa* by a merchant called Bodha Seḷḷi at the temple of Śāntinātha. The death of a Jain saint named Śuchacandra belonging to the Kāṇūra-gaṇa is mentioned in a Banda like inscription of AD 1213. *Jaina Śilālekha Saṃgraha*, II, Nos. 140, 207; III, Nos. 448-9.

Bandūra: Ancient Bandavura, findspot of an epigraph of AD 1168 in the Arsikere taluk of the Hassan district, Karnataka, which mentions Hoysala Ballāla II and records the construction of a Jain temple dedicated to Pārśvanātha by two merchants, Mādirāja and Saṅka-Seṭṭi. Monks of the Aruṅgala-anvaya including Malleṣena, Śrīpāla Traividya and Vāsupūjya II are mentioned here. The image of Pārśva was made by Puṣpasena-muni, a disciple of Vāsupūjya II. *Jaina Śilālekha Saṃgraha*, III, No. 373.

Baniawadi: Site of a Jain temple in Dhar, Madhya Pradesh, where inscribed images of the fourteenth and fifteenth centuries are preserved.

Baṅkāpura: Jain centre in the Dharwar district, Karnataka, founded by Baṅkeyarasa, a feudatory of Amoghavarṣa I of the ninth century. It is a holy place in the *praśasti* of Guṇabhadra's *Uttarapurāṇa*. Jain inscriptions of later times have been discovered here. In an epigraph of AD 925 we have a reference to Dhora Jinālaya of Baṅkāpura. Another Jain temple of this place is mentioned in an inscription of the twelfth century. An epigraph of śaka 977 mentions Prince

Vikramāditya VI, whose feudatory Harikeśari of the Kadamba Bankapura had built a Jain temple at this place. *Bombay-Karnatak Inscriptions* I (1) No. 34; *Jaina Śilālekha Saṃgraha* IV, No. 144.

Bankura: District in West Bengal where Jain sites are scattered in Ambikanagar on the confluence of the Kaṃsāvatī and Kaumārī, Chitgiri opposite Ambikanagar, Chiada, opposite Pareshnath, Kendua on the bank of the Kamsavati Barkola celebrated for Coumukhas of *rekhā*-deul type, etc. The sites of Bankura yielded a good number of Jina images of the tenth-eleventh centuries. Also findspot of a twelfth-century Mahāvīra image in Kotulpur, Bankura district, West Bengal, which is locally worshipped as Śītalā-Ṣaṣṭhī. It is nearly 2 feet in height and stands in *kāyotsarga* with the emblem lion. Historically Bankura and its adjoining districts, Purulia and Burdwan (Vardhamāna, after Mahāvīra) formed the original Jain culture-complex in Bengal. Subsequent migration of Jainism was probably from this culture-complex to north Bengal on the one hand (the earliest Jain epigraph from Bengal has been discovered at Paharpur) and to the Midnapore district in the south. The sites of Bankura have been individually mentioned in this volume.

Banpur: Jain site near Tikamgarh in central India where an interesting shrine of Nāgara style is found which is built on a square basement, about 1 metre high. Its entire composition, the decorated pillars, ceilings, *garbhagṛha* and tapering *śikhara* are remarkable. The decorative arrangement of the river goddesses, the *navagrahas* and foliage-work are also exquisitely done. The images of Ādīnātha, Sarasvatī and other deities are also nicely carved.

Banpur Hoard: Bronze image, Buddhist and Jain, discovered at Acutarājapura or Banpur in Puri district. The Orissa State Museum collection of Jain images of this hoard comprises a seated Ambikā with a child in her lap under a mango-branch; standing Asokā or Mānavī, holding the branch of a tree, a bear on pedestal; seated Pārśvanātha with seven hoods of a serpent; standing Pārśvanātha with the snake emblem on a pedestal; and an image of Ādīnātha with matted hair, bearing an inscription recording that it was the gift of one Śrīkara. The images belong to the eleventh century.

Bappabhaṭṭi: A Śvetāmbara Jain activist who was responsible for promotion of Jainism in different places of northern India in the eighth century. He set up in his lifetime Jain shrines at Mathura, Gopagiri, Anahillapura, and other places. *Prabandhakośa* 41. His patron Āma of Kanauj is not known from epigraph sources. It has been conjectured that he should be identified either with Nāgabhaṭa II or with Indrayudha Indrarāja. Some scholars hold that he was the son and successor of King Yaśovarman of Kanauj. Bappabhaṭṭi was the author of *Sarasvatī-stotra* and *Caturviṃśati-Jinastuti*. His life-stories are found also in the *Prabhāvakacarita* and *Bappabhaṭṭi Suri Caritra*.

Barabhuji Gumpha: See Khaṇḍagiri Caves.

Barabhum-Jina: Jina image from Barabhum in Midnapur district, West Bengal, now in the Indian Museum, Calcutta. It is a medieval composition, the principal image in the centre being surrounded by miniature figures of twenty-three Jinas and other auxiliary divinities.

Bare Baba: Site at Kundalpur in Damoh district, Madhya Pradesh, which has yielded a large number of loose sculptures representing the Tīrthaṃkaras and Yakṣīs.

Barkola: Findspot of a Pārśvanātha image in the Bankura district in a ruined temple. The main image is lost but the feet are extant on a pedestal. The Nāga figure below identifies the lost figure with that of Pārśva. An Ambikā image from Barkola, about 1 foot 6 inches in height stands on a lotus. Its right hand, slightly bent, holds a child. She is clad in a *sārī* and ornaments, and over her head there are hanging mangoes in branches. There is a female attendant on the right and a lion below. Two eleventh-century Caumukhas are found. These are of *rekhā*-deul type. There are four Jinas on the four sides, identified as Ṛṣabha, Candraprabha, Śāntinātha, and Padmaprabha.

Barmer: Site in Rajasthan where two inscriptions of the time of Samantasiṃha of the Jalor house of the Cāhamanas dated VS 1352 (AD 1294) contain Jain elements. The temple of Ādinātha of Barmer was visited by the Kharatara Ācārya Jinesvara in VS 1283 (AD 1225).

Basavanapura: Findspot of a Jain inscription of AD 1183 in Narasipur taluk, Mysore district, which gives a list of the spiritual predecessors of Candraprabha Muninātha belonging to the Drāviḍa-saṅgha, Aruṅgala-anvaya and Nandi-saṅgha. The inscription mentions Samantabhadra, Kumārasena, Cintāmaṇi, Cūḍāmaṇi, Maheśvara, Śāntideva, Akalaṅka, Puṣpasena, Vimalacandra, Indranandī, and Paravādimalla. Then some portion is effected after which come the names of Maladhārī, Ajitasena I, Candraprabha, Ajitasena II, Samayadivākara, and Sūri Candraprabha. *Epigraphia Carnatica*, III, Narasi 105.

Basti-Halli: Site of Pārśvanātha temple in Hassan district, Karnataka. It is of the Hoysala style with fourteen fine polished black-stone pillars in the *sabhā-maṇḍapa*. Two carved elephants stand at the sides of the entrance. Close to this site is an Ādinātha-basti and a Śāntinātha-basti. There is also a *mānastambha* with a horse galloping eastwards.

Bastipur: Findspot of a Jain inscription of AD 1383 in Srirangapatna taluk of Mandya district which refers to the construction of a Pārśvanātha temple and to the monks of Tintiṇi-gaccha and Kāṇūra-gaṇa. *Epigraphia Carnatica*, III, Seringa 144.

Bateshwar: Site of the remains of a Jain shrine in Agra district.

Bāwā-Pyārāś Math: Caves near Junagarh. The prevalence of Jain faith in Saurashtra in the early centuries of the Christian era can be deduced from the occurrence of the religious symbols in this place. The site consists of a group of about twenty monastic rock-cut cells. H.D. Sankalia, *Archaeology of Gujarat*, Bombay, 1941, 166ff.

Bayana: Anciently known as Śāntipura or Śrīpatha, it is in the Bharatpur region. This place was once a stronghold of Jainism and yielded an inscribed Jain image of AD 994, recording that it was dedicated at the instance of one Surasena of the Vāgoḍa-saṃgha. A fourteenth-century mosque, known as the Ukhā-masjid, and five other mosques at Bayana were built with material obtained from the demolition of Jain and Hindu temples as is attested to by the re-used old carved pillars and other architectural members.

Begur: Site of Cokimayya Jinālaya in Bangalore taluk and district, managed by one Śubhacandra of Pustaka-gaccha, mentioned in an inscription of AD 1427 found therein. *Epigraphia Carnatica* IX, Bangalore 82.

Belur: A Jain centre in the Hassan district, Karnataka. Among the epigraphs found here, one belonging to AD 1137 eulogizes the achievement of Viṣṇu Daṇḍādhīpa, general of the Hoysala Viṣṇuvardhana. This general built a magnificent Jina temple named after his master Viṣṇuvardhana Jinālaya in Dorasamudra. His *guru* was the great logician Śrīpāda Traividyadeva. It should be noted in this connection that the writing on the specimens of paintings of the Hoysala period (preserved in the manuscript library of the temple in Mudbidri) may be compared with those of the flowery lines on the metal plates of the Belur temple. *Epigrahia Carnatica*, V, Belur, No. 17. *Jaina Śilālekha Saṃgraha* II, No. 305.

Bellūr: Site of Vimalanātha-basti in Mysore district, Karnataka.

Belūru: Findspot of a Jain inscription of AD 1022 in Mandya Taluk, Karnataka which refers to the construction of a Jina temple in the reign of Gaṅga Permanadi. *Jaina Śilālekha Saṃgraha*, II, No. 172.

Benisāgar: An unexplored Jain site in the Singhbhum district of Jharkhand.

Besnagar: Historical site in Madhya Pradesh, modern Vidisha, which is the findspot of an interesting sculpture of a standing Tīrthaṃkara, having two flying garland-bearers near the head, in front of the circular halo with a lotus in the centre and two half-seated headless devotees near the legs. It is now in the Gwalior Museum. The sculpture seems to belong to the late sixth century.

Betūrū: Site of Lakṣmī Jinālaya in Devangar taluka of Citradurga district, Karnataka, wherefrom an inscription of AD 1271, during the reign of Yādava Rāmacandra, mentions its construction by Kucirāja, a feudatory of the Yādava king. Kucirāja was the disciple of Padmasena Bhaṭṭāraka. The temple was given to the monks of Mūla-saṅgha, Sena-gaṇa and Pogala-gaccha. *Epigraphia Carnatica* XI, Deva, No. 13.

Bhadrabāhu: Patriarch who became the head of the Jain order in 317 BC. Last of the *śrutakevalins* (q.v.), Bhadrabāhu was born in a Brāhmaṇa family at Koṭikapra in Puṇḍravardhana. He was the last to master knowledge of the fourteen *pūrvas* (q.v.) which contained the canon in the original. His tenure is remarkable for events which led ultimately to the Śvetāmbara-Digambara split. In the *Bhadrabāhucarita* of Ratnanandin it is said that Bhadrabāhu had foreseen that a famine of twelve years' duration would ravage northern India. So leaving his colleague Sthūlabhadra (q.v.) in charge of the monks who did not wish to follow him, he left Magadha for southern India. When he reached Sravanabelgola (q.v.) Bhadrabāhu felt his end approaching, and after designating Viśākha, he ended his life by starvation. Mean-while the northern monks adopted several modifications in the rules of their conduct, of which the southerners did not approve. Another cause of division was the council of Pāṭaliputra to fix the canon, under the lead of Sthūlabhadra. The work of this council was repudiated by the followers of Bhadrabāhu. According to a different version of the Bhadrabāhu legend, he returned from south India at the end of the famine to be the head of the whole community and his party declined to accept the work of the Pāṭaliputra council. A third account says that Bhadrabāhu resigned his position as leader to Sthūlabhadra and retired to

Nepal for the rest of his life. When Stūlabhadra went to Nepal to consult him on the canon and its preservation by the council of Pāṭaliputra he learnt from his predecessors all the fourteen *Pūrvas* but was forbidden to reveal to others more than the first ten of them. Bhadrabāhu preached in different parts of India and four of his disciples Agnidatta, Godāsa, Jinadatta, and Somadatta attained celebrity, but none of these disciples succeeded him. Besides the *Kalpasūtra* attributed to him, Bhadrabāhu is said to have composed *niryuktis* or commentaries on ten canonical books and another work, *Upasarga Harastotra*, is praise of Pārśva. His name can, however, be associated with these texts only conventionally and not actually because, according to one tradition he passed away 170 years after the demise of Mahāvīra and according to another after 162 years. So the year of his death should be 297 or 289 BC, too early for these works. It is likely that these were authored by a second Bhadrabāhu whose existence is acknowledged in Jain tradition. Kundakunda (q.v.) who lived in the first century AD called himself a pupil of Bhadrabāhu, perhaps referring thereby to Bhadrabāhu II.

***Bhadrabāhucarita*:** See Ratnanandin.

Bhadrakali: Findspot of a tenth-century unidentified Jina image in the Hoogly district, West Bengal, now in the Asutosh Museum, Calcutta University. It is an extremely sensitive figure with *Uṣṇīṣa* and curling hair, truncated at the waist, a nude bust with the face registering the dedicative calmness and straight arm stretched downwards strongly suggesting *kāyotsarga* pose. It is unidentifiable in the absence of *lāñchana* or emblem.

Bhadra-Śāla: Mythical forest encircling the Sudarśana Meru (q.v.). It has five divisions called Bhadra-śāla, Mānasottara, Deva-ramaṇa, Nāga-ramaṇa and Bhūta-ramaṇa. It has four Caityālayas.

Bhadreśvara: Jain centre in the Kutch district of Gujarat. The Pārśvanātha temple of this place is well-known. In the *Jagaḍucarita* there is a reference to the Viranatha shrine of this place. Jagaḍu is said also to have built a temple consisting of image of all the Jinas.

***Bhagavatī*:** Also known as *Vyākhyāprajñapti* (Prakrit *Viyāhapannati*) this bulky text, regarded as the fifth Aṅga (q.v.) deals with the dogmatics of Jainism, partly in the form of questions and answers, Mahāvīra replying to the questions of his disciple Indrabhūti Gautama, and partly in the form of dialogue-legends (*itihāsa-saṃvāda*). The life and personality of Mahāvīra, his relationship to his disciples and contemporaries, his parables intended for religious education, details about his predecessors, the earlier Tīrthaṃkaras, accounts of his difference with Jamāli and others, descriptions of the heavenly worlds of the gods and those of the hells, etc., from the subject-matter of the *Bhagavatī*. The voluminous text extends to 41 Śatakas. The fifteenth Śataka, called Gośālaka, gives an elaborate account of the career of Gośāla Maṅkhaliputta, the famous Ājīvika (q.v.) teacher. Edited with Abhayadeva's com. Āgamodaya, 3 vols, Bombay, 1918-21; Gujarati trans. by Bechardas Jivaraj Doshi and Pandit Bhagavandas, 4 vols., Jināgama Prachār Sabhā, Ahmedabad, vs 1974-88; J. Deleu.

***Viyāhapannatti*:** Rijks University of Ghent 1970.

***Bhagavatī Ārādhanā*:** See Mūlārādhanā.

***Bhairava-Padmāvatī-Kalpa*:** Jain Tantric text composed about AD 1047 and available in a Gujarati edition. The author of this work was Mallisena who was a member of the Drāviḍa Saṅgha. It deals with Tantric rituals meant for hypnotism, success in love, creating bad blood, healing, and so forth and refers to the processes of making herbal preparations, drawing diagrams, performing bodily gestures, uttering syllables and allied magical practices.

***Bhaktāmara Stotra*:** See Mānatuṅga.

Bhaktilābha: See *Uttama-caritra-kathānaka*.

***Bhaktaparijñā*:** Prakrit *Bhattaparinnā*, the second of the Prakīrṇa (q.v.) series which signifies dispensing with food. In 172 verses it describes legends of grievous sinners who did penance and became saints. Bhavanagar edn. 1908; Agamodaya edn., Bombay, 1925.

Bhaṇḍāri-Basti: A large temple at Sravanabelogola (q.v.) measuring 81 by 23 m on plan. It houses all the Tīrthaṃkaras, to whom it is dedicated. The images are about 1 m in height. There are three gateways. The middle door is well-carved and the figure right in front is that of Vāsupūjya. The temple was built in AD 1159 by Hulla, the treasurer of the Hoysala Narasiṃha I (AD 1141-73). *Epigraphia Carnatica*, II, No. 349.

Bhāṇḍasar Temple: The oldest Jain shrine of Bikaner dedicated to Pārśvanātha. It was constructed by a merchant named Bhāṇḍa in the sixteenth century. The architectural design of this temple shows Islamic influence. The exterior of the tall *śikhara* is decked with *uraḥ-śṛṅgas*, turrets attached to the central projection, besides the double-storeyed projection balconies. Above the cella with its circumambulatory are two storeys each opening into four balconies and interconnected by narrow stairs.

Bhaṇḍ-Dewal Temple: Jain temple at Arang in Raipur district Chhattisgarh. It belongs to the late eleventh century and represents the Bhumija mode of architecture in regional Kalacuri style. It is west-facing and preserves only the sanctum preceded by an *antarāla*, with no remains of a *maṇḍapa*. The sanctum is stellate on plan with six offsets and carries a five-storeyed *śikhara*. The sanctum stands on a high *pīṭha*. The basement rising above the *pīṭha* consists of the usual mouldings, and these are heavily ornamental with scrolls and geometrical designs. The *kalaśa*-moulding is adorned by niches containing figures of Jain deities. The sanctum enshrines three standing Jina images of black basalt representing Śāntinātha, Kunthunātha, and Aranātha recognized by their cognizances.

Bhanpura: Site with Jain art relics in Mandsaur district, Madhya Pradesh.

Bhāraṅgi: Findspot of Jain epigraph in Sorab taluk, Shimoga district, Karnataka. One of these inscriptions of AD 1415 refers to a Pārśva temple at this place under the control of two Jain teachers of Gopaṇa, namely, Paṇḍitācārya and Śrutamuni. The other of AD 1466 describes Bhāraṅgi as an important Jain centre run by the monks of the Pustaka-gaccha and Deśī-gana. *Epigraphia Carnatica*, VIII, Sorab 329-30.

Bharata: The first Cakravartin (q.v.), mentioned both in Jain canonical and non-canonical literature who gave the name Bhāratavarṣa to this country after his own name. His career began with obtaining fourteen jewels while marching on his adventurous conquests. The *cakra*-jewel was generated in his palace which showed him the way to his conquests. He crossed the river Sindhu, marched towards Veyaḍḍa mountains and being guided by *carma*, *cakra*, *daṇḍa*, *hasti*, *maṇi*, and *kākinī* jewels, he visualized the territories to be occupied by him which he had done with success. After accomplishing his conquests he marched through the Himavanta mountain and arrived at Ṛṣabhakūṭa which come under his domain. Thereafter he came to the Vaitāḍhya mountain inhabited by the Vidyādharas and received their submission who offered him Subhadrā who was consecrated as his consort. Bharata thus came to rule over the entire continent, giving Bharahavāsa (Bhāratavarṣa) its name.

***Bharatādikathā*:** See Śubhaśīla Gaṇin.

***Bharateśvara-Bāhubali-Ghora*:** Gujarati Jain work composed in AD 1170 by Vajrasena which narrates the mythological incident of war between the kings Bharata and Bāhubali, sons of the first Jain Tīrthaṃkara Ṛṣabha. It has five sections and the sequel is characteristically Jain in which the merit of virtue and renunciation is focused.

***Bharateśvara-Bāhubali-Rāsa*:** An extension of Vajrasena's (q.v.) work composed in AD 1185 by Śālibhadra in Gujarati. It is in fifteen sections, each composed after a specific metrical pattern. Gujarati edn. by L.B. Gandhi, Baroda, 1940.

***Bharatpur Jina Image Inscription*:** Belonging to VS 1051, that is, AD 994, this inscription refers to a preceptor called Śrī Surasena of Vāgaṭa Saṅgha. It occurs on the pedestal of a Jina image: *Journal of the Asiatic Society of Bengal* (Letters), 1953, XIX, 109-10.

Bhartṛpura: Modern Bhatvera in Mewar, Rajasthan which contains the temple of Ādīnātha built by Rāṇā Bhartṛbhaṭa in the first half of the tenth century.

***Bhāṣyas*:** Commentarial literature composed in Prakrit verses. These in some cases have been so intermingled with the *Niryuktis* (q.v.) that it is now very difficult to separate them. The Bhāṣyas carry the systematization and elaboration further. These texts, of which there are eleven available, are mostly anonymous. The elaborate Bhāṣya on the *Āvaśyaka-Niryukti* is, however, attributed to Jinabhadra Kṣamāśramaṇa and that on the *Kalpasūtra* (q.v.) to Saṅghadāsagaṇi. There are altogether ten Bhāṣyas on the following texts—*Āvasyaka*, *Dasavaikālika*, *Uttarādhyayana*, *Bṛhatkalpa Vyavahāra*, *Niśītha*, *Jitakalpa*, *Oghaniryukti* and *Piṇḍaniryukti*.

Bhatkal: Jain temple site in North Kanara district. Known as Nāyakana Candranātheśvara-basti, it consists of two blocks of buildings joined together by an intervening porch. The western block is in two storeys, the ground floor containing the principal hall supported upon six pillars. The eastern block has a plan somewhat similar to that of the contemporary *gopurams* of south Indian temples. It is also the findspot of a Jain inscription of AD 1410. Ratnatra-vasadi of this place, dedicated to Aranātha, Mallinātha and Suvrata, was built in the sixteenth century. *Jaina Śilālekha Saṃgraha* IV.423.

Bhatewar: Town founded by Guhila Bhartṛbhaṭa I of Mewar in *c.* AD 930 which has yielded Jain relics including an image of Pārśvanātha.

***Bhattaparinna*:** See Bhaktaparijñā.

Bhaṭṭāraka: Superintendants possessing religious learning and character engaged by a section of the Diagambaras to look after the relations between the monks and the lay followers, to act as religious teachers (*dharma-gurus*) and to lead the community. The system of Bhaṭṭāraka was constituted for the religious divisions of society like *saṅgha*, *gaṇa* or *gaccha*. Thus at Karanjia in Berar there were three Bhaṭṭārakas, each of Kāṣṭha-saṅgha, Balātkāra-gaṇa and Sena-gaṇa. Later on a Bhaṭṭāraka came to be intimately associated with a particular caste and he was given an important position in the organization of that caste. The Bhaṭṭārakas were especially patronized by the Bisapanthīs, while the Digambara Terapantha arose as a revolt against the Bhaṭṭāraka system. Not all Digambara Jain castes have Bhaṭṭārakas of their own. The Hummaḍa Mevāḍa, Narasimhapurā, Khandelvāla, Saitavāla, Caturtha, Pañcama, Bogāra, Upādhyāya, Vaiśya, and Kṣatriya castes have their separate Bhaṭṭārakas while the Kaṭhanera, Budhelā, Agravāla, Golāpūrva, Jaisavāla, Nevi, and Mahārāṣṭra-Hummaḍa castes have no Bhaṭṭāraka system at all. Besides in some castes, the Paravāra, Bannore, Dhākaḍa, and Bagheravāla, the system formerly prevalent is now extinct. The principal duty of a Bhaṭṭāraka is *dharmarakṣā*, that is, protection of religion. Along with religious duty he has to look after the interest of his caste members and help them in social matters. The procedure of appointing a Bhaṭṭāraka is that of *Śiṣyaparamparā* in which the existing Bhaṭṭāraka selects his successor from his disciples. Once a Bhaṭṭāraka is appointed he cannot generally be removed from his position, even though he fails in his duties or misuses his authority. Though he has to remain celibate through life and to live according to the religious principles, he is allowed to possess property. Whatever power the Bhaṭṭārakas are said to possess in theory they hardly exercise in practice. In reality they take contributions from their followers, but do not disturb their quotidien life. Formerly as part of his duties, a Bhaṭṭāraka could control the working of the caste-*pañcāyats*. But now this is not the position. The central places of residence of the Bhaṭṭārakas of Hummaḍa-Mevāḍa are Surat, Sojitra, Karol, Narasiṃhapur, and Dungarpur; of Narasiṃhapurā Surat, Sojatra and Kesariaji; of Khandelavāla Gwalior, Sonagira, Nagora, Ajmer, and Mahāvīraji; of Saitavāla Latur and Nagpur; of Caturtha Nandani, Kolhapur, Hosur, and Terdal; of Pancama Kolhapur, Rayabag, Hosur, and Humacha; of Bogara Humacha, Mysore, Sravanabelgola and Narasimharajpur: of Upādhyāya Mudabidri and Karakal; of Vaisya and Kṣatriya Mudabidri, Karakal, Mela-Sittamur, Sravanabelgola, Jinakāñci, and Narasimharajpur.

Bhāva-Bandha: One of the two major classes of the Jain concept of *bandha* (q.v.) or bondage caused by the union of the soul with *pudgala* (q.v.). The states of thought which condition the accumulation of *karma* (q.v.) are called *bhāva-bandha* on account of which the actual connection between *karma* and Jīva (q.v.) takes place *Dravyasaṃgraha*, vṛtti 30ff; *Vardhamāna Purāṇa*, XVI. 44.

***Bhavabhāvanā*:** See Maladhārī Hemacandra.

Bhavadeva Sūri: See *Pārśvanātha-carita*, *Kālakācārya Kathānaka*.

Bhāvanā: See Anuprekṣā.

Bhāvanā: Attendant meditations in connection with each of the five *mahāvratas* (q.v.) or great vows which are *ahiṃsā*, *satya*, *asteya*, *brahmacarya*, and *aparigraha*.

Bhavanavāsin: One of the four orders of the celestial beings or Devas. As their name suggests, they belong to the residential category. They have their residence in *manuṣya-loka* or the human world, the central part of the cosmos consisting of island continents or *dvīpas*, each encircled by an ocean. They also live in *naraka-loka*, especially in the highest infernal region called Ratnaprabā. They have Jina-caityālayas as a component of their mansions which are thought of as natural and eternal. They are of ten classes: Asura, Nāga, Vidyut (Vijju), Suparṇa (Suvaṇṇa), Agni (Aggi), Vāta (Vāyu, Vāu), Stanita (Thaniya), Udāḥi, Dvīpa (Diva), and Dik (Diśā). *Prajñāpanā* 84. They all have youthful appearances and are described as male, though some of them, according to various descriptions, seem to be female. Their size is seven cubits and they differ in colour. The Asuras are black, the Nāgas and Udāhis whitish, the Suparṇas, Diśās and Stanitas are golden, the Agnis, Divas and Vidyuts orange and the Vātas dark. Cf. *Tattvārtha* IV. These colours indicate their activities, seats, and emblems. They act also as Lokapālas. In Jain tradition the Asuras (q.v.) are not the sworn enemy of the gods. The *Bhagavatī* describes them as gods of the lower world. But they may go down into the deep beyond the Ratnaprabhā and reach any place. Barring fifteen extremely wicked ones, the Asuras are of good temperament. The Nāgas (q.v.) being water-gods are connected with the rain-clouds, while the Udāhis seem to command the sea. The Suparṇas or Suvaṇṇas correspond to the Buddhist and Hindu Suparṇa-Garuḍa. Their enmity with the Nāgas as found in the Brahmanical and Buddhist tradition is also stressed in the Jain texts. Their fight with the Nāgas is said to be the cause of an earthquake. The Diks or Diśās are elephant-spirits often conceived of as females. They had a role in the consecration ceremony of the Tīrthaṃkaras. The Divas are unspecified gods having a connection with lions. Agni and Vāyu are Vedic gods who have found their way into the Jain pantheon, while Vidyut seems to be a Jain adaptation of the Vedic Parjanya and Maruts. They are all described in the plural. The Vāyus occupy submarine caves and they cause the movement of the wind. The following *caitya* trees have been assigned to the Bhavanavāsī gods: *aśvattha*, *saptaparṇa*, *śālmalī*, *udumbara*, *śirīṣa*, *dadhiparṇa*, *vañjula*, *palāśa*, *vapra*, and *karṇikāra*.

Bhavaprabha Sūri: See *Nemibhaktāmaram*.

***Bhāvasaṃvara*:** One of the two classes of *saṃvara* (q.v.) or stoppage of the influx of *karma* (q.v.). It comprises observance of the following rules and restraints: the five vows, the *samitis* (q.v.) consisting of the avoidance of the killing of insects (*iryā*), gentle and holy talk (*bhāṣā*), receiving proper alms (*iṣaṇā*), etc., *guptis* (q.v.) or restraint of body, mind, and speech; *daśalakṣaṇa dharmas* (q.v.) consisting of ten virtues; *anuprekṣā* (q.v.) consisting of meditations of various forms; *pariṣahājaya* (q.v.) consisting of conquering of all kinds of external conditions, and *cāritra* or right conduct.

Bhāvāsrava: One of the two classes of *āsrava* (q.v.) denoting thinking by which the *karma* particles enter the soul. It is of five kinds, namely, *mithyātva* or delusion, *avirati* or want of control, *pramāda* or inadvertence, *yoga* or activities of body, mind and speech, and *kaṣāya* or passions (qq.v.).

***Bhavavairāgyaśataka*:** A collection of a hundred verses on the vanity of existence in Prakrit. Edited and trans. by L.P. Tessitory in *Giornale della Societa Asiatica Italiona* XXII, 179-211.

***Bhavisayatta Kahā*:** A romantic epic in Apabhraṃśa by Dhanavāla, a Digambara Jain layman, who belonged to the merchant caste of Dharkaṭā. It relates the story of Bhavisatta, i.e., Bhaviṣyadatta glorifying certain *vratas* and the methods of performing them. The hero, Bhaviṣyadatta, was stranded on a lonely island and his wife was taken away by his step brother. He regained his former position and wife with the help of a Yakṣa, and this was possible because of his firm devotion to the faith and vows. The author cannot be precisely dated but he seems to have used Haribhadra's (q.v.) *Samarāiccha-Kahā* as a model. The author is distinct from Dhanapāla, the author of *paiyalacchi*. Partly edited by C.D. Dalal and completed with introduction, notes, glossary, etc., by P.D. Gune in Gaekwad's Oriental Series, Baroda, 1923.

Bhāva-Worship: Worship of the Tīrthaṃkaras in their actual nature with the type of reverence accorded to them when they were living on the earth as omniscient beings.

***Bhayahara Stotra*:** See Mānatuṅga.

Bhelupura: Jain site at Vārāṇasī supposed to be the birthplace of Pārśvanātha. The temple is stated to date to the period of Akbar as a text dated vs 1619 refers to it. But it is actually a late-medieval construction. There is a good collection of late medieval Jain sculptures in this temple.

Bhīma I: Cālukya king of Gujarat during whose reign in AD 1031 the magnificent temple of Abu (q.v.) was constructed by Vimala (q.v.). The earliest known inscription of the temple-complex at Abu is of AD 1062 at the time of when Bhīma I was ruling. Bhīma's patronage of Jain religion is attested by the Poliyad plates and also by the *Prabhāvakacarita*.

Bhīma II: Cālukya king of Gujarat (AD 1178-1241) in whose reign Jainism flourished as is proved by the evidence of literary materials and inscriptions. His reign coincided with the religious activities of two great Jain ministers of Gujarat, Vastupāla and Tejaḥpāla. Among the two important Mount Abu inscriptions of his reign, only one mentions him by name. An inscription of his reign from Veraval refers to his patronage of Digambara Jains. In a good number of dated Jain manuscripts his name occurs with such attributes as *samastarājāvalivirājita, mahārājādhirāja, umāpativaralabdhaprāsāda, jaṅgamajanārdana, pratāpacaturbhuja* and *śrīmad-bhīmadeva*.

Bhīma Jinālaya: A Jain temple at Kaidal, originally Kāydāḷa, in the Tumkur taluk of the district of the same name in Karnataka, erected by Bācideva, a feudatory of Hoysala Visnuvardhana (AD 1106-52), according to an inscription of AD 1150. *Epigraphia Carnatica*, XII, Tumkur 9.

Bhīmapalli: Jain centre in Gujarat, 10 miles south-east of Patan, famous for a temple of Mahāvīra and associated with the activities of the monks of the Kharatara-gaccha.

Bhinmal: Jain centre in the Jalor district of Rajasthan. The place was also known as Bhinnamāla, Śrīmāla, etc. As early as the eighth century it was regarded as a place of pilgrimage according to the evidence of the *Kuvalayamālā*. The Jain temple of this place is mentioned by both Dhanapāla and Jinaprabha. Siddharsi's teacher was associated with this *tīrtha* apparently in the last quarter of the ninth century. Temples dedicated to Śāntinatha and Pārśvanātha also adorned this place. The former temple was reconsecrated by Hīravijaya in AD 1576. The medieval work *Śrīmāla-māhātmya* refers to the Jain association of this city.

Bhogapabhogamana: See Caritra.

Bhogapuram: Jain site between Vizianagaram and Bhimunipatnam. It was famous for the temple of Pārśvanātha called Rājarāja Jinālaya built by Mannama Nāyaka in 1187 during the reign of Anantavarman Rājarāja. There now survives only a sculpture of the deity, about 1 m high.

Bhojpur Inscriptions: Belonging to the first quarter of the eleventh century, issued during the reign of Paramāra Bhoja and found in Bhojpur in Raisen district of Madhya Pradesh, this inscription records the installation of a colossal statue of Śānti Jina. This was due to the efforts of a householder named Sāgaranandin, while the ceremony was performed by a Jain monk called Nemicandrasūri. Another inscription incised on the pedestal of an image of Pārśvanātha refers to a person called Cillaṇa, a devout Jain of the Vemaka family. *Epigraphia Indica*, XXXV, 185ff.

Bhoktā: Enjoyer of the fruits of all its *karmas*; characteristics of a Jīva.

Bhṛgukaccha: Barygaza of the Greek writers. Bhārukaccha of the Buddhist texts, it is modern Broach in Gujarat, which is associated with Jainism from a very early period. The Śakunikāvihāra of this town, eulogized in numerous Jain texts, was one of the greatest and most celebrated Jain shrines of western India. This vihāra is supposed to have been built in the Gupta period. The *Vyavahārabhāṣya* describes Bhṛgukaccha as a sacred place. A bronze image of Pārśva dated śaka 908 (AD 986), discovered here refers to the Mūlavasati of Bhṛgukaccha. *Lalit Kalā*, Nos. 1-2, 1955-6, plate XII, fig. 10A.

Bhṛkutī: Attendant Yakṣa of Neminātha (q.v.). He is described as having four faces and eight hands, and a bull as his vehicle. Hands carry the usual emblems. This Yakṣa is called Nandiga, and has a mysterious affiliation with Nandī, the attendant of Śiva. Bhṛkutī is also the name of the Śāsanadevatā (q.v.) of Candraprabha (q.v.). She is thought of as riding a cat or swan and her hands are adorned with a sword, club, spear, and axe, according to the Śvetāmbara tradition.

***Bhūpāla Kavi*:** Author of the hymn *Jinacaturviṃśatikā*, he seems to have flourished in the fourteenth century. Pub. Kāvyamālā, Pt. VII.

Bhūtabali: See *Satkhandagama, Dhavala.*

Bhūtaga II: Also known as Nanniya Gaṅga, he was the king of the Gaṅga main line who ascended the throne around AD 937. The Kudlur plates describe him as a devout Jain. In the Sudi plates, dated śaka 860, it is said that during the Nandīśvara festival at Purikara he made gifts to six female mendicants. He washed the feet of Nāgadevapaṇḍita of the Vadiyūr-gaṇa at Suṇḍi and donated sixty *nivartanas* of land to the Jain caityālaya built by his wife Divalāmbikā. This inscription may be spurious. An undated fragmentary stone inscription of this king refers to his grant to a Jain temple and a long time of Jain teachers belonging to the Krāṇura-gaṇa. They include Bālacandrabhaṭṭāraka, Meghacandra, Guṇanandī, Śabdabrahma, Akalaṅka, Meghanandī, Prabhācandra, Śāntakīrti, and Municandrasiddhāntadeva. From the Kudlur grant it is known that Bhutaga II was a Jain scholar and defeated the Buddhists in debate. *Mysore Archaeological Report*, 1923, No. 113; *Mysore Gazetteer*, II, 675.

Bhūtamahā: Festival of Bhūta mentioned in Jain literature. It is one of the four great festivals, celebrated on the full-moon day of Caitra. It is meant for people seized by evil spirits (*bhūta*) to be treated. The offering (*bali*) was made to the *bhūtas* and soothing rites were performed. The *bhūtas* are described as dancing with spear, javelin, club, and axe in their hands. There are references to ghost-houses (*bhūta-gṛha*) situated on the corner of the road. Details about the festival of the ghosts are found in the *Bṛhadkalpabhāṣya* and Haribhadra's *Āvaśyaka-ṭīkā*.

Bhūtas: Ghosts, goblins, etc. In Jain demonology the Bhūtas have a very interesting role. Exorcists are supposed to be possessed by them. They are invoked to avert terrible cyclones and are regarded as one class of the *vyantara* gods. They have the power of granting offspring to deserving candidates if properly propitiated. In most cases they are mentioned along with Yakṣas, Rākṣasa, and Piśācas. The festival of the Bhūtas was celebrated on the full-moon day of the month of Caitra. It is interesting to note that during the reign of king Pradyota there were shops (*Kuttiyāvana*) in Ujjayinī and Rājagṛha where Bhūtas were sold. The Bhūtas are described as dancing with spear, javelin, club, and axe. They wear the skin of deer. Their yellow hair is dishevelled. They are covered with black serpents. They have protuberant bellies and large faces. Ghost-houses (*bhūta-gṛha*) were situated on road crossings. *Bhūtabali* or offerings made to the Bhūtas were a common practice. There were special festivals in honour of the Bhūtas. *Nāyādhamma* 1. 23; 2.49-50; 17.201; *Uttarādhyayana* 3, *Vasudevahiṇḍi* 386.4-7, etc.

Bhubanesvara Caves: A number of caves, all Jain in religious affiliation, in the Udayagiri and Khaṇḍagiri Hills near Bhubanesvara in Orissa contain sculptured friezes and panels which though belonging to the common denominator of the art of Madhyadeśa, speak nevertheless a distinct local or provincial dialect. The approximate period of these excavations may be ascertained from the inscriptions of Khāravela, king of Kaliṅga, in the Hathigumpha and that of his chief queen in the Manchapuri nearby. Khāravela flourished in the first century BC. These two caves and possibly a few others were excavated about that period. But not all the caves were produced at one and the same time. Activity in the two hills, apart from the medieval excavations in the Khaṇḍagiri was carried for about a century, the latest in the series possibly falling in the first century AD. The caves are not laid out on definite and regular plan, but located at convenient places according to the physical configuration of the rock. The Manchapuri cave relief in Udayagiri and Ananta-gumpha reliefs in Khaṇḍagiri, though characterized by a robust vitality and vigorous movements, are marked by poor workmanship. The long friezes of the Rāṇī-gumpha and Gaṇeśa-gumpha came much later, probably in the first or early second century AD. They are also equally provincial in outlook, but very much advanced in theme and conception, treatment, and composition, though the workmanship is crude and coarse. The Khaṇḍagiri caves contain some standing and seated Jina images of the later Gupta and early medieval periods which are interesting from the iconographic point of view. The northernmost cave known as Satghara or Satbakhra contains on its rear wall two rows of carvings. The upper one represents the first seven of the Tīrthaṃkaras, all in *samādhimudrā* distinguished by their individual symbols beneath their lotus seats, and the lower consisting of seven female figures guarded by Gaṇeśa, a Jain version of the Brahmanical Saptamātṛkā. These female deities are variously depicted—ten-armed, four-armed, and two-armed. They have for their cognizances the Garuḍa and swan, elephant, bull, indistinct object, peacock, vase and lotus, and lion respectively. A few of them carry a small child in their arms. All of them, with the exception of the first one seated on the lotus seats, sit in *ardhaparyaṅka* or *lalitāsana*. Another section of the same cave contains two rows of figures, the upper showing the 24 Tīrthaṃkaras, the lower, 24 female figures, most probably the corresponding Śāsanadevatās of the former. The iconography of these female figures is extremely varied, some of them are endowed with eight, ten, twelve, or even twenty arms, their corresponding textual descriptions being hardly available.

Biharinath: Findspot of an eleventh-century Pārśvanātha image in the Bankura district which is fixed on the wall of a modern temple. It is a much abraded stone slab representing the standing Jina in *kāyotsarga* on a double lotus *chowri*-bearers are on further right and left. Tiny figures of *navagrahas* are on both sides and garland-bearing flying Gandharvas are on the upper corners.

Bija: The seed-*mantra* described in Jain Tantras. These are invocatory formulae consisting of mystic syllables aiming at invoking the deity and not at communicating any desires. These are more unintelligible than the prayer *mantras* (q.v.) for these consist of only *bīja* or seed words. For example, *uu kaumārī namaḥ āṅ krōṇ svāhā* aims at invoking the goddess Kaumārī. Such *bīja-mantras* are met with in chapter six of the *Jvālinīkalpa* which deal with the propitiation of the eight mothers. They consist of two *bīja* prefixed, to the name of the mother. The name of the mother in its twin is suffixed by the invocation *namaḥ āṅ krōṇ svāhā*. The invocation remains the same even when the *bīja* differs.

Bijolia Rock Inscription of Someśvara: Refers to a great temple, dedicated to Vardhamāna, built in the first half of the twelfth century at Ajayameru or Ajmer, by several members of a Jain family, belonging to the Prāgvaṭa kula. This temple has also been mentioned in an inscription of AD 1163 found at Phalodhi, ancient Phalavardhikā in Rajasthan. The Bijolia rock inscription of Someśvara (AD 1168-76) also says that Pṛthvīrāja II donated a village called Morajhari to the Jain temple of Pārśvanātha at Bijolia. It also says that Someśvara himself had donated to the temple of Bijolia, ancient Vindhyavalli or Vijayavalli, now in the Bhilwara district of Rajasthan, a village called Revaṇā. *Epigraphia Indica* XXVI, 84ff; Jinavijaya, *Prācīna Jaina Lekhasaṃgraha* II, No. 445.

Bikaner: District in northern Rajasthan which has yielded more than 2,500 Jain inscriptions, mostly on metal icons. They give the names of the prominent monks of different *gacchas*. An inscription from the Ādinātha temple of Bikaner, constructed during the reign of King Bikaji in AD 1503, says that the original icon of Ādinātha was installed by Kharatara Ācārya Jinakuśala in

AD 1322 at Maṃḍavara. Another inscription refers to Kamran's destruction of this temple in AD 1533 and its subsequent restoration by Varasiṃha, minister of Jayantasiṃha. This temple is now known as the Cintāmaṇi temple and has a collection of 1,050 metal images. Well-known monks like Merutuṅga, Jayakīrti, and Jayakeśara of Añcala-gaccha, Kakkasuri I, II and III of Upakeśa-gaccha, Nannasuri of Koramtaka-gaccha, Jinapati, Jineśvara, Jinaprabodha, Jinacandra I-V, Jinakuśala, Jinabhadra, Jinasamudra, Jinahaṃsa, Jinamāṇikya and others of the Kharatara-gaccha, and several Dhaneśvaras Śāntisūris and Siddasenasūris of Nāṇaka-gaccha, are mentioned in these inscriptions as also prominent monks of the well-known Tapā-gaccha like Munisundara, Ratnaśekhara, and Lakṣmīsāgara. Inscriptions from other temples of Bikaner mention royal personalities such as Akbar and Luṇākaraṇa. Before AD 1600 there were as many as five temples in the town of Bikaner, namely, those of Ādinātha, Sumatinātha, Vāsupūjya, Neminātha, and Mahāvīra. Jain inscriptions are also found in other places in Bikaner district: like Napasar, Rajaldesar, Ratangarh, Sardarsahar, Rini, etc. A.C. and B.L. Nahata, *Bikaner Jainalekha-saṃgraha*, Calcutta, 1954.

Biligi: A great Jain centre in North Kanara district, Karnataka. Two Jain epigraphs have been found in Ratnatraya-basadi, one of which is of AD 1587. It refers to a Jain monk called Bhaṭṭa Akalaṅka who belonged to the Pustaka-gaccha. His spiritual predecessors were Vijayakīrti III, Akalaṅka I, Vijayakīrti II, Srutakīrti II, Vijayakīrti I, Śrutakīrti I and Cārukīrti. The other of AD 1581 refers to the construction of the said basadi and of the *maṇḍapa*, *muni-vāsa*, *candra-śālā*, etc., by a certain chief and a Gandhakuṭi-basti for Śāntīśvara by a royal lady. There is also a Pārśvanātha-basti, built in the sixteenth century. *Jaina Śilālekha Saṃgraha* IV, No. 490; *Epigraphia Indica* XXVIII.292.

Biliyur Inscription: Found in Biliyur in Virajapet taluk of Coorg district, the stone inscription of the Gaṅga King Rājamalla II who ascended the throne in AD 870, refers to his grant of twelve villages to the Jain monk Sarvanandideva, disciple of Śivanandī-siddhānta Bhaṭāra for the maintenance of a temple called Satyavākya Jinālaya at Pennegaḍaṅga. It should be mentioned in this connection that Satyavākya was an epithet of Rājamalla II. *Epigraphia Carnatica*, Rev. edn. 1972, I. No. 96.

Bina-Barha: Jain centre situated in Sagar district, Madhya Pradesh, on the banks of the river Sukhchain. It has two temples and a *gandha-kuṭi*. The first temple is that of Candraprabha whose image was installed in 1775 by Bhaṭṭāraka Mahendra-Kīrtti. It also houses a Mahāvīra image about 4 m high. The second temple is that of Śāntinātha built in 1746. His image enshrined here is over 5 m in height.

Binaikiya: Also known as Laharisena or Laghuśreṇī, it is a branch of the Jain caste known as Paravāra (q.v.). This caste is said to consist of the offspring of irregular unions and widows who have remarried. The Binaikiyas are divided into four groups, two of which are known as Purāne (old) and Naye (new). The latter is rapidly increasing owing to its capacity of incorporating within its body various backward Jain communities.

Biographical Literature: There is a vast biographical literature in Prakrit written by Jains. It consists of the lives of Tīrthaṃkaras, Cakravartins, Baladevas, Vāsudenvas, and Prativāsudevas, besides a large number of narratives of legendary heroes, ascetic heroes, eminent post-Mahāvīra teachers, patriarchs, renowned saints, outstanding authors, royal patrons, merchant-princes and others who served the cause of Jain religion at different periods. In this context mention may be made of such works as *Taraṅgavaikahā*, *Vasudevahiṇḍi*, *Paumacariya*, *Harivaṃśacariya*, *Cauppanna-mahāpuriṣacariya*, *Kahāvali*, *Tiloyapannatti*, etc. The *Kahāvali*, for example, besides narrating the lives of 63 great personalities (*śalākā-puruṣa*) gives an account of eminent teachers from Kālakācārya to Haribhadrasuri. Besides there are numerous works dealing with the biography of individuals, such as the *Sura-sundarīcariya*, *Rayanacuḍācariya*, Guṇacandra-gaṇi's *Pāsanāhacariya*, and *Mahāvīracariya*, Laksmaṇagaṇi's *Supāsanāhacariya*, Devendra-suri's *Sudaṃsaṇācariya*, etc. The historical and mythical biographies of the Tīrthaṃakaras form an important section of Jain religious literature in Sanskrit, Prakrit and Apabhraṃśa. The titles of these works contain names of the Tīrthaṃkaras to which the suffixes *catritra*, *carita*, and *cariu* are added. The tendency of narrating the lives of great personalities and celebrated persons continued in Sanskrit, Apabhraṃśa, Kannaḍa, Tamil, old Hindi, and old Gujarati. Jinasena, Guṇabhadra and Hemacandra were prolific writers of biographical literature in Sanskrit, Puṣpadanta in Apabhraṃśa, and Cāmuṇḍarāya in Kannaḍa.

Birudur Temple: Situated in Birudur, North Arcot

district, this temple has an earlier stone image of Vardhamāna. It is now broken and kept in a front *maṇḍapa*. A later image is placed in the sanctum.

Bīsapanthī: A major subsect of the Digambaras who are idol-worshippers. Their leaders or heads are known as Ācāryas and their religious teachers are known as Bhaṭṭārakas who are ascetics below the rank of *yatis*. They worship the Tīrthaṃkara images along with the idols of Bhairava, Kṣetrapāla and other demi-gods. Their mode of worship resembles that of the Hindus. The priests perform *āratī*, waving lights around the image, and worship with flowers, fruits, and sweetmeats. After the completion of worship the devotees are given shares of the offered food as *prasāda* or grace. The Bīsapanthīs remain seated when they worship. Bīsapanthīs are found in large numbers in Rajasthan and Gujarat.

Bistolā: Śvetāmbara subsect. See Sthānakavan.

Bodhan: Originally a Jain centre in the Nizamabad district, Andhara Pradesh, it has now lost importance owing to the destruction of the great Jina temple of this place by the Muslims. A teacher called Municandra Siddhāntadeva is mentioned in a damaged inscription found from this place.

Bogāḍi: Findspot of a Jain inscription of AD 1145 in Nagamangala taluk, Mandya district, Karnataka, which refers to a Jain shrine called Karaṇa Jinālaya at Bhogavati, modern Bogāḍi, under the spiritual line of Ajitasena and Śrīpāla Traividya. Another inscription of AD 1173 from this place records a grant to the monk Padmaprabha, the donor Heggaḍe being an officer of the Hoysala King Ballāla II. *Epigraphia Carnatica* IV, Naga 100; *Jaine Śilālekha Saṃgraha* III, No. 319; IV, No. 268.

Bogāra: A Jain caste of the Deccan and south India. In Kannaḍa Bogāra means one who deals in brass or copper vessels. They are known as Kāsāras in Maharastra. The Bogāras claim to have originally been Kṣatriyas. Among them cross-cousin marriage is allowed. Divorce and widow remarriage are allowed in their society. They are mostly dealers in acrticles made of metal. Their teacher has his centre in Malkhed. A section of the Bogāras living in the North Kanara district is known as Tagara-Bogāra.

Botany: Early Jain philosophers divided all living beings into immovable and movable ones The immovable ones are of three kinds—earth-lives, water-lives, and plants. Each of these three categories is again subdivided into subtle and gross from the viewpoint of appearance and into developed and undeveloped from the viewpoint of condition. The gross and fully developed plants are of two kinds—those having one body in common and those having their bodies. To the former category belong *guccha* or shrubs, i.e. those in which a single root or bulb gives rise to many stalks, e.g. *vṛntaka* (solanun melongena), *gulma* or shrubs which are similar to the preceding class but which bring forth twigs or stems instead of stalks, e.g. *navamālikā* (jasminum sambac), *latā* (creepers as lotus, pandanus, etc.); *valli* or creeping plants, as gourds, piper-betel, etc.; and *tṛṇa*, i.e. grass. Palms, plants with knotty stems or stalks, mushrooms, water plants, annual plants and herbs possess their own bodies. Those plants of which many have one body in common are of many kinds A list of them is given in *Uttarādhyayana* XXXVI.93-106. As regards the origin of plant life, the *Sūyagaḍa* II.3 refers to the seed as its material cause. At the same time it is stated that the souls on account of their *karma* are to be born as trees were previously embodied in the earth whence they are transferred by their *karma* to the seed which brings forth the tree. 'According to the seed and place (of growth) of these plants some beings—born in earth, originated in earth and grown in earth, having in it their birth, origin and growth, being impelled by their *karma*, and coming forth in it on account of their *karma* growing there in particles of earth, the origin of various things—come forth as trees. These living beings feed on the liquid substance of these particles of earth, the origin of various things; these beings consume earth-bodies, water-bodies, fire-bodies, wind-bodies and the bodies of plants; they deprive of life the bodies of manifold movable and immovable beings; the destroyed bodies which have been consumed absorbed (are) digested and assimilated (by them). And the bodies of these (trees) which bring forth their different parts, are of manifold colour, smells, tastes, touches, forms and arrangement of corporeal particles.' *SBE* XLV.388-9. The *Sūyagaḍa* II.3 mentions four different kinds of seeds generated respectively at the top, bottom, knots, and stem—as the source of plant life.

Trees sprung from shoots, sprouts aerial roots, etc., are considered a class different from those whose offshoots they are. Just as the trees themselves originate in earth and are sustained by the substances of the earth, so also these parasites are born in the trees and nourished by the sap of the trees. In the same way the watery plants like *avaga* (a grassy plant growing in marshy land), *paṇaga*, *śevāla* (the aquatic plant *vallisneria*), *kalambuya* (*kodamba*), *kaseruya* (*scirpus kysoor*), *kacchabhānīya*, *utpala*, *pauma*, *kumuya*, *nalina* (four varieties of lotus), *subhagasonīya poṇḍariya*, *sayavatta*, *kalhāra*, *kokanada*, *and tāmarasa* (these are all varieties of lotus), are born in water and sustained by the substances of water. The same process holds good in the case of creepers, herbs, and grains. They are all born from seeds in earth or water and develop by consuming earthly or watery substances. The medicinal texts classify all trees and plants into four groups: *vanaspati* which produces fruits without producing flowers, *vanaspatya* which produces flowers as well as fruits, *oṣadhi* which dies after producing the fruits and *virudha*, the stems of which scatter all around. To the fourth category also belong *latā* (creepers) and *gulma* (shrubs). Grass (*tṛṇa*), and shrubs (*avatāna*) are included in a separate category. In Guṇaratna's commentary on the *Ṣaḍdarśanasamuccaya* the following aspects of plant life are recorded : infancy, gradual development, sleep and waking, response to external stimuli, healling of wounds, and assimilation of food in accordance with the nature of soil.

Botika Sect: See Digambara-Śvetāmbara split.

Brahmā: Brahmanical deity conceived of as the Dikpāla (q.v.) or guardian of the upper regions. He is described as four-handed, riding a swan and holding a book and a lotus. The symbols tally exactly with what is noticed in the Brahmanical originals.

Brāhma: One of the eight forms of Jain marriage adapted from the Brahmanical legal texts with some modifications. In this form of marriage the daughter is given by the father to a bridegroom who is learned and well-behaved, after calling him and decorating him as well as the bride with valuable ornaments. *Trivarṇikācara* XI.71; *Nītivākyāmṛta* XXXI.4.

Brahmacarya: Celibacy, the fourth vow, which the Jain monk must observe. He is not to give way to sensuality and has to renounce all sexual pleasure in a threefold way, i.e. acting, commanding, and consenting in mind, body and speech. To the householder *brahmacarya* means abstaining from adultery, matrimonial offences, unchastity, addiction to prostitutes, and sexual intercourse in forbidden relationships. Unnatural sexual gratification, indulging in oral sex or sexual talk, visiting immoral married and unmarried women, etc., are forms of matrimonial offence to be avoided.

Brahmacarya Pratimā: Maintaining sexual purity assuming the stricter aspect of celibacy and also not decorating one's person.

Brahmadeva Stambha: Columns or pillars associated with Jain architectural constructions. The Brahmadeva-stambhas have a figure of Brahmadeva on the upper part. Examples of Brahmadeva-stambhas are found near the Gommaṭa figures at Karkal and Venur.

Brahma-Jinālaya: Jain religious establishment at Lakkundi, district, Dharwar, Karnataka. The temple is built of schist, similar to the later Hoysala temples. Its plan is of multi-*ratha* layout and its central projection is well maintained. In an inscription of AD 1007 from Lakkundi, gifts to this Jinālaya by the pious lady Attiyabbe are recorded. In Amarapuram of the Anantapur district there is another Brahma-Jinālaya on the Thailagiri fort. This temple received Āḷūpā-devī's munificence in 1228 according to an inscription. A third Brahma-Jinālaya is at Kuppaturu in the Shimoga district, Karnataka, which was dedicated to Pārśvanātha. This temple had received a grant from Mālaladevī, queen of the Kadamba prince Kīrtideva, who was a disciple of Padmanandin. There were many more Brahma-Jinālayas, a few of which are mentioned in inscriptions as well. *Epigraphia Carnatica*, VIII, Sorab No. 262; *Annual Report on South Indian Epigraphy*, 1961-2, No. 21.

Brahmanasvāmin Temple: Situated at Varman it is an early Jain temple of Rajasthan with an interesting variety of ceiling decoration.

Brahmasūri: Author of the drama *Jotiṣprabhānāṭaka* which was written in the fourteenth century. His two other works are *Pratiṣṭhātilaka* and *Trivarṇācāra*. See *Jinaratnakośa* 137, 163, 261. *Jotiṣprabhānāṭaka* was published from Bangalore, 1893-4.

Brahma Yakṣa: Attendant Yakṣa of Śītalanātha (q.v.) who is modelled after Brahmanical Brahmā having four faces and a lotus seat. His eight hands have the citron, club, noose, *abhaya*, mongoose, mace, goad and rosary respectively.

Bṛhaspati: The planet Jupiter conceived of as a Jyotiṣka or stellar god by the Jains. He holds a book and rides on a swan. According to some iconographic texts he carries a rosary and a waterpot, often a staff, and shows boon-giving posture. He is the ruler of the north-eastern quarters.

***Bṛhatkalpa*:** Also known as *Kalpa* and *Bṛhat-Sādhu-Kalpa-Sūtra*, it is the fifth Chedasūtra (q.v.), the principle work on the rules and regulations for the monks and nuns. The work is divided into six sections. Edited with the *Bhāṣya* of Saṅghadāsa and *Ṭīkās* of Malayagiri and

Kṣemakīrti by Punyavijaya, Bhavnagar, 1933-42; ed. W. Schubring with notes, etc., in German, Leipzig, 1905; cf. his *Drei Chedasūtras des Jaina-Kanons*; rpt. Hamburg, 1966.

***Bṛhatkathākośa*:** Written by the Digambara author Harisena (q.v.) in the first half of the tenth century. It is a treasury of tales written in Sanskrit. It is an extremely informative work, not only pertaining to the Jain tradition but to the early medieval in Indian social life as well. Ed. A.N. Upadhye, Bombay, 1943.

***Bṛhat-Svayambhū-Stotra*:** A hymn of praise of the 24 Jinas composed by Samantabhadra (q.v.). It is also known as *Caturviṃśati Jinastavana*. Pub. in Digambara Jaina Granthabhaṇḍāra, Kashi, I; with Hindi trans. and intro. by Jugalkeshor Mukhtar, Virasevā Mandir, Sersava, 1951.

British Museum Plate of Amma II: Undated copper plate of Eastern Cālukya Amma II, the find-spot of which is not known. It registers the grant of a village named Kulucuṃbarru in the Attilinānḍuviṣaya to a Jain teacher called Arhanandin belonging to the Valahari-gaṇa and Aḍḍakali-gaccha for the purpose of providing for repairs to the charitable dining hall of a Jain temple called Sarvalokāśraya Jinabhavana, named after one of Amma II's predecessors who bore the title Sarvalokāśraya. The making of the grant was inspired by a lady called Cāmekāmbā who was a mistress of the king and a lay pupil of Arhanandin. *Epigrahia Indica* VII, 177ff.

Buddhi-Rāsa: A collection, in four sections, of moral sayings, proverbs, pithy maxims and religious instructions given as a summary list of do's and don'ts. It was composed by Śālibhadra about AD 1200 in Gujarati.

Buddhism: In the earlier Jain works like the *Sūyagaḍa* I.I.17, I.2.25-8, II.6.26-9 the Buddhists are described as fools believing in the doctrine of the momentariness of the five *skandhas* or aggregates of existence. The Jains criticise the Buddhists saying that those who hold that there is nothing really permanent in the universe and that everything changes from moment to moment are one-sided because change and permanence are both parts of the same reality which consists of three factors—permanence, origin, and decay, *utpāda-vyaya-dravyayaktaṃ-sat*. If everything is taken to be momentary it will be impossible to explain memory, recognition, the immediate feeling of personal identity. Accordingly the concept of liberation will not be able to stand in the absence of any permanent soul to be liberated. Moral life will not be possible then, since it is impossible for a momentary person to make any attempt to attain any end. The Jains do not subscribe to the Buddhist view that all knowledge by perception of external objects is in the first instance indefinite and indeterminate. The Jains hold that perception reveals the external objects as they are, with most of their characteristics of colour, form, etc., and deny the existence of any indeterminate stage of perception preceding to the determinate one. The Jains reject the Buddhist view that reality consists in causal efficiency, i.e. an object is real if it is capable of causing any effect. The Jains reject this approach saying that even an illusory snake must be called real as it can cause effects like fear. Jainism rejects the Buddhist Śūnyavāda and Vijñānavāda because the latter do not accept the competence of the sense-organs. It rejects the Buddhist theory of dependent origins saying that this theory conceives in its own distinctive manner the series of qualities and attributes that originate or perish, but posits no permanent substance in form of the substance of these qualities and attributes. On the problems of knowledge in general, the Jains are in agreement with the Buddhists belonging to the Vijñānavāda school on the point of the self-revelatory character of cognition, but while the Vijñānavādins hold that there exists no object apart from the cognition, and a particular piece of cognition is possessed of a particular form, the Jains posit the existence of external objects and treat cognition as a generated phenomenon. Although the systems differ on specific points, in their incipient stages, they stood for the same or similar principles. Both deny the existence of an intelligent first cause, adore deified saints, insist on moral values, right conduct, and self-discipline, oppose the authority of the Vedas and the supremacy of the Brāhmaṇas, and think it sinful to take the life of animals.

Buddha: The planet Mercury conceived as a Jyotiṣka or stellar god by the Jains. He is known as the son of the Moon and the ruler of the north. He rides on a swan and holds a book in his hand.

Burdwan: District of West Bengal named after Mahāvīra Vardhamāna which has yielded a few Jina images, the exact findspots of which are unknown. Among these a Candraprabha image is now in the Asutosh Museum, Calcutta University. This four-handed seated stone image belongs to the eighth-ninth centuries. Two hands of the image are placed upon the centre of the two upturned soles of the feet. Two other hands are placed on the knees with palms hanging down and touching the lotus seat. Two ends of the crescent moon emblem, touch the two palms like a girdle. An eleventh-century Pārśvanātha image, now in the Asutosh Museum is of black stone with arch-shaped top. It stands in *kāyotsarga* on a double-petalled lotus placed on a *triratha* pedestal carved with floral designs. The mutilated face has long ear-lobes. Many Jain images have been found in specified sites, of this district.

Būtaga I: Younger brother of the Gaṅga King Rājamalla II. He married a daughter of the illustrious Amoghavarṣa I. That he was a devout Jain is attested by the Kudlur inscription and the Gattivādipura plates dated AD 904. *Epigrahia Carnatica* XII.135.

C

Caccari, Carcari: See Jinadatta Sūri.

Caityālaya: Religious building of the Tāraṇapanthīs which means to them *granthālaya*, or house of books as well. Here they perform their religious duties, especially *sāmāyika*, *jinastuti* and *vandanā*. In the middle of the Caityālaya is erected a pulpit and on it the fourteen books of Tāraṇasvāmī, the founder of the Tāraṇapantha, are placed.

Caityavāsins: A prominent Jain sect. See Durlabharāja. For details see *Kathākośa*, ed. Jinavijaya, intro. 3ff.

Caitya-Vṛkṣas: Ancient cult of trees which had received a new dimension in Jainism which held that all its Tīrthaṃkaras obtained enlightenment under *caitya*-trees. The Jains were attracted to this idea probably under the influence of the Yakṣa cult. In the *Aupapātika-sūtra* description of the *caitya* of Pūrṇabhadra there is no mention of a structural shrine, and here possibly the tree itself with *śilā-paṭṭa* or stone slab symbolizing the seat of the deity, is the Yakṣa-*āyatana*. The erection of a *pīṭha* with *śilā-paṭṭa* on each of the four sides of a tree served as the fundamental conception of the early *caitya*, open on four sides, the *caturmukha* shirne, and that of *pratimā-sarvatobhadrikā* (qq.v.). In the *Ādi Purāṇa* XXII.184-204 it is said that the *samavasaraṇa* or the auditorium of Ṛṣabhadeva contained *caitya-vṛkṣas*. The *Tiloyapannatti* III.33-9 refers to the *caitya*-trees of the Bhavanavāsin (q.v.) gods. A list of trees associated with the Bhavana-vāsins is given in *Sthānāṅga*, X.3 (766). The *caitya*-trees were introduced on relief sculpture of Tīrthaṃkaras as foliage spread over the head. Originally perhaps the Jina image was placed under a *caitya*-tree. That the *caitya*-tree was given special importance is best illustrated by a type of Tīrthaṃkara images where the Jina is shown sitting under a big prominent tree, almost all other *pratihāryas* being either eliminated or subdued. The *Samavāya* records the list of *caitya-vṛkṣas* of all the 24 Tīrthaṃkaras. The *Kalpasūtra* refers to the *caitya*-trees respectively of Ṛṣabha, Nemi, Pārśva, and Mahāvīra. The earliest reference to the *caitya*-tree of Mahāvīra is found in the second book of the *Ācārāṅga*. The Jains have assigned the spirits connected with the tree-worship to the class of Vyantara (q.v.) gods. Each of this group has on its crest the symbol of a tree in the following order—*kadamba*, *sulasa*, *vaṭa*, *khaṭvāṅga*, *aśoka*, *campaka*, *nāga*, and *tumburu*.

Cakrabhiseka: A stage in the career of the Tīrthṃ-akara in which he celebrates his conquest.

Cakralābha: A stage in the career of the Tīrthaṃkara which is the acquiring of *cakra*, that is, nine stones and fourteen jewels.

Cakravartin: 'Sovereign who abides in wheel or discus' which means 'universal monarch'. According to the Jains, twelve Cakravartins are counted among sixty-three great men (*śalākāpuruṣa*). They are Bharaha or Bharata, Sagara, Maghava, Saṇakkumāra or Sanatkumāra, Śānti, Kunthu, Ara, Subhoma, Mahāpauma, or Mahāpadma, Heriṣena, Jaya and Bambhadatta or Brahmadatta. Out of these Śānti, Kunthu, and Ara became Tīrthaṃkaras. Bharata (q.v.) was the first king after whose name this continent was designated.

Cakreśvarī: Śāsanadevatā (q.v.) of Ṛṣabhanātha (q.v.) whose symbol is disc and vehicle. In Śvetāmbara conception she has eight hands with the *varada-mudrā*, arrow, disc, noose, bow, thunderbolt, disc and goad. The Digambaras attribute to her either four or twelve hands. In the case of the former there are two discs and in that of the latter, eight. Other attributes are conventional. A good number of Cakreśvarī images, either independent or together with Ṛṣabha, have been found.

Cāmarājanagara: Findspot of a Jain epigraph of AD 1117 in the Mysore district which records that Punisa, minister of the Hoysala King Viṣṇu-vardhana, built at this place a Jina temple of the name of Trikūṭa-basadi and donated some land for it. An inscription of AD 1482 from Harave in Chāmrajnagar mentions a grant to the Ādinātha temple. Another inscription of AD 1518 mentions Vijaya-Pārśva temple. *Epigraphia Carnatica* IV, Charm 83, 189.

***Caṃḍā-Vijjhaya-Vijjhaga*:** See Candrakavadhyaka.

Campa: Capital of ancient Aṅga-Janapada, the extensive ruins of which are found scattered near the modern town of Bhagalpur in Bihar. The twelfth Tīrthaṃkara Vāsupūjya was born here. It was also the place of his demise. Mahāvīra spent three years of his missionary life at Campā where he met king Ajātaśatru as well. This city also had a Yakṣa shrine of Pūrṇabhadra according to the *Aupapātika*. The Vāsupūjya temple-complex of this city is mentioned in Jinasena's *Harivaṃśa*. Śayyambhava composed his celebrated *Daśavaikālika* in this city. Jinabhadra in his *Vividhatīrthakalpa* has given a brief history of this place. It was destroyed by Sutan Shamsuddin in AD 1302.

***Campakaśreṣṭhī-Kathānaka*:** See Jinakīrti.

Cāmuṇḍā: Śāsanadevatā (q.v.) of Neminātha (q.v.) according to the Digambara tradition in which she is conceived of as riding on a dolphin and carrying in her hands a rosary, a staff, a shield, and a sword. The name is an adaptation of the Brahmanical Cāmuṇḍā.

Cāmuṇḍa-Mahārāja: A pupil of Jinasena (q.v.) who wrote the *Cāritrasāra*, a manual of morals and the path of salvation according to the faith of the Digambaras. He is to be distinguished from the author of the *Cāmuṇḍarāya Purāṇa* and the founder of the Gommaṭa statue, though both had the same epithet *raṇaraṅgasiṃha*, 'lion on the stage of battle'. *Cāritrasāra*, ed. with explanation in Hindi by Lala Ramaji in Sanatana Jaina Granthamala 20.

Cāmuṇḍarāya: Minister and general of the Gaṅga princes Mārasiṃha II and Rācamalla or Rājamalla II of the tenth century. He devoted himself to pious work in his later years, erected the famous colossal satue of Gommaṭa at Sravanabelgola in Karnataka in about AD 980, and wrote the *Cāmuṇḍarāya Purāṇa* in Kannaḍa in AD 978. He mentions Ajitasena and Nemicandra as his teachers. Cāmuṇḍarāya's other name was Gommaṭarāya in whose honour Nemicandra's *Gommaṭasāra* (q.v.) received its name. Cāmuṇḍarāya himself had written a commentary on this work in Kannaḍa. It should be noted in this connection that there were political personages named Cāmuṇḍarāya in the eleventh century who were distinct from the founder of the Gommaṭa statue.

Cāmuṇḍarāya-basadi: Also Cāvuṇḍarāya-basti, it stands at some distance to the north of Candragupta-basti on the Candragiri Hill at Sravanabelgola. Built by Cāmuṇḍarāya, the Gaṅga minister of Rācamalla in the last quarter of the tenth century, it is the largest and finest example among the Jain temples of the period. The temple complex consists of a three-storeyed square Drāviḍa *vimāna*, 11.5 m square at the base with two lower storey. The *vimāna* has five bays. The first storey is marked by a string of miniature shrines. Each part of this great shrine has its own characteristics. According to the foundation-inscription, the temple was constructed in AD 982. The consecration of Pārśvanātha in the upper shrine, as attested by the minister's son on the pedestal of the image, took place in AD 995. The front *agramaṇḍapa* is perhaps an addition in the time of Hoysala Viṣṇuvardhana.

Caṇḍā: Also called Pracaṇḍā, she is the Śāsanadevatā (q.v.) of Vāsupūjya (q.v.) according to the Śvetāmbaras. She has a horse as her vehicle and her hands have the *varada mudrā*, the spear, flower, and club.

***Candanabālā-Rāsa*:** Gujarati poem written by Āsiga in AD 1201 which deals with the life-story of Candanabālā who is known to the Jain tradition as the first *pravartinī* or head-nun in the first monastic order founded by Mahāvīra. *Prācīna Gurjara Kāvya Saṃgraha*, ed. C.D. Dalal, Gaekwad's Oriental Series, No. 13, Baroda, 1920.

Candanavihāra: Jain centre situated near Svarṇagiri, a hill near Jalor in Rajasthan, where Yaśovīra, minister of the local king, Udayasiṃha, of the thirteenth century, had built an image of Mahāvīra according to the *Purātanaprabandhasaṃgraha*.

***Canda-Pannatti, Candraprajñapti*:** See Sūrya-prajñapti.

***Candra*:** Moon-god of the Jains described as driving a chariot of ten white horses and holding an urn of nectar. He is the master of stars and ruler of the north-western quarters.

Candragupta: Founder of the Mauryan empire (324-300 BC) who according to the Jain tradition renounced the throne in his old age under the influence of his teacher Bhadrabāhu, whom he followed towards the south till both teacher and pupil settled down at a place in Mysore known as Sravanabelgola (q.v.). Bhadrabāhu is said to have led this Jain migration towards the south to escape from Magadha, then in the grip of a severe famine. Some local inscriptions and monuments also refer to the same tradition. An inscription of about AD 600 mentions Muni Candragupta and Bhadrabāhu as a *yugma* or pair. Their association is also repeated in a few other local inscriptions and one deifies them both. A small hill at Sravanabelgola is called Candragiri, because Candragupta lived and performed austerities there: on the same hill is a temple called Candragupta-basadi, believed to have been erected by Candragupta. The tradition of Candragupta's conversion is recorded in later works like the *Tiloyapaṇṇati* and Hariṣena's *Bṛhatkathākośa*.

Candragupta-basti: Group of three simple *vimānas* on the Candragiri Hill or Chikkabetta at

Sravanabelgola in the Hassan district of Karnataka, each about 2 m square on the base, standing on either end of a common rectangular basement. In the intervening space betwen the two *vimānas* is a third shrine with a flat roof. The platform and the other lateral walls of both the exteme *vimānas* are extended forward to form a square *ardha-maṇḍapa* in front of the respective shrines, turning the whole complex into a large square. This seemingly triple shrine, traditionally associated with Candragupta, is the earliest extant monument of Sravanabelgola and its surrounding area atributable to the middle of the ninth century.

***Candrakavedhyaka*:** Prakrit *Caṃda-vijjhaya* or *Caṃda-vijjhaga*, the seventh Prakīrṇa(q.v.) which deals in 174 verses with teachers and pupils and with discipline in general. The name means 'the apple of the eye which is to be bored through', that is, 'hitting the mark'. Cf. the colloquial *cāndmārī*. Agamodaya edn., Bombay, 1925.

Candramahattara: Thirteenth-century author of the sixth Karmagrantha known as *Saptaṭīkā*. It is composed in 70 verses to which his teacher Devendra Sūri added a further 19. Candramahattara is also the author of *Pañcasaṃgraha*, a compendium of the whole doctrine of *karma*. *Saptaṭīkā* with Malayagiri's com., published by Śrī Jaina Prasāraka Sabhā, Bhavnagar 1911; *Pañcasaṃgraha* with Malayagiri's com., ed. Hiralal Hamsaraj, Jamnagar, 1909.

Candranātha Temple: Situated in Mettuppudur hamlet of Vijayamangalam, an ancient Jain centre in Coimbatore district of the Koṅgumaṇḍalam, it is a Gaṅga structure with its brickwork *vimāna*. The cella inside contains an idol of Candranātha. The stone *ardha-maṇḍapa* is more or less of the same width as the first storey of the *vimāna* with a larger *mahāmaṇḍapa* in front. The outer additions to this temple complex are of the Vijayanagara period.

Candranāthasvāmin Temple: A flat slab-roofed Jain structure at Haduvalli or Sangitapur 118 km east-north-east of Bhatkal (q.v.) in North Kanara district.

Chandranātheśvara-basti: See Bhatkal.

Chandraprabha: The eighth Tīrthaṃkara whose parents were Mahāsena and Lakṣmaṇa of Candrapura, tentatively identified with Candravati near Kashi. He had the height of 150 bow-lengths and life span of a million years. Dinna and Sumanā were his chief disciples. He had liberation on the Sammeya mountain. His sacred tree was *nāgavṛkṣa*. His cognizance is the moon or the crescent, attendants are Vijaya and Bhṛkuṭī/Jvālāmālinī, and the *chowrie*-bearer Dānavīrya. Regarding the origin of his name it is said that before his birth his mother wanted to drink the moon. To assuage her craving a plate of water was one night handed to her in such a way that the moon was reflected on it. When the child was born he was found to possess the lustre of the moon. Many good specimens of this Jina image have come to light in northern India. An inscribed image of Candraprabha standing with other Tīrthaṃkaras is in the Deogarh Fort. In the same fort may be seen a seated image of his Jina. In Madanpur in the Jhansi district five Jina figures have been found, of which one represents Candraprabha. An erect figure of Candraprabha from Gwalior is in the Indian Museum, Calcutta. The Aluara collection of the Patna Museum contains two bronze images including Candraprabha on lotus pedestal in *kāyotsarga* with his emblem, the crescent moon. The Chausa hoard has also two bronze images in which he is represented in *dhyāna-mudrā*, a crescent moon on the top of the round beaded *śiraścakra*.

***Candraprabha-Carita*:** Idealized biography of the Tīrthaṃkara Candraprabha written in 8,000 verses by second Haribhadra of the twelfth century. There is another *Candraprabha-carita* written by Vīranandin about AD 1000 in 18 cantos and 1,611 verses.

***Candraprabhacaritamahākāvya*:** See Vīranandī.

Candraprabhamahattara: Prakrit poet who had written in Jain Maharastri in the second half of the eleventh century the life of Vijayacandrakevalin. It contains 1,063 *gāthās* and gives eight stories describing the eight different ways of worshipping the Jinas.

Candraprabha Temple: Situated in the Jain temple comlex at Tirupparuttikkunram or Jina-Kāñcī, a suburb of Kanchipurm, the Candraprabha temple is the northernmost structure in the existing complex of four major temples and three minor shrines within a huge enclosure. It is a three-storeyed square *vimāna* with a *mukha-maṇḍapa* in front. Of the three storeys the lowermost is built solid and forms the platform for the second storey which contains the real shrine. There is another Candraprabha temple in the Jaisalmer Fort which seems to be an abridged version of the great Caturmukha temple at Ranakpur.

Candrapuri: Birthplace of the eighth Tīrthaṃkara Candraprabha which is a few miles from Varanasi and is identified as the place of the same name, also sometimes called Candramādhava.

Candraśālā: Name of a cave near Girinagara (Girnar) in which Ācārya Dharasena taught Puṣpadanta

Bhūtabali the scriptures. It is often identified with the caves of Bāwā-Pyāra's Math.

Candrasena: See *Dhavalā*.

Candravāḍa: Place sacred to Candraprabha on the Yamuna near Firozabad in the Agra district, Uttar Pradesh. A temple of this Tīrthaṃkara was constructed here in AD 996.

Candravatī: An ancient town near Abu in Sirohi district of Rajasthan associated with the Tīrthaṃkara Candraprabha. According to the *Tīrthamālā* composed in AD 1443 there were 1,800 Jina temples in this town, including the great temple of Ṛṣabha. That in the eleventh century Candravatī was a Jain centre is suggested by the fact that in AD 1038 Dhaneśvaramuni wrote his *Kathāsurasundarī* at Candravatī. The Jhaloḍi inscription of Dhārāvarṣa mentions the Vīra temple of Candravatī. This place was also connected with the activities of the monks of the Kharatara-gaccha. *Prācīna Jaina Lekhasaṃgraha* II.430.

Candrikāyāṭa: Seat of a line of the Digambara Jain teachers of the Sena-saṅgha, modern Candakavaṭi in the Sindgi taluk of Bijapur district of Karnataka. It contains a few Jain epigraphs. The earliest teacher of this line who had his seat at this place was Dharmasena of the ninth century. The name of his disciple is also found in the inscriptions.

Caranāgare: Also known as Samaiya, it is the name of a subcaste of the Jain Paravāra (q.v.) caste. They reside mainly in the Damoha and Chindwara districts of Madhya Pradesh. Caranagare is one of the six castes that follow Tāraṇapantha (q.v.) or Samaiya-pantha, a subject of the Digambaras. Like other Bania or mercantile subcastes the Caranāgares are divided into Viśā (twenties) and Daśā (tens).

***Caraṇānuyoga*:** The fourth Digambara Veda which deals with the rituals and of conduct prescribed for the householder as well as the homeless ascetic. This Veda includes Vaṭṭakera's *Mūlācāra* and *Trivarṇācāra* and Samantabhadra's *Ratnakaraṇḍa-Śrāvakācāra* (qq.v.).

Cāranti-Math: Group of temples at Aihole in the Bijapur district, Karnataka. The main temple is dedicated to Vardhamāna Mahāvīra. It has *garbhagṛha*, *ardha-maṇḍapa*, *sabhā-maṇḍapa*, and *mukha-maṇḍapa* carrying a southern *vimāna*-tower on the roof. There is a super-structural shrine on the roof in typical Jain requirement, itself with a cella and *mukha-maṇḍapa*. This temple may be dated to the eleventh century, though allied temples have different dates.

***Caritra*:** Certain rules of moral behaviour recorded in Hemacandra's *Yogaśāstra* in which we have an interpretation of the five vows. There are *irryā* (precaution while walking to prevent oneself from treading on insects, etc.), *bhāṣā* (to talk pleasantly), *iṣaṇa* (to beg alms in proper monastic manner), *dānasamiti* (inspection of seats to avoid transgressions), *utsargasamiti* (careful movement of the body), *manogupti* (to remove all false thoughts), *vāggupti* (absolute silence), *kāyagupti* (steadiness of the body), etc. Duties for householders are *digvirati* (to desist from injuring living beings), *bhogapabhogamāna* (to desist from drinking alcohol), *anarthadaṇḍa* consisting of *apadhyāna*, *pāpopadeśa*, *hiṃsopakāridāna* (desisting from evil, injurious and violent acts directly or indirectly), *pramādācarana* (desisting from excitement) and *Śikṣāpadavrata* consisting of *sāmāyikavrata* (to treat all beings equally), *deśāvakāśikavrata*, *poṣadhavrata* (different kinds of restrictions) and *atithisaṃvibhāgavrata* (to make gifts to guests). No kind of asceticism (*tapas*) can be of any good until the mind is purified. When a man learns to look upon all beings with equality (*samatva*) he can conquer *rāga* and *dveṣa*. In order to effect this equality he should have to think of the transitoriness (*anityta*) of all things. He should think that even the gods are subject to death. The world is full of misery and men are differentiated from one another by the *karma* they acquire individually. He should think that the practice of ten virtues of self-control (*saṃyama*), truthfulness (*sunṛta*), purity (*śauca*), chastity (*brahma*), absence of greed (*akiñcanatā*), asceticism (*tapas*), forbearance (*kṣānti*) mildness (*mārdava*), sincerity (*ṛjutā*) and emancipation (*mukti*) can alone help in the achievement of the highest goal.

***Cāritra*:** Five kinds of the right conduct required for *saṃvara* (q.v.) or stoppage of the influx of karmic matter into the soul. These are *sāmāyika*, equanimity; *chedopasthāpanā*, recovery of equanimity after a fall from it; *parihāravisuddhi,* pure and absolute non-injury; *sūkṣmasampradāya*, complete freedom from passion; and *yathākhyāta*, ideal and passionless conduct.

***Caritrasāra*:** See Cāmuṇḍa Mahārāja.

Caritrasundara: See *Śīladūta*, *Kumārapālacarita*, *Mahīpālacaritra*.

Carucandra: See *Uttama-Carita-Kathānaka*.

Carudatta: A popular character of Jain narrative literature. Son of a well-off Jain merchant at Campa, he was robbed of all his wealth by a cunning prostitute Vasantatilakā. His family-house was sold and his mother and wife lived miserably in the slums. A repentant Cārudatta promised to revive his fortune and travelled far and wide with his trade goods, faced many difficulties and disasters and eventually after passing through much hardship returned with huge profit. The story of his life resembles that of Sindbad of the *Arabian Nights*, with the difference that Cārudatta was a devout Jain in all conditions. When he was on his journey to Ratnadvīpa or 'treasure-island', the caravan leader instructed the merchants to kill their goats, eat their flesh and cover their bodies with the skin so that the huge flesh-eating *bharuṇḍa* birds would mistake them for raw meat and carry them off to the 'treasure island' in their beaks. Devout Jain that he was, Cārudatta refused to obey this command. His previous acts of compassion and religiousness were rewarded. He was reunited with the family, honoured by the citizens, and blessed with wealth. Details of the story of Cārudatta are to be found in the *Bṛhatkathā-ślokasaṃgraha* and *Vasudevahiṇḍi*.

Cārūpa: Site of the Pārśvanātha temple in Patan taluk of the Mehesana district of Gujarat. Other Jina temples dedicated to Ṛṣabhanātha, Śāntinātha, etc., were later erected here, but they do not exist now. This place has been referred to as a Jain centre of pilgrimage by Sumatisāgara in the sixteenth century.

Caste Names: The number of castes in the Jain community is so large that their investigation in detail is expected to form a separate matter for research. The following caste names along with their variant readings are provided here on the basis of V.A. Sangave's investigation: Agravāla, Ajamerā, Andāluia, Ajaudhiyā, Aḍāliyā, Avakathavāla, Acitavāla, Athasamaya Paravāra, Anadorā, Akanā, Ayodhyāpārva, Aṣṭaki, Aṣṭadhāra, Anāndi, Aneravāla, Āḍhavaraji, Auravāla, Ausavāla, Aṇḍaurā, Aṣṭavāra, Ānande, Ayodhyāvāsī, Asāsti, Anyadharmī, Bagheravāla, Badaneurā, Baramākā, Baugāra, Bhavanage, Bhūṅdaḍavāra, Basākamakomaṭi, Bajava, Bhaṭanāgara, Barihiyā, Baramorā, Bhuṅgerivāla, Brahmatā, Beduja, Bāharīyā, Bhangela, Bimoṅgai, Berasāri, Bogośrī, Bamāriya, Baṭivarā, Barūrī, Bāisa, Bhuṅgaḍa, Bhārijā, Bhuṅgaravāla, Bāvariyā, Brahmāka, Baḍhai, Bhavanageha, Bhākarīyā, Bāgaraurā, Buḍhela, Binaikyā, Baḍale, Baraiyā, Buḍhela, Badanere, Bhavasāgara, Bogāra, Brāhmaṇa, Bhāvasāra, Bhojaka, Brahmabhāṭa, Caturtha, Cītauḍā, Coraṇḍiyā, Cakauḍa, Citorā, Cakkicape, Citravāla, Cauraḍiyā, Cakkacapā, Citoḍā-Daśā, Citoḍā-Biśā, Caughale, Dhūñsara, Dasaurā, Dhavalakauṣṭhī, Dhākaḍa, Dusare, Dasarā, Dhūdhatavāla, Dosavālā, Daśārā, Poravāra, Deḍhu, Deḍhagraha, Danderavāla, Dhaktha, Dhakkacāla, Dhavalijoti, Dīḍū, Dīnḍoriyā, Dīsāñvāla, Dasārā, Doilavāla, Dhākaḍā, Dhanvalā, Dhavala-Jaina, Dasā-Hūmaḍa, Dīśāvāla-Daśā, Daraji, Gaṅgarāḍā, Gāhilavāla, Gaulavāla, Gogavāra, Gindoḍiyā, Guruvālā, Golāpūraba, Golālāre, Golasiṅghāre, Gahapātāyā, Ghanorā, Gaṅgarānī, Ghaḍī, Goḍha, Golāla, Gajapūrvi, Gahakhaṇḍuja, Goguvāla, Gogayya, Gaṅgarda, Gundoriya, Gasaura, Gujaravāla, Gauyalavāla, Gailavāḍā, Gaulapura, Gaṅgeravāla, Gaugavāra, Gindauḍiyā, Gurjara, Gāndhi, Harasaurā, Halada, Hākariyā, Haradorā, Himmāragujarāti, Harasola, Haradara, Harada, Hakariyā, Hūmada, Hummada-Viśā, Hummada-Daśā, Indra-Jaina, Jaisavala, Janaurā, Jālaurā, Jāraulā, Jiraṇavāla, Jelavāla, Jemā, Jambū, Jhaliyāra, Jannara, Jolura, Jeharānā, Jayalavāla, Jālorā, Jambusarā, Kaṭanerā, Kapulā, Khaḍāyata, Khaṇḍelavāla, Kaṭhāḍā, Kakasthana, Kāṅkariyā, Kharavā, Khemavāla, Karohiyā, Karanasiyā, Khaḍabaḍa, Kāralāla, Kānthaḍa, Kajapuri, Khaṇḍoya, Kabaliya, Kapola, Kāhari, Khandarya, Koraghāriya, Katheravāla, Karavera, Kākaliya, Kājutivāla, Kauraṭavāla, Kambauvāla, Khadāyatā, Khatāravāla, Khici, Kharavā, Kākarīyā, Kapaula, Kandoiyā, Khurasāla, Khaṇḍavarata, Karavastana, Kamāiyā, Kacchiyā, Kāregarāyā, Khairobā, Kṛṣṇapakṣi, Kāmbhoja, Kṣatriya, Kanabi-pāṭidāra, Kandoi, Khatri, Koli, Luvāra, Luvānā, Lāḍa, Lohiyā, Lāmecū, Lavecū, Lāḍisāka, Liṅgāyata, Lambusarā, Medatavāla, Mauḍa, Māṇḍaliyā, Magalavāla, Mūrivāra, Māli-Poravāla, Majhavārā, Māḍāhāḍa, Mothiya, Mandakya, Mārakeya, Moṭavāla, Mānatavāla, Mehavāḍā, Māḍa, Mihiriya, Maṅgaurā, Mauṭha, Medaurā, Māyā, Maṭiyā, Mauḍamāṇḍaliyā, Mahatā, Mevāḍā, Mevāḍā-Daśā, Miśra, Maheśrī, Modha-Maṇḍliya-Daśā, Mahātmā, Māru, Moḍha-Ghāñci, Nimā-Daśā, Nimā-Viśā, Nāi, Nemā, Narasiṃhapura-Daśā, Narasiṃhapura-Viśā, Nāgadā-Daśā, Nāgadā-Viśā, Nutana, Narāyā, Narasiyā, Nagaurī, Nauṭiyā, Nāchelā, Nāthacalla, Naphāka, Nāgara, Nāgendrā, Nāghaurā, Nemilāra, Nariścya, Naṭila, Nadilā, Nivā, Nārāyaṇa, Naṭerā, Nānāvāla, Navāñbharā, Nāranagaresā, Osavāla, Osavāla-Viśā, Osavāla-Daśā, Pāṇḍe, Pañcā, Poravāḍa-Viśā, Poravāḍa-Jaṅgāḍa-Viśā, Poravāla, Pouravāla, Pauravāra, Poravāḍa-Daśā, Pokara, Purohita, Papaḍivāla, Pañcama, Phatehapuriyā, Pallivāla, Palibāla, Paravāra, Padmavati-Paravāra, Paravāra-Cosaka, Pavārachiya, Pehāsayā, Pausarā, Padamoura, Puskaravāla, Pañcamavāla, Pākhastya,

Pāvarābhi, Paukarā, Pausarā, Rajapurā, Rājiyā, Rāyakavāla, Rājapūta, Śrīmāla, Śrīmāla-Daśā, Śrī-Śrīmāla, Śrīmālī, Śrīmālī-Viśā, Śrīmālī-Daśā, Śrīmālī-Laḍavā, Śrīmālī-Māravāḍi, Sāḷavī, Sāṇḍasarā, Sutāra, Saṃkavāla, Sukura, Samaiyya, Saitavāla, Selāvāra, Śrāvaka, Sādara, Singāra, Saradiyā, Sareḍavāla, Śrīguru, Svarindra, Saunaiyā, Stavī, Suraravāla, Sirakera, Sauni, Saujatavāla, Sācaurā, Sekasantānya, Somavaṃśibogāra, Surendra, Soniya, Sorāthiya, Svetavāla, Sahelava, Śrīgodha, Sārathiya-Poravāra, Sohora, Sācorā, Śrīkhaṇḍa, Śrīguru, Sāṃbharā, Saḍauiyā, Saredavāla, Sauvathavāla, Sauhitavāla, Surendra, Saunaiyā, Saurandiya, Ṭinṭauḍā, Ṭanṭauriyā, Tattora, Thākaravāla, Thagara-Bogara, Terauḍa, Tipaura, Takacāla, Tagara, Upādhyāya, Vogadiya-Viśā, Vaiśya, Vahaḍa, Vadvaiya, Vañsavāla, Vaugārā, Vadela, Vapuchavāra, Vidiyādi, Vagheravāla, Vacaḍa, Vāgrīva, Vāvaravāla, Vāmanavāla, Vālamivāla, Vahaura, Veḍanaurā, Vidyavya, Vikriya, Vidiyādā and Yavapaḍa. The list cannot be complete, but contains all the major caste-names. Sometimes names with variant readings denote the same caste, the variation in spelling or pronunciation being due to regional differences.

Caste System: See Jāti and Varṇa.

***Catuḥ-Śaraṇa*:** Prakrit *Caüsaraṇa*, the first of the Prakīrṇa (q.v.) series which deals in 63 verses with the prayers by means of which one may take the fourfold refuge, namely that of the Arhat, Siddha, Sādhu, and Dharma. The text is authored by Virabhadra. Bhavnagar edn., 1908; Agamodaya edn., 1925.

***Caturhārāvalī-Citrastava*:** A hymn composed by Jayatilaka Sūri in which the syllables are to be read in a special way.

***Stotraratnākara*:** II, Bombay, 1913.

Caturindriya Jīvas: Four-sensed Jīvas (q.v.) possessing the organs of touch, smell, touch and sight. To this class belong wasps, scorpions, mosquitoes, flies, locusts, and butterflies.

Cāturmāsa: Four months of rain from Āṣādha to Kārttika.

Caturmukha: See Caumukha.

Caturmukha: Attendent Yakṣa of Vimalanātha (q.v.) according to the Digambars. His mount is peacock. Caturmukha has twelve arms according to one version and eight arms according to another.

Caturmukha Shrine: See Caumukha, Quadruples, Ranakpur.

Caturmukha-Vimāna: The monolithic Jain *camukha* (q.v.) standing in the forecourt of the Indrasabhā at Ellora. It is a *vimāna* of three storeys, square on plan but with the crowning *grīvā* and *śikhara* octagonal. The ground floor is open on the four cardinal sides. The projected porches have advanced pillars, each with a square base. The sanctum contains a central stele with Jina sculptures on its four sides facing the four entrance. The second storey is a lesser square of shorter height than the first. The third storey is a still smaller square and of much less height.

Caturtha: Southern Jain caste belonging to the Digambara stream. They are mainly concentrated in northern Karnataka and southern Maharashtra. Whence the name Caturtha has come is not definitely known. They are mostly agriculturists and settled in villages unlike the urbanized Bania castes. Among them widow-remarriage is allowed. Their religious teacher or Bhaṭṭāraka has his headquarters at Nāndani near Kolhapur. They often call themselves Sat-Śūdra or pure Śūdra.

***Caturviṃśati-Jinālaya*:** A set of twenty-four *devakulikās* or *devakoṣṭhas*, small sanctuaries, each with a Tīrthaṃkara serially installed in it. They form three rows of eight each, the central one facing the main sanctuary in the temple.

***Caturviṃśati Jinastuti*:** Hymns to the 24 Jinas composed by Bappabhaṭṭi (q.v.) in 96 Sanskrit verses. Edited in *Stutisaṃgraha*, Nirnaya Sagara Press, Bombay, 1912. Another Stuti was composed by Jinaprabha Suri, Kāvyamālā VII. See also Dharmaghoṣa.

***Caturviṃśati Paṭa*:** A panel depicting the 24 Tīrthaṃkaras. This may be taken to be a miniature *Caturviṃśati Jinālaya* (q.v.) which type became very popular from the medieval period to modern times.

***Caturviṃśatitīrthaṃkarapurāṇa*:** See Dāmanandin.

Caubara-Dera: Jain temple of the twelfth century situated in Un, West Nimar district, Malwa, constructed in Paramāra style of architecture which is an extension of the Cālukya style. The temple faces the north. The sanctum is a *pañca-ratha* on plan with the central *ratha* having three facets and the remaining ones only two. The *śikhara* over the sanctum is now lost. The temple is entered through three *ardha-maṇḍapas* of one bay each. The *trika-maṇḍapa* has six pillars and the same number of pilasters. The *gūḍha-maṇḍapa* is a fairly large octagonal hall supported on eight pillars.

Caumuha: Extolled by Svayambhū (q.v.) in his *Paumacariu* who said that it was from him that the poet derived his style of *paddhaḍiā* metre with *duvai* and *dhruvaka*. Obviously Caumuha was either the originator of the Apabhraṃśa style or he was the first to make extensive use of it. In a few old verses found prefixed in the *Paumacariu*, Caumuha is praised for his excellent diction. We also find Caumuha extolled for his *Goggahakahā*.

Caumukha: Quadruple, which is a feature of Jain sculptural representations. It also has the name Sarvotobhadra Pratimā, that is, auspicious from all sides. It is a based obelisk representing the figure of a Tīrthaṃkara on each of the four sides. The Sanskritized form is Caturmukha. There seems to be no regularity as to the particular Jina to be sculptured there. Miniature Caumukha shrines are numerous. Besides usual caumukha slabs containing representations of four Tīrthaṃkaras on four sides, there are well-known Caturmukha temples such as the Caturmukha shrine of Ranakpura or Camurmukha-Vimāna of Ellora or Caumukha-basti of Karkal (qq.v.). See Quadruples.

Caumukha-basti: Situated in Karkal in South Kanara, this structure was built in AD 1586-7. Each of its four doors opens on three black-stone figures of three Tīrthaṃkaras—Aranātha, Mallinātha, and Munisuvrata—of identical size and shape. The temple has pillars of simple workmanship. It has the sloping caves made of long overlapping stone slabs. It has no superstructure and therefore is an example of *muṇḍa-prāsāda* of the *sarvatobhadra* class.

***Caüsarana*:** See Catuḥśaraṇa.

Cave Temples: Jain monks of the earliest period being mostly forest recluses and wandering ascetics depended on natural caves for shelter, which later began to be given shape in the form of cave temples. Side by side was developed the custom of excavating caves for religious and monastic purposes as also for artistic inspiration. Examples of the caves of the second category are to be found in those of Udayagiri and Khaṇḍagiri (qq.v.) near Bhubaneswar in Orissa which began to be excavated since the time of Khāravela, *circa* first century BC. The Tamil country comes up with an interesting series of natural caverns on hills, suitably altered to render them habitable for ascetics. The caverns together with early Brahmi inscriptions are found in several spots on the Eastern Ghats, particularly in the region surrounding Madurai. These inscriptions provide authentic evidence of the early spread of Jainism in the Tamil country. The sites are Anaimalai, Arittapatti, Mankulam, Muttuppatti, Tirupparankunram, Varichchiyur, Karungalakkudi, Kilavalavu, Tiruvatavur, Vikkiramangalam, and Mettupatti in the Madurai district, Pillaiyarpatti and Kunnakkudi in the Ramnathapuram district, Marukaltalai in Tirunelveli district, Tiruchirapalli, Pugalur, Sivayam, Sittannavasal, Narttamalai and Tenimalai in the Tiruchirapalli district, Aracchalur in Coimbatore district, Mamandur and Sedarampattu in North Arcot district and Tirunatharkunru and Solavandipuram in the South Arcot district. Sittannavasal is the most important among all these which was in continuous occupation of the Jains from about the second century BC to the ninth century AD. Most of these pertained to the Jains but a few to other sects. There are also instances of occupation and conversion of some of these caves. The large cave temple at Tirupparankunram is an instance of conversion of an original Jain temple to a Śaiva one. The same holds good in the case of a cave temple at Malaiyadikkurichi in Tirunelveli district. The Pabhosa cave (q.v.) near Allahabad belonging to *circa* first century BC contains an inscription. The Son-Bhandara cave of Rajgir contains a standing figure of Sambhavanātha. Four cave temples excavated in the northern scarp of the Badami (q.v.) cliff is the solitary Jain example excavated in the middle of the seventh century. Three of these caves are Brahmanical and the topmost one belongs to the Jains. It is the most lavishly embellished. The Nanabasti (q.v.) Jain cave temple on the south-east face of the Meguti Hill at Aihole is slightly different in plan, belonging to the close of the seventh century or the begining of the eighth century. Just below the brow of the same hill at Aihole and close under the Meguti temple is a two-storeyed cave-temple, partly structural and partly excavated or rather a natural cavern so fashioned. The minor Jain rock-cut temple on the western slope of the Meguti Hill consists mainly of a sanctum and front *maṇḍapa*, cut into the hill-side with a shrine doorway. Next in the Jain series of cave temples come those of Elapura or Ellora (q.v.). There is a small series of Jain rock-cut caves and a specimen of monolithic cut-out *vimāna*, the Chotā Kailāśa (q.v.) and the still smaller one, the Indra Sabhā (q.v.) occupying the northern horn of the Ellora ridge. These were excavated in the eighth-ninth centuries. The Indra Sabhā (cave 32) and Jagannātha Sabhā (q.v., cave 33) are the most noteworthy and elaborate excavations in the Jain series. The rock-cut cave-shrine in the south cell of the court is Chotā Kailāśa (cave 30), consisting of a shrine, *antarāla* and front *maṇḍapa*. Tringalvadi and Chandor in the Nasik district contain two Jain cave temples. The former which has an incription of AD 1344 consists of a *garbhagṛha*, *antarāla*, and *maṇḍapā*. Along the front of the *maṇḍapa* is a low parapet wall from which rise pillars, one on the either side of the entrance, supporting the outer cave of the verandah. The Chandor cave, which seems to be later in date, has a small room supported by rough square pillars. See Arcthitecture.

Cedaga, Ceṭaka: Maternal uncle of Mahāvīra who was the chief or president of 36 republican states of eastern India comprising nine Mallaki, nine Licchavi and eighteen *gaṇarājyas* of Kashi and Koshala. Mahāvīra's mother Triśalā was his sister. It is therefore natural to expect that the Master at the initial stages of his career as religious teacher had received great patronage from Cedaga. Kuṇika or Ajātaśatru, king of Magadha, planned to overthrow the confederacy and declared war against it. Cedaga assembled the republican chiefs and they resolved to fight Ajātaśatru. The Buddha encouraged them saying that so long as they held full and frequent assemblies, maintained internal concord in assembly and administration, followed old traditions, honoured the elders of the community, old institutions and shrines, saints and women they would remain invincible. Ajātaśatru thereupon resolved to destroy their inner unity and deputed his minister Vassakāra on the nefarious mission of sowing seeds of disunion among the republican tribes. His work for three years eventually bore fruit. The war broke out. Cedaga had also brought on his side the king of Sindhu-Sauvīra, Vatsa, and Avantī, who married his daughter. The Jain texts indicate a period of more than 16 years for this war. Gośāla (q.v.) who died in *c*. 484 BC saw the war in progress, while the confederation of these republics was still going strong up to 468 BC, the date of Mahāvīra's death which they celebrated by a joint illumination to mark the disappearance from their midst of the light that was in their Mahāvīra. The war, which must therefore have lasted from at least 484 to 468 BC ended in complete victory for Ajātaśatru. Unable to bear the humiliation caused by his defeat as the head of the republican confederacy Cedaga committed suicide. Mahāvīra was the sister's son of Cedaga and Ajātaśatru, Halla, and Vehall were his grandsons. Their mother was Cedaga's daughter Cellanā who was given in marriage to Bimbisāra. Hoernle, *Uvasagadasāo*, II. App.

Ceiyajattā: Caityayatra, festival of Caitya. It was celebrated on the day of moonlight festivity (*kaumudikā caturmāsī*) in the Aṅgamandira garden of Campā. The worship of the *Caitya*-tree is of an age-old tradition. The Jain Tīrthaṃkaras are provided with a holy tree under which they are said to have attained omniscience. The Bhavanavāsī and Vyantara gods have been assigned the *caitya*-trees. Jain temples are also known as Caityālayas. See Caitya Vṛkṣa.

Cennanna-basti: A late Jain shrine at Sravanabelgola constructed in AD 1673. It consists of a *garbhagṛha*, porch, and varandah, and enshrines a seated figure of Candraprabha.

Cenna-Pārśva-basadi: A Jina temple, dedicated to Pārśvanātha, which was constructed by Bittideva, feudatory of Hoysala Narasiṃha I, mentioned in an epigraph from Heggera in Chiknayakanhati taluk in Chikmagalur district, Karnataka. One Māṇikanandin Siddhāntadeva, disciple of Guṇacandra, was recipient of a grant given to this temple. *Epigraphia Carnatica*, XII, Chik 21.

Cetana Dravya: Same as Jīva (q.v.), the nature of which is *cetana* or *citsvarūpa*, that is, conscious. In itself, it is incapable of being measured by material units or space units. In the concrete world, it is always found associated with a body and has all the characteristics of a living being. It is a knower (*jñātṛ*), an actor (*kartṛ*), and an enjoyer (*bhoktṛ*) and as an active part figures as the operative cause of its own *karmas* and in turn enjoys or suffers the fruits of such *karmas* (q.v.).

Chahardi: Jain site in Dhulia district which has yielded the elaborate bronze *caturviṃśati-paṭṭa* of Ṛṣabhanātha which is recorded to have been installed by a disciple of Pradyumnācārya of the Candra-*kula*.

Chakkammovaesa: See Amarakīrtigaṇi.

Chandakāvate: Jain site in Bijapur district wherefrom a *niśīdhi* pillar in memory of the death of Māghanandī-Bhaṭṭāraka of the Surāsta-gaṇa is found.

Chandakedi: Jain site in Kota area where a temple of about the seventeenth century is of an underground type, probably to offer protection to Jain images from the fanatic followers of other faiths.

***Chandonuśāsana*:** See Hemacandra.

Chamdor: Site of a Jain cave temple in Nasik district, Maharashtra.

Chandwar: Findspot of a good number of fine Jain sculptures of the eleventh and twelfth centuries near Agra.

Chansma: Site of a Jain temple in Gujarat which now houses the Pārśvanātha image from Bhatewar (q.v.).

Charampa: Jain centre in Balasore district of Orissa, some miles to the north of Bhadrak, wherefrom several Jain images have been found. Four of the these images—of Ṛṣabhanātha, Ajitanātha, Śāntinātha, and Mahāvīra—are now in the State Museum at Bhubaneswar. The face of the image of Mahāvīra is badly mutilated. The images of Ajitanātha and Śāntinātha are in *dhyānāsana* having on either side a *chowri*-bearer at the bottom and a flying Gandharva with a garland at the top. The Ṛṣabhanātha image is accompanied by Bharata and Bāhubali.

Chatra: Jain site in Purulia district which has yielded an eleventh-century Ṛṣabhanātha image standing in *kāyotsarga* on lotus pedestal relieved with bull. The figure has *jaṭāmukuṭa* on head and is flanked by two attendants on each side of his legs. Above the attendants there are eight miniature Jinas four on each side in a row of two, one row above the other. The emblem is indistinct and a flying *gandharva* is on the top left corner. There is an umbrella on Jina's *jaṭāmukuṭa*. A tenth-century Pārśvanātha image found here stands in *kāyotsarga* on a lotus seat relieved with snake design and canopy of seven-hooded snake over the head and standing attendants on each side. Another sculpture of the same Jina is found, similar to the one mentioned above with the exception that the pedestal does not show a relief of the snake. A tenth-century colossal Mahāvīra image on a large slab with arch-shaped top has been also found in this place which stands in *kāyotsarga* on a double-petalled lotus placed on a *pañcaratha* pedestal. There are two attendants on either side and miniscule figures of the 24 Tīrthaṃkaras, twelve on each side in six compartments. Another Mahāvīra image from Chatra is also in *kāyotsarga* on a lotus seat with indistinct figure of lion and flanked by attendants on two sides. Four miniature Tīrthaṃkaras are above the attendants on two sides of the Jina. Two Caumukhas of the twelfth century were found here at the gate of R.K. Mission and are now in the State Archaeological Gallery. They contain representations of the 24 Jinas in *kāyotsarga* with their respective symbols and are divided into segments by incised lines.

Chausa Hoard: Collection of Jain Metal images from Chausa in Bihar now preserved in the Patna Museum. This hoard contains four bronze images of Ṛṣabhanātha. Two of these images are in *kāyotsarga* pose with long wavy hair covering shoulders and back, while the remaining two are seated in *dhyāna-mudrā* and *vajraparyaṅka* posture with hair parted in the middle, locks on shoulders and on the back of the head. It has two bronze images of Candraprabha in which he is represented as seated with *dhyāna-mudrā* crescent moon on the top of the round beaded *śiraścakra*. There are two large *makara* heads on either side of the throne. The hoard also contains two bronze images of Pārśvanātha, one standing in *kāyotsarga* with serpent coil, curly hair, and three lines on each side of the pelvic region, while the other, the lower portion of which is lost, shows his standing figure whose head is protected by a seven-hooded serpent.

***Chedasūtra*:** Prakrit Cheyasutta, belonging to the Śvetāmbara canonical literature. Six texts of this series comprise *Niśītha* (Nisīha) *Mahāniśītha* (Mahānisīha), *Vyavahāra*, *Dasaśrutaskandha*, *Bṛhatkalpa* and *Pañcakalpa* (qq.v.). *Bṛhatkalpa* is also known as *Kalpa* (Kappa). The *Pañcakalpa* is now lost and replaced by *Jita-kalpa* (Jiyakappa). The eighth section of the *Ācāra-dasāo* or *Dasaśrutaskandha* is known as the *Kalpasūtra* (q.v.) of Bhadrabāhu (q.v.) which is a combination of three different works—*Jina-carita* dealing with the lives of the Tīrthaṃkaras, *Sthavirāvali* (Therāvali) dealing with the schools, sub-schools and teachers, and *Sāmācārī* (Sāmāyāri) dealing with the rules observed by ascetics during the rain-retreat. Two other texts, the *Piṇḍaniryukti* (Pindanijjuti) and *Oghaniryukti* (Ohanijjuti) are sometimes included in the Chedasūtra group.

Chettipatti: Jain site in the Tiruchirapalli district, Tamil Nadu. Among the findings of this place the most interesting are the excavated remains of an all-stone temple revealing the *adhiṣṭhāna* with *prākāra* and *gopura*-entrance on the east. The site yielded also two pillars with couchant lions, two more without the shafts over the lion-head and other architectural fragments. A good number of Tīrthaṃkara images have been found at this site. From an inscription it is known that the *gopura* of this temple, which belonged to a merchant guild, was built by one Jayavīra Perilamciyam. This inscription is in the characters of the tenth-eleventh centuries.

Cheyasutta: See Chedasūtra.

Chhani: Site of a Jain Bhaṇḍāra near Baroda.

Chiada: Jain site in Bankura district, opposite Pareshnath, in West Bengal. Some Tīrthaṃkara images are found here.

Chilukuru: Findspot of a colossal figure of Pārśvanātha, 3.25 mm height. It is a famous Jain basadi, about 20 km from Hyderabad. The image is carved on sandstone, shown with curly hair, elongated ear-lobes, and snake-hood canopy over the head. The left hand is damaged. The same site also yields another image of Mahāvīra in seated *padmāsana* with his hands in *dhyāna-mudrā*. It is carved on a highly polished black basalt and is about 1 m in height. The two *chowri*-bearers carrying fruit and flywhisk are carved separately for installation on either side of the main image. They wear crowns and *cakra-kuṇḍalas*.

Chippagiri: Jain centre in Bellary district said to have close association with the Kalacuri King Bijjala's life who is said to have erected a Jain temple, the layout of which comprises the *gardhagṛha*, *ardha-maṇḍapa* and *mahā-maṇḍapa*. In 1528 the Vijayanagara King Kṛṣṇadevarāya (AD 1509-20) made a gift to the Jain basadi of Chippagiri. The site has also yielded a few tomb-stone figures of Jain saints.

Chirwa Epigraph of VS 1330: Belongs to the time of Samarasiṃha, the Guhila chief and son of Tejasiṃha (q.v.). This inscription refers to the fact that the Jain saint Ratnaprabha was honoured by both Viśāladeva and Tejasiṃha (qq.v.).

Chitaral Inscription: Belongs to the 28th year of the reign of the Pāṇḍya King Varaguṇa I (*circa* AD 765-815) *alias* Nedunjaḍayan which records a gift of golden ornaments to the Bhaṭāriyār of the sacred hill of the Cāraṇas, made by a lady named Guṇandāngi Kurattigal, disciple of Ariṣṭanemi Bhaṭāra of Perayakkudi. *Travancore Archaeological Series*, I.193ff.

Chitgiri: Findspot of a ninth-century Śāntinātha image in Bankura district which was found lying in temple ruins. It is about two feet in height, standing in *kāyotsarga* on a double-petalled lotus with attendants on either side of the legs. The slab shows in high relief two more Tīrthaṃkaras in the same pose. There are flying figures on the top corners and a deer emblem on the pedestal.

Chitor: See Citrakūṭa.

Chittamur: Site of an interesting group of rock-cut sculptures in South Arcot district, assignable to the ninth-tenth centuries or the middle and late Cola periods in which structural temples came up. Notable among these sculptures are those of Bāhubali, Pārśvanātha with his attendants, and Mahāvīra with his Yakṣī Siddhāyikā. Chittamur is the headquarters of a *maṭha* of the Tamil Jains.

Chotā Kailāśa: Constituent of Jain rock-cut caves at Ellora, excavated on the model of the larger and earlier Brahmanical Kailāśa. It is hewn out of the central mass of rock, but is unfinished. The temple faces west. The main *vimāna* has two superposed storeys as in many Jain structural temples. The lower storey has a large Mahāvīra attended by Yakṣas and Yakṣīs enshrined in the sanctum, and the upper has Sumatinātha with his attendants. On the side walls flanking the entrance into the lower shrine are other images of Jinas and also an eight-armed goddess on the north wall. The shrine is preceded by a small *antarāla* and a large *mahā-maṇḍapa* with sixteen pillars arranged in groups of four at the four corners of the hall which has three entrances on the west, north, and south, with pillared porches fronting them as in the greater Kailāśa.

Cikka Hanasoge: Situated in the Mysore district, it is the findspot of a number of Jain inscriptions. A tradition that this place had once contained 64 Jina temples is attested by an epigraph of about AD 1100. A tenth-century inscription records the death of Śrīdharadeva of the Panasoge-śākhā and another of the Jain queen Jakkiyabbe. A third-one mentions the death of the Jain saint Elācārya, while a single line inscription of about AD 1025 mentions a Jina temple called Rajendra Cola Jinālaya. Among other inscriptions, one of AD 1060 refers to the erection of a Jina temple dedicated to the monks of the Pustaka-gaccha by Vīra Rājendra Nanni Caṅgālva. The latter's religious activities are also mentioned in another inscription from Hanasoge. An inscription of AD 1080 mentions Dāmanandi Bhaṭṭāraka of Deśiya-gaṇa, Pustaka-gaccha and Kondakunda-anvaya in charge of 64 Jina basadis of Panasoge (Hanasoge). *Epigraphia Carnatica* IV, Yeda 21-6; VII, Shik. 219; *Jaina Śilālekha Saṃgraha* II, Nos. 175, 195-6, 239, 249; IV, 74-6, 195-6.

Cintāmaṇi Temple: Jain temple of Bikaner erected by Cintāmaṇi Rao Bikāji completed after his death in AD 1505. The original form comprised a *garbhagṛha* and an attached *maṇḍapa*. Later it was enlarged and another *maṇḍapa* with two side-porches and a *mukha-maṇḍapa* were added. It enshrines a large marble image of Ādinātha. In 1583 Jain images looted from Sirohi by Rao Raisingh were deposited in a vault of this temple. It is a collection of 1,050 metal icons stored in the underground chamber. According to a different tradition, these images were taken from Sirohi to Fatehpur Sikri by a Muslim general of Akbar and were kept in the royal treasury. Afterwards at the request of Raisingh these were handed to him by the emperor.

Citrakūṭa: A great centre of Jainism in Rajasthan from the eighth century AD. It is the same as Chitor. The celebrated logician and philosopher Haribhadra was a native of Citrakūṭa which had also produced a good number of Jain scholars. From the eleventh century this place became the centre of the activities of monks of the Kharatara-gaccha. The temples of Mahāvīra and Pārśva are two of the earliest temples of this city. There were also temples dedicated to Ādinātha and Candraprabha. A *kīrti-stambha* of Digambara affiliation is also found here. According to a mutilated epigraph, this *stambha* was started by a person called Jiju and completed by his son Pūrṇasiṃha. It was consecrated by Dharmacandra. An epigraph refers to the erection of a temple of Śāntinātha at this place by a treasury officer under King Kumbha whose name was Velāka. An epigraph from Ghagsa near Chitor of AD 1265 refers to the name of Ratnaprabha Sūri of Caitra-*gaccha*. The Chitor epigraph of Tejaḥsiṃha dated vs 1324 (AD 1267) originally belonged to the Mahāvīra temple connected with the activities of Kharatara-*gaccha*. These two inscriptions are directly associated with Tejaḥsiṃha, the Guhila king of Rajasthan. Another Chitor inscription of the time of Samarasiṃha records the construction of a Pārśvanātha temple at that place by the queen mother Jayatalladevī in vs 1335. The inscription further records the grant of land by King Samarasiṃha for the construction of a monastery by Pradyumna Suri. Among the Jain monuments here the most remarkable is the soaring *kīrti-stambha*. The Jain temple beside the *kīrti-stambha* seems to be a fourteenth-century construction. The Śāntinātha temple referred to above which has a *garbhagṛha*, *pañcaratha* on plan and an attached *catuṣki* on the north and west was built in AD 1448. Another Jain Shrine at Chitorgarh is the Sātbis-deoḍi of the fifteenth century. It is dedicated to Ādinātha and has the following constituents: *garbhagṛha*, *antarāla*, *gūḍha-maṇḍapa*, *nava-caukī*, *octagonal maṇḍapa* and *mukha-maṇḍapa*. *Rajputana Museum Report*, 1927, 3; *Journal of the Asiatic Society of Bengal* LV (1) 46-8; M.A. Dhaky in *Journal of the Indian Society of Oriental Art*, Calcutta, Special Number, 1965-7, 7-8.

Classification of Beings: The primary Jain classification of beings was made on the basis of the number of sense-organs the Jīva (q.v.) is supposed to possess, from *ekendriya* or one to *pañcendriya* or five (qq.v.). The five-sensed Jīvas are classified into four divisions—demons, lower animals, human beings and demi-gods. Other modes of classification lead to the following divisions: (1) Siddha and Saṃsārin (male, female, neuter), (2) Nārakī (born in hell), Tiryak (lower animals), Manuṣya (human beings) and Devatā (spirits, gods, demon); (3) Hell-beings, male lower animals, female lower animals, male human beings, female human beings, male demi-gods and female demi-gods; (4) The five sub-divisions of the one-sense Jīvas as well as the two-, three-, four-, and five-sensed Jīvas, thus making a total of nine classes; (5) The aforesaid five divisions of one-sensed, etc., subdivided into two groups, *paryāpta* and *aparyāpta*, thus making a total of ten classes; (6) first four orders of the Jīvas one-sensed, etc., three subdivisions of the five-sensed Jīvas (Nārakī, Tiryak, Manuṣya) and four subdivisions of gods (Bhavanapati, Vyantara, Jyotiṣka and Vaimānika), making a total of eleven classes; and (7) combination of all these in different ways making a total of twelve, thirteen and fourteen classes. There is another classification into six divisions on the basis of *lesyās* (q.v.), an abstract principle pertaining to the doctrine of *karma* (q.v.) making a coloured grading of beings.

Cognizances: *Lāñchanas*, the identifying marks of the Jinas. All the Tīrthaṃkaras look alike and it is on the basis of the *lāñchanas* or symbols inscribed on the seat or pedestal identification is possible. The Mathura images of the Tīrthaṃkaras belonging mostly to the Kuṣāṇa period do not contain any *lāñchana*. The first datable and the earliest known sculpture with a *lāñchana* is the partly mutilated sculpture of Neminātha from Rajgir, belonging to the Gupta period. In the centre of the pedestal is the beautiful figure of a standing *cakra-puruṣa* with a wheel on his back, and on either side of the wheel is a conch-shell, the mark of Neminātha. The *Abhidhānacintāmaṇi* supplies the following list of identifiers: Ṛṣabha: bull; Ajita: elephant; Sambhava: horse; Abhinandana: monkey; Sumati: *krauñca* bird; Padmaprabha: lotus; Supārśva: *svastika*; Candraprabha: moon; Suvidhi: *makara*; Śītala: *śrīvatsa*; Śreyāṃśa: rhinoceros; Vāsupūjya: buffalo; Vimala: boar; Ananta: falcon; Dharma: thunderbolt; Śānti: deer; Kunthu: goat; Ara: *nandyāvarta*; Malli: pitcher; Munisuvrata: tortoise; Nami: blue lotus; Nemi: conch-shell; Pārśva: snake; and Mahāvīra: lion. According to the Jain writers the *lāñchana* is to be placed in the centre, below the *pāda-pīṭha*, while the attendant Yakṣa and Yakṣī are to be on the right and left the pedestal. There are points of difference with regard to the identifiers between the Śvetāmbaras and the Digambaras. The fourteenth Jina Ananta as stated above has the falcon symbol according to the *Abhidhānacintāmaṇi*, while the Digambaras hold it to be a bear. The *śrīvatsa* symbol of Śītala has been replaced by the *svastika* in the *Tiloyapannattī* and by *śrīdruma* in the *Pratiṣṭhāsaroddhāra*. Aranātha's *nandyāvarta* is replaced by a fish in the Digambara texts.

Cokimayya Jinālaya: A Jina temple mentioned in an epigraph dated AD 1427 found at a place called

Begur in Bangalore taluk of the district of the same name. *Epigraphia Carnatica* IX, Bangalore 82.

Cosmography: The main sources of information of the general plan of the cosmos in the Jain tradition are the cosmographic sections of the *Ṭhāna* and *Samavāya*, the first and second *payas* of the *Paṇṇavanā*, the third section of *Jīvābhigama* with the supposed interpolated text *Divasāgara-pannatti* which opens with a description of Jambūdvīpa and deals in particular with the ring continents and oceans, and the *Jambud-dīvapannatti* which deals with Jambūdīpa in general, its enclosure and gates, and the continent of Bharata and the remaining continents of Jambūdvīpa, the geographical details of Jambū-dvīpa, and so on. Descriptions of the universe (q.v.) and its measurement are found in Vinayavijaya's *Lokaprakāśa*; heaven and hell (qq.v.), are described in *Uttarādhyayana*, the 16 inner and 16 outer island-continents (q.v.) are mentioned in the *Tiloyapannattī*.

Cosmology: That framework of concept and relations which is erected for the purpose of bringing a descriptive order into the universe as a whole. It treats of the universe as an ordered system, and as such is confined to a description of the salient features of the observed universe in terms of such categories as time, space, and matter. Cosmogony, ontology and teleology are related branches of cosmology dealing respectively with the questions concerning the origins, inner nature, and purpose of the universe. In Jainism the scope of cosmogony is limited since the Jains hold that the universe has neither beginning nor end and that its production is not due to any intelligent agent. Regarding ontology or the inner nature of the universe the Jains have a well-defined approach, revealed in their treatment of metaphysics (q.v.) while the major portion of Jain teleology is related to its ethics (q.v.). The entire cosmos is composed of substances (q.v.) of different kinds. These substances are possessed of some unchanging essential characters (*guṇas*, q.v.) and changing modes (*paryāyas*, q.v.). These are broadly classified into two groups, that which has a body and that which is devoid of it. To the second category belongs time which is non-extended. The substances having a body and possessing extension are of two kinds, animate and inanimate. The former consists of various classes of living beings divided on the basis of the number of sense-organs. The inanimate or non-living objects having extension are divided into four categories. There is space (*ākāśa* q.v.) which makes room for the existence of all extended substances, the substratum of motion (*dharma* q.v.) which is the principle of mobility, the substratum of non-motion (*adharma* q.v.) which is the principle of immobility, and matter (*pudgala* q.v.) which is liable to integration and disintegration. The smallest form of matter which cannot be further divided is the *paramāṇus* or atom (q.v.). Two or more atoms may combine to form compounds (*saṃghāta*). Time or *kāla* is the only substance which is devoid of extension, indivisible, and present everywhere. It makes possible the continuity, modification, movement, newness and oldness of other substances. Space is supposed to embrace the perceptible universe and beyond. All the inanimate entities are classified into *rūpa* or those with form (*pudgala* or matter) and *arūpa* or those without form (space, motion, rest, and time). These five categories constitute the world or *loka* (q.v.) and beyond is the immeasurable infinite called *aloka*. The latter is not properly defined in the Jain texts but is described as an absolute void impenetrable to anything. The space belonging to the preview of *loka* contains the visible universe which looks like a human being standing with feet apart and arms akimbo. Things left together hanging in space would lead to chaos which is why the substrata of motion and rest, mobility and immobility, are required. They represent the laws by which the cosmic bodies are set up in order. See Universe.

Courtesanship: See Prostitution.

Cross-Cousin Marriage: According to the *Tri-varṇikācāra* XI, 37-38, he who marries his paternal aunt's daughter, the daughter of his mother's brother, or his wife's sister commits no sin, but if he marries the daughter of his mother's sister, a girl of his own *gotra* (q.v.), or a sister of his mother-in-law he commits sin. The custom of marrying the maternal uncle's daughter was in vogue among the Buddhists and among the Hindus in certain parts of India. This practice was observed by the early Jains also. Among the Jains marriage between cross-cousins was not illegal, but marriage between parallel cousins in which the bride belongs to the same *gotra* as the bride-groom was forbidden. In actual practice the rule is controlled by local usages. Cross-cousin marriage is neither allowed nor practised in northern India but in the south it is much in vogue. Marriage between maternal uncle and the niece is found among the Kannadiga Brāhmaṇas, Liṅgāyatas, and Jains. According to Jain mythology Ṛṣabha married his sister and gave his daughters, Brāhmī and Sundarī, in marriage to his sons, Bāhubali and Bharata respectively. King Agrasena's grandsons and granddaughters married among themselves and their progeny are known as the Agravālas.

Cūḍakarma: See Kṣurakarma.

Culagiri: Jain centre in the West Nimar district, Madhya Pradesh, celebrated for the colossal image of Ṛṣabhanātha. There is also an interesting large image of Śāntinātha. Some Jain temples are also found. Several epigraphs of the twelfth from this place are known. *Jaina Śilālekha Saṃgraha*, III, Nos. 370-1.

Culikā-Sūtras: See *Nandī-sūtra* and *Anuyogadvāra*.

Cūrṇis: Commentarial literature which are prose glosses with a curious admixture of Prakrit and Sanskrit. Cūrṇis on twenty texts are available. Some of the them contain valuable historical information as well. The *Āvaśyaka-cūrṇi*, for example, makes mention of a flood in Śrāvastī, thirteen years after Mahāvīra's enlightenment. The *Niśītha-cūrṇi* contains a reference to Kālakācārya who invited a foreigner to invade Ujjain. All the Cūrṇis are indiscriminately ascribed to Jinadāsagaṇi. Unlike the Niryuktis and the Bhāṣyas the Cūrṇis are written in prose. The following Cūrṇis are generally attributed to Jinadāsa—*Niśīthaviśeṣacūrṇi*, *Nandīcūrṇī*, *Anuyogadvārācūrṇi*, *Āvaśyakacūrṇi*, *Dasavaikālikacūrṇi*, *Uttarādhyayanacūrṇi* and *Sūtrakṛtāṅgacūrṇi*.

***Cūrṇisūtra*:** See Yativṛṣabha.

D

Dabhoi: Site of a great Jain temple constructed by Tejahpala (q.v.).

Dadaga: Situated in the Mandya district, Karnataka, it is the findspot of an undated Jain inscription which refers to five temples of which one, dedicated to Bāhubali, received a grant from two generals of the Hoysala King Viṣṇuvardhana (AD 1106-52) namely Bharata and Mariyana. The recipient was Meghaeundra, disciple of Munibhadra, who belonged to the Kanura-gaṇa and Tintriṇika-gaccha. The ancient name of this place was Daḍiganakere. *Jaina Śilālekha Saṃgraha* IV, No. 212.

Daddala: Site of a Jain temple called Girigotemalla-Jinālaya mentioned in an inscription dated śaka 991 (AD 1069) of the time of Cālukya Someśvara II. This temple was constructed by Maleyamarasa Girigoṭemalla, a feudatory of the Cālukya ruler. *Epigraphia Indica*, XXXVII, 113-16.

Dadhabhūmi: Dhalbhum in Singhbhum district, Jharkhand, visited by Mahāvīra.

Dadhipadra: Jain centre in the Panch Mahals of Gujarat with a twelfth-century Śāntinātha temple.

Dahala Sculptures: See Karitalai.

Dahigaon: Once a Jain centre in the Sholapur district of Maharashtra. It has now a modern Mahāvīra temple amidst old ruins.

Daiva: One of the eight forms of Jain marriage adopted from the Brahmanical legal texts with modification. It is the marrying of one's daughter at the conclusion of the worship of the Jina to the person who conducts the ceremony. Here the daughter is given as a gift. *Trivarṇikācāra* XI. 72; *Nītivākyāmṛta* XXXI.5.

Dāmandandin: Author of *Purāṇasārasaṃgraha* in which the lives of Ādinātha, Candraprabha, Śāntinātha, Neminātha, Pārśva and Mahāvīra are treated, and *Caturviṃśatitīrthaṃkara-purāṇa*. He was probably from Karnataka. His date may be placed between AD 1100 and 1300. *Purāṇasārasaṃgraha*, Bhāratīya Jñānapīṭha, Varanasi, 1954.

***Dānakalpadruma*:** See Jinakīrti.

Dānas: Giving gifts, which is one of the six daily duties of the Jain laymen. The gifts have been classified into four kinds, namely, food, protection, medicine, and learning. These are known as *āhāra-dāna*, *adhaya-dāna*, *auṣadha-dāna*, and *śāstra-dāna*.

Dānasamiti: See *Caritra.*

Dānavulapadu: Jain centre in the Jammalmadugu taluk of the Cuddapah district. There were Jain temples previously, fragments of which now remain. The site has yielded a good number of images of beautiful workmanship. Some of these, and a few architectural fragments are now in the Government Museum of Madras. Two pillars, a water-chute, and some *niśīdika*-stones are inscribed. These belong to the Rāṣṭrakūṭa period. An undated inscription belonging to the time of Indra III refers to one general Śrīvijaya who voluntarily resigned this world and became a Jain ascetic in order to attain eternal bliss. *Epigraphia Indica* X, 147ff.

Dānsale: Situated in Tirthahalli Taluk in the Shimoga district, it is the findspot of an inscription of AD 1103 which refers to Caṭṭaladevi and Tribhuvanamalla Sāntara and mentions the erection of a Jain temple by the former. It refers to Ajitasena Bhaṭṭāraka belonging to Drāviḍa Saṅgha and Arungala-anvaya. *Epigraphia Carnatica* VIII, Tirth No. 192.

Darbat Śāntinātha Image Inscription: Dated VS 1132 (AD 1074) and found at Darbat in Hamirpur district, the epigraph records the installation of an image of Śāntinātha by *Sresthins* Pahila and Jiju, belonging to a group of hereditary ministers in the reign of Candella Kīrtivarman (*circa* AD 1070-1100). It also refers to the Digambara saint Vasavendu. *Indian Historical Quarterly* XXX, 183-5.

Darbhavatī: Situated in the Vadodara district in Gujarat, this place is famous for two Pārśvanātha temples. Darbhavatī is regarded as a *tīrtha* in medieval Jain texts. The Pārśva temple-complex of this place is called Lodana-Pārśvanātha. There are also epigraphic references to it. *Prācīna Jaina Lekhasaṃgraha* II, Nos. 38, 39, 41, 43.

Darsana Pratimā: Possessing the perfect, intelligent and well-reasoned faith in Jainism, that is, having a sound knowledge of its doctrines and their applications in life.

Darsanasāra: See Devasena.

Darśanāvaraṇīya: That which prevents beholding the faith. It is an obstruction arising from *ghātin karma* (q.v.).

Dasabhakti: See Pūjyapāda.

Daśalakṣaṇa Dharma: Ten observances required for

saṃvara (q.v.) or stoppage of the influx of karmic matter into the soul. These are: *uttama-kṣamā*, supreme forgiveness; *uttama-mārdava*, supreme-tenderness; *uttama-śauca*, supreme purity; *uttama-satya*, supreme truth, *uttama-saṃyama*; supreme self-restraint; *uttama-tapa*, supreme austerities; *uttama tyāga*, supreme renunciation, *uttama akiñcanya*, supreme humility, and *uttama brahmacarya*, supreme celibacy.

Dasalakṣaṇa Parva: See Paryuṣana.

Daśapura: Modern Mandasore in Madhya Pradesh, famous for the Jīvantasvāmin image. This town which was the seat of the earlier Jain Ācāryas and which witnessed the schism of Ninhava Goṣṭhāmāhila was visited by the celebrated philosopher Samantabhadra. According to *Vividhatīrthakalpa* there was an old temple of Supārśvanātha at this town.

Daśapūrvī: Leaders of the Jain church who knew the ten Pūrvas (q.v.) of the twelfth Aṅga. The first three apostles after Mahāvīra were *kevalins* who obtained omniscience and liberation in their lifetime. The next six *gaṇadharas* were *śrutakevalins* who lacked omniscience but had complete knowledge of the scripture. They were followed by the *dasapūrvīs*.

Dasarā: Festival held in common with the Hindus by Jains as part of regional culture.

Daśaśrutaskandha: Prakrit *Dasāo*, also known as *Āyāradasāo*, the fourth Chedasūtra (q.v.) supposed to have been composed by Bhadrabāhu (q.v.). The earlier sections of the *Daśaśruta-skandha* deals with the disciplinary rules of the Jain monks. The eighth section of this *Dasāo* is known by the title *Kalpasūtra* (q.v.) of Bhadrabāhu. In the ninth section Kuṇika is represented as meeting Mahāvīra in the Pūrṇabhadra shrine at Campā. The last section refers to Śreṇika's meeting with Mahāvīra at Rājagṛha. Edited with *Niryukti* and *Cūrṇi*, Bhavnagar, 1953. See Kalpasūtra.

Daśavaikālika: Prakrit *Dasaveyaliya*, the third Mūlasūtra which according to the tradition was composed by the Brāhmaṇa Nirgrantha ascetic Sayyambhava (Sajjaṃbhava) for his son Mānaka. It has twelve *adhyayanas* including two Cūrlikās. It consists of sayings pertaining to monastic life, some of which remind us of the sayings in the *Dhammapada*, whilst others contain only rules for monastic discipline. *Niryukti* by Bhadrabāhu; Cūrṇi by Jinadasāgaṇi Mahattara, Ratlam, 1933; *Cūrṇi* by Agastyasiṃha, Ahemdabad, 1973; com. by Haribhadra, Bombay, 1918. *Sūtra* and *Niryukti* ed. E. Laumann in *Zeitschrift der Deutschen Morgenlandischen Gasellschaft*, XLVI, 1893, 581-662; with introduction and notes by W. Schubring, Ahmedabad, 1932; Index by Ānandasāgara Sūri, Bombay, 1928.

Dasaveyaliya: See Daśavaikālika.

Daughter: unmarried daughters and sisters are entitled to maintenance out of the family property, according to Jain law. It is the responsibility of the family to give them in marriage. The Brahmanical law-givers hold that after the father's death the sons shall divide property among themselves and the daughters receive a fourth part of the sons' share. But they do not make any clear statement whether this one-fourth share is for natural succession or a moral obligation. The Jain law-givers too hold that in the event of their father's death the daughters are entitled to one-fourth part of the shares of their brothers. In the absence of the father, the guardianship of the sisters up to the time of their marriage devolves on their elder brothers. Daughters who are given in marriage by their father cannot claim share of their father's property after his death. However, during marriage what the daughters receive from their parents, friends, husband, in-laws and relations become their five kinds of Strīdhana (q.v.), which are exclusively theirs.

Dedā: A merchant of Gujarat hailing from Avanti during the reign of the Vaghelas, was a great patron of Jainism and came to be called as Kaṇakagiri for his generosity. At Devagiri he built a Pauṣadhaśālā for the Jain monks. His achievements are recorded in a fourteenth-century work called the *Upadesataraṅgiṇī*.

Delavada: Situated in the Junagarh district, Gujarat, this place is well-known for its Pārśvanātha temple complex.

***Delhana*:** See *Gayasukumāla-rāsa*.

Deogarh: A good number of inscriptions from Deogarh on the Betwa in Lalitpur district, Uttar Pradesh which have been found on the temple sites and assigned between AD 800 and 1000, refer to various Jain shrines, teachers and their sectarian affiliation. Probably some of the temples here were built in the Gupta period. An inscription of Pratihāra Bhoja has been found in the temple of Śāntinātha. Another inscription of AD 958 mentions Tribhuvanakīrti, disciple of Devendrakīrti, grand-disciple of Ratnakīrti of the Sarasvatī-gaccha of Śrī Mūlasaṅgha. Nāgasenācārya and other eminent Jain teachers are mentioned in certain inscriptions. In the ninth century the place was called Luacchāgira.

Afterwards, it was given the name Kīrtigiri. The temple complexes of Deogarh offer an interesting study. The eastern sector of the fort has a group of about 31 Jain temples dating from the ninth to the twelfth centuries and even later. With the exception of temples 11,12, and 28, all of them are structurally unpretentious and small in size. They are either square or rectangular on plan and comprise a hall with or without a projecting cella at the back but normally containing a frontal portico. To the ninth-century belong temples 12 and 15, to the tenth hall-temples made of large blocks, viz., 9, 13, 16, and 20, to the eleventh 2, 3, 11, and 19, and to the twelfth 18, 21, 25, 26, 27 (i), and 30. Only two temples, 10 and 15, show architectural embellishment. Deogarh also abounds in sculptures and *mānastambhas*. Images of Jinas including one of Ajitanātha and of Kṣetrapālas and Yakṣas, a few belonging to the Gupta period, deserve mention. The sculptures of the Tīrthaṃkaras and other Jain divinities found in the Deogarh Fort fully answer the characteristic descriptions given in the iconographical texts and as such they are frequently cited by scholars dealing with Jain iconography. See Klaus Bruhn, *The Jina Images of Deogarh*, Leiden, 1969.

Deoli: Jain site in the Purulia district, West Bengal, which had a *pañcāyatana* group of temples. From this area was discovered to life-size statue of Aranātha or Śāntinātha. This eleventh-century image standing in *kāyotsarga* on a lotus is enshrined in a temple. The top section contains rows of other Tīrthaṃkaras.

Deolia: Findspot of an unidentified Jina image in Burdwan district, West Bengal, which is now in the Asutosh Museum, Calcutta University. The upper portion of the image is broken. It stands in *kāyotsarga* under a five-tiered *chatra*. There are representations of other Tīrthaṃkaras in miniature, but only two visible on the right and on the left garland-bearing Gandharvas are at the level of Jina's ears. The emblem is absent.

Deopara: Findspot of a fragmentary sculpture in the Rajshahi district, Bangla Desh, now in the Varendra Research Museum. Here one finds a male and a female seated in *lalitāsana* on two sides of a tree, each with a child on the lap. The upper part of the sculpture is missing, but on analogy with other sculptures of this type it is evident that the missing upper section had the representation of the Jina seated on the outspread foliage of the tree, the trunk of which survives in the lower section.

Derāvasī: Śvetāmbara subsect. See Mūrtipūjaka.

***Deśavrata*:** Taking a vow to limit worldly activity for a limited area.

***Deśavirati*:** The fifth *guṇasthāna* (q.v.) ascending on which the Jīva realizes the great importance of conduct and becomes mentally prepared to follow the twelve prescribed vows of right conduct.

***Deśināmamālā*:** See Hemacandra.

Deulbhira: Findspot of a tenth-century Pārśvanātha image in Bankura district. Housed in the Indian Museum, Calcutta, it is a seated Jina in *dhyāna* pose under the canopy of seven spread-out hoods of a snake. *Chowri*-bearing attendants are on either side.

Devabhadra: Author of *Pārśvanātha-carita* in Prakrit written about AD 1108 at Bhṛgukaccha.

Devacandra: Teacher of the famous Hemacandra (q.v.). His *Śāntinātha-carita* is in Prakrit, though it contains many Apabhraṃśa verses. He belonged to the Pūrṇatalla-gaccha and wrote his work in AD 1103.

Devacandra Suri: see *Kālakācārya-kathā*. The author of the same name of a five-act play *Candralekhāvijaya-prakaraṇa* seems to be a different person. This play was enacted during the spring festival in the temple of Ajitanātha at Patan before Kumārapāla and his courtiers.

Devagati: Celestial form which a Jīva (q.v.) receives owing to its *karma* (q.v.).

Devagiri: Same as Daulatābad in the Aurangabad district, Maharashtra; this place is described as a Jain *tīrtha* in Jinaprabha's *Tīrthakalpa*. Śrībhūṣaṇa of Kāṣṭhā-saṅgha and Nanditaṭa-gaṇa composed his *Pārśvanātha Purāṇa* in AD 1596 in the Pārśvanātha temple at Devagiri, often described as a *mahāsthāna*.

Devanandā: Brāhmaṇa woman in whose womb Mahāvīra was first conceived. She was the wife of Ṛṣabhadatta and of Jālandhara lineage. Her husband was of Koḍala lineage and an inhabitant of the Brahmanical part of Kuṇḍagrāma. But Indra, finding that a Jina ought not to, according to tradition, take his birth in a poor Brāhmaṇa family, transferred the foetus to the womb of Triśalā (q.v.), a kṣatriya woman of royal birth. According to the *Kalpasūtra*, Devanandā saw the following in her dreams—an elephant, a bull, a lion, an anointment, a garland, the moon, the sun, a flag, a vase, a lotus lake, the ocean, a celestial abode, a heap of jewels and a flame. According to the *Bhagavatī*, Devanandā was alive to see her son attaining the status of *kevalin*. Mahāvīra met her at Brāhmaṇa-Kuṇḍagrāma. When Devanandā saw him milk oozed from her breasts. When asked Mahāvīra explained that she was his mother and because of her motherly affection that had happened.

Devanandin: See Pūjyapāda.

Devapattana: Also known as Prabhāsa Pāṭana in Junagarh district, Gujarat, this place was famous for the Candraprabha temple, which, according to Jinaprabha, was founded after the destruction of Valabhi. Merutuṅga in his *Prabandha-cintāmaṇi* has referred to this place as a great Jain centre. This is also attested by Hemacandra and Kumārapāla.

Devardhi-Gaṇi Ksamāśramaṇa: Saint and scholar who was responsible for preserving and editing the Jain canon at the council of Valabhi held in AD 453. The so-called fourteen Pūrvas might have consisted of traditions handed down orally from teacher to pupil. Some part of this tradition might have been compiled by Sthūlabhadra (q.v.) in the Pāṭaliputra council and the council of Valabhi under Devardhi made use of the current oral tradition as well as such texts as might have been already reduced to writing. The authorship of *Nandisūtra* is attributed also to Devardhi.

Devarhalli Plates of Śrīpuruṣa: Found at Devarhalli in the Nagamangala taluk of Myore district and dated in śaka 698 (AD 776) and fiftieth year of Śrīpuruṣa's reign, this inscription refers to a line of *gurus* belonging to the Nandī Saṅgha and Mūla Gaṇa. The name of the Gaccha is given as Pulikal, probably connected with Puligere or Pulikara, the ancient name of Lakshmeśvara, famous for its Jain temples. The *gurus* are Candranandin, Kumāranandin, Kirtinandin, and Vimalacandra. The inscription also refers to Kundācci, wife of a feudatory, who built a Jain temple called Lokatilaka on the northern side of Śrīpura, near Gudlur to the west of the Nilgiris and made an endowment for its maintenance. *Epigraphia Carnatica*, IV, Nagamangla No. 5.

Devas: See gods.

Devasena: Tenth-century author who wrote a manual of the Digambara faith entitled *Darśanasāra* in AD 933. In the same year he composed *Śrāvakācāra*, a manual of rules for the life of the layman. He is also the author of an *Ārādhanāsāra*, 'essence of worship' and of the *Tattvasāra*. All these are written in Prakrit verses. His *Alapapaddhati* is a short manual of dogmatics in Sanskrit verses with commentary. *Darśanasāra*, ed. Nathuram Premi, Bombay, 1920; *Ārādhanāsāra* and *Tattvasāra* edn. in Manikcandra Series Nos. 6 and 13; *Ālāpa-paddhati*, pub. in Digambara Jaina Grantha-bhandar, No. 1.

Deva Suri: Author of *Śāntinātha-caritra* (q.v.) written in AD 1282 in Sanskrit verses. Deva Suri was the teacher of Tilakaprabha whose pupil was Vīraprabha. His disciple Ajitaprabha also wrote a great epic under the title *Śāntinātha-carita*. Deva Suri's work was revised by Pradyumna Suri.

Deva Suri: See Śrīdeva.

Devavijaya Gaṇin: Pupil of Rājavijaya Sūri who in AD 1603 had rendered Maladhārin Devaprabha Sūri's (q.v.) *Pāṇḍavacarita* (q.v.) in prose with inserted verses. Among the verses many have been taken literally from Devaprabha's work, whilst many others belong to the gnomic poetry and are known from other sources. Edited by Hargovind Das and Becher Das in Yaśovijaya Jaina Granthamālā, Benares, 1911.

Devendragaṇin: Author of the *Sukhabodha* commentary on the *Uttarādhyayana* (q.v.), which was completed in AD 1073. The interesting tales from this commentary were rendered into Sanskrit by Lakṣmīvallabha whose date is not known. Devendragaṇin also composed a *Mahāvīracariyam* in Prakrit. Edited in Devachand Lalbhai Series, 1929.

***Devendrastava*:** Prakrit *Devindatthaya*, the ninth Prakīrṇa (q.v.) which in 300 verses contains a classification of the kings of gods according to their groups, residences, etc. Āgamodaya edn., Bombay, 1925.

Devendra Suri: Pupil of Jagaccandra who flourished in the thirteenth century. His major works are the *Vandāru-vṛtti*, which is a commentary on the *Śrāddhapratikarmaṇa-Sūtra, Siddhapañcāśikā*, which is an extract of the *Dṛṣṭivāda* (q.v.) in 50 stanzas and *Upamitibhavaprapañca-kathāsāroddhāra* which is an extract from Siddharsi's famous poem. But his most important work is the first five of the six Karmagranthas, which cover all aspects of the Jain *karma* doctrine. These are *Karmavipāka, Karmastava, Bandhasvāmitra, Ṣaḍaśiṭīkā, Śataka* and *Saptaṭīkā, Vandāruvṛtti* ed. in Devachand Lalbhai Series, No. 8, and Bombay, 1912. Karma-granthas, ed. in Vol. IV of *Prakaraṇa-Ratnākara*, Bombay, 1880; with the author's com. on Books 1-5 by Śrī Jaina Dharma Prasāraka Sabhā, Bhavanagar, 1909-11.

***Devindatthaya*:** See Devendrastava.

Dhāhila: See *Paumasiri-cariu*.

***Dhamma-Parikkhā*:** A specimen of an interesting branch of Apabhraṃśa short-story literature meant for entertainment as well as moral and religious instruction. It is written by Hariseṇa (q.v.) who acknowledges his debt to the work of his predecessor Jayarāma in *gāthā* metre. Hariṣena's work is satirical and is composed in the tenth century in eleven *sandhis* comprising in all 234 *kadavakas*, equal to more than 2,000 *ślokas*.

Dhanaicha: Findspot of several Jain images, each bearing on its pedestal an inscription mentioning its installation on the same date (*Caitra*, su 15, Thursday, vs 1390) in Morena district.

Dhanañjaya: Well-known author of *Rāghava-Pāṇḍavīya* or *Divisandhāna*, an epic in 18 cantos which is based upon the *Rāmāyaṇa* and the *Mahābhārata* with a remote Jain touch. Bhāratīya Jñānapīṭha edn., Varanasi, 1970. He himself was a Jain and his preceptor was one Dasaratha. He flourished probably in the eighth century. His other works are *Nāmamālā*, *Anekārth-anāmamālā,* and *Viṣāpaharastotra*. His works were quoted by subsequent Jain authors.

Dhanapāla: Śobhana's (q.v.) brother and commentator of his hymn who flourished in the second half of the tenth century and was born in a Brāhmaṇa family. He himself also composed a hymn to Ṛṣabha entitled *Ṛṣabha-Pañcāśikā*. This is a Prakrit poem in 50 stanzas. In the first 20 verses there are allusions to events in the life of Ṛṣabha, while the rest is exclusively devoted to his praise. Probably this Dhanapāla is the same author who wrote the Prakrit dictionary *Pālyalacchi* in AD 972 and also the *Tilakamañjarī* (q.v.) *Ṛṣabha-Pañcāśikā*, ed. and trans. into German by Klatt in *ZDMG* XXXIII, 1879, 445 ff; text with Sanskrit trans. In Kāvyamālā Pt. VII, Bombay, 1890; with *Avacūrṇi*. Devachand Lalbhai, Bombay, 1933.

***Dhaneśvara*:** Author of the *Śatruñjaya-Māhātmya* (q.v.) who, according to his own statement, wrote this work in Valabhi at the desire of Śilāditya, king of Saurāṣṭra. He probably flourished about the eighth century AD. He is described as the 'moon in the ocean of the moon-*gaccha* (*śaśigacchāmbudhiśaśī*)'. A Dhaneśvara of the Candra-gaccha is mentioned in the list of teachers by Abhayadeva, the teacher of Āṣaḍa. The last-named lived in about AD 1191. Hence, this Dhaneśvara lived about AD 1100. This Dhaneśvara was probably the author of the *Surasundarīcariya* (q.v.)

Dhanavala: See *Bhavisatta-kahā.*

Dhandhuka: Birthplace of Hemacandra (q.v.) where King Kumārapāla constructed the Jotikha Vihāra in AD 1163.

Dhaneśvara: See *Surasundarī-cariyam.*

Dhank: Site of Jain caves in Saurāṣṭra in which sculptures belonging to the second century of Ṛṣabha, Pārśva, Mahāvīra, and others have been definitely identified. A group of rock carvings of a later period has also been found here.

***Dhanyakumāracarita*:** A poem dealing with the idealized biography of Dhanyakumāra written by Guṇabhadra, a disciple of Nemisena in the twelfth century. Ed. Pannalal Sahityācārya, Vīra Samvat 2499. See also *Jinaratnakośa* 187.

Dhārā: Capital of the Paramāras, which was associated with Jainism from a very early period. The Pārśvanātha temple of Dhārā which was constructed in AD 933 is mentioned in the works of Devasena, Madanakīrti, and others. There was also a temple of Śāntinātha in this town and a Jinavara vihāra. Jinapatisūri of the Kharataragaccha flourished at Dhārā. An image of Ṛṣabhanātha from Dhārā bearing an inscription of vs 1626 is now in the Jaisinghapura Jaina Archaeological Museum, Ujjain. A few inscribed images of the fourteenth and fifteenth centuries from this place are also preserved in a temple at Baniawadi. A very beautiful Sarasvatī image from Dhārā is in British Museum.

Dharaṇapriyā: Śāsanadevatā of Mallinātha according to a different version of the Śvetāmbara tradition. See Aparajitā, Vairoti.

Dharaṇavihāra: Temple of Ādīśvara at Rānakpur (q.v.) in the Pali district of Rajasthan, named after its builder Dharaṇa. It was built in AD 1438 and also known as Trailokyadīpaka. The temple contains inscriptions. Jinavijaya, *Prācīna Jaina Lekhasaṃgraha* II, Nos. 307ff.

Dharaṇendra: King of the Nāgas. Pleased with his services Ṛṣabha appointed him as the moral governor of the Vidyādharas who had installed his images in their cities. His queens were Allā, Akkā, Saterā, Sayāmaṇi, Indā, and Ghanavijjuyā. He cured Jain Ācārya Abhayasūri by licking his body and had shown him the *stambhanaka* of Pārśva, according to the *Prabandhacintāmaṇi.* He also rescued King Ceṭaka when he fell into a well. Dharaṇendra is also known as the Yakṣa of Pārśva. In connection with the origin of Dharaṇendra, there exists in Jain literature a story as to how he was saved by Pārśvanātha from being burnt in the sacred fire of a false ascetic Kaṭha (afterwards Meghamālin) and when attacked by Meghamālin, in his *kāyotsarga-āsana*, Pārśvanātha was greatefully waited upon by the same serpent, born next as Dharaṇendra or Nāgendra Yakṣa of Pātāla. Apart from this mythology, the very name Dharaṇendra or Dharaṇīdhara clearly signifies his identity with Śeṣanāga, the king of the serpents. It is said in the *Vasudevahiṇḍi* that he is going to be reborn as a future Tīrthaṃkara in a descending age.

Dhāraṇī: Śāsanadevatā (q.v.) of Aranātha (q.v.) according to the Śvetāmbara tradition. She is conceived as seated on a lotus and holding in her four hands a citron, two lotuses, and a rosary. Dhāraṇī is a class of Buddhist *mantra* texts from which the name of this Yakṣiṇī seems to have been inspired.

Dharaṇī Vihāra: Same as Dharaṇa Vihāra constructed at Ranakpur near Sadari in Mewar, Rajasthan, in AD 1438 which is an epitome of the grandeur and magnificence of the northern building style. See Caturmukha shrine, Ranakpur, Ādīśvara temple, Yugādiśvara temple.

Dharāpat: A Jain site in Bankura district. Here a Ṛṣabhanātha image has found grafted on a temple wall. It is about five feet in height, in *kāyotsarga* and pointed *jaṭāmukuṭa* in a double-petalled lotus placed on a *triratha* pedestal and flanked by two kneeling devotees. Above the attendants there are tiny figures of 24 Tīrthaṃkaras, twelve in each panel and in pair in six sections on both sides. The topmost portion of the slab has at its centre a three-tiered umbrella. The uppermost row of the tiny Tīrthaṃkaras is occupied by a flying Gandharva couple. A Pārśvanātha image from this place is turned Vaiṣṇavite by grafting on two extra hands and Viṣṇu's attributes. The original image is in *kāyotsarga* under the canopy of a seven-hooded snake. The image is locally worshipped as Manasā.

Dharasena: See *Dhavalā.*

Dhārāśiva: A Jain place of pilgrimage, about 3 miles from the town of Osmanabad in Maharashtra. The site has yielded a few very old Pārśva images. The account of this *tīrtha* is given in Hariṣena's *Bṛhatkathākośa* and Kaṇakamāra's *Karakandacariyu.* The caves of this place were excavated between AD 500 and 560. It is likely that they were originally Buddhist and were later used by Jains.

Dhārāvarṣa: See Ārāsaṇā, Jhaloḍi.

***Dharma*:** Principle of motion, one of the five constituents of the Ajīva (q.v.) category. While life and matter are both capable of moving of their own accord determined by appropriate operative causal conditions, their movement is dependent upon the presence of the non-operative principal called *dharma.* Remaining in itself non-operative, *dharma* serves as a condition for making movement possible. The illustration generally given is the presence of water for the movement of fish. When a fish swims, the movement is due to an imperative cause. Just as water helps the fish to move about, even so *dharma* makes the movement of soul and matter possible. *Dharma* is imperceptible, though it fills the entire universe, life, and matter. It has none of the characteristic qualities of life or matter, but forms the medium of motion, which is possible only through its existence. It has three divisions—*skandha* (whole), *deśa* (part), and *pradeśa* (portion of a part) and as a condition of motion it is pervasive. *Dharma*, here, should not be confused with righteousness. *Tattvārtha* V. 17-18.

***Dharma*:** see *Jambusvāmī-Cariya.*

***Dharmābhyudaya*:** 'Dharma on compassion', written around VS 1273 by Meghaprabhācārya. Of one act and often enacted as a shadow play (*chāyānāṭaka*) it is based on the life of a sage called Daśārṇabhadra. Bhavangar, Jaina Ātmānanda Granthamālā, No. 61, 1918.

***Dharmābhyudaya Mahākāvya*:** Written in the thirteenth century by Udayaprabha, it is a poem in 15 cantos and over 5,000 verses describing the achievements of Vastupāla. Cantos 10-14 is almost a separate work called the *Neminātha-carita.* Ed. by Puṇyavijaya, Bombay 1949.

***Dharmabindu*:** See Haribhadra.

***Dharmacakra*:** See *Malayasundarī-kathā*

Dharmadāsagaṇi: Author of the Prakrit *Upadesamālā* which consists of over 500 stanzas in *gāthā* metre. The work is of early origin and a commentary on it was written by *Jayasiṃhasūri* in AD 857.

Dharmādhikārī: Village high priest among the southern Jains. He is the religious head. He appoints the Grāmopādhyāyas (q.v.) or village priests and has the power to dismiss them if they do not work satisfactorily. He receives a subscription from the village priests by which his office is maintained. This office is selective: a high priest chooses his successor from among his favourite disciples. The high priest of Kolhapur has his headquarters at Nāndani. The high priest of Sittamur in South Arcot district who is called Maṭhādhipati, is elected by representatives of the chief Jain villages.

Dharmaghoṣa: Pupil of Devendra of the thirteenth century, author of a *Yamaka-stuti* and probably also of a *Caturviṃśati-Jinastuti* ed. in *Stotraratnākara*, part I, 1913. Whether it is the same or a much earlier Dharmaghoṣa who is the author of *Isimaṇḍala* or *Ṛṣimaṇḍala Stotra* has not been settled. A commentary on this work in AD 1496 by Padmamandira contains numerous legends of the Jain teachers honoured in *Ṛṣimaṇḍala.* It is in Prakrit stanzas.

***Dharmakalpadruma*:** 'The wish-tree of faith', a

bulky narrative in Sanskrit verse written by Udayadharma in about AD 1450.

Dharmakumāra: Jain poet of the thirteenth century whose *Śālibhadracarita* tells in seven cantos the legend of Śālibhadra. Ed. in Yaśovijaya Jaina Granthamālā, Benares, 1910.

Dharmalakṣmī Mahattara: A great female exponent of Jainism, of Gujarat, in the fifteenth century. She had many disciples and was greatly respected even by her male counterparts.

***Dharmāmṛta*:** See Āśādhara.

Dharmanātha: The fifteenth Tīrthaṃkara who was the son of Bhanu and Suvrata of Rayanapura. He had a height of 45 bow-lengths and a life-span of a million years. Ariṣṭa and Śivā were his chief disciples. He achieved salvation on Mount Sammeya. His sacred tree was the *dadhiparṇa*. His symbol is the *vajradaṇḍa* or thunderbolt. The Yakṣa couple attending to him are Kinnara and Kandarpā/Mānasī. The one who fans him is Puṇḍarīka-Vāsudeva. Images of Dharmanātha are not rare, and the Nagpur Museum has two perfect images. The story of Dharmanātha is treated by the poet Haricandra in the epic *Dharmaśarmābhyudaya*.

***Dharmaparīkṣā*:** See Amitagati.

Dharmapura: Findspot of a Jain inscription of AD 1410 in Hiriyur taluk of Chitradurga district, Karnataka, which refers to a Śāntinātha temple, patronized by Gopa Camupa, general of the Vijayanagara Emperor Devarāya I. *Epigraphia Carnatica* IX, Hiriyur 28.

Dharmapuri Inscription: Among the two inscriptions from Dharmapuri (ancient name Tagaduru), which is the headquarters of the district of the same name in Tamil Nadu, the earlier one, dated śaka 800 (AD 878) records the grant to a Jain temple. The other, dated śaka 815 (AD 893) records that two citizens, Candiyaṇṇa and Nandiyaṇṇa, after receiving the gift of the village of Mullapalli from the king, gave it to Kaṇakasena Siddhānta, pupil of Vinayasena Siddhānta of the Pogariya-gaṇa, Sena-anvaya, and Mūla-saṅgha for repairing the basadi at Dharmapuri. *Epigraphia Indica* X. 54ff.

Dharmasāgara: See *Kupakṣakauśikasahasrakiraṇa*.

Dharmasāgara Gaṇin: See *Gurvāvalī-sūtra*.

Dharmaśālās: Rest houses for pilgrims in every big town and places of pilgrimage. These are typical Jain institutions though other religious sects have emulated them. With the exception of a very few, all are open to people free of cost. Some of them provide utensils, bedding, etc., for a nominal fee.

***Dharmaśarmābhyudaya*:** A *mahākāvya* in 21 cantos dealing with the life-story of Dharmanātha, the fifteenth Tīrthaṃkara, written by Haricandra probably in the twelfth century in imitation of Māgha's *Śiśupālavadha*. Nirnaya Sagar Press, Bombay, 1888; also ed. P.L. Jain in Bhāratīya Jñānapīṭha, with Hindi trans., Varanasi.

Dharmavaram: Jain centre in Andhra Pradesh. A temple called Kaṭakābharaṇa Jinālaya was built here by Durgarāja during the reign of the eastern Cālukya Amma II. Durgarāja also granted to this temple a village to provide for worship, as is known from a copper plate inscription. A number of sculptures were found at Dharmavaram, of which a *caumukha* deserves special mention. Each of its facets is divided into three panels, each panel showing two Tīrthaṃkaras. The total number thus comes to twenty-four, making it a *caturviṃśati paṭṭa*. The images are cut in low relief *Annual Report on South Indian Epigraphy*, 1906-7, copper plate VII.

***Dharmottaratippanaka*:** See Mallavādin.

Dhātaki-Khaṇḍa: The second island-continent between the two oceans, Lavaṇa and Kāla. It is divided into east and west by two mountains running from north to south. The two divisions have two different sets of mountains, rivers and other geographical items.

***Dhātuvidyā*:** The *Vasudevahiṇḍi* has referred to a mendicant who, it is said, smeared a piece of iron with elixir, put it in burning charcoal, blew it with bellows and thus produced gold. More details are provided in the *Kuvalayamālā* about alchemy. The art of making artificial gold was practised in a secluded place of the Vindhya forest. It is stated that the red colour of flames of the fire indicates the making of copper, yellow of gold, white of silver, black of iron, and a colourless flame indicates bronze. The text *Yoniprābhṛta* is mentioned as the source of this branch of knowledge. The art of mining is also described in the *kuvalayamālā*.

***Dhavalā*:** Commentary on the *Ṣaṭkhaṇḍāgama* (q.v.) written by Vīrasena about AD 816. Virasena has described himself as a disciple of Āryanandin and a grand disciple of Candrasena of the Pañcastūpānvaya and one who studied the Siddhānta under Elācārya. According to Vīrasena after the death of Lohacārya when the knowledge of the Śāstra became extinct, only the saint Dharasena of Girinagara still retained the knowledge. Puṣpadanta and Bhūtabali were sent to learn from him. These two monks composed the *Ṣaṭkhaṇḍāgama* about the second century AD. The commentary written by Vīrasena is based, according to his own statement, on the earlier commentaries including the one written by

Kundakunda (q.v.). See Hiralal Jain's ed. of *Ṣaṭkhaṇḍāgama*, 16 vols., Amraoti, 1939-59.

Dhavala-Jinālaya: A Jina temple in Laksmeśvara in Dharwar district, Karnataka, which was repaired in the time of Cālukya Vikramāditya II mentioned in an inscription of AD 734, on the occasion of which some land was granted to Vijayadeva Paṇḍita of Mūla-saṅgha and Deva-gaṇa. *Indian Antiquary* VII, 106-7.

Dhavalakapura: Dholkā in the Ahmedabad district, Gujarat, which contains a few Jina temples including the Kalikunda Pārśvanātha shrine. The *Purātanaprabandhasaṃgraha* mentions the Simandharasvāmin temple, popularly known as Uda-vasti and named after its founder Uda, a merchant. It was consecrated by Devācārya in the first quarter of the twelfth century. This town was associated with the celebrated commentator Abhayadeva, the great religious activists, Vastu-pāla and Tejaḥpāla and Kamalaprabhasūri, the author of the *Puṇḍarīkacarita.*

Dholaka: Site of a Jain temple in west India built by Udayana which was consecrated by Vaidyadeva Sūri. Śreṣṭhin Dhavala constructed here a Muni-suvrata temple in AD 1137. Dholaka also contains a Neminātha temple.

Dhora Jinālaya: A Jina temple in Bankapur in the Dharwar district, Karnataka, mentioned in an inscription of AD 925. Another Dhora Jinālaya of Dharwar district is mentioned in an epigraph of AD 1060. *Bombay Karnataka Inscriptions* I(1), No 34; *Jaina Śilālekha Saṃgraha*, IV, No. 144.

Dhṛti: Sacrament performed in the seventh month after conception. Music and other entertainments are to be offered to keep the pregnant woman happy.

Dhuleva: Situated in the Udaipur district of Rajasthan, this place is known for its famous Ṛṣabhadeva temple, popularly known as the Keśariyaji temple.

Dhuṇḍiyā: Śvetāmbara subsect. See Sthānakavāsī.

***Dhūrtākhyāna*:** A satirical work by the celebrated Haribhadra (q.v.) written in Prakrit in which stories are told by five rogues called Mūlaśrī, Kandarika, Elāṣāḍha, Śaśa, and Khaṇḍapānā. Ed. A.N. Upadhye, Bombay, 1944.

***Dhuttākkhāna*:** See Dhūrtākhyāna, Haribhadra.

Didactic Narratives: Didactic literature composed by the Jains with a large number of narratives, giving prominence to ritualistic practices, virtues of self-restraint, chastity, charity, worship, penance, renunciation and so forth. The *Uvaesamālā* of Dharmadāsagani (fourth-fifth centuries), the *Uvaesapada* of Haribhadra Sūri (eighth century), the *Dharmopadeśamālā-Vivaraṇa* by Jayasiṃha-Sūri (ninth century), the *Silavaesamālā* by Jayakīrti (fourteenth century AD), the *Bhavabhāvanā* and *Upa-desamālāprakaraṇa* by Maladhārī Hema-candrasūri (twelfth century), the *Saṃvegaraṅga-śālā* by Jinacandrasūri (twelfth century) the *Uvaesarayanāyara* by Municandrasūri (before fourteenth century), etc., are note-worthy. Numerous popular tales explaining the teaching of Mahāvīra have been incorporated in these works. Apart from witty tales and anecdotes, eloquent speeches, witty sayings, didactic verses, riddles, and questions and answers are found in most of these narratives. New literary forms are also present. Maladhārī Hemacandra's *Bhavabhāvanā* deals with the stories related to the twelve meditations considered essential for the development of detachment from worldly objects. The *Saṃvegaraṅga-śālā* records a dislogue between a king and a queen emphasizing the desire for attaining emancipation from things of the world. The *Uvaesarayanāyara* illustrates its point through the examples of birds, animals, insects, trees, plants and so on.

***Digambara-Śvetāmbara Split*:** The great schism resulting in the official separation of the Digambaras and Śvetāmbaras took place during the patriarchy of Vajrasena. Jain tradition records as many as eight schisms, the first of which took place as early as the days of Mahāvīra under the leadership of his son-in-law, Jamāli (q.v.). The second was caused by Gośāla (q.v.) who actually did not belong to the order, the third by Āṣāḍha Ācārya, the fourth by Aśvamitra, the fifth by Gaṅga, the sixth by Rohagupta and the seventh by Goṣṭha. But the last schism was of a far greater dimension and had a permanent impact on the history of Jainism. Various causes have been attributed to this split. According to one, the monks, who went to the south with Bhadrabāhu (q.v.) during the famine of Magadha, returned to find that those who were staying in Magadha under Sthūlabhadra had begun to wear white robes (*śveta-ambara*) as also a peculiar headdress known as *ardhaphalaka*. Notwithstanding disapproval by the followers of Bhadrabāhu, they continued their new rules about dress, and came to be known as Ardhaphalakas and then Śvetāmbaras. According to another tradition Bhadrabāhu did not die in the south. During his absence a council was summoned at Pataliputra to fix the canon under the lead of Sthūlabhadra (q.v.). The council fixed it as eleven Aṅgas and fourteen Pūrvas. The books were not committed to writing at that time but were orally transmitted. The work of the council, however, was repudiated by Bhadrabāhu or his followers. The differences with regard to the content of the canon and its authoritative text exemplified in stories like this became another marked point of difference between the two great sects. According to a Śvetāmbara version, there was in Rathavīrapura, a teacher called Śivabhūti, also known as Sahasramalla and Botika. One day Śivabhūti received a costly garment from the king and his *guru* Āryarakṣita tore it to tatters. Śivabhūti understood the significance of his master's action, resolved to wear no clothes thereafter, and began to preach nudity. When his sister Uttarā wished to follow his example, he dissuaded her, saying that women could not attain final deliverance on any account. Thus was founded the Botika or Nagnatā sect which grew into the order of the Digambaras. The points on which the Digambaras are opposed to the Śvetāmbaras and lay greater emphasis are that the Tīrthaṃkaras must be represented as nude and with downcast eyes, that women cannot attain *mokṣa*, that the *kevlajñānins* require no food, that Mahāvīra was never married, that the compiled canonical works are not valid since they are man-made, that the ascetics must be entirely nude and that the Ācāryas after Jambusvāmin do not represent the entire community. The immediate cause of the great split is not known, but there are grounds to hold that there had always been more than one party in the community. Different modes of monastic life too became opposed to each other. The enmity was nourished for a long time, but suddenly, probably on some minor issue, it burst open. By the end of the first century the division was complete.

***Digvijaya*:** A stage in the career of the Tīrthaṃkara in which he starts for the conquest of the whole universe.

***Digvrata*:** Taking a lifelong vow to limit worldly activity to fixed points in all directions.

***Dikpālas*:** Guardians of the quarters, taken from the Brahmanical pantheon and given a rank subservient to that of the Tīrthaṃkaras. The Dikpālas in some cases, such as in those of Indra, have introduced their own spouses in the Jain pantheon. This has happened also in the case of Buddhism. They are also known as Lokapālas, rulers and protectors of people, and worshipped as Vāstudevatā or household deities. Some texts make them function as Kumāras who are also regarded as protectors.

***Dikṣādya*:** Sacrament; taking up pro-ascetic life.

Dilwara Images: Images in the group of marble temples at Mount Abu displaying some of the finest examples of Jain figure sculpture chiefly from the viewpoint of their delicacy and severe simplicity. These images are very similar in appearance, 'representing nothing more than skilled realization of a formula'. Notwithstanding the artificiality, the workmanship is unsurpassed. It must be remembered that the decorations are worked out of white marble, which required chiselling and scraping in a delicate and minute manner. It should also be stated in this connection that the Mount Abu figure sculpures betray undoubted medieval characteristics, some of which persist in Rajput sculpture through the subsequent centuries.

Dilwara Temples: Jain temple complexes on Mount Abu. The group consists of four principal temples, and their accessory structures, each enclosed within a quadrangular court. Two of them, built respectively by Vimala and Tejaḥpāla (qq.v.) and known as Vimala Vasahi and Luṇā Vasahi, are noteworthy for the exuberance of ornamental detail. The Ādinātha temple complex consists of the sanctum, placed near the western end of the court, and preceded in front by *maṇḍapa* and a portico, the three surrounded by a colonnaded cloister of image-cellas aligned round the enclosing wall. All these adjuncts, however, do not seem to have been of the same period.

The halls in front were erected in AD 1031 by Vimala, an officer of the Cālukya King Bhīma I. The second temple, the Luna Vasahi, is dedicated to Neminātha. Generally it follows the plan of the Ādinātha temple. The front halls were put up in AD 1230 by the banker Tejaḥpāla, brother of Vastupāla (q.v.).

These temples are situated at a height of 4,000 feet. Externally they are plain, but a splendid display of sculptors' skill is spread over the interior decoration of the pillars, ceilings, doorways and cloistered cells. The central structure is a cell, containing the statue of a Jina, with a pyramidal roof, and connected with this is a closed hall. In front of the hall is an extensive open portico adorned with free-standing columns. In each of the domed halls of both temples, the central feature is the octagonal nave supporting the dome over a ring of eight pillars with light cusped ornamental arches in between. The carving of the pillars is delicate and minute. In the Vimala Vasahi they are of a uniform pattern while in the Luna Vasahi they exhibit varieties.

The exuberance of sculptural magnificence reaches its climax in the treatment of the vaulted ceilings of the halls. Each of the ceilings is built of concentric rings, each of which carries a beautiful motif. Oblique to the lower rings is a series of sixteen brackets with representations of the Jain Vidyādevīs. In both the temples the splendid wealth of intricate ornamentation had been executed with a perfection seldom achieved by human endeavour. Both the temples are constructed entirely of white marble on which Cousens observed: 'The crisp, thin, translucent, shell-like treatment of the marble surpasses anything seen elsewhere, and some of the designs are veritable dreams of beauty.' For a general account J. Fergusson, *History of Indian and Eastern Architectures,* 2nd edn. revised by J. Burgess and R.S. Spiers, London, 1910, II 36-43; Henry Cousens, *Archaeological Antiquities of Western India*, London, 1926, 46-9; Percy Brown, *Indian Architecture*, 3rd edn., Bombay, 1956, 147-9.

Dinnasuri: Patriarch who headed the Jain church after Indradinna (q.v.). See Suhastin.

***Dīpāvali*:** Also known as Divālī, this festival is celebrated alike by Jains and Hindus. The origin of the festival is to be sought in the event of Mahāvīra's *nirvāṇa* when the assembled people instituted an illumination saying that 'since the light of intelligence is gone, let us make an illumination of material objects'. From that time the followers of Mahāvīra celebrate the festival of lamps in honour of his liberation. He is worshipped and sweet balls known as *nirvāṇa-lāḍu* are distributed. Besides decorating the residences with lamps, there are other ceremonies like Lakṣmī-Pūjan and Bhāu Bīja. These are, however, local customs.

Dīpikās: See Ṭīkās.

Diśās: See Bhavanavāsin.

Disposal of the Dead: Early Jain texts have laid down elaborate rules for the disposal of the dead. The *Bhagavatī Ārādhanā, Āvaśyaka Niryukti, Āvaśyaka Cūrṇi, Niryukti-Dīpikā*, etc., may be mentioned in this connection. The *Bṛhatkalpa-sūtra*, a part of the early portion of Jain canonical literature, has laid down the following prescription: if a monk dies, fellow-monks should borrow the wooden frame of a layman for carrying the dead and keep the body at a solitary place, away from living beings, and return the frame to the owner. Regarding the disposal of the dead the *Bhagavatī Ārādhanā* says that first of all the *nisihīyā* or the place of disposal of the body has to be inspected. It should be a calm, quiet, and solitary place. The frame for the dead is called in this text *siviyā*. The south-western, southern, and western directions are considered auspicious. It is laid down in the Āvaśyaka literature that three pieces of cloth are needed, one to spread below, another to cover the body and a third one to cover the entire body. There is however, a controversy with regard to the use of cloth.

The *Bhagavatī Ārādhanā* is silent on this point since its author Śivārya belonged to the Yāpanīya sect, whose followers went about naked, and hence perhaps could not entertain the idea of cloth even for covering the dead. About the time, it is said that the body is to be taken out as soon as possible. The *Bṛhatkalpa-bhāṣya* says that under exceptional conditions the body may be preserved for a longer period, but thereafter it has to be taken to the place of disposal. Instead of burying or cremating the body, the *Bhagavatī Ārādhanā* prefers to abandon it in an open space to be devoured by birds and beasts. For lay persons, however, the body is to be taken to the cremation ground and cremated according to local rules, with recitals from sacred texts. But the problem was with the monks. The *Vyavahāra-bhāṣya* says that in case no suitable site or space for abandoning the dead body of the monk is found, the body is to be taken for cremation. If the guardian of the crematorium asks for tax he should be pacified by sermons or by giving him a few pieces of cloth procured from the villages. The body should be carried by monks or by laymen, or in a bullock cart by Mallas. In the cases of laymen, besides cremation, the custom of burial was also prevalent. The place of burial was called *mataga-giha.*

***Ditthivāya*:** See Dṛṣtivāda.

Diva: Jain *tīrtha* situated in the Junagarh district of Gujarat, sacred to Pārśvanātha.

Divas: See Bhavanavāsin.

Divorce: In Jainism marriage is conceived of as a permanent union, but there are certain circumstances in which there are provisions to dissolve the wedlock. According to *Trivarṇikācāra* XI.171-3, if after the marriage either partner finds defect in the other within a stipulated period and complains of it, the marriage is cancelled. The Jain law-givers, following the Brahmanical *smṛti* passage *naṣṭe mṛte pravrajite,* etc., ordain that a wife is allowed to remarry with the permission of the caste-*pañcāyat* if the husband becomes a sinner, or an ascetic, or impotent, if he dies, and if no information is available regarding his whereabouts. Rules regarding divorce are governed by local customs and the Jains in general do not favour divorce, and it is possible only in exceptional cases. In the south divorce is permitted among the Bogaras on the ground of a wife's unchastity, barrenness, or ill-temper. Such divorced wives may remarry by following the rites of widow-remarriage. Divorce is also recognized among the Saitavālas. Phattelalji, *Jaina Vivāha Paddhati,* 3ff. See Widow-remarriage.

Diyāṇā: Situated in the Sirohi district of Rajasthan, this place is known for the temple of Jīvitasvāmī Mahāvīra. It was known as Nāṇā in ancient times. Numerous epigraphs have been discovered from this place. P.C. Nahar, *Jain Inscriptions* I, Nos. 885ff.

***Dohās*:** Couplets of varying measure. In the available Apabhraṃśa poetry the Dohā verses are more universal and less grammatically regulated than other forms of poetic composition. *Dohās* fall into two classes, romantic and ascetic. The latter class is represented by a large number of works composed by the Jain and Buddhist saints. *Paramappāsaru* and *Yogasāru* of Joindu (sixth century), *Pahuḍa-dohā* of Rāmasiṃha Muni, *Savayadhamma-dohā* of Devasena (tenth century) and *Vairāgyasāra* of Suprabhācārya are some of the best examples of *Dohā* in Jain literature. In Devasena's *Nayacakra,* a Prakrit work on logic, it is said that the work was originally composed in *Dohā* metre, but it was subsequently transformed into *gāthās* by Mailladeva.

Dokalyāṇadharī: See Arhanta.

Dolgaon: Findspot of an eleventh-century Caumukha in the Dinajpur district, now in the Asutosh Museum, Calcutta University. It is of miniature *rekhā* deul type with four Jinas on four sides identified respectively with Ṛṣabhanātha, Candraprabha, Pārśvanātha and Mahāvīra.

Dorasamudra: Ancient Dvārasamudra and modern Halebid in the Hassan district, Karnataka. A twelfth-century inscription of the time of Hoysala Viṣṇuvardhana mentions his general Gaṅgarāja as the rebuilder of numerous dilapidated Jain temples of Gaṅgavādi and his son Boppa as the builder of the great Jain temple of Doraramudra consecrated by Nayakīrti Siddhānta Cakravartī. King Viṣṇuvardhana changed the name of this temple from Drohagharaṭṭa Jinālaya to Vijaya-Pārśvadeva-basadi. A temple of Śāntinātha is mentioned in an inscription, according to which a gift was registered for this temple in AD 1196 by some merchants of Dorasamudra when Ballālá II was the reigning king. Other inscriptions from Halebid refer to these temples, to one built by the merchant Govinda in the first half of the twelfth century, and to another called Puṇiśa Jinālaya built in the eleventh century. *Jaina Śilālekha Saṃgraha* II, No. 301; III, Nos. 426, 499, IV, No. 309; V, Nos. 66-7.

Dostaṭīkā: A city of Gujarat mentioned in Jinasena's *Harivaṃsapurāṇa* as the site of a great temple of Śāntinātha.

***Draupadīsvayamvara*:** Well-known play in two acts written by Vijayapāla of the twelfth century. It was enacted before the Cālukya King Bhīma II during the spring festival. Ed. Jinavijaya, Bhavnagar, 1918.

***Dravya*:** Substance. *Dravya* is that which is capable of becoming this or that. The different senses of the word *dravya* are but different ways of conveying the aforesaid idea. In Jainism the word *dravya* is used differently. The *Tattvārtha* (I.5; V.31) divides the *nikṣepas* into *dravya, nāma, bhāva, sthāpanā*, etc., the *Nayas* into *dravyārthika* and *paryāyārthika,* and so on. The *Bhagavatī* (III. 19) speaks of aspects like *dravya, kṣetra, kāla, bhāva*, etc. In other cases we come across such expressions as *dravyakarma, dravyācārya*, etc. In all the cases, however, notwithstanding their functional significance, the term conveys the idea of capacity to become this or that. In Jain metaphysics the word *dravya* is normally used in the sense of the basic types of entity found in the universe. For example, *jīva, padgala, dharma, adharma, ākāśa*, and *kāla* (qq.v.) are six *dravyas*. In Vaiśeṣika philosophy the word *dravya* stands for the substratum of qualities. In this very sense the old Āgamas like the *Uttarādhyayana* (XXVIII.6) put forward the Jain thesis of six *dravyas*. The word *dravya* is variously interpreted in Patañjali's *Mahābhāṣya.* According to one of these interpretations a *dravya* is defined as that whose basic character remains unimpaired even in the midst of newer qualities. Apart from the non-soul *dravyas*, in a narrow sense *dravya* denotes material substance. In *Tattvārtha* (V.4ff.) the atom is described as substance and it is said that the qualities of touch, smell, taste or colour that characterize a material substance are possessed by the atoms and their compounds. See substance, qualities.

***Dravya-Bandha*:** One of the two main classes of *bandha* (q.v.) or bondage. It denotes the real connection between *karma* (q.v.) and Jīva (q.v.), which is like dust sticking on oily cloth. If oil is spilled on a cloth, dust will easily adhere; the cloth represents the Jīva, the oil the passions, transgressions, and activities and the dust, the *pudgala* (q.v.) *Dravyasaṃgraha*, Vṛtti 30ff.; *Vardhamāna Purāṇa* XVI.44; *Tattvārtha* VII.1.

Dravyānuyoga: The third Digambara Veda dealing with metaphysical questions, the nature of life, matter and other primary categories of reality. Philosophical works of Kundakunda (q.v.), Umāsvāti's *Tattvārthādhigama* (q.v.) with its commentaries, Samantabhadra's *Āptamīmāṃsā* (q.v.) with its commentaries, etc.

Dravyasaṃgraha: See Nemicandra Siddhānta-cakravartin.

Dravyasaṃvara: One of the two main classes of *saṃvara* (q.v.) or stoppage of the influx of *karma* (q.v.). It is connected with the reactions of the external objects which in the form of infra-atomic particles of matter soil the soul through the five senses and four passions.

***Dravyāsrava*:** The substratum of *karmāsrava* (q.v.) which is concerned with the influx of *karma* particles into the soul through external agencies.

Dravya-worship: Adoring those souls who are to become Tīrthaṃkaras in future.

Dreams: Dreams are looked upon as communion with the spirits. When Mahāvīra was conceived his mother saw fourteen great dreams. The *Bhagavatī* contains an entire section devoted to dreams. At the time of her conception queen Dhāriṇī had in her dream a big elephant entering her mouth, which indicated that she would give birth to an illustrious son. The *Āvaśyaka Cūrṇi* says that 'drinking the moon' in a dream is an indication of the new-born child's elevation to the rank of a universal monarch.

Drohagharaṭṭa Jinālaya: Jina temple at Dorasamudhra, modern Halebid built by Boppa and consecrated by Nayakīrti Siddhānta Cakravarti in the twelfth century. King Viṣṇuvardhana, a patron of this temple, renamed it Vijaya-Pārśvadeva-basadi.

Dronagiri: A *siddha-kṣetra* in Chhatarpur district, Madhya Pradesh, which has thirty Jain shrines on hillocks. The temples were built between AD 1483 and 1539. The earliest, dedicated to Ādīnātha, has an inscription of vs 1549.

***Dṛṣṭa*:** The 'evil-eye' that causes harm to human beings in many ways. There are various methods of averting its influence, among which one is to imprison it (*najarabandī*) by means of spells.

***Dṛṣṭivāda*:** Prakrit *Ditthivāya*, the twelfth of the Aṅga (q.v.) category which is lost for ever. According to the Jain tradition, the lost text had five divisions known as *Parikarmāni*, *Sūtrāṇi*, *Pūrvāgata*, *Anuyoga*, and *Cūlikā*. Whether or not these divisions and their subdivisions formed the subject-matter of the lost text is a different question, but the fact is that these constitute the basic categories of the Jain thought complex. *Parikarmāni* deals with cosmology, *Sūtrāṇi* with contemporary philosophical schools, *Anuyoga* with facts of remote antiquity, *Pūrvāgata* with the problems of birth, death and continuity, *Utpāda* with substances, *Āgrayāṇī* with exposition of nature, *Vīryānanupravāda* with potential of the soul and other substances, *Astināsti-pravāda* with substances of nature from the viewpoint of infinite qualities and forms, *Jñāna-pravāda* with epistemology, *Satyapravāda* with expiatory rites, *Vidyānuvāda* with the exposition of various sciences, *Kalyāṇavāda* with astrology, omens and portents, *Prāṇavāda* with physical and medical sciences, *Kriyāviśāla* with seventy-two fine arts, *Lokabindusāra* with worldly professions and *Cūlikā* with charms and magic.

Dubkund: Findspot of an inscription dated vs 1145 (AD 1088) in Morena district in a ruined Jain temple. Belonging to the time of Vikramasiṃha, the last known prince of the Kacchapaghāta dynasty, it describes the temple as very high and white-washed with a thick lime-solution. It further states that the moon is the mark of the Tīrthaṃkara Candraprabha and refers to Śruta-devatā or the goddess of learning as residing on the lotus.

Duggamāra: Brother of the Gaṅga King Sivamara II whose inscription discovered in Hebbalaguppe, in the Haggadade Vankote taluk in Mysore district, reveals that he donated land, about AD 825, for the maintenance of a Jain temple constructed by the architect Nārāyaṇa. *Mysore Archaeological Report*, 1932, 240-1.

Dungarpur: Belonging to the district of the same name in Rajasthan, it became a Jain centre from the fourteenth century onwards. The Pārśva temple of this town belonged to the Śvetāmbaras and the Ādinātha temple to the Digambaras. Jayānanda's *Pravāsagītikātraya*, composed about AD 1370, mentions that there were five Jina temples at this town. Two inscriptions from the Abu region belonging to AD 1468 mention the saint Lakṣmīsāgara in connection with Duṅgarasiṃha or Dungarpur. The saint is also mentioned along with the Dungarpur chief Somadāsa in an image inscription found in the same place. Two fifteenth-century manuscripts were copied here and they mention the local king, Gaipaladeva or Gajapāla. Jinavijaya, *Jaina Pustakapraśasti Saṃgraha*, 143-5; Velankar, *Jinaratnakośa*, 106.

Duritāri: Śāsanadevatā (q.v.), of Sambhavanātha

(q.v.), who is known as Prajñapti in Digambara tradition. Duritāri rides a ram and is four-handed. Prajñapti has a bird as her mount and is six-handed. The objects, which they hold are conventional.

Durlabharāja: Cālukya king of Gujarat during whose reign in AD 1024 a great debate had taken place in his court at Anahilapāṭaka in which the Śvetāmbara logician Jineśvara (q.v.), disciple of Vardhamānasūri defeated the Caityavāsins. After this debate the group led by Jineśvara came to be known as the Kharatara sect. King Durlabharāja seems to have been a disciple of Jineśvara, which is attested to in Hemacandra's *Dvyāśraya-kāvya.*

***Dvatriṃśatika*:** See Amitagati.

***Dvātriṃśika-Stotra*:** Also known as *Vardhamāna-Dvātriṃśikā*, it is a hymn addressed to Mahāvīra in 32 Sanskrit stanzas by Siddasena Divākara (q.v.). Ed. A.N. Upadhye in Jain Sāhitya Vikās Maṇḍal, Bombay, 1971.

Dvīndriya Jīvas: Two-sensed Jīvas (q.v.) possessing the organs of taste and touch. To this category belong worms, things living in shells, leeches, earth-worms, etc.

Dwarahat: Site of the Jain *devakulikās* of *circa* fourteenth century in the Mānyā temple complex in Almora district. This solitary group of tiny shrines, is marked by heavy and stylized *devakulikās* of the Nāgara variety in the form of a quadrangle with no ornamentation. The *devakulikās* are on three sides of a platform. Some of the temple-lintels and platform bases bear crude figures of the Jinas. Probably these were raised during the reign of the Katyuri-rājas of this area about the fourteenth century. The complex is the only representative of Jain structural art in the Himalayan belt. From epigraphical evidence it may be held that there was at least one Jain establishment in Dwarahat in the tenth century.

E

Echiganahalli: Findspot of a Jain inscription of AD 1370 from Mysore district, Karnataka, which praises two monks, Bāhubali and Pārśvadeva, and records the death of Meghacandra. The inscription was found in the Neminātha temple complex. *Epigraphia Carnatica* III, Nan 43.

Ekasambi: Situated in the Belgaum district, Karnataka, it is the findspot of an inscription dated śaka 1087 (AD 1165) of the time of the Śīlāhāra rulers which records the gift of land for the temple of Neminātha, built by one Kalyāṇa, a commander of Vijayaditya. The recipient of the gift was Vijayakīrti II, disciple of Kumārakīrti belonging to the Yāpanīya Saṃgha and Punnagavṛkṣamūla. *Jaina Śilālekha Saṃgraha* IV, No. 259.

Ekendriya Jīvas: One-sensed Jīvas (q.v.) possessed of only the sense of touch. They are subdivided into earth-bodies, water-bodies, fire-bodies, air-bodies, and vegetative bodies. Evidently there are being connected with the categories of elements. Life manifested in vegetative forces is also taken into account in this connection.

***Ekībhāva-Stotra*:** Philosophical hymn composed by Vādirāja II. Pub. in Kāvyamālā VII.

Elācārya: Jain savant who was a native of Citrakūṭa, modern Chitor, and a contemporary of Haribhadra (q.v.). See Dhavalā.

Elapura: See Ellora.

Ellora Caves: Notable group of Jain caves at Ellora, in the northern horn of the ridge. These caves are not earlier than AD 800. Among these, the Indra Sabhā (No. 32, q.v.), particularly the upper storeys of the cave, is one of the most perfect specimens at the site. The monolithic shrine in the centre of the courtyard and the gateway of the court are both shaped out of the rock. Behind the monolithic shrine rises the facade of the cave in two storeys, each of which is roughly of the plan of a pillared hall with a cella at the back end and range of cells on either side. The Jagannātha Sabhā (No. 33 q.v.) follows the Indra Sabhā in general principles and in the treatment of its essential elements, but lacks the balanced character of latter. The Chotā Kailāśa (No. 30, q.v.), as its name implies is a smaller imitation of the famous Kailāśa temple.

Embryology: See physiology. In the *Bhagavatī* embryology has been treated in detail. The *Sūyagaḍa* II.2 describes the functions of the embryo in terms of its consumption of the menstrual blood, a theory which finds parallel in the views of ancient naturalists like Aristotle and Pliny. The *Tandulaveyāliya* and *Prajñāpanā* hold that the margin of fertility is 55 years with the woman and 75 years with men. The fruit remains in the womb for about 278 days. It has four stages of development, each of which has been characterized by the names *kalada*, *abluya*, *peśi*, and *ghaṇa*. 'Its weight amounts to 3 *kariṣa* (3/4 *pala*) in the first month, in the second it gets solid, in the third it rouses lust within the mother, in the fourth it makes the limbs swell, in the fifth its extremities and its head develop (*pañca piṇḍiyāo*) in the sixth its gall and its blood, in the seventh its veins, muscles, vessels, nerves, pores, hairs and nails, and in the eighth the child is complete. The sex depends on the preponderance of either sperm or blood, in case neither prevails sexlessness will result. A sexless fruit lies in the centre of the mother, but a male on the right and a female on the left side. Its position and its condition are in accordance with the mother.' Schubring, *DJ*, 141.

Endogamy: Marriage within the same caste which is practised by the Jains and the Hindus as well. A Jain caste in itself is endogamous and is composed of a number of exogamous groups or *gotras* (q.v.). A man is to marry within his caste (*varṇa* or *jāti*) but outside his group (*gotra*). Again there are many castes in Jain society which have counterparts in other societies. The Agravālas, Śrīmālīs, Poravāḍas, etc., are also among the Hindus and matrimonial relations exist between them, though they follow different religions. There is also local and factional endogamy among the Jains which is conditioned by the distribution of the castes, slackening of internal contacts, the rise of factionalism, and so forth. Rise of factional endogamy can be illustrated with reference to the Saitavālas who were split up into two endogamous groups over the question of accepting Bhaṭṭārakas (q.v.) as Gurus. Again in the constitution of the Viśā Śrīmālī subcaste of Saurashtra, it has been laid down that their members should keep matrimonial relations only with Viśā Śrīmālīs of Bhavanagar, Veraval, Porbunder, Jamnagar, and Mangrol.

Epistemology: Jainism admits five kinds of knowledge: *mati* or ordinary cognition obtained by means of sense-perception; *śruta* or testimony derived from scriptures, teachings, etc., *avadhi* knowledge by clairvoyance; *manaḥparyāya* or telepathic knowledge of other's mind; and *kevala* or perfect knowledge independent of senses. The fourth and fifth kinds are characterized as *pratyakṣa* or direct knowledge, which cannot be wrong while the first two or three are *parokṣa* or indirect knowledge and hence liable to error. The original Jain conception of *pratyakṣa* and *parokṣa* was the reverse of the traditional Indian conception, but later the Jain thinkers changed their original position and brought their *pratyakṣa-parokṣa* concepts on par with other systems. The two manifestations of consciousness are perception (*darśana*) and intelligence (*jñāna*). In the former we have simple apprehension, and perception of the generalities (*sāmānya*) of things, while in the latter we have conceptual knowledge. The Jains believe that external objects exist and they are knowable. Cognition is a generated phenomenon capable of being perceived and inferred. It is self-revelatory. Knowledge of a thing as it is in itself is *pramāṇa* and knowledge of a thing in its relation is *naya*. According to Siddhasena and Samantabhadra (qq.v.), the immediate effect of a *pramāṇa* is removal of ignorance, but the remote effect should possibly be the decision to accept or reject or ignore the object. The *nayas* or standpoints are divided into seven categories and distinguished into *dravyārthika* from the viewpoint of substance and *paryāyārthika* from that of modification. The most important use of these standpoints is of course Syādvāda or Śaptabhaṅgī-naya (qq.v.). Although it is said that *mati-jñāna* should come under *indriya-pratyakṣa* or sense-perception and *śtruta-jñāna* under verbal testimony, the Jain authors were constantly faced with the question as to whether *anumāna* (inference), *upamāna* (analogy), and *arthāpatti* (implication) which the other traditions accept as *pramāṇa*, should be regarded as valid. It was Umāsvāti (q.v.) who for the first time clearly suggested that *anumāna*, etc. should fall under the category of *parokṣa* or non-perceptual *pramāṇa*. Akalaṅka holds that *parokṣa-pramāṇa* consists of five species—*anumāna* or inference, *pratyabhijñā* or recognition, *smaraṇa* or memory, *tarka* or knowledge of invariable concomitance, and *āgama* or verbal testimony. The Jains are of the view that the number of steps for formulating an inference should not be fixed, and that they may be more or less according to their requirements. They hold that *pratyabhijñā* or recognition is a form of *mati-jñāna* and an independent *pramāṇa*. Likewise, *smaraṇa* or memory ought to be treated as a *pramāṇa* because it is true of facts. Akalaṅka (q.v.) seems to be the first to determine the nature, objects, and utility of *tarka* and he has been followed by all later Jain logicians. The Jain tradition is one with the Mīmāṃsaka in treating *tarka* as a cognition of the nature of *pramāṇa*. Regarding the aspects of the nature of probans, the type of probans, pseudo-probans, the nature of the terms, the fallacies and other allied problems of inference, Jain logicians hold different views from others and they have differences among themselves.

Eradukaṭṭe-basti: Situated in Śravaṇabelgola (q.v.). The double-storeyed approach to which has given it this name, has in the sanctum a figure of Ādinātha whose pedestal carried the record that the temple was built by Lakṣmī, wife of the general Gaṅgarāya, in AD 1118.

Erambarage: Old name of Yalbargi in the Raichur district of Karnataka which was a flourishing Jain centre. An inscription of the time of the Sinda Prince Vīra Vikramāditya of the twelfth century mentions the temple of Pārśvanātha at this place. It was the seat of the Jain Ācārya Māghanandi Siddhānta Cakravartī and monks of Mūla-saṅgha and Deśīya-gaṇa. This place was also known as Erambarapuram.

Eraṃḍavela: Situated in the Jalgaon district of Maharashtra, this place is known for two Jain temples dedicated respectively to Neminātha and Dharmanātha.

Erotic Tales: Though the Jain authors did not favour any contact with women at all, Kāmakathā or erotic tales were also used by them for the purpose of teaching in an inverted way as they were fascinating to the people. Rājaśekhara Maladhārī records the story of a merchant's son who was brought in into a life of religion by a monk by means of such stories. Dharmadāsagaṇi Mahattara, author of the *Majjhimakhaṇḍa*, keen to make his work delightful to the readers, affirms that people listening to popular love stories take delight in them. According to him, just as a physician administers his own nectar like medicine to an unwilling patient under the pretext of giving what the patient desires, so should a virtuous story be told under the pretext of a love story. The *Kuvalayamālā* and Haribhadrasuri's

Samarāicchakahā accomplish such a purpose. The *Kahānayakośa* of Jineśvarasūri records a beautiful tale of Sundarī, wife of a merchant Yaśobhadra, making adultery with a handsome prince. The *Rayaṇaseharikahā* tells a story how a king in the disguise of a female ascetic made love with a handsome girl and eventually married her; the *Taraṅgalolā* records the love-story of Taraṅgavatī and Dhanadeva. We read the love-story of Prince Kuvalayacandra and Princess Kuvalayamālā. The *Vasudevahiṇḍi* of Saṅghadāsagaṇi and *Mejjhimakhaṇḍa* of Dharmadāsagaṇi Mahattara play an important role in bringing out the love theme. The former narrates how the hero, not satisfied with one wife, goes on marrying one woman after the other, delighting in love-sports and enjoying unrestrained sensual pleasures. The *Taraṅgavaikahā* of Pādaliptsūri (second-third centuries AD) is a pioneering work but it is lost to us. Its abridged form is Nemicandragaṇi's *Tarangalolā*. The *Naravāhanadattakahā* is counted among popular love-stories. Erotic elements are also found in the Tamil epic *Jīvakacintāmaṇi*. Like the Dharmakathā and Arthakathā, the importance of Kāmakathā was understood by Jain authors, who argue that only the one who studies the science of the erotic, gives delight to his consort, who in turn can bear him a son, and can then later on lead a virtuous life.

Eruvadi: A natural cavern on the Irattaipottai rock in Tirunelveli district. An overhanging boulder over the cavern bears a series of Jain bas-reliefs accompanied by votive inscriptions in Vaṭṭeḻutter script.

Ethics: *Samyag-darśana-jñāna-caritrāṇi mokṣa-mārgaḥ*, the path to salvation is constituted by right faith, right knowledge, and right conduct, says the *Tattvārthādhigama*. These three requirements—*samyak-darśana*, *samyak-jñāna* and *samyak-caritra* (qq.v.), collectively called *ratnatraya* (q.v.), form the basis of Jain ethics. There are two courses of moral discipline or conduct in Jain ethics, one prescribed for householders (q.v.) and the other for ascetics (q.v.). In both cases the codes are the same, but the ascetics should follow them more rigorously than the householders. Complete abstinence from violence, worldly things, sensuality, falsehood and attachment in speech, thought, behaviour and action cannot be expected of the ordinary householders. Thus gross offence against living beings is understood by fettering, overloading, beating, wounding and other forms of cruelty to domestic animals; gross untruthfulness is understood by falsely accusing a person, by forgery, by passing wrong judgements, etc.; gross appropriation consists in receiving of, or dealing in, stolen goods, in theft and other illegal economic transactions; gross sensuality consists in offences against matrimonial faith; and gross greed is understood in terms of attachment to gold, cattle, estate and so forth. Abstinence from all these is demanded of householders. Meanwhile supreme importance is given to the doctrine of *karma*, which rests on the maxim, as you sow, so you reap. Because of good or evil *karma* a living creature will be reborn into any species, particularly suited to and measured by the action, from the vilest insect to a god. The moral values are so strongly upheld in Jainism that *pāpa* (vice) and *puṇya* (virtue) have become two important categories of nine fundamental truths.

In order to possess an unwavering faith the individuals are expected to get rid of three types of superstitious ignorance and eight kinds of haughtiness or arrogance. The superstitions are belief in the sanctity and miracle-working power of certain places, rivers, lakes, mountains and so forth; belief in the power of gods and goddesses; and devotion to false ascetics. The ascetics on the other hand, have no need to associate themselves with the ordinary social occupations. The whole discipline of an ascetic aims at the conquest of the environment including his own self. He completely abandons all worldly possessions and ceases to dwell under a roof. The five vows of non-injury to living beings, truthfulness, non-stealing, celibacy and non-possession are observed by him in their strictest forms.

Certain features of Jain ethics may especially be noted: both lay persons and ascetics are required to have religious and secular knowledge. Supreme emphasis is laid upon the observance of the five main vows. Utmost importance is given to *ahiṃsā* (q.v.) or avoidance of *hiṃsā*, injury and violence. Jain ethics lays down very elaborate rules of conduct, both for laymen and ascetics and its significant feature is the prescription of one ethical code for all people irrespective of their position and stage of life.

Evambhūta: See Naya.

Evil Spirits: The Jains believe in spirit possession and call their family spirits *pitrad* or fathers. Diseases of children are supposed to be caused by evil spirits. They dread the *jakhims* (q.v.), ghosts of women who die with unfulfilled wishes. There is no professional exorcist among the Jains, but when sickness is believed to be caused by spirit possession, the priest is consulted. He gives the patient *tīrtha* or holy water to drink and ties a *tāita* or charmed casket round the sick person's arm or neck. In certain places of Karnataka a regular worship of *bhūtas* (q.v.) or devils is undertaken. Women are supposed to be possessed by the spirits when they have just bathed, when their colour is brightened, when their hair is loose, when they are gaily dressed or when they go alone to the well or river. Often disease is supposed to be due to *dṛṣta* or the evil eye. In order to remove the evil eye a detailed process known as *najara-bandī* is undergone. Magical (q.v.) practices are required to avert the evil eye, for giving protection against malignant men or spirits and allied purposes. Professionals experienced in magical skills are found in Rajasthan and they were known as *vidyāvān*.

Exogamy: Prohibition of marriage between near relatives, especially agnates. This custom is followed by Jains and Hindus. There are several exogamous groups within an endogamous group and the exogamous group is known as the *gotra* (q.v.). The *gotras* of the bride and bridegroom should be different at the time of marriage which means that *sagotra* marriage is forbidden. *Samavibhāvābhijanayoḥ asamagotrayośca vivāhasambandaḥ—Nītivākyāmṛta*, XI.20.

F

Fast: Fasts are observed by the Jains in connection with important events and festivals like Paryuṣana, Aṣṭāhnika, etc., for the purpose of self-purification and spiritual upliftment. In addition to these devout Śvetāmbaras fast on the two second, two fifth, two eighth, two eleventh, two fourteenth and the bright and dark fifteenth of each month. The Digambaras observe as fasts the second, fifth, eighth, eleventh and fourteenth days of both bright and dark halves of the month. Those who cannot do these throughout the year fast only during *Cāturmāsa* (q.v.). Less devout Śvetāmbaras fast for only five days, Digambaras only for four. Moreover, four full-moon days during the year in the months of Kārttika, Phālguṇa, Caitra, and Āṣāḍha are observed as special fasts by the Śvetāmbaras.

Female Ascetics: *Sādhvīs* who follow the five great vows strictly. In the *Kalpasūtra* it is stated that 3,000 female ascetics became liberated under the guidance of Neminātha. During the Jinahood of Pārśvanātha 20,000 nuns attained liberation. In the time of Mahāvīra their number increased to 36,000. Brāhmī was appointed head of the nuns by Ṛṣabha. Candanabālā was the first woman disciple of Mahāvīra. She headed the order of the nuns and achieved liberation. The head of the female ascetics was known as Gaṇinīs. At the initial stages of monastic life female and male ascetics had to follow the same rules of conduct. But they were subject to discriminatory treatment. They were placed under a more rigorous discipline than monks. They are prohibited to read certain texts. It is said that a monk of 3 year's practice can become a teacher of a nun of 30 years' practice. Still their position was better than their Buddhist sisters, because the Buddhist code says that a nun though 100 years old must stand in reverence before a monk though he may be just initiated as a novice. Though according to the Jain rules nuns could under no circumstances preach to monks, some like Sādhvī Rājimatī (q.v.) did. The Digambaras hold the view that women are not entitled to liberation in this life. For that they will have to be reborn as men, which is why they maintain that the 19th Tīrthaṃkara Malli was a male. Against many odds female Jain ascetics made a great struggle for their worthy survival and spiritual uplift in consequence of which we hear of a large number of women in the history of Jainism who distinguished themselves as teachers and preachers.

Female Education: Female education was emphasized by the early Jains. The Śrāvikās or lay women formed an integral part of the community, which is why their welfare and spiritual upliftment were matters of great concern for the community. The Ācārya admitted them freely into the order, no matter whether the candidates for admission were royal consorts, members of the aristocracy, or women belonging to the common run of society. The formation of a community endowed with a spirit of idealism requires some sort of mental enlightenment among its members, both male and female, which is not possible without education. The founder of the system, Ṛṣabhadeva, realized the importance of educating women, which is why he advised his daughters, Sundarī and Brāhmī, to obtain academic brilliance. The Jains were the first to introduce the cult of the Vidyādevīs or the goddesses of learning. The Vedic Vāk, later identified with Sarasvatī, found her most magnificent expression in Jainism. In the Jain texts it is stated that a woman is expected to know the 64 arts of dancing, painting, music, aesthetics, medicine, domestic science, etc. As a result many women used to enter the teaching profession. We also come across enlightened Sādhvīs who had had a good education. There are numerous instances of highly educated and cultured Jain women from the earliest times to the end of the Hoysala Period. From the late-medieval period female education among the Jains declined under diverse historical circumstances.

Female Nurse: The *Niśītha Cūrṇi* and *Piṇḍaniryukti* refer to five kinds of female nurses engaged in bringing up children—the wet-nurse, the bath-nurse, the toilet-nurse, the play-nurse, and the lap-nurse. It is said that if the oozing of milk from the breast of the wet-nurse were scanty the child would be lean and thin; if her breasts were large they hit the mouth of the child shaping its nose flat; if her breasts were flat the child's teeth protruded. If the bath-nurse put the baby in water it would develop a fear. If the play-nurse's voice was loud the child would also speak loudly and if low its voice would become indistinct.

Likewise the child's bodily frame depended on the figure, slimness, or corpulence of the lap-nurse. The toilet-nurse had, however, no such problem because her function was to apply various marks on the body of the child to save it from the evil eye.

Festivals: A very common affair among the Jains, performed to commemorate important events of the past. They are intended to divert the attention of laymen from their worldly activities to their ultimate goal and serve to strengthen the devotion of laymen. The festivals are observed mainly as religious ceremonies to be performed at proper time and place determined through the help of astronomy. Important Jain festivals are Paryuṣaṇa or Daśalakṣaṇa-parva, Siddhacakra-pūjā or Saint-wheel worship, Aṣṭāhnika, Mahāvīra Jayantī, Vīraśāsana Jayantī, Śruta-pañcamī, Bathing of Gommaṭeśvara, Divālī or Dīpāvalī, Rakṣā-bandhana, Akṣayatṛtīyā (qq.v.) etc.

Fallacies: Early Jain logicians insisted on *nayābhāsa*, fallacies of *naya* which were concerned *naigoma*, *saṃgraha*, *vyavahāra*, *ṛjusūtra* and *śabda* moods of statements. Later the scope became more wide. Beside the fallacies of inference the Jains admitted logical fallacies (*ābhāsas*) of a general nature such as those of perception (*pratyakṣa*), recollection (*smaraṇa*), recognition (*pratya-bhijñā*), argumentation (*tarka*), minor term (*pakṣa*), middle term (*hetu*), example (*dṛṣṭ-ānta*), and verbal testimony (*āgama*). To the former category belong those of the unproved middle (*asiddha*), contradictory middle (*viruddha*), irregular middle (*savyabhicāra*), inferentially contradicted middle (*sapratipaks*), non-inferentially contradicted middle (*vādhita*), etc. Jain conceptions of logical fallacies derived their main impulses from corresponding dev-elopments of the Nyāya school. *Asiddha* or *sādhyasama* is the fallacy of the unproved, which occurs when the middle term is wrongly assumed in any of the premises. Thus when one argues: 'The sky-lotus is fragrant because it has *lotusness* in it like the natural lotus', middle has no *locus standi* since the sky-lotus in non-existent, and is, therefore, *asiddha* or a merely assumed but not proved fact. *Viruddha* or the fallacy of the contradictory middle occurs when the middle term instead of proving the existence of the major in the minor, proves its non-existence therein; in other words when it disproves the very proposition it is meant to prove. If one argues: 'Sound is eternal because it is produced' we have this fallacy, because the middle term *produced* does not prove the *eternality* of sound, but just the reverse. *Savyabhicāra* or *anaikāntika* or the fallacy of the irregular middle occurs when the ostensible middle term becomes an inconstant concomitant of major term. If one argues: 'All knowable objects are fiery', in this case the middle term *knowable* is indifferently related to both fiery objects like the kitchen and fireless objects like the lake. All knowable objects being thus not fiery, we cannot argue that a hill is fiery because it is knowable. The middle term should be universally concomitant and universally related to the major term. *Vādhita* or *kālātīta* is the fallacy of the non-inferentially contradicted middle, typical instance of which is such a proposition as 'Fire is cold because it is a substance' or 'Sugar is sour because it produces acidity'. In the first example, coldness is *sādhya* or a major term and substance is the middle term. Here the non-existence of the major term, i.e. coldness, is flatly negated by a stronger instrument of valid knowledge, namely excep-tion, which already proves to be hot instead of being cold. There are other fallacies like *prakaraṇasama* or *satpratipakṣa*, fallacies of allowing scope for a counter inference. *Pakṣā-bhāsa* or the fallacy of the minor term arises when one attributes to it as a proved fact what is yet to be proved. *Dṛṣṭāntābhāsa* or fallacies of example may arise in homogeneous and heterogeneous forms from a defect in the major or middle term or both or from doubt about them.

Folk Festivals: The *Nāyādhammakahāo* furnishes the following list of local festivals celebrated in honour of folk deities: Indamaha (Indramaha), festival of Indra; Khandamaha (Skandamaha) festival of Skanda; Ruddajattā (Rudrayātrā), festival of Rudra; Śivajattā (Śivayātrā), festival of Śiva; Vesamanajattā (Vaiśravaṇa-yātrā), festival of Vaiśravaṇa; Nāgajattā (Nāgayātrā), festival of Nāgas; Jakkhajattā (Yakṣayātrā), festival of the Yakṣas; Bhūyajattā (Bhūtayātrā), festival of the Bhūtas; Naijattā (Nadīyātrā), festival of rivers; Talayajattā (Taḍāgayātrā), festival of tanks; Rukkhajattā (Vṛkṣayātrā), festival of trees; Caiyajattā (Caityayātrā), festival of Caitya; Parvayajattā (Parvatayātrā), festival of mountains; Ujjanajattā (Udyānayātrā), festival of garden; and Girijattā (Giriyātrā), festival of hills. The *Rāyapasenijja* furnishes the following list; Indamaha, Khandamaha, Ruddamaha, Maundamaha, Śivamaha, Vesamanamaha, Nāgamaha, Jakkhamaha, Bhūyamaha, Thuva-maha, Ceityamaha, Rukkhamaha, Girimaha, Darimaha, Agadamaha, Naimaha, Śaramaha and Sāgaramaha. The following are recorded in the *Niśīthasūtra*, Inda, Khanda, Rudda, Maunda, Bhuya, Jakkha, Nāga, Thuva, Ceiya, Rukkha, Giri, Dari, Agada, Tadaga, Daha, Nai, Sara, Sāgara, and Ākāśa.

Four Gifts: See *Dāna*.

Forms of Marriage: The traditional eight forms of marriage described in the Brahmanical Dharmaśāstras have been accepted by the Jains with some modification. These are Brāhma, Daiva, Ārṣa, Prājāpatya, Āsura, Gāndharva, Rākṣasa, and Paiśāca (qq.v.). Among these the first four are called *dharmya* and *ārya*, that is, meritorious and valid, while the last four are considered to be *adharmya* and *pāpa*, that is immoral and sinful for obvious reasons. Asura marriage involves the sale of the bride and Gandharva marriage is performed stealthily and as such both these forms are condemned. Rākṣasa marriage involves forceful abduction of the girl and Paiśāca marriage intentionally perpetrates violence on a helpless girl. Obviously Jainism cannot recognize these forms as valid. The names of the last four forms may have a greater significance, which both the Brahmanical and Jain law-givers failed to comprehend. These might stand for the system of marriage as found among the peoples or tribes known as Asura, Gandharva, Rākṣasa, and Piśāca. Nowadays only one form survives which is a combination and elaboration of the Brāhma and Prājāpatya forms. *Trivarṇikācāra* XI.71-78; *Nītivākyāmṛta* XXXI.4-11.

G

Gabbur: Situated in the Raichur district of Karnataka this place had a Jina temple called Nagara Jinālaya or Brahma Jinālaya in the twelfth century.

Gaccha: A collective body, a branch or subdivision of the *saṃghas* and *gaṇas* (qq.v.). It is said that during the tenth century Uddyotana started 84 *gacchas* through his disciples. Most of these *gacchas* have become extinct in course of time and some new ones like Tapa, Kharatara, Añcala, etc., have come into existence. The *gacchas* originated from different teachers who became heads of their own groups. The following is a list of the names of the *gacchas*; Āgama, Añcala, Anpuri, Aḍḍakali, Bagheravāla, Baherhā, Bapanā, Barhagaccha, Barodiya, Belia, Bhārati, Bhartṛpriya, Bharuyaccha, Bṛhad, Bhaṭanera, Bahavaharṣa, Bhavendra, Bhavarāja, Bhīmapalli, Bhīmasena, Bhinmāla, Birajivāla, Boresiṃgha, Brāmhaṇa, Caitra, Candra, Chapasa, Candrakapāṭa, Chitourhā, Citravāla, Desiya, Dekacharha, Dhandhuṣa, Dharmaghoṣa, Dobandanika, Dokarha, Dhaneśvara, Gacchapāla, Gaṇadhara, Gaṅgesara, Ghanghodharā, Ghoghera, Ghoṣavāla, Gubela, Guptauba, Haṃsaraka, Hastikuṇḍīya, Harsapuriyā, Jalori, Jalihora, Jamaṇakiya, Jamgorhā, Javāharaka, Jherantiya, Jirāvala, Jirāpalli, Jittara, Kachela, Kamalakalasa, Kamboja, Kandobiya, Kapurasimha, Kāsadraha, Kattakapura, Kavala, Khambhyata, Kharatara, Korantavela, Kosipura, Kṛṣṇarṣi, Kucora, Kutubapura, Lumpaka, Madhukara, Maladhārī, Maladhora, Mandaliya, Mandharaṇa, Maṇḍitāla, Mandovara, Manghoṣa, Masena, Māthura, Meṣapāsana, Moḍha, Muhasorarha, Muramdavāla, Nādola, Nāgadraha, Nagapuriya, Nagarakaṭa, Nagaravāla, Nāgendra, Nagori, Nanavāla, Nānakīya, Nandī, Nandītaṭa, Narhiya, Nigama, Palanapura, Palli, Pallikiya, Pallivala, Pañcabahali, Pārśvacandra, Pippalaka, Pogala, Pogiri, Pūrṇatalla, Pūrṇimā, Pustaka, Pulikal, Rāja, Rājakula, Rāmasena, Raṅgavijaya, Revatī, Rudrapalliya, Sāgara, Sañcara, Sanderaka, Sañjātā, Sarasvatī, Saravāla, Sardhapunamīya, Sevantara, Siddhānta, Siddhapura, Soraṭha, Suraṇa, Tagarila, Tanavāla, Tapā, Thanbhana, Tintrini, Treṅgaliya, Tirbhaviya, Upakeśa, Ustavāla, Utabiya, Vakra, Vāyaḍa, Vidyādhara, and Vijaya. The list is not complete. Some of the names are synonymous, such as Pustaka and Sarasvatī. In some cases again two names seem to be one, both having minor variations in pronunciation. A good number of names of the *gacchas* indicate geographical regions. Their differences were meagre, but the *gacchas* had mutual rivalries. Books like *Kupakṣa-Kusikasahasrakiraṇa, Tapomatakuṭṭa*, and *Añcalamatadalana* indicate this spirit of rivalry. We have later lists of teachers (*gurvāvalī, paṭṭāvalī*) of different *gacchas*, which give a summary account from Mahāvīra down to the founder of the sect in question, and then a more detailed one of the line of descent from the latter downwards, and with particulars of subsequent heads of the sect called Śrīpūjya. See Saṅgha, Gaṇa, Śākhā, Kula, Bali, Anvaya.

Gadag Inscription: An inscription dated śaka 847 (AD 925) discovered from Gadag taluk, Dharwar district, of the time of Rāṣṭrakūṭa Govinda IV, refer to a Jinālaya built by one Nāgayya. It also mentions another Jinālaya called Dhora Jinālaya at Bankapura with the preceptor Candraprabha Bhaṭāra as its head. *Bombay Karnataka Inscriptions*, I(1), No. 34.

Gadarmal Sculpture: Situated in Badoh (Videsha) the Gadarmal temple contained a gigantic sculpture which represents the mother of Tīrthaṃkara attended by the Dik-kumārikās. It shows a woman reclining on a couch with an ornamental bed-sheet and a pillow. A child lies beside her on a small pillow. The woman has a halo behind her head and is attended by four female attendants on her right and one behind bent head. This sculpture is now in Central Archaeological Museum, Gwalior.

***Gadyacintāmaṇi*:** Religious novel written at the beginning of the eleventh century AD by Oḍeyadevavādibhasiṃha (q.v.) which is based on a legend of the *Uttara Purāṇa*, ed. T.S. Kuppuswami Sastri, Madras 1902.

Gajapaṃtha: A Jain centre in the Nasik district of Maharashtra which is acclaimed by Jain authors like Guṇabhadra, Asaga, Sumati, Jayasāgara, etc.

Gaṇa: School or sect. The term basically denotes *samūha* or a collective body and often equated with *saṃgha* (q.v.) meaning 'tribe' and applied to a 'religious order' or 'monastic order' or 'congregation of brethren'. In Jainism the 'head of the order' is known as *gaṇadhara*, but in the sectarian sense the term *gaṇa* means a subdivision of a *saṃgha*. Among the principal *gaṇas* mentioned in the Jain inscriptions along with their association with the *saṃghas*, especially with the Mūla, Nandī, Drāviḍa and Sena *saṃghas*, reference may be made to Kandura, Balātkāra, Deśī, Deśīya, Kāreya, Koṭika, Krānura, Punnagavṛkṣamūla, Sena, Puṣkara, Surāṣṭa, Surastha, Vadiyur, Kaṇḍura, Pogariya, Koṭimaḍuva, Valahari, Vidyā, Desiga, and Kanura. According to Indranandin's *Nītisāra* the *gaṇas*, *gacchas* and others have arisen from the *saṃghas*. There is no difference between them whatever in their monastic and other practices. In them there is no difference of images or of penitential observances or in their rules and readings. The *gaṇas* comprise smaller subdivisions of *gacchas*, *śākhās*, *kulas* (qq.v.), etc.

Gaṇadhara: 'Tribal heads', 'apostles', 'leaders', 'patriarchs' of the Jain church. After the death of Mahāvīra, the leadership of the four orders of the Jain community—monks, nuns, laymen, and laywomen—fell on his disciple Indrabhūti Gautama who was the *gaṇadhara* for twelve years. According to a different tradition since Indrabhūti obtained *kevalajñāna* in his lifetime, he was not the official pontiff, as was his successor Sudharman who also held office for another twelve years. Sudharman was succeeded by Jambusvāmin who led the community for twenty-four years. Subsequent leaders were Prabhava, Syambhava, Yaśobhadra, Sambhūtavijaya, Bhadrabāhu and Sthūlabhadra. Subsequent *gaṇadharas* were Mahāgiri, Suhastin, Susthita, Supratibuddha, Indradinna, Dinnasūri, Siṃhagiri, Vajrasvāmin, and Vajrasena. After Vajrasena the church was led by the following patriarchs: Puṣyagiri, Phalgumitra, Dhanagiri, Śivabhūti, Bhadra, Nakṣatra, Rakṣa, Nāga, Jehila, Viṣṇu, Kālaka, Sampalita, Bhadra (J), Vṛddha, Saṅghapālita, Hastin, Dharma (J), and Śāṇḍilya. The *Kalpasūtra* list begins with Sudharman and ends with Śāṇḍilya or Skandila. In most of the cases their names and *gotras* are given, but there is an expanded list from Bhadrabāhu to Vajrasena which adds more details (the disciples of each patriarch and of the sects and branches (*gaṇa*, *kula* and *śākhā*) originating with them). We have also later lists of teachers (*gurvāvalī*, *paṭṭāvalī*) of different sects (*gaccha*, etc.), which give a summary account from Mahāvīra down to the founder of the sect in question, and then a more detailed one of the line of descent from the latter downwards, and with particulars of subsequent heads of the sect called Śrīpūjya. These lists are useful so far as the later and regional history of Jainism is concerned.

Ganavaram: Findspot of an inscription in the Guntur district, Andhra Pradesh, of the time of Kulottuṅga Rājendra, which refers to a shrine, called Candraprabha Jinālaya. *Jaina Śilālekha Saṃgraha*, IV, No. 224.

Gandharatīrtha: A Jain *tīrtha* in the Broach district of Gujarat, which achieved importance in sixteenth century. It elevated position was due to Hīravijaya. The place contains temples of Pārśvanātha and Mahāvīra. A temple dedicated to Ādinātha is also found here. Gandharatīrtha contains an interesting image of Hīravijaya.

Gāndhārī: Śāsanadevatā of Vāsupūjya (q.v.) according to the Digambara tradition. She is represented as riding a crocodile and carrying a club and two lotuses and showing *varada* pose. Gāndhārī is also the name of the Śāsanadevatā of Neminātha according to the Śvetāmbara tradition in which she is conceived of as riding a swan, holding a sword, a citron and a spear and showing *varada-mudrā*. Gāndhārī is also a Vidyā-devī (q.v.) and represented as seated on a lotus with conventional attributes.

Gāndharva: One of the eight forms of Jain marriage adopted from Brahmanical legal texts. It is the union of the two in mutual love and consent, without the permission of their parents or guardians. This form of marriage is regarded as unethical, though frequent in Prakrit narrative literature. *Trivarṇikācāra* XI.76; *Nītivākyāmṛta* XXXI.9.

Gandharvas: See Vyantara.

Gandharva-Yakṣa: Attendant of Kunthunātha (q.v.). The Digambara account makes him ride a bird and bear with four hands holding a snake, noose, bow, arrow. The Śvetāmbara representation shows a swan as his vehicle and his four hands holding *varada* pose, noose, citron and goad. This Gandharva is a personal name and has nothing to do with the Gandharvas who are a class of demi-gods, heavenly musicians and possessed of wonder-working faculties.

Gandhawal: Situated in Dewas district in Malwa, it is a prolific site for Jain images, assignable to *circa* ninth century. The site has a colossal standing Jina image flanked by Indra and Upendra as *chowri*-bearers in addition to sculptures of other Jinas like Śāntinātha, Sumatinātha and Suvidhinātha and figures of Vidyādevīs, Yakṣas, and Yakṣiṇīs.

Gaṇeśa: Brahmanical divinity who has made his way

into Jainism. The conception of this god is same in both the systems. According to description of *Ācāradinakara* Gaṇeśa is pot-bellied holding in his hands an axe, *varada-mudrā*, *modaka* (sweetmeat-ball) and *abhaya-mudrā*. His mount is a mouse.

Gaṇeśa-Caturthī: Festival held in common with the Hindus by the Jains of Karnataka but in a changed perspective.

Gaṇeśa-Gumphā: Cave No. 10 of the Udayagiri Hill near Bhubaneswar. Its front wall seems to represent Jain themes.

Ganga-Kandarpa-Jinālaya: One of the most prominent Jain temples at Lakshmeswar in Dharwar district, Karnataka. It was probably built during the reign of the Western Gaṅgas.

Gaṅgarāja: Famous general of the Hoysala King Viṣṇuvardhana of the twelfth century. Gaṅgarāja was a devout Jain and his religious activities have been recorded in numerous Karnataka inscriptions. His wife Lakṣmī was also a devout Jain as is attested by inscriptions from Sravanabelgola (q.v.). Apart from his construction of temples, his donations for Jain establishments and lavish gifts to celebrated teachers are worthy of mention. His son Boppa was also a devout Jain and constructed a temple at Halebid in memory of Gaṅgarāja in AD 1133.

Ganigitti Jinālaya: Jain temple at Hampi, the capital of Vijayanagara, built in 1385 by Iruga, the minister of Bukka II. There is a lofty *māna-stambha* in front of the temple with an inscription. The temple is described as a *caityālaya* of Kunthu-Jinanātha. This all-stone structure has a *garbha-gṛha*, *antarāla*, *ardha-maṇḍapa*, and *mahā-maṇḍapa* with an attached sub-shrine facing east. The pillars are of the early heavy cubical variety. The superstructure is a stepped pyramid of six diminishing *talas*. The low square *śikhara* is domical.

***Gaṇividyā*:** Prakrit *Gaṇivijjā*, the eighth Prakīrṇa, which is an astrological treatise in 86 verses. Agamodaya edn., Bombay, 1925.

***Gaṇivijjā*:** See Gaṇividyā.

Gaṇopagrahaṇa: Taking the role of the protector of the community as preacher and religious activist in the advanced stage of life.

Garbhādhāna: Also known as *ādhāna*, it is the sacrament of conception. The woman and her husband go to the temple and worship in the prescribed way. Then they cohabit at night for the sake of progeny. The Śvetāmbaras perform it in the fifth month after conception. A priest is invited to chant sacred hymns and bless the couple.

Gardabhilla: See Kālakācārya.

Garh Jaipur: Jina site in Purulia district, west Bengal, which has yielded an interesting Ṛṣabhanātha image. The Jina stands in *kāyotsarga* between two attendants with the bull, shown on the pedestal. He is seen installed within a shrine, which is fronted by a trifoliate arch and surmounted by a roof in tiered stages, crowned by an *āmalaka*. There are representations of the 24 Tīrthaṃkaras in six rows of two each on either side. This image is now in the Asutosh Museum, Calcutta University.

Garoli: Findspot of two Śāntinātha images in Madhya Pradesh, which are now housed in State Museum, Dhubela.

Garuḍa Yakṣa: Attendant Yakṣa of Śāntinātha (q.v.). His vehicle according to *Pravacanasāroddhāra* is a boar and according to Hemacandra an elephant. His four hands hold, according to the Śvetāmbara view, a citron, lotus, mongoose and rosary. To the other sect they are known to have a lotus, fruit, *vajra*, and discus.

***Gāthākośa*:** Anthology of moral sayings in Prakrit verses compiled by Municandra Sūri in the twelfth century.

***Gāthāsāhasrī*:** A comprehensive anthology of moral saying compiled in AD 1630 by Samayasundara in one thousand stanzas partly in Sanskrit and partly in Prakrit.

***Gatis*:** Gradation of Jīvas (q.v.) according to place where they are born or their condition of existence. The *gatis* are of four kinds: *narakagati* or hellish beings, *tiryaggati* or subhuman beings, *manuṣyagati* or human beings, and *devagati* or celestial beings. The Jīvas are born in these four *gatis* according to their merits and demerits.

Gaurī: Śāsanadevatā (q.v.) of Śreyāṃśanātha (q.v.) according to the Digambara tradition. She rides an antelope and holds a club, lotus, and urn, her fourth hand in *varada-mudrā*. Gaurī is also a Vidyā-devī (q.v.) whose mount is *godhikā*, which also holds good in the case of her Brahmanical counterpart.

Gautama Ṛṣi: Tīrthaṃkara locally called by this name whose image in the inner shrine of the Bhagavatī temple on the Singikulam Hill in the Tirunelveli district suggests that it was originally a Jain temple.

Gawarwad: Situated in the Dharwar district of Karnataka it is the findspot of an inscription in four parts and two dates (śaka 993, 994 = AD 1071, 1072) of the time of the Western Cālukya King Someśvara II. The first part describes a Jain temple at Annigere, which was constructed by Gaṅga Permaḍi, generally identified with Bhūtaga II. The temple was in charge of Guṇakīrti, belonging to the Balātkāra-gaṇa of the Mūla-saṅgha. It was repaired by the Governor Lakṣmarasa who gave some grant to Muni Tribhuvanacandra who is also mentioned in the second part of the inscription as a recipient of grant from a chief named Kātarasa. The third and fourth parts also refer to grants to temples. *Jaina Śilālekha Saṃgraha* IV, No. 154.

Gayā: Regarded as a scared place of the Jains in Jñānasāgara's *Sarvatīrthavandana.* It is associated with the Jain philosopher Akalaṅka who is said to have constructed here temples of Sambhava, Nemi, and Supārśva.

***Gayasukumāla Rāsa*:** Gujarat composition by Delhaṇa in AD 1250 which deals with the life-story of Gajasukumāra who was the younger brother of Kṛṣṇa-Vāsudeva according to the Jain tradition and adopted all the hardships of ascetic life and attained omniscience.

Gerasoppe: Findspot of Jain inscription in the North Kanara district, Karnataka. It is also well-known for its Jain temples. One inscription from this place dated AD 1378 mentions King Haiveya, his ministers, and his favourite merchants, all of whom were excellent Jains. Another inscription refers to a devoted Jain woman called Ramakka, wife of the merchant Yojanaseṭṭi, who constructed a temple of Anantanātha. The third inscription of AD 1401 found at this place, records the death of a dedicated Jain. A fourth inscription of AD 1421 records some grant for local Pārśvanātha temple. The temples of Neminātha and Vardhamāna are also known from inscriptions of this place. *Jaina Śilālekha Saṃgraha* IV, Nos. 397, 400, 674; *Mysore Archaeological Report* 1928, 97.

Ghanerao: Site of the celebrated Mahāvīra temple, district Pali, Rajasthan. The temple comprises a sanctum with ambulatory, a *gūḍha-maṇḍapa*, a *trika-maṇḍapa*, and an entrance porch. In front was a pillared hall open on all sides with 24 *devakulikās* or small shrines. The entire complex is within a boundary wall. The sanctum has an apparently simple plan, though the structure displays a difficult and attractive execution. It is regarded as a notable example of the Madapāṭa (Mewar) school of the Maru-Gurjara style.

Ghantai Temple: Jain temple of Khajuraho. It is so called on account of the chain-and-bell motifs carved on its tall conspicuous pillars. The extant portion shows that it was essentially of the same design as the Pārśvanātha temple, but nearly twice as large. All that has survived is the *ardha-maṇḍapa* and the *mahā-maṇḍapa*, each resting on four pillars and supporting a flat but ornate ceiling. Like all other local Jain temples the Ghantai also belonged to the Digambaras.

Ghaṭeśvara: Findspot of a tenth-century damaged stone image of Ṛṣabhanātha found at Kulpi in 24-Parganas, West Bengal. The image, now in the Asutosh Museum, Calcutta University, is 3 feet 5 inches in height and 1 foot 9 inches in breadth. Its left side is broken. The image stands in *kāyotsarga* or a double-petalled lotus placed on a *triratha* pedestal. Below the lotus seat is the bull emblem flanked on either side by kneeling devotees. To the left of the bull is a female figure. The Jina is flanked by two standing *chowri*-bearers in *tribhaṅga* pose. The top corner of the pedestal slab depicts *navagraha* figures. Above the *grahas* are 24 miniature Jinas in eight rows of three. On the uppermost row flying Gandharvas are seen carrying garlands.

***Ghātin Karma*:** one of the two groups of obstructive *karmas*, which is subdivided into four categories, namely *jñānāvaranīya*, *darśanāvaranīya*, *mohanīya*, and *antarāya* (qq.v.).

Ghaṭiyālā inscription: Dated VS 918, that is, AD 861, and found at Ghatiyala, some 20 miles north of Jodhpur city, this inscription of Kakkuka, belonging to the Gurjara Pratihāra lineage, refers to his establishment of a Jain temple and its handing over to a Jain community of Dhaneśvara-gaccha. *Epigraphia Indica* IX.280-1.

Ghoghā: Jain *tīrtha* in Bhavnagar district, Gujarat, well-known for the temple of Pārśva referred to as Ghoghāmandira in a literay record of VS 1575, it is also mentioned in an image inscription of VS 1513.

Ghora Jinālaya: A Jina temple mentioned in an epigraph of AD 1168 from Halsangi in the Bijapur district. *Jaina Śilālekha Saṃgraha* IV, No. 263.

Ghoṭārsi: Site of Pārśvanātha temple near Pratapgarh in Rajasthan.

Ghumli: Site of Pārśvanātha temple in Gujarat of which the *maṇḍapa* has survived. It is stylistically akin to the better known Navalākhā temple at the same place and, like the latter, belongs to the end of the twelfth century.

Girigoṭemalla Jinālaya: A Jina temple mentioned in an inscription from Daddala in Raichur district, Karnataka, of the time of Śomesvara II which gives the date śaka 991 corresponding to AD 1069. This temple was apparently built by Someśvara's feudatory Maḷeyamarasa Girigotemalla. *Epigraphia Indica*, XXXVII, 113-16.

Giripura: See as Dungarapura (q.v.).

Girnar: Temple city on a great cliff some 900 m above the sea level. Not far from Junagarh, Girnar contains some sixteen temples. The Neminātha temple built by Daṇḍanāyaka Sajjana, is the largest and perhaps also the oldest of all. It bears an inscription recording its restoration in AD 1278 and hence its original erection must have been considerably earlier than this date. A few temples belonging to a later period are also found and among them the more important ones are the temples of Samarasimha, Samprati-Rāja and Mekala-vasahi, all belonging to the fifteenth century. J. Fergusson, *History of Indian and Eastern Architecture*, London, 1910, II, 27-33.

Godasa: Disciple of Bhadrabāhu I from whom came into existence the *śākhās* connected with Bengal, such as Tāmraliptika, Koṭivarsīya, and Puṇḍravardhanīya.

Godi: Site of a Pārśvanātha temple and findspot of a twelfth-century Jain epigraph in Sirohi district, Rajasthan.

Gods: The traditional Vedic gods are incorporated in the Jain pantheon. Gods in Jainism have an inferior position and mortals can easily excel them in merit. The good gods are described as Daivī and Āsurī while the evil ones are known as Kudevas or Kadamras. Demons and ghosts are also indicated by the term Kudeva. Neither the state of a god or that of a demon is permanent. Whether they would continue as gods depends on the merit or demerit of their *karmas* (q.v.). The gods are of four orders, namely, Bhavana-vāsin or residential, Vyantara or the peripatetic, Jyotiṣka or the stellar, and Vaimānika or the heavenly ones. Among these, the Bhavana-vāsins have their residence in the *manuṣya-loka* or the human world and partly in the *naraka-loka* or the nether world. More categorically, they reside in the upper half of the Ratnaprabhā, the highest of the seven nether worlds. They have Jina *caityālayas* or component parts of their mansions, which are *akṛtrima* or natural and *śāśvata* or eternal. They are of ten classes, namely, Asura, Nāga, Vidyut, Suparṇa, Agni, Vāta, Stanita, Udadhi, Dvīpa, and Dik, each with the suffix *kumāra*. They are all reformed demons and have received the position of gods. The Vyantaras include demons, goblins, ghosts and spirits living above or below the earth who are divided into eight classes, namely, Kinnaras, Kiṃpuruṣas, Mahoragas, Gandharvas, Yakṣas, Rākṣasas, Bhūtas, and Piśācas. Previously they were malevolent, but owing to the grace of the Jinas their characters were absolutely changed and they were transformed into gods. But there were some among them who did not change and were not converted into the creed. They are often called *duṣṭa-vyantaras*. They have their dwelling places in the upper hard part of the first earth beyond the innumerable islands and oceans, but the Rākṣasa class of them resides in the *paṅka-bahula* or muddy part of the same earth. The Jyotiṣka or stellar gods are of five classes, namely, of the sun, moon, planets, constellations and scattered stars. They are characterized by incessant motion around the Merus (q.v.), whereas outside the Mānusottara they are stationary. The sun and moon (in Jain concept there are more than one) have Jina-*caityālayas* in their *vimānas*. The Vaimānikas or the heavenly ones are the only celestial beings to reside in the upper world (*svarga-loka*) which comprises sixteen *kalpa-vimānas*, nine *graiveyaka-vimānas* and five *anuttara-vimānas*—altogether thirty-nine. Those which make the beings residing in them feel as possessing merit are called *vimānas*. Besides these four categories of gods, the Jain texts refer to four Lokapālas namely, Soma, Yama, Varuṇa, and Vaiśravaṇa or Kubera, the god Śūlapāṇi or Śiva, described as *vṛṣabha-vāhana*, one hundred Indras enumerated as *bhavanālaya-cālīsā vyantara-devāṇa hoṃte-battisā, kappāmara-caubisā sūro ṇaro tireyo*, Agni, Skanda, Gaṇeśa, Kṣetrapālas, Bhairavas, Vidyā-devīs, Lakṣmī, Sarasvatī, Gaṅgā, Yamunā, etc. In the *Aṅgavijjā*, Vaiśravaṇa is pictured as the god of merchants and Śiva as the lord of cows, buffalos, and sheep. Kārttikeya is associated with the cock, peacock, and Viśākha with sheep, ram, boy, and sword. In the list of the female deities, in which the major Purāṇic goddesses have an importance, some foreign ones occur as well, such as Apalā who is the Greek Pallas, Athene, Anāditā who is same as the Iranian Anahita, Airāṇī, who is equated with the Roman goddess Irene, and Sālimālinī who is none other than the moon goddess Silene. There is Hariṇegamesi who was responsible, according to the *Kalpasūtra*, for transferring the embryo of Mahāvīra from the womb of Devanandā to that of Triśalā. An inscription from Mathura refers to Bhagavat Nemesa who is sculpted as a goat-headed deity. He is no other than Hariṇegamesi of the Jain canonical texts. Many Jains, following local customs, allow the existence of the Hindu gods and goddesses and place their idols in Jina temples. Among the Hindu gods who have received a share of Jain worship special mention should be made of Hanumān, Bhairava, Skanda-Kārttikeya, and Gaṇeśa.

Godapuram: A ruined site near Alathur, Palghat district. Locally known as Śākkayār Bhagavatī temple, the site has yielded two Jain images, now in the Trichur Museum. Mahāvīra is seated on a throne with a three-tiered umbrella over the head. There is an attendant figure on either side holding a fly-whisk in the right hand. The Pārśvanātha image recovered from the site is in *kāyotsarga* pose, standing on a double lotus *pīṭha* with a three-hooded cobra over his head.

Goggiya-basadi: One of the most prominent Jain temples at Lakshmeswar in Dharwar district, Karnataka. It was probably built during the reign of the western Gaṅgas.

Gokak Plates: These grants from Belgaum district record a gift of 50 *nivartanas* of land in Jalāsagrāma of Kasmāṇḍi-viṣaya for the worship of the divine Arhat and maintenance of learned Jain ascetics. Ācārya Āryanandin, belonging to the Jambukhaṇḍa-gaṇa, received the gift from King Indrananda, son of Vijayānanda Madhyamarāja of the Sendraka family. This inscription is supposed to be dated in the ninth century. *Epigraphia Indica*, XXI, 291ff.

Golden Age: in Jain tradition as recorded in the *Samavāya, Jambudvīpaprajñapti, Āvaśyaka Cūrṇi*, etc. Ṛṣabha, the first and foremost ruler, was the founder of the rules of morality. While he was ruling, people were happy; there was no mistrust or jealousy amongst them; hence there was no provision for punishment. At that time the desire-yielding trees effortlessly provided all kinds of comforts to people: delicious food, excellent costumes, precious ornaments, utensils, dwelling houses, pleasant music, and so on.

Golla: The Godāvarī plain which has been mentioned in Jain texts. The *Ācārāṅga-cūrṇi* says that here in cold weather the Jain monks were allowed to wear two garments instead of one. The *Bṛhatkalpabhāṣya* says that this place was full of goblins. One Gollacārya is mentioned in a Sravanabelgola inscription.

Gomedha: Attendant Yakṣa of Neminātha or Ariṣṭanemi (qq.v.). He has three faces and six hands with ususal attributes. Some aspects of Kubera are reflected in his conception. Like Kubera he is *naravāhana*, having man as his mount and *puṣpayāna*, having the *puṣpaka* chariot as his vehicle. A fairly good number of Gomedha images are found.

***Gommaṭasāra*:** See Nemicandra Siddhānta-cakravartin.

Gommaṭeśvara-Anointing: The bathing of Gommaṭeśvara or Bāhubali at Sravanabelgola in Karnataka. It is one of the rare festivals of the Digambaras at intervals of twelve years. The image was made by about AD 983, a colossal statue of 57 feet in height carved out of one stone. The consecration is made by milk and other coloured liquids.

Gommaṭeśvara Colossi: One of the largest free-standing images in the world. It is in Sravanabelgola, Hassan district, Karnataka. The topmost section of granite hill Indragiri was fashioned into this gigantic statue of Gommaṭeśvara, the son of the first Jina Ṛṣabhanātha, who resigned his kingdom to become an ascetic. Gommaṭa here is represented as one practising the *kāyotsarga* austerity, undisturbed by the serpents about his feet, the ant-hills rising to his thighs, or the growing creeper that has already reached his shoulders. This 57-foot high sculpture was carved at the orders of Cāmuṇḍa Rāya (q.v.) about AD 983. Another colossal statue, about 42 feet in height, is found at Karakala, modern Karkal, in the South Kanara district, Karnataka. It was built by Vīra Pāṇḍya in śaka 1353 (AD 1432). Estimated to weigh about eighty tonnes, the figure is made to lean against a slab which reaches up to its wrists. The Venur colossus, also in South Kanara district, about 35 feet high resembles the Karkal. According to inscriptions it was set up at Enuru by Timmarāja of the family of Cāmuṇḍa in AD 1603-4. Another beautiful sculpture representing Gommaṭa is found on the hill called Gommaṭagiri situated to the right of the Mysore-Hunsur Road at a distance of 25 km from Mysore. Like other figures this also represents the saint standing with creepers going round the legs, thighs and arms and showing at the shoulder. Stylistically this figure may be assigned to the fourteenth century.

Gomukha: Yakṣa attached to Ṛṣabhanātha (q.v.) who is described according to Vasunandin's *Pratiṣṭhāsāroddhāra* as showing *varada-mudrā* and holding a rosay and a noose or axe. His mount is an ox or elephant and his complexion golden. The Digambaras assign a *dharmacakra* symbol to his head. Images of Gomukha are found in two types, one detached and larger in size and the other a miniature, an attendant to Ṛṣabha. The latter type is more abundant as images of Ṛṣabha are met with in numerous Jain sites.

Gopācala, Gopagiri: Modern Gwalior, a celebrated centre of Jainism since the Gupta period. Quite a good number of Jina images of the fourth century have been recovered from this place. Particular interest attaches to an inscribed image of Pārśvanātha dated Gupta era 106. According to the tradition recorded in the *Prabhāvakacarita* and the *Prabandhakośa*, Bappabhaṭṭi of the eighth century built a Mahāvīra temple here. The kings of the Tomara dynasty of Gwalior actively supported the Digambara Jain saints and scholars. The name of the Apabhraṃśa poet Raidhu may be mentioned in this connection. Literary works mention monks belonging to the Kāṣṭha-saṅgha and Mathurā-gaccha in this region. Kuśarāja, minister of the Gwalior king, Virāmadeva, was the patron of the Jain poet Padmanābha, disciple of Guṇakīrti, and author of the *Yaśodharacarita* and builder of the Candraprabha temple. The fifteenth century was the golden age of Jainism in Gwalior. A copy of the *Samayasāra*, made at Gwalior, describes the place as full of Jinālayas. During the reign of Kīrtisiṃha and his successor Mānasiṃha Jainism received special patronage in Gwalior.

Gopinātha Guṭṭa: Low Hill at the north-eastern base of Nandi-drug in Chikballapur taluk of Kolar district which contains an inscription, probably of the eighth century, which opens with a homage to Ṛṣabha and refers to a Jain shrine said to have been formerly built by the mythical Rāma and rebuilt by Kuntī. *Epigraphia Carnatica*, X, CB.29.

Gorur: Findspot of a Jain inscription in Belur taluk, Hassan district, Karnataka which refers to a twelfth-century Jain basadi at Goravura, the earlier name of the findspot. *Mysore Archaeological Report*, 1943, 74.

Gośāla Maṅkhaliputta: A senior contemporary and close associate of Mahāvīra who, according to the Jain tradition, was responsible for creating the second schism in the Jain church. Historically, however, he was one of the greatest exponents of the Ājīvika (q.v.) creed which, as a religio-philosophical complex, was able to maintain its independent existence in Indian history. Jainism and Ājīvikism have many elements in common, especially in their structural, conceptual and ritual aspects, but the systems differed widely in regard to the basic approach to life and worldly problems. The main sources of information regarding Gośāla Maṅkhaliputta, who in the Buddhist Pali texts is called Makkhali Gośāla, and his doctrines are the Jain *Sūyagaḍa* I.1. 2.1-14, IV.7-9, II.1.29.6 with Śīlāṅka's com., *Bhagavatīsūtra* XV with Abhayadeva's commentary, and *Aupapātikasūtra*, sec. 118, 12, the Buddhist *Sāmaññaphalasutta* of the *Dīgha Nikāya* with Buddhaghoṣa's com. *Saṃyutta Nikāya* III.69, *Aṅguttara Nikāya* I. 286, *Majjhima Nikāya* I.36, I.231, Chinese and Tibetan versions of the *Sāmaññaphalasutta*, *Milindapañho*, *Mahābodhi Jātaka* and the Tamil *Nīlakeci*, *Manimekalai* and *Civañānacittiyār*. Gośāla's father was probably a *maṅkha*, an exhibitor of religious pictures and a bard. According to the Jain tradition he was born in a cowshed in a village called Śaravana. Before his meeting with Mahāvīra, he maintained himself by the profession of a *maṅkha*, according to the *Bhagavatīsūtra*. It is not known why and how Gośāla resorted to asceticism. When he met Mahāvīra for the first time at Nālandā he was already a recluse. They lived together for six years and travelled extensively in northern India often suffering humiliation and even imprisonment. But then arose ideological differences and the mental gulf between the two could not be bridged. Gośāla left Mahāvīra and declared himself a Tīrthaṃkara. He had made his headquarters in Śrāvastī in the workshop of a potter-woman called Hālāhālā. Like Buddha and Mahāvīra he travelled from place to place, towns and villages, preaching and gathering converts. Sixteen years thereafter the two teachers met once again and had an exchange of words. Mahāvīra charged Gośāla for his treacherous behaviour as a disciple, and the same charge was levelled against Mahāvīra by Gośāla. It appears that the main cause of the difference between Gośāla and Mahāvīra was the former's insistence on the doctrine of *niyati* or fate and *akriyā* or non-action to which Mahāvīra was not ready to contribute. According to Gośāla, 'all beings, all that have breath, all that are born, all that have life, are without power, strength or virtue, but are developed by destiny, chance and nature, and experience joy and sorrow in the six classes of existence' (*Sāmaññaphalasutta*). All beings are subject to a fixed and unchangeable series of existence, each of which has its own unchangeable characteristic. He denies the effects of action and energy, since he holds that every being is helpless, unable to either help himself or others. Gośāla not only succeeded in popularizing his religion in different parts of northern and eastern India before long, but was also able to produce a number of remarkable Ājīvika teachers before his death. According to one account Gośāla died 16 years before the Nirvāṇa of Mahāvīra. Another account makes his death coincide with the Mahāśilākaṇṭaka war between Ajātaśatru and the Vajjians. He died of high fever during which he proclaimed a list of eight finalities in his delirium which were suggestive of the social realities of his time.

Gotra: One of the four constituents of the *aghātin karma* (q.v.) which is designated after the specific conditions, such as country, tribe, caste, etc., by which the gods, human beings, animals and hell-beings are characterized.

Gotras: Exogamous groups. The word *gotra* literally means 'an enclosure for cows' but gradually came to mean a kin group as the limit within which marriage relations were denounced. The basic concept of the Hindu and Jain *gotra* is the same. The exact number of *gotras* prevailing among the Jains is not known. The traditional number is 84. Different castes have their own lists of *gotras*. The Agravālas have 18 *gotras*, but for some reason the last *gotra*, known as Goina is considered a half. The Osavālas had originally 18 *gotras*, but later, due to further additions caused by conversion the original 18 was split into 498 sub-*gotras*. Afterwards the number was multiplied and the total number was settled at 1,444 *gotras*. The Khaṇḍelavālas have 84, Śrīmālas 135, Poravādas 24, Hummaḍas 18, Saitavālas 44, etc. The surviving Jain *gotras* are said to be 140. There is no fixed rule regarding the avoidance of particular *gotras* in contracting a marriage. For example, the Saitavālas are supposed to possess many *gotras* of which the names of only 44 are available at present, but they regulate their marriage by the custom of family surname, that is, matrimonial contract between two parties having the same surname is avoided. Again there are castes which have no *gotras* at all, and in the case of such castes avoidance of the same *gotra* has no meaning. Though *gotra* denotes in an ordinary sense 'an exogamous group within one endogamous caste', in course of time the term acquired a philosophical connotation. It signifies the conduct of the soul coming down from generation to generation, and its ranks depend on the *karma* that determines a high or low birth for the soul. It should be remembered in this connection that there is no underlying principle in the formation of these *gotras*. These were often named after individuals, clans, towns, regions, birds, animals, professions, and objects. Original *gotras* are often split up and new ones are created. In some cases *gotra*-names show totemic affiliations. Originally marriage in *sagotra* or same *gotra* was disallowed, but later the custom of avoiding a number of *gotras* came into vogue. *Gotras* among the Jains, unlike the Hindus, are liable to be discarded, changed or newly created.

Grāmopādhyāya: Hereditary village priest among the southern Jains who conducts their ceremonies and is paid either in cash or kind. These priests are usually married and have families. They are under a high priest called the Dharmādhikārī, an ascetic, by whom they are appointed. The Dharmādhikārī (q.v.) has the power to dismiss any priest who breaks religious rules or caste customs. The Grāmopādhāya keeps a register of all marriages and thread-girdings in the village. See Upādhyāya.

Grantha Bhāṇḍāras: 'Book-houses'. The Jains possess a large number of books written on paper or on palm-leaves. These have been assiduously preserved by the Jains for so many centuries, especially in Rajasthan, Gujarat and Karnataka. In fact, every big Jain temple possesses a *grantha-bhāṇḍāra*. Catalogues of manuscripts of the Jain centres of Mudabidri in South Kanara district, Karanja in Maharashtra, Patana in Gujarat and Jaisalmer in Rajasthan have been published.

Granthālaya: See Caityālaya.

Great vows: See Mahāvrata.

Gṛhatyāga: Sacrament of renunciation after fulfilling the duties of a householder.

Gṛhīśitā: Sacrament for excellence in layman's duties.

Gudar: Findspot of a Jain inscription of AD 1149 in Sivapuri district, Madhya Pradesh, which refers to the installation of the image of Śāntinātha, Kunthunātha, and Aranātha.

Gudigere: Findspot of an inscription dated śaka 998 (AD 1076) in Dharwar district, Karnataka, which mentions the monk Śrīnandī, his female disciple Aṣṭopavāsakanti and a temple of Pārśvanātha. It also refers to the Anesejjaya basadi of Purigere which was constructed by Kumkumadevī, the sister of Cālukya Vijayāditya. There is also reference to the Bhuvanaikamalla Śāntināthadeva temple, apparently built by Someśvara II. *Indian Antiquary* XVIII.35ff; *Jaina Śilālekha Saṃgraha* II, No. 210.

Gudivāḍa: Site of a medieval Pārśvanātha temple in the Krishna district, Andhra Pradesh.

Guhanandin: Mentioned in the Paharpur Copper Plate inscription (q.v.) of Gupta year 159 as belonging to the Pañcastūpanikāya. He probably lived in the last quarter of the fourth century AD at Kashi. The Jain Vihāra at Vaṭagohāli near Paharpur was originally founded by the disciples and grand-disciples of Guhanandin. *Epigraphia Indica* XX.61ff.

Gulbarga: Findspot of a Pārśvanātha image which is in *kāyotsarga* posture. Besides the five-hooded snake-canopy the image includes *chowri*-bearers and a triple umbrella. The identifying inscription belongs to the twelfth century.

Gumānapaṇthī: A minor Digambara subsect which flourished in the late eighteenth century.

It was designated after his founder Gumāna Rāma.

Guṇa: Quality. A common term in Indian religio-philosophical tradition which is generally understood to mean some unchanging essential characters of a substance, although the term is variously interpreted. The Nyāya-Vaiśeṣikas single out 24 kinds of qualities such as colour, taste, smell, touch, sound, number, magnitude, distinctness, conjunction, disjunction, remoteness, nearness, cognition, pleasure, pain, desire, aversion, effort, heaviness, fluidity, viscidity, tendency, merit and demerit, as inherent in substance and dependent on it. At the same time they are also conceived as distinct from substance because they can by themselves be known and are thus independent. The Jains hold that in the sense of qualities, such as existence, enjoyability, substantiveness, knowability, specific characters, the capacity of possessing forms, etc., the *guṇas* adhere to specific substances and cannot exist by themselves. They maintain that substance and quality are inseparable inasmuch as the latter cannot exist in itself, but there is also an element of difference in the nature of a substance, in its acquiring new qualities, leaving the old ones and maintaining some permanent qualities. In all changes some collection of qualities appears to remain unchanged (*dhruva*), some new qualities are generated (*utpāda*) and some old qualities are destroyed (*vyaya*). In Jain texts both the words *guṇa* and *paryāya* (q.v.) are used sometimes in identical and sometimes in different meanings. See Dravya, Paryāya, Qualities, Substance.

Guṇabhadra: Disciple of Jinasena II (q.v.) and the author of the last portion of the *Ādipurāṇa* (q.v.) and the whole of the *Uttarapurāṇa* (q.v.). The latter which was composed in the ninth century runs into 8,000 verses and deals with the notable characters of early Jain history and mythology except Ṛṣabhanātha. Guṇabhadra also wrote an ethical poem, *Ātmānuśāsana*, in 270 stanzas. *Uttarapurāṇa* published in Bhāratīya Jñānapīṭha, Kashi 1968; *Ātmānuśāsana*, ed. in Digambara Jaina Granthabhandara, I, 55ff.

Guṇacandragaṇi: Reputed author of the last quarter of the eleventh century who belonged to the Kharatara-gaccha and whose other name was Devabhadrasūri. His teacher was Sumati Upādhyāya who was the disciple of Jineśvara I (q.v.). Guṇacandra's first work *Saṃvegaraṅgaśālā* is not now available. His second work, *Pārśvanāthacarita*, is divided into five parts (*parstavas*) giving, *inter alia*, stories of his three births. A few of the details are taken from the *Kalpasūtra* of Bhadrabāhu (qq.v.). His *Mahāvīra Caritra* (q.v.), like its predecessor is written in Prakrit in eight chapters. It also contains 50 Apabhraṃśa verses and a few Sanskrit passages. The sixth chapter dealing with Gośāla follows the fifteenth book of the *Bhagavatī*. The seventh chapter deals with the master's attainment of *kevalajñāna* and the eighth, his missionary life, including the rebellions of Jamālī and Gośāla. Guṇacandra's fourth work *Kathāratnakośa* or *Akahyanakosa* contains fifty stories. Like his other work here too Guṇacandra has freely used both Sanskrit and Prakrit, and there are also Apabhraṃśa passages. See *Jinaratnakośa*, 241ff., 306; *Pārśvanātha Carita*, Allahabad, 1945; *Mahāvīracarita*, Devachand Lalbhai, 1929; *Kathāratnakośa*, ed. Puṇyavijaya, Bhavanagar, 1944.

Guṇadharācārya: See Kaṣāyaprābhṛta.

Guṇaratna: See *Tarkarahasyadīpikā*.

Guṇasthānas: Fourteen steps to liberation from *karma* thought of as a ladder by which a *jīva* may reach its desired goal. The first is known as *mithyātva*, at which the *jīva* is completely under the influence of *karma*, knowing nothing about what is real and what is false. The second step is known as *svāśvāsadana*, climbing on which a *jīva* begins to distinguish between what is real and what is false. But this sense of distinction does not produce any lasting effect. On the third step, which is *miśra*, he is still in an uncertain condition, still tormented by hopes and doubts. This inbalance, however, ceases when he reaches the fourth step known as *aviratisamyagdṛṣṭi*. He feels the urge within himself to control anger, pride, and greed, but he cannot free himself completely from their influence. From the fifth step, known as *deśavirati*, a qualitative change takes place. The *jīva* now realizes the great importance of conduct and becomes mentally prepared to follow the twelve prescribed vows of right conduct. At this stage, too, anger, deceit, pride and greed are not completely controlled. On the sixth step of the ladder, which is known as *pramatta*, slight passions are controlled but negligence remains. At the seventh stage known as *apramatta* anger is more or less controlled but pride, deceit, and greed remain in a small degree. The process continues in the next higher stage known as *apūrvakaraṇa*, in which pride is controlled and the fetters of *karma* begin to loosen. The ninth step is known as *aniyatibādra*. At this stage deceit disappears while greed persists until the *jīva* reaches the tenth step which is known as *sūkṣmasamparyāya*. But complete annihilation of greed requires two more stages—*Upaśāntamoha* and *Kṣīṇamoha*—after which *jīva* becomes free of all *kaṣāyas*. The last stages are known as *sayogikevalin* and *ayogikevalin* and then all *karma* is purged.

Guṇavarma I: A later contemporary of Amoghavarṣa (q.v.) who composed a Purāṇa on Neminātha in Kannaḍa.

Guṇavarma II: Kannaḍa author who wrote *Puṣpadanta Purāṇa* on the life of the ninth Tīrthaṃkara.

Guṇavijaya Gaṇin: Author of *Caturviṃśatijinabhavastava* of the fourteenth century. Printed in *Jainastotrasaṃgraha*, II, Yaśovijaya Jaina Granthamālā IX.

***Guṇavratas*:** First three of the seven *śilāvratas* (q.v.). The *guṇavratas* are multiplicative vows which purport to raise the value of five *mahāvratas*. These are *digvrata*, taking the lifelong vow to limit worldly activity to fixed points in all directions; *deśavrata*, taking a vow to limit the above also for a limited area; and *anarthadaṇḍavrata*, taking a vow not to commit purposeless sins.

Gundlupet: Findspot of an inscription of AD 1196 in Mysore district, Karnataka, which mentions the erection of a Jinālaya by Goravagavuṇḍa, a feudatory under Ballāla II at Tuppura, which was given to the monks of Aruṅgala-anvaya and Nandī-saṅgha. *Epigraphia Carnatica* IV, Gundlu 27.

***Gupti*:** Means of *saṃvara* (q.v.) or stoppage of the influx of karmic matter into the soul. It is the control of mind, speech, and body and is of three kinds: *manogupti* by which the mind is to be controlled in the shape of giving room only to pure thoughts; *vāg-gupti*, which is the regulation of speech and consists in observing silence for a particular period or in speaking only as much as is essentially necessary; and *kāyagupti*, regulation of bodily functions.

Gurugala-Basti: Jain temple at Mudabidure to which grants were made according to an inscription dated in AD 1390.

***Gurupujana*:** Worship of the child-Tīrthaṃkara by Indra.

***Gurusthānābhyapagama*:** Acceptance of the post of a teaching ascetic with the consent of one's preceptor at an advanced stage of life.

Guruvayanakare: Findspot of a Jain inscription of AD 1484 in the South Kanara district, Karnataka, which mentions a Jina temple called Kannaḍibasadi dedicated to Śāntinātha. *Jaina Śilālekha Saṃgraha* IV, Nos. 445, 457.

***Gurvāvalī-sūtra*:** A list of teachers of the Tapāgaccha prepared by Dharmasāgara Gaṇin.

Gwaleswar Temple: An old Jain temple with Nagara-*śikhara*, now renovated, situated in the Un region, West Nirmar.

Gyaraspur: Site of Mālādevī temple in Vidisha district, Madhya Pradesh. A finely executed image of Pārśvanātha from Gyaraspur is now in the Victoria and Albert Museum, London.

H

Huduvalli: Saṅgītapura in South Kanara district, 18 km north-east of Bhatkal, which is known for its Candranāthasvāmī temple. The temple a flat slab-roofed structure and it is of little architectural interest. A few examples of Jain sculpture are known from this place. One of these, a metal image of Ṛṣabhanātha, deserves special mention.

Halasangi: Findspot of an epigraphical record of AD 1168 in Bijapur district which refers to a local Jain temple called Ghora Jinālaya. *Jain Śilākekha Saṃgraha* IV, No. 263.

Halebid: Jain site in Hassan district, Karnataka. There are three large temples in one compound, the westernmost is for Pārśvanātha with a 4.3 m high statue in fine black stone in the *sabhāmaṇḍapa*. The middle temple, smallest in the group is for Ādinātha, flanked by Gomukha and Cakreśvarī. There is also a seated Sarasvatī. The easternmost temple is dedicated to Śāntinātha. See Dorasamudra.

Hallur: Site of the Megudi Jain temple in Dharwar district, Karnataka, which is both in its name and characteristics analogous to the Meguti (q.v.) temple of Aihole. The temple has the provision of a regular stone-cut monolithic stairway to the roof. It is attributed to the second half of the seventh century AD.

Halsi Grants: A few Jain grants have been found at Halsi, ancient Palasika, in the Belgaum district. The one of Kakusthavarman begins with homage to the holy Jinendra and refers to land in Khetagrāma possessed by the Arhats. An indirect reference to the Jinendra temple at Palassika is also found in this epigraph. Another inscription of Mṛgeśavarman of the last quarter of the fifth-century records his construction of a Jinālaya and his grant of 33 *nivartanas* of land, between the river Mātṛsarit and Ingini-saṅgama for the Yāpanīyas, Nirgranthas and Kurcakas. Of the two grants of Ravivarman of the sixth century, the first refers to the eight-day festival of Lord Jina at Palasika in which the king himself participated. It also refers to the Yāpanīya monks and their chief Kumāradatta. The Jain element in his second grant is not so pronounced. Of the two grants of his son Harivarman, the first refers to an Arhat temple at Palasika, built by Mṛgeśa, for the maintenance of which a grant was received by Candrakṣānta, head of the Kurcaka Saṅgha named after Vāriṣenācārya. The second says that on a request from the Sendraka chief Bhānuśakti, he made a grant of a village called Maradi for a Jain Caityālaya at Palasika. This was the property of the Sramaṇa Saṅgha called Ahariṣṭi under Ācārya Dharmanandin. *Indian Antiquary*, VI, 24-32; *Epigraphia Carnatica*, IV, 130, VIII, 12; *Epigraphia Indica* XIV, 165.

***Hammīra-Madamardana*:** Drama in five acts written by Jaysiṃha in AD 1229 which describes how the pride of Hammīra (the Turkish Amir Shikar) was humbled and his attack on Gujarat was repulsed. It has nothing Jain in it except that the brothers Vastupāla and Tejaḥpāla, ministers of the Cālukya King Vīradhavala, who played a part in the drama, were devout Jains. Ed. C.D. Dalal, Gaekwad's Oriental Series, No. 10, Baroda, 1920.

***Hammīra-Mahākāvya*:** A historical poem by Nayacandrasūri written in the fifteenth century in 14 cantos and 1,564 verses. The first three cantos deal with the history of the Cāhamānas and the war between Pṛthvīrāja and Muhammad of Ghur. The fourth canto describes the birth of Hammīra and the next four are conventional. The ninth canto deals with the conquests of Hammīra. The rest deals with Hammīra's wars with Alāuddin, in which he was finally defeated and killed. Nayacandra has paid Hammīra a fitting tribute by calling him an immortal hero. Ed. Kirtane, Bombay 1879; Jinavijaya, Jodhpur.

Hampi: Site of the capital of Vijayanagara in the Bellary district, Karnataka, which has yielded a few Jain inscriptions. An inscription of AD 1386, of the time of Harihara II, records the construction of a temple of Kunthunātha by Iruga, son of an officer named Caicapa and disciple of Siṃhanandī of Mūla-saṅgha, Balātkāra-gaṇa and Sārasvata-gaccha. A second temple dedicated to Kunthunātha at a place called Kundanavrolu constructed by Immadi-Bukka, son of the minister Baicapa, is mentioned in an inscription of AD 1395, in which connection occurs the name of the Jain saint Dharmabhūṣaṇa. Another inscription of AD 1426, of the time of Devarāya II, records the construction of a temple of Pārśvanātha by the king himself. The temples in

Hampi are stepped pyramidal superstructures. The Gaṇigitti Jinālaya (q.v.) is a typical example of Hampi architecture. Jain sculptures from Hampi are also known to exist. A very early group of Jain sculptures is found carved on the rock-surface at Anegondi on the northern bank of the Tungabhadra just opposite Hampi. *South Indian Inscriptions* I, 152-3; *Jaina Śilālekha* III, Nos. 585, 620; IV, No. 404; *Annual Report on South Indian Epigraphy*, 1933-6, 41; A.H. Longhurst, *Hampi Ruins*, Delhi, 1933, 94ff.

Hanumakonda: Site of the Jain Kadalāya-vasadi in the Warangal district, Andhra Pradesh, which was built during the reign of Kākatīya Prola under the patronage of his wife Mailamadevī. The *śikhara* of the temple, also known as Padmavasi temple, is built of brick, the sanctum formed by natural cavern, and with a closed hall adjoining the cella, all facing north. Sculptures carved on the rock nearby include Pārśvanātha on the lotus and a female holding up an umbrella for him. The temple belongs to *circa* AD 1117.

Hantūru: Findspot of a Jain inscription in Mudigere taluk of Chikmagalur district, Karnataka, dated śaka 1052 (AD 1130). It praises the Hoysala King Viṣṇuvardhana's (AD 1106-56) daughter Hariyabbarasi who was converted to Jainism by the teacher Gandavimukta Siddhāntadeva, disciple of Māghanandī Siddhāntadeva belonging to Mūla-saṅgha, Kundakunda-anvaya, Deśī-gaṇa and Pustaka-gaccha. It is said that she reconstructed the temple at Hantiyūra, modern Hanturu, and donated rent-free land to her teacher. *Epigraphia Carnatica*, VI, Mudi 22.

Haribhadra: The great eighth-century philosopher who belonged to the Śvetāmbara school but had no special sectarian bias who had the candour to say that he had no special fondness for Mahāvīra or hatred for Kapila and others who were not Jains. Being a Brāhmaṇa by birth he was thoroughly acquainted with the Brahmanical philosophical systems as is attested in his masterly work *Ṣaḍdarśanasamuccaya*, a summary of six philosophical systems, Buddhist, Nyāya, Sāṅkhya, Jaina, Vaiśeṣika, and Pūrva-mīmāṃsā. Although he has not dealt with the Yoga and the Vedānta systems, there is a short section on Cārvāka philosophy in this work. His another work, *Lokatattvanirṇaya*, a philosophical text in Sanskrit, investigates the true nature of the world and has no bearing on any particular system. He was also well-versed in Buddhism. His commentary on Diṅnāga's *Nyāyapraveśa* is a classic in this field. Because of this commentary the great work of Diṅnāga could survive. The earliest writer who quotes from Haribhadra is the Buddhist Śāntarakṣita. Udyotanasūri, in his *Kuvalayamālā*, says that he had learnt logic from Haribhadra. In his *Anekāntajayapatākā*, composed in four chapters, he has refuted the doctrines of the Brahmanical and Buddhist philosophical schools. Other works of Haribhadra such as the *Yogavindu* and *Yogadṛṣṭisamuccaya* present Jain doctrines. The former, composed in 526 verses, deals largely with the disciplinary aspects while the latter is more philosophical in nature. The *Dharmabindu* is a manual on practical morals and asceticism in three sections, the first of which treats of the duties of the laymen, the second the rules for monks, and the third on the bliss of the saint in Nirvāṇa. In *Śāstravārtāsamuccaya*, which deals with doctrinal matters, he has also referred to the view of the Buddhist logicians. Among his other works in Prakrit are the *Dhuttākkhāna*, *Samaraiccakahā,* and *Upadesapada*. Hairbhadra was born in Citrakūṭa (Chitor) and was a pupil of Jinabhadra (or Jinabhaṭa) and Jinadatta of the Vidyādhara dynasty. Besides this famous Haribhadra there were at least eight other Jain writers of the same name. *Ṣaḍdarśanasamuccaya*, ed. with Guṇaratna's com. by L. Suali, Bib. Ind., Calcutta, 1908; in Ātmānanda Granthamālā, Bhavnagar, 1917; with *Aṣṭaka-prakaraṇa*, Surat, 1918; *Lokatattvanirṇaya*, ed. L. Suali in *Giornale della Societa Asiatica Italiana*, XVIII, 263ff., text, Bhavnagar, 1902; *Anekāntajayapatākā*, pub. in Yaśovijaya Jaina Granthamālā No. 40, Vīra Saṃvat 2436-9, *Yogabindu*, ed. with com. by L. Suali, Bombay, 1912; *Dharmabindu*, ed. with Italian trans. by L. Suali in *Giornale* XXI, 223ff., with Municandra's com. Bib. Ind., Calcutta, 1912; *Yogadṛṣṭisamuccaya*, ed. L. Suali, Bombay 1912; *Śāstravārtāsa-muccaya* 1913; *Dhuttākkhāna*, ed. A.N. Upadhye, Bombay, 1944; *Samarāiccakahā* ed. H. Jacobi, Calcutta, 1926; *Upadesapada*, Baroda, 1923-5.

Haricandra: Author of *Jīvandhara-campū* (q.v.), probably same as the author of *Dharma-śarmābhyudaya* (q.v.).

Hariṇegamesi: A deity and a very interesting image type, also known as Naigameṣa. He was one of the generals of Devarāja Indra, who transferred the embryo of Mahāvīra from the womb of the Brāhmaṇa woman Devanandā to that of Triśalā, a Kṣatriya woman, on orders from Indra. He is depicted with the head of an antelope or goat, and reminds us of the goat-headed Dakṣa-Prajāpati of the Brahmanical pantheon. His character as general of the gods is also reminiscent of Kārttikeya, one of whose names was Naigameya. One of the earliest sculptural representations of this god is to be found in a broken frieze from Mathura in the collection of the Lucknow Museum. It shows on its obverse the animal headed deity 'seated in an easy attitude on a low seat, turning his head to the right, as if addressing another personage whose image has been lost'. He is described as *bhagavā nemeso* in bold characters of the first century AD, and is accompanied by one child and three female figures on his left, his companions on the right being broken. Traces of letters below the attendants seem to show that the obliterated inscription might have contained their names. The reverse of the ornamental slab represents female dancers and musicians probably rejoicing at Naigameșa's successful transference of the foetus. Smith suggests that the scene of the composition is Indra's heaven where Naigameșa had gone after succeeding in his mission. V.A. Smith, *Jain Stūpa and Other Antiquities from Mathura*, Allahabad, 1901, 25-6, pl. XVIII. J.N. Banerjee, *Development of Hindu Iconography*, Calcutta, 1956, 561-3.

Harișena: Author of *Bṛhatkathākośa* (q.v.) who flourished in the first half of the tenth century. He was a disciple of Bharatasena and belonged to the Punnāṭa Saṅgha.

Harișena: Author of the *Dhammaparikkhā* who was originally a resident of Chitor and later migrated to Acalapura or Ellichpur where he studied metre and rhetoric and composed the said work in AD 987.

***Harivaṃśa Purāṇa*:** Composed in AD 783 in 66 Sargas by Jinasena it narrates legends of Kṛṣṇa and Balarāma in a Jaina setting with sermons and doctrines inserted in many places. The legend of Ṛṣabhanātha is told by way of introduction, and connected with the story of Kṛṣṇa, we have that of his cousin Nemi or Ariṣṭanemi. The story of the Kauravas and Pāṇḍavas and their conversion into Jainism along with Karṇa, are described. Another *Harivaṃśa* in 39 Sargas was written by Sakalakīrti and his pupil Jinadāsa in the fifteenth century. Jinasena's *Harivaṃśa Purāṇa*, ed. Pandit Darbarilal Nyāyatīrtha, Sahityaratna, Manikacandra Digambara Jaina Granthamālā, 32-3; Sanskrit text with Hindi trans. by Pannalal Jain, Bhāratīya Jñānapītha, 1962.

Harmashra: Findspot of a mutilated tenth-century Pārśvanātha image in Taldangra P.S., Bankura district, West Bengal. It stands in *kāyotsarga* on a double-petalled lotus seat placed on a *pañcaratha* pedestal. The central pedestal has two lions back to back. On the next two *rathas* there are kneeling devotees. *Chowri*-bearers are on either side with a miniature *rekhā*-deul design behind. Above them are four planets. Even higher are flying Gandharvas. The canopy of the Jina is formed by a seven hooded snake. A Nāga couple are shown as devotees below.

Hastagiri: Jain *Tīrtha* situated near Śatruñjaya and associated with Ādinātha.

Hastikundi: Site of a tenth-century Ṛṣabha temple in Pali district, Rajasthan.

Hastimalla: Jain dramatist of south India and a pupil of Guṇabhadra. His *Vikrānta-Kaurava* in six acts is based on the theme of the *Mahābhārata*, while his *Maithilī-kalyāṇa* is a Rāma-Sītā drama based on the *Rāmāyaṇa* story. These two plays have been edited in Manikacandra Digambara Jaina Granthamālā, Nos. 1 and 6. His other works are *Anjañā-Pavanāñjaya* and *Subhadrāharaṇa*. He flourished in the thirteenth century.

Hastinapura: Ancient site in the Meerut district, Uttar Pradesh. A huge statue of Śāntinātha found here contains an inscription of AD 1179 stating that it was a gift of one Devapāla Soni of Ajmer. The image is in *kāyotsarga* pose.

Hatadiha: Findspot of a Ṛṣabhanātha image in the Jaypore subdivision of Cuttack district, Orissa. The image belongs to the tenth century.

Hatana: Findspot of a Jain epigraph of AD 1178 in Nagamangala taluk, Mandya district, Karnataka, which records the construction of temple of Pārśvanātha by a merchant called Sovisețți during the reign of the Hoysala Ballala II and a grant to the teacher Bālacandradeva who belonged to the Pustaka-gaccha. *Epigraphia Carnatica* IV, Naga 70.

Hathigumpha Inscription: Issued by Khāravela (q.v.) of the Mahāmeghavāhana dynasty of Kaliṅga, a devout Jain who lived in the first century BC. It opens with homage to the Arhants and Siddhas. The inscription seems to suggest that King Khāravela had set up in his capital the Kalinga Jina (q.v.) which was taken away from Kaliṅga by a Nanda king. The reading of the relevant passage is, however, doubtful. The inscription says that after accomplishing his conquests with success, Khāravela directed his energy to religious affairs and as a lay devotee he served the Jain monks. *Epigraphia Indica* XX. 71ff.

Hathundi Inscription: Dated vs 1345 (AD 1287) and found at Hathundi in the Godwar district of Rajasthan, this inscription of Sāmantasiṃha of the Jalor house of the Cāhamānas refers to a temple of Mahāvīra. Nahar, *Jaina Lekha Saṃgraha*, No. 897.

Haṭṭana: Findspot of an important Jain epigraph dated śaka 1000 (= AD 1078), in Tiptur taluk, Tumkur district, Karnataka, which records a land grant, during the time of Someśvara II and his Hoysala feudatory, for the Nakhara Jinālaya of Haṭṭana. It refers to monks belonging to the Mūla-saṅgha, Deśīya-gaṇa, Pustaka-gaccha and Kundakunda-anvaya. Another inscription of the time of Hoysala Ballāla (AD 1101-8) mentions the Jain Ācārya Subhacandra. *Epigraphia Carnatica* XII. Tiptur No. 101; *Jaina Śilālekha Saṃgraha* II, No. 118; IV, 183; *Mysore Archaeological Report*, 1918, 45.

Heavens: According to the Jain conception, above the earth are situated the heavenly regions, *vimānas*, consisting of twelve *kalpas*, namely Saudharma, Aisāna, Sanatkumāra, Mahendra, Brahmaloka, Lantaka, Mahāsukha, Sahasrāra, Ānata, Pranata, Āraṇa, and Acyuta; the nine *graiveyakas*, that is, the heaven forming the neck of the human-shaped universe comprising Sudarśana, Amogha, Subuddha, Payodhara, Subhadra, Suviśāla, Sumanasa, and Priyaṅkara; and five *anuttaras*, namely Vijaya, Vaijayanta, Jayanta, Aparājita and Sarvārthasiddha. Thus there are 26 heavens placed one above the other. Above the highest heaven called Sarvārthasiddha is situated Iṣatpragbhāra, the place which is the final resort of all souls. According to another account there are forty heavens pervading the top section of the human-shaped universe just above the Sudarśana Meru (q.v.). These are Saudharma, Aisāna, Sanatkumāra, Mahendra, Brahman, Brahmottara, Lāntava, Kāpiṣtha, Śukra, Mahāśukra, Satāra, Sahasrāra, Ānata, Pranata, Āraṇa, Acyuta, nine *graiveyakas*, nine *anudiśas* and five *anuttaras*, thus making a total of thirty-nine. The names of the *graiveyakas* and *anuttaras* have been given above. The *anudeśa* heavens are known as Lakṣmī, Lakṣmī-mālika, Vairavaka, Rocanaka, Soma, Soma-rūpya, Aṅka, Palyaṅka and Āditya. The Vaimānikas are the only celestial beings who reside in these heavens. Among the one hundred Indras or chiefs, ninety-eight look after these heavenly regions.

Heggere: Findspot of a Jain inscription of AD 1161 in Chiknayakanhali taluk of the Tumkur district, Karnataka, which records the construction of a Jina temple, called Cenna-Pārśva-basadi by Biṭṭideva, feudatory of Hoysala Narasiṃha I. It also refers to Mānikanandi Siddhāntadeva, disciple of Guṇacandra, belonging to the Mūla-saṅgha, Deśīya-gaṇa, Pustaka-gaccha, and Kundakunda-anvaya. *Epigraphia Carnatica* XII, Chik. No. 21.

Hells: Situated below the earth-disc according to the Jain conception. These are Ratnaprabhā, Śarkarāprabhā, Valukāprabhā, Paṅkaprabhā, Dhūmraprabhā, Tamaḥprabhā, and Mahātamaḥprabhā. They are otherwise called Dharmā, Vaṃśā, Śailā, Añjanā, Ariṣtā, Mādhayā, and Mādhavī. Denizens of hell are called Nārakīs or Nārakas. They have although a demonic nature they cannot leave the place where they are commissioned to stay or cause harm to anyone except their fellow Nārakas. The souls of those who have committed grave sin are removed to one of the seven netherworlds which contain different hells. There the soul of the condemned is fitted out with an enormous ugly body. They possess superhuman power which they waste by fighting among themselves. In addition to the pains produced by the wounds they inflict on one another and by the tortures they have to undergo, they continually suffer from extreme heat or cold, intolerable smells and horrid sounds. However, the lower world is not only a place occupied by hell-beings, but its uppermost region known as Ratnaprabhā is also the seat of gods of both the *bhavanavāsins* and *vyantara* categories.

Hemacandra: Jain polymath of the twelfth century who lived in the court of the Cālukya King Kumārapāla of Gujarat and earned the title *Kalikālasarvajña*, 'the all-knower of the Kali age', for his scholarship. His *Laghu-Arhannītisāra* is a treatise on the science of polity. His *Triṣaṣtiśalākā-puruṣacaritra* describes in ten cantos the lives of 63 best men according to the Jain belief. He has narrated the life of king Kumārapāla of Anahilapāṭaka in his *Kumārapālacarita*, which is also known as *Dvāśraya-kāvya*, either because it is written both in Sanskrit and Prakrit or because, besides being a history, it also serves the purpose of illustrating the rules of grammar. He has written four lexical works: *Abhidhānacintāmaṇi*, *Anekārthasaṃgraha*, *Nighaṇṭuśeṣa*, and *Deśināmamālā*. The first two deal respectively with synonyms and homonyms; the third is a botanical *nighaṇṭu*; and the fourth is a Prakrit lexicon. His grammatical work *Śabdānuśāsana* has eight chapters of four sections each, the total number of Sūtras being 4,500. In the field of poetics his *Kāvyānuśāsana* written in the form of Sūtra and Vṛtti, along with its commentary called *Viveka* deals with the doctrines of *dhvani*, *rasa*, *guṇa*, *doṣa*, and *alaṅkāra*. In the field of metrics his *Chandānuśāsana* is a very extensive work in Sanskrit, Prakrit and Apabhraṃśa in metre. Composed in AD 1150, it consists of three parts, namely the Sūtras, the Vṛtti and illustrations by Hemacandra himself. It is really Hemacandra who gave final shape and sanctity to Apabhraṃśa language and literature. In his *Siddhahemacandra* he deals with Mahārāṣṭrī, Saurasenī, Māgadhī, Paiśācī, Culikapaiśācī, and Apabhraṃśa. Besides, he composed *Vītarāga* and *Mahāvīra Stotras*. Hemacandra was born in Dhandhuka in AD 1088 and died in AD 1172. He was patronized by the Cālukya King Jayasiṃha Siddhirāja and was responsible for the conversion of his successor Kumārpāla. *Kumārapālacarita*, Sanskrit, Cantos I-XX, ed. A.V. Kathvate, 2 parts, Bombay, 1886, 1915; Prakrit, Cantos XXI-XXVIII, ed. S.P. Pandit, Bombay, 1900; rev. edn. P.L. Vaidya, Poona, 1936; *Laghu-Arhannīti*, Ahmedabad 1906; *Abhidhānacintāmaṇi*, ed. B. Rama and V. Misra, Calcutta, 1907; ed. Böhtlingk and Rieu, St. Pitersburg, 1847; ed. Hargovindadas, Bechardas and Jinavijaya, 2 vols. Bhavnagar, 1914-19; *Anekāntasaṃgraha*, Vienna 1893; *Deśīnāmamālā*, ed. R. Pischel and G. Bühler, Bombay Sanskrit Series XVII, 1880, by P.V. Ramanujaswami, Poona, 1938; *Dhātupāṭha*, ed. J. Kirste, Vienna, 1899; *Siddhahemacandra* and *Śabdānuśāsana*, Sri Jain Yaśovijaya Series, Benares, 1905; ed. Sri Vijaya Gaṇi, Botad, 1952; *Siddha-hemaśabdānuśāsana*, ed. R. Pischel in two parts, the second part contains a German trans. expl. and comp. study, Halle Amzar, 1877-80, ed. P.L. Vaidya, BORI, Poona, 1936, rev. edn. 1958, *Chandānuśāsana*, Bombay, 1912; Chs. IV-VII. ed. H.D. Velankar, in *Journal of the Bombay Branch of the Royal Asiatic Society* XIX, 27-74, XX.1-46; in *Jayadaman* by H.D. Velankar, Bombay, 1949; *Kāvyānuśāsana*, ed. Sivadatta and Parab, Bombay, 1901, ed. R.C. Parikh and R.B. Athavale, 2 vols. Bombay, 1936. *Triṣaṣṭiśalākāpuruṣacaritra*, Bhavnagar, 1903-13; Eng. trans. by Helen M. Johnson, 6 vols., Baroda, 1931-62; *Pariṣiṣṭaparvan*, ed. H. Jacobi, Bib. Ind., Calcutta, 1891; extracts trans. into Garman by J. Hertel, Leipzig, 1908; *Yogasāra*, Bhavnagar, 1926, *Vītarāgastotra*, Devachand Lalbhai, 1911; *Mahāvīra-stotras*, ed. in Kāvyamālā VII.

Hemavati Inscriptions: Found of Hemavati in Anantapur district, Andhra Pradesh, one of the inscriptions records donations to a local Jain temple by Nolamba Mahendra and his son Ayyapa. Another inscription of the latter found on the same site refers to the gift of a village called Buduguru to Lokayya, an illuminator of the doctrine of the Arhats. These belong to the ninth and tenth centuries AD. *South Indian Inscriptions* IX (1), No. 19; *Epigraphia Indica*, X.70.

Hemavijayagaṇi: See *Kathāratnākara*.

Heragu: Jain centre in the Hassan taluk of the Hassan district, Karnataka. According to an inscription of AD 1155, a temple named Cenna-Pārśvanātha was built during the reign of Hoysala Narasiṃha I by Jakkabbe, wife of the General Cābimayya. Another inscription from this place, of AD 1174, records a gift for the said temple by King Ballāla II himself. Grants to this temple are recorded also in other inscriptions. *Jaina Śilālekha Saṃgraha* III, Nos. 339, 385, 390; *Epigraphia Carnatica* V, Hassan 57-9.

Herle Inscription: Found at Herle in Kolhapur district, Maharashtra, this inscription, of the time of Śilāhāra Gaṇḍarāditya dated śaka 1040 (AD 1118), reveals the name of some of the Digambara luminaries of Kolhapur area such as Tribhuvanacandra, Nāgacandra Saiddhāntika, Bālacandra-vrati, Śāntivīramunīndra, etc. The temple-complex, dedicated to Candraprabha at Herle was built by Nemagavuṇḍa and was popularly known as Tribhuvanatilaka, an epithet of Śilāhāra Gaṇḍarāditya. *Corpus Inscriptionum Indicarum* VI, No. 46.

Hetu: *Liṅga* or reason, which serves the most important purpose as the middle term in the formation of a syllogism (q.v.). Early Jain logicians equated *hetu* with *anumāna* (q.v.) or inference itself. Later Jain logicians, however, consider *hetu* as exclusively the middle term, that which cannot occur otherwise than in connection with the major term (*sādhya*). Thus in the proposition 'the hill (minor term, *pakṣa*) is full of fire (major term, *sādhya*) because it is full of smoke' smoke is the middle term (*hetu* or *liṅga*) which cannot arise from any other things than *fire* which is the major term. The middle term is either perceptible (*upalabdhi*) and imperceptible (*anupalabdhi*). Each of these again may occur in the form of affirmation (*vidhi*) or negation (*pratiṣedha*). The fallacies (q.v.) arising from the deflections of *hetu* are known as *hetvābhāsa*. Among these, three are frequent: (1) The unproved (*asiddha*): 'This is fragrant, because it is a sky lotus'; here the middle term, the sky-lotus, is unreal. (2) The contradictory (*viruddha*): 'This is fiery, because it is a body of water'; here the reason alleged is opposed to what is to be established. (3) The uncertain (*anaikāntika*): 'Sound is eternal, because it is always audible'; here the middle term is uncertain because audibility may or may not be a proof of eternity.

Without an inseparable connection or invariable concomitance (*vyāpti*) between the major and the middle term the formation of any syllogism (q.v.) is impossible. If the middle term and the major term exist simultaneously, the former is called *vāpya*, pervaded or contained, and the latter *vyāpaka*, pervader or container. But if the middle term follows the major term, the former is called effect (*kārya*) and the latter, cause (*kāraṇa*).

***Hiraṇyajanmatā*:** Entering of the soul to the embryo of a woman who is to give birth to a Tīrthaṃkara.

Hire-Abli: A Jain centre of Sorab taluk in Shimoga district, Karnataka. An epigraph from this place refers to the name of a local Pārśvanātha temple which received a grant in AD 1142 during the reign of Jagadekamalla. The donor was Pergade Mayduna. The epigraph mentions Vīrasena and Māṇikasena, belonging to the Mūla-saṅgha, Sena-gaṇa and Pogari-gaccha. Two short inscriptions of AD 1366 and 1371 mentions the Vijayanagara Emperor Bukka I. In one of the inscriptions of the time of the next King Harihara II there is reference to Pārśva-Jina of this place. The next emperor, Devarāya I, is mentioned in several Jain memorial tablets. *Epigraphia Carnatica* VII, Sorab 125; VII, Sorab 102-3, 115.

Hīravijaya: A great sixteenth-century Jain activist (AD 1527-96) of Gujarat. He was a pupil of Vijayadānasuri belonging to the Tapā-gaccha. Contemporary inscriptions refer to the installation of Jina images by him. Several literary works record his achievements, the important ones being *Hīrasaubhāgyakāvya* by Devavimala and *Hīravijayasūrirāsa* by Ṛṣabhadāsa. The most important event in Hīravijaya's life was his contact with Emperor Akbar. Owing to his influence the Emperor made some concessions to the Jains and conferred on him the epithet *jagadguru*. Hīravijaya's famous pupils were Bhānucandra and Śānticandra. A work called *Jagadgurukāvya* was composed in VS 1646 by Padmasāgara of the Tapā-gaccha, which also gives an account of Hīravijaya's life. Numerous inscriptions from Gujarat, Rajasthan and even U.P. mention Hīravijaya and his disciples and associates. *Epigraphia Indica* II.50ff.; Nahar, *Jain Inscriptions* III, Nos. 1762, 2370-1, 2448.

Hirehalli: Findspot of a Jain inscription of AD 1248 in Belur taluk, Hassan district, Karnataka, which mentions the construction of a shrine dedicated to the Jain monk *Perumāledeva* by a chief called *Ādi-gavuṇḍa*. Another inscription of AD 1257 from this place mentions a Jinālaya built by the same Ādi Gāvuṇḍa. *Jaina Śilālekha Saṃgraha*, III, Nos. 496. 504.

Hisugala-basadi: Jain temple built by the saint Munibhadra during the reign of Harihara II of Vijayanagara mentioned in an epigraph from Tavanandi in Sorab taluk of the Shimoga district Karnataka. *Epigraphia Carnatica*, VIII, Sorab, Nos. 196, 200.

Hogekeri: Findspot of a few fifteenth-century Jain inscriptions and a Pārśvanātha temple in Bijapur district, Karnataka.

Holy Trees: In Jain tradition each Tīrthaṃkara is provided a holy tree, called *aśoka*, under which the attained omniscience. Trees assigned to the Vyantara (q.v.) gods are known as Caitya-trees. The Piśācas have been assigned the *kadamba* tree (with orange-coloured rounded blossoms), the Yakṣas the *vaṭa* (banyan), the Bhūtas the *tulasī* (basil), the Rākṣasas the *kandaka* (reed), the Kinnaras the *aśoka* (belonging to the leguminous class with magnificent flowers), the Kiṃpuruṣas, the *campaka* (*Michelia champaka* bearing a yellow fragrant flower), the Mahoraga the *nāga* (big tree with colourful flowers, the middle portion of which looks like a serpent-hood, also called *nāgakeśara* cognizance of the Buddhist Mañjuśrī) and the Gandharvas the *tinduka* (*Dyospyros embryopteris*). These names are recorded in the *Sthānāṅga* which also assigns the following trees to the Bhavanapati gods: *aśvattha*, *saptaparṇa*, *śālmali*, *udumbara*, *śiriṣa*, *dadhiparṇa*, *vañjula*, *palāśa*, *vapra*, and *karṇikāra*.

Hollakere: Findspot of a copper-plate inscription of AD 1154 in Chitradurga district, Karnataka, which records the existence of a temple of Śāntinātha associated with Pārśvasena Bhaṭṭāraka of the Mūla-saṅgha. *Epigraphia Carnatica*, XI, Hol, No. 1.

Honnenahalli: Findspot of a Jain inscription of AD 1303 in Hunsur taluk, Mysore district, which records a grant to a Jina temple through the monk Padmanandī of the Hansoge branch who was a disciple of Bāhubali Maladhārīdeva. *Epigraphia Carnatica*, IV, Hunsur 14.

Honnur Inscritption: Incised on an image of Pārśvanātha, found from the Jain temple at Honnur, 2 miles to the south-west of Kagal in Kolhapur district, Maharashtra, this inscription refers of Mahāmaṇḍaleśvara Ballāla's (AD 1100-8) and his brother Gaṇḍarāditya's contribution to a Jain basadi constructed by Bamagāvuṇḍa, disciple of Rātrimatikanti of the Punnagavṛkṣa-mūlagaṇa of the illustrious Mūla-gaṇa. *Corpus Inscriptionum Indicarum*, VI, No. 44.

Honwad: Findspot of an inscription dated śaka 976 (AD 1054) of the time of the Western Cālukya king Someśvara I in the Bijapur district. The inscription refers to the building of a Jain temple called Tribhuvanatilaka, presumably named after Someśvara I who bore the title Trailokyamalla, dedicated to Śāntinātha. It was built by Cānkirāja, an officer of Ketaladevī, the wife of Someśvara I. The latter requested by this queen, granted some land for the maintenance of this temple. Cānkirāja has been described as a sincere Jain layman and a disciple of Mahāsena, who belonged to the Mūla-saṅgha, Sena-gaṇa and Pogari-gaccha, and was disciple of Brahmasena and grand disciple of Āryasena. The epigraph further informs us that Cānkirāja also built an image of Supārśva at the request of his father Kommarāja in the temple-complex of Śāntinātha. Another disciple of Mahāsena, namely, Jinavarman, built a temple of Pārśva near the main shrine. *Indian Antiquary* XIX, 268ff.

Hosahoḷḷu: Findspot of a Jain epigraph, assigned to AD 1125, in Krishnarajapet taluk of the Mandya district, Karnataka, which records that during the rule of Hoysala Viṣṇuvardhana, Nolabi Setti donated a village, a tank and a *dānaśālā* for the Trikūṭa Jinālaya, consturcted by Dambikabbe, to his teacher Subhacandradeva. *Epigraphia Carnatica* IV, Krishna 3.

Hoskote Inscription: Western Gaṅga inscription of the 12th year of the reign of Avinīta, discovered in Hoskote in Bangalore district which records that a *devāyatana* or temple, dedicated to the Arhats, was constructed by the mother of the Pallava overlord Siṃhaviṣṇu at the village of Pulligere in Karikunda division for the exclusive use of the Yāvanika or Yāpanīya Saṅgha. The mother of Siṃhaviṣṇu constructed this temple with a view to enhancing the glory of her husband's family. This inscription belongs to the second half of the sixth century AD. *Mysore Archaeological Report*, 1938, 80ff.

Householders: In Jainism asceticism is a continuation of house-holder's life. Lay persons, males and females, are known respectively as *śrāvakas* and *śrāvikās*, and these lay devotees, the householders are the source of the strength of the religion. Thirty-five rules of good conduct are enjoined on a householder. He should follow an honest profession; marry a girl of a pious family; avoid dangerous pursuits like gambling, etc.; control sensuality; avoid places of difficulties, settle in a peaceful country; have the company of virtuous people; live in a decent locality; be properly dressed; spend according to his income; honour regional customs; aviod undesirable habits slandering anybody and bad company; resist cultivating ill-feeling; maintain dependants: render service to deserving persons; give up excessive eating and drinking; take proper medicine; avoid travelling in unprotected areas; live peacefully with others; impress lower people with high ideal; abstain from too much intimacy; mix with the right kind of people; try to achieve the four-fold objective of life; make right estimate of himself; attempt to rise higher and higher; do the proper thing at the proper time; read the scriptures; give up obstinacy; be partial to virtues and develop the right attitude towards religion and get doubts solved. Besides these thirty-five rules of right conduct, the householder has to perform twelve *vratas* or vows comprising five *anuvratas* and seven *śīlavratas* (qq.v.), pass through eleven *pratimās* (q.v.) or stages of life, and perform six *āvaśyakas* (q.v.) or daily duties. Among the five *anuvratas*, the observance of *ahiṃsā* (q.v.)., that is, not doing violence to any living being, presents many difficulties. Since violence cannot be absolutely avioded in the ordinary business of life, it is said that violence is of four kinds—accidental, occupational, protective, and intentional. The householder is required to abstain fully from the fourth kind of injury, and he should take as much care and caution against loss of life in the other forms as is possible for him. The same kind of concession is enjoyed by the householder in the observance of the other four vows also. He should neither speak falsehood himself, nor spread false ideas, divulge the secrets of others, forge documents, and so forth. These are all *anṛta* or falsehood, which the householder should avoid. Likewise, appropriating to oneself what another man has forgotten or dropped, or accepting what he knows to be stolen property, instructing another person in stealing, adulteration, the use of false weights and measures, etc., are all forms of theft and should be avoided. A householder should be satisfied with his own wife. By commiting adultery he violates the vow of *brahmacarya*. The fifth vow recommends that a householder should fix before hand, the maximum limit of his belongings and in no case exceed it. Apart from these *anuvratas*, the householder should practise *śīlavratas* wich comprise three *guṇavratas* (q.v.) and four *śikṣāvratas* (q.v.).

Hoysala Jinalaya: Jina temple erected by Vinayāditya, a general of the Hoysala King Viṣṇuvardhana, mentioned in an epigraph from Muttatti in the Hassan taluk of the district of the same name in Karnataka. *Epigraphia Carnatica*, V, Hassan, 112.

Huli: Findspot of Jain inscriptions in Belgaum district, Karnataka. One inscription in three plates of the time of King Mangaleśa (*circa* AD 600) of the Badami Cālukya house records a grant of land to a Jain monastery by the Sendraka chief Raviśakti, son of Kannaśakti. Huli continued to be a Jain centre whence we have other inscriptions of Jain character. The first part of a two-fold inscription dated śaka 966 (AD 1044) tells that one Lacchiyabbe, wife of a district governor, constructed a Jain temple and gave some grants to its priest Bālacandra Bhaṭṭāraka of the Yāpanīya Saṅgha and Punnagavṛkṣamūla-gaṇa. The second part, dated śaka 1067 (AD 1145), mentions Jagadekamalla as the reigning king and records a grant in favour of the said Jain temple, *Indian Archaeology: A Review*, 1968-9, 47, pl. 52B; *Epigraphia Indica* XVIII, 172ff.; *Indian Antiquary*, VII.161-2; *Jaina Śilālekha Saṃgraha*, IV, No. 130.

Huligere Saṅkha-basadi: Jain establishment managed by a monk named Candraprabha mentioned in two copper plates of AD 1522 from Sonda in the North Kanara district of Karnataka. *Annual Report on South Indian Epigraphy*, 1939-40, 22.

Huluhalli: Findspot of a Jain inscription of AD 1372 in Mysore district, which mentions a number of monks of the Pustaka-gaccha and Deśīya-gaṇa, the earliest of whom was Abhayendu. This place had two Jina temples, Parameśvara Jinālaya and Trijajammangala dedicated to Māṇikyadeva or Pārśvanātha. *Jaina Śilālekha Saṃgraha* III, No. 571.

Humbaḍa, Hummaḍa: Jain Bania or mercantile caste of western India and Deccan. They are mostly Digambaras but the Śvetāmbaras are also among them. Their original habitat was probably Pāṭana. The Humbaḍas are divided into 18 exogamous *gotras*: Kheraja, Kamaleśvara, Kākadeśvara, Utreśvara, Mātreśvara, Bhīmeśvara, Bhadreśvara, Viśveśvara, Śaṅkheśvara, Gaṅgeśvara, Ambeśvara, Māmaneśvara, Someśvara, Rājiyāṇa, Laliteśvara, Raṅgeśvara, Kāśyapeśvara and Budheśvara. They are said to have received their name from Humaḍa, their spiritual ancestor. Like other Bania castes they are also divided into two groups, Viśā and Daśā, 'twenties' and 'tens'. They are also called Vāgadiya, after the Vāgaḍa or wild regions of Rajasthan.

Humcha: Jain centre in Shimoga district of Karnataka which has yielded a large number of Jain epigraphs. The earlier name of this place mention Jain temples of Pāliyakka, Paṭṭana-svāmī, Nokkiyabba, Urvitilaka, etc. The earliest epigraph is dated śaka 819 (AD 897) mentions the erection of a Jain temple by Tolapuruṣa Vikramāditya Śāntara for his *guru*. Maunī Siddhānta Bhaṭṭāraka, belonging to Kondakundaanvaya. Another inscription mentioning the building of a temple is of the said Tolapuruṣa's wife Pāliyakka. The Paṭṭanasvāmī Jinālaya was erected by Paṭṭanasvāmī Nokkaya Setti, officer of Vīra Sāntara, a provincial governor under Someśvara I according to an inscription of AD 1062. Nokkaya Setti's teacher Divakaranandia and his spiritual colleague Sakalacandra Paṇḍita are also mentioned in this inscription. But another inscription of the same date says that the Nokkiyabba temple was originally built by Jinadatta. It also says that Vīra Sāntara and his wife Cāgaladevī were devout Jains and that the latter added a *toraṇa* to the said temple. The epigraph also mentions a Jain teacher called Mādhavasena. In the time of the next Sāntara ruler Bhujabala we have a Jinālaya after his name as we find from an inscription of AD 1065 which also refers to his teacher Kaṇakanandīdeva. Another inscription of the time of the same feudatory, assigned to AD 1077, records some grant for Tīrthada-basadi built by Paṭṭanasvāmī. One long epigraph of AD 1077 belonging to the brother of the Bhujabala mentions the gifts made to Jain establishments by the female members of the family, in which connection the Urvitilaka Jinālaya and the spiritual lineage of the teacher Vijaya-Bhaṭṭāraka are mentioned. This and another inscription of the same date refer to the queen-mother Caṭṭalādevī's religious constructions and endowment. The Humcha inscription of AD 1147 refers to Vikrama Sāntara II and his sister Pampādeva as lay disciples of Ajitasena Paṇḍita. It mentions the celebrated Jain teacher Vāsupūjya Siddhāntadeva and endowments made in favour of Urvitilaka Jinālaya. An inscription of AD 1530 describes the achievements of the Jain logician Vidyānanda who defeated his philosophical opponents in debate. In the court of the Vijayanagara Emperor Kṛṣṇadeva Rāya (AD 1509-29) he established his eminence as a logician. Two spiritual predecessors of Vidyānanda, namely Siṃhakīrti and Viśālakīrti, are mentioned in this inscription. His disciple Devendrakīrti was held in high esteem by the Vijayanagara King Acyuta Rāya. A colleague of Vidyānanda, named Nemicandra, built a big temple of Pārśvanātha at Humcha. As late as the seventeenth-century Humcha was a Jain *tīrtha*. Some of the surviving temples of this place are important for historians of Indian architecture. *Epigraphia Carnatica* VIII, Nagar 35, 45, 47, 58-60; *Jaina Śilālekha Saṃgraha* II, Cos. 132, 212-16, 226; III, No. 326, 667.

Hunasi-Hadagali: Eight miles to the west of the town of Gulabarga in Karnataka, it is the findspot of an inscription of the time of Vikramāditya VI, dated in Cālukya Vikrama Year 23 (AD 1097-8) which mentions two temples of Śāntinātha and Pārśvanātha situated therein. One Rakkasayya, a feudatory and disciple of Bālacandra described as 19th in the spiritual descent from Kundakunda, is the donor in the epigraph. It also contains an incorrect list from Kundakunda (spelt as Kondakunda) to Bālacandra.

Hūnasikaṭṭi: Site of a Jain temple called Māṇikya-deva-basadi in Belgaum district, Karnataka, which is mentioned in an inscription of AD 1130 during the reign of Someśvara III. The temple is dedicated to Pārśvanātha. *Jaina Śilālekha Saṃgraha* II, No. 292.

Hungund: Jain centre in Bijapur district, formerly known as Ponnugunda. One inscription from this place of AD 1074 of the time of the Western Cālukya Someśvara II refers to Arasara-basadi, a Jain temple. The other belonging to the time of Vikramāditya VI refers to a Jain temple built by one Bāhubali Ācārya, belonging to Mūla-saṅgha, Deśīya-gaṇa and Pustaka-gaccha. *South Indian Inscriptions* XI, III, 141; *Jaina Śilālekha Saṃgraha* IV, Nos. 158, 171.

I

Iconography: Although a few references to images and shrines of Arhats are found in the Aṅga texts *Nāyādhammakahāo*, *Uvāsagadasāo*, and *Bhagavatī*, the earliest dated evidence laying down standards for a Tīrthaṃkara image so far known is supplied by the *Bṛhatsaṃhitā*. The torso and legs of a Tīrthaṃkara sculpture from Lohanipur (q.v.) near Patna show that during the Maurya age worship of Jina images had already come into vogue. Jain texts show in their classification of the Jain gods and goddesses that many of the subsidiary divinities were mere adaptations from the Brahmanic pantheon. The principal class of Jain divinities are the 24 Tīrthaṃkaras or Jinas characterized by their respective marks, Upāsakas and Śāsana-devatās. Subsidiary divinities are of four classes—Bhavanavāsin, Vyantara, Jyotiṣka, and Vaimānika—divided on the basis of their natural and individual affiliation. Hindu deities such as Śrī-Lakṣmī, Gaṇeśa, Kubera, etc., as also group of divinities such as the Navagrahas, Dikpālas, Śruta or Vidyādevīs, Mātṛkās, etc., also grace the Jain pantheon.

Canons of Jain iconography seem to have come into existence about the beginning of the Christian era when the Mathura images were produced. Early Jina images are all nude. The *Mānasāra*, assigned to the sixth century AD, supplies important information on Jina images (q.v.). More details are found in Vasunandī Siddhāntikā's *Pratiṣṭhāsārasaṃgraha* and Āśādhara's *Pratiṣṭhāsāroddhāra*, both the texts having Digambara affiliation. Different Tīrth-aṃkaras are identified with the help of *lāñchanas* (qq.v.) carved on or below their seats. Images of the Tīrthaṃkaras were made of various articles and the rules for selecting them have been laid down in the *Ācāra Dinakara*. Vasunandī in his *Śrāvakācāra* says that images of the Jinas, Siddhas, Ācāryas, and others should be made according to the iconographic formulae, the materials used, etc. Vasubindu in his *Pratiṣṭhāpāṭha* has also dealt with the materials with which the image is to be made. It is said that defective images should not be installed. The *Ācāra-Dinakara* prohibits the worship of images less than 12 *aṅgulas* high in public shrines. From the *Āgama* texts it is possible to obtain a fairly early conception of the Jina image from the stock descriptions of *śāsvata-jinapratimās*. Traditions of the Śvetāmbaras and Digambaras refer to Siddhāyatanas containing images of the Tīrth-aṃkaras known as Śāsvata Jinas. The images of the Jinas are characterized by their long hanging arms, the *śrīvatsa* symbol, the youthful body and nudity.

According to the Śvetāmbara canon, the Jina images are partially clad. The Yakṣas and Yakṣiṇīs are shown to the right and left of their respective Jinas, sometime depicted beneath their particular *bodhi* trees. Several of the other *pratihāryas* or marks are occasionally carved on the *prabhāvalī*. It is said that at the back of the Jina images there should be figures of umbrella-bearers, on each side of the main image two figures of fly-whisk-bearers, in front a pair of Nāga and Yakṣa figures, one on each side, besides various articles. From such Agamic descriptions the *aṣṭa-mahāpratihāryas* (q.v.) prescribed for Jina images by both Śvetāmbara and Digambara *pratiṣṭhā* texts of the medieval period may be anticipated. It should be pointed out that in the case of Mathura Jina images we find on each side an attendant *chowri*-bearer or a Nāga figure with folded hands, and occasionally a garland bearer at the top and an umbrella above the head. But there is no *lāñchana*, nor the figures of Śāsanadevatās (q.v.), the attendant Yakṣas and Yakṣīs. The text describing the Śāsvata Jinas do not refer to their garments. According to the *Aupapātika* description of Mahāvīra's body, his height was 7 cubits. The front of his head is attractive, hair dark, thick, and curly, scalp smooth like gold, the head shaped like an umbrella, his forehead clear and his face perfect, ears proportionate, nose long, straight and uplifted, lower lip red, rows of teeth white, unbroken and smooth, beard and moustache well-dressed, chin well-set, shoulder broad and rounded, palms soft, red and endowed with auspicious marks, showing emblems of sun, moon, conch, *cakra*, *svastika*, etc., chest broad with a *śrīvatsa* mark, sides well-developed and symmetrical, hair on the body measured and charming, abdomen excellent, navel deep and spiral and the soles of his feet soft and red, showing auspicious marks. It is said that brilliant like a glowing fire, Mahāvīra possessed all the one thousand and eight marks of the best of human beings. These bodily marks were standardized into the *mahāpuruṣa-lakṣaṇas*. The Tīrthaṃkaras have certain extra-ordinary qualities which are known as *atiśayas*. They include the group of eight *mahā-pratihāryas* well known as the *parikara* of the Jina image, the Yakṣas and Yakṣiṇīs, when they are separately represented can be distinguished not only by their individual attributes and emblems, but also by the miniature figures of their respective Jinas either on their crown or on the topmost part of the stele. The iconography of many of these subsidiary divinities also differs according to their affiliation to one or other of the major Jain sects. Apart from the Jain Purāṇas, Āgama Texts, *stotra* literature and specific iconographical texts, non-Jain works on *Śilpa-śāstras* also throw welcome light on Jain iconography. See Cognizances, Jina Images, Sculpture, Śāsanadevatās, Yakṣas, Yakṣiṇīs.

Idar: Jain centre in Sabarkantha district of Gujarat which is referred to in Jinapati's *Tīrthamālā*. Jain authors like Munisundara, Somasundara, Śrutasāgara, etc., flourished in this holy place which was associated with Śāntinātha and contained a temple of Ādīśvara.

Idar Manuscript: Palm-leaf manuscript containing thirty-four miniatures illustrating the *Kalpasūtra* which is in the collection of Anandji Mangalji in Pedhina Jñān Bhāṇḍār at Idar.

Idol Worship: See Image Worship.

Ilango-Adigaḷ: Author of the Tamil epic *Silappadikaram*, composed about the second century AD. He was a Cera prince who renounced his claims to the Cera throne and took to asceticism. In all probability he became a Jain monk and retired to Guṇavāyirkoṭṭam.

Image Worship: Apart from the Tāranapanthis among the Digambaras, and the Sthānakavāsīs among the Śvetāmbaras, most Jains are image worshippers. The Digambara and Śvetāmbara images differ in certain respects. Images are either standing or seated, postures being *kāyotsarga* and *padmāsana*. The seated image has its feet close to each other, the hands left straight down and the half-closed eyes pointed to the end of the nose. In contrast with the simple nude, unadorned Digambara images, the Śvetāmbara are often adorned with golden ornaments and jewels and are represented as wearing a loin cloth. The images of the Tīrthaṃkaras are practically of the same type and can be identified only with the help of their respective emblems. Image worship is conducted through eight processes known as *jala-pūjā*, bathing the image with water; *candana-pūjā*, marking or sprinkling the idol with sandal-wood-paste and saffron or turmeric; *puṣpa-pūjā*, offering flowers before the image or garlanding it; *dhūpa-pūjā*, burning incense sticks before the image; *dīpa-pūjā*, waving of a light near the image; *akṣata-pūjā*, offering rice in front of the image; *naivedya-pūjā*, offering sweetmeats before it; and *phala-pūjā*, offering of fruits before the image. The idol worshippers are known as *mandiramārgīs* (q.v.).

Indirakula-Gṛha: Temple in Sravanabelgola, Hassan district, which was caused to be erected by Gaṅgarāya around AD 1117. It is so called due to a record which is set up near its entrance.

Indra: Chief of the Vedic gods regarded as the guardian of the eastern quarter in Jainism who, however, retains his Vedic characteristics. His elephant is Airāvata and *vajra* or thunderbolt is his chief weapon. His wife is Sacī. Often he is described as possessed of one thousand eyes.

Indrābhiṣeka: Consecration as an Indra by Gods as a result of ascetic merit.

Indrabhūti Gautama: Direct disciple of Mahāvīra (q.v.) who, after his master's death became the spiritual leader of the Jain church for twelve years though, according to a different tradition having become a *kevalin* he never held office. In the *Uttarādhyayana* XXIII there is a conversation between Keśin, a follower of Pārśva's church, and Indrabhūti on doctrinal matters. Indrabhūti was a Brāhmaṇa and Gautama (Prakrit Goyama) was his *gotra* surname. His two brothers, Agnibhūti and Vāyubhūti, were also eminent Jain leaders. It was Indrabhūti who learnt directly from Mahāvīra that the latter was originally conceived in the womb of the Brāhmaṇa woman Devanandā. In the *Kalpasūtra* it is said that just before Mahāvīra's death on the early morning emerging from the dark fortnight of Kārttika when the moon was in conjunction with the *Svāti* star Indrabhūti obtained *kevala* knowledge. At Nalanda Indrabhūti had doctrinal conversation with Udaka Pedhalaputta, from which we learn that some of the followers of Indrabhūti were known as Kumāraputras. In the *Bhagavatī* it is said Indrabhūti received major instructions from Mahāvīra in the Guṇaśila shrine which was situated near Rājagṛha.

Indragiri: Hill in Sravanabelgola on which the colossus figure of Gommaṭeśvara (q.v.) has been fashioned.

Indradinna: Also known as Indradatta. He headed the Jain church after Susthita (q.v.). In his time the celebrated Kālakācārya flourished. It was in the second century BC. See Suhastin.

Indramaha: Festival celebrated according to the *Niśītha Cūrṇi* on the full moon day of Āṣāḍha (June-July). The festival is said to have celebrated by King Durmukha in Kāmpilyapura with raised flagstaff, amidst the beating of auspicious musical instruments. In this festival there was dancing, poetic recitation, demonstrations by jugglers, and rejoicing. This festival was celebrated in the country of Lāṭa (Saurashtra) on the full moon day of Śrāvaṇa and in Mahārāṣṭra on the fifth day of Bhādrapada. Elsewhere the festival of Indra was celebrated after the rainy season. Indra's banner was specially erected in the city of Mahāpura. The festival was also celebrated in Dvārakā and Hemapura. Hundreds of town-girls are said to have gathered around the banner erected in honour of Indra, carrying oblations. During the Indra festival people spent their time eating, drinking, singing, dancing, merry-making, and visiting friends.

Indra Maṇḍapa: One of the temples at Śatruñjaya (q.v.).

Indranandin: Teacher of the celebrated Nemicandra (q.v.) of the tenth century who was a Digambara scholar and author of the *Śrautāvatāra* in which facts relating to the commentaries on the important philosophical treatises have been supplied. For example, he has ascribed the *Ṣaṭkhaṇḍāgamaṭīkā* (q.v.) which has been repeatedly mentioned by Vīrasena in his *Dhavalā* (q.v.), to Kundakunda. A number of earlier commentaries on this text were mentioned by him, but none of these has survived. He has also referred to two commentaries on the *Kaṣāyaprābhṛta* (q.v.) which were composed before the monumental *Jayadhavalā* (q.v.) by Vīrasena and Jinasena.

Indras: Priests who are Brāhmaṇas. Among the southern Jains, Indras, Bogāras, Pañcamas, and Caturthas are equated respectively with the traditional four *varṇas*. The members of the first caste call themselves Jain Brāhmaṇas. They study Jain scriptures and become Arcakas (q.v.) or priests. They are styled Indras. They are hereditary, have a family life, live on offerings made to deities and income from their teaching, perform the function of astronomers and astrologers, and form an intermediate class between Yatis or ascetics and the Śrāvakas or laymen. They may eat with lay persons but cannot have intermarriage with them. If they fail to get suitable brides for their sons they pay a bride-price.

Indra Sabhā: Cave No. 32 of Ellora which is an elaborate excavation in the Jain series. It is the earliest of the group, double storeyed and south-facing. In front of the main two-storeyed cave is a courtyard containing a monolithic *vimāna* with an elephant to its east. The lateral walls of the entrenched open court have two smaller excavations containing sculptures of the Tīrthaṃkaras, gods and Yakṣas. The lower storey of the main excavation is unfinished. It has a front verandah with four pillars and four pilasters of the square type. One of them has a nude Tīrthaṃkara. The upper storey consists of a central hall, with two additional sanctuaries thrown forward of each wing with the balconies of all the three overlooking an open-entrenched court. The hall proper has twelve pillars of four different types. The principal shrine is dedicated to Mahāvīra. Spaces are dedicated to other Tīrthaṃkara images, but those of Sumatinātha have received special preference.

Indratyāga: Abandoning the pleasures of heaven for a higher purpose.

Indropapada: Receiving the status of Indra after death by virtue of merit.

Inference: See Anumāna.

Ingalgai: Findspot of an inscription in Chitapur taluk, Gulbarga district, Karnataka, dated Cālukya-Vikrama year 18 (AD 1094), which mentions Jākaladevī, one of the queens of Vikramāditya VI Tribhuvanamalla, who was a devout Jain and under the inspiration of the king himself constructed a magnificent Jain temple of Mahamāṇikyadeva, i.e. Mahāvīra, at Inguṇije, the present site of the epigraph, and asked her family teacher Indrasena Bhaṭṭāraka of Mālanura-*amnāya* (Drāviḍa-saṅgha Sena-gaṇa), the disciple of Mallasena Bhaṭṭāraka, to took after its maintenance. *Jaina Śilālekha Saṃgraha* V, No. 58.

Iṅgaleśvara: Jain centre after which the Iṅgaleśvara-bali of the Mūla-saṅgha and Pustaka-gaccha was named. It is in Bijapur district, Karnataka.

Inter-Caste Marriages: Through *savarṇa* marriage in which the partners belong to the same caste, is preferred to *asavarṇa*, marriage in which the partners belong to different castes, there are many instances of the latter system in Jain literature such as those of Gajakumāra and Somā, Guṇavatī and Dhanyakumāra, Teyaliputta, Gayasukumāla, Jayasattu, Bambhadatta, etc. Of the two categories of *asavarṇa* marriage the *anuloma*, in which the bridegroom is of higher caste than the bride was preferred to *pratiloma* in which the caste of the bride is higher than that of bridegroom. There are instances when non-Jains were considered suitable for marriage purposes. In ancient times marriages were contracted by Jains with non-Aryans and Mlecchas or foreigners. Examples are Vasudeva, Upaśreṇika, Candragupta, Bharata, Śālibhadra, Jinadatta, etc. Any suitable girl from any position was welcome. The wives of Cārudatta, Cārucandra, Nāga-kumāra, Vasudeva and many other eminent Jains of the past came from the families of prostitutes. Later, new rules were formed to suit changing conditions. In the first place, though the *asavarṇa* marriage was allowed, the *pratiloma* system, i.e. marriage in descending order, was discarded. In Jinasena's *Ādi Purāṇa* XVI. 247 it is said that a Brāhmaṇa can have wives from all the four *varṇas*, the Kṣatriya from three, the Vaiśya from two and the Śūdra from one, i.e. a woman of his own *varṇa*. Even this freedom in *anuloma* order was not allowed for a long time. With the rise of the endogamous professional castes the sphere became much more limited. There are several *gotras* (q.v.) or exogamous groups within an endogamous caste and people have to select their marriage partners from outside the exogamous group. This is the present situation. Inter-religious marriage, but within the same caste, is, however, allowed.

Irryā: See Caritra.

Isaṇa: See Caritra.

Īśāna: Guardian deity of the north-east quarters, he is described in the Jain texts as riding a bull, joined by Umā and holding a bow and a trident. He also wears matted hair and snakes on his person. He is no other than the Brahmanical Śiva who has been directly imported into the Jain pantheon.

Isibhāsiyāim: See Prakīrṇa.

***Isimaṇḍala-Stotra*:** See Dharmaghoṣa.

Island-Continents: Constituents of the earth-disc according to the Jain conception. These are Jambbūdvīpa, Dhātakī, Puṣkara, Vāruṇivara, Kṣīravara, Ghṛtavara and Kṣudravara. These are surrounded respectively by seven oceans known as Lavaṇoda, Kāloda, Puṣkaroda, Varuṇyoda, Kṣīroda, Ghṛtoda, and Kṣaudroda. It appears that originally the Jain authors thought of seven island continents in accordance with Hindu Puranic cosmography but their number increased later. The *Tiloyapannattī* V.11-16 speaks of 16 inner and 16 outer islands forming the earth and each of them has an ocean beyond it. Besides the seven continents mentioned above, the said text refers to the following: Nandīśvara, Aruṇavara, Aruṇabhāsa, Kuṇḍalavara, Śaṅkha-vara, Rucakavara, Bhujagavara, Kusavara, and Krauñcavara. The last two names are borrowed from the Puranic lists. The 16 outer islands are Manaḥśīla, Haritāla, Sindūra, Śyāma, Añjanavara, Hiṅgula, Rūpya, Kāñcanaka, Vajravara, Vaidūrya, Nāgavara, Bhūtavara, Yakṣavara, Devavara, Ahindravara, and Svayambhūramaṇa. In later Jain works more names were artificially added by suffixing *vara* and *varāvabhāsa* to Aruna Kundala, Śaṅkha, Rucaka, Hara, Kaṇakavali, Ratnāvali, Muktāvali, Ajina, Sūrya, etc.

***Iṣṭopadeśa*:** A didactic poem by Pūjyapāda (q.v.) ed. in Manikacandra Digambara Jain Granthamala, No. 13 with Āśādhara's (q.v.) commentary, Eng. trans. by C.R. Jain, Hardoi, 1925.

Isur: Findspot of an inscription in Shimoga district, Karnataka, of the time of Western Cālukya Vikramāditya VI which mentions the construction of a Jain temple and a grant by Bineya Bammi Setti. *Epigraphia Carnatica*, VII, Shik. No. 8.

Īśvara-Yakṣa: Attendant Yakṣa of Śreyāṃsanātha (q.v.) who has a bull vehicle, three eyes, and four hands. The Digambara canon places on his hands the attributes of trident, staff, rosary, and fruit. The Śvetāmbara icon of the same Yakṣa holds a mongoose, rosary, staff, and fruit. An independent image of this Yakṣa is in the Indian Museum. This Yakṣa represents a borrowed form of the Brahmanic Śiva or Īśvara.

J

Jabalpur: Findspot of a number of Jain images dating from *c.* ninth to eleventh centuries. Of these, a seated image of Jina Dharmanātha, with an elaborate *parikara*, is now in the Central Museum, Nagpur.

Jagadekamalla Jinālaya: Jina temple named after the illustrious Western Cālukya monarch Jayasiṃha II (AD 1015-43) whose title was Jagadekamalla. This information has been obtained from an inscription from Maski in Raichur district, Karnataka. *Jaina Śilālekha Saṃgraha* IV, No. 251.

Jagaḍu: A wealthy merchant and Jain layman whose pious activities have been told in a fourteenth-century work, *Jagaḍucarita*. His achievements are also related in another fourteenth-century work called the *Upadeśataraṅgiṇī*, composed by Ratnamandira. His centre of pious activities was at Bhadreśvara in Kutch where he built a temple containing 24 images of the Tīrthaṃkaras, gave a gold covering for the image of Pārśvanātha, adorned the temple of Vīranātha with a golden knob and a gold staff, repaired the tanks built by King Kumārapāla and Mūlarāja, made a garden for supplying flowers, built a Pauṣadhaśālā and a mosque for the Muslims. At Vardhamāna, modern Wadhawan in Saurashtra, Jagaḍu built two Jain temples and made three pilgrimages to Girnar and Śatruñjaya.

***Jagaḍucarita*:** An historical work written towards the close of the thirteenth century by Sarvānandasūri, pupil of Dhanaprabhasūri, in 338 verses which contains valuable details regarding the history of Gujarat, ed. M.D. Khakkar, Bombay, 1896.

Jagannātha-Sabhā: Constituent of Jain Ellora (q.v.) is essentially similar to the Indra-Sabhā (q.v.) but lacks the regularity of plan. The ground floor is a complex of three asymmetrically disposed sanctuaries, each a complete unit. Access to the upper floor is provided through a passage cut through the south-east corner of the upper shrine on the lateral wall of the adjoining Indra-sabhā complex. The upper floor has a *nava-raṅga* hall with twelve massive pillars—central four and peripheral eight—some with square bases and *kalaśa* capitals. The shrine at the rear has an ornate entrance, flanked by a Jina with Kubera and Ambikā. The lateral walls contain reliefs of other Tīrthaṃkaras, and there are also relics of ancient paintings on the ceiling of the hall.

Jagat: Site for the Ambikā temple at Udaipur, Rajasthan.

Jagatsāgar: A tank near Mau in Chatarpur district, which has yielded some images of granite with inscriptions on their pedestals. Particular interest attaches to a Śāntinātha image standing in *kāyotsarga* with *śrīvatsa* in the chest. It has on its pedestal a four-line inscription dated *saṃvat* 1203 stating that is was installed by Devasvāmin of Golapūrva-*kula* and his sons. It was regularly worshipped by Lakṣmīdhara of the Dumbara family. It is in the State Museum, Dhubela Palace.

Jaina Mahārāṣṭrī: The language of the Śvetāmbara Jain canon was Ardhamāgadhī (q.v.), but there is no uniformity or homogeneity in the dialect. Since in many cases it is closer to the Mahārāṣṭrī, some scholars like to designate it as Jaina Mahārāṣṭrī. It is not pure Mahārāṣṭrī, but later it came under the influence of south-western Mahārāṣṭrī. The most important texts of the Jaina Mahārāṣṭrī comprise the non-canonical commentarial literature including the Āvaśyaka legends and the stories narrated by Devendragaṇi in his *Uttarādhyayana* commentary. At the time of the composition of *Vasudevahiṇḍi* (q.v.) Jaina Mahārāṣṭrī, separated from Ardhamāgadhī, was taking the shape of a distinct dialect about the third century AD. It continued in use as late as about the fourteenth century AD.

***Jainendrayajñavidhi*:** See *Śrutasāgara*.

Jaisalmer: District with principal town of the same name western Rajasthan which became an important Jain centre owing to the organizing ability of the Kharatara Ācārya Jinapati. The Pārśvanātha temple of Jaisalmer was constructed by Jagaddhara before AD 1218. During the reign of Lakṣmaṇa in the early fifteenth century this temple was rebuilt. During the reign of Lakṣmaṇa's son and successor Vairasiṃha the temple of Sambhavanātha was constructed here in AD 1437. The Kharatara Ācārya Jinabhadra, whose name occurs in numerous inscriptions of Gujarat, Rajasthan and other parts of northern India, installed 300 images in this temple. Subsequent kings, Cacigadeva, Devakarṇa, Jaitrasiṃha, Umākarṇa, Jaitrasiṃha II, Bhīmasena, etc., were patrons of Jainism. The temples of Śāntinātha, Candraprabha, Śītalanātha,

Ṛṣabhanātha, and Mahāvīra were built here in the fifteenth century. The epigraphs of this place have been edited by P.C. Nahar in his third volume of *Jaina Inscriptions*, Calcutta 1929.

Jakhin: Ghosts of women who die with unfulfilled wishes. They plague the living by attacking children with diseases. In many cases Jain parents make to the Jakhin a vow that if the child recovers from sickness, they will offer worship to her.

Jakhoda: Site of a fourteenth-century Śāntinātha temple in Pali district, Rajasthan, mentioned in Megha's *Tīrthamālā*.

Jalayātrā: See Siddhacakra Pūjā.

Jalolli: Findspot of a Jain inscription of AD 1545 in North Kanara district, Karnataka, which mentions a temple of Pārśvanātha. *Jaina Śilālekha Saṃgraha* V, No. 240.

Jalor Inscriptions: Ancient Jāvālipur in Rajasthan wherefrom some important Jain inscriptions are found. One stone inscription of AD 1163 of the Cālukya King Kumārapāla of Gujarat refers to the building of a Jain vihāra containing an image of Pārśvanātha at the request of Prabhu Hemasūri, that is Hemacandra, on the fort of Kāñcanagiri belonging to Jāvālipur. One inscription of Cāhamāna Samarasiṃha of AD 1182 opens with an invocation to Nābheya or Ṛṣabhanātha, the pupil of Candrasūri, the founder of Candragaccha and the erection of *maṇḍapa* by Yaśovīra, a merchant of the Jain Śrīmāla family. The second epigraph which has four dates says that the temple of Pārśvanātha on Kāñcanagiri which was originally built by Kumārapāla was rebuilt by Yaśovīra on the orders of Mahārāja Samarasiṃha. The next important inscription is a record of the reign of King Cāciga of AD 1224 which refers to a gift given by Mahottara Narapati to the well-known Candra-vihāra of Jāvālipur. Another inscription mentions the temple of Pārśvanātha on the Suvarṇagiri, the same as the one mentioned above, which received some grant from a chief during the reign of Sāmantasiṃha of this dynasty. *Epigraphia Indica* XI.54ff; P.P. Nahar, *Jaina Lekha Saṃgraha*, I.240, Nos. 902-3.

Jamāli: Son-in-law of Mahāvīra according to late commentaries such as the *Āvaśyakacūrṇi* and *Kalpasūtravṛtti* of Dharmasāgara. He was born in a rich Kṣatriya family, and having passed a few happy years of married life under the influence of his illustrious father-in-law, renounced the world and joined the creed. The Digambaras do not count him as Mahāvīra's son-in-law because they hold that the Master never married. But like Devadatta of the Buddhist texts, Jamāli was a born rebel. He publicly announced his difference with his teacher and founded his own sect at Śrāvastī. From the *Bhagavatīsūtra* it is learnt that from the very beginning Jamāli behaved as a rival of Mahāvīra and started wandering with his followers to different places, much against Mahāvīra's wish. Afterwards there developed further doctrinal differences between the two and Jamāli declared himself a Jina at Śrāvastī. He, along with his disciples, stayed in the Koṣṭhaka shrine of that town. When Mahāvīra was staying in the Pūrṇabhadra shrine at Campā he had occasion to meet Jamāli, and defeated him publicly in a debate. Even after this Jamali continued to defy Mahāvīra's authority till his death. According to the Jain texts *Sthānāṅga* 587, *Āvaśyakaniryukti* 780, etc. Jamāli was the first *ninhava* or propounder of wrong doctrines.

Jamaṇapura: Site of a Candraprabha temple in the Mehsana district of Gujarat.

Jambūdvīpa: Central continent which, according to the Jain tradition, covers half the continental ring. Its diameter is 100,000 *yojanas*. It is surrounded by some sort of wall, 8 *yojanas* in height, built with stone slabs each 1/2 *yojanas* in height and 506 *dhaṇus* in breadth. The base is made of diamond, the support of *riṣṭa*, the beams of gold bars and the bolts of rubies. The wall has four gates—Vijaya, Vaijayanta, Jayanta, and Aparājita. Jambūdvīpa is divided by six mountains, called *varṣa-parvata* or *kula-parvata*, and known by the names of Himavat, Śikharin, Mahāhimavat, Rukmin, Niṣadha, and Nīla. Each range has a number of peaks. Every mountain had at its first or eastern summit a temple known as Siddhāyatana or Siddhakūṭa and in the middle a vast lake. That which lies in the middle of the Himavat is known as Pauma or Padma. Jambūdvīpa is watered by 14 big rivers. Among these the Gaṅgā, Sindhu and Rohita flow from the aforesaid Padma lake on mount Himavat; the Rohitāṃśā and the Harikrāntā from the Mahāpadma lake on the Mahāhimavat; the Haritā and Sitodā from the Tiṅgiccha lake on the Niṣadha; the Sitā and Nārī from the Kesarin lake on the Nīla; the Narakāntā and Rupyakulā from the Mahāpuṇḍarīka lake on the Rukmin; and the Suvarṇa Kulā, Raktā and Raktodā from the Puṇḍarīka lake on the Śikharin. The Jain writers who apparently depended on the Puranic conception of Jambudvīpa held that it was divided into seven *varṣas* which were Bharata, Airāvata, Haimavata, Hari, Hiraṇyavata, Ramyaka and Videha. Airāvata which is watered by Raktā and

Raktodā, stands next to Bharata. Haimavata, is watered by Rohitā and Rohitāmrā, lies to the north of Himavat. Its central mountain is Śabdapati. Hairaṇyavata, the central mountain of which is Malayavat and which watered by Suvarṇakulā and Rupyakulā, lies to the south of Śikharin. Harivarṣa also contains a mountain called Vikaṭapati and it is watered by Haritā and Harikrānatā. Ramyaka contains the Gandhapati mountain and is watered by the Narakāntā and Nārī. The middle and biggest *varṣa* is Videha, at the centre of which stands Mount Meru or Mandara, which has sixteen names. To the north of Meru, between the Gandhamādana and Malayavat is the Uttarakuru country and to the south, between the Saumanasa and Vidyutprabha, is Devakuru. To the east of Meru lies Pūrva Videha and to the west Apara-Videha. These four divisions contain a number of provinces, each having a town, a number of mountains and a few rivers. Bhāratavarṣa or India proper lies to the south of Himavat.

***Jambuddiva-Pannatti*:** See Jambūdvīpaprajñapti.

***Jambūdvīparajñapti*:** Prakrit *Jambuddiva-Pannatti*, the sixth text of the Upāṅga (q.v.) category, which is the description of Jambūdvīpa, the central continent. It is the mythical geography of the Jains in which the description of Bhāratavarṣa and the legends of King Bharata occupy much space. Ed. with Śānticandra's com. in Devchand Lalbhai Jaina Pustakoddhara, Bombay, 1920.

Jambunada: See Apraticakrā.

***Jambusvāmī-Cariya*:** Gujarati composition by Dharma in AD 1210 which deals with life-story of Jambusvāmī, the third pontiff of the church established by Mahāvīra.

Jambusvāmin: The third *gaṇadhara* (q.v.) of the Jain church, his predecessors being Sudharman and Indrabhūti Gautama (qq.v.). He led the community for 24 years. He was the last of the *kevalins*, for after him both *mokṣa* and omniscience were closed to men. Besides the *Āvaśyaka Sūtra* and its commentarial literature, there is a hymn in Prakrit stanzas in Jambusvāmin's praise. This is Dharmaghoṣa's *Isimaṇḍala* or *Ṛṣimaṅgala-stotra*. Jambusvāmin attained *mokṣa* according to one reckoning in 403 BC, but it should be remembered that dates given for events in the history of Jainism are only approximations.

Jananāthapuram: Jain site in Thanjavur district.

Jāṅgalu: Village in the Bikaner district, Rajasthan. Inscription found from this place indicate that in the twelfth century it was a Jain centre containing temples of Mahāvīra and others.

***Janma*:** Birth ceremony of a child which is in itself a sacrament to be felicitated with the presence of the preceptor and astrologer for preparing the horoscope. It is the Śvetāmbara pattern.

Janna: Kannaḍa author who wrote a Purāṇa on the 14th Tīrthaṃkara and also the tragically rich poem *Yaśodhara-caritra*.

***Jasahara-Cariu*:** Sanskritized name *Yaśodhara Carita*, an Apabhraṃśa poem of high merit written in four Sandhis by Puṣpadanta (q.v.) of the tenth century. The story of Yaśodhara was a favourite theme of the Jain poets. Somadeva, Vādirāja, and others have written on it, ed. P.L.Vaidya, Karanja 1931.

Jati: Caste. Though theoretically opposed to social divisions and inequality, the Jains had to acknowledge the functional caste system of India which has the following characteristics. Every caste had a special caste-profession; is endogamous; is autonomous and guided by its own social laws and customs; has a specific status—high, middle or low—in the social hierarchy, with exclusive rights and privileges of its own. Regarding the Jain caste system the following observation of V.A. Sangave is instructive. In the first place the exact number of Jain castes is not available, though the traditional number is 84. Secondly, apart from the exclusive Jain castes, that is, castes in which all members are Jains, there are Jain sections or divisions in several Hindu castes. These are mainly occupational castes, some members of which happen to follow the Jain religion and as such they form into distinct groups or sub-castes in those castes. Third, excepting a few castes like Osavāla, Śrīmālī, Agravāla, Khaṇḍelvāla, Saitavāla, Paravāra, Caturtha, and Pañcama, all other Jain castes have a meagre strength. Fourth, along with the decline of Jain population, we find the assimilation of one caste into another. Fifth, only a few Jain castes like Osavāla, Poravāda, Humbaḍa, Narasiṃgapura, and Nemā are common to both the Digambaras and the Śvetāmbaras.

There are as many as 87 castes and subcastes recorded among the Digambaras and 38 among the Śvetāmbaras. Sixth, there are different places where different Jain castes have been concentrated. Thus Śrīmālīs are found mainly in Gujarat and Kathiawar, Osavāla in Gujarat and Marwar, Khaṇḍelavālas in Marwar and Malwa, Agravāla in Uttar Pradesh and Delhi, Humbaḍas in Marwar, Paravāras in Bundelkhand, Saitavāla in Madhya Pradesh, and Caturthas and Pañcamas in Karnataka.

Not all Jain castes follow the same rules or social norms. While the Jain castes of the north do not allow widow remarriage, some of those of the Deccan do, and have practised it. There are different rules and regulations for each caste regarding birth, marriage, death and other ceremonies. No overall order of social precedence like that claimed by Hindu Brahmaṇas is found among the Jains, despite the existence of Jain Brāhmaṇas. Again, in some castes like Śrīmālīs, Poravāḍas, Humbaḍas and others there are subdivisions like Viśā, Daśā, Pañca, and Adhica and these are treated in a descending order of social respectability. Among the six castes of Terapanthīs, the Charanāgare caste is considered more respectable than others. In the Deccan the Śrāvagis are regarded as superior in rank to the Poravāḍas because of the great regard the former entertain for animal life. Among the Lamechū caste members there are two divisions—*ūñcā* and *nīcā*—high and low. In Karnataka the Caturthas and the Pañcamas look upon Tagara-Bogaras as inferior. Originally there was no restriction in relation to inter-dining and other forms of social intercourse among the Jain castes, but later restrictions were introduced.

In spite of the fact that Jainism allows any person to follow the religion and observe its religious practices, in reality we find that many have been debarred form certain rites. In some castes which are divided into Viśās and Daśās, at certain places the latter are not allowed even at present to perform worship in the temples. Along with civil and religious restrictions there were restrictions on the choice of occupations. The occupations were considered hereditary and it was not proper for a person to abandon one in favour of another. Among Daśā Śrīmālīs there is a division by name Caṇāpahua which suggests that its members might be following in the past the occupation of selling grains and parched rice. Moreover, there are a few castes among the Śvetāmbaras which are known after their occupation, viz., Kaṇḍvi (sweetmeat seller), Sutāra (carpenter), Darji (tailor), Moḍha-ghāñci (oil-crusher), Kachia (vegetable dealer), etc. In some cases, however, castes were named after places of their origin. Śrīmālīs were so called because they came from Śrīmāla; Osavālas from Osia, Agravālas from Agroha, Khaṇḍelvālas from Khandela., etc. One of the important restrictions observed by members of a caste is regarding the extent to which the members are allowed to contract their matrimonial alliances. For this purpose, a caste is generally divided into smaller groups known as subcastes and members are enjoined to choose their partners from their own subcastes. The Jain castes in the Deccan differ in many respects from those in the north. In the first place, there are only four main castes in the Deccan, namely Saitavāla, Caturtha, Pañcama, and Bogara and three small castes, namely Upādhyāya, Kāmbhoja, and Harada. Secondly many castes in the north have their counterparts in other non-Jain communities. But this is not the case in the south. Third, while in the north, in some Jain castes Digambara and Śvetāmbara divisions are found, in the south there is no such division. While a large number of northern castes are divided into Viśās and Daśās and sometimes further into Pañcās and Aḍhāiyās, in the south there are no such divisions. Jain castes in the south have their own Jain priests, and they do not employ Hindu Brāhmaṇas as priests as is done by the northerners. Each of the four castes in the Deccan has its own Bhaṭṭāraka as religious head or Svāmī who has even the final power to fine or excommunicate any caste member. This system is absent in the north.

Jaṭṭappa Nāyakana Candranātheśvara-basti: See Bhatkal.

Jāvālipura: Same as Jalor (q.v.) in Rajasthan which yielded many Jain inscriptions as also was the venue of temples dedicated to various Tīrthaṃkaras.

Javāri: Temple at Khajuraho.

Jayacandra: Jain teacher belonging to the Tapāgaccha, whose name occurs in the fifteenth-century image inscriptions from Gujarat and Rajasthan. *Jainadhātupratimālekhasaṃgraha* II, Nos. 3, 53, 103, 358, 510, 629, 655, 731, 479.

***Jayadhavalā*:** Commentary on the *Kaṣāyaprābhṛta* or *Kaṣāyapāhuḍa* (q.v.) of Guṇadharācārya composed by Vīrasena and his disciple Jinasena. It is a bulky work, the first 20,000 *ślokas* of which were composed by Vīrasena. It was afterwards completed in 60,000 *ślokas* by Jinasena. This great commentary was written in the ninth century in Saurasenī Prakrit. During the tenth century its subject-matter was compressed by Nemicandra Siddhāntacakravartin in his *Gommaṭasāra* (Jīvakāṇḍa and Karmakāṇḍa), The *Labdhisāra* and the *Kṣapanasāra* in about 2,400 *gāthā* verses. Published in several volumes from Mathura 1944-63.

Jayadhīra Jinālaya: Jina temple constructed by Śaṅkaragaṇḍa, Rāṣṭrakūṭa governor of the tenth century, at Kopana mentioned in an inscription from Uppina-Betgiri in Raichur district, Karnataka. Jayadhīra was the title of the governor.

Jayakīrti: See *Silovaesamālā*.

***Jayantavijaya*:** See Anhayadeva.

Jayasiṃha: Śvetāmbara author of the ninth century who was the author of *Dharmopadeśamālā* on morals illustrated by 156 stories. There was a second Jayasiṃha who composed the drama *Hammīra-Madamardana* (q.v.) in the thirteenth century.

Jayasiṃha: See *Kumārbhūpālacarita*.

Jayasiṃha Siddharāja: Cālukya king of Gujarat who ruled for a period of nearly 50 years (AD 1092-1142) and was a great patron of Jainism. It is said that he set up golden knobs on the Jain temples out of deference for Maladhārin Hemacandra (q.v.). The great Jain philosopher Devasūri (q.v.) was also patronized by him. His patronage was extended to Abhayadeva Maladhārī, Vīrācārya, etc. Although Jayasiṃha was basically a Śaiva, he had a great respect for the religion of the Jainas. According to Hemacandra, Jayasiṃha built at Siddhapura a temple of Lord Mahāvīra. Hemacandra (q.v.) himself received his patronage. Probably in the last year of his reign Jayasiṃha visited the Jain *tīrthas* on Girnar and Śatruñjaya. He granted twelve villages for the maintenance of Ādinatha at Śatruñjaya.

***Jayatihuyana-Stotra*:** See Abhayadeva Sūri.

Jayatilaka: See *Malayasundarī-kathā*.

Jaya-Vijaya: Jain *gumphā*, cave No. 5, in Udayagiri near Bhubaneswar, Orissa.

Jaypur: Findspot of an eleventh-century Ṛṣabhanātha image in Purulia district, now in the Asutosh Museum, Calcutta University. It is made of standstone and was placed within a miniature *rekhā*-deul of Orissan type. The figure stands in *kāyotsarga* on a lotus seat upon a *pañcaratha* pedestal, flanked by two *chowri*-bearers. There are standing miniature Jinas on both sides in six pairs each. A twelfth-century Caumukha from this place is also in the Asutosh Museum. Its height is about 20 inches and is of *rekhā* variety and contains Jina figures on four sides among which Candraphabha and Mahāvīra can be recognized from their emblems. See also Garh Jaipur.

Jeśala Shah: Fourteenth-century exponent of Jainism in Gujarat. He belonged to Stambhatīrtha or Cambay and erected there in AD 1310 a temple dedicated to Ajitanātha and also a *pauṣadhaśālā*.

Jhagaḍiyā: A village in Broach district of Gujarat which has yielded many Jain icons of twelfth century.

Jhagaḍu: See Mātṛkā.

Jhājoli: Jain *tīrtha* in Sirohi district, Rajasthan, well-known for Ādīśvara temple wherefrom Jain epigraphs of the twelfth century have been discovered.

Jhalda: Findspot of a tenth-century Ṛṣabhanātha image in Purulia district which is now in the Asutosh Museum, Calcutta University. It resembles one from Jaypur (q.v.) in Purulia which is made of sandstone and placed within a miniature *rekhā*-deul of Orissan type, also in the same museum.

Jhalodi Inscription: See Candravati.

Jhālrāpatan: See Candravati.

Jhanjhana: Son of Pethaḍa (q.v.) and grandson of Dedā (q.v.), a wealthy Jain merchant of Gujarat whose ancestors came from Avantī and received favours from the Vaghela rulers. Like his father he was also the disciple of Dharmaghoṣasūri. He built several Jina temples and visited along with his teachers several Jain *tīrthas*. His meeting with the Vāghela King Sāraṅgadeva in AD 1282 is recorded in the *Upadeśataraṅgiṇī*.

Jholika Vihāra: Jain monastery constructed by King Kumārapāla in AD 1163 at Dhandhuka, the birthplace of his *guru*, Hemacandra.

Jina: One who is endowed with infinite knowledge, perception, power, and bliss, the omniscient Tīrthaṃkara (q.v.) symbolizing absolute perfection, after which name the Nirgrantha religion is often designated. A Jina is not a supernatural being nor an incarnation of an all powerful god. The term means 'conqueror'—one who has conquered worldly passions by one's own strenuous efforts, who has attained supreme knowledge, subjugated passions, and become free from all attachment. Human beings are entitled to become Jinas. The 24 Jinas who were responsible for the development of Jianism or Nirgrantha way of life were all human beings who had acquired omniscience and self-control by their own personal efforts.

Jinabhadra: Jain teacher belonging of the Kharatara-gaccha whose name occurs in image inscriptions of the fifteenth century including one dated VS 1505 and two dated VS 1509. *Jainadhātu-pratimālekhasaṃgraha*, II, Nos. 258, 495, 530, 589, 608, 739.

Jinacandra: Fourteenth-century exponent of Jainism in Gujarat and Rajasthan. He belonged to the Kharatara-gaccha and was the head of the Saṅgha from VS 1341 to 1376. He visited the Jain *tīrthas* of Rajasthan, Gujarat, Haryana, and other parts of north India when the Jain shrines were being systematically destroyed by the Muslim iconoclasts (*mlecchakaṭakakopa*). In this worst of times (*viṣamaduḥsamakāle*) he, with great effort, succeeded in obtaining a *farman* from Qutbuddin Mubarak Shah (AD 1316-20), Sultan of Delhi, to save a number of Jina establishments from annihilation.

Jinacandra Gaṇin: Author of Jain philosophical treatises who called himself Devagupta. In AD 1015 he wrote the *Navapaya* in Prakrit with a Sanskrit commentary. He was also the author of *Navatattvaprakaraṇa* which deals with the nine fundamentals of Jain metaphysics. It was commentary upon by Abhayadeva (q.v.) in AD 1063 and by Yaśodeva between AD 1108 and 1117. *Navatatta* ed. with both coms. in Atmananda Series, No. 10, Bhavnagar 1912.

Jinadatta Sūri: A pupil of Jinavallabha Sūri who flourished between AD 1075 and 1154 and wrote *Upadeśarasāyanarasa*, a didactic poem in the form of a dancing song in 80 verses, *Kāla-svarūpakulakam* a didactic poem in 32 rhymed verses in Apabhraṃśa, and a *Caccari (carcari)*, kind of dancing-song in praise of his teacher. All edited with a Sanskrit introduction by L.B. Gandhi; with commentaries in Gaekwad's Oriental Series, No. 37, Baroda, 1927. A *Gana-dharasārdhaśataka* and *Sugurupāratantrya* are also ascribed to him. Another Jinadatta, who lived in the first half of the thirteenth century, wrote an encyclopaedia called *Vivekavilāsa.*

Jinahakṣa: Jain teacher belonging to the Kharatara-gaccha whose name occurs in the fifteenth-century image inscriptions from Rajasthan and Gujarat. *Jinadhātupratimālekha-saṃgraha* II, Nos. 77, 148, 313, 410, 443, 487, 597, 690, 707, 719, 985.

Jinaharṣa: Thirteenth-century author of *Vastu-pālacarita*, which eulogizes Vastupāla, a statesman, warrior, philanthropist, constructor of temples, poet, patron of poets and founder of big manuscript libraries.

Jina Images: The *Bṛhatsaṃhitā* of Varāhamihira is the earliest text which lays down the standards for a Jina image. Here it is said that the Jina is to be represented as young and beautiful, with no garment on his person. He should have the *śrīvatsa* mark on his chest and arms reaching his knees. This formula refers to Digambara images, through the Śvetāmbara images are not nude. The Jivantasvāmin image representing Mahāvīra meditating in *kāyotsarga* posture has a *dhotī*, crown, and ornaments on his person. The *Māna-sāra* says that the Jina figure should be in a straight and its two long hands should be in the same posture, the whole image being in a stiff attitude and bearing a meditative look. The image should further be accompanied by Nārada and other sages, as well as by gods and goddesses, Yakṣas, and Vidyādharas. The attendant gods, especially Nārada, are not represented in the *parikara* of any Jina image known hitherto, but Yakṣas, Nāgas, *chowri*-bearers, Gandharvas, Vidyādharas, elephant-riders, drum-beaters are represented. In the *Pratiṣṭhā-sāroddhāra* of Āśādhara it is stated that the eyes of the Jina image should be centred on the tip of the nose and that the image should be accompanied with the eight *pratihāryas* (q.v.) and the Yakṣas. Vasunandī in his *Pratiṣṭhāsārasaṃgraha* says that there shall be no hair on the body or beard on the face of the Tīrthaṃkara, that the image must contain the *śrīvatsa* symbol on the chest and that the arms are to reach the knees. Twenty-one Tīrthaṃkaras are said to have obtained salvation while engaged in meditation in the *kāyotsarga* posture, while three Tīrthaṃkaras—Ṛṣabha, Nemi and Mahāvīra—obtained salvation while seated hands in the *dhyāna-mudrā.* So far as the complexion of the Jinas is concerned it is to be noted that Padmaprabha and Vāsupūjya are red, Munisuvrata and Neminātha are dark-blue, Supārśva and Pārśva are greenish, Candrprabha and Puṣpadanta are white and the rest are golden. Different Tīrthaṃkaras are to be identified with the help of *lāñchanas* (q.v.) carved on or below their seats. The *Ācāra Dinakara* lays down certain rules for the selection of materials for the construction of the Jina images. Vasunandin in his *Śrāvakācāra* says that images of the Jinas should be made according to the iconographic formulae. Defective images are not to be installed or worshipped.

Jina-Kāñci: Jain centre near Kañchipuram in Chengalpattu district, Tamil Nadu. Some 17 epigraphs ranging from the twelfth to sixteenth century have been found in the Vardhamāna temple at this place. See Tirupparuttikkunram.

Jina-Kāśī: See Mudbidri.

Jinakīrti: Author who flourished in the middle of the fifteenth century. Of his three known works the *Campakaśreṣṭhī-kathānaka* relates the story of the merchant Campaka containing as well inserted stories of the defiance of fate, deception, saving of life and so forth under the shadow of Jain morals. His second work, *Pāla-Gopāla Kathānaka*, gives the story of two brothers who after many years of wandering achieved fame and prosperity having overcome many temptations. The same Jinakīrti is also the author of a didactic poem *Dānakalpadruma* in which the importance of making gifts is upheld. The *Campaka-śreṣṭhīkathānaka* was first analysed by A. Weber in 1883. It was edited and translated into English by Hertel in *ZDMG* 1911, 1-51, 425-70 who also made a German translation of it in 1922. Rep. with intro. by Ronal Beer, Berlin, 1975. The story is also to be found in the *Kathākośa*, translated by C.H. Tawney, and in Merutuṅga's *Prabandhacintāmaṇi* (qq.v.). Also published by Vidyavijaya Yantralaya, 1915. G. *Pālagopālakathānaka* was treated by J. Hertel in 1917. It was published by Atmananda Jain Granthamālā, Dabhoi, vs 1974. The *Dānakalpadruma* was published in Devchand Lalbhai, Bombay, 1919.

Jinakuśalasūri: Fourteenth-century exponent of Jainism in Gujarat who succeeded Jinacandra III (q.v.) of the Kharataragaccha in vs 1376. He visited the Jain *tīrthas* of Gujarat in particular and north India in general, saw the devastated and depopulated Jain centres, and eventually his followers in Delhi succeeded in obtaining a *farman* from the Emperor Ghiasuddin Tughluq (AD 1320-5) assuring safety to some Jina temples. Jinakuśala continued ceaselessly to work for the promotion of Jainism undertaking repeated journeys by inducing his followers to build or repair temples and *pauṣadhaśālās*. According to the *Kharataragacchabṛhadgurvāvalī* he and his disciples worked hard to restore the lost Jain shrines of Sind. Jinakuśala passed away in vs 1389 at Devarajapura, a town in Sindhu-maṇḍala. He was succeeded by Jinapadmasūri.

Jinamaṇḍana: Thirteenth-century author of a historical narrative named *Kumārapālaprabandha*, which is a loose compilation of material collected from unreliable sources and lacks any critical merit.

Jinapāla: See *Kharataragaccha-bṛhadjurvāvalī.*

Jinapatisūri: Saint-scholar, born in AD 1152, who belonged to the Kharatara spiritual lineage and defeated Padmaprabha, another Śvetāmbara teacher belonging to Ukeśa or Upakeśa lineage in a great debate in the court of Pṛthvīrāja III, the Cāhamana ruler of Śakambharī arranged by his Governor Rāmadeva. The king bestowed the *jayapatra* title of victory on him.

Jinaprabha Suri: Fourteenth-century exponent of Jainism in Gujarat who travelled all over India, visited Jain shrines and recorded the accounts in his *Vividhatīrthakalpa* or simply *Tīrthakalpa* which was composed between vs 1364 and 1389. He maintained a good relation with Muhammad Bin Tughluq (vs 1325-51) and thus saved many Jain temples from Muslim depredations. Vidyatilakasuri has furnished additional information that the Sultan was respectful towards the Jains. He is the author of *Caturviṃsati Jinastuti* and several other hymns. Pub. in Kāvyamālā VII and also in *Stutisaṃgraha.* In AD 1309 he wrote a commentary on Mānatuṅga's (q.v.) *Bhayaharastotra.* See *Vividhatīrthakalpa.*

***Jinapravacanarahasyakośa*:** See Amṛtacandra.

***Jinarūpatā*:** Sacrament. It consists of throwing off clothes and taking on the life of an ascetic without any bondage.

Jinas: See Tīrthaṃkaras.

Jinasāgara: Jain teacher belonging to the Kharataragaccha, whose name occurs in the fifteenth-century image inscriptions from Gujarat. *Jinadhātupratimālekhasaṃgraha* II, No. 916.

Jinsena I: See *Harivaṃśa Purāṇa.*

***Jinasena* II:** Digambara poet and scholar of the ninth century who was the author of *Pārśvābhyudaya* (q.v.) and *Ādipurāṇa* (q.v.) and co-author of *Jayadhavalā*, done with his teacher Vīrasena (q.v.) the vast commentary on the *Kaṣāyaprābhṛta* (q.v.). The *Ādipurāṇa* deals with the life of Ṛṣabha who is also known as Ādinātha. The poet calls it both Purāṇa and Mahākāvya. The *Ādipurāṇa* was completed by his disciple Guṇabhadra (q.v.) who wrote the last 1,620 *ślokas* while the entire work runs to 12,000 verses. Jinasena's *Pārśvābhyudaya* was written in his early years. The *Jayadhavalā* (q.v.) commentary was completed in 60,000 *ślokas* in AD 837, the first 20,000 of which were composed by Vīrasena.

***Jinastotraratnākara*:** See Munisundara Suri.

***Jinastutiśataka*:** See Samantabhadra.

Jinavallabha: See *Ajita Śānti-Stava.*

Jinavallabha Suri: Teacher of Jinadatta Sūri who flourished in the eleventh-twelfth century and composed *Saṅghapaṭṭaka.* App. to Gaekwad's Oriental Series, No. 37, Baroda, 1827.

Jinavara-vihāra: Jain monastery at Dhar where Nayanandī composed the *Sudarśana-Carita* in AD 1043.

Jineśvara: Disciple of Vardhamāna, first head of the Kharataragaccha, author and philosopher, who flourished in the eleventh century AD. His *Līlāvatī-kathā* in Prakrit is no longer available in original, although we have a good Sanskrit imitation by Jinaratna made in the thirteenth century at Jāvalipattana or Jalore. Jineśvara's *Kathānakakośa* or *Kathākośa* is one of the most celebrated works in Prakrit and contains several popular stories known through tradition. Ed. Jinavijaya, Singhi Jaina Granthamālā, No. 11, Bombay, 1949.

***Jineśvara-Sūri-Samyamaśrī-Vivāha-Varnaṇa-Rāsa*:** A specimen of the *Vivāhala* form of Gujarati poetry composed by Somamūrti about

AD 1275. In such compositions the occasion of ordination of some well-known person is metaphorically described as his wedding with the lady "Self-control". This poem relates to the ordination of one Ambaḍa who as Ācārya Jineśvara Sūri (AD 1189-1275) become well-known in Kharatara-gaccha.

Jirāpalli: Village in Sirohi district, Rajasthan, which contains the Jirāvālā Pārśvanātha temple.

Jīrnadurga: Same as Junagarh, a well-known Jain centre.

***Jitakalpa*:** Prakrit *Jiyakappa* by Jinabhadra which is sometimes called the sixth Chedasūtra (q.v.). It is a detailed metrical compilation of the cases in which the individual transgressions are valid. Basically it is a later work on monastic discipline. Edited with extracts from Siddhasena's *Cūrṇi* by E. Leumann, Berlin 1892.

Jīva: Living beings. Although there is a tendency among scholars to explain Jīva in terms of 'soul'—and in Jain tradition this explanation is approved, etymologically the term stands for 'what lives or is animate'. Originally conceived as a vital principle, later the Jīvas were theoretically arranged in a continuous series according to the degrees of consciousness. On the top of this series were placed the perfect souls that had overcome all *karmas* and attained omniscience and at the bottom were placed imperfect soul inhabiting the bodies on earth, water, fire, air and vegetable. *Tattvārthādhigama* II.23-23. The material and biological considerations were gradually thrown aside, and the Jīva was conceived of as existing permanently, acting and being acted upon, as an experient (*bhoktā*) and agent (*kartā*). *Dravyasaṃgraha* 2. It was supposed to know things, perform activities, enjoy pleasure, suffer pain, and illumine itself and other objects. In the subsequent stage of the development of this process, the intrinsic nature of Jīva was conceived as one of perfection, and it was characterized by infinite intelligence, infinite peace, infinite faith, and infinite power. Though it has no form, it acquires, like a lamp which remaining the same illumines the whole of the space of a room, the size and form of the body wherein it lives. *Syādvādamañjarī* 8. Owing to the inclinations generated by its past actions a Jīva comes to inhabit different bodies successively. Whilst the knowledge possessed by the Jīva may be boundless, that which it actually possesses is fragmentary, due to the obscuration caused by *karma*. That is why it suffers and enjoys the fruits of its deeds, and then, in consequence of the *karma* it has acquired, goes through a succession of rebirths and finally obtains liberation through the destruction of its *karma*. So long as it feels hatred, desire, and other detachments and is fettered by *karma*, it undergoes continual reincarnations. Jiva is either emancipated or fettered. There are also various other classifications of the Jīvas on the basis of different standards. See Baddha Jīvas, classification of Beings, Caturīndriya Jīvas, Dvīndriya Jīvas, Ekendriya Jīvas, Gatis, Leśyās, Mukta Jīvas, Pañcendriya Jīvas, Samsārin Jīvas, Siddha Jīvas, Sthāvara Jīvas, Trasa Jīvas, Trīndriya Jīvas.

***Jivadayā-Rāsa*:** Written by Āsiga in Gujarati, it consists of fifty-three stanzas on religious instructions. Edited by Jina Vijaya Muni in *Bhāratīya Vidyā* III, 1944.

***Jīvājīvābhigama*:** Third text of the Upāṅga (q.v.) category, containing 272 Sūtras. The title, upholding the doctrine of living (*jīva*) and lifeless (*ajīva*) things, gives in 20 sections a comprehensive classification of living creatures and a description of the universe in all its details. Edited with Malayagiri's com. in Devchand Lalbhai Jaina Pustakoddhara, Bombay, 1919.

***Jīvakacintāmaṇi*:** Tamil epic written by Tiruthakkathivar. It is based on the *Uttarapurāṇa* of Guṇabhadra (qq.v.). It was written in the tenth century and is undoubtedly one of the finest poems in Tamil. It describes how Jīvaka regained his father's throne after killing a usurper and thereafter in his forty-fifth year renounced the world, lived the life of Jain ascetic and finally attained liberation. Konguvelir's *Perunkathai*, detailing the story of Udayanan, bears marked resemblances to the *Jīvakacintāmaṇi*.

***Jivandhara-Campū*:** Religious novel in the form of Campū written by the Digambara Jain poet Haricandra (q.v.) on the basis of the Jivandhara legend of the *Uttarapurāṇa*. An earlier form of the legend is founded in Tamil *Jīvakacintāmaṇi* (q.v.). Edited by T.S. Kuppuswami Sastri, Tanjore, 1905.

Jīvasamāsa: See Maladhārī Hemacandra.

Jivantasvāmin: Lifetime image of Mahāvīra; an appellation.

***Jñānabinduprakaraṇa*:** See Yaśovijaya.

***Jīvavicāra*:** Prakrit Jīvaviyāra, 'investigation in regard to the living beings' composed by Śānti Sūri of the eleventh century in 51 Āryā verses. In this work beings are classified into such as are in the state of release, and such as are still in the cycle of rebirths; the latter are again classified into lifeless and living, these being in their turn subdivided into denizens of hell, animals, human beings, and gods. The work is therefore at one and the same time a treatise on theology, zoology, botany, anthropology, and mythology. Edited and translated into French by A. Guérinot in *Journal Asiatique*, 1902, XIX, 231ff.; with Pāṭhaka's Ratnākara's com. in Yasovijaya Series, Ahmedabad, 1915.

***Jñānālocana-Stotra*:** Philosophical hymn composed by Vādirāja II. Pub. in Manikacandra Digambara Jaina Granthamālā, No. 21.

***Jñānapañcamīkathā*:** Written by Maheśvara, pupil of Sajjana Upādhyāya, in the eleventh century in 2,800 verses. It contains ten stories of religious significance and glorifies the fifth day of the bright fortnight of the month of Kārttika which is known as *jñāna* or *saubhāgya pañcamī*. It is heavily influenced by the language of the Ardha-Māgadhī canon and also by Apabhraṃśa language. Ed. A.L. Gopani, Singhi Jaina Granthamālā, No. 25, Bombay, 1949.

***Jñānārṇava*:** See Subhacandra.

Jñānasāra: See Yośovijaya.

***Jñānāvaraṇīyā*:** That which hides all aspects of knowledge and its five sources—*mati*, *śruti*, *avadhi*, *manaḥaparyāya*, and *kevala* (qq.v.). It has four constituents, namely *utpātikī*, *vaināyakī*, *pariṇāmikī*, and *kāmikī* (qq.v.). It is an obstruction arising from *ghātin karma* (q.v.).

***Jñātṛdharmakathā*:** Prakrit *Nāyādhammakahāo*, the sixth text of the Aṅga (q.v.) series, which probably means 'examples and religious narratives'. The work is divided into two Śrutaskandhas, of which the first is divided into twenty-one chapters (*adhyayanas*). The second Śrutaskandha is almost a repetition of the first. Each chapter as a rule presents a complete, independent narrative. Most of these tales lay stress on a parable incorporated in them obviously for a didactic purpose. It also contains novels, tales of travellers' adventures, mariners' fairy-tales, robber tales and the like. In the eighth chapter the legend of Mallī, the only female Tīrthaṃkara (q.v.), is told. A fabricated version of the Draupadī legend is also found in this text. Edited with Abhayadeva's com. in Āgamodaya, Bombay, 1916; by N.V. Vaidya, Poona, 1940; Gujarati trans. by Bechardas Jivaraj Doshi, Ahmedabad, 1931; with Abhayadeva's com. Anandacandra-grantha-ratnākara, Bhavnagar, 1951-2.

Jorapukur: Site in Purulia district, West Bengal, a place adjacent to Deoli (q.v.), which has yielded a good number of Jain images.

Junagarh Inscription: Belonging to the grandson of Jayadāman of the second century AD, this inscription refers to those who have obtained *kevalajñāna* and conquered disease and old age. This inscribed slab is found in a cave, one of a group of about twenty monastic cells arranged in three lines near the town. *Epigraphia Indica* XVI.241; Lüders, *List*, No. 966.

Jvālāmālinī: Also known as Jvālinī she is the Śāsanadevatā of Candraprabha (q.v.) according to the Digambara tradition. She rides a buffalo and holds in her hands disc, arrow, noose, shield, trident, and bow. Jvālāmālinī is also the name of a Vidyādevī (q.v.). The *Ācāra-dinakara* describes her as riding a cat, but mentions no attributes. The *Nirvāṇakalikā* describes her as riding a boar and holding many weapons without description.

***Jvālinī-Kalpa*:** Jain Tantric text, still unpublished. It was brought out in AD 939 by Indranandin who was a member of the Drāviḍa Saṅgha and meant for Jvālāmālinī, the Yakṣiṇī of the Jina Candraprabha. The Tantric form of her cult was introduced by one Helācārya of Karnataka, who flourished in the beginning of the ninth century. The texts refer to various Tantric rituals and herbal preparations for curing sterility, becoming invisible, abducting women, successful coition, securing fertility to women, and preventing conception. It refers to practices regarded as the means by which the devotee or aspirant identifies himself with his chosen deity. A few essentials mentioned herein include prayer and formulae (*mantra*) syllables of mystic significance peculiar to each deity (*bījas*), diagrams drawn on papers, leaves, stones and metals (*yantra*, *maṇḍala*), special ritual positions for fingers and movements of the hands (*mudrā*), and placing the deity on different parts of the body by touching them with the fingers tips (*nyāsa*).

Jyotiṣa: Astrology which was quite popular among the Jains who had written numerous treatises on the subject. Astrologers and fortune-tellers were consulted often while attending ceremonies and for day-to-day work. *Ramala* or *pāśakavidyā* is the art of foretelling events by casting dice, which is said to have brought by Ācārya Kālaka from the country of the Yavanas. Jyotiṣa is mentioned as one of the fourteen branches of learning along with arithmetic (*saṅkhāna*), phonetics (*sikkhā*), ritual (*kappa*), grammar (*vāgarana*), metre (*chanda*), and exegesis (*nirukta*). Astrology has been dealt with in *Jyotiṣasāra* by Ṭhakkara Pheru, *Jyotiṣasāra* by Hīrakalasa, etc.

Jyotiṣka Devatā: The Jains following the earlier Brahmanical tradition reduced the planetary system to a group of iconic representations which constitute an important class of gods known as

Jyotiṣka Devatā

Jyotiṣka-devas. Sūrya or the sun-god has been described as riding a chariot drawn by seven steeds and holding in his hands two lotuses. He is known as the deity of the east and husband of Ratnā Devī. Candra or the moon-god drives a chariot of ten white horses and holds an urn of nectar. He is the master of stars and rules over the north-western quarters. Maṅgala or Mars is known as the son of the earth and ruler of the south. Budha or Mercury is the ruler of the north-western quarters while Sukra or Venus is the teacher of the demons and ruler of the south-east region. Saturn or Śani is the ruler of the west. The features of these gods in sculpture mostly follow Brahmanical originals, though some Jain attributes have been given to them. From the ritualism attached to these gods we may well infer that individually and collectively their worship was much in vogue among the Jains. It is noticeable that stress has been given to the supremacy of stellar deities over the different quarters.

K

Kacholi: Jain *tīrtha* in the Sirohi district of Rajasthan, the antiquity of which is attested by an inscription of AD 1285 found at this place.

Kadaba Plate Inscription: Dated śaka 735 (AD 814) and found in Tumkur district of Karnataka, this inscription, which refers to the reign of Prabhutavarṣa, that is, Rāṣṭrakūṭa Govinda III, tells about the existence of a line of Jain monks of the Nandī Saṅgha of the Yāpanīyas. The name of the Gaṇa is given as Punnagavṛkṣamūla. The line of teachers comprises Śrīkīrti, Kuli-Ācārya, Vijayakīrti, and Arkakīrti. *Epigraphia Indica* IV.332ff. *Indian Antiquary* XII.11ff.

Kāḍakol: Jain *tīrtha* in the Dharwar district of Karnataka which is attested by a good number of inscriptions found at this place.

Kadalāya-basadi: See Hanumakoṇḍa.

Kadamras: See gods.

Kadaṅgala: Findspot of an epigraphic record in the Bijapur district of AD 1230, belonging to the time of Yādava Siṅghana, which refers to a temple of Pārśvanātha and a monk called Sakalacandra Bhaṭṭāraka of Mūla-saṅgha and Kānura-gaṇa. *Jaina Śilālekha Saṃgraha* IV, No. 326.

Kaḍavaka: Characteristic feature of Apabhraṃśa epic poem. The Kadavaka, consisting of about eight rhymes in *allihaka* or *pajjhaṭīkā* metre, followed by a *ghaṭṭa* or *duvai* verse, is the normal unit. This style could easily be recognized as the forerunner of the *Caupai-dohā* of Hindi poetry. A number of Kaḍavakas, normally ten to fifteen, constitute a *sandhi* or canto, which sometimes opens with a *dhruvaka* verse, and the metre and style frequently change in consonance with the movement of the narrative, so as to match the sentiment to be expressed.

Kaḍavanti: Situated in the Chikmagalur district, Karnataka, it is the findspot of an epigraph of AD 1060 which mentions a temple called Niravadya Jinālaya and records some grants for it. *Epigraphia Carnatica* VI, Chik. No. 75.

Kahaum Inscription: Belonging to the reign of Skandagupta this inscription, found at Kahaum in Gorakhpur district, Uttar Pradesh, and dating to AD 461, refers to the setting up of five Jina images by a person called Madra, who traced his descent from one Somila. The images were probably of Ṛṣabha, Śānti, Nemi, Pārśva, and Mahāvīra. *Corpus Inscriptionum Indicarum* III, 67; Bhandarkar, *List*, No.1278.

Kaidal: Findspot of a Jain inscription of AD 1150 in the Tumkur taluk of Tumkur district, Karnataka, which records the establishment of a Jina temple of the name of Bhīma Jinālaya at Kaydāḷa, modern Kaidal, by Bācideva, a feudatory of the Hoysala Viṣṇuvardhana, which along with its adjoining tank (excavated by the same person), was dedicated to Pārśvanātha. *Epigraphia Carnatica* XII, Tumkur 9.

Kākandi: Jain *tīrtha* associated with the birth of the ninth Tīrthaṃkara Puṣpadanta which is generally identified with Kakan in the Monghyr district, Bihar.

Kakatpur: Site near Konarak in Puri district, Orissa, wherefrom a good number of Jain metal sculptures have been found. These are in the Indian Museum and Asutosh Museum of Calcutta. They seem to belong to the twelfth century, and comprise mostly Tīrthaṃkara images. A Candraprabha image of this collection, now in the Asutosh Museum, deserves mention. The Jina stands in *kāyotsarga* on a lotus supported on a square pedestal which bears his emblem, the cresent moon.

Kakkasūri III: Spiritual descendant of the author of the *Nābhinandanoddhāraprabandha*, this Kakkasūri belonged to the Upakeśa-gaccha and was a well-known monk of the fifteenth century whose name is mentioned in a large number of published inscriptions.

***Kāla*:** One of the five Ajiva (q.v.) categories which implies that which makes possible the continuity, modification, movement, newness and oldness of substances—*vartanā-pariṇāma-kriyāḥ paratvāparatve ca kālasya*. It falls within the *anastikāya* (q.v.) group because it is not extended in space. It is an indivisible substance present everywhere at the same time. In a general sense *kāla*, however, bears the connotation of time and is divided and subdivided into seconds, minutes, hours, days, or years. This is empirical or conventional time, *vyavahārika kāla*, also called *samaya*. But in the real sense *kāla* is indivisible, and it is that which is continually making old things new and new things old. For example, a child grows up into a young man, and finally dies in old age, and the Jiva is forced to inhabit the body of another infant. The Jīva remains the same, but the power that made its covering body at one time old and then young is *kāla*. Thus the distinction between the old and the new cannot be explained without time. This is the grounds on which the existence of time can be inferred. Like space, time is also inferred, though not perceived. Of other grounds of inference it may be said that modification or change of states cannot be conceived without the supposition of time. The real time or *paramārthika kāla* is formless and eternal. It cannot have the divisions of *skandha*, *deśa*, or *pradeśa* (denoting whole, part, or portion of a part respectively). *Kāla* as *dravya* (q.v.) consists of moments or *kāla paramāṇus* which constitute a time series having only the relation of before and after. There can be no simultaneous moments in the time series. The *vyavahārika* or conventional time is that which we use in our social life, the duration being measured by the movements of the sun and the moon. This is of different durations, according to different measures, and ranges from the shortest *nimeṣa* to the longest *yuga*. Some Jain thinkers do not admit time as a separate substance, but regard it as a *paryāya* or mode of other substances. *Tattvārtha* V.22; *Dravyasṃgraha* 21; *Ṣaḍdarśana-samuccaya* 49.

Kālakācārya: Saint who flourished during the patriarchy of Indradinna (q.v.). The story of Kālaka has many versions. According to one version, Gardabhilla, king of Ujjain, insulted Kālakācārya by abducting his sister who was a nun. Kālakācārya then approached a Śaka king for help. Gardabhilla was protected by the goddess Rāṣabhī but she failed to save him because of the magic power of Kālaka. The Śaka army captured Gardabhilla, and Kālaka's sister was released. Gardabhilla thereupon repaired to a forest where he was finally devoured by a tiger. Gardabhilla's son Vikramāditya, according to some versions of the story, then came from Pratiṣṭhāna to Ujjain, drove away the Śaka invaders, and ruled for a long time and established an era that goes by his name (58 BC). The historical foundation of this story is doubtful. Kālaka was on good terms with Vikramāditya who himself, according to the Jain sources, was a patron of Jainism.

***Kālakācārya Kathā*:** Written by Devacandrasūri in the eleventh century, it narrates the story of Kālaka who brought the Śakas to punish the tyrant Gardabhilla, who wanted to molest his sister Sarasvatī. This story was so popular with the Jains that we have no less than 38 versions of it. See N.W. Brown, *The Story of Kālaka*, Washington, 1933.

***Kālakācārya Kathānaka*:** A Prakrit poem in prose and verse which is generally recited by monks at the end of the recital of the *Kalpasūtra*. It is the story of Kālaka who converted to the Jain religion and attained a high degree of spiritual merit. His sister, the nun Sarasvatī, was abducted by Gardabhilla, ruler of Ujjayinī, and Kālaka rescued her with the help of the Sāhī rulers of Śakakula and conquered Ujjayinī after defeating Gardabhilla. The date of the work is unknown and the name of its author has not come down. Ed. and trans. by H. Jacobi in *ZDMG* XXXIV, 247ff., XXXV, 675ff., and Leumann, ibid. XXXVII, 493ff. There is also a *Kālakācārya-kathānaka* by Bhavadeva Suri in 102 Prakrit verses.

Kalakeri: Site of a Jain temple of Tīrthaṃkara Ananta in the Bijapur district mentioned in an inscription of AD 1245 of the time of Yādava Siṅghana. It is also mentioned in an inscription of the time of Yādava Kṛṣṇa. *Jaina Śilākekha Saṃgraha* IV, Nos. 329, 336.

***Kālasvarūpakulakam*:** A didactic poem in 32 rhymed verses, written in Apabhraṃśa by Jinadatta Sūri (AD 1075-1154).

Kalāvasati: Findspot of a Jain inscription of AD 1529 in Koppa taluk of Chikmagalur district, Karnataka, which records a grant for a Pārśvanātha temple by Kālaladevī, sister of the King Bhairarasa Boḍeyara. *Epigraphia Carnatica*, VII, Koppa 47.

Kalbhāvi: A place in Belgaum district, Karnataka, which was known as Kumudavāḍa in the eighth century and had a Jain temple of that time under the supervision of the monks on the Maitapa *anvaya* and the Kāreya-gaṇa belonging to the Yāpanīyasaṅgha. An epigraph mentions a Gaṅga chief Saigaṭṭa Gaṅga Permāndi *alias* Śivamāra as being favoured by the goddess Padmāvatī and records the construction of a Jain temple by him. The Jain establishment was in the hand of Devakīrti, disciple of Śubhakīrti and grand-disciples of Jinacandra. *Indian Antiquary*, XVIII, 309ff.

Kalegere: Situated in the Mandya district, Karnataka, it is the findspot of a Jain inscription of the time of Narasiṃha III which refers to the Śāntinātha temple of Dorasamudra (q.v.). This temple received a grant from the king himself and was entrusted to Meghanandī, disciple of Kumudacandra, who belonged to the Balātkāra-gaṇa and Mūla-saṅgha. *Jaina Śilālekha Saṃgraha*, IV, No. 376.

Kālī: See Vajraśṛmkhalā and Śānta. Kālī in Jainism is also a Vidyā-devī (q.v.), conceived as riding a deer and holding a staff and sword. In Śvetāmbara conception she sits on a lotus with hands in *varada* and *abhaya mudrā*, holding the conventional attributes.

Kalholi: Situated in Belgaum district, Karnataka, and known as Kalpole and Sindana-Kalpole in early times, it was the site of a temple of Śāntinātha which was under the supervision of the monks of the Hanasoga section of the Pustaka-gaccha, the Mūla-saṅgha and the Kundakunda-anvaya as is known from an inscription of AD 1204. *Jaina Śilālekha Saṃgraha* III, No. 449; *Journal of the Bombay Branch of the Royal Asiatic Society* X.173ff.

Kaliṅga-Jina: A Jina image said to have been brought back from Magadha to Kaliṅga by Khāravela (q.v.) of the Mahāmeghavāhana dynasty. There is a possible reference in the Hathigumpha inscription to the removal of a Jina image from Kaliṅga to Pāṭaliputra by the Magadhan King Nanda at the time of his invasion of Kaliṅga, and its subsequent recovery by Khāravela who invaded Magadha in the first century AD. According to K.P. Jayaswal's version of the Hathigumpha text, the booty lifted by Khāravela from Magadha included an image of Śītalanātha, the Jina of Kaliṅga, which had been carried away by King Nanda. According to B.M. Barua, however, the correct reading should be Kaliṅga-jana, people of Kaliṅga, and not Kaliṅga Jina.

Kallil: Jain rock-shelter near Peruṃbavur in Ernakulam district which was transformed into a Bhagavatī shrine in later times. On the facade of this rock-shelter is carved an unfinished seated figure of Mahāvīra, as also in the back wall of the shrine. A stone image of Padmāvatī stands near the figure of Mahāvīra and is now worshipped as Bhagavatī.

Kalpa Druma: Wish-fulfilling tree, Hemacandra refers to ten kinds of such trees which are *madyāṅga, bhṛṅga, turyaṅga, dīpaśikhā, jyotiṣka, citrāṅga, citrarasa, mānyaṅga, gehakāra,* and *anaṅga*. These are described in detail in the *Jambūdvīpaprajñapti* XX.

***Kalpasūtra*:** The eighth section of *Dasaśrutaskandha*, popularly known as the *Kalpasūtra* of Bhadrabāhu (q.v.). In the history of Jainism there is a Bhadrabāhu problem because there was more than one person of this name. Three different texts form the body of the *Kalpasūtra* and it does not seem feasible that Bhadrabāhu was the author of all three. The first section contains the *Jinacarita*, the main portion of which is the biography of Mahāvīra told in great deatail with descriptions in the *kāvya* style. The biographies of Mahāvīra's predecessors have also been given. The second section consists of the *Therāvalī*, a list of schools, their branches and heads. The list goes far beyond Bhadrabāhu, and hence is not written by him. The third section is probably the oldest nucleus of the *Kalpasūtra* which contains the *Sāmācārī* or rules for the ascetics. The *Kalpasūtra* is also known as *Paryuṣaṇakalpa*. Critical edition by H. Jacobi, Leipzig, 1879; and Eng. trans. by the same author in Sacred Books of the East, XXII, Oxford, 1884; ed. with Samayasundara's com., Bombay, 1939; ed. Muni Puṇyavijaya with *Kalpa-Niryukti, Kalpa-Cūrṇi* and Pṛthvīcandra's *Tippanaka,* Ahmedabad, 1952.

***Kalpāvataṃśikā*:** Prakrit *Kappavadamsiāu*, ninth text of the Upāṅga (q.v.) series which is the second part of the text *Nirayavạli Suttam*. It gives an account of the fate of ten princes of the dynasty of Cedaga after their death who like their grandmothers reached different heavens after their conversion in true religion. *Nirayavalikasūtram* with Candrasena's com. Agamodaya edn. Ahmedabad, 1922.

Kalpetta: Jain settlement in Kerala.

Kalvan Plates: Belonging to the time of Paramāra Bhoja, that is, early eleventh century, this undated inscription refers to a Śvetāmbara monastery at Muktapali in Nasik district, the temple of Suvratasvāmin in the same region, the migration of the monks of Draviḍa Saṅgha, and the grant of six villages to the Jain monastery of Uriamma. *Epigraphia Indica* XIX, 69-75.

Kalya: Findspot of a Jain inscription of AD 1368 in the Bangalore district, Karnataka, of the time of the Vijayanagara Emperor Bukka I, which refers to an agreement signed by Jains and Vaiṣṇavas for mutual protection. *Epigraphia Carnatica*, IX, Magadi 18.

***Kalyāṇamandirastotra*:** Set of hymns (composed by the celebrated Siddhasena Divākara (q.v.) edited and translated into German by H. Jacobi in *Indische Studien* XIV, 376ff.; text published in Kāvyamālā Series, part VII. The *Paramajotistotra*, an old metrical translation in the old Braj dialect of the *Kalyāṇamandirastotra* was published by L.P. Tessitory in *Indian Antiquary* XLII, 1913, 42ff.

***Kāmaghātakathā*:** See *Pāpabuddhi-Dharmabuddhi-Kathānaka*.

Kamaṭha Pārśva Basti: An old Jain temple-complex patronized and adorned with a dancing hall by Nāgadeva, the *pattanasvāmī* of the Hoysala King Ballāla II, as is known from an inscription from Belgola of AD 1195. *Epigraphia Carnatica* (rev.). II, No. 335.

Kambadahaḷḷi: Findspot of a number of Jain inscriptions in Nāgamangala taluk, Mandya district, Karnataka. An inscription of AD 1118 mentions the gift of Gaṅgarāja (q.v.) to his teacher Subhacandra. An epitaph of Rukkmabba and Jakabbe, lay women disciples of Prabhācandra, is found in an inscription of AD 1120. An epigraph of about 1,130 records the construction of a Jina temple dedicated to Śāntinātha at this place by Boppa, the son of Gaṅgarāja. Another epigraph of AD 1155 mentions a grant to the said temple by two generals of the Hoysalas, Manyane and Bharatimayya, disciples of Gandavimukta. Another of AD 1167 shows that the temples of this place remained under the control of the monks of Mūla-saṅgha, Deśīya-gaṇa, Pustaka-gaccha, and Kondakunda-anvaya. *Jaina Śilā-lekha Saṃgraha* II, Nos. 269, 294; III, 372; IV, No. 213; *Epigraphia Carnatica* IV, Naga, 19-21, V, Belur 124; *Mysore Archaeological Review,* 1939, 193.

Kambadur: Jain single-towered temple site in Andhra Pradesh.

Kāmbalikā Tīrtha: A place in western India where the use of drapery by some Jain monks seems to have started according to the evidence furnished by the *Bṛhathathā* of Hariṣeṇa.

Kāmeśvara: Jain temple at Auwa in north India.

Kamikī: That which impedes intellectual stimulus, a constituent of *jñānāvaraṇīya* (q.v.). It is an obstruction arising from *ghātin-karma* (q.v.).

Kampilya: Modern Kampil in Farrukhabad district, Uttar Pradesh, birth-place of the thirteenth Tīrthaṃkara, Vimalanātha. Jinaprabha in his *Vividhatīrthakalpa* refers to this place as an important Jain *tīrtha.*

Kanaji Pantha: A Digambara subsect consisting of the followers of Kanaji Svāmī. This sect is of recent origin. Its founder originally belonged to the Śvetāmbara Sthānakavāsī sect but later, after going through the works of Ācārya Kundakunda very thoroughly, he changed his line and re-interpreted the Ācārya's doctrine in a new perspective giving more prominence to the *niścaya-naya* or realistic viewpoint in preference to *vyavahāranaya* or practical viewpoint. But the Digambaras in general did not approve the stand of Kanaji Svāmī, since they held both viewpoints as equally important. So a need was felt for the introduction of this new sect, the chief centre of which is Sonagaḍha town in Gujarat.

Kanakāmara: Author of the Apabhraṃśa *Kara-kaṇḍa-cariu* (q.v.) written in the tenth century. He was a Brāhmaṇa of the Candrarṣi Gotra and adopted the Digambara Jain faith on account of a feeling of renunciation.

Kanakasena Vādirāja: Jain poet of the tenth century who composed the epic *Yaśodhara-carita* in Digambara perspective. It was composed about AD 950, ed. T.A. Gopinatha Rao, Sarasvati Vihara Series, Tenjore, 1912.

Kāñcī: Jina-Kāñcī or Tirupparuttikkunram (qq.v.), a suburb of Kanchipuram. The Candraprabha temple of this place is the northernmost structure in the existing Jain complex of four major temples and three minor shrines, within a huge enclosure. It is a three-storeyed square *vimāna* with a *mukha-maṇḍapa* in front. The ground floor of this structure is built of local sandstone. The second storey contains the real shrine. The temple as a whole belongs to the eighth century although the upper parts appear to be a faithful reconstruction of a much later period.

Kandarpā: Śāsanadevatā (q.v.) of Dharmanātha (q.v.), also known as Pannagadevī, according to the Śvetāmbara tradition. She rides on a horse or fish, holds two lotuses and a goad, and shows *abhaya-mudrā.* Her Digambara variant Mānasī is described as riding a tiger and holding in her six hands two lotuses, a bow, the *varada* pose, a goad, and an arrow.

Kaṅkālī Ṭīlā: An early form of the structural architecture of the Jains at Mathura. It is a large and beautiful Jain stūpa believed in the beginning of the Christian era to have been conceived by the gods in the time of the seventh Tīrthaṃkara and renovated in that of the twenty-third Tīrthaṃkara. This form was extant till probably the beginning of medieval times. The *Vyava-hārabhāṣya* (V.27) refers to a bejewelled stūpa in Mathura, probably in an idealized view of this stūpa. Excavations at Kaṅkālī Ṭīlā have brought to light the remains of a brick stūpa, images of Tīrthaṃkaras, fragments of sculpture depicting incidents from the lives of the Tīrtha-ṃkaras, *āyāgapaṭas*, *toraṇas*, and railing pillars with sculptures mostly belonging to the period of the Kuṣāṇas. The dismembered slabs give an idea of the architectural and sculptural splendour of the magnificent monuments raised by the affluent and pious Jain community. Inscriptions on many of the slabs and images furnish not only the names of the rulers, but throw a flood of light on the organization of the Jain

Saṅgha with its teachers and ascetics grouped into various *gaṇas*, *kulas* and *śākhās*.

Kannaḍi-Basadi: A Jina temple, probably dedicated to Śāntinātha, mentioned in an inscription (AD 1484) from Guruvayanakara in South Kanara district, Karnataka. *Annual Report on South Indian Epigraphy*, 1928-9, 45.

Kannangarakkudi: Site in Coimbatore district, Tamil Nadu which has vestiges of Jain structural temples. Tīrthaṃkara images have also been recovered in this place.

Kantabania: Findspot of an eleventh-century Pārśvanātha image in 24-Parganas, West Bengal, enshrined in Viśālākṣī temple *in situ* and worshipped as Pañcanan Ṭhākur. It is similar to one in the Siddheśvara temple at Bahulara (q.v.). Standing in *kāyotsarga*, the figure is flanked by male *chowri*-bearers in *kaṭihasta* pose. Miniature figures of 23 seated Tīrthaṃkaras are depicted. Hairs and *uṣṇīṣa* are well marked. The canopy is formed by seven snakehoods.

Kanyānayana: A Jain *tīrtha* near Delhi mentioned by Jinaprabha in *Vividhatīrthakalpa*.

Kāpa: Findspot of a Jain copper-plate inscription of AD 1556 in South Kanara district, Karnataka, which records a grant for the Dharmanātha temple in the time of the Vijayanagara Emperor Sadāśivarāya. Monks like Devakīrti, his disciple Municandra, and the latter's disciple Devacandra are mentioned in this inscription which also refers to Bhānumunīśvara of the Tintrini-gaccha. The imprecatory passage at the end mentions Gommaṭeśvara of Belgola, Candranātha of Kopana and Neminātha of Girnar. *Epigraphia Indica* XX.89.

Kāparḍā: Jain *tīrtha* in Jodhpur district of Rajasthan where stands a seventeenth-century temple of Pārśvanātha.

***Kappāvaḍamsiāu*:** See Kalpāvataṃśikā.

Kārakala: Popularly known as Karkal, this place in South Canara district of Karnataka was a great Jain centre. There were several temples in this place, including one dedicated to Gommaṭeśvara and another to Pārśvanātha. The local kings of this area gave full patronage to Jain constructions. Karakala is extremely well known for its famous Jain *mānastambha*, 59 feet in height and fashioned out of a single stone. The great statue of Bāhubalī of this place was constructed by Pāṇḍārāya in AD 1432. This is known from an epigraph of this place which also mentions the Jain monk Lalitakīrti belonging to the Panasoge-śākhā. A detailed account regarding the Jain shrines of this place is given in an epigraph of AD 1589. It not only mentions Sommetīśvara of this place that reveals the construction of Tribhuvanatilaka Jina Caityālaya on the hill Cikkabetta by King Bhairava II who installed in it the images of Aranātha, Mallinātha, and Suvrata. The sixteenth-century writers Jñānasāgara has mentioned the famous statue of Gommaṭeśvara and also a temple of Neminātha here. *Jaina Śilāekha Saṃgraha* III, Nos. 624, 680.

***Karakaṇḍa-Cariu*:** Written in Apabhraṃśa by Kanakamāra (q.v.) and admittedly inspired by the poetry of Puṣpadanta (q.v.), it narrates in ten sandhis, in easy and lucid style, the life of Karakaṇḍa who is recognized as a Pratyekabuddha by the Jains and Buddhists. The hero's campaign to the south is occasion for the description of Jain caves at Terapur which are identifiable with the existing caves at Dhārāśiva in the vicinity of Osmanabad. According to the details furnished by the poet, these may belong to the time of early Śilāhāra princes. The work may be assigned to the tenth century AD. Edited with intro., trans., glossary, etc., by H.L. Jain, Karanja, 1934.

***Karaṇānuyoga*:** The second Digambara Veda which deals with cosmological issues. This Veda includes the *Sūrya* and *Candra-prajñaptis* (qq.v.) and also a text called *Jayadhavalā* (q.v.).

Karandai: Findspot of three inscriptions of Rājarāja II (AD 1146-73) in the North Arcot district, Tamil Nadu, referring to grants to local Jain temples. *Jain Śilālekha Saṃgraha* IV, Nos. 248-50.

Karanja: Jain *tīrtha* in Akola district of Maharashtra described by Jñānasāgara and Śīlavijaya. It contained the famous Candranātha or Candraprabha temple.

Karitalai: Centre of Jain sculpture of the tenth and eleventh centuries in the Jabalpur district. The Dāhala sculptures a all from this site. Among the large number of Jain images of the Kalacuri period, thirty-three have been acquired by the Raipur Museum and comprise Ṛṣabhanātha, Śāntinātha, Pārśvanātha, Mahāvīra, four unidentified Jina images, Dvi-mūrtikās, Sarvatobhadrikā, Sahasrakūṭas, Ambikā, and Sarasvatī.

Karkala: See Gommaṭeśvara.

Karkyala Inscription: Inscribed on a hillock called Bommalagutta at Kurkyala, 13 miles west of Karimnagar, Andhra Pradesh, this epigraph, belonging to the Cālukyas of Vemulavāda and to the time of Arikeśari II (AD 930-58), refers to a Jain devotee called Jinavallabha, brother of the poet Pampa (q.v.), who constructed a vasadi called Tribhuvanatilaka. The inscription records the installation by Jinavallabha of the images of Ṛṣabha and Vardhamāna and his construction of a Caityālaya dedicated to Ṛṣabha at Vṛṣabhādri. He was a disciple of Jayamgonda Siddhānta Bhatāra of the Deśīya-gaṇa and Kondakunda-anvaya. The inscription also says that King Arikeśari II of Vamulavāda gave Pampa, as a mark of his appreciation of *Pampabhārata*, the village of Dharmavura as an *agrahāra*. The details given in this epigraph regarding Pampa tally generally with those given by the poet in his works. *Epigraphia Andhrica* II.21ff.

Karma: The doctrine according to which all actions, good or bad, produce their consequences in the life of the individual who acts. In the early Vedic ideas *karma* denotes sacrifice. In the later Vedic texts and in the Upaniṣads, the simple form of the doctrine of *karma* is that just as good seeds bring a good harvest and bad seeds bad, so also man becomes good by good deeds and bad by bad deeds. At the sophisticated level, however, *karma* is regarded as a blind unconscious principle governing the whole universe. It is not the subject to the control even of God, according to Buddhism, Sāṅkhya, and Mīmāṃsā, through the Nyāya-Vaiśeṣikas hold that *karma* is under the guidance and control of god. It is inextricably blended with the doctrine of transmigration of the soul and rebirth.

The Buddhist law of *karma* is only a special form of the more general law of causation. Since life is thought of as an unbroken stream of successive states which are causally connected, the present existence of an individual is in accordance with that of *karma*, the effect of the past. The Mīmāṃsakas think that the world is composed of living bodies wherein souls reap the consequences of their past deeds, the *indriyas* or organs which are instruments for sufferance or enjoyment of those consequences and the objects which constitute the fruits to be suffered or enjoyed. According to the Vedānta the bondage of the soul to the body is due to its *karma*. This is of three kinds—those that have borne their effects (*prārabdha*), those still lying accumulated (*sañcita*), and those stored in the present life (*sañcīyamāna*). In Jainism, unlike other systems, *karma* is conceived as material and permeating the Jīvas (q.v.), weighing them down to the mundane level. Through the actions of body, speech, and mind, *karma* is formed as a subtle matter.

Not to speak of animals and plants, the Jains think that everything of the world, even the four elements, are bodies of the soul and hence can be obscured by the defilement of *karma*.

Things perceived consist of gross matter, while subtle matter is supersensuous. It is this subtle matter that gets transformed into different kinds of *karma*. 'The defilement of the soul takes place in the following way. Subtle matter ready to be transformed into *karma* pours into the soul (i.e. Jīva); this is called influx (*āsrava*). In the usual state of things a soul harbours passion (*kaṣāya*) which acts like a viscous substance and retains the subtle matter coming into contact with the soul; the subtle matter thus caught by the soul enters, as it were, into a chemical combination with it; this is called binding (*bandha*) of *karma*-matter. The subtle matter "bound" or amalgamated by the soul is transformed into eight kinds of *karma*, and form a kind of subtle body (*kārmaṇa-śarīra*) which clings to the soul in all its migrations and future births and determines the individual state and lot of that particular soul. . . . Now when a particular *karma* has produced its effects in the way described, it is discharged or purged from the soul. The process of "pouring off" is called *nirjarā*. When the process goes on without interruption, *karma* matter will, in the end, be discharged from the soul, and the latter now freed from the weight which had kept it down before the time of its liberation (for matter is heavy and *karma* is material) goes up in a straight line to the top of the universe where the liberated souls dwell.' Jacobi in *ERE*, VII.468-9.

This conception of *karma* directly follows Jain ethics. Meritorious actions are needed for extinguishing the existing *karma* and to stop its further influx. The actions of mind, speech, and body continually produce certain subtle *karma* matters which pour themselves into the Jīva and stick to it coming into contact with its passions, collectively known as *kaṣāya* and consisting of the four sins of anger, conceit, intrigue, and greed. The *Kaṣāyas* (q.v.) result in tying men to the cycle of rebirth. The influx of *karma* particles, constituted by certain sorts of infra-atomic particles of matter, into the soul is called *āsravas*. There are seventeen major ways and twenty-five minor ways in which *karma* is acquired. The actual influx of *karma* affects the soul in eight ways in accordance with which it is divided into eight kinds. The way in which the influx of *karma* can be checked is called *saṃvara*. 'As a large tank, when the supply of water has been stopped, gradually dries up by the consumption of water and by evaporation, so the *karma* of a monk, which he acquired in millions of births, is annihilated by austerities, if there is no influx of bad *karma*.' Jacobi in SBE, XLV, 174. The ideal

of liberation can thus be realized only by the stoppage and shedding of *karma*. *Saṃvara* (q.v.) is that which stops. By it the channels through which *karma* finds entrance into the soul can be blocked.

Just as water flows into a boat through a hole in it, so also the *āsravas* represent the channels or modes through which the *karmas* enter the soul. By means of *saṃvara* the process may be arrested, but the *karmas* which have already soiled the soul become responsible for its bondage to *karma*. It is what binds the soul to the body. It is caused by the union of the soul with *pudgala*. The process of arresting the influx of new *karma* and shedding of the stored *karma* which starts with the observances and austerities associated with the practice of *saṃvara* reaches a distinctly higher level with the arrival of the stage of *nirjarā* (q.v.) which is the purging of the *karmas*. It is of two kinds, *bhāva* and *dravya*, the former meaning change in the soul by virtue of which *karma* particles are destroyed, and the latter, the actual destruction of *karma* particles either by reaping their effects or by penances, before their time of fruition. One of the chief ways of annihilating *karma* is the practice of austerities which are of two kinds—exterior and interior—when the Jīva is freed from all bondage to *karma* and has passed far beyond the possibility of rebirth, it is said to have *mokṣa* or liberation.

Karma has four sources. It springs from (1) *avirati* or attachment to worldly pleasures, (2) *kaṣāya* or passions in the form of anger, pride, deceit, and greed, (3) *yoga* or the employment of body, mind, and speech to material and sensual things and (4) *mithyātva* or false belief. There are eight kinds of *karma* which the Jains classify broadly under two groups—*ghātin* and *aghātin*. Each group is further subdivided into four categories. To the former belong *jñānāvaraṇīya* (knowledge-obscuring) *darśanāvaraṇīya* (cognition-obscuring), *mohanīya* (deluding), and *antarāya* (obstructive). To the latter belong *vedanīya* (feeling), *āyu* (the age), *nāma* (body-making) and *gotra* (family determining). Besides, there are three tenses—*satta*, *bandha*, and *udaya*—and two types—*nikācita* and *śithila*—of *karma*.

Jñānāvaraṇīya hides all aspects of knowledge from us. It is concerned with the five sources of knowledge—*mati*, *śruti*, *avadhi*, *manaḥparyāya*, and *kevala*. That which hides these five sources of knowledge prevents our making the right use of knowing what is passing in the minds of others, what is happening at a distance, and what is the right way of attaining liberation. *Darśanāvaraṇīya* prevents our beholding the faith, *vedanīya* causes us to experience the pleasures of happiness and the pains of misery, and *mohanīya* generates attachment and passion. Of the *karmas* belonging to the *aghātin* group, *āyu* determines the length of time which a Jīva must spend in the form his *karma* has endowed him. The conditions by which various classes of beings are governed are collectively known as *nāma*; their country, caste, etc., determining the specific conditions are likewise known as *gotra*. Individual differences are due to *antarāya*.

The *karma* accumulated in the past life is called *sattā*; that which is being accumulated in the present life is named *bandha*; and that which will concern the future life is *udaya*. The *karma* which has already been stored up is known as *nikācita*, and that, the influx of which may be evaded, is called *śithila*. There are fourteen steps to liberation from *karma*. These steps are known as *guṇasthānas* (q.v.) and conceived like a ladder by which a Jīva may mount to liberation. These steps are *mithyātva*, *svāśvāsadana*, *miśra*, *aviratisamyagdṛṣṭi*, *deśavirati*, *pramatta*, *apramatta*, *apūrvakaraṇa*, *aniyatibādra*, *sūkṣmasamparyāya*, *upaśāntamoha*, *kṣīṇamoha*, *sayogikevalī*, and *ayogikevalī* (qq.v.).

Karmagranthas: See Devendra Suri.

***Kārmaṇa Śarīra*:** The *karmic* body. According to Jain conception, the soul is always surrounded by a large volume of fine matter called *karma*. This contact leads to the formation of what is called the *kārmaṇa-śarīra*, body of subtle *karma* matter, corresponding to the *liṅga* or *sūkṣma śarīra* of the Sāṅkhya, which accompanies the soul throughout life as well as in its migrations from one body to another. That this *kārmaṇa-śarīra* is formed of actual matter particles is evident from the fact that it has both weight and colour. The light soul which has a tendency to fly at once into space is actually kept down by the weight of its *kārmaṇa-śarīra*. The latter also imparts to it a *leśyā* or complexion that may be dark blue, grey, yellow, red, or white. The *kārmaṇa-śarīra* binds the soul in eight different ways, according to the nature of forces developed in it when the inflow of *karma* takes place. Thus the *karmic*-body forms the nucleus around which the grosser bodies are built up. According to this conception the building up of the *kārmaṇa-śarīra* forms the foundation of life in *saṃsāra* or worldly existence and its disintegration constitutes the final liberation of the Jīva. The Jīva cannot cast away

the *kārmaṇa śarīra* during its worldly existence. Conscious activities such as desires and emotions act as cause of the building up of the *karmic* body which then becomes the vehicle for good or evil, and in its turn affects the nature of the psychic experience. Thus the interdependence between Jīva and the *karmic* body, acting as cause and effect, each in its turn, continues to keep up the show of the worldly drama.

***Karmaprābhṛta*:** See Ṣaṭkhaṇḍāgama.

Karmaprakṛti: See Śivaśarma Sūri.

Karmā Shāh: Originally a cloth merchant of Citrakūṭa who was a sixteenth-century Jain activist in Gujarat and later became a minister of King Ratnasiṃha. He made the seventh restoration of the famous temple of Ādinātha in Śatruñjaya (q.v.). The temple of Puṇḍarīkasvāmin situated just opposite the temple of Ādinātha on Śatruñjaya was built by him. Information on Karmā Shāh or Karmarāja is found in an inscription of AD 1531. *Epigraphia Indica* II, 42ff.

***Karmāsrava*:** One of the two classes of *āsravas* (q.v.) the process of the actual entrance of *karma* particles into the soul. The effect on the soul of the actual influx of *karma* is of eight kinds: *jñānāvaraṇīya*, *darśanāvaraṇīya*, *vedanīya*, *mohanīya*, *āyu*, *nāma*, *gotra* and *antarāya*.

Karmic Body: *Karmāṇa-śarīra* (q.v.) which is associated with every Jīva (q.v.) till the time of its liberation or *mokṣa* (q.v.) and produced from *karmaprayoga-pudgala*, subtle material aggregates. It is inevitably associated with every worldly Jīva throughout its career in the cycle of births and deaths and the Jīva cannot cast it away. Its intrinsic purity is lost because of its association with the *karmic* body built up by the psychic activities of the soul itself.

Karṇa: Caulukya king of Gujarat who succeeded his father Bhīma I (q.v.) around AD 1064. According to a statement of Rājaśekhara he was a patron of Abhayadevasūri and conferred upon him the title Maladhārin. We learn from *Prabandhacintāmaṇi* that at the city of Karṇāvatī, founded by him, there was a well-known temple of Ariṣṭanemi. But Hemacandra says that he was a devout Vaiṣṇava.

Karṇapārya: Author of the *Neminātha Purāṇa* in Kannaḍa which was composed in the twelfth century in the Tribhuvanatilaka Jinālaya and dedicated to Candraprabha at Herle. His patron was Lakṣmīdhara, an officer of King Vijayāditya. Published by the Madras University, 1940.

***Karnavedha*:** Śvetāmbara sacrament of piercing the lobes of the ears of the child when it is either three, five or seven years old.

***Kartā*:** Agent, responsible for all action; characteristic of a Jīva (q.v.).

***Kārttikeyānuprekṣā*:** Prakrit *Kattigayānupekkhā* written by Svāmī Kārttikeya or Kumāra of the Digambara tradition who belonged to the late centuries of the first millennium AD. The work treats in 12 chapters of the 12 *anuprekṣās* or meditations. In the twelfth chapter it deals with the doctrine of *karma*, and how its influx on the soul is to be stopped and the various stages of the attainment of liberation. Printed with Pandit Jayachand's *Bhāṣā-ṭīkā*, Gandhi Natharang, Bombay, 1904; Pandit Mahendra Kumar Jain Palni, Khandwa, 1974; with Śubhacandra's Sanskrit com., Hindi trans. by Pandit Kailash Chandra Jain Siddhāntaśastrī and A.N. Upadhye's intro. Raycand Shastramala, Agas, 1960.

Kuruṅgalakkudi: A village on a hill called Pāñcapāṇḍavarkuṭṭu in Madurai district where Ācārya Ajjanandi saw some Jain sculptures. It was a resort of Jain ascetics as attested by inscriptions.

Karugund: Findspot of a Jain inscription of AD 1158 in Arsikere taluk, Hassan district, Karnataka which states that a local chief named Śantiyana built a Jina temple at Karikunda, i.e. Kargund during the reign of Hoysala Narasiṃha I. A grant for this temple was entrusted to Mallisena Paṇḍita, disciple of Vāsupūjya II and grand-disciple of Śrīpāla Traividya. *Epigraphia Carnatica* V, Arsi 141; *Jain Śilālekha Saṃgraha* III, No. 347.

***Karuṇā-Vajrāyudha*:** Drama written by the Jain teacher Bālacandra who also known as a writer of commentaries. In this drama the legend of the compassionate King Śibi, who protected the dove from the falcon it treated. Here Śibi is known as Vajrāyudha. Ed. Muni Chaturvijaya in Jaina Ātmānada Granthamālā, No. 56, Bhavnagar, 1916.

Kāruṇya: Compassion for the afflicted, one of the four virtues to be cultivated in connection with the observance of the five *mahāvratas* (q.v.).

Karupannasami: Rock at Uttampalaiyam in Nilkottai taluk, Madurai District, Tamil Nadu, which has rows of Jain sculptures, mostly of the Tīrthaṃkaras.

Kāsahrada: A Jain *tīrtha* in Sirohi district, Rajasthan, which contained an eleventh-century Śāntinātha temple. The *Vividhatīrthakalpa* refers to other Jina temples of this place.

Kasalageri: Findspot of a Jain inscription of AD 1142

in Nagamangala taluk of the Mandya district, Karnataka, which records the construction of a big Jinālaya by a feudatory of Hoysala Viṣṇuvardhana, known as Ekkoṭi Jinālaya, dedicated to Pārśva. The grant of a village is recorded for its maintenance and the recipient was Brahmadeva belonging to Mūla-saṅgha and Surastha-gaṇa. *Epigraphia Carnatica* IV, Naga 94-5.

Kaṣāya: A concept closely associated with the nine fundamentals of Jainism. Human actions of all sorts produce certain subtle *karma* matters which defile souls and harbour *kaṣāya* or passions which act as a viscous substance and retain the subtle matter coming into contact with the souls. The *kaṣāyas* consist of four sins—anger (*krodha*), conceit (*māna*), intrigue (*māyā*), and greed (*lobha*). In some cases these sins are nourished throughout life (*anantānubandhī*), in other cases for one year (*apratyākhyāna*), or for four months (*pratyākhyāna*), or for a while (*sañjavalana*). There are nine other categories of *kaṣāya* which are laughter (*hāsya*), pleasure (*rati*), disgust (*arati*), fear (*bhaya*), grief (*śoka*) and other minor faults. Such moods as laughing, pleasure, fear, grief, and loathing do not, however, count among the chief passions and are called *nokaṣāya* for that reason. Sexual consciousness as man or woman or neuter has also been referred to in this connection. The *kaṣāyas* result in tying men to the cycle of rebirth. They cannot be removed except by the control of senses. Their motives are said to be space, object, and body. They depend on impressions made by all colours, different kinds of tastes and smells, and four sensations—warmth, cold, softness, and roughness—and these they have in common with the central offences and all other sins. To get rid of the stains of *kaṣāya* twelve prescribed vows of right conduct, the processes of which are laid down in the steps or stages of *guṇasthāna* (q.v.), are required. The effects of the *kaṣāyas* are given in detail in *Dasav* VIII.37-9; cf. *Sūyagaḍa* I.1.4.11ff; I.2.2.29; 9.11. They are also recorded in scattered passages of other Aṅgas.

Kaṣāyaprābhṛta: Also known as *Kaṣāyapāhuḍa* and composed by Guṇadharācārya, it is a philosophical work of the second century AD which has come down to us with huge Prakrit-Sanskrit commentaries. It is a work on the Jain doctrine of *karma* in 233 *gāthā-sūtras* which has been elaborated in the *Cūrṇisūtras* of Yativṛṣabha (q.v.) who probably flourished in the last quarter of the sixth century AD. Afterwards, according to Indranandin two other commentaries were written on it, and finally the great *Jayadhavalā* (q.v.) composed on it during the ninth century by Vīrasena and Jinasena. Edited with the *Cūrṇi* of Yativṛṣabha by Hiralal Jain, Calcutta, 1955.

Kaṭakābharaṇa Jinālaya: Jain temple in the Andhra region of the time of the Eastern Cālukyas which was built by Durgarāja at Dharmavaram. A village was granted to this temple for worship and maintenance. *Annual Report on the South Indian Epigraphy*, 1906-7, Copper Plate VII.

Kathākośas: Jain authors compiled treasuries of stories from time to time, not only in Prakrit, but also in Sanskrit, Apabhraṃśa, Kannaḍa, Tamil, Old Hindi, and Old Gujarati. A.N. Upadhye has mentioned several *kathākośas* written in Prakrit and Sanskrit in his introduction to *Bṛhatkathākośa*: (1) *Kathākośa* in Sanskrit interspersed with Prakrit *gāthās*; author unknown; composed in the last quarter of the eleventh century; translated in 1895 into English by C.H. Tawney. (2) *Kathākośas*, under which title ten manuscripts are available in the government collection of the Bhandarkar Oriental Research Institute, Pune. No information is available about their authors. Some have small stories in Apabhraṃśa and old Gujarati; Sanskrit prose mixed with Prakrit quotations; and Sanskrit stories interspersed with Prakrit and Apabhraṃśa verses. (3) *Kathāmahodadhi* (or *Karpūraprakāśa* or *Sūktāvalī*) by Hari or Hariṣena in Sanskrit. Date not settled. Commentaries were written on this work. (4) *Kathāratnasāgara* by Naracandrasūri in Sanskrit. The Patan MS is dated samvat 1319. (5) *Kathārṇava* (or *Iṣimaṇḍala*, that is *Ṛṣimaṇḍalastotra*) by Dharmaghoṣa of the thirteenth century. More than a dozen commentaries on this text are available. (6) *Kathāsamāsa* (*Upadeśamālā*) by Jinabhadra in Prakrit. Date is not definite. (7) *Kathāsaṃgraha* under which title seven works by Hemācārya, Ānandasundara, Sarvasundara, and others are noted in the *Jinaratnakośa*. Some works are anonymous or we do not know much about them. All the works are in Sanskrit interpersed with Mahārāṣṭrī and Apabhraṃśa quotations. (8) *Kathākośa* by Śrīcandra of the eleventh century written in Apabhraṃśa. (9) *Kathākośa* by Prabhācandra (there were many writers of this name) of the eleventh century in Sanskrit prose. (10) *Kathākośa* by Nemidatta of the sixteenth century in Sanskrit verses. (11) *Vaḍḍarādhanā* in eleventh-century Kannaḍa prose. It contains quotations in Prakrit (with Apabhraṃśa),

Sanskrit, and Kannaḍa. (12) *Puṇyāsrava Kathākośa* by Nāgarāja composed in AD 1331 in Kannaḍa. It is based on a Sanskrit work of the same name composed by Ramacandra Mumukṣu and has been translated into Marathi 1821 by Jinasena. Apart from all these, the *Kahānayakośa* (*Kathānakakośa* or *Kathākośaprakaraṇa*) is a storehouse of popular tales told by Jineśvarasūri in the eleventh century. The *Ākhyānamaṇikośa* or *Kathāmaṇikośa* by Nemicandrasūri of the eleventh century with a commentary of Amaradeva of the twelfth century is collection of didactic stories. The *Kahārayanakośa* or *Kathāratnakośa* by Guṇacandra of the early twelfth century is another collection of narratives. The *Kumāravālapadiboha* (enlightenment of Kumārapāla) by Somaprabhasūri (twelfth century) is another important compilation of stories narrated by the celebrated Hemacandra to teach King Kumārpāla. The *Bṛhatkathākośa* of Hariṣena is in Sanskrit but has its origin is Prakrit. The *Kathākośa* (or *Kathāsaṃgraha* or *Antarakathāsaṃgraha*) by Rājaśekhara Maladhārī (fourteenth century) and the *Kathākośa* (or *Bhadreśvara-Bāhubali-Vṛtti*) by Śubhaśīla (fifteenth century AD) should also be mentioned in this connection.

Kathāmahodadhi: 'The Great Ocean of Stories' compiled in 1448 by Somacandra which contains 157 stories partly in Prakrit and partly in Sanskrit with Prakrit verses.

Kathānakas: Short stories, so many of which were included in the commentaries and also written down frequently as independent works, and sometimes they were elaborated into ornate poems. These were collected from a variety of sources, many of which were originally secular but later were given Jain tone and colour.

Kathānakakośa: Collection of stories written by Jineśvara (q.v.) pupil of Vardhamāna, in AD 1992.

Kathāratnākara: Also known as *Kathāratnasāgara*, it is written in 15 cantos by Naracandrasūri, pupil of Devaprabhasūri of the Maladhārī-gaccha at the request of Vastupāla in the thirteenth-century.

Kathāratnākara: A book of 258 stories written in AD 1600 by Hemavijaya. With the exception of a very few metrical narratives, the work is written in elaborate Sanskrit prose. Into this are interspersed stanzas in Sanskrit, Mahārāṣṭrī, Apabhraṃśa, old Hindi, and Old Gujarati. Most of the narratives are similar to those in the *Pañcatantra* and other books of stories of this kind. Ed. Hiralal Hamsraj, Jamnagar, 1811; trans. into German by J. Hertel, Munchen, 1920; revised and modernized under the title *Das Perlenmeer* (The Sea of Pearls), Berlin, 1979.

Kaṭṭale-basti: The largest temple in the Candrabetta Hill, Sravanabelgola, being about 38 m by 12 m on plan with a *garbhagṛha*, an open *andha-maṇḍapa*, a *mukha-maṇḍapa* and an outer verandah. Dedicated to Ādinātha, it is also known as Padmāvatī-basti. It is without a tower. The pedestal record states that it was carved AD 118 by Gaṅgarāya for the merit of his mother Pocchive.

Kauśāmbī: Kosam in the Allahabad district, Uttar Pradesh, which according to the Jain tradition is the birth-place of Padmaprabha, the sixth Tīrthaṃkara.

Kavirājamārga: See Amoghavarṣa.

Kāvyānuśāsana: Written by Vagbhata about AD 1300, it is a work on rhetoric. The author was the son of Nemikumāra, a Śrāvaka who built a Jain temple at Medapāṭa or Mewar.

Kāvyānuśāsana: See Hemacandra.

Kāyotsarga: Standing meditating posture in which Jina images are made. Monks practising penance stand in this posture. We are told of Bāhubalī that while he was practising austerities, the vines grew up around his legs and covered his body, and ants prepared a mound at his feet. He is stated to have remained in this posture for an entire year. This motif is noticed in the *Mahābhārata* story of the sage Cyavana who assumed the standing posture and stood quiet and still like a post for a long time.

Kendua: Eleven km north of Ambikanagar in the Bankura district, it was once a flourishing centre of Jainism as it attested by the religious relics scattered over this village. The whole area is littered with the fragments of a stone temple, and a beautiful image of Pārśvanātha broken at the top lies near by. The figure stands in *kāyotsarga* on a lotus *triratha* pedestal. Three-hooded snakes are on the immediate right and left on the feet of the Jina, the one on the right holding a *ghaṭa* and the other a stick. There are *chowri*-bearers further right and left, and miniature Tīrthaṃkaras in rows of three on either side of the central image.

Keravase: Findspot of two Jain inscriptions, respectively of AD 1450 and 1510 , in South Kanara district, Karnataka, which refer to the Vardhamāna temple of this place. *Jaina Śilālekha Saṃgraha* V, Nos. 201, 230.

Kesavāra: Site of a dilapidated Jain temple of Pārśvanātha in the Gulabarga district, Karnataka, which was repaired in AD 1385 according to an inscription found therein. *Jaina Śilālekha Saṃgraha* V, No. 181.

Keśavāpa: Sacrament. It is the ceremony of keeping

the hair after shaving for the first time.

Kesoraipaton: Also known as Āsramanagara, it lay in the Malwa region where Nemicandra wrote his *Laghudravyasaṃgraha* during the reign of Paramāra Bhoja.

Ketu: Jyotiṣka or stellar deity conceived by the Jains as having the symbol and attribute of a snake. He has no direction to rule over. He is the opposite point of Rāhu (q.v.).

***Kevala Jñāna*:** Knowledge that unobstructed, unconditional, and absolute, which is to be acquired by yoga or concentration. It belongs to the *pratyakṣa* or direct category because it is not acquired through the medium of the senses. *Tattvārtha* I, 9.12, 21-9. See Epistemology.

Khajuraho Jain Inscription: Dated in VS 1215 (AD 1157), it records the dedication of an image of Sambhavanātha in the reign of Candella Madanavarman by Sādhu Sālha, son of Pāhila of Grahapati Vaṃśa. *Epigraphia Indica* I, 152-3.

Khajuraho Temples: Among the six Jain temples at Khajuraho erected by merchants, with Jina images installed therein by individual donors, the largest, now called the Pārśvanātha, bears an inscription of Pahila ' who was respected by King Dhaṅga'. Erected about AD 950, his temple is adorned with graceful Surasundarin and Hindu gods. The other Jain temples are the Ghaṇṭai (*c.* tenth century) the Śāntinātha (*c.* AD 1027) and Ādinātha (about AD 1075). The other two are insignificant. The Ghaṇṭai temple, as it now stands, is in extremely fragmentary state, and a few pillars that remain represent but a shell of what was apparently a great conception. The pillars are arranged in two blocks, the frontal one constituing the portico and the rear sillar the *maṇḍa*. The *garbhagṛha* or sanctum is no more. The Ādinātha temple represents a small structure. Its *maṇḍapa* and other adjuncts either did not exist originally or were removed and replaced in modern times by a brick construction. Rising on a high *adhiṣṭhāna*, the sanctum is *saptaratha* on plan and correspondingly has a sevenfold division of the *bāḍa*. The sanctum walls are decorated by three tiers of sculpture. The elongated *śikhara* rises stepwise and is richly fretted with delicate interlacings of *caityas*. The Pārśvanātha temple, the holiest of the Jain group at Khajuraho, is one of the most elaborate productions. Its construction was financed by Pahila who alone gifted seven gardens in the names of various persons including the one called Dhaṅga-vāḍi in honour of King Dhaṅgadeva. Graceful divine couples adorn the Pārśvanātha temple. It should be noted in this connection that the *vyāla surasundarī*, *mithuna*, etc., were regarded as auspicious ornaments of medieval temples irrespective of their sectarian affiliation. The temple comprises an oblong structural scheme with a projected portion at each end of the sanctum—the one in front forming the *maṇḍapa* hall and the other at the back an attached shrine. There is an enclosed passage around the sanctum cella. It exuberant wealth of sculptural elegance had been referred to above.

Khambhat: Digambara Jain centre in western India where Tejaḥpāla (q.v.) constructed a temple for the merit of his mother.

Khaṇḍagiri Caves: Fifteen caves in Khaṇḍagiri near Bhubaneswar in Orissa are of Jain affiliation. Among them Anantagumpha contains a single Tīrthaṃkara image; Navamuni has ten Tīrthaṃkaras and seven Śāsanadevatās; Bārabhuji has twenty-five Tīrthaṃkara images and twenty-six Śāsanadevatās; Triśūla has twenty-four Tīrthaṃkara images; unnamed cave no. 10 has two Tīrthaṃkara images and one Śāsanadevatā; and the Latalendukeśarī gumpha has eight Tīrthaṃkara images. The carvings mostly belong to the eleventh and twelfth centuries, excepting Triśūla which is later. On the back wall of the Anantagumpha to the right of a *nandipāda* on a stepped pedestal, an unfinished Tīrthaṃkara image is relieved. In the Navamuni Tīrthaṃkara, image have been carved of Ṛṣabha, Ajita, Sambhava, Abhinandana, Vāsupūjya, Neminātha, and Pārśvanātha, in high relief, in a row within niches that are rounded on the top. They are flanked on either side by standing fly-whisk bearers. Beneath the row of Tīrthaṃkaras are carved, in another row, their respective Śāsanadevatās. Besides these rows of images on the right hand wall of the cave are carved two nude figures of Ṛṣabha and Pārśva. Further on the left wall there is a small figure of Candraprabha, seated on a lotus. The Bārabhuji gumpha contains 24 seated Tīrthaṃkaras on three sides of the antechamber, and one standing image of Pārśvanātha on the back wall in the left. All Tīrthaṃkaras are seated in *yogāsana* on double-petalled lotuses. All the images are flanked by standing attendants holding fly-whisks. Below the Tīrthaṃkara images are carved in a row their respective Śāsanadevatās. All of them are shown in *ardhaparyaṅka*, except Nirvāṇī, shown seated cross-legged and Naradatta shown recumbent. A standing Pārśvanātha image carved on the back wall is larger in size than the rest in the group. Two twelve-armed figures of Cakreśvarī (q.v.) and Ajitabalā (q.v.) are carved on the left and right walls of the verandah. Three relief figures, two of Ṛṣabhanātha and one of Āmrā, are carved on the back wall of cave No. 10. Near this cave is the damaged Lalātendukeśarī gumpha. It contains a few images of Ṛṣabhanātha and Pārśvanatha. Adjacent to Bārabhuji gumpha is the Triśūla which contains in its three sides of antechamber the images of 24 Tīrthaṃkaras. The carvings in this particular cave, unlike that of the others, are crude.

Khandelavāla: Important Digambara Jain mercantile caste spread over in north India which received its name from Khaṇḍela in Jaipur ruled by King Khaṇḍelagira of Cauhāna dynasty. According to tradition, after an epidemic the king along with his subjects became converted into Jainism under the influence of Ācārya Jinasena who gave them the caste named Khaṇḍelavāla and created 84 *gotras* out of 84 towns of the kingdom. According to another tradition, four Kṣatriya brothers killed a hermit's pet deer in a hunting expedition. The hermit forgave them on condition that they would give up violence for ever. The Khaṇḍelvālas sprang from these four brothers. From this legend it appears that the Khaṇḍelvālas were originally Kṣatriyas, but later they became Vaiśyas when they took to commerce. They are not divided into Viśā and Daśā sections. Khaṇḍelavālas are not rare among the Hindus, but they are mostly Jains. The Khaṇḍelavāla caste is also known as Śrāvagī or Saravagī.

Kharatara Sect: See Durlabharāja.

***Kharataragaccha-Bṛhadgurvāvalī*:** An important work dealing with the activities of the *gurus* of Kharatara-gaccha from Vardhamānasūri to Jinapatisūri, including a part of the activities of Jineśvara II, written originally by Jinapāla in the thirteenth century. Thereafter the activities of other chiefs up to the middle of the fourteenth century were recorded by an unknown writer belonging to this gaccha. Ed. Jinavijaya, Singhi Jain Granthamālā, No. 42, Bombay, 1956.

Kharatara-vasahi: *Caturmukha* temple of fifteenth century in the Dilwara group of temples, Mount Abu.

Khāravela: Cedi king of Orissa who adopted the usual eclectic policies of Indian monarchs, but showed a decided inclination towards Jainism, as can be seen from his own record and the inscription of his chief queen dedicating a cave for the use of the Jain monks. He seems to have ruled in the first century BC. The events of his life are recorded in considerable detail in the Hathigumpha inscription (q.v.). He was a great conqueror and builder, and for his devotion to Jainism he was called *bhikṣu-rāja*, that is, the monk king. He excavated a number of Jain caves in the Kumārī Parvata or Khaṇḍagiri Hill. Probably he also built a monastery at a place called Pabhāsa not far from these caves. In the twelfth year of his reign he invaded Magadha, humbled its king, Bṛhasvātimitra or Bṛhaspatimitra, and carried away much booty together with certain Jina images previously taken away by a Nanda king from Kaliṅga. See Kalinga Jina.

Khedabrahmā: A Jain *tīrtha* in Sabarkantha district of Gujarat which contained a medieval Mahāvīra temple.

Khenora: See Yakṣendra.

Khimvsar: Findspot of very fine specimen of Jīvantasvāmin image of tenth-eleventh century in Nagaur district, now in the Jodhpur Museum.

Kidangil: Findspot of a bronze image of Mahāvīra in Tindivanam taluk, South Arcot district, now housed in a government Museum, Madras. It bears a twelfth-century inscription in Tamil.

Kilavalavu: Situated in Melur taluk, Madurai district, Tamil Nadu. A Brahmi inscription records the foundation of a monastery by a lay devotee from Toṇṭi. Later sculptures of Tīrthaṃ-karas are found on the boulders.

Kil-Sattamangalam: A rock inscription from this place in the Wandiwash taluk of North Arcot district in Tamil Nadu records an endowment for feeding monks. This belongs to the time of Nandivarman II Pallavamalla. Two more inscriptions from the same place also refer to similar endowments. The name of the grantee saint is Pavanandivar who had received it for the merit of Pūṇḍi Muppavai, daughter of Jinadiyār of Vilukkam in the Tindivaram taluk. *Annual Report of Indian Epigraphy*, 1968-9, 60; Nos. B. 219-20, 268.

Kinnara Yakṣa: Attendant Yakṣa of Dharmanātha (q.v.). He has three faces and six arms. According to the Śvetāmbaras he has tortoise as his mount and his attributes are the citrus, mace, lotus, and rosary. One hand is in *abhaya*. The Digambaras describe him as carrying a disc, *vajra*, goad, club, rosary, and one hand in *varada-mudrā*.

Kiradu Inscription of Alhanadeva: A stone inscription dated Vikrama Samvat 1209 (AD 1153), obtained from Kradu, the ancient Kirātakūpa in Western Rajasthan, records that Maharaha Alhanadeva, a feudatory of the Cālukya King Kumārapāla (q.v.) of Gujarat, had given protection to the lives of animals on certain specified dates, obviously on the approval of his overlord. *Epigraphia Indica*, XI.44ff; *Bhavnagar Inscriptions* 172-3.

Koḍehala-basadi: Name of a twelfth-century Jain

temple situated at Kyātanahalli, Srirangapatna taluk, Mandya district, Karnataka, mentioned in an inscription from the same place. *Jaina Śilākekha Saṃgraha* III, No. 387.

Kogali: Findspot of Jain inscriptions in Haḍagalli taluk, Bellary district, Karnataka. An inscription of AD 992 mentions a Jain pontiff called Gaṇadharadeva Bhaṭṭāraka. Another inscription of AD 1055 informs of a Jain temple dedicated to Pārśva, originally constructed by the western Gaṅga King Durvinīta. It mentions Indrakīrti of Kondakundanvaya. Two thirteenth-century epigraphs from this place refer to a number of Jain donors hailing from different places and Kogali as a *tīrtha*. An incomplete inscription on the wall of the Pārśvanātha temple at Kogali mentions Sāmana Jinālaya of Kolhapur. *South Indian Inscriptions* IX(1), Nos. 77, 346-7, 362; *Epigraphia Carnatica*, rev. edn. II, No. 380; *Jaina Śilālekha Saṃgraha*, IV, Nos. 141, 363.

Kojarā: A Jain *tīrtha* in Sirohi district, Rajasthan, the antiquity of which is attested by an epigraph of AD 1166.

Kolanupaka: Findspot of an inscription of AD 1125, of the time of Vikramāditya VI in Nalgonda district, which mentions a Jain temple of the goddess Ambikā. *Annual Report on the South Indian Epigraphy*, 1961-2, No. 92.

Kolhapur Plates: Dated śaka 1037 (AD 1115), the plates refer to the existence of a feudatory family named Nigumba, who were great patrons of a Jain Saṅgha with special reference to one named Nolamba. Besides there is a stone epigraph dated śaka 1040 (AD 1118) of the reign of Śilāhāra Gaṇḍarāditya found at the Pārśvanātha temple of Kolhapur, which was founded by his feudatory Nimbadevarasa at Kavaḍegolla and records gifts to Śrutakīrti Traividyadeva of the Pustaka-gaccha in the Deśīya-gaṇa of the Mūla-saṅgha, who officiated as the priest of the Jain temple called Rūpanārāyaṇa in Kolhapur. An undated inscription of the time of Gaṇḍarāditya, found in the *maṇḍapa* of the shrine of Seṣāśāyī in the backyard of the Mahālakṣmī temple at Kolhapur, records the construction of an Ādinātha temple built and financed by the same Nimbadevarasa. Mention may also be made in this connection of an inscription of Śilāhāra Vijayāditya (AD 1138-75) recording a grant for a Pārśvanātha temple, constructed by one Vāsudeva who was in the service of his feudatory Kāmadeva and disciple of Māghanandin Siddhāntadeva. *Corpus Inscriptionum Indicarum*, VI, Nos. 45, 49-50, 53.

Kollipāka Temple: Built by Kumāra Tailapa, this temple now lies in a ruined state. It was seemingly destroyed during Cola invasions. Vestiges of *pūrṇa-ghaṭas* on some door-jambs of some of the smaller shrines, *māna-stambha*, carvings of Ādinātha, Padmāvatī, and a high stone *toraṇa*, etc., testify to the importance of this temple.

Konakoṇḍala: Findspot of an eleventh-century epigraph in the Anantapur district, Andhra Pradesh, which mentions the erection of a Jinālaya in the birth place of Kundakunda (q.v.) the great Digambara Jain philosopher. *Annual Report on the South Indian Epigraphy* 1915-16, No. 565.

Kongar-Puliyangulam: A hill-site in the Tirumaṅgalam taluk of Madura district which contains an image of the Jain saint Ajjanandī.

Konnur Stone Inscription: Dated śaka 782 (AD 860) of the time of the Rāṣṭrakūṭa Amoghavarṣa I and found at Konnur on the south bank of the Malaprabha in Nawalgund taluk of Dharwar district, this inscription refers to the emperor's patronage of an officer Bankeśa (Bankeya). A land-grant was given for the benefit of a Jain sanctuary founded by the said officer himself at Kolanura to the sage Devendra, disciple of Trikālayogīśa, belonging to the Pustaka-gaccha, Deśīya-gaṇa and Mūla-saṅgha. *Epigraphia Indica* VI, 25ff.

Kopana: Also known as Kopbal in Raichur district, Karnataka, this place had yielded a number of Jain inscriptions. An inscription of AD 881 states that Sarvanandin Bhaṭāra, pupil of Ekacattugada Bhaṭāra of the Kundakunda lineage, practised austerities here and attained liberation by performing the vow of *sallekhanā*. Another inscription refers to the saint Jaṭāsiṃhanandin. As a place of Jain pilgrimage Kopbal is mentioned in inscriptions found elsewhere, e.g. Sravanabelgola. The death of Sukumārasena Muni on the hill of Kopana is mentioned by Cāmuṇḍarāya in his *Purāṇa* (qq.v.). We have references to some Jain shrines of this place including Kusa Jinālaya. An inscription of the first year of Vikramāditya V's reign, assigned AD 1008, refers to the voluntary death of Siṃhanandī, who belonged to the Kondakunda-anvaya of Deśīya-gaṇa. Five of his spiritual predecessors, Ravicandra, Guṇasāgara, Guṇacandra, Abhayanandī, and Māghanandī are mentioned. A monk called Kalyāṇakīrti and a temple of Śāntinātha are eulogized. An inscription of AD 1240 of the time of Yādava Singhana records a charitable endowment of land in favour of the Jain temples of Kopana. One inscription refers to a Jain teacher called Candrasena. Another inscription of the thirteenth century mentions a Jain temple named after Sāntaladevī, the queen of the Hoysala King Viṣṇuvardhana. It also refers to three other Jain temples, namely Arasiya-basadi, Tirthada-basadi, and Timamba-basadi. *Epigraphia Carnatica*, II, Nos. 127, 191, 345, 384, P.B. Desai 350-65.

Kopbal Inscription: Dated śaka 887 (AD 964), found near Kopbal at Uppina Betgiri in the Raichur district, this inscription refers to a feudatory of Rāṣṭrakūṭa Kṛṣṇa III named Sankaragaṇḍa II who erected a Jain shrine called Jayadhīra Jinālaya P.B. Desai, *Jainism in South India and Some Jain Epigrapha*, Sholapur, 1957, Part III, No. 48.

Koppa: Town in the Chikmagalur district, Karnataka, which is the findspot of a Jain inscription of AD 1599 referring to Sādhana-Jinālaya dedicated to Pārśvanātha. *Epigraphia Carnatica* VII, Koppa, 50.

Koppa Jinālaya: Jina temple dedicated to Pārśvanātha, which was situated at Adak, in the Gulbarga district, Karnataka. It was named after a general called Kopparasa of the time of the Western Cālukya Vikramāditya VI as stated in an inscription of AD 1126. Another inscription of AD 1243 belonging to the time of Yādava King Siṅghana mentions a gift to Koppa Jinālaya by local merchants.

Koraga: Findspot of an inscription of AD 1419 from South Kanara district, Karnataka, which records a grant to a Jina temple by the Pāṇḍya-Bhūpāla, chief of Keravasa and refers to a monk called Vasantakīrti belonging to the Balātkāra-gaṇa. *Jaina Śilālekha Saṃgraha* IV, No. 442.

Koṭivarṣa: Bengarh in West Dinajpur district in West Bengal after which a *śākhā* of the Jains was designated.

Kovilangalam: Findspot of an inscription of the Cola King Kulottuṅga I (AD 1070-1120), dated in his 48th year, in the Ramanathapuram district, Tamil Nadu. It shows that the Jains of Kumbnur in that district were quite affluent. *Inscriptions of Madras Presidency*, No. 17.

Kriyāvāda: One of the four major philosophical schools current in the days of Lord Mahāvīra according to the Jain texts which mention its 180 forms. Kriyāvāda is the doctrine according to which the soul acts and is acted upon. The term Kiriyam or Kriyāvāda, with some reservations, also applies to the Jain doctrines. According to the *Sūyagaḍa* I.12. 11-12, the followers of this doctrine maintain that misery is caused by oneself and not by an external agent. Liberation may be attained by knowledge and good conduct (*vijjācaraṇam pamokkham*). Fools are unable to stop the influx of evil actions, but the wise can do so by abstaining from wrong doing (*nakommaṇā kamma khavemti bālā, akammaṇā kamma khavemti dhiro*). Contemporary philosophical schools were not ready to accept the view of the Kriyāvādins that human suffering is not conditioned by, or dependent on, external conditions. Cf. *Aṅguttara* III.440.

Kṛṣṇa II: Rāṣṭrakūṭa emperor of the ninth-tenth century who was a patron of Jainism according to the Saundatti inscription of AD 897 and Mulgund inscription of AD 902. He was probably a patron of Guṇabhadra, author of the *Uttarapurāṇa*. Guṇabhadra himself claimed that Kṛṣṇa II was his disciple. A Sravanabelgola inscription connects a Jain saint Paravāḍimalla with Kṛṣṇarāja. The latter is often identified with the Rāṣṭrakūṭa monarch Kṛṣṇa II.

Kṛṣṇadāsa: See *Vimala Purāṇa*.

***Kṣapaṇasāra*:** See Nemicandra Siddhāntacakravartin.

***Kṣatracuḍāmaṇi*:** See Oḍeyadeva Vādibhasiṃha.

Kṣetrapāla: Protector of the arable land conceived of in terms of a deity in all the religious systems of India. The Jain Kṣetrapāla has twenty hands, matted hair, and a snake as his holy thread. He is surrounded by Ānanda and other Bhairavas and leads the sixty-four Yoginīs. Kṣetrapāla himself is a Bhairava and seems to be a master of the Yoginīs. As the name suggests, he is the deity whose function is to protect the field. Hence the dog is his companion. The Brahmanical Bhairavas such as Kālabhairava and Vaṭukabhairava are always associated with a dog. The relation of Kṣetrapāla and Vaṭuka is clearly mentioned in the *Ācāradinakara*.

***Kṣīṇamoha*:** The twelfth *guṇasthāna* (q.v.) in which greed completely disappears.

***Kṣīrāsana*:** Sacrament which consists of sprinkling of holy water on a child by the preceptor when mother's milk is given to it. It is a Śvetāmbara ritual.

***Kṣurakarma*:** Also known as *cūḍākarma* it is the tonsure ceremony of the child, a Śvetāmbara sacrament.

Kubera: Protector of the northern regions who has been conceived of by the Śvetāmbaras as a deity riding a man and wearing gems and a club. He is the king of the Yakṣas who rules over Kailāśa and possesses the *puṣpaka* chariot flying on the air as his vehicle. He is also the lord of wealth, which is why he had become an important deity, far above the others, among the Jain mercantile communities.

Kubera-Yakṣa: Attendant of Mallinātha (q.v.). He has an elephant as his vehicle. In Śvetāmbara tradition he holds the axe, spear, citron, *śakti*, club, rosary with two hands in *abhaya* and *varada, mudra*. In Digambara tradition the attributes are shield, bow, staff, lotus, sword, axe, noose, and *varada* pose. Kubera as the god of wealth and the lord of the Yakṣas has, however, a separate entity and position in Jainism with which the concept of Kubera-Yakṣa does not seem to tally.

Kudeva: See gods.

Kudlur Inscriptions: Two inscriptions dated śaka 884 (AD 962-3) distributed in plates of the Gaṅga King Mārasiṃha III (AD 960-74) found at Kudalur in Mandya taluk, Mysore district, the earlier of which presents a line of Jain teachers beginning with Prabhācandra of Mūla-saṅgha and Surasta-gaṇa. Other teachers are Kalaneledeva, Ravicandra and Elācārya. The last named teacher received the gift of the village Kadalur (Kudlur) in Koṅgal-deśa for maintaining the Jinālaya constructed by the king's mother Kallabbā. The second inscription refers to the religious leanings of his predecessors who were mostly devout Jains. Mārasiṃha is described in this inscription as one 'who washed out all taints with the water of the daily bath of Jina and one who was devoted to the worship of his *gurus*.' The inscription refers to an Ācārya named Muñjārya Vādighanghala whose 'eloquence in the exposition of literature made Gaṅga Gāṅgeya Satyavākya (title of Bhūtaga II, q.v.), a cuckoo in the grove of delighters of all learning, his pupil.' He was given as Śrutaguru's fee a village called Bagiyur. *Epigraphia Indica* IV.281; XXXVI. 97ff.; *Mysore Archaeological Report*, 1921, 18ff.

***Kula*:** Clan or family, also known as *sambhoga*, functioning as subdivision of *śākhā* or branch of the *gaṇa* (qq.v.) or school. Like the *gaṇa* and *śākhā*, the term *kula* has no fixed definition. According to the traditional accounts pertaining to the line of patriarchs, the Uddehāgaṇa of Rohana comprised four *śākhās* and six *kulas*, Uduvaṭika-gaṇa of Bhadraśas four *śākhās* and three *kulas*, Veśavāṭika-gaṇa of Kāmardhi four *śākhās* and four *kulas*, Caraṇa-gaṇa of Śrigupta four *śākhās* and seven *kulas*, Mānava-gaṇa of Ṛṣigupta four *śākhās* and three *kulas*, and Kauṭika-gaṇa of Susthita, Kotika and Supratibuddha four *śākhās* and four *kulas*. In the Mathura inscriptions Nāgabhutikīya and Paridhāsika *kulas* are associated with the *śākhās* of the Odehikiya-gaṇa; Hālakīya, Puṣyamitra, Āryaciṭiya, Petavamika and Ayyabheṣṭa *kulas* with those of Vāraṇa-gaṇa; and Brahmadāsika, Sthāniya, Vairi, Uccenāgari and Vidyādharī with those of Koliya-gaṇa. A Mehika-*kula* finds an independent mention in the Mathura inscriptions. In some later manuscripts of Vāgbhaṭa's *Neminātha-kāvya* the author has been described as belonging of the Prāgvaṭa-*kula* of Ahicchatrapura. Rājaśekhara, author of the *Prabandhakośa*, was a pupil of Śrītilaka of Maladhārī or Harṣapurīya gaccha, belonging to the Praśnavāhana-*kula* and Kotika-gaṇa. Jain inscriptions from Orissa refer to Aryasaṃghagraha-*kula*. The Vidyādhara-*kula* belongs to Rajasthan. See Saṅgha, Gaṇa, Gaccha, Anvaya, Śākhā, Bali.

***Kulacaryā*:** Sacrament. It is the performance of the six daily duties of a householder.

Kulugamalai: An important stronghold of Jainism in Tinnevelly district. This hill has yielded a good number of sculptures and inscriptions.

Kulagāṇa Inscription: Undated inscription of the time of the Gaṅga King Śivamāra I (AD 670-713) found at Kulagaṇa in Camarajanagar taluk of Mysore district which refers to individual grants to Jain institution with the permission of the king. Śivamāra himself made a grant to the Jain Candrasenācārya, the *kartārar* or manager of a temple complex. *Mysore Archaeological Report*, 1925, 90ff.

Kumāra: Attendant Yakṣa of Vāsupūjya (q.v.) whose mount is a swan and who has a white complexion. The Digambara view makes him three-headed and six-handed, hands carrying the bow, ichneumon, fruit, club, and in *varada* pose. In Śvetāmbara conception he is four-armed holding citron, mongoose, arrow, and bow respectively. It is rather curious that this Yakṣa, who bears the analogous name to Kumāra or Kārttikeya, should have a swan instead of a peacock for his vehicle while the next Yakṣa Caturmukha, an epithet of Brahmā, has a peacock as his riding animal.

***Kumārabhūpālacarita*:** Legendary and partly historical biography of King Kumārapāla of the Cālukya house of Gujarat written in 6,000 verses by Jayasiṃha in AD 1364. Pub. by Hiralal Hamsaraj, Jamnagar, 1915; also Bombay 1926.

Kumārapāla: Cālukya king of Gujarat who ruled from the middle of the twelfth century AD. Originally he was a Śaiva but later was converted to Jainism under the influence of Hemacandra. This happened about AD 1160 according to the *Mahārājaparājaya*. From Hemacandra's *Mahāvīracarita* we learn that Kumārapāla did his best to make his kingdom a model Jain state. He laid greatest emphasis on practising *ahiṃsā* or non-violence and non-injury to animals in public life. Exaggerated versions of his insistence on non-violence are given in such works as the *Prabandhacintāmaṇi*, *Prabhāvakacarita*, and

Kumārapālapratibodha (qq.v.). Two magnificent temples, dedicated respectively to Pārśvanātha and Neminātha, were built by him in the capital Pattana. Rāmacandra in his *Kumāravihāraśataka* has given a grand description of the former. A temple dedicated to Ajitanātha was built by Kumārapāla on the Tarangā Hills, some 26 miles north-east of Siddhapura. Inscriptions found in Kiradu, Ratanpur, and Jalor (qq.v.) testify to his religious activities. A devoted Jain, Kumārapāla made a pilgrimage to two great *tīrthas*, Girnar and Satruñjaya. He passed away in AD 1173.

***Kumarapalacarita*:** Written by the celebrated Hemacandra (q.v.) on his patron and disciple King Kumārapāla, the work actually purports to illustrate the rules of Prakrit grammar. The last two cantos are written in various Prakrit dialects, Śaurasenī, Māgadhī, Paiśācī, and Apabhraṃśa. Rev. edn. by P.L. Vaidya, Poona, 1936.

***Kumārapālacarita*:** A poem in ten cantos which runs to 2,032 verses, on the great Jain King Kumārapāla written in *kāvya* style in the early fifteenth century by Caritrasundara, the disciple of Ratnasiṃhasūri. Bhavnagar, 1913.

***Kumārapālaprabandha*:** A work on the Jain King Kumārapāla written in mixed Sanskrit prose and verse in the fifteenth century by Jinamaṇḍaṇagaṇi, pupil of Somasundara of the Tapāgaccha, Bhavnagar, 1915.

***Kumārapālapratibodha*:** See Somaprabha.

***Kumārapālapratiboshacarita*:** Idealized biography of the Cālukya King Kumārapāla written in AD 1366 by Somatilakasuri of the Rudrapalliya-gaccha who was a disciple of Sanghatilakasuri. See *Jinaratnakośa* 93.

Kumāravihāra: Pārśvanātha temple complex built by the Cālukya King Kumārapāla (q.v.) of Gujarat in his capital, Pattana. This temple consisted of a large inner and 24 adjoining temples, each dedicated to a Tīrthaṃkara. In the central shrine there was an image of Pārśvanātha made of white marble. Descriptions of this temple complex are to be found in the works of Somaprabhācārya, Merutuṅga, and Prabhācandra (qq.v.). According to Prabhācandra the opening ceremony of this temple was performed by Hemacandra. The latter's disciple Rāmacandra has written a nice description of this complex under the title *Kumāravihāraśataka*. Vardhamānagaṇi also has written a eulogy of this temple complex, entitled *Kumāravihārapraśasti*.

Kumārī Hill: See Udayagiri caves.

Kumaras: See Dikpālas.

***Kumāravihārapraśasti*:** Written by Vardhamānagaṇi, pupil of Hemacandra, (q.v.) in Sanskrit *ślokas* in which Kumārapāla, Hemacandra, and the minister Vāgbhaṭa have been praised. This poem has been published in Anekārtha Sāhitya Saṃgraha, Puṣpa 2, Ahmedabad.

Kumbharia Temples: Situated in southern Rajasthan, here stand a number of Jain temples among which the Nemināthа temple with double-*āmalakas* crowning the *aṅgaśikharas* and the main *śikhara* stands unique. The Pārśvanātha temple at Kumbharia is also identical in form and design, and both structures belong to the eleventh century AD. The *maṇḍapas* of both temples, especially of the latter, are exquisite. 'The *maṇḍapa* of Pārśvanātha temple in Kumbharia puts to unique use white Makrana marble of Rajasthan. The gleaming spaciousness of the hall, within the internal cloister of cells—evolved particularly in Jain temples—is without equal.' Stella Kramrisch, *Art of India*, London, 1954, 210.

Kumkumadevī: Queen of the Western Cālukya King Vijyāditya who constructed a Jina temple at Puligara which is recorded in a copper plate from Dharwar district belonging to the eleventh year of the king and śaka 630. *Annual Report of Indian Epigraphy*, 1945-6, A. 49.

Kumudacandra: A great Digambara dialectician of Karṇāṭa country who was the preceptor of Jayakeśin, the maternal grandfather of Jayasiṃha. It is said that he was defeated in a theoretical debate with the Śvetāmbara scholar Devasūri (q.v.) in AD 1123 at Pattana in the court of Jayasiṃha Siddharāja. According to the *Prabhāvakacarita* 174ff., the Śvetāmbara supporters of Devasūri did not follow the ethics of debate in this case. Hemacandra observed: 'If truly the snowbright Devasuri had not conquered Kumudacandra, not a single Śvetāmbara in this world would have worn a covering of his loins.' Another account is found in the *Mudritakumudacandra* (q.v.).

Kuṇāla: Same as northern Kosala. The river Sarayu divides Kosala into north and south. Śrāvastī is known as Kunālanagarī which was its capital. Kunāla country was frequented by Jain monks. In the Jain texts it is mentioned as a holy place along with Aṣṭapada, Ūrjayanta (Girnar), Hastināpura, Dharmacakra, etc.

Kundakunda: Celebrated Jain philosopher of the Digambara tradition who was also held in esteem by the Śvetāmbaras. He seems to have flourished in the first century AD. and composed as many as 88 treatises in Prakrit of which more than a dozen texts called *pāhuḍas* (*prābhṛtas*) are now available. They are on the subjects of *Darśana* (36 verses), *Cāritra* (44), *Sūtra* (27), *Bodha* (62), Bhāva (163), *Mokṣa* (106), *Liṅga* (22), *Śila* (40), *Ratna* (162), *Dvādaśānuprekṣā* (91), *Niyamasāra* (187), *Pañcāstikāya* (180), *Pravancanasāra* and *Samayasāra* (415). *Pancasttiyasārā* (*Pancastikayasara*) and *Samayasara* (415). *Pañcatthiyasara* (*Pañcastikāyasāra*) or *Pravayanasāra Pañcatthiyasaṃgaha* (*Pravacanasāra Pañcastikāyasaṃgraha*) consists of two parts, which are really independent works. The first and longer section contains the doctrine of five *astikāyas* or groups of existence: soul (*jīva*), non-souls (*pudgala*), principles of motion and rest (*dharma* and *adharma*) and space (*ākāśa*). The second section treats of the path of liberation. This work together with *Pravacanasāra* and *Samayasāra* forms a trilogy. The *Pañcāstikāya* is preserved in two recensions, one by Amṛtacandra which has 173 verses and the other by Jayasena which has 181 verses. The *Parvacanasāra* has 275 and 311 *gāthās* and the *Samayasāra* has 415 and 439 verses according to Amṛtacandra and Jayasena respectively. The *Pravacanasāra* is a much prized work on Jain dogmatics, psychology and ethics. On *Samayasāra* there are commentaries by Prabhacandra and Amṛtacandra. To Kundakunda is also attributed Chappāhuḍa (*ṣaṭprābhṛta*) 'six chapters on Jain doctrine' but this attribution is doubtful. *Pañcastikāya* with Amṛtacandra's and Jayasena's Sanskrit commentaries and Hemaraja Pande's *Balāvabodha bhāṣyaṭīkā* and Hindi trans. by Manoharlal, Sri Rajcandra Jain Sastramala, Bombay, 1904; Eng. trans. by A. Chakravarty in *Sacred Books of the Jains*, Arrah, 1920; *Pravacanasāra* with Amṛtacandra's and Jayasena's Sanskrit commentaries, and Hemarāja Pande's *Ṭīkā*, ed. and Eng. trans. by A.N. Upadhye, Sri Rajacandra Series, Bombay, 1935; *Dasabhatti*, included in the *Kundakundaprābhṛtasaṃgraha* (Collection of Kundakunda's *Pāhuḍas*), ed. K.C. Jain Siddhāntaśāstrī, Jivraj Jain Granthamala, Sholapur, 1960. *Chappāhuḍa*, com. by Amṛtacandra Sūri and Śrutasāgara, edited with a Hindi com. by Surajbhan Vakil. Benares, 1910.

Kundalpur: Jain centre in Damoh district. Here at Bare Baba numerous Jain sculptures have been discovered.

Kunthunātha: The seventeenth Tīrthaṃkara who was the son of Śūra and Śrī of Hastinapur. His height was 35 bow-lengths and his sacred tree was the *tilaka*. His disciples were Svayambhū and Amjuyā. He attained liberation on Mount Sammeya after living for 95,000 years. His symbol is a goat. He has as his Yakṣa Gandharva and yakṣiṇī Balā/Vijayā. His *chowrie*-bearer is Kunāla. His father belonged to the Kuru race.

***Kupakṣakauśikasahasakiraṇa*:** A polemical treatise against the Digambaras written in Prakrit in AD 1573 by the Śvetāmbara Dharmasāgara. It is also known as *Pravacana-Parīkṣā*.

Kupbal: Findspot of an elaborately carved Jain stone sculpture in Mysore. This twelfth-century sculpture of Pārśvanātha as the central figure with other 23 Jinas, Dharaṇendra and Padmāvatī, is now in the Salar Jung Museum, Hyderabad.

Kuppataru: A Jain centre in Shimoga district of Karnataka well-known for its Pārśvanātha temple known as Brahma-Jinālaya. An inscription from this place dated śaka 997 (AD 1075) mentions Mālaladevī, queen of a Kadamba prince, who washed the feet of the Jain teacher Padmanandī of Bandanika and made a grant for the said Brahma Jinālaya. Padmanandī belonged to Kundakunda line, Kanura-gaṇa and Tintrini-gaccha. An inscription of AD 1367 from Kuppataru mentions the restoration of a dilapidated Jain temple by one Ādideva, disciples of Devacandra of Deśī-gaṇa. Another inscription of AD 1408, of the reign of the Vijayanagara Emperor Devarāya I, records the erection of a Jina temple by a feudatory known as Gopipati II who was a disciple of Siddhāntācārya belonging to the Mūla-saṅgha and Deśi-gaṇa. A few other Jain inscriptions have also been found from this place. *Epigraphia Carnatica* VIII, Sorab 261-3.

Kurikyal: Site in Karimnagar district, Andhra Pradesh which has yielded some Jain sculptures.

Kurugodu: Site of a Jain temple in the Bellary district, Karnataka, which was constructed by Rāmarāya in the time of the Vijayanagara Emperor Sadāśiva, according to an inscription of AD 1545. *Jaina Śilālekha Saṃgraha* IV, No. 473.

Kuśa Jinālaya: Jain temple at Kopana in the Raichur district, Karnataka mentioned in two medieval inscriptions found therein.

Kuṣmāṇḍī: Ambikā.

Kusuma: Also known as Puṣpa Yakṣa he is the attendant of Padmaprabha (q.v.) whose characteristic symbol is an antelope. According to the Śvetāmbara tradition he had four hands holding a fruit and *abhaya* pose in his right hands and a rosary and a mongoose in his left hands. According to the Digambara it is, however, the *varada* pose, shield, *abhaya* pose and lance. His name Kusuma or Puṣpa has direct connection with the red lotus, the flower of his master.

***Kuvalayamālā*:** Written by Udyotanasūri (q.v.) about AD 779 at Javalipura, modern Jalor in Rajasthan, it is a love story in Mahārāṣṭrī Prakrit. The author calls the work primarily a *dharmakathā*, though it has become *saṅkīrṇakathā*, or mixed story owing to its varied content. It has erotic elements. The *Kuvalayamālā*, though a religious story, is compared to a newly married woman in form and beauty. The poet has shown his power of observation in the description of romantic episodes, in the presentation of life and character of the people of different *janapadas*, and in providing information on things of material interest. The tale concerns the passionate desire of prince Kuvalayacandra to possess the beautiful Princess Kuvalayamālā. He impatiently entertains all kinds of wild schemes to obtain her and finally manages to win her heart. Then comes the wedding ceremony and fulfilment. This part has been described vividly with greatest emphasis on erotic affairs. Of course the story eventually ends with both renouncing worldly life and sensual pleasures. In this work the author had been able to adjust a tale of gross sensuality with an ascetic, edifying, and religious way of life. Ed. A.N. Upadhye in two parts, Bombay, 1959 and 1970.

Kuvara Vihāra: Jain temple in Rajasthan built in AD 1164 by Cālukya Kumārapāla and renovated in AD 1185 by Cāhamāna Samarasiṃha according to an inscription from Jalor which also says that a golden flagstaff was installed on the *mūla-śikhara* in AD 1199 and a golden *kalaśa* was installed in the *madhya-maṇḍapa* in AD 1205.

Kyatanahalli: See Kodehala-basadi.

L

Labdhisāra: See Nemicandra Siddhāntacakravartin.

Lachagir: Findspot of the representation of a Jain tutelary couple datable to the eighth century in the Allahabad district. Carved on a standstone slab, it shows seated male and female divinities in *ardhaparyaṅka* under an *aśoka* tree which has a small Jina figure just above the trunk. The right hand of the two deities is in the *abhaya mudrā* and they have the usual ornaments on their bodies and a striped *dhotī* in the lower part. The female, who also wears a sacred thread, carries a child in her lap and above the basal band are depicted six figures.

Lodol: Findspot of a marble image of an unidentified Tīrthaṃkara in district Mehsana in Gujarat which shows him standing in *kāyotsarga* and wearing a *dhotī*, suggestive of the fact that the image was made for the worship of the Śvetāmbaras. The image has been assigned to the twelfth century. A *chowri*-bearer is shown on the right and a *makara-śārdūla* above it.

***Laghiyastraya*:** See Akalaṅka.

***Laghu-Arhannītisāra*:** See Hemacandra.

Laghuśreṇī: See Binaikiya.

Laharisena: See Binaikiya.

Lāja: An ancient Jain *tīrtha*, sacred to Ādīśvara, situated in the Sirohi district, Rajasthan. Some Jain antiquities have been found here.

Lakkhana: See Aṇuvaya-Rayaṇa-Paiu.

Lakkundi: Also known as Lokkigundi, it is the site of an eleventh-century Jain temple situated 7 miles to the south-east of Gadag in Dharwar district. It seems to represent an earlier stage in the formation of the Cālukyan style. It consists of the *vimāna*, an intermediate vestibule and *maṇḍapa* with a forward open pillared hall, all axially aligned. A greater ornamental effect has been introduced in the treatment of exterior surfaces. H. Cousens, *Calukyan Architecture of the Kanarese Districts*, Calcutta, 1926, 77-9.

Lakṣmadeva: See *Nemināha-carin.*

Lakṣmaṇagaṇi: Author of the Prakrit *Supāsanāha cariya* (q.v.) in 8,000 *gāthās* which was composed in AD 1142.

Lakṣmaṇa-Vihāra: Temple dedicated to Pārśvanātha at Jaisalmer, Rajasthan. It possesses a fine *toraṇa*, an open porch, various *maṇḍapas*, and fifty-two *devakulikas* or chaplets surrounding the complex. It was constructed in AD 1417. The pillars and ceilings of the hall preserve some decorative features that remind us of the older architectural style of this region.

Lakṣmaṇi: Mentioned as a Jain centre in Jayānanda's *Pravāsagīti*, composed about the fifteenth century. It is in Jhabua district of Madhya Pradesh.

Lakṣmeśvara: Jain centre in the Dharwar district of Karnataka where lived the famous Śaṅkha Jinendra. A few stone inscriptions of the seventh century refer to the grant of land to the caitya of Śaṅkha Jinendra at Puligere, grant to an Ācārya of Mūla-saṅgha Anvaya and Deva-gaṇa sect, to Udayanadevapaṇḍita or Niravadyapaṇḍita who was the home-pupil of Śrī Pūjayapāda and so forth. One inscription of AD 734, of the time of Vikramāditya II, refers to Saṅkhatīrthabasati and Dhavala-Jinālaya and the grants made to them. The donee's name is Vijayadevapaṇḍita, a disciple of Jayadevapaṇḍita and the latter of Rāmadeva Ācārya belonging to Mūla-saṅgha and Deva-gaṇa. An inscription referring to Permādi Caityālaya or Basadi of Puligere as also to the Tribhuvancandra is found here which has the date śaka 999 (AD 1074). The Ānesajjaya-basadi dedicated to Śāntinātha is referred to in the Ablur inscription. It was originally built by Kumkumadevī, the younger sister of Cālukya Vijayāditya. Another inscription of AD 1081 from Lakṣmeśvara refers to a grant to Jain Muni Narendrasena II, disciple of Nayasena and grand-disciple of Narendrasena I of Mūla-saṅgha and Sena-gaṇa. One inscription of AD 1539 records the settlement of a dispute between the Jains and the Śaivas, in which Jain saints Śaṅkhana and Hemācārya of the Sankha-basadi and Śaiva ācāryas Kālahasti and Śivarāma were parties. Among the prominent Jain temples of this place mention may be made of the basadis of Tīrtha, Mukkhara, Śrī Vijaya Marudevī, Dhavala, Goggiya, and Ānesajjaya. Besides there are Gaṅga-Kandarpa Jinamandira as also Permādi Caityālaya. This place was previously known as Puligere or Purigere. *Indian Antiquary* VII.101ff; XVIII.37f., *Jaina Śilālekha Saṃgraha*, IV, Nos. 157, 165, 471.

Lakṣmī Jinālaya: Jain temple at Beturu, situated in Devangere Taluk of Chitradurga district, Karnataka, constructed by Kucirāja, an officer of a feudatory of Yādava Rāmacandra and a pupil of Padmasena Bhaṭṭāraka, mentioned in an epigraph of AD 1271. *Epigraphia Carnatica*, XI, Devanagere 13.

Lakṣmīsāgara: Jain teacher belonging to Tapāgaccha whose name occurs in the fifteenth-century image inscriptions from Gujarat and Rajasthan. He is specially mentioned in inscriptions from Abu of AD 1468. He was a contemporary of the great Kumbha of Mewar. He was the teacher of Sumatisādhu, author of the *Somasaubhāgya-kāvya*. *Jainadhātu-pratimālekhasaṃgrah* II, Nos. 31, 149, 214, 257, 415, 439, 595; Jinavijaya, *Prācīna Jaina-lekhamālā*, Nos. 264-5, 267.

Lal Mandir: Jain temple at Delhi established in AD 1656. Structurally it is ordinary in character.

Lalrai Inscriptions of Kelhana: Two inscriptions of the Nadol Cāhamāna King Kelhana, dated VS 1233 (AD 1175) found at Lalrai near Bali in South Rajasthan refer to the existence of a temple of Śāntinātha at this place. *Epigraphia Indica* XI.49ff.

Lavaṇakheṭaka: Also known as Kheṭanagara or Khednagar, this place in Marwar region of Rajasthan has been described as a Jain *tīrtha* with temples of Ṛṣabha, Śāntinātha, and Mahāvīra by Siddhasena of the twelfth-century.

Lesser Vows: See Anuvrata.

***Leśyā*:** A principal of the classification of beings. By the term *leśyā* is understood the different conditions produced in the Jīva by the influence of different *karmas*. The *leśyās* are six in number, the first three bad and the others good. An individual is always a *saleśī* because he is swayed by any of the three good or three bad *leśyās*. Only the Siddhas are free of the influence of the *leśyās* and so they are called *aleśī*. In between the two there are six classes of Jīvas, each of the classes being swayed respectively by the influence of black, blue, gray, red, yellow, and white *leśyās*. Of the three bad *leśyās*, *kṛṣṇa* or black is the worst of all. Its taste is as bitter as a *nim* tree and it smells like a dead cow. As far as touch is concerned it is rougher than a saw. Jīvas under the influence of this *leśyā* are of bad temper, cruel, and violent. Any kind of misdeed can be performed by them. The *nīla* or blue *leśyā* tastes more pungent than pepper. Its odour and roughness are the same as those of the former. Jīvas under the influence of this *leśyā* become envious of others, lazy, gluttonous and wanting in modesty. They think about their own happiness and prevent others from acquiring merit. The *kapota* or grey *leśyā* tastes like an unripe mango, as bad in odour and touch as its predecessors, A Jīva under its influence becomes a thief, a liar, an intriguing person who delights to expose the bad qualities of others and to conceal his own. Of the good *leśyās*, the first is *tejaḥ* or red, which is like a fragrant flower to smell, a ripe mango to taste, and butter to touch. It removes all evil thoughts from the Jīva. The *padma* or yellow *leśyā* is sweeter than honey as far as taste is concerned. Through its influence a Jīva controls anger, pride, deceit, and avarice. The *śukla* or white *leśyā* is the best of all. Its taste is sweeter than sugar. Under its influence a Jīva becomes completely stainless. This classification according to the *leśyās* applies to the Jīvas in general, but was really meant for human beings for the justification of the doctrine of *karma*. According to the Jain texts, the *leśyās* are not dependent on the nature of Jīva, but on *karma* which accompanies it. Thus the classification is based not on that of nature or the inherent qualities of the thing concerned, but on an extra substance supposed to infiltrate it from outside. It is said that the alteration produced on the Jīva, just as on a crystal by the presence of the black things, etc., is denoted by the word *leśyā*: *kṛṣṇādidravyasācivyāt pariṇāmo ya ātmanaḥ; sphaṭikasyeva tatrāyaṃ eśyāśabdaḥ pravartate*. Thus according to the above explanation, what produces *leśyā* is a subtle substance accompanying the Jīva to which are attributed the qualities. The word *leśyā* appears to have been derived from *kleśa*. See *Uttarādhyayana* XXXIV.

Liberation: See *Mokṣa*.

***Līlāvatī-kathā*:** See Jineśvara.

***Lipisaṅkhyānasaṃgraha*:** Sacrament. In the fifth year a child is taught to write at the hands of a learned layman after performing worship.

Lodrava: Situated in Jaisalmer district, Rajasthan, this place, a Jain *tīrtha* which had an eleventh-century temple of Pārśvanātha, has yielded a good number of Jain inscriptions. Nahar, *Jain Inscriptions* III, Nos. 2498, 2530, 2543, 2560-1, 2572, etc.

Logic: Jain logic begins with the dictum that every judgement expresses one aspect of reality and is therefore relative and subject to some conditions. It is due to the fact that every object has innumerable characters. Thus a thing should be comprehended from different standpoints and the method of such comprehension is called Nyāya (q.v.). In the *Sthānāṅga* knowledge is divided into *pratyakṣa* (direct) and *parokṣa* (indirect), the former being subdivided into *kevala* (perfect) and *akevala* (imperfect)—to which category belong *avadhi* and *manaḥparyāya* (qq.v.). In Māṇikya Nandī's *Parikṣāmukhasūtra* objects of valid knowledge have been classified into general (*sāmānya*) and particular (*viśeṣa*). The general is of two kinds, homogeneous (*tiryak*) and heterogeneous (*ūrdhvatā*), Siddhasena divides direct knowledge into practical (*vyavahārika*) and transcendental (*paramārthika*). The former, according to Deva Suri, is characterized by inversion (*viparyaya*), doubt (*saṃśaya*), and uncertainty (*anadhyavasāya*). The term *pramāṇa* (q.v.) is generally understood as the means of valid knowledge which is also classified under the two traditional categories *pratyakṣa* (direct) and *parokṣa* (indirect). The latter has been divided by Siddhasena Divākra into inference (*anumāṇa*, q.v.) and verbal testimony (*śabda* or *āgama*). *Anumāna* (q.v.) or inference, along with its two forms *svārtha* and *parārtha* and its traditional five *avayavas* or members—*pratijñā*, *hetu*, *udāharaṇa*, *upanaya*, and *nigamana*. This five-membered syllogism (q.v.) adopted from the Nyāya school, was a modification of Bhadrabāhu's ten-membered syllogism (q.v.). The Jains also accepted the ways and means of the Nyāya school to detect the argument fallacies (q.v.). Not only the material fallacies of inference like *asiddha* (unproved middle), *viruddha* (contradictory middle), *savyabhicāra* (irregular middle), *satpratipakṣa* (inferentially contradicted middle) and *vādhita* (non-inferentially contradicted middle) were accepted, but fallacies of a general nature like those of perception (*pratyakṣābhāṣa*) of recollection (*samaraṇābhāṣa*) of recognition (*pratyabhijñānābhāṣa*) of argumentation (*tarkābhāṣa*), of minor term (*pakṣābhāṣa*) of middle term (*hetvābhāṣa*) of example (*dṛṣṭāntābhāṣa*) and of verbal testimony (*āgamābhāṣa*) had as well been taken into account. *Hetu* (q.v.), also known as *liṅga*, which is the reason or middle term, was in the earlier stages of the development of Jain thought equated with inference or *anumāna* (q.v.). Later Jain logicians, however, consider *hetu* as exclusively the middle term. The semblance of reason or fallacy (q.v.) of this *hetu* or middle term (*hetvābhāsa*) arises from doubt, misconception or non-conception about it. It is of three kinds: the unproved (*asiddha*), the contradictory (*viruddha*), and the uncertain (*anaikāntika*). Without an inseparable connection or invariable concomitance (*vyāpti*) between the major and the middle term the formation of any syllogism is impossible. The major term is called *sādhya* or that which is to be proved, and the middle is called *sādhanā* or that by which it is to be proved. The minor term is called *pakṣa*, the place in which the major term abides. In an inference the minor term must be explicitly set forth, otherwise the reasoning may be misunderstood. The middle, major and minor terms are the parts of an inference, but example (*dṛṣṭānta* or *udāharaṇa*) is not. Nevertheless, for the sake of explaining matters, the example (*dṛṣṭānta*) and even application (*upanaya*) and conclusion (*nigamana*) are admitted as features of inference.

The most important viewpoint of Jain logic is, however *syādvāda* (q.v.) or the doctrine of conditional proposition. The word *syād* means 'may be' which signifies that everything of the universe can be looked at from many points of view, and that each viewpoint yielded a different conclusion. This is known as *anekāntavāda* (q.v.). Every proposition is therefore conditional, and there is nothing called absolute affirmation or absolute negation. The Jains illustrate this position by means of the story of a number of blind people examining an elephant and arriving at varying conclusions regarding its form while in truth each observer gets at only a part of it. They hold that any dogmatic claim of a particular viewpoint (*ekāntavāda*) amounts to the fallacy of exclusive predication which is why it is desirable to qualify a judgement explicitly by a word like 'may be'. See Anekāntavāda, Anumāna, Fallacies, *Hetu*, Logicians, *Naya*, Non-Absolutism, Pramāṇa, Syādvāda, Syllogism.

Logicians: The early Jain writers who discussed specific problems of logic were Bhadrabāhu and Umāsvāti or Umāsvāmī. In his commentary on *Dasaveyāliya* and *Sūyagaḍa* Bhadrabāhu elaborated a syllogism (q.v.) consisting of ten parts (*daśāvayava-vākya*) and also a principle called 'the assertion of probabilities (*syādvāda*, q.v.) or the sevenfold paralogism (*saptabhaṅgīnaya*)'. Umāsvāti or Umāsvāmī dealt with the doctrine of *pramāṇa* or right knowledge and also with different kinds of Nyāya or 'the mood of statement'. The first Jain writer of systematic logic was, however, Siddhasena Divākara of the sixth century, in whose *Nyāyā-vatāra* we come across a comprehensive treatment of the valid sources of knowledge, terms of syllogism, various types of logical fallacies, and methods of judgement. Siddhasena Gaṇi and Samantabhara commented on the *Tattvārthādhigama*. The former's work is known as *Tattvārthaṭīkā* in which the sources of knowledge and the method of comprehending things from particular standpoints are fully discussed. The latter's work, known as *Āptamīmāṃsā*, consists of 115 stanzas in Sanskrit in which a full exposition of the seven parts of *syādvāda* has been given. Akalaṅka of the eighth century wrote a commentary on the *Āptamīmāṃsā* under the title *Aṣṭaśatī*. His independent work of logic is known as the *Nyāyaviniścaya*, which was the source of Māṇikya-Nandi's *Parīkṣāmukha Sūtra*. In the latter we come across exhaustive analysis of the characteristics of valid knowledge (*pramāṇasvarūpa*) direct apprehension (*pratyakṣa*), indirect apprehension (*parokṣa*) objects of valid knowledge (*viṣaya*), result of valid knowledge (*phala*) and semblances or fallacies (*ābhāsa*). Vidyananda of the ninth century wrote a commentary on Samantabhadra's *Āptamīmāṃsā* which is known as *Aṣṭasāhasrī* and in which non-Jain doctrines are severely criticised. Another logical treatise called *Pramāṇaparīkṣā* is attributed to him. Prabhācandra's *Prameyakamalamārtaṇḍa* is a commentary on Māṇikya Nandī's work. He is also the author of *Nyāyakumāracandrodaya* which is a commentary on the *Laghiyastraya* of Akalaṅka. Of other Jain logicians of the ninth-tenth centuries, we mention Ṛṣabhasanandī who wrote a commentary on the *Sambandhaparīkṣā* of the Buddhist logician Dharmakīrti entitled *Sambandhoddyota*. Mallavādin wrote *Dharmottaratippanaka* on the Buddhist *Nyāyabindu-ṭīkā*. Amṛtacandra Suri wrote *Tattvārthasāra* and Devasena Bhaṭṭāraka *Nayacakra*. Abhayadeva Suri of the eleventh century was the author of *Vādamahārṇava* and of a commentary on the *Sammatitarkasūtra* called *Tattvārthabodhavidhāyinī*. His contemporaries were Laghusamantabhadra, author of a commentary on the *Aṣṭasāhasrī* of Vidyananda called *Aṣṭasāhasrīvisamapadatātparyaṭīka*, Kalyanacandra, author of *Pramāṇavārtikaṭīkā* Anantavīrya, author of a commentary on the *Parikṣāmukha* of Māṇikya Nandī called *Parīkṣāmukhapañjikā* or *Prameyaratnamālā* as also a commentary on Akalaṅka's *Nyāyaviniścaya* called *Nyāyaviniścayavṛtti*. Deva Sūri who flourished in the twelfth century was the author of the well-known treatise on logic called *Pramāṇanayatattvalokālaṅkāra* on which he himself wrote an elaborate commentary named *Syādvādaratnākara*. The former consists of eight chapters dealing with the determination of the nature of recollection, recognition, argumentation and inference, determination of thc nature of valid knowledge derived from verbal testimony and scripture, determination of the nature of objects of knowledge, determination of the consequences and fallacies of knowledge, determination of nature of one-sided knowledge and determination of the right procedure of a disputant and his opponent. Deva Sūri's contemporary was the great Hemacandra, author of *Pramāṇamīmāṃsā*, on which he himself wrote a commentary. Of other logicians of the twelfth century mention should be made of Candraprabha Suri, author of *Darśanaśuddhi*, *Prameyaratnakośa* and *Nyāyāvatāravivṛti*; Haribhadra Suri (there were more than one Jain scholar of this name) author of *Daśavaikālikaniryuktiṭīkā*, *Nyāyapraveśakasūtra* and *Nyāyāvatāravṛtti*; Pārśvadeva Gaṇi, author of a commentary on *Nyāyapraveśa* called *Nyāyapraveśapañjikā*, Śrīcandra, author of *Nyāyapraveśaṭippana* which is a super-commentary on the *Nyāyapraveśavṛtti* of Haribhadra; Devabhadra, author of *Nyāyāvatāraṭippana*; Candrasena Suri, author of *Utpāda-siddhiprakaraṇa*; and Ratnaprabha Suri, author of *Syādvādaratnākarāvatārikā*. Of the Jain logicians flourishing between the thirteenth and seventeenth centuries, the following deserve special mention: Tilakacarya, author of *Āvaśyakalaghuvṛtti*; Mallisena Suri, author of *Syādvādamañjarī* which is a commentary or Hemacandra's *Vītarāgastuti* or *Dvātriṃśikā*; Rājaśekhara Sūri, author of *Ratnāvatārikāpañjikā*; Jñāna Candra, author of *Ratnākarāvatārikāṭippana*; Guṇaratna, the celebrated author of *Tarkarahasyadīpikā* which is a commentary on Haribhadra's *Ṣaḍdarśanasamuccaya*; Śrutasāgara Gaṇi, author of *Tattvārthadīpikā*; Dharmabhūṣana, author of *Nyāyadīpikā*; Vinayavijaya, author of *Nyāyakarṇikā*; and Yaśovijaya Gaṇi, author of *Nyāyapradīpa*, *Tarkabhāṣā*, *Nayāyarahasya*, *Nyāyamṛtataraṅgiṇī* and *Nyāyakhaṇḍakhādya*.

Lohācārya: See Dhavalā.

Lohanipur Image: One of the earliest stone images in the round to be associated with Jainism. It is the torso of a nude figure unearthed from Lohanipur in Patna, the high polish of which enables us to date it in the Maurya or early Śuṅga period. Its nudity, the stiff straight pose of its arms hanging down by its sides indicative of the *kāyotsarga* attitude characteristic of the Jinas, and its general outlook unmistakably prove that it was originally the image of one of the Tīrthaṃkaras. The upper and lower portions being unfortunately lost, there is no means to ascertain which of the 24 Jinas it represented. *Journal of the Bihar and Orissa Research Society*, XIII, 130-2 and plates.

Loka: Jain term for universe. It is the mutual association of the two fundamental principles of Jīva (the principal of consciousness) and Ajīva (unconscious matter). These two are eternal entities, which are neither born nor will ever perish. The substance that has its supreme influence on the principle of consciousness in its worldly career is only the *pudgala* (material atoms) which comes into association with the soul in a number of ways and also delimits its various capacities. But the principle of consciousness has intrinsic and fundamental potencies which, when properly directed, eventually emancipate the consciousness from the influence of material atoms. The atom of the Jains undergoes transformations like the Prakṛti of the Sāṅkhya, and is not absolutely unchanging like the atom of the Nyāya-Vaiśeṣika.

The Jains do not agree with the Nyāya-Vaiśeṣikas in admitting that the material atoms of earth, water, etc., belong to fundamentally different types. The Jains like the Sāṅkhyas and Mīmāṃsakas regard the universe as beginningless and endless from the standpoint of the chain of unbroken successions. The cosmos is, according to Jainism, shaped like a man standing arms akimbo with legs spread out. The space inside the cosmos is called Lokākāśa and that outside it is called Alokākāśa. The *siddha-śilā* or the space of the liberated souls is the summit of the cosmos. The space below this region down to the waist-like part of the cosmos is inhabited by *trasa-jīvas* (q.v.) or mobile beings. The cosmos is 343 *rajju* cubes in volume. A *rajju*, literally a rope, is indicative of the distance a celestial being traverses in six months. The cosmos has in its central 100 *yojana* portion the *manuṣya-loka* or the area of human habitation. The *svarga-loka* above the *manuṣya-loka* is meant for celestial beings while below it are seven earths constituting *naraka-loka* for the hellish beings. The central part of the cosmos, that is, *manuṣya-loka*, consists of numerous continents or *dvīpas*, each enriched by an ocean. These are of double the diameter of the preceding ones. The concept of island-continents is evidently based on the cosmography of the Purāṇas. The concept is popular also with the Buddhists. See Cosmography, Triloka, Universe.

***Lokākāśa*:** See *Ākāśa*.

***Lokapālas*:** See *Dikpālas*.

***Lokaprakāśa*:** A comprehensive encyclopedia of Jainism written in AD 1649 by Vinayavijaya, son of Tejaḥapāla (q.v.). Ed. Hiralal Hamsaraj in 3 vols., Jamnagar, 1910.

Lokasena: Jain poet who added further continuation to *Adipurāṇa-Uttarapurāṇa* about AD 898.

***Lokatattvanirṇaya*:** See Haribhadra.

***Lokavibhāga*:** A work on cosmography belonging to the Digambara tradition. It was composed by Sarvanandī of the village Paṭalika in the Pāṇḍya kingdom who flourished about the fifth century AD. The original work is now lost, but it has been referred to by Yativṛṣabha (q.v.) in his *Tiloyapannatī*.

Lokkigundi: Modern Kakkundi in Dharwar district, Karnataka, which contained a good number of medieval Jain temples as suggested by epigraphical evidence. *South Indian Inscriptions*, X. 39; *Jaina Śilālekha Saṃgraha*, IV, No. 274.

Loṅkā: A reformist sect founded in AD 1474 by Loṅkā Sāha, a rich and scholarly merchant of Ahmedabad. This sect was for religious puritanism and raised a passionate outcry against idolatry. This sect was responsible for the emergence of the Sthānakavāsīs or Dhundhiya at a later period. For a detailed account of Loṅkā Sāha, his personality and preaching see B.L. Nahata in *Shrimat Rājendrasūri Smāraka Grantha*, 470-7; D. Malvania in *Gurudeva Śrī Ratnamaṇi Smṛtigrantha*, 365-85.

Lotus Ponds: Constituents of the Saumanasa (q.v.) forest, the third from the bottom encircling Meru (q.v.). Each of these *puṣkariṇīs* or lotus-pools accommodates in the centre a *vihāra-prāsāda* or palace for enjoyment. The sixteen lotus ponds are Utpala-gulmā, Nalinā, Utpalā, Utpalotpalā, Bhṛṅgā, Bhṛṅganibhā, Kajjalā, Kajjalaprabhā, Śrī-bhadrā, Śrī-kāntā, Śrī-mahitā, Śrī-nilayā, Nalinā, Nalina-gulmā, Kumudā, and Kumudaprabhā.

Luna-vasahi: The marble temple of Neminātha built in AD 1231 by Tejaḥpāla (q.v.) on Mount Abu (q.v.). Like the Vimala-vasahi, its sanctum and *gūḍha-maṇḍapa* are plain and have a superstructure of horizontal tiers. Reliefs on corridor-ceiling show scenes from the life of Neminātha. See Dilwara temples.

M

Macherla Slab Inscription: A record of the reign of the Eastern Cālukya Jayasiṃha II (AD 696-709) found near Macherla in Palnad taluk of Guntur district which refers to Sarvalokāśraya Jayasiṃhavallabha and registers a grant of land by Kalyāṇavasantulu to Arahanta Bhaṭṭāra, to be maintained by the family of Raṭṭagudis of Koṃbhuru. *Annual Report on South Indian Epigraphy*, 1941-2, No. 181.

Madalapura: Findspot of a Jain inscription of AD 1080 in Arkalgud taluk, Hassan district, Karnataka, which refers to a temple called Arakere-basadi and associates Amalacandra Bhaṭṭāraka and his teacher Kālacandra Siddhāntadeva with it. *Epigraphia Carnatica* V, Arkal 102.

Madalura: A village in the Kolhapur district of Maharashtra where the existence of a Pārśvanātha temple is indicated by a twelfth-century inscription.

Madanpur: Findspot of a twelfth-century Mahāvīra image in Bankura district. The image is two feet in height, standing in *kāyotsarga* with the emblem lion. Locally it is worshipped as Kālabhairava.

Maddagiri: Findspot of a Jain inscription of AD 1531 in Tumkur district, Karnataka, which refers to a Mallināthasvāmī temple and an endowment to it. *Epigraphia Carnatica* XII, Madda 14.

Mādhavacandra Traividyadeva: Author of a *vṛtti* on Nemicandra's *Kṣapanasāra* composed in AD 1203 at a place called Dullakapura during the reign of Śilāhāra Bhoja of Kolhapur. See *Jinagrantha Praśastisaṃgraha*, No. 11.1, Part I, Delhi 1954.

***Mādhyatha*:** Tolerance or indifference to those who are uncivil or ill-behaved, one of the four virtues to be cultivated in connection with the observance of the five *mahāvratas* (q.v.).

Magadha: Centre of activities of Mahāvīra. He preached his religious tenets in the local dialect known as Ardhamāgadhī. Magadha was considered a holy place in the east. In the *Thānāṅga* and *Āvaśyaka Cūrṇi* it is stated that when Bharata, the first sovereign king, was installed on the throne, holy water was brought from this land for his consecration. In the *Vyavahāra-bhāṣya* the inhabitants of Magadha are called wise. The capital was Rājagṛha where Mahāvīra passed fourteen rainy seasons. It was frequented by Mahāvīra's disciples and other Ācāryas. As the city was surrounded by five hills it was called Girivraja, the Vaibhāra and the Vipula hills being more popular among the Jains.

Māghanandi Siddhāntadeva: Originally the priest of the Jain temple called Rūpanārāyaṇa in Kolhapur during the reign of Śilāhāra Gaṇḍarāditya (AD 1108-38) and Vijayāditya (AD 1138-75), he was the teacher of Nimbadevarasa (q.v.), feudatory of Gaṇḍarāditya. He was also the teacher of Śrutakīrti Traividyadeva belonging to the Pustaka-gaccha in the Deśīya-gaṇa of the Mūla-saṅgha according to the inscriptions found at Kolhapur, Tridal and Sravanabelgola. In the Mahālakṣmī temple inscription Māghanandi is described as a disciple of Kulacandra belonging to the lineage of Kondakunda. In an inscription of the time of Vijayāditya, one Vāsudeva, who built a temple of Pārśvanātha and was in service of a feudatory known by the name Kāmadeva, is mentioned as the disciple of Māghanandi Siddhāntadeva. Two other disciples of Māghanandi are also known from inscriptions. They are Māṇikyanandi Paṇḍita and Arhanandi-Siddhāntadeva. *Corpus Inscriptionum Indicarum* VI, Nos. 39, 45, 49-50, 53.

Magical Practices: Magical beliefs and practices which go back to the primitive tribal life, pertain to all forms of religious systems and Jainism is no exception. But while in the Vedic religion we come across beliefs and practices of a simpler type, from which their original purpose can easily be detected, and are by nature plainly imitative or contagious, the magical practices as found in Jain commentarial and narrative literature are very complex. In them the ancient tribal lore is mixed with traditional ritualistic details and brewed with abstruse metaphysical concepts. In Jain texts like the *Aṅgavijjā* magic spells are mentioned under the names of birds and animals such as *mayūrī, vṛścika, nākuli, sarpa, biḍālī, mūṣaka, vyāghrī, mṛgī, siṃhī, vārāhī, ulukī, kākī, ulāvakī, śakunikā*, etc., bringing in totemic elements also. Jain magical practices are often named after specific tribes referring to the source of their origination such as Pulindas, Śabaras, Taṅganas, Mataṅgas, Kirātas, Svapākas, etc. Mountains have been referred to as places for accomplishing the magic lore and the Vidyā-

***Malayasundarī-Kathā*:** A romantic epic in Prakrit dealing with the fate of the Prince Mahābala and Princess Malayasundarī, their love, separation, and final union, eventually resulting in their conversion and omniscience. The author is unknown, but the popularity of this work is attested to by its Sanskritized extract made by Dharmacakra in the fourteenth century under the title *Malayasundarīkathoddhāra*, the *Mahabala-Malayasundarīkathā*, written by Māṇikyasundara in the fifteenth century which, in its turn, served as a prototype of Jayatilaka's Sanskrit *Malaya-sundarī-caritra*.

Maleyakheda: Malkhed in the Gulbarga district, Karnataka, described as a Jain *tīrtha* by Jñāna-sāgara and Viśvabhūṣaṇa. There was a Nemi-nātha temple here.

Maleyūr: An important Jain centre sacred to Pārśvanātha situated in the Chamrajnagar taluk of Mysore district. It has yielded a number of epigraphs, the earliest of which is dated śaka 1103 (AD 1181). It mentions the Pārśvanātha temple at Kaṇakācala and records the gift of a village by a lady called Cikkatāyi. The name of the granted village was Kinnaripurā. An epigraph of AD 1422, of the time of the Vijayanagara Emperor Devarāya II, refers to Harihara's grant of the entire village of Maleyūr for the temple of Vijayadeva. *Epigraphia Carnatica* IV, Cha. 144, 158, 159.

Malkhed: Situated in the Gulbarga district, it was the capital of the Rāṣṭrakūṭas where there was a Jain basti in the twelfth-thirteenth centuries. Jain images of later times have been found here.

***Mallavādin*:** Jain logician of the eighth century who has been referred to in Haribhadra's *Anekāntajayapatākā* and in the Śvetāmbara tradition as nephew of the last Śilāditya of Valabhī. He wrote a commentary called *Dharm-ottaraṭippanaka* on the *Nyāyavindu* of the Buddhist Dharmakīrti. He may also be identified with his namesake mentioned in the Surat plates of Karka dated AD 821. *Dharmottaraṭippanaka*, ed. Th. Stcherbatsky, St. Petersburg, 1909.

Mallinātha: The nineteenth Tīrthaṃkara born of Kumbha and Prabhāvatī/Prajāvatī of Mithila. According to the Śvetāmbara tradition Mallinātha was a woman and in the Digambara tradition a man. The *Nāyādhammakahāo* gives an account of Mallinātha's life. The female Mallinātha was exceedingly beautiful and had a height of 25 bow-lengths. Kings of six countries wanted to marry her. She refused them and converted them into great Jains. Her sacred tree was the Aśoka. She had a life of 45,000 years. Indra and Bandhumatī were her chief disciples. She attained salvation on Mount Sammeya. The male Mallinātha of the Digambara tradition has a water-jar as his emblem, Kubera and Dharaṇapriyā/Aparājitā as attendants, and Suluma as *chowri*-bearer. Sculptures of Mallinātha are not rare and, together with the masculine suffix *nātha*, go in favour of the Digambara conception. There is a *Mallinātha-carita* in Prakrit, the author of which was one Haribhadra of twelfth century.

***Mallinātha-carita*:** Prakrit idealized biography of the nineteenth Tīrthaṃkara Mallinātha written by a second Haribhadra of the twelfth century.

Malliṣena: Author of the *Syādvādamañjarī*, written in collaboration with Jinaprabhasūri in AD 1202. It is a philosophical treatise in which, besides the establishment of the Jain viewpoint, the Buddhist Śūnyavāda has been criticised. Actually it is a commentary on the 32 verses of Hemacandra's (q.v.) *Anuyogavyavacchedikā*. *Syādvādamañjarī* ed. in Chowkhamba Sanskrit Series, Benares, 1900, with and Eng. trans. by A.B. Dhruva, Bombay 1933; Hindi trans. by J.C. Jain, Bombay, 1935; 3rd edn. 1760; F.W. Thomas, *The Flower-spray of the Quodammode Doctrine*, Berlin, 1960.

Malliṣena: Digambara author from Karnataka who lived in the first half of the eleventh century and composed the *Mahāpurāṇa*, *Nāgakumāra-kāvya*, *Bhairava-Padmāvatīkalpa*, *Sarasvatī-Mantrakalpa*, *Jvālinīkalpa*, *Kāmacaṇḍālikalpa*, etc. Of these the *Mahāpurāṇa* has 2,000 verses and gives a short account of all the 63 remarkable persons of Jain mythology. The *Nāgakumāra-kāvya* glorifies Śrīpañcamī in 507 verses and five cantos. The *Bhairava-Padmāvatīkalpa* deals with the legends of Padmāvatī, the Śāsanadevatā of Pārśvanāth. Malliṣena was a disciple of Jinasena.

Maliyapūṇḍi Grant of Amma II: Originally discovered in Madanur, 10 miles from Ongole in Andhra Pradesh it is a grant, the donee being a Jinālaya called Kaṭakābharaṇa, founded by Durgarāja, an officer of the Eastern Cālukya Amma II. The temple was located south of Dharmavuramu (Dharmapurī) in Nellore district. At the request of this officer Amma II made a gift of the village of Maliyapūṇḍi to the temple in AD 945. The temple was in charge of Śrī Mandiradeva, disciple of Divākara and grand-disciple of Jinanandin belonging to the Yāpanīya-saṅgha, Nandi-gaccha and Kotimaduva-gaṇa, *Epigraphia India* IX.47ff.

Mamandur: One of the hill caverns in North Arcot district where early Jain foundations later came to be remodelled into Śaiva ones.

***Manaḥparyāya*:** One of the five kinds of knowledge. It is derived from reading the thoughts of others. By concentration of mind and cultivation of intellectual faculties it is possible for a person to read the thoughts of others. It belongs to the category of *pratyakṣa* or direct knowledge. *Tattvārtha* I.9ff. See Epistemology.

Mānasī: See Kandarpā. She is a Vidyā-devī (q.v.) with either swan or a lion as vehicle and four hands holding the conventional attributes.

Mānatuṅga: Author of the famous *Bhaktāmarastotra* which enjoys a great reputation among both the Śvetāmbaras and the Digambaras, as both sects class the poet among their own writers. Mānatuṅga is generally assigned to the third century, but some scholars place him later. In this hymn the Jina Ṛṣabha is extolled as incomparable, a saint on level with the highest deities, and his name is invoked as a protection in all perils. Mānatuṅga is also the author of *Bhayahara-stotra*, a hymn to Jina Pārśvanātha, in Prakrit, *Bhaktāmara-stotra*, ed. and trans into German by H. Jacobi in *Indische Studien*, XIV, 359ff. A com. on the *Bhayahara-stotra* was made by Jinaprabha Suri in AD 1309.

Mānavī: Śasanadevatā (q.v.) of Śītalanātha (q.v.) according to the Digambara tradition. She rides a hog and possesses the conventional attributes. Mānavī or Śrīvatsā Devī is the Śvetāmbara variant of Gaurī (q.v.), the Śāsanadevatā of Śreyāṃśanātha. She rides a lion and her hands hold the *varada* pose, club, and goad. Mānavī is also a Vidyā-devī (q.v.) who sits on a lotus showing *varada*, rosary, and the bough of a tree. In Digambara conception she is of blue colour, rides a boar, and bears a trident.

Mānavijaya: Author of the *Dharmasaṃgraha*, a bulky work on the duties of the householder and the ascetic, written in 1681 and revised by Yaśovijaya (q.v.). Devachand Lalbhai, 26, 45, Bombay, 1915, 1918.

Manchapuri: See Bhūbaneśvara Caves.

***Maṇḍala*:** Magic-circles prepared for attaining occult powers, described in certain Jain texts. The *Samarāicchakahā* relates how one night the Vidyadhara Cakrasena sat in *padmāsana*, drew a *maṇḍala*, performed *mudrās* (q.v.) and recited *mantras* for fulfilling his own desires. The Yakṣiṇī Ajitabalā is invoked with the help of the magic-circle (*maṇḍala*). The *Supārśvanātha-carita* refers to Siddhaputra Yaśodhara who, accompanied by his Uttarasādhikā or female partner went to a cremation ground where he drew a *maṇḍala*, lit. a fire of *khadira* wood, and recited *mantras*. In the fourth chapter of the *Jvālinī-kalpa* the worshipper is enjoined to draw the magic circle called *sāmānya maṇḍala* in a secluded place. The circle to be drawn on plain ground should measure 8 hands and have four gates and should be adorned with flags, mirror, bells as well as arches prepared from Aśvattha leaves.

Mandarendrābhiṣeka: Worshipped by Indra on Mount Meru after taking birth as a Tīrthaṃkara.

Māṇḍavagaḍha: Tīrtha sacred to Supārśvanātha, in Dhar district, Madhya Pradesh, which contained temples dedicated to Śāntinātha and Mahāvīra.

Mandiramārgī: The idol-worshippers (q.v.), that is, those who go to temples for their spiritual upliftment. See Mūrtipūjaka.

Mandoil: Findspot of a tenth-century Ṛṣabhanātha image in the Dinajpur district, Bengal, which is now in the Asutosh Museum of the Calcutta University. It is a stone image, 32 x 22 inches, standing in *kāyotsarga* on lotus, placed on a pedestal with the characteristic *lāñchana* bull. The image is flanked by profusely bejewelled attendant *chowrie*-bearers. Nine *grahas* and Gaṇeśa are distributed around the image. The head of the Jina is lost, probably struck off with a sharp weapon. Behind the lost head is the *prabhāmaṇḍala* on which is a *chatra*. On both sides of these are flying Gandharvas carrying garlands.

Māṇḍu: Ancient Māṇḍavyapura near Dhar. Several Jain scholars occupied prominent positions in the royal courts. Among them mention may be made of Pethaḍa Shāh, Jhanjhana and Maṇḍana who patronized Jain religion and art. Peṭhada Shāh is credited with the building of eighty-four Jain temples in important Jain centres including Śatruñjaya, Prabhāsa, Dholaka, and Salakṣaṇapura around AD 1264. Excellent illustrated Jain manuscripts were also prepared from Mandu.

Maṅgala: The planet Mars conceived as a Jyotiṣka Devatā by the Jains. He is known as the son of the earth and the ruler of the south. He is conceived of as having four hands holding *varada, śakti*, trident, and club.

Maṅgalapura: Jain *tīrtha* in the Malwa region dedicated to Abhinandana. It is mentioned in Jinaprabha's *Vividhatīrthakalpa*.

Maṅgāyi-basti: A Jain temple in Sravanabelgola, Hassan district, Karnataka, which dates to about AD 1325. The inscriptions in the temple state that it was sponsored by Maṅgāyi of Beḷugula. It is a plain structure. A standing figure of Pārśvanātha is known from the inscription on its pedestal to have been donated by Bhīmādevī, a lay-disciple of Paṇḍitācārya and the queen of Devarāya I of Vijayanagara.

Māṅgi-Tungi: An ancient Digambara *tīrtha* in the Nasik district of Maharashtra mentioned in the *Tīrthavandanasaṃgraha*.

Māṇikyacandra: Author of *Pārśvanātha-caritra* (q.v.) written about AD 1217. He had also written a *Śāntinātha-carita* and a commentary on the *Kāvyaprakāśa*. He was patronized by Vastupāla (q.v.)

Māṇikyadolalu-Basadi: Name of a Jain temple of the twelfth century situated at basti in Krishnarajpet taluk, Mandya district, Karnataka, mentioned in an inscription from the same place. *Jaina Śilālekha Saṃgraha* III, No. 328.

Māṇikyanandin: Ninth-century Jain logician whose celebrated work is the *Parikṣāmkhasūtra*. Composed in 207 Sūtras it is based on Akalaṅka's *Nyāyaviniścaya* (qq.v.) Prabhācandra's *Prameyakamalamārtaṇḍa* (qq.v.) is the well-known commentary on Māṇikyanandin's work.

Māṇikyasūri: Jain poet of the eleventh century who composed the epic *Yaśodharacarita* (q.v.) in Śvetāmbara perspective. Ed. Hiralal Hansaraj, Jamnagar, 1910.

Māṇikyatīrtha-basadi: Jain temple at Huli in the Belgaum district, Karnataka, mentioned in a twelfth-century epigraph from Huli itself. The priest of this temple was Prabhācandra Siddhāntadeva. *Epigraphia Indica* XVIII, 201.

Manki: Findspot of a Jain inscription in North Kanara district which refers to an Ananta Tīrthaṃkara temple. It belongs to AD 1514. *Jaina Śilālekha Saṃgraha* V, No. 231.

Manne Plate of Yuvarāja Mārasiṃha: Found at Manne in Bangalore district, this inscription of Yuvarāja Mārasiṃha, son of Śivamāra II, dated śaka 719 (AD 797) refers to a commander (*senādhipati*) called Śrīvijaya who is described as holding 'Arhat as supreme' and the builder of a Jain temple at Mānyanagara, i.e. Manne. It also refers to the grant of a village called Kiruvekkura by Mārasiṃha for the maintenance of this temple. Jain teachers such as Toraṇācārya, Puṣpanandin, and Prabhācandra are mentioned. *Epigraphia Carnatica*, IX, No. 60.

Mannera Masalevāḍa: Findspot of a Jain epigraph of AD 1297 in Bellary district, Karnataka, which refer to a Jina temple at Masalevāḍa which received a grant from a feudatory named Bhairavadāsa. The recipient was one Vinayacandra belonging to Mūla-saṅgha and Deśī-gaṇa and described as a disciple of Nemicandra. *Jaina Śilālekha Saṃgraha* IV, No. 359.

***Manoramā-Carita*:** Idealized biography Manoramā written in Mahārāṣṭrī Prakrit comprising 15,000 *gāthās* in AD 1083 by Vardhamāna Sūri (q.v.).

Manovegā: See Acyutā.

Maṇṭaniḍugallu: Findspot of a Jain inscription of AD 1232 in Pavagada taluk, Tumkur district, Karnataka, which records the construction of a Jina temple called Jogavaṭṭiga-basadi at Nidugalla by a chief called Gaṅgena Māreya. Dedicated to Pārśvanātha, this temple was asociated with Padmaprabha Maladhārīdeva, disciple of Vīranandī, belonging to Mūla-saṅgha, Deśīya-gana, Kondakunda-anvaya and Pustaka-gaccha. Another inscription of AD 1450 mentions the death of the wife of a Jain merchant, called Candrava, whose father-in-law was the disciple of a Jain saint called Vṛṣabhasena Bhaṭṭāraka, belonging to the Mūla-saṅgha, *Epigraphia Carnatica* XII, Pavagada 51, 55.

***Mantra*:** Prayers and formulae, syllables of mystic significance peculiar to the deities. These are the means by which the devotee invokes and identifies himself with his chosen deity. The *mantras* constitute esoteric words of mystic significance. Intense meditation on certain mystic words sacred to the chosen deities is supposed to produce phonetic phenomena and bring before the worshipper's eyes an image of the divinity concerned. Various kinds of *mantras* are found in the *Jvālinī Kalpa* and the *Bhairava Padmāvatī Kalpa*. Some *mantras* are used, according to the Jain texts, to placate evil spirits. Each of the *mantras* is offered to divinities for protection against death, disease, accident, etc., as also for health, prosperity, and longevity. Some *mantras* are characterized as invocatory formule. See Bīja.

Manuṣyagati: Human form which a Jīva (q.v.) receives owing to its *karma* (q.v.)

Manya Temple: See Dwarahat.

Markuli: Findspot of a Jain inscription of AD 1173 in the Hassan taluk of the Hassan district, Karnataka, which refers to a temple called Trikūṭa Jinālaya erected by Bucimayya, a dignitary of the court of Hoysala Ballāla II. It mentions Aruṅgala-anvaya, Vāsupūjya II and Śrīpāla Traividya as well. *Jain Śilālekha Saṃgraha* III, 379: *Epigraphia Carnatica* V, Hassan 119.

Mārsiṃha III: See Kudlur Inscriptions. His Sravanabelgola stone pillar inscription says that 'he maintained the doctrine of Jina and erected *Vasatis* and *mānastambhas* at various places' and that, keeping the vow of *sallekhanā* in the presence of Ajitasenabhaṭṭāraka, he died at

Bankapura in śaka 896 corresponding to AD 974.

Marriage: Among the Jains, the main purpose of marriage is to maintain the continuity of the race by begetting legitimate children. There are eight forms (q.v.) of marriage, Brāhma, Daiva, Ārsa, Prājāpatya, Āsura, Gāndharva, Rākṣasa, and Piśāca (qq.v.). These are adapted from Brahmanical legal texts with modifications from the Jain viewpoint. The last four forms are condemned as unethical and sinful. The following nine things are to be marked in a bridegroom before giving daughter to him in marriage: his caste, health, age, character, education, bodily stature, parental wealth, and members of the family. One should marry a girl who is of one's own caste, but not the same *gotra* and who is endowed with indication of long life, virtues, and learning. As in Jain literature we come across many instances of marriage contracted according to Gāndharva or Svayamvara system, it may be presumed that marriage partners were sufficiently mature at the time of marriage in the earlier period. But later the age of marriage was lower and child marriage came into vogue. Recently, however, there has been an enhancement in the age of marriage.

In the earlier periods of Jain history *asavarṇa* or inter-caste marriages (q.v.) both hypergamous and hypogamous, were allowed. Later, however, new rules were formed to suit changing conditions. At present marriage is performed within the circle of the endogamous castes and marriage partners do not belong to the same *gotra* (q.v.). Cross-cousin marriage (q.v.) is allowed, but marriage between parallel cousins (father's brother's son or daughter) is prohibited. Marriage by capture is not approved as the right form of marriage, and seldom happens. There are however, instances of marriage by exchange. We have the story of Devadatta who married the sister of Dhanadatta and in exchange gave his own sister in marriage to the latter. There are several instances which sufficiently testify to the prevalence of the practice of giving a daughter in marriage in exchange for money. Though the Prakrit narrative literature is full of the stories of Gandharva marriages, free love is not encouraged by the conservative Jains. In most cases marriage is settled through negotiation between the kin of the bridegroom and bride. Elaborate nuptial rituals (q.v.) are performed. According to the Śvetāmbaras there are 16 main rites in the marriage ceremony. For the Digambaras 20 rites are prescribed. Five of such rites are important which are *vāgdāna* (engagement), *pradāna* (presentation of ornaments), *varaṇa* (nuptial consecration) *pāṇipīḍana* (taking the hand of the bride), and *saptapadī* (circumambulation of the sacred fire). During circumambulation the couple are required to understand that mere pleasure-seeking is not the purpose of marriage. The officiating priest is required to remind the bridal pair at this time that the aim of life is to rise above sensual pleasure. See Cross-Cousin Marriage, Divorce, Endogamy, Exogamy, Forms of Marriage, *Gotras*, Inter-Caste Marriage, Nuptial Rituals, Polygamy, Wife.

Marudevī-basadi: One of the most prominent Jain temples at Lakshmeswar in the Dharwar district of Karnataka. It was probably built in the time of the Western Gaṅgas.

Marukoṭṭa: Situated in the desert area of Marwar in Rajasthan this place contained a medieval Candraprabha temple. It was a centre of the Kharatara-gaccha activists.

Maruru: Findspot of a Jain inscription of AD 1598 which refers to a Pārśvanātha temple at that place. *Jaina Śilālekha Saṃgraha* IV, Nos. 494-5.

Maruttuvakuḍi: Place in the Thanjavur district whence an epigraph of the time of Cola Kulottuṅga I (AD 1070-1120), dated his 16th regional year, has been found. It mentions two Jain shrines at Janaṇāthapuram. *Inscriptions of Madras Presidency,* No. 1003.

Marutu: Site of a late-medieval Pārśvanātha temple in South Kanara district, Karnataka.

Maski: Findspot in Raichur district, Karnataka, of an epigraph dated śaka 953 (AD 1032) of the time of Jagadekamalla, a title of Jayasiṃha II (AD 1015-43), the western Cālukya King of Kalyāṇa. It refers to a Jain shrine called Jagadekamalla Jinālaya which suggests that the temple was named after the monarch. *Jaina Śilālekha Saṃgraha* IV, No. 125.

Masulipatnam Grant of Amma II: It refers to a Jain Ācārya Jayasena who bore the surname Nāthasena and was the disciple of the illustrious Candrasena, was well-versed in the Siddhānta and attained proficiency in *parasamaya*, and was honoured by the Śrāvakas, Kṣapaṇakas, Kṣullakas, and Ajjakas. In his honour two nobles, Bhīma and Naravāhana II, constructed two Jina temples (Jinabhavana) at Vijayavāṭika (Bezwada), for which purpose King Amma II granted the village of Pedda-Galidiparru, having converted it to a *devabhoga* and exempted it from tax. *Epigraphia Indica*, XXIV.268ff.

Mātaṅga: Attendant Yakṣa of Supārśvanātha (q.v.),

who is otherwise known as Varanandī. The Śvetāmbaras give him an elephant as a mount while the Digambaras make him ride a lion. His hands contain the wood-apple, noose, mongoose, and goad according to the former, while the latter tradition endows him with staff, spear, *svastika*, and flag. The *Pratiṣṭhāsārasaṃgraha* speaks of this Yakṣa as two-armed and having a crooked face.

Mātaṅga: Attendant yakṣa of Mahāvīra. He is two handed and riding on elephant. The Śvetāmbara school gives the mongoose and citron as his attributes while the Digambara makes them a *varada-mudrā* and a citron. There is a *dharma-cakra* symbol for his head.

Mātaṅga Spells: Magical spells named after the Mātaṅga tribe that has been ranked with the Ḍombas, Śvapākas, Cāṇḍālas, Paṇis, and the other so-called degraded classes. They are mentioned in the narrative literature of the Jains as also in the commentaries of the *Uttarādhyayana, Niśītha, Āvaśyaka,* etc. They belonged to the Vidyādhara clan indicating their skill in magic lore. The Mātaṅgī and Śvapākī lore are noted along with the Pārvatī, the Vaṃśalatā and the Vṛkṣamūlikā. It is said that a certain Mātaṅga was in possession of *vidyā* which could not be transferred to King Śreṇika Bimbisāra unless the king agreed to give up his throne and occupy the Mataṅga seat below. *Daśavaikālika-cūrṇi* 45. As the Ghaṇṭika Yakṣa belonged to the Ḍombas so the Aḍambara or Hiriddikka Yakṣa was related to the Mātangas. The Mātaṅgī-spell is grouped with Gaurī and Gandhārī which were despised as they were difficult to acquire, though we are told in the *Bṛhatkalpabhāṣya* that once acquired they fulfilled all desires. The Mātaṅgas were evidently tribal people whose magical practices received attention in Jainism and gave them a better position. This enhanced status is symbolized by the appointment of a personalized and deified Mātaṅga as attendant of the seventh and twenty-fourth Jinas.

Mātaṅgeśvara: Caturmukha Jain temple at Khajuraho. It has four openings on four sides, but only that in the east has been treated as the entrance to the shrine.

Materialism: Two materialistic theories are spoken of in the *Sūyagaḍa*, in the first of which it is said that there is no soul apart from the body, while the second is concerned with the doctrine of elements. Jain atheism has some features in common with that of the materialists known in Indian tradition as the Cārvākas or the Lokāyatas who hold that the assumption of god as creator is unnecessary since the world comes into existence by the spontaneous combination of material elements. According to the Jains neither perception nor inference can prove god. But in other respects the Jains, notwithstanding their realistic world-view, have differences with the Cārvākas. In accepting non-perceptual sources of knowledge like inference and testimony, the Jain philosophers felt it necessary to justify their view by refuting the Cārvāka theory that perception is the only source of valid knowledge. The Jains agree with the Cārvākas on the point that perception reveals the reality of material substances composed of four elements. But they add that for the establishment of the concepts of space and time and also of motion and rest, inferential knowledge is necessary. They point out that in some cases even the Cārvākas have to depend on inferential knowledge, e.g. when they say that consciousness is due to the combination of material substances. Moreover, according to the Jains, when the Cārvākas deny the existence of non-perceptible objects like life-after-death, they go beyond perception and infer the non-existence of the objects from the fact of their non-perception. The Jains are not ready to accept the Cārvāka view that there is no soul apart from the body, or that consciousness is the effect of matter, resulting out of the combination of material elements that constitute the body. This on the ground that there is no concomitance between the body and consciousness, the development and decay of the former not being invariably followed by corresponding changes in the latter. The Jain criticism of the Cārvākas was directed mainly against their theory of knowledge.

Maṭhādhipati: Title of the high priest at Sittamur in the South Arcot district. He is elected by representatives of the chief Jain villages. He has supreme authority over the Jains of this region. He travels round in a palanquin to the chief centres, the expenses being paid by the communities he visits. He settles disputes and inflicts punishment on the erring. His control over his people is real.

Mathura: Particularly sacred to the Jains from early times. Jain literary tradition ascribes a hoary antiquity to Jain religion and culture in this region. The existence of *pāsādas* or Jain shrine in Mathura as early as the middle of the second century BC is attested by epigraphical evidence. The Jain antiquities of Mathura can be divided into a few categories, the foremost of which is the Kaṅkālī Ṭīlā (q.v.) and its components. This is the main site within the orbit of Mathura which has yielded an overwhelmingly large number of sculptures, *āyāgapaṭas*, pillars, capitals, umbrellas, railing-posts, cross-bars, copings, component parts of gateways, bracket-figures and other architectural pieces. Shrines and monasteries were also part of the Jain culture of Mathura of which we have, besides epigraphical evidence, architectural remains and sculptural evidence. The *āyāgapaṭas* (q.v.) are important features of the Jain culture of Mathura and form a class by themselves. The representations of Jinas and *stūpas* on them tend to prove that these slabs did not serve merely as offerings to the Jinas or *stūpas* but were also themselves objects of worship. Of the Kuṣāṇa period there are numerous images from Mathura, several bearing the dates of the Kuṣāṇa rulers. Since the custom of attaching distinguishing *lāñchanas* were yet to be evolved, apart from Pārśvanātha who is marked by a canopy of snake-hoods and Ṛṣabhanātha who has some locks of hair falling on his shoulders, individual Tīrthaṃkaras cannot be identified with certainty. There are *caturmukhas* or *sarvatobhadrikas* which represent the figure of a Tīrthaṃkara on each of the four sides of the stone-block. An interesting type of image is that of Neminātha or Ariṣṭanemi flanked by Balarāma and Vāsudeva Kṛṣṇa. Among other figures that are important, one is the relief of Āryavatī attended by three women holding an umbrella, a *cāmara* and a garland and the other is the earliest Jain image of Sarasvatī. It is headless and dated in the year 54 (AD 132). Inscriptions from Mathura are no less important for the study of history of Jainism in this region.

Mathura Inscriptions: The earliest Jain inscription from Mathura, assigned to the first century BC, tells of a shine raised in honour of the Arhat Vardhamāna and also of the dedication of seats for teachers. Other pre-Kuṣāṇa Jain inscriptions from Mathura record the setting up of an *āryavati* by Āmohini, a female lay-disciple, together with her sons for the worship of Arhats; the erection of a shrine or *devakula* with necessary accessories for the Nirgranthas by a few courtesans; establishment of a tablet of homage by Śivayaśa, wife of a dancer called Phaguyaśa; and similar dedications by others. A characteristic production of the Jains of Mathura was the *āyāgapaṭa* or 'tablet of homage'. These were sculptured tablets containing inscriptions. One important pre-Kuṣāṇa inscription refers to Bhagavat Nemesa. A second-century inscription of Kaṅkāli Ṭīlā says that the stūpa was built by the gods, indicating its legendary antiquity. Such inscriptions suggest that the Jains had erected stūpas since long, as the canon refers to them. The stūpas upon which the figures of the Arhats were depicted were supposed to have been the work of gods, suggesting that they had been standing since time immemorial.

A large number of dedicatory inscriptions of the Kuṣāṇa age from Mathura have come to light. They are all on the pedestals of statues. In many of them the dedicators gave not only their own names, but also those of the teachers to whose communities they belonged. The teachers were of two classes—*vācaka* or ordinary teachers and *gaṇin* or heads of schools. The names of the schools to which the teachers belonged are also specified in the inscriptions which are in many cases dated. The larger groups were called *gaṇas*, and their subdivisions, *kulas* and *śākhās*. Exactly the same division into *gaṇa*, *kula*, and *śākhā* is found in the *Kalpasūtra*. The discoveries made in Mathura prove by the nakedness of the sculpted figures that the schism of the order into the Digambara and Śvetāmbara dates as early as the first century AD. Besides, the inscriptions show that in the first and second centuries the tradition of the 24 Tīrthaṃkaras with their distinctive emblems and attributes was firmly established, that an order of nuns was in existence, and that some canonical works were already composed by that time. An inscription of AD 433 refers to a monk called Datilācārya who belonged to the Vidyādharī-śākhā and Koliya-gaṇa. His disciple Samādhya had built a Jina image at his command. Another inscription dated in the year 299 of an unknown era refers to the erection of an image of Mahāvīra and a temple by Okha, Sarika, and Sivadinā. Mathura continued to be a Jain centre and even in the tenth century we come across Jain epigraphs from Mathura. Notwithstanding Sultan Mahmud's destruction of the city, the Jains were able to rebuild their fortune in Mathura during the medieval period. *Epigraphia Indica* I.373ff. 381-2, 390, 396, II.199-202, 206-7; *Indian Antiquary,* XXXIII. 142ff; H. Lüders, *List,* Nos. 17ff, 59, 78, 94, 99ff. *Journal of the Royal Asiatic Socity*, 1905, 635-55; 1962, 57ff., 153ff.

Mathura: Post-Kuṣāṇa Finds: In post-Kuṣāṇa Mathura, the *āyāgapaṭas* and independent figures of Jain deities like the Śāsanadevatās, Yakṣas, Sarasvatī, Balabhadra, Dharaṇendra, etc., are conspicuous by their absence. The Archaeological Museum of Mathura and the State Museum at Lucknow, which house the bulk of Jain antiquities, respectively possess only 38 and 21 Jain sculptures that can be attributed with certainly to the Gupta age. These may be classified under the following categories: 25 seated Jina figures in meditation; 6 Jina figures in standing pose; 23 detached heads of the Tīrthaṃkaras; and some fragmentary pieces. Among the seated Jina images two are of Ṛṣabha. The one of Neminātha is mutilated.

Others are difficult to identify. Three of them bear inscriptions. Four standing images have been identified—one of Neminātha, one of Pārśvanātha and two of Ādinātha. The finds suggest that even in the Gupta age the Jains had an establishment at Mathura and that Jain images did not cease to be made and enshrined.

Mathura Remains: From the first century onwards Mathura became the centre of Jain artistic activities. We have here remains of a Jain shrine dating back to the pre-Christian period and a large number of small dedicatory inscriptions engraved on the image of the Jinas, votive tablets and arches, dating from the first two centuries of the Christian era. Their references to the teachers of the donors, their *gotra*, *kula*, *śākhā*, etc., offer welcome confirmation of similar information found in the *Sthavirāvalī*. The Kaṅkāli Ṭīlā yielded a variety of Jain specimens, including railing pillars with reliefs of demi-gods and goddesses and a few sculptures containing scenes from the lives of the Tīrthaṃkaras. A few specimens like the Āmohinī relief, the Loṇaśobhikā-*āyāgapaṭa* (q.v.), the Kaṅkāli-Tīlā-*āyāgapaṭa*, etc., probably belonging to the pre-Kaṇiska decades, show traces of heavy physicality, emphasizing the stature of the main figure by raising its height and grading the subsidiary figures accordingly. But this style gradually changed: the heaviness of form was partly replaced by introducing new elements. Almost all the seated Tīrthaṃkara images in the Mathura Museum, which can be dated on the basis of their pedestal inscriptions in the Kuṣāṇa period, show below their seat a wheel of law, a *dharmacakra* on a pillar in the centre, flanked by numbers of devotees, male and female, with a lion at each end. But none of them appears to bear on their *pīṭhikā*, their individual cognizances, which are invariably present in later Jain reliefs. An image of Ṛṣabhanātha dated in 84 Kaṇiṣka era has wheel and devotees but not his bull emblem. A sculptured panel representing the ascetic Kanha, dated in the year 95, has on its top section four Jinas, two on each side of a stūpa, seated in *samādhi-mudrā*, who can reasonably be identified with the last four Tīrthaṃkaras—Nami, Nemi, Pārśva, and Mahāvīra. Another composite relief, probably to be dated in the early Gupta period on the basis of its extremely fragmentary inscription, shows Mahāvīra seated in the *dhyāna* pose on his lion-throne underneath a tree, surrounded by the miniature figures of the 23 other Tīrthaṃkaras. It is noteworthy that none of these miniatures bears on its seat its special mark. Of other specimens of the Kuṣāṇa period, mention may be made of a headless image of Sarasvati of the year 79 on which probably stood the 18th Jina Aranātha, as is indicated by his distinctive symbol and a broken frieze showing on the obverse the animal-faced Naigameṣa. So far as the Aranātha image is concerned, the symbol in the centre of the pedestal composition is a wheel, resting on a *nandipāda* placed on a lotus and flanked by two fish. The inscription above it records the setting up of the image of the Arhat Nandyāvarta. This proper name also indicates the emblem of a sort of geometrical pattern typical of the 18th Jina. Some early Yakṣa sculptures are in the Mathura Museum, a few of which seem to have Jinistic affiliation. The figure of a dryad, modelled almost in the round, of an architrave support from Kaṅkāli Ṭīlā anticipates the charming dryads of the Sanchi *toraṇas*. Thus Mathura, the home of one of the most important and prolific artistic movements in early India, has supplied significant examples of early Jain artistic activities, inspired by the same impulse that characterized the production of the central Indian school, and having many things in common with it. G. Bühler, *The Indian Sect of the Jainas*, App. A; V.A. Smith, *Jaina Stūpa and other Antiquities of Mathura*, Allahabad, 1901; J. Ph. Vogel, *Mathura Museum Catalogue*, Allahabad, 1910, 41-3, 66-82.

***Mati*:** The first among the five kinds of knowledge. It refers to the ordinary process of sense-experience which is generally conditioned by perception through the sense-organs and the inferential knowledge based thereon. It is also called *abhinibodha-jñāna* and placed in the *parokṣa* or indirect category of knowledge. It is due to the fact that in *mati-jñāna* knowledge is obtained through the senses and mind. It is considered an obstruction arising from *ghātin karma* (q.v.). Later Jain writers, however, for the sake of uniformity with other philosophical traditions of India, declare it to be a form of *pratyakṣa* or direct knowledge. *Tattvārtha* I.13-14. See Epistemology.

***Mātṛkā*:** A form of early Gujarati poetry which gives moral and religious instructions in verses, each of which begins with a letter of the Sanskrit syllabary, in serial order. There are three such early specimens composed before the end of the thirteenth century which *Mātṛkā-caüpai*, *Saṃvega-mātṛkā*, and *Samyaktyamai-caüpai* of Jagaḍu.

***Mātṛkā-Caüpai*:** See *Mātṛkā*.

Mattāvara: Ancient name Mattvūra. Situated in the Chikmagalur distict, Karnataka, it is the findspot of a number of Jain inscriptions, the principal one belonging to śaka 991 (AD 1069). It holds that the Hoysala king Vinayāditya built a temple originally outside the village Mattavura, but at the request of a merchant constructed a new vasadi in the village itself. The other Jain epigraphs from Mattavara belonging to AD 1116, 1120 and 1143 are inscribed on memorial tablets. A fourteenth-century epigraph from this place refers to a local Jain temple. *Mysore Archaeological Report*, 1932, 171; *Jaina Śilālekha Saṃgraha* IV, Nos. 152, 410.

Matter: See Pudgala.

Matya: Findspot of a tenth-century Ṛṣabhanātha image in the Midnapur district, West Bengal. It is a small statuette in grey-white stone, standing in *kāyotsarga* on a double-petalled lotus placed on a *triratha* pedestal and flanking his legs *chowri*-bearing attendants standing face to face. The central *ratha* is relieved with the miniature figure of a bull flanked by lions. Above the *chowri*-bearers are shown two Jinas, one below the other, each standing in *kāyotsarga* on lotus.

***Maunādhyayanavṛtti*:** Sacrament for concentrated scriptural study.

Māya-Mṛsa: See Pāpa.

Medical science: The traditional Indian system of medicine are also followed by the Jains. In the *Ācārāṅga Sūtra* I.6.1, sixteen different diseases are mentioned. These are boils, leprosy, sickness, consumption, blindness, stiffness, lameness, humpbackedness, dropsy, dumbness, apoplexy, eye-disease, trembling, crippledness, elephantisis and diabetes. A similar list is found in the *Vipākaśruta*. The *Sthānāṅga* refers to eight main subjects of therapeutics which are pediatrics (*kumārabhicca*), internal diseases like those of heart, etc. (*kāya-tigicchā*), surgical cases (*salāi* and *sallahattā*), toxicology (*jangoli*), psychotherapeutics (*bhūya-vijjā*), cautery (*kharatanta*), and elexirology (*rasāyana*) and nearly conform with the eight limbs of Āyurveda. The same text refers to nine causes of diseases which are a sedentary way of living, bad food, too much sleep, too little sleep, constipation, anuria, marching, sitophobia, and addiction to sensual enjoyment. The Ayurvedic concept that the root of all diseases is to be sought in the functions of the wind, gall-bladder, and heart (respiration, growth of phlegm, etc.) is entertained by the Jains who hold that the eaten food becomes a pulp in the stomach, and by the action of *samāna* wind goes to the gall-bladder where it is saturated by acid coming out from the gall-bladder, and thus becomes the vital fluid which ultimately transforms into blood circulated by the heart and purified by the lungs. Side by side insistence on the doctrine of *karma* is also given. The story of Umbaradatta, as recorded in the *Vipākaśruta*, shows that the cause of his ailments was the actions of his past life.

Meghaprabhācārya: See *Dharmābhyudaya*.

Megudi Temple: See Hallur.

Meguti Temple: Jain temple at Aihole erected in śaka 556, i.e. AD 634, by one Ravīkirti during the reign of the Cālukya King Pulakeśin II. It belongs to the category of those temples that are flat-roofed, with a covered ambulatory around the sanctum and preceded by a porch in front. It is a perfect example of the series and displays refinement and delicacy in the ornamental treatment of the temple as a whole. The decoration of the outer walls by means of narrow pilasters with little bracket capitals exhibits a distinct progress in artistic execution. In plan the temple is a long rectangular building consisting of two parts, the shrine with its surrounding gallery and the forward hall with its roof supported on pillars and probably originally open all around. The two are joined together by a narrow vestibule or antechamber in between.

Melaka Vasahi: A temple on Mount Girnar which was erected in AD 1455.

Menā-basti: Site of a Jain cave-temple on the Meguti Hill at Aihole. It was excavated towards the close of the seventh or the beginning of the eighth century. It has a narrow verandah behind the plain square-pillared facade with bays, except the central one. The left end wall of the verandah has a relief of Pārśvanātha with Dharaṇendra and Padmāvatī and a host of other attendants. The inner *maṇḍapa* is a hall with two side shrines, the one on the left dedicated to Mahāvīra and his attendants. It is incomplete. The inner entrance to the shrine behind has three openings formed

to a basadi dedicated to 24 Tīrthaṃkaras, *Jaina Śilālekha Saṃgraha* V, No. 234.

Mote Bennur: Situated in Dharwar district of Karnataka, it is the findspot of an epigraph which mentions a monk called Śāntinandī Bhaṭṭāraka described as belonging to the Candrikāvaṭa-vaṃśa of the Mūla-saṅgha. A short epigraph recording the death of a monk called Māghanandi of Surastha-gaṇa has been found in this place. *Jaina Śilālekha Saṃgraha* IV, Nos. 147-8.

Mountains: Mountains have been assigned a holy place in Jainism. A majority of the Tīrthaṃkaras attained liberation on some mountain or the other. The Himalaya mountain is said to have been the dwelling place of the Vidyādharas. It is divided into two mythological regions. According to the Jain tradition when Nami and Vinami approached Ṛṣabha, Dharaṇendra (q.v.), king of the Nāgas, bestowed upon them two Vidyādhara territories situated on both sides of the Veyaḍḍha mountain. The mountain Sīmaṇaga which was situated at the confluence of five rivers had a shrine of Ṛṣabha and was famous for omniscience of Acala, one of the Baladevas. The mountain Hrimat was another holy place where the image of Dharaṇendra was installed. Śrīparvata was another holy place assigned for practising meditation. Besides we have numerous other mountains such as Sammedaśikhara (Paresnath Hill), Rajgir, and Mandargiri in Bihar; Udayagiri and Khaṇḍagiri in Orissa; Śatruñjaya, Girnar, Taraṅgagiri, and Pavagarh in Gujarat; Abu in Rajasthan; Daśārṇapura, Kuñjaravarta, Rathāvarta, and Siddhavarakūṭa in Malwa; Muktagiri and Kunthalagiri in Mahārāṣṭra; Droṇagiri, Nainagiri, and Sonagiri in Madhya Pradesh; Sravanabelgola and Karkal in Karnataka, etc.

***Mṛgavati Caritra*:** See Maladharin Devaprabha Suri.

Mūḍabidri: An important Jain centre in South Kanara district of Karnataka and also known as Bidure and Bedari. This Jain site is very important for its thousand-pillared temple, tombs of priests, and metal images comprising those of individual Jinas, *caturmukhas* and *meru*, constructed with the images of the Tīrthaṃkaras. A copper-plate of AD 1504 from this place refers to a Jain monk called Cārukīrti. Another of 1546 mentions a grant for the Tribhuvanacūḍāmaṇi temple of this place dedicated to Candraprabha or Candranātha. The temple of Pārśvanātha is mentioned in a copper-plate grant of AD 1563. An inscription of AD 1622 mentions one Tribhuvanatilaka temple of this place. In this town were discovered the manuscripts of *Dhavalā* and *Jayadhavalā* (qq.v.). The seventeenth-century Jain writer Śīlavijaya has mentioned 19 Jain temples of this place. *Jaina Śilālekha Saṃgraha* IV, Nos. 455, 475, 478, 520, 577.

Mūdahalli: Findspot of a short mutilated Jain inscription of AD 1170 in Nanjangud taluk, Mysore district, Karnataka, which praises the *anvaya* of Aruṅgala, belonging to Nandi-saṅgha. *Epigraphia Carnatica*, III, Nanjan 133.

Mūḍha: Superstitious ignorance from which a true believer must be free in order to develop *samyag-darśana* (q.v.), that is, right belief. These are *loka-mūḍha* which refers to superstition regarding attachment of sanctity to certain places, e.g. belief that a bath in the Ganga will wash off the sins; *deva-mūḍha* which refers to superstitions like propitiation of the so-called gods and goddesses for the fulfilment of worldly and spiritual desires; and *pāsandhi-mūḍha* which refers to regard for false ascetics and their teachings. Freedom from these three types of superstition is the essential condition of right faith.

***Mudrā*:** Special position of fingers and movements of hands. In Chapter Three of the *Jvālinīkalpa* we come across a detailed account of the different forms of *mudrās*. These may be enumerated as the *jaṭharabhedana-mudrā* for piercing the belly, the *galamocana-mudrā* for cutting the throat, the *antaracchedana-mudrā* for cutting the intestines, the *vidyun-mudrā* for striking with lightning, the *majjana-mudrā* for drowning in the deep seas, the *śikhi-mudrā* or the *gadā-mudrā* for giving a blow of the mace, the *akṣisphoṭana-mudrā* for piercing the eyes, the *curcikā-mudrā* for striking with a knife, and so on. The *Bhairava Padmāvatīkalpa* refers to *aṅkuśā-mudrā* for attracting persons, *saroja-mudrā* for controlling a person, *jñāna-mudrā* for curing of disease, the *pallava-mudrā* for creating enmity between persons, the *śaṅkha-mudrā* for paralysing persons, and the *vajra-mudrā* for killing enemies.

***Mudritakumudacandra-prakaraṇa*:** A drama in five acts written by Yaśascandra. It tells how the Digambara teacher Kumudacandra was defeated by the Śvetāmbara teacher Devasūri in a disputation in the presence of king Jayasiṃha. The author was a contemporary of King Jayasiṃha who reigned in Gujarat from AD 1094 to 1142. Edited in Yaśovijaya Jaina Granthamālā, No. 8. Benares, 1905.

Mugulūr: A Jain centre in the Hassan district, Karnataka. An inscription from this place records the death of Vāsupūjya who belonged to the spiritual lineage of Śrīpāla Traividyadeva. The Muglur inscription of AD 1147 records that at Muguli, that is, Muglur, a merchant called Govinda built a Jina temple. His father had also built a Jina temple at Dorasamudra, *Jaina Śilālekha Saṃgraha*, II, No. 265; III, No. 327; *Epigraphia Carnatica,* V, Hassan, Nos. 130-1.

Mukkara-basadi: One of the most prominent Jain temples at Lakshmeswar in the Dharwar district of Karnataka. It was probably built during the reign of the Western Gaṅgas.

Muktagiri: Situated near Achalpur in Amaravati district, Maharashtra this hill is mentioned as a Jain *tīrtha* in the works of Jñānasāgara, Sumatisāgara and others. It is also known as Medhagiri.

Mukta Jīva: Liberated soul, also called *siddha-jīva.* Mukta Jīvas are those who have accomplished absolute purity. They dwell in the state of perfection at the top of the universe and have nothing to do with worldly affairs. They have attained *nirvāṇa*, also known as *nivṛtti* or *mukti.* They have four enjoyments which are unlimited perception, absolute knowledge, infinite power, and unhounded happiness. Liberated souls are absolutely pure and they are supposed to be disembodied. But from another point of view liberated souls may also be embodied. The Jinas or Tīrthaṃkaras were all liberated souls but maintained their physical bodies for imparting beneficial knowledge to mankind. In Jain tradition they are superior to gods. The latter are meritorious beings, enjoying the fruit of their merit as belonging to a class of higher beings. But they are not Mukta Jīvas or liberated souls. They are subject to endless rebirth in various forms. *Tattvārtha* II.21-3.

***Mukti*:** See *Mokṣa.*

***Mūlācāra*:** Text on ethics belonging to the Digambara tradition composed by Vaṭṭakera (q.v.). It contains 1,252 verses and is divided into twelve parts. Some of the rules are directly taken from the Śvetāmbara canon. In one manuscript the *Mūlācāra* is ascribed to Kundakunda. There is a commentary named *Ācāravṛtti* on it written by Vasunandin who observes by way of introduction that Vaṭṭakera intended to give in his work a brief summary of the *Ācārāṅga*. Published in Manikchand Digambara Jaina Granthamālā, in two parts, VS 1977, 1980; K. Okud, *Eine Digambara Dogmatik*, Wiesbaden, 1975; Phoolchand Jain Premi, *Mūlācāra kā Samīkṣātmaka Adhyayan*, in Hindi, Varanasi, 1987.

Mūlaguṇas: Eight basic or primary virtues of a householder. These are the five *anuvratas* (q.v.) and refraining from the use of wine, flesh and honey for minimizing injury to living beings.

Mulanātha Jinadeva Temple: Śvetāmbara temple at Anahila Patan built by Cālukya Mūlaraja I (AD 942-95).

***Mūlārādhanā*:** Also known as *Bhagavatī Ārādhanā* it is the earliest Digambara work on Jain ethics. Composed by Śivārya, it contains 2,166 Prakrit verses giving an exposition of the four devotions, faith, knowledge, conduct, and austerities but at the same time dealing with practically all aspects of Jainism. The *Mūlārādhanā* seems to have close affinities with the *Mūlācāra* (q.v.) of Vaṭṭkera (q.v.) as well as with the Āgama texts of the Śvetāmbaras. Published with Pandit Sadāsukha's *Bhāṣāvacanikā* in Muni Anantakirti Digambara Jaina Granthamālā, VS 1989; with com. of Aparājita and Āśādhara, Sholapur, 1935; with Aparājita's com. *Vidyodaya*, Karanja, 1935; with Hindi trans. and intro. by Pandit Kailash Chandra Jain Siddhāntaśāstrī, Sholapur, 1977.

***Mūlasūtra*:** Prakrit Mulasūtta, a collection of four texts belonging to the Śvetāmbara canonical tradition. Of these the *Uttarādhyayana* (Uttarajjhāyā, q.v.) which consists of 36 chapters is said to have been spoken by Mahāvīra himself. The *Dasavaikālika* (Dasaveyaliya, q.v.), said to have been composed by Sejjambhava, deals with monastic life in general. The *Āvaśyaka* (*Āvassaya*, q.v.) is a *gāthā* taking its name from the six *āvassaya* or formulae to be recited daily. The *Piṇḍaniryukti*, often mentioned as the fourth Mūlasūtra, is a text on discipline, food habits, and mistakes made by the almsgiver and receiver.

Mūla-Vasatika: Digambara church built by Cālukya Mūlarāja (AD 942-95) in Anahila-Patan.

Mulgund Inscriptions: Dated śaka 824 (AD 902) and found at Mulgund in the Gadag taluk of Dharwar district, one inscription of the time of the Rāṣṭrakūṭa Kṛṣṇa II refers to Arasārya, a governor's son who was proficient in logical Āgama (*Nayāgamakuśala*) texts, making an endowment for the maintenance of a Jinālaya established by his father, the Governor Cikārya. The gift was entrusted to Kanakasena Sūri, disciple of Vīrasena who was a disciple of Kumārasena Ācarya Candikavāṭa. Several inscriptions of later times with Jain contents have come from Mulgund. One belonging to the time of the Western Cālukya Someśvara, dated śaka 975 (AD 1053) records a land grant by Kāñcarasa of the Sinda house to Nayasena Paṇḍita, fourth in the spiritual lineage from Ajitasena belonging to the Mūla-saṅgha and Sena-anvaya. An inscription of the time of

Someśvara I claims that his feudatory Bhavanagandhavāraṇa was a benefactor of Jain establishments in Mulgund. *Epigraphia Indica* XIII.190ff; *South Indian Inscriptions*, XI.99f.; *Jaina Śilālekha Saṃgraha* II, No. 137; IV, Nos. 346, 432, 514.

Mullur: A Jain centre in the Somavarapet taluk in Karnataka. The Pārśvanātha-basadi of this place was established by the Kongāḷva feudatory rulers according to epigraphical evidence. Queen Pochabbe, mother of Rājādhirāja Kongāḷva, was a lay disciple of Guṇasena Paṇḍita of Nandisaṅgha and Arungala-anvaya. An undated epigraph from this place records that Mallisena of the same saṅgha and anvaya had the basadi of Śāntinātha reconsecrated. *Epigraphia Carnatica,* rev. edn. I, Nos. 6, 71-2, 77.

Muṇḍasthala: Situated in the Sirohi district of Rajasthan, this Jain *tīrtha* contained a celebrated Jīvantasvāmī Mahāvīra temple according to Jinaprabha's *Vividhatīrthakalpa.*

Muni: Advanced spiritual aspirants who hold a high position in Jainism. This postion is acquired through a prescribed process. An individual aspiring for this position has to observe the five *mahāvratas* (q.v.), five *anuvratas* (q.v.), four *śikṣāvratas* (q.v.) and eleven *pratimās* (q.v.) very strictly. Thereafter, receiving permission from his relatives to renounce mundane affairs and worship the *pañca-parameṣṭhins* (q.v.) he requests the Gaṇin to admit him into the order. Munis represent the highest stage in the spiritual hierarchy, especially of southern Jainism. This stage can be achieved either directly or through promotion, from Arcaka to Anuvratī and from Anuvratī to Muni (qq.v.). Achieving this stage is open to all Digambara Jains irrespective of whether they stay in the north or in the south. The Munis have to live a celibate life, away from the world. There are, however, other kinds of Munis also, like those who are attached to various religious divisions of the Sthānakavāsīs known as Saṃghādās, such as Limadi-Saṃghādā, Goṇḍala-Saṃghādā, Rajkot-Saṃghādā, etc. These Munis are appointed and removed by the Saṃghādās. They are not allowed to own property and do not exercise control over the people, or authority over the caste pañcāyats.

Municandra: Commentator on Haribhadra's *Upadeśapada*. The commentary is in Prakrit written in AD 1116 at Anahilapāṭaka. It contains a good number of illustrative stories, for details regarding various commentaries see *Jinaratnakośa* 48ff.

Municandra Sūri: See *Gāthākośa.*

Muniratna: Jain poet of the thirteenth century whose *Amāmacarita* describes the life of Amamasvāmin in thirty cantos. *Munisuvratacarita* is his other work.

Munisundara: Disciple of Somasundara who was not only a great writer of Gujarat in the fifteenth century but also an active exponent of Jainism. He was also honoured by the Muslim Naik of Cambay. *Somasaubhāgyakāvya* X.2-3.

Munisundara Suri: Author of a large collection of hymns entitled *Jinastotraratnakośa*. The first *prastāva* contains 23 *stotras* in praise or various Jinas in connection with their monuments in various sacred places. Munisundara flourished in the fourteenth century. Edited in *Jaina Stotra Saṃgraha* II; Yaśovijaya Jaina Granthamālā IX.

Munisuvrata: The twentieth Tīrthaṃkara, the son of Sumitra and Padmāvatī of Rājagṛha. His sacred tree was the *campaka* and he had a life-span of 30,000 years. His height was 20 bow-lengths. Kumbha and Puṣpavatī were his chief disciples. He attained liberation on Mount Sammeya. His emblem is the tortoise, attendants Varuṇa and Nagadattā/Bahurūpiṇī, and *chowri*-bearer is Ajitā. His images are not absolutely rare.

***Munisuvratacarita*:** See Arhaddāsa.

Muni Suvrata Temple: Temple built in Dholaka by Śreṣṭhin Dhavala.

***Mūrtipūjaka*:** Śvetāmbara subsect also known as Pujerā, Derāvāsī, and Mandiramārgī. They worship idols with flowers, fruits, etc., adorning them with rich clothes and ornaments. Their ascetics cover their mouths with strips of cloth while speaking. Their ascetics often wear yellow robes.

Musinikonda Grant: An inscription according to which Ayyana Mahādevī, wife of Kubja-Viṣṇuvardhana (AD 624-41) of the Veṅgī Cālukya lineage, made a grant of the village of Musinikonda in Tonka Notavāḍi Viṣaya to the Jain saint Kalibhadrācārya for the maintenance of Nadumbi-vasati at Bezwada which was probably built by the queen herself. The grant was renewed in the reign of Viṣṇuvardhana III. *Annual Report on South Indian Epigraphy,* 1916-17, CP. No. 16; *Journal of the Andhra Historical Research Society*, XIII.185ff.

Mutsandra: Findspot of a Jain inscription of *c.* AD 1000 in the Nagamangala taluk of Mandya district, Karnataka, which refers to a temple called Coka-Jinālaya. *Jaina Śilālekha Saṃgraha* II, No. 170.

Muttatti: Findspot of an inscription of AD 1120 in Hassan taluk, Hassan district, Karnataka, which says that Vinayāditya, a general of Hoysala

Viṣṇuvardhana, built a Jina temple in this place and gave it the name Hoysala Jinālaya. A grant for this temple was given to Prabhācandra Siddhāntadeva, disciple of Meghacandra of Pustaka-gaccha, Kundakunda-anvaya, Deśī-gana and Mūla-saṅgha. *Jaina Śilālekha Saṃgraha* II, No. 275.

Muttupatti: A village in the Nilakkotti taluk of Madurai district where inscriptions bearing on Jainism have been found.

N

Nachna: Site in Panna district, Madhya Pradesh, wherefrom two beautiful Jina images of the Gupta age, now preserved in the Rājendra Udyān, have been found. Near the Brahmanical centre at Nachna was the Jain centre of Sira Pahari in the Gupta age whence a group of Jain sculptures have been found. They were lying in two caves on a hill by the side of a lake near the Brahmanical shrines at Nachna. From the site of Nachna itself come two seated images of Ādinātha and a standing figure of Pārśvanātha of *c.* eighth century AD.

Nandana: Forest encircling the Meru (q.v.) at its second level. Characteristically it is akin to Bhadraśāla, Saumanasa, and Pāṇḍukā (qq.v.) forests.

Nadlai: Findspot of five inscriptions of the Nadol Cāhamāna King Rāyamalha, found in this place, 8 miles to the north-west of Desuri in Rajasthan, all belonging to the twelfth century, speak of a variety of topics pertaining to Jainism. The first records a gift by queen Mānaladevī and two princes of a regular supply of oil for the Jain saints in or outside Naḍulaḍāgikā; the second records the gift of lamps, incense, offering, flowers, etc., for the worship of Neminātha; the third records a gift by *rauta* Rājadeva in the presence of others for the spiritual merit of his mother; the fourth records a gift to the temple of Mahāvīra; and the last records the pious deeds of Rājadeva for the sake of the Mahāvīra temple of Nadlai. The place is situated in the district of Pali and was known by the names Naḍūlaḍāgika, Nandakulavatī, Nāradapurī, etc. The famous Vijayasena, disciple of Hīravijaya was born at this place. *Epigraphia Indica* XI.28ff.

Nadol: Findspot of copper-plate grants in the Pali district of Rajasthan. The first of the two copper-plate grants dated VS 1218 (AD 1161), of the Nadol Cāhamāna King Alhanadeva, records a donation of five *drammas* by the king to the temple of Mahāvīra, belonging to Sanderaka Gaccha at Naddūla Mahāsthāna. The second records a grant of the royal family to the Jina Mahāvīra of Naḍḍūla. The place is situated in the Pali district and is called a *mahāsthāna* in a twelfth-century epigraph. Its principal Jina temple was dedicated to Mahāvīra. At present, however, the principal deity of this holy place is Padmaprabha. There is also an old Neminātha temple here. *Epigraphia Indica* IX.63ff.

Nadumba-vasadi: Jain temple-complex at Vijayawada in Andhra Pradesh. A copper-plate inscription of the time of the Eastern Cālukya King Viṣṇuvardhana III records the renewal of the grant of the village Musinikonda which had been earlier granted to this temple by Ayyana-mahādevī, the queen of Kubja-Viṣṇuvardhana. *Annual Report on South Indian Epigraphy*, 1966-7, CP IX.

Nāga: Dikpāla (q.v.) or guardian deity of the lower regions. This god in Jainism is conceived as seated on a lotus and having a snake in his hand. He rules over Pātāla or the netherworld. The name also denotes a serpent, the cult of which was widespread in ancient India with an elaborate mythology. The Nāga cult owing to its tribal base was not hostile to Jainism and the Nāgas form the canopy of Pārśvanātha. The Nāga King Dharaṇendra has an important role in Jain myths and legends. In the field of Jain art the serpents serve excellent decorative purpose. See Nāgamaha.

Nagacandra: Also known as Pampa II or Abhinava Pampa, he was one of the greatest personalities in Kannaḍa literature who wrote *Mallinātha Purāṇa*, the life-story of the nineteenth Tīrthaṃkara and a Jain version of the *Rāmāyaṇa* with the title *Ramacandracarita Purāṇa*, popularly known as *Pampa-Rāmāyaṇa*. He flourished in the twelfth century.

Nagahrada: Modern Nagda in Udaipur district, Rajasthan, which is mentioned as a *tīrtha* containing the temples of Śāntinātha and Pārśvanātha in medieval Jain texts.

Nagamaha: Festival of the Nāgas (q.v.). Mathura was a large centre of Nāga worship where a number of Nāga sculptures have been recovered. There was a Nāga shrine built outside the city of Sāketa in which the deity was worshipped by queen Padmāvatī. The *yātrā* in honour of the Nāga deity was celebrated with pomp and ceremony. We come across another Nāga shrine in Kusāgrapura in which the deity was worshipped by Nāgadattā with her attendants. These are mentioned in the *Nāyādhammakahāo*. The *Vasudevahiṇḍi* refers to the Nāga shrine on the bank of the Varadā River wherefrom

Rukmini, in the pretext of paying homage to the Nāga, eloped with Vāsudeva Kṛṣṇa. A festival in honour of Nāgavana is referred to in the *Bṛhatkathāślokasaṃgraha*. In Jain tradition King Bhagiratha is said to have been the founder of Naga-*bali*. When the dwellings of the Nāgas were disturbed, the Nāga King Jvalanaprabha reduced the sons of King Sagara into ashes. He was thereafter appeased by Bhagīratha and the sons of Sagara were restored to life. Dharaṇendra (q.v.) was another powerful king of the Nāgas whose images were installed in the cities of the Vidyadharas (q.v.). Evidence of the powerful existence of Nāga cults in all parts of India is found alike in Jain, Buddhist, and Brahmanical sources.

Nagapura: Nagaur in Rajasthan which contained a temple of Nemināthа of about AD 1100. Medieval Jain texts refer to this town as a holy place associated with the activities of Kharatara Ācārya Jinavallabha.

Nagara Jinālaya: Jina temple constructed by Nāgadeva, the *paṭṭanasvāmī* of the Hoysala King Ballāla II, as is known from an inscription from Belgola of AD 1195. *Epigraphia Carnatica* (rev.) II, No. 335.

Nāgaraja Temple: An originally Jain temple which was later transformed into a Brahmanical one at Nagercoil, district Kanyakumari. It contains many Jain reliefs carved on pillars.

Nagarakoṭṭa: Jain *tīrtha* in the Dharmashala district of Himachal Pradesh which contained a great Śāntinātha temple complex in the thirteenth-century.

Nagara-Mahāsthāna: Situated in the Jaipur district of Rajasthan, it was connected with Yugādideva or Ṛṣabhanātha according to the testimony of the *Prabandhacintāmaṇi*.

Nāgas: Gods of the Bhavanavasin (q.v.) category. The term Nāga denotes serpents. In Hindu mythology Nāga denotes a serpent-demon belonging to the race of Kadru or Surasā inhabiting the waters, or the city of Bhogavatī under the earth. They are supposed to have a human face and to assume human form. Nāgas like Śeṣa and Vāsuki attained celebrity for their wisdom and valour. In Buddhist mythology also we have anthropomorphic conception of the Nāgas. In the Jain *Jambudvīpaprajñapti* the Nāgas are described as water-gods and associated with rain-clouds. Their fight with the Suparṇas is supposed to be the cause of earthquakes. The legends of King Sagara's sacrifice, destruction of his sixty thousand sons, the bringing of the river Gaṅgā by Bhagīratha, etc., as narrated in the Hindu epics and Purāṇas, are brought in relation to the Nāgas in the Jain tradition. There it is said that king Bhagīratha, the grandson of Bharata, was the founder of the Nāgabalī. When the dwellings of the Nāgas were disturbed Jvalanaprabha, their king was annoyed and by his poisonous eyes burnt the sons of King Sagara to ashes. Then in order to pacify the king of the Nāgas, Bhagīratha visited the Aṣṭapada mountain and presented a respectful offering consisting of garlands, perfumes, and incense. From that time onwards people started offering *bali* to the Nāgas, according to the commentary on *Uttarādhyayana*. Dharaṇendra (q.v.) was another powerful king of the Nāgas who was given the position of the moral governor of the Vidyādharas by Lord Ṛṣabha himself. His name signifies his identity with Śeṣanāga, lord of the serpents. Pārśvanātha's association with the Nāga cult is well-established in Jain history.

Nagda: Findspot of a Jain inscription of AD 1436 in Mewar, Rajasthan, which records the installation of an image of Śāntinātha at Devakulapāṭaka in Medapāṭa-deśa, i.e. Mewar, during the reign of Kumbha, by a rich person called Sāraṅga. The consecration ceremony was done by Jinasāgara of the Kharatara-gaccha Nahar, *Jain Inscriptions* II, No. 1958.

Nagda Temples: Nagda in Rajasthan has a few interesting medieval Jain temples. The Padmāvatī-mandir seems to be a shrine of Pārśvanātha according to the inscriptions of AD 1298 and 1333 in its *garbhagṛha*. It contains a *mūlaprāsāda* with towering central *śikhara* decked with *aṅgaśikharas* and a domed *maṇḍapa*. One of the three interior sanctuaries has a *sarvatobhadrikā* image. The Adbhudji temple (q.v.) dedicated to Śāntinātha was set up in AD 1437. The Pārśvanātha temple datable to the fifteenth century consists of a cella, a closed hall and three other halls, of which the last is separated from the others by means of a flight of steps. It has well-carved concave ceilings with floral and figure decoration.

Nagnatā Sect: See Digambara-Śvetāmbara split.

Naigama: See Nāga.

Naigamesa: See Hariṇegamesi.

Nairṛta: Guardian-god of the south-west direction, conceived in the Śvetāmbara tradition as riding a goblin, wearing a tiger's skin, and holding a club or sword and a bow. The same is told in Digambara tradition which substitutes a boar for the goblin.

Nakhara Jinālaya: Jain temple at Haṭṭana in Tiptur taluk, Tumkur district, Karnataka, mentioned in an inscription of AD 1078. *Jaina Śilālekha Saṃgraha* II, No. 218.

Nākodā: Situated in the Barmer district of Rajasthan this place is mentioned in inscriptions as containing temples of Śāntinatha, Pārśvanātha, and Mahāvīra.

Nalgora: A village in the 24-Parganas, West Bengal which has yielded an exquisitely-carved bronze figure of Ambikā, the Yakṣī of Neminātha. The deity in graceful moulding, stands on a lotus, holding with her left hand on a child at her waist, under the bent bough of a tree. A nude child is shown standing on her right side. At the bottom of the tree is Ambikā's symbol, the lion. The image is attributed to the tenth century. It is in the State Archaeological Gallery, West Bengal.

Nalajanampadu Stone Inscription: Found at Nalajanampadu in the Nellore district, Andhra Pradesh, this inscription refers to the Pallava King, Parameśvaravarman I (AD 670-95) as a devout Jain meditating at the feet of the supreme master, the lord Arhat. *Epigraphia Indica*, XXVII, 203ff.

***Nāma*:** One of the four constituents of the *aghātin karma* (q.v.) which is designated after the conditions by which the gods, human beings, animals, and hell-beings are governed.

***Nāmakarma*:** Sacrament, naming of the child, which may be on any auspicious day twelve days after birth. The Śvetāmbaras do it generally on the same day on which *sucīkarma* (q.v.) is performed. The horoscope of the child is also prepared.

Nāma-Worship: Uttering or hearing the name of the Tīrthaṃkaras.

Naminātha: Twenty-first Tīrthaṃkara, son of Vijaya and Vappā of Mithila. He had a height of 15 bow-lengths and a life-span of 10,000 years. Subha and Amalā were his chief disciples. He attained salvation on Mount Sammeya. His sacred tree was the *bakula*. His emblem is blue lotus or *aśoka* tree; attendants are Bhṛkuṭī and Gandārī/Cāmuṇḍī; and *chowri*-bearer is Vijaya.

***Nammayasundarikahā*:** Written in Prakrit in AD 1130 by Mahendrasūri, it describes the trials and tribulations of Narmadāsundarī, wife of the Jain merchant Mahesvaradatta who deserted her in a foreign country when he became suspicious of her fidelity. But in spite of many provocations and temptations she was able to maintain her chastity. Edited in Singhi Jaina Granthamālā, Bombay, 1958.

Nāṇa: Situated in the Pali district of Rajasthan, it has a Mahāvīra temple, on the door of which is incised a Jain inscription of AD 960.

Nandibevuru: Findspot of a Jain inscription of AD 1054 in Bellary district, Karnataka, which mentions the Jain saint Astopavāsi Bhaṭāra and a Jina temple constructed by a Nolamba-Pallava chief called Brahmadhirāja. In another epigraph from the same place there is a reference to a monk called Vīranandī, belonging to the Pustaka-gaccha and Deśī-gaṇa. *Jaina Śilālekha Saṃgraha*, IV, No. 139; *South Indian Inscriptions*, IX(1), No. 115.

Nandiṣena: See *Ajita-Śānti-Stava.*

***Nandīsūtra*:** Independent treatise, not strictly a canonical work, but regarded as a sacred text from very early times. The original *Nandīsūtra* has 90 *gāthās* and 59 *sūtras*. According to tradition it was written by Devardhi. Its subject matter is not solely religious, but pertains to many branches of knowledge. It also gives details of Jain epistemology. Edited with Malayagiri's *Vṛtti* in Agamodaya, Bombay, 1924; by Puṇyavijaya with the *Cūrṇi* of Jinadāsa Gaṇi, Prakrit Text Society, Varanasi, 1966 and published with *Ṭīkā* of Haribhadra by Ṛṣabhadevji Kesarimalji, Śvetāmbara Samstha, Ratlam, 1928.

Nandīśvara-Dvīpa: The eighth continent in the middle world. There are four mountains, styled *añjanas* for their dark complexion, in this continent. They are Devaramana in the east, Nityodyota in the south, Svayamprabha in the west, and Ramaṇīya in the north. Each of these mountains has again, in each direction, a square lake which accommodates a mountain called Dadhimukha. In each of the outer corners of the four lakes is a golden mountain called Ratikara. Each of the lakes in each direction has a forest containing mansions for the Vyantara-devas. On the top of the fifty-two mountains are *caityālayas* where the gods assemble to celebrate *aṣṭāhnika-parvan* or eight-day function thrice a year. Nandīśvara-dvīpa has various representations in art. A few temples based on the Nandīśvara-dvīpa model have recently been built up. Miniature representations are also made by putting 52 small Tīrthaṃkara figures on a four-tiered platform or constructing miniature shrines in four groups of thirteen each.

Nāndiyā: Situated in the Sirohi district of Rajasthan, the great Mahāvīra temple of this place is mentioned in a manuscript of *Pārśvanāthacaritra* of Raṇasiṃha.

Nannarāja-vasati: Pārśvanātha temple at Wadhwan in Gujarat where Jinasena wrote his *Harivaṃśa-purāṇa* in AD 783.

Naracandrasūri: See *Kathāratnākara.*

Naradatta: Śāsanadevatā (q.v.) of Munisuvrata (q.v.) according to the Śvetāmbara tradition in which she is conceived as seated in *bhadrāsana* posture, holding a rosary, citron, and trident, and showing *varada-mudrā*. For Digambaras she is seated on a serpent, holds a shield, fruit and sword, and shows the *varada-mudrā*.

Naraiṇa: About 40 miles north-east of Ajmer this place is described as a Jain *tīrtha* by Siddhasena, Dhanapāla and other authors. A twelfth-century Mahāvīra temple at this place is recorded in the Bijolia inscription.

Naraka, Niraya: See Hells.

Narakagati: Hellish form which a Jīva (q.v.) receives owing to its *karma* (q.v.).

Narasapura Inscription: Found in Narasapura in the Kolar taluk of the district of the same name, this inscription of the Gaṅga King Rajamalla II, dated śaka 824 (AD 903), refers to a grant for the Jain basadi at Konamaṅgala, erected by Megante-Nandāka Gādeya. It mentions a female disciple called Kamuṅgare Kanti of Uttanandipuri Mandalabhaṭāra. Another Jain basadi, built by one Śrīvarmayya is also mentioned in this inscription. *Epigraphia Carnatica*, X, No. 90 (text), 25ff. (trans.).

Narasiṃharājapura Plates: Five copper plates found at Narasiṃharājapura in Belur taluk of the Chikmagalur district, a considerable portion of which contains the inscription of the Gaṅga King Śrīpuruṣa referring to his grant to a Jain Caityālaya. It opens with an invocation of Jina: 'Victorious is the sole sun of the world, who has witnessed all the worlds and who by the rays of Syādvāda has illumined the veil of darkness of the other creeds.' *Mysore Archaeological Report*, 1920, 27ff.

Naravara: Modern Narhad in Jhunjhunu district of Rajasthan whence a few Jain icons have been discovered. The Pārśvanātha temple of this place is mentioned by Vinayaprabha in his *Tīrthayātrāstavana*.

Naregal: Situated in Ron taluk of Dharwar district this site has yielded an inscription of AD 950, pertaining to the time of Rāṣṭrakūṭa Kṛṣṇa III, which refers to a grant to a Jain establishment by a subordinate chief Namayara Mārasiṃghayya. The gift was received by Guṇacandra, pupil of Vīranandī, grand-pupil of Mahendra Paṇḍita belonging to the Kondakunda-anvaya of Deśika-gaṇa. *Bombay-Karnataka Inscriptions* I (1), No. 38.

Narendraprabha Suri: See Alaṅkāramahodadhi.

Narrative Literature: Jain narrative literature comprises all sorts of tales and anecdotes about artisans, tradesmen, witch-doctors, fortune-tellers, beggars, mendicants and so on. Many of these narratives are pieces of genuine didactic tales, depicting the life of common people. There are fables, fairy tales, legends, parables, illustrations, romantic and adventurous tales, moral stories, and sayings drawn from the common stock of Indian folklore. The *Sūyagaḍa*, one of the ancient portions of Jain canon, in order to exhort monks to keep away from sins and passions and devote themselves to the right conduct, employs parables. The *Nāyādhammakahāo*, a collection of stories believed to be narrated by Mahāvīra himself, deals with various illustrations and tales tinged with religious sermonizing. The *Uttarādhyayana*, an important ancient work of ascetic poetry, has recorded some interesting parables. The pro-canonical literature is represented by *Niryukti* (*c.* fourth century AD), *Bhāṣya* (*c.* fourth-fifth centuries), *Cūrṇi* (seventh century AD) and *Ṭīkā* (eighth to sixteenth centuries). These are storehouses of narrative reflecting the social and cultural life of the people. Among these, the *Niśītha-bhāṣya, Bṛhatkalpa-bhāṣya* and *Vyavahāra-bhāṣya* are to be particularly mentioned. The *Cūrṇi* literature, the *Niśīthaviśeṣa-cūrṇi* and the *Āvaśyaka-cūrṇi* are informative, containing a large number of fascinating stories preaching moral lessons. A number of long and short commentaries have been composed on Jain canonical literature by renowned authors such as Haribhadrasūri (eighth century), Vādivatāla Śāntisūri (eleventh century), Nemicandrasūri or Devendragaṇi (eleventh century), Malayagiri (twelfth century), Abhayadevasūri (twelfth century), Maladhāri Hemacandra (twelfth century), Kṣamākīrti (thirteenth century), and others. The commentaries of the *Āvaśyaka Sūtra* by Haribhadrasūri and Malayagiri, and on the *Uttarādhyayana Sūtra* by Vādivatāla Śāntisūri and Nemicandrasūri are particularly noteworthy, as they contain material based on old traditions of stories recorded faithfully. Here the old *kathānakas* are retained in Prakrit though the major part of the commentary is in Sanskrit. Post-canonical Jain literature is a mine of narratives. There are numerous compilations of narratives not only in Prakrit but also in Sanskrit, Apabhraṃśa, Kannaḍa, Tamil, Old Hindi and Old Gujarati. The author of the *Prabandhacintāmaṇi* has remarked that the mind of learned men is not pleased by listening to mythological stories of the Purāṇas again and again, which is why by incorporating realistic stories in their literature, of various shades, colours and contrasts, the Jains made a considerable contribution to this field. See *Kathākośas.*

Narwar: Ancient Nalapura, 40 km north-east of Shivpuri, Madhya Pradesh, where several Jain temples and statues were built. White stone used for temples and images here was highly polished and thus gave the appearance of marble. Kings Yajvapāla, Gopāladeva, and Asalladeva of Narwar largely contributed to the development of Jain art in this region. Jain sculptures from Narwar are mostly preserved in the Shivpuri Museum.

Nāsikya: Nasik in Mahārāṣṭra where existed the famous Jain Jīvitasvāmī Tribhuvanatilaka Candraprabha temple.

***Nāṭakasamayasārakalaśāḥ*:** See Amṛtacandra.

Naunia: Jain centre from the eleventh to the fourteenth centuries near village Barhatta in Narasinghpur district, Madhya Pradesh, where colossal statues of Ādinātha, Candraprabha and Mahāvīra are found.

Nava-Devatā: The Digambara version of the Śvetāmbara Siddhacakra (q.v.). Navadevatā comprises the Five Dignitaries (Arhat, Siddha, Ācārya, Upādhyāya, and Sādhu) along with *caitya* (the Jina image), *caityālaya* (temple enshrining the Jina image), *śruta* (scripture), and *dharmacakra* (wheel of law). The last four are substitutions for the Śvetāmbara *jñāna, darśana, cāritra,* and *tapas.* These nine items are represented in the forms of diagrams on stone, metal, canvas, or paper. This conception is nicely illustrated in the bronze Navadevatā, now in Trailokyanātha temple at Tirupparuttikunram (q.v.). In the *Nityasandhyā-kriyāvidhi* of the *Jinasaṃhitā* ascribed to Indranandī of tenth century the Navadevatās are invoked.

Navalakha Temple: Jain temple of Ghumli in west India which was constructed in the eleventh century.

Navamuni Gumpha: See Khaṇḍagiri caves.

Navapaya: See Jinacandra Gaṇin.

Navasari: Site of a Jain temple in west India constructed by Tejaḥpāla.

***Navatattvaprakaraṇa*:** See Jinacandra Gaṇin.

Naya: Method of comprehension of a thing or subject from different standpoints. In the *Bhagavatī* and the *Prajñāpanā* this *Naya*, which is also interpreted as partial knowledge about any of the innumerable aspects of an object or judgement, is divided into seven kinds. Among these *naigama* is the non-analytical method by which an object is regarded as possessing both general and specific properties. Thus we may conceive the rose either as a flower possessing the attributes common to all flowers or as a thing possessing the specific attributes of the rose as distinguished from other flowers. *Saṃgraha* is a collective method which takes into consideration generic properties only and ignores particular properties. *Vyavahāra* is quite its opposite and takes into account only particulars, ignoring the general. *Ṛjusūtra* is the method which considers only the momentary entity without reference to time and space. *Śabda* is the method of correct nomenclature. It is of three kinds, namely *samprāta*, the suitable, *samābhirūḍha*, the subtle, and *evambhūta*, the such-like. The last two form the sixth and seventh categories of Naya. In Siddhasena's *Nyāyāvatāra* this classification is maintained while in Deva Sūri's *Pramāṇanaya-tattvalokālaṅkāra* the fallacies arising out of the misapplication of each of these several kinds of Naya are elaborately discussed with the help of examples.

Nayacandrasūri: See *Hammīra-Mahākāvya.*

***Nāyādhammakahāo*:** See Jñatṛdharmakathā.

***Nayakumāra-Cariu*:** *Nāgakumāra-carita*, a short work in Apabhraṃśa composed by Puṣpadanta (q.v.), who flourished in the tenth century, in ten sandhis. It was composed in the palace of Nanna, the son of his patron Bharata, the minister of Kṛṣṇa III. Edited by H.L. Jain Karanja, 1933.

Nayanandī: See *Sudarsana-carita.*

Nayasena: Kannaḍa twelfth-thirteenth-century author of the ethical work *Dharmāmṛta.*

Nellikara: Findspot of a Jain inscription of AD 1552 in South Kanara district which mentions a temple dedicated to Anantanātha. *Jaina Śilālekha Saṃgraha* IV, No. 466.

***Nemibhaktāmaram*:** Hymn to Neminātha with allusions to the legend of Nemi and Rājimati, written by Bhavaprabha Sūri in imitation of Mānatuṅga's *Bhaktāmarastotra* (qq.v.). Edited in *Stotraratnākara*, Pt. I, Bombay, 1913.

Nemicandra Siddhāntacakravartin: Teacher and minister of Cāmuṇḍa-Rāya (q.v.) of Karnataka who flourished in the tenth century. He was the author of many celebrated works. His *Dravyasaṃgraha*, 'Compendium of Substances' in 58 Prakrit verses, deals not only with the cosmological substances but also with principles leading to the final release. His *Gommaṭasāra*, written in honour of Gommaṭa Rāya or Cāmuṇḍa Rāya, consists of two parts, the *Jīva-kāṇḍa* dealing with the Jīvas or souls and *Karma-kāṇḍa* dealing with the doctrine of *karma*, Prakrit verse.

The text is also known as *Pañcasaṃgraha*. Cāmuṇḍa Rāya himself wrote a commentary on this work in Kannaḍa. The *Labdhisāra*, 'the essence of attainment' of the things which lead to perfection, and *Kṣapanasāra*, 'the essence of annihilation of the *kaṣāyas* which are connected with each other, form a sequel to *Gommaṭasāra*. His *Trilokasāra*, 'the essence of the three worlds' is on cosmology. Nemicandra is also said to have written *Pratiṣṭhāpāṭha* on the installation and consecration of statues. *Dravyasaṃgraha*, ed. with intro., trans., notes and com. by S.C. Ghoshal, Arrah, 1917; *Gommaṭasāra*, ed. with intro., trans. in Sans. and Eng. by J.L. Jaini, Lucknow, 1927; ed. along with *Labdhi* and *Kṣapana* with Sans. and Hindi com. in Gandhi-Haribhai-Devakarana-Jaina Granthamālā, Calcutta.

Nemicandrasūri: Śvetāmbara writer of the eleventh century whose *Ākhyānamaṇikośa* 'treasure-house of stories' was published in AD 1073 and was commented upon by Āmradeva-sūri (q.v.). His *Ratnacūḍarājacarita* describes the love-affair of Ratnacūḍa and Tilakasundarī. His *Mahāvīra-carita* was composed in AD 1083. Like the preceding one it is also written in Prakrit and has 2,385 verses. He has also written a Vṛtti on the *Uttarādhyayana* called by the name *Sukhabodha* which is based upon the commentary of Śāntācārya called *Śiṣyahita*. See *Jinaratnakośa* 43ff; *Ākhyānamaṇikośa*, Prakrit Text Society, ed. Punyavijaya, Varanasi, 1962; *Ratnacūḍarājacarita* also known as *Tilaka-sundarī-Ratnacūḍa-Kahānaka*, Ahmedabad, 1942; *Mahāvīracarita*, Bhavnagar, 1915; *Sukha-bodha*, pub. from Valad in Atmavallabha Granthavali 1937.

Nemidatta: Sixteenth-century author of *Ārādhanā-Kathākośa*, *Śrīpālacaritra* and *Neminātha Purāṇa*.

Nemidatta: See *Ārādhanā-Kathākośa.*

***Nemidūta*:** A late-medieval work composed by Vikrama, the son of Sāṅgaṇa. The theme of the poem is the lament of Rājimatī, after her husband had become a monk. The last line of each verse is taken from the *Meghadūta* of Kālidāsa, while the first three lines are composed by the poet himself. Ed. in Kavyamala, Part II, 85-104.

***Nemi-Jina-Stava*:** A hymn addressed to Neminātha in which consonants are rare. *Stotraratnākara*, II, Bombay, 1913.

***Neminātha-Cariu*:** Written by Haribhadra, it is an Apabhraṃśa poem in *raḍḍā* metre, as distinguished from the normal *paddhadia*. A portion of the work, edited in München with German translation and notes in 1921 by H. Jacobi, is known as *Sanakumāra-cariu*. It contains 343 *raḍḍā* verses which constitute verses 443 to 785 of the original. The whole book contains more than 8,000 *ślokas*. The hero of the poem is one of the twelve Cakravartins and the poet names his teacher Candra, and mentions the date of his work as vs 1216. *Neminātha-cariu* is the idealized biography of Neminātha. The author was a contemporary of Hemacandra (q.v.) and did the work under the patronage of Pṛthvīpāla, the minister of Kumārapāla. The entire first half of the poem treats only of the previous births of Nemi and Rājimatī. Haribhadra had also written *Mallināthacarita* in Prakrit. There is yet another *Nemināha-cariu* by Lakṣmadeva or Lakṣmaṇadeva in four cantos. The poet was the son of Rayana, i.e. Ratnadeva, and was born at Gonanda in Malava. The work does not mention the year of its composition though the days of commencement and completion are given. The MS records that it was a gift made in AD 1453 (vs 1510) so that it was composed earlier. We have a *Nemināthacarita* also in Sanskrit by Surācārya composed in the eleventh century and another by Maladhāri Hemacandra.

Neminātha: Also known as Ariṣṭanemi, he is the twenty-second Tīrthaṃkara who was the son of Samudravijaya and Śivā. His father was the king of Sauripurī or Dvārakā. His ancestry is in the Harivaṃśa and he belonged to the Yādava tribe. The most interesting fact about him is that he was a cousin of Kṛṣṇa and Baladeva. His emblem, the conch, may be accounted for as being symbolic of his residence in a sea-side place or because of his kinship with the clan of the Vāsudeva Kṛṣṇa. He had a height of 10 bow-lengths and his sacred tree was the *vetasa*. His name was Ariṣṭanemi because before his birth her mother saw a wheel of black jewels. According to the Śvetāmbara tradition, Neminātha's marriage was settled with Raimai, a daughter of Ugrasena. While going to marry he saw several animals in cages, ready for slaughter for the marriage feast. So he renounced the world and resorted to asceticism. Eventually he became a Jina. His chief disciples were Varadatta and Yakkinī and he attained liberation on the summit of the Girnar Hill. It is interesting to note that both Kṛṣṇa and Neminātha are given life-span of 1,000 years in the Jain canonical texts. His attendants are the Yakṣa Gomedha and Yakṣiṇī Ambikā/Kuṣmāṇḍinī. Neminātha has numerous epigraphical references as well as temples and images all over the country. The legends of Neminātha have been made the theme of numerous poetic versions beginning with the early one in the *Uttarādhyayana*. In later times there were at least a dozen life-stories of Neminātha. Thus in the eleventh century we have a *Neminātha-carita* in Sanskrit by Surācārya and one by Maladhārin Hemacandra. In AD 1159 Haribhadra completed his *Nemināhacariu* in Apabhraṃśa. The life-story of Neminātha is also treated by the poet Vāgbhaṭa in his *Nemi-Nirvāṇa*, a *mahākāvya* in 15 cantos. The poem *Nemidūta* by Vikrama is an imitation of Kālidāsa's *Meghadūta*. There is a *Nemi-Jina-stava* in Prakrit. The name Ariṣṭanemi occurs in the *Mahābhārata* but it does not refer to the Jina of the same name. Celebrated Neminātha temples are in Mt. Abu, Dholaka, Girnar, Kumbharia, and Tirumalai.

***Neminātha-Catuṣpadikā*:** Composed by Vinayacandra at the end of the thirteenth century, it makes a better and fuller treatment of the story of Prince Nemi and Rājimatī as given in Pālhaṇa's *Nemi-Rājula-Bārahamāsā* (qq.v.).

Neminatha Temple: See Kumbharia Temples, Dilwara Temples.

***Nemi-Nirvāṇa*:** A *mahākāvya* in 15 cantos and 958 verses written by Vāgbhaṭa which deals with the life history of Neminātha. The poet lived in the eleventh-twelfth centuries. Ed. in Kavyamala, LVI, 1896.

***Neminirvāṇamahākāvya*:** See Vāgbhaṭa.

***Nemi-Rājula-Bārahamāsā*:** See Pālhaṇa.

Nidigi: Situated in Shimoga district, Karnataka, it is the findspot of an inscription of AD 1117 which records the erection of a Jain temple by one Barmi-setti. Several monks belonging to Kranura-gana, Meṣapāsāṇa-gaccha, including Prabhācandra and Śubhakīrti are also mentioned in this epigraph. *Epigraphia Carnatica*, VII, Shim. No. 57.

***Nighaṇṭuśeṣa*:** See Hemacandra.

Niḥsaṅgatvātmabhāvanā: Devotion of time to self-meditation in the advanced stage of life.

Nijjuti: See Niryukti.

Nikācita: *Karma* that has been stored up.

Nīlakaṇṭha: Also known as Rajorgarh and Paranagar, this is an old town in Alwar district of Rajasthan, famous for the colossal image of Pārśvanātha. It was a reputed centre of medieval sculpture and temples, Jain and Brahmanical. An inscription dated 923 of the time of King Sāvata records the construction of a Śāntinātha temple and the installation of the main image therein by Sarvadeva of the Dharkaḷā family. The Pārśvanātha image is locally called Naugajā and there are three other large Jina figures. Temple remains of the tenth century have been discovered in this place. *Indian Archaeology: A Review*, 1961-2, 85.

***Nīlakeci*:** Tenth-century Tamil work written mainly to rebut a Buddhist Tamil work *Kuntalakeci*. The anonymous author has taken Nīli or Kāli of Palayanur as the heroine of his dream story. She was requested by other spirits to tame a Jain monk who obstructed animal sacrifice by advocating *ahiṃsā*. Nīli was so impressed that she became a disciple of the Jain monk and began to propagate Jainism. Her first target was the Buddhist Kunlatakeci whom she conquered in a debate. The preceptor of this Buddhist nun, and his preceptor, were defeated and converted by her. Finally she defeated the Buddha himself. The Jain monk Municandra Bhaṭṭāraka expounded to Nīlakeci Jain cosmology and metaphysics, the three divisions of the universe, heaven and hell, four kinds of beings *narakar, vilaṅku, mentitar,* and *tevar*—their organic classifications, categories of beings—good, bad, *kumānuār* and human beings—Devas and divine beings such as *pavaṇar, viyanatarar, cotiṭar, karpadevar,* and *vaimanikar,* suffering of beings, *astikāya* and *anastikāya* categories, liberation, epistemology and its *vaippu, nayam* and *pukuvail* categories; *uyiriyalpu* or *kuṇatthānam*, that is fourteen *guṇasthānas* (q.v.), fourteen kinds of *markkaṇai* comprising *gati, indriya, kāya, yoga, veda, kaṣāya, jñāna, saṃyama, darśana, leśyā, bhavya, samyaktva, sañjnā* and *ākāra*. The text then deals with right perception in terms of *jñāna, pūjā, kula, jāti, śakti, ṛddhi, tapas,* and *deha*. Duties of monks and nuns are described and also *lokākāśa* and *alokākāśa*, visible and invisible space. *Nīlakeci* refutes the Buddhist doctrines of *anātma*, the five *skandhas,* doctrine of momentariness and causation. The Vedavāda, Sāṅkhya and Bhūtavāda are also refuted. But the most interesting chapter is concerned with the refutation of Ājīvikism. The refutation in itself is conventional but it provides information that provides a wider dimension to Ājīvikism. It refers to a number of Ājīvika teachers who are otherwise known in the religio-philosophical tradition of India, but whose links with Ājīvikism was not previously known. The *Nīlakeci* is thus not only a valuable guide to the southern Jainism, it also provides useful sources for the reconstruction of Ājīvika history.

Nimbadevarasa: A feudatory of Gaṇḍarāditya, Śilāhāra ruler of the Kolhapur region, who is described in the Kolhapur stone inscription of śaka 1040 (AD 1118) as the builder of the Pārśvanātha temple of Kolhapur. The temple was situated at Kavadegolla suburb of the city. Nimbadeva is said to have been favoured by Padmāvatī, the Śāsanadevatā of Pārśvanātha. In the Tendal inscription of Goṅka dated śaka 1045 (AD 1123). Nimbadevarasa has been described as a disciple of Māghanandī Siddhāntadeva, the priest of the Rūpanārāyaṇa temple of Kolhapur. The Mahālakṣmī temple inscription of the time of Gaṇḍarāditya refers to the construction of an Ādinātha temple by Nimbadevarasa. 'Thus flourished the excellent Nimbadeva, who has made the whole land full of the temples of Jinanātha, the entire country full of Jineśvaras . . . the entire excellent village full of pleasingly good Jains, the whole surrounding full of the pervasive influence of the words, meanings and the essence of (Jaina) *tattva.*' *Corpus Inscriptionun Indicarum* VI, Nos. 39, 45, 49-50.

Nimittaśāstra: Science of prognostication by reading signs and symbols, a branch of Śrutajñāna (q.v.). The Ājīvika teacher Maṅkhali Gośāla was well-versed in the eight branches of *mahānimitta.* Kālakācārya, Bhadrabāhu, and Dharasena also knew this subject well. Among the eight branches of the Nimitta, the first is *aṅga* or movements of the limbs of the body. It has been dealt with in the *Aṅgavijjā.* Nemicandrasūri, in his commentary on the *Uttarādhyana,* has quoted Prakrit verses related to *aṅga.* The second is *svara* or notes of birds or seven notes of music which has been treated by Abhayadeva in his commentary on *Ṭhāṇāṅga* with Prakrit verses. The third is *lakṣaṇa* or science of interpreting bodily signs, elaborately discussed in the 37th chapter of the *Aṅgavijjā.* The fourth is *vyañjana* or marks treated likewise in the same text. The fifth is *svapna* or auspicious and inauspicous dreams discussed in the *Aṅgavijjā* and *Uttarādhyayana* commentary. The sixth is *chinna* or the rending of clothes, the seventh *bhauma* or that which is related to the earth, e.g. earthquakes, and the eighth is *antarikṣa* or that which is related to space, e.g. rain, thunderstorms, fog, etc. These have been treated sporadically in different texts and commentaries. Later works on prognostication are *Jayapāhuḍa, Cūḍāmaṇi, Nimittapāhuḍa, Jonipāhuḍa, Nimittaśāstra, Riṭṭhasamuccaya,* etc.

Niralgi: Situated in Dharwar district, Karnataka, this place had a Mallinātha Jineśvara temple in the twelfth century. An epigraph of AD 1147 from this place refers to an Ācārya of Mūla-saṅgha, Surastha-gaṇa and Citrakūṭa-anvaya.

***Nirayāvalikā*:** Prakrit *Nirayāvaliyāo,* the eighth text of the Upāṅga (q.v.) series, which is the first part of a text entitled *Nirayāvali-suttam.* It means the 'series of hells' and relates how the ten half-brothers of King Kuṇika or Ajātaśatru were reborn in various hells. *Nirayāvalikasūtram* with Candrasena's com. Agamodaya, Ahmedabad, 1922.

***Nirayāvaliyāo*:** See *Nirayāvalikā.*

***Nirbhaya-Bhīma-Vyayoga*:** A drama composed by Rāmacandra (q.v.), on the giant Baka being killed by Bhīma. The story is taken from the *Mahābhārata.* Edited in Jaśovijaya Jaina Granthamālā, No. 19.

Nirgrantha: Followers of Jainism, though the term is sometimes applied to the Buddhists as well. The term denotes 'one who is free of all ties and hindrances', 'one who is without possessions', or a 'saint who has withdrawn from the world and lives either as a hermit or a religious mendicant wandering about naked'.

***Nirjarā*:** Purging the *karmas* which is of two kinds, *bhāva* and *dravya,* the former meaning a change in the soul by virtue of which the *karma* particles are destroyed, and the latter, their actual destruction, either by reaping their effects or by penances before their time of fruition, called *savipāka* and *nirvipāka nirjarās* respectively. One of the chief ways of annihilating *karma* is the practice of austerities, which are of two kinds—*bāhya-tapa* (q.v.) or exterior and *abhyantara-tapa* (q.v.) or interior. The former consists of taking a vow to fast, taking food a mouthful less everyday, limiting food, intake, abstinence from tasteful food, physical suffering, and avoidance of temptations. The latter consists of penance, reverence, service to others, study, meditation and absolute indifference to the body and its needs.

***Nirvāṇa*:** See *Mokṣa.*

***Nirvāṇakṣetra*:** See Siddhakṣetras.

Nirvāṇī: Śāsanadevatā (q.v.) of Śāntinātha (q.v.). According to the Śvetāmbara tradition she is seated on a lotus and holds a book, a lotus, a *kamaṇḍalu* and a lotus bud. Her Digambara variation, Mahāmānasī, has the vehicle of a peacock, holds in her hand a disc, a fruit and a sword, and has one hand in *varada-mudrā.*

***Niryuktis*:** A class of commentarial literature, the authorship of which has been attributed to Bhadrabāhu. There was undoubtedly more than one Bhadrabāhu (q.v.). In the Digambara tradition it is said that the first Bhadrabāhu died 162 years after the Nirvāṇa of Mahāvīra and the second 515 years after. The ten Niryuktis attributed to Bhadrabāhu are on *Ācārāṅga, Sūtrakṛta, Sūryaprajñapti, Uttarādhyayana, Āvaśyaka, Daśavaikālika, Dasaśruta, Kalpa-sūtra, Vyavahāra,* and *Ṛṣibhāṣita-sūtra*. These are very concise explanations in Āryā verses and Jain Mahārāṣṭrī. At a later date, these Niryuktis were extended to form exhaustive commentaries in Prakrit, such as *Bhāṣyas* and *Cūrṇis* (qq.v.). These in their turn formed the foundation for the Sanskrit commentaries—*Ṭīkās*, *Vṛttis*, and *Avacūrṇis*—which were compiled in the eleventh and twelfth centuries.

***Niṣadyā*:** Sacrament in which the child is made to sit after performing the worship.

***Nisīha*:** See *Niśītha.*

***Niśītha*:** Prakrit *Nisīha*, the first Chedasūtra (q.v.) which is the largest text of this group, having a *Niryukti* by Bhadrabāhu, a *Bhāṣya* by Siṃha-dāsagaṇi and a *Cūrṇi* by Jinadāsa. It contains regulations for punishment for various transgressions against the rules of daily life and has embodied a major portion of the *Vavahāra* (q.v.) in its later sections. Ed. W. Schubring, Leipzig, 1918; with *Niryukti, Bhāṣya* and *Cūrṇi*, Sanmati Jñānapītha, ed. Upadhyaya Kavi Amar Muni and Muni Kanhaiyalal Kamal, Agra, 1957-60; Madhu Sen, *A Cultural Study of Niśīstha-cūrṇi*, Varanasi, 1975.

***Niṣkrānti*:** A stage in the career of the Tīrthaṃkara when he gives his empire to his eldest son and becomes an ascetic.

Niṣkriya Dravya: Dravyas (q.v.) that are incapable of action. These are Dharma, Adharma, Ākāśa, and Kāla (qq.v.), devoid of intrinsic activity.

Nītimārga I: Son of the Gaṅga King Rājamalla I. He ruled between AD 853 and 870. He is described in the Kudlur plates of śaka 884 of Narasiṃha III as 'a bee in the lotus feet of adorable Arhat Bhaṭṭāraka'. His other well-known name was Eregaṅgadeva. *Mysore Archaeological Report*, 1921, 18ff.

Nītimārga II: Gaṅga king of the main line who ruled between AD 907 and 935. In the Kudlur plates he is described as a Jain. An inscription of his reign refers to the setting up of a tomb-stone for a Jain teacher named Elācārya. *Mysore Archaeological Report*, 1921, 22.

***Nītivākyāmṛta*:** A book on polity written by Somadeva, which is largely based on the *Arthaśāstra* of Kauṭilya. It was written in prose in the tenth century. According to its commentator it was written at the request of Mahendrapāla, king of Kannauj. Ed. in Manikacandra Digambara Jaina Granthamala, Bombay, 1921.

Nitoḍā: Situated in the Sirohi district, Rajasthan, wherefrom an epigraph of AD 1142 refers to an ancient temple of Nemināth.

Nittur: Site of Śāntīśvara-basti in Tumkur district. This temple of the mid-twelfth century has a *garbhagṛha, ardha-maṇḍapa, mukha-maṇḍapa,* and *nava-raṅga*. The original image is now lost but a fresh one has been installed. The outer wall contains Jina figures.

Non-Absolutism: The first and foremost Jain contribution to Indian thought is the systematic exposition of *pramāṇa-śāstra* or logic standing on two pillars, *anekāntavāda* or doctrine of non-absolutism, and *nayavāda* or the doctrine of partial truths. The Jain logicians from their non-absolutist standpoint hold that all particular theories based on logic are true to a certain extent and from a certain point of view. So also all cognition, be it of identity or of diversity, is valid to a certain extent and from a certain point of veiw. That the seemingly contradictory cognitions should reveal in their respective ways the nature of reality is exemplified in terms of forest and trees. One person may take note of the trees in the form of particular entities while another may take note of the forest in general. Neither of these two cognitions can be regarded as solely true, and both are partly true within their respective spheres. From the aforesaid viewpoint the Jains attempt to reconcile the special controversy between eternalism and momentarism by postulating that a thing is eternal insofar as it is of the form of a continuous flow, and momentary insofar as it undergoes a change or modification (*paryāya*) every moment. The non-absolutist standpoint also eliminates the controversy between the doctrines of definability and indefinability of postulating that the gross entities of medium duration and extension are capable of definition, while the innumerable subtle aspects of an entity's nature are not. Again, a thing is never cognized either solely through its positive traits or solely through its negative traits. Thus it is not self-contradictory to view a thing as a positive and also negative entity. The opposition between the doctrines of absolute presence of the effect in the cause and that of absolute absence of the effect in the cause can also be eliminated from the non-absolutist point of view, for it holds that the effect may be present but also absent in the material cause. For example, in the case of a gold bangle, the gold itself has the capacity to turn into a bangle, and from this viewpoint the effect can be said to be present even before it is actually produced. But since this effect is not there to be seen because of the absence of necessary accessories, it is absent before its actual production. In the same way the Jain non-absolutist standpoint bridges the gulf between the Buddhist doctrine of conglomeration of atoms and the Nyāya-Vaiśeṣika doctrine of an altogether novel composition. The Jain texts speak of types of judgement, *dravyārthika* and *paryāyārthika*, the former denoting that line of thought which takes substance into account in terms of what is general, common, non-distinct or unitary about things. The latter is the name of that line of thought which takes modes or changing phases into account. When the two views are sought to be synthesized and as such judgements are formed to give expression to the positive as well as negative aspects of the subject-matter in question, the result is a complex seven-fold judgement, the *saptabhangīnaya* (q.v.).

Nonamangala Grants: Found at Nonamangala in Kolar district and belonging to the first half of the sixth century AD, this inscription refers to *parama-arhat* Vijayakīrti, the preceptor of the king, on whose advice Avinīta granted land to the Uranur Arhat temple established by Ācārya Candranandin of the Mūla-saṅgha. The same inscription refers to another Jain temple, the Perur Evani Adigal Arhat. Another inscription of the Western Gaṅga King Mādhava III, belonging to the last quarter of the fifth century, refers to the name of Ācārya Vīradeva and to a Jain temple erected by the monks of the Mūla-saṅgha at Pebbolalagrāma of Mudukottura-viṣaya. *Epigrahia Carnatica*, X. Melur, No. 72-3.

Nṛpatuṅga: See Amoghavarṣa.

Nuns: See Female Ascetics.

Nuptial Rituals: Though the rites and customs of marriage among the Jains vary according to regional influence, some features are maintained both by the Śvetāmbaras and Digambaras. According to the Śvetāmbaras there are 16 main rites in their marriage ceremony: Mātṛkasthāpana, Saptakulakarasthāpana, Varaghoḍāna Śāntimantra, Hastamelapa, Agnisthāpana, Homa, Prathamābhiṣeka, Gotraccāra, Maṇḍapavedīpratiṣṭhā, Toraṇapratiṣṭhā, Agnipradakṣiṇā, Kanyādāna, Vāsakṣepa, Dvitīyābhiṣeka, Karamocana, and Āśīrvāda. The Digambaras have 20 rites: Vāgdāna, Vināyakavidhāna, Kaṅkanabandhana, Gṛhasaṃskāra, Toraṇavidhi, Vivāhavidhi, Parasparamukhāvalokana, Varamāla, Varapratijñā, Kanyādāna, Devaśāstragurupūjā, Homāhūti, Granthibandhana, Pāṇigrahaṇa, Saptapadī, Puṇyāhavacana, Śāntimantra, Āśīrvāda, Svagṛhagamana, and Jinagṛhe-Dhanārpaṇa. Among these, five are considered to be main parts of the marriage ceremony: *Vāgdāna*, engagement which takes place usually one month before the marriage ceremony; *pradāna*, presentation of ornaments by the bridegroom's father to the bride; *vraṇa* or *kanyādāna*, consecration and gift of the bride; *pāṇigrahaṇa* or *pānipīḍana*, joining of the hands of the bride and bridegroom; and *saptapadī*, circumambulation of the sacred fire which is the culmination of the marriage ceremony. During circumambulation the bridal pair have to desire their attainment of *saptaparamasthāna* (q.v.), i.e. the seven high states of life. According to the Śvetāmbaras, the newly married pair departs for consummation of marriage on the same day on which the Āśīrvāda, the last item of the marriage rituals, is performed. According to the *Ādipurāṇa* XXXVIII.131-33 of the Digambaras, the bride and the bridegroom should observe the vow of celibacy for seven days after the marriage ceremony. Thereafter they should proceed on a pilgrimage to a sacred place and then enjoy the wedded life in their own place.

***Nyāyakumudacandrodaya*:** See Prabhācandra.

***Nyāsa*:** Tantric practice adopted by some Jain worshippers according to which the deity is to be felt in different parts of the body by touching them with finger and palm. The *Bhairava-Padmāvatī Kalpa* refers to what is known as *svakīya aṅganyāsa*, whereby the devotee places the divinities in different parts of his body by uttering *mantras* sacred to each divinity. The *Jvālinī Kalpa* states that without *nyāsa*, the worshipper cannot be successful in rites relating to the torture of evil spirits. The entire ritual of *nyāsa* is referred to as *sakalikaraṇa*. The ritual starts with the *nyāsa* of the fingers of both hands with the Bījas *vaṃ, maṃ, haṃ, saṃ, taṃ,* etc. This is followed by the *nyāsa* of the left hand. In the Hindu Tantras the *nyāsa* does not generally follow a descending or ascending order. But in the *Jvālinī-kalpa* it starts at the legs and follows an ascending order.

Nyāya-Vaiśeṣika: Although the main target of the Jain attack was the theistic standpoint of the Nyāya-Vaiśeṣikas, so far as logic is concerned the Jains drew heavily from them. Again the Nyāya-Vaiśeṣika conception of atomism has a significant bearing on the same conception developed among the Jains. The Jain philosophical literature testifies to a gradually developing clarity with regard to the descriptions (*vyākhyā*), definitions (*lakṣaṇa*) and logical justification (*upapatti*) of the categories (*padārtha*) like 'organ of valid knowledge' (*pramāṇa*), etc., in accordance with the corresponding developments of such ideas in Nyāya-Vaiśeṣika literature. Jain and Nyāya-Vaiśeṣika conceptions of substances have much in common. The material substances in both cases can be reduced to *paramāṇus* or atoms, but while in the Nyāya-Vaiśeṣika view all the atoms are not homogeneous in quality, the Jains hold them to be homogeneous. In Jainism quality or *guṇa* is the essential character of the substance. In the Nyāya-Vaiśeṣika, the *guṇas* are conceived as inhered in and dependent upon substance. At the same time they are also conceived as distinct from substance, because they can by themselves be known and are thus independent realities. The Jains, admitting that different qualities are perceived by different sense-organs, argue that since a quality is non-distinct from the substance of which it is a quality, all the sense-organs are competent to perceive qualities as well as substances. But the Nyāya-Vaiśeṣikas hold that the visual sense-organ and the tactile sense-organs are alone competent to perceive substance. The Jains are advocates of the self-revelatory character of cognition. The Nyāya-Vaiśeṣikas on the other hand do not regard cognition as self-revelatory in the sense of being perceptually cognizable by something than itself. As regards perception, the Jains share with the Nyāya-Vaiśeṣikas the ideas of indeterminate and determinate perceptions. According to the Nyāya-Vaiśeṣikas, the material cause of the sense-organs are the *bhūtas* or material elements. The Jains also maintain that the material cause of the sense-organs is in a particular kind of *pudgala* or matter. Regarding the technique of inference, the Nyāya-Vaiśeṣikas admit the necessity of establishing a five-member syllogism. Although the Jains adopt this in practice, they hold that the number of steps in an inference should not be fixed. The Nyāya-Vaiśeṣikas and the Jains agree in holding that an effect is a proper probans and that a probans is valid when it is free of all helerologues irrespective of whether or not it is present in a homologue. This position has been defended in great details by the Naiyāyikas and Jains alike.

***Nyāyāvatāra*:** Logical treatise composed by Siddhasena Divākara (q.v.) of the Gupta period in which we come across a comprehensive treatment of the valid sources of knowledge, rules of syllogism, various types of logical fallacies, and the methods of judgement. The topic of *pramāṇa* has been critically discussed in this work which also deals with the methods of comprehending things from a multiple viewpoint (*naya, anekāntavāda*) in 32 Sanskrit verses. It is a fundamental work on Jain logic which forms a part of *Dvātriṃśad-Datriṃsikā*. Ed A.N. Upadhye, Jain Sahitya Vikas Mandal, Bombay, 1971; ed. with Eng. tans. by S.C. Vidyabhusan, Calcutta, 1909.

***Nyāyaviniścaya*:** See Akalaṅka.

O

Occupations: The *Aupapātika Sūtra* gives a list of various occupations. Jainism lays special emphasis on trade and commerce and manufactures. It has been a religion of the mercantile community. Next in importance were agriculture and cattle-rearing. Besides those who were employed in cultivation and tending cattle, there were a large number of people who, though not labourers, had different avocations and played an important role in society. Amongst those who accepted the professions of learning, teachers, physicians, those expert in testing the foundations of a house, those versed in the science of prognostication and fortune-tellers are mentioned. Amongst those in public entertainment, there were musicians, acrobats, dancers, rope-walkers, wrestlers, boxers, jesters, story-tellers, leaders, ballad reciters, narrative-tellers, pole-dancers, picture-showmen, pipers, lute-players, clappers, snake-charmers, bards, buffons, flatterers and mime actors. Besides, the texts refer to royal attendants, military men, carriers, and craftsmen.

Odalavadi: Site of the Arhat temple in Polur taluk, North Arcot district. The Tīrthaṃkara image enshrined here is given the name *aṇiyād-alagiyār.*

Oḍeyadeva Vādibhasiṃha: Eleventh-century author of *Gadyacintāmaṇi* and *Kṣatracūḍāmaṇi* (qq.v.), both based on the legend of Jīvandhara of the *Uttara Purāṇa* (q.v.). His teacher was Puṣpaṣena, a fellow-pupil of Vādirāja, author of the *Yaśodharacarita* (qq.v.). Both were pupils of Somadeva Suri, author of the *Yaśastilaka* (qq.v.).

Ogha Niryukti, Oha Nijjuti: See Piṇḍa-Niryukti, Chedasūtras.

Omens: Sign of some future event, either good or bad. Eight auspicious objects are mentioned in Jain texts: *svastika, śrīvatsa, nandāvarta, vardhamāna, bhadrāsana, kalasa, darpaṇa* and *matsyayugma*. See Aṣṭamaṅgalas. Animals, birds, trees and plants are said to bring good or bad luck. The *Triṣaṣṭiśalākāpuruṣacarita* which gives a list of unfavourable omens, says that lunar days (*tithis*), astrological division of days (*karaṇa*) and constellations (*nakṣatra*) are to be examined in terms of their capability for bringing good or bad effects before performing any ceremony, setting out for a sea-voyage and so on. In the *Samarāiccakahā* it is said that when King Guṇasena proceeded to the battlefield, water-pitchers were set and auspicious musical instruments were sounded. Good and bad omens are mentioned in the *Kuvalayamālā* with regard to the throbbing of different parts of the body. It refers to the howlings of jackals, notes of a crow and the chirping of a lizard. *Śakunaruta*, or knowledge of birds also help to foretell events. The *Pariśiṣṭaparvan* refers to various omens to be observed at the birth of a child and says that Cāṇakya was born with a complete set of teeth, whereupon a monk foretold that he was likely to become a king.

Ontology: A branch of cosmology (q.v.) dealing with the questions of the inner nature of the universe (q.v.). In the Jain scheme all the substances having body or extension are divided into the categories of living (*jīva*, q.v.) and non-living (*ajīva*, q.v.). The term *jīva* stands for that 'which lives or is animate'. The concept bears a clear mark of formulation from observing the characteristics of life and not through search after a metaphysical principle underlying individual existence. Thus the word in the original sense stood for the vital principle rather than for the soul. Later on, however, the question of consciousness was emphasized. *Tattvārtha* II.8; Guṇaratna on *Ṣaḍdarśanasamuccya* 47. The *jīvas* thus were theoretically arranged in a continuous series according to degree of consciousness. On the top of this series were placed perfect souls that had overcome all *karmas* and attained omniscience and at the bottom were placed imperfect souls inhabiting the bodies of earth, water, fire, air or vegetation. *Tattvārtha* II.22-3. But this classification was originally biological and from the purely empirical point of view on the basis of sense-organs, such as those that have one sense, two senses, etc. Guṇaratna on *Ṣaḍdarśana* 49. In a subsequent stage of the development of the concept of *jīva,* it is thought of as existing permanently, acting and being acted upon, as an experiment (*bhoktā*) and agent (*kartā*). *Dravyasaṃgraha* 2. It is thought of as capable of expansion and contraction according to the dimensions of the physical body. It is associated with the latter for the time being. That explains its capacity to contain all the powers and potentials of life on the one hand and the problem of its relation with the body on the other. It fills up the latter from top to bottom just as a lamp illumines a room of any size. Its identification with the soul makes it formless, but it is said to occupy space or possess extension though its non-spatial character is affected by its association with matter. It is said that by ignorance it identifies itself with matter which accounts for all its troubles and degradation. A classification of the *jīvas* as mundane and liberated subsequently came into existence. While the liberated soul possesses infinite perception, knowledge, power, and happiness, the mundane *jīvas* are embodied souls of living beings and subject to the cycle of endless rebirths because of their association with subtle matter. They are graded according to the place where they are born or their condition of existence which is of four kinds, viz., hellish, subhuman, human, and celestial. The *ajīva* or inanimate substances consist of objects responding to sense-organs. Among its five categories *kāla* or time is indivisible and continually makes old things new and new things old. For example a child grows into a young man, and finally dies in old age, and the *jīva* is forced to inhabit afresh the body of another infant. The *jīva* remains the same, but the power that makes its covering body at one time old and then young is *kāla*. Like space, time is also inferred, though not perceived. Of the grounds of inference it may be said that modification or change of states cannot be conceived of without time. Similarly movements also cannot be thought of without the supposition of time. Real time, *paramārṭhika-kāla*, is beyond comprehension. It is the empirical or conventional time, *vyavahārika-kāla* or *samaya*, that holds the field. Space or *ākāśa* makes room for the existence of all extended substances, which are of two kinds—*lokākāśa* or space containing the world where the *jīvas* beyond it. *Dharma* is the principle of motion, the accompanying circumstance or cause which makes motion possible. Just as water, itself indifferent or neutral, is the condition of the movement of fish, so *dharma*, itself non-motive, is the *sine qua non* of motion. *Adharma* is the reverse. It is the substance that helps the immobility of objects, just as the shade of a tree helps a traveller to rest. Without space substances cannot be extended; so also without the principles of motion and rest, which work on space, things cannot stay or move in the right order. Both are complementary principles, eternal and formless, pervading space. Matter is called *pudgala*. In Jainism, whatever is perceived by the senses, the mind, the *karmas* and other material objects is known as *pudgala* which is liable to integration and disintegration and possesses colour, smell, taste, and form, is perceptible to the touch, can be consumed or destroyed, and may decay or alter its form. All six categories from *jīva* to *pudgala* are known as *dravyas* or substances. A *dravya* has three characteristics—the quality of existence, the quality of permanence through origination and destruction, and the quality of serving as the substratum of attributes and modes. It has some essential and some accidental characters, the former remaining in it so long as it remains, and it is through the accidental characters that a substance undergoes change or modification.

Orambakkam: A village in Chingleput district, Tamil Nadu, which contains Jain elements in its natural caverns and chiseled rock-beds. Near one of them are found reliefs of Ādinātha, Pārśvanātha, and Mahāvīra.

Orissa: See Bhubaneśvara caves, Kaliṅga Jina, Khāravela, Khaṇḍagiri Caves, Orissan Cave Inscriptions, Podasingidi, Udayagiri Caves.

Orissan Cave Inscriptions: Apart from the Hathigumpha (q.v.), inscriptions in the Udayagiri-Khaṇḍagiri caves disclose the names of a few Jain devotees. One records the establishment of a cave (*leṇa*) in honour of Arhamta by Khāravela's (q.v.) chief queen, who like her husband was a worshipper of the Jinas. A few other inscriptions disclose the existence of devotees like Vakadeva, Vadhuka, etc. One inscription records the donation of a servant named Kusuma. Lüders, *List*, Nos. 1342-53.

Osavāla: Important Jain caste in Rajasthan, Malwa and Gujarat. The name Osavāla is derived from the town of Osia or Osiyanagara in Marwar. It is said that the king of this town obtained a son through the grace of the ascetic Ratnaprabha Sūri. The latter converted the king to Jainism by performing a miracle at the behest of Osadevī, the guardian-deity of that place. According to another legend the city was founded by a few discontented merchants under King Jayacandra and the preceptor Ratna Sūri. Osavālas are of Rajput origin and have eighteen *gotras*: Tātahaḍa, Baphaṇā, Karṇāta, Balaharā, Morākṣa, Kulahaṭa, Birahaṭa, Śrīśrīmāla, Śreṣṭhi, Sucinti, Āicananga or Adiyanama, Bhuri or Bhaṭevarā, Bhādra, Cicaṭa Kumbhaḷa, Dindu, Kanoja, and Laghu-śreṣṭhī. Later a few more were added and the original *gotras* were split into 498 sub-*gotras*. Like other mercantile castes, the Osavālas are divided into Viśā (twenties)and Daśā (tens). They

Osia

also have Pañcā (fives) and Āḍhāiyā (two-and-a-half) divisions. They are the most important trading caste in Rajasthan. They also hold important public offices. The Osavālas are mostly Śvetāmbaras. They marry with other Baniya castes so long as both the parties are Jains. Again, a Jain Osavāla boy can marry a Vaiṣṇava Osavāla girl.

Osia: Site of the Mahāvīra temple, one of the few Jain temples at this straggling village about 32 miles to the north-west of Jodhpur in Rajasthan. This temple represents a stage in the evolution of the *nāgara* style and the appearance of regional characteristics. According to a fragmentary inscription, the original shrine of Mahāvīra seems to date back to the period of Vatsarāja, the Gurjara Pratihāra king of the last quarter of the eighth century AD. It was subsequently repaired in AD 956 by a merchant named Jinodaka. The ornament *toraṇa* was set up in AD 1018. The style of the temple, with the *śikhara* of the sanctum surrounded by clusters of *aṅga-śikharas*, belongs to the eleventh century AD, though evidence of an earlier history are fully supported by the varied forms of pillars of the *maṇḍapa*, of the porch, and of the *toraṇa* in front. Osia was also known as Upakeśapura which has been regarded as a çelebrated place of pilgrimage by Siddhasena and Jinaprabha. *Archaeological Survey of India: Annual Report,* 1908-9, 108; *Indian Antiquary* XIX.233ff.; Bhandarkar, *List* No. 73; P.C. Nahar, *Jaina Lekha Saṃgraha* I. 192ff.

P

Pabhosa Cave Inscriptions: At Pabhosa near Allahabad, there are two caves, bearing inscriptions in Śuṅga characters, recording their dedication by one Āṣāḍhasena from Ahicchatra for the use of the Kāśyapīya Arhats, the *gotra* to which Mahāvīra belonged. According to D.C. Sircar the inscriptions refer to the monks of Ahicchatra. That the Pabhosa cave was sacred to the Jains from pre-Christian times is proved by the discovery of Jain images therefrom. Three standing Jina images, cut in the rock, are also to be found there. *Epigraphia Indica* II, 242f; D.C. Sircar, *Select Inscriptions*, 95ff.

Pādaliptapura: Ancient name of the famous Palitana near Śatruñjaya (q.v.). It was a celebrated Jain centre named after the saint Pādaliptasūri (q.v.). According to the *Prabandhacintāmaṇi* the Mahāvīra temple of this place was in existence in Vastupāla's time who also built a *pauṣadhaśālā* there.

Pādaliptasūri: Prakrit Pālitta, author of the earliest Śvetāmbara non-canonical literary text, *Taraṅgavatī*. The text is missing but an abridged version of this work is Nemicandra's *Taraṅgalolā*, written about 1,000 years after the original. According to tradition Pādalipta was a contemporary of the Sātavāhana King Hāla. He is mentioned to in the *Prabhāvakacarita* and *Prabandhakośa*, and his work is mentioned to in the *Anuyogadvāra* and the *Viśeṣā-vaśyakabhāṣya* of Jinabhadra. Pādalipta thus belonged to the early centuries of the Christian era, probably the third century, and is also mentioned by later writers like Jinadāsagaṇi Ksamāśramaṇa, Udyotana Suri, Dhanapāla and others.

Padhvali: Site in Morena district, which has yielded a number of Tīrthaṃkara images now in the Central Archaeological Museum, Gwalior.

Padmakīrti: Author of *Pāsanāha-cariu* composed in AD 942. It is in 18 Sandhis. He refers to Candrasena, Mādhavasena, Jinasena, and Padmakīrti of the Sena Saṅgha as his spiritual precursors.

***Padmānanda Kāvya*:** See Amaracandra.

Padmaprabha: The sixth Tīrthaṃkara whose parents were King Dhara and Queen Susimā of Kausambi. His sacred tree was the *chatrābha* and his disciples were Suvrata and Rati. He lived for 3,000 thousand years and had a height of 250 bow-lengths. He attained liberation on Sammeya. His symbol is the red lotus and his attendant spirits, Kusuma and Syamā/Manovegā. Two interpretations of his name are given, that his colour was that of the red lotus, or that his mother, while the Jina was in her womb, expressed a desire to sleep on a bed of red lotuses, which was fulfilled. His symbolism and the name of his Yakṣa attendant, Kusuma, express the same fact. Padmaprabha images are not abundant, but at the same time not rare.

***Padmapurāṇa*:** Composed by Raviṣena in AD 678, it is a slightly extended recession of Vimala Suri's *Paumacariya* (q.v.) in Sanskrit, agreeing with it on all essential points. It begins with a description of the world, especially the world of the Vidyādharas and a glorification of Ṛṣabhanātha. Canto 20 deals with the Tīrthamkaras, and the actual story begins in canto 21. Here, too, Padma is the name given to Rāma, and Kuśa and Lava are called Aṅkuśa and Lavaṇa respectively. In canto 26 are given the dreadful consequences of killing and of eating flesh, with a description of the hells. Ed. Pandit Darbarilal Nyayatirtha Sahityaratna in Manikacandra Digambrara Jaina Granthamālā, Nos. 29-31, 1928; with Hindi trans. in three parts in Bhāratīya Jñānapīṭha, Kashi, 1958-9.

Padmasundara: Author of the *Pārśvanātha-kāvya* which was written in AD 1565.

Padmāvatī: Śāsanadevatā (q.v.) of Pārśvanātha (q.v.). She is conceived of in the Śvetāmbara traditon as riding a snake and holding a lotus, noose, fruit, and goad. Padmāvatī of the Digambaras is described as of four types according to the number of hands. She is the goddess of the snakes living in the nether regions. Her Hindu counterpart is Manasā, also known by the name Padmāvatī.

Padmāvatī-basti: See Kattaḷe-basti.

Padmāvatī Mandira: An interesting Jain temple of Nagda (q.v.). It seems to be a shrine of Pārśvanātha according to the inscriptions of vs 1356 and 1351 in its main *Garbhagṛha.* It contains a simple *mūla-prāsāda* with towering central *śikhara* decked with *aṅga-śikharas* and a domed *maṇḍapa.* The interior has three sanctuaries, one of them with a *sarvatobhadrikā* image while the other two are empty.

Paharpur Copper Plate: The earliest Jain record from Bengal, dated in Gupta year 159, obtained from Paharpur in the Rajashahi district which records an endowment for the worship of Arhats to a vihāra in Vaṭagohali in the same region, presided over by the disciples descended from the Nirgrantha Ācārya Guhanandin (q.v.) of Kashi, by a Brāhmaṇa named Nāthaśarman and his wife Rāmī. The Jaina vihāra referred to above was situated in the Nāgiratta-*maṇḍala* of Puṇḍravardhana-*bhukti*. Vaṭagohali is the present village Goalbhita, where the ruins of a big temple and a Jina image have been unearthed. *Epigraphia Indica* XX.61ff.; Bhandarkar, *List*, No. 2037; R.C. Majumdar (ed.), *Dacca History of Bengal*, vol. I, Calcutta, 1943, 410ff.

Painna: See Prakīrṇa.

Paintings: The Jain cave-temple at Sittanavasal (q.v.) in the Tiruchirapalli district, Tamil Nadu, contains mural paintings of the ninth century. Notwithstanding the pronounced Jain character of the cave, the paintings are secular, depicting a royal couple, a danseuse, *apsarases*, flower-gatherers, animals, birds, fish, lotus pools, etc. The paintings are on the cave ceiling, pillars and architraves. The Indra-sabhā (q.v.) at Ellora (q.v.) contains paintings of the ninth-tenth centuries on the entire surface of its ceiling and walls. The scenes illustrate Jain texts, divine and semi-divine mythical beings, flying celestials, and floral, animal, and bird designs.

The Cola style is reflected in the paintings of the Jain Tirumalai temple. The manuscripts of the temple library at Mudbidri (q.v.) contain paintings of the Hoysala period. These are on palm-leaves and important for the beauty of the letters and the illustrations that accompany them. It is interesting to compare the writing in these manuscripts with the nicely executed lines on metal plates from the Belur temple. Jain paintings on the *saṅgītamaṇḍapa* of the Vardhamāna temple at Tirupparuttikkunram (q.v.) near Kanchipuram of the Vijayanagara period show themes chosen from the life of Vardhamāna. To the subsequent Nayaka phase belong the later paintings in the Mahāvīra temple at Tirupparuttikkunram. Scenes from the life of Ṛṣabhadeva, Vardhamāna, Neminātha, and his cousin Kṛṣṇa are all graphically portrayed in a long series with elaborate painted labels in Tamil explaining each scene.

Side by side we have the tradition of miniature paintings on *paṭtas*, palm-leaf, and paper. It is not unlikely that the early manuscripts containing painted illustrations have perished, since they could not be safely stored. But from the eleventh cenury onwards the situation seems to have changed. There is another theory that the beginning of the art of palm-leaf manuscript illustration is a later development, of which the earliest known example is a manuscript of AD 1060 preserved in a Jain Bhandara at Jaisalmer. Then there are *paṭli* illustrations. A *paṭli* is a wooden manuscript-cover. On these are depicted the Vidyādevīs, teachers delivering sermons and their disciples, lay disciples, trading caravans, birds and beasts, aquatic animals, trees, creepers and floral designs. In one *paṭli*, also belonging to the Jaisalmer Bhandara, we find a giraffe and a rhinoceros in the roundels of the meandering creepers, birds, aquatic monsters, antelope, boar, flute-player and bare-breasted girls. One *paṭli* depicts the famous disputation between the Śvetāmbara logician Vādiveda Suri and the Digambara scholar Kumudacandra at the court of Siddarāja Jayasiṃha in AD 1124. *Paṭlis* of later periods, however, appear to be increasingly formal. An illustrated manuscript of AD 1127 in the Śāntinātha temple Bhandara at Cambay has an attractive figure of Sarasvatī, precursor of the characteristic Jain style of subsequent manuscript-illustration. By the thirteenth century the Jain palm-leaf illustration-style developed certain mannerisms which were to remain for centuries. Another development was that the illustrators, even in the limited format at their disposal, began increasingly to give expression to the subject-matter of the text in a narrative form. A manuscript of AD 1288 in the collection of the Sanghvi Bhandara, Patan, contains as many as 23 illustrations. Here the method of continous narration is employed. The events which comprise an incident in the life of Neminātha are all placed in the picture-space of a single illustration. A palm-leaf manuscript belonging to the Anandji Mangalji Bhandar at Idar, containing 34 miniatures, shows the use of gold to highlight the colour-effects. This is probably the Persian influence. From the fourteenth century onwards illustrated Jain manuscripts on paper came into vogue. The main centres for the production of the late-fourteenth and early-fifteenth century illustrated paper manuscripts were the towns of Gujarat and Rajasthan, but the style of painting was not confined to these areas. At Mandu during the middle of the fifteenth century, two excellent manuscripts were produced which adhered to tradition and hieratic requirements, but revealed innovation and a better colour-treatment.

Provincial developments are also found in the Jaunpur manuscripts in which numerous vignettes and decorative patterns were introduced under the influence of Persian painting. Apart from serving religious and aesthetic purposes, these illustrated Jain manuscripts provide valuable clues to the understanding of trends in pre-Mughal painting.

***Paiśāca*:** One of the eight forms of Jain marriage adopted from Brahmanical legal texts with some modification. It is about violating a senseless, helpless, or sleeping girl and is considered as the worst form of marriage. *Trivarṇikācāra* XI.78; *Nītivākyāmṛta* XXXI. 11.

***Pajjuṇṇa-Kahā*:** Sanskrit name *Pradyumna-kathā*. This Apabhraṃśa poem in fifteen cantos narrates the life of Pradyumna Kumara, son of Kṛṣṇa and the 21st Kāmadeva out of the 24 recognized in the Jain hierarchy of great persons. The first eight cantos were composed by Siddha, who probably flourished in the early part of the tenth century. The work was completed by Siṃha who added the last seven cantos.

Pajnari: Medieval Jain temple site at Sagar, Madhya Pradesh.

Pakbira: An important Jain site in the Purulia district, West Bengal, which seems to be the most prolific in Jain shrines and images. One of the colossal images is that of an eleventh-century Padmaprabha with a height of 7 feet 6 inches and carved in the round in chlorite. It stands in *kāyotsarga* on a low pedestal on which the lotus emblem is carved. Flanked by *chowri*-bearers, this image is locally worshipped. An eleventh-century Śāntinātha image has been found in the same place and is now in the State Archaeological Gallery of West Bengal. The upper half of this image is lost. The lower portion on a double-petalled lotus is placed on a *pañcaratha* pedestal on which the deer emblem is carved, flanked by lions on the extreme right and left. Two *chowri*-bearers are on either side of the image. The blank portion is occupied by four female devotees in *añjali-mudrā* and a goat-headed male figure who must be Naigamesa. There is an inscription on the top portion of the central projection of the pedestal. An eleventh-century Ambikā image standing on lotus and placed on a *pañcaratha* pedestal, holding a child by her hanging left hand is found here. The right hand is broken at the elbow. There is an attendant near the right leg. Branches of a mango tree with pendant mangoes over the head are represented. A miniature representation of a Jina is seen amid the branches. Two other eleventh-century Ambikā images along with her consort are found at Pakbira. The first one is a broken sculpture in which the male is seated in *ardhaparyaṅka* to the left of the goddess with right hand in *abhaya*. The goddess is also in a similar posture. Both are profusely ornamented. Below their feet are seven miniature male figures seated in row, their left leg being bent at knee and hands raised in *abhaya*. Flying Gandharvas are on the top corners. There is a miniature figure of a Jina seated in *yogāsana* on a lotus pedestal at the top of a bifurcated tree hanging over the head of the central figure. The second figure features almost the same as the above. The right hands are broken in both, the right legs hanging down and the left placed upon the seat. The left leg of the goddess is on the lotus. In between the two hanging legs are shown in relief a bowl-on-stand and a *ghaṭa*. More than one branch in semi-circular curve are seen on each of the main figures. Seven miniature figures exist on the pedestal, each kneeling with folded hands. Images of Ṛṣabhanātha, Kunthunātha, Neminātha, and Mahāvīra have also been found. The Mahāvīra image contains an inscription of the ninth century.

Pakṣa: Minor term: See logic.

Pakudha Kaccāyana: Apparently an Ājīvika (q.v.) teacher who was a contemporary of Mahāvīra. In the Jain Aṅga text *Sūyagaḍa* I.1.1.15-16 his philosophy is described as the 'doctrine of the soul as the sixth', *ātma-saṣṭhavāda*, which the commentator Śilāṅka identifies with the doctrine of *Bhagavadgīta* as well as with the Sāṅkhya and some aspects of the Śaiva system. In the Buddhist *Sāmaññaphalasutta*, Pakudha's philosophy has been described as the doctrine of seven categories, *sattakāyavāda,* comprising earth, water, fire, air, pleasure, pain and being, which are uncreated, barren, steadfast, and fixed. These are eternal and immutable. In the Buddhist *Majjhima Nikāya* I.513ff. Pakudha's doctrine has been incorporated into Gośāla's (q.v.) fatalistic creed. The southern Ājīvikas held a theory of elements very similar to that of Pakudha. According to the *Manimekalai,* the Ājīvikas believe in five immutable atomic elements—earth, water, fire, air and life, but the text adds two more, joy and sorrow. The *Nīlakeci* leaves the total of the elements at five, but the *Civañāṇa-cittiyar* insists on seven elements—earth, water, fire, air, life, good, and evil. This is surely the seven element theory of Pakudha with more moral categories good and evil substituted for the ordinary pleasure and pain.

Pāladi Inscription of Kelhaṇa: Dated in vs 1249

(AD 1192) this inscription of the Nadol Cāhamāna king Kelhaṇa found at Pāladi in Sirohi district, Rajasthan, refers to a temple of Mahāvīra. P.C. Nahr, *Jaina Lekha Saṃgraha* I, 265f, No. 955.

***Pālagopāla Kathānaka*:** See Jinakīrti.

Pala Jain Inscription: An inscription from Pala in Pune district Maharashtra, which refers to the excavation of a cave by a monk called Indrarakṣita. It begins with the typical Jain expression *namo araṃbatānam* and may be assigned to the beginning of the Christian era. *Jaina Śilālekha Saṃgraha,* Bharatiya Jnanapitha. V. 3.

Palaśikā: Modern Halsi in the Belgaum district, Karnataka, it was once a Jain centre. At present, however, there is no trace of Jainism at Halsi.

Palghat: Well-known place in Kerala. Palghat proper has a Jain temple dedicated to Candraprabha which stylistically belongs to ninth-tenth century.

Pālhaṇa: See *Abu-Rāsa.* He also composed the *Nemi-Rājula-Bārahamāsā* which describes nature in the order of months, from the angle of love-lorn Rājimatī, whose wedding with Prince Nemi failed to come off because the latter decided at the eleventh hour to renounce the world and become a monk.

Pāli: Mentioned by Jinaprabha as a great Jain *tīrtha* sacred to Vīra or Mahāvīra. It is situated in the district of the same name in Rajasthan. The earliest Jain inscription from this place belongs to the eleventh century.

Palitana: Hill in Gujarat which is known as Śatruñjaya (q.v.) considered sacred to the Jains from a very early period. It sprang into prominence after the tenth century AD. It is ancient Pādaliptapura.

Pallankovil Copper Plate: Found at Pallankovil in Tirutturaipundi taluk of Tanjore district, Tamil Nadu, this inscription, supposed to be of the late tenth century, refers to the existence of a Jain temple founded by Śaletti Kuḍiyan. The name of the temple is given as Sundaraśolapperumbaḷḷi, apparently named after Sundara Cola (AD 956-73). *Annual Report on Indian Epigraphy*, 1961-2, 4-5; *Transactions of the Archaeological Society of South India,* 1958-9, 84ff.

Pallava-Jinālaya: Temple at Pudur established by Kaṇakasena Bhaṭṭāraka of the Drāviḍa Saṅgha under the patronage and land grant of Hallakarasu, a feudatory of Tribhuvanamalla Vikramāditya (AD 1076-1126), the Kalyāṇī Cālukya king.

Pallava Jain Inscriptions: A few Jain Pallava inscriptions of the reign of Nandivarman II Pallavamalla (AD 730-800) are known, among which a rock-cut inscription from Kil-Sattamaṅgalam (q.v.) is important. Another Jain shrine is mentioned in his Agalur inscription from Gingee taluk of South Arcot district while one from Kanchi which records a grant to an Arhat temple, interestingly refers to an Ācarya of the Ājīvika-*darśana.* Inscriptions of his son Kampavarman, also known as Dantivarman, are also suggestive. One of them gives us a clear idea regarding a Jain temple complex. It records the renovation of a temple, originally established by Pavanandi, and the addition of a *mukha-maṇḍapa* to it, the construction of a Yakṣī temple, the installation of a bell, and so forth. The entire temple complex was called *palli* in this record which is again mentioned in an inscription from the same site, belonging to the reign of Rajaraja I, dated in his 13th Tīrthaṃkara Vimala. The Noḷamba-Pallavas ruled parts of Karnataka in the ninth and tenth centuries as is attested to by their inscriptions, especially the Dharmapuri and Hemavati inscriptions of Mahendra. *Annual Report on Indian Epigraphy*, 1954-5, B.221, 360, 1968-9, B.219-20, 223, 268; *Epigraphia Indica* X.54ff.; *South Indian Inscriptions* IX, Pt. I, No. 19.

Pallava Inscription of Simhavarman II: Issued from Kanchi about the middle of the sixth century AD, this inscription records the grant of a village to the Jain sage Vajranandin of Nandi Saṅgha at Vardhamāneśvara Tīrtha for performing the worship of the Jina. The land regarding the grant was at a place called Puruttikkanru which was a locality near Kanchi. *Transaction of the Archaeological Society of South India*, 1958-9, 41ff.

Pampa I: See Ādi Pampa.

Pampa II: See Nāgacandra.

Pañcakūṭa-basti: Jain temple in Kambadahalli at the outskirts of Sravanabelgola. It is a perfect specimen of southern *vimāna* architecture. Three of the *vimānas* of this complex form an unmistakable illustration of the three forms defined in southern architectural texts—the Nāgara, Drāviḍa, and Vesara. There is another Pañcakūṭa-basti at Markuli in the Hassan district of Karnataka. It was erected by Bucchimayya, the minister of the Hoysala Ballāla II in AD 1173. It is for Ādinātha, Neminātha, Pārśvanātha, Puṣpadanta, and Supārśvanātha. It has a twelve-armed figure of Cakreśvarī.

***Pañcakalpa*:** Prakrit *Paṃcakappa*, the sixth Chedasūtra (q.v.). It does not appear to be in existence any longer. There is a work called *Pañcakalpa-mahābhāṣya* which was formerly a part of *Bṛhatkalpabhāṣya.*

Pañcakalyāṇa: See Arhat Parameṣṭhin.

Pañcakalyāṇadhārī: See Arhanta.

Pañcama: One of the important Jain castes of the Deccan, of Digambara affiliation. Various interpretations as to the significance of this name and theories in regard to the origin of this caste have been given, none satisfactory. In the Jain hierarchy the position of the Pañcamas is not high. They are mainly agriculturists and petty merchants. Their religious leader lives in Kolhapur. They claim to be Vaiśyas and are of good conduct.

Pañca Parameṣṭhins: See Parameṣṭhins.

Pañcasaṃgraha: See Candramahattara, Nemicandra Siddhāntacakravartin.

Pañcasāra Pārśvanātha Temple: Also known as Vanarāja-vihāra, it is said to have been built by Vanarāja Cāpotkaṭa in Patan, Anahilwara, Gujarat.

***Pañcaśati Prabandha-sambandha*:** See Subhaśila Gaṇin.

***Pañcāstikāya*:** See Kundakunda.

Pañcastūpanikāya: The Nirgrantha Ācārya Guhanandin (q.v.) of Kashi, mentioned in the Paharpur Copper-Plate Inscription (q.v.), belonged to his school. The name of this school occurs in the canonical literature of the Digambaras. In Hariṣena's *Bṛhatkathākośa* we have an account of the founding of five stūpas at Mathura. In south Indian inscriptions we come across Pañcastūpanikāya monks. Vīrasena, author of the *Dhavalā* (qq.v.) and Jinasena, author of the *Ādipurāṇa* (qq.v.), belonged to the *Pañcastūpanikāya* sects. It appears that with the propagation of Digambara viewpoints in Bengal this school had found an expression in the Jain centre at Paharpur.

Pañcendriya Jīvas: Five-sensed Jīvas (q.v.) possessing the organs of touch, smell, taste, hearing, and sight. In this category are included mainly the bipeds and quadrupeds. The animals which possess five organs of sense are of two kinds, those which originate by *generatio acquivoca* (*samucchedanā*, coagulation) and those which are born from the womb. Each of these are again of three kinds—aquatic, terrestrial, and aerial. Fishes, tortoises, crocodiles, *makaras* and Gangetic porpoises are five kinds of acquatic animals. Quadrupeds and reptiles are two kinds of terrestrial animals. The former are of four kinds—solidungular animals such as horses, etc., biungular animals like cows, etc.; multiunglar animals as elephants, etc., and animals such having toes and nails as lions, etc. The reptiles are of two kinds—those which walk on their arms (lizards) and those which move on their breast (snakes). Both are again of many kinds. Winged animals are of four kinds—with membranous wings, with feathered wings, with wings in the shape of a box, and outspread wings. Men are of two kinds—originating by coagulation (to which category belong gods and other supernatural beings) and born from the womb. Those who are born from the womb are of three kinds—those living in the *karmabhūmi*, those living in the *akarmabhūmi* and those living in minor continents. *Uttarādhyayana* XXXVI. 171ff.

***Pāṇḍavacarita*:** Composed about AD 1200 by Maladhārin Devaprabha Suri in 18 Sargas it deals with the contents of the 18 Parvans of the *Mahābhārata* in Jain perspective. Some episodes of the original *Mahābhārata* are maintained in this work, especially those having a bearing on Jain ethics. The legend of Jina Ariṣṭanemi in connection with the Pāṇḍavas is narrated. The last Sarga relates how Baladeva reached heaven and Ariṣṭanemi and the Pāṇḍavas attained Nirvāṇa. It was rendered in prose with inserted verses by Devavijaya Gaṇin in AD 1603. Published in Kāvyamālā Series, No. 93, Bombay, 1911. Earlier editions appeared in the Jaina Śāstra Kathāsaṃgraha and Caritrasaṃgraha, Ahmedabad 1884.

***Pāṇḍava-Purāṇa*:** Also known as the Jaina *Mahābhārata* it was written by Śubhacandra (q.v.) in AD 1551. In the opening verses the author of this poem makes salutation to the celebrated Ācāryas Kundakunda, Samantabhadra, Pūjyapāda, Akaṅlanka, Jinasena, and Guṇabhadra. There is also a second *Pāṇḍava-Purāṇa* in 18 Sargas by Vādicandra.

Paṇḍitarahalli: Findspot of a Jain inscription of AD 1150 in the Tumkur taluk of the Tumkur district in Karnataka which mentions the reconstruction of a dilapidated Jina temple at the time of Hoysala Narasiṃha I. It also mentions the Jain Gaṇḍavimuktadeva of Pustaka-gaccha, Deśīgaṇa, Kondakunda-anvaya and Mūla-saṅgha. *Epigraphia Carnatica* XII, Tumkur No. 38.

Pāṇḍuka: Forest encircling the Meru (q.v.) at its highest level. It is itself encircled by railings and contains mansions. There are four crescentic slabs in the four directions, each a hundred *yojanas* in length. The one in the north is called Pāṇḍukaśilā. At the centre of this slab is a throne and two other seats. The throne is meant for the consecration of the infant Tīrthaṃkara from the Bharata region by the Indras—Saudharma and Aiśāna. The three other slabs, known respectively as Pāṇḍukambala-śilā, Rakta-śilā and Raktakambala-śilā meant for the consecration of the infant Tīrthaṃkaras from Apara Videha, Airāvata, and Pūrva-Videha regions. In the east of the forest near the *culika* or crest there is a very large circular palace named Lohita, occupied by Soma, the Lokapāla of the eastern horizon. Likewise there are three other places—Anjana in the south, Haridrā in the west and Pāṇḍuka in the north—inhabited by Yama, Varuṇa, and Kubera. The Pāṇḍuka forest also has in each direction four Jinendraprāsādas, each 100 *krosas* long and 75 *krosas* high.

Paṇhā-vagaranaim: See *Praśnavyākaraṇa*.

Pāñjarāpolas: Shelters for animals. Various kinds of birds and animals are looked after in the Pāñjarāpolas. The sick animals are given treatment and medicine. The Pāñjarāpolas or Piñjrāpols are typically Jain institutions.

Paṇṇagadevī: See Kandarpā.

Pannavaṇā: See *Prajñāpanā*.

Pāpa: One of the nine fundamentals of Jainism which comprises sinful acts of eighteen kinds: *hiṃsā* (violence), *asatya* (untruthfulness), *adattadāna* (stealing), *abrahmacarya* (sensualism), *parigraha* (attachment), *krodha* (anger), *māna* (egoism), *māyā* (hypocrisy), *lobha* (greed), *rāga* (personal attachment), *dveṣa* (hatred) *kleśa* (quarrelsomeness), *abhyakhyāna* (scandals), *paiśunya* (gossiping), *paraparivāda* (telling ill of others), *rati-arati* (sexuality), *māyā-mṛṣa* (sinful acts under the pretext of goodness) and *mithyādarśanaśalya* (ascribing reality to unreal) respectively. There are eighty-four consequences of sin. It has evil effects on knowledge, intellect, sight and sense organs. It affects beings to be born in the next incarnation in many ways. It also results in personal lightness of many kinds, in the loss of bodily strength and in various deformities in the human body. Certain sins condemn the soul that commits them to be born in next life in the class of degraded species. Other sins prevent the soul from acquiring the full number of powers and senses of the class to which it is born. The actions of mind, speech and body continually produce certain subtle *karma* (q.v.) matters which pour themselves into the *jīva* (q.v.) and thereby come into contact with its passions. These passions are collectively called *kaṣāya* (q.v.). They act like viscous substances in retaining and impouring *karma* matter. They consist of four sins—anger, conceit, intrigue and greed (*krodha, māna, māyā* and *lobha*). Each of these is taken into account from four viewpoints, namely *anantānubandhī* (when the sin is cherished throughout thc whole life), *apratyākhyāna* (when it is cherished for a year), *pratyākhyāna* (when it is cherished only for four months) and *sañjavalana* (when it is cherished for a while). Beside these sixteen categories of *kaṣāyas* there are nine others, making a total of twenty-five. These tie human beings to the cycle of rebirth. The *āsravas* are also conducive to sin. The *bhāvāsravas* (q.v.) are generally of five kinds, namely, delusion (*mithyātva*), want of control (*avirati*), inadvertence (*pramāda*), activities of the body, mind, and speech (*yoga*), and passions (*kaṣāya*).

Pāpabuddhi Dharmabuddhi Kathānaka: The story of an evil-minded king and a pious minister. The former who believed in power and wealth was going to his doom while the latter by virtue of his pious deeds was going to have a great spiritual and material upliftment. Finally a monk enlightened both of them as to their destinies in their former incarnations, and both the king and his minister became Jain monks. Its date and author are not known. It was edited and translated into Italian by R. Lovarini in *Giornale della Societa Asiatica Italiana,* III, 94-127. Two recessions of the story in Sanskrit prose, one of these entitled *Kāmaghaṭakathā*, have been edited by Hiralal Hamsaraj, Jamnagar, 1909.

Paramāṇu: See Atomism, Ajīva, *Pudgala*.

Paramāra Bhoja: Though an ardent follower of Brahmanical Hinduism, Paramāra Bhoja who started ruling from about AD 1000 was a patron of Jain saints, scholars and establishments. According to the *Prabandhacintāmaṇi*, under the influence of the Jain writer Dhanapāla, he gave up hunting. A Sravanabelgola inscription says that the Jain monk Prabhācandra was honoured by Bhoja of Dhārā. Another inscription from Dubkund describes him as patron of the Jain scholar Śāntisena. Jain scholars like Amitagati, Śrīcandra, Nayanandin, Nemicandra, Śrutakīrti, etc., were based in Bhoja's capital Dhārā and many of them were directly patronized by him. Later Paramāra kings were also patrons of Jain scholars and many great Jain authors wrote their works in Dhārā.

Parameṣṭhins: Beings who are supposed to have attained the ideal of Jina (q.v.). The term *parameṣṭhin* means 'the supreme one'. There are five such beings—*siddha, arhat* (Tīrthaṃkara), *ācārya, upādhyāya,* and *sādhu*—collectively called *pañca-parameṣṭhins* who are objects of worship. An omniscient being who has conquered *saṃsāra*, that is, the cycle of births and deaths is called the *siddhaparameṣṭhin* (q.v.).

The *arhat* or *Tīrthaṃkara-parameṣṭhins* (q.v.) represent a lower stage than the former. They are embodied souls who have attained omniscience, but have not yet discarded the body. In one sense they are superior: they are great teachers, who maintain their human form for the sake of the benefit of the world leading human beings to the path of salvation. The remaining three *parameṣṭhins* are the *ācārya, upādhyāya*, and *sādhu* who do not, however, represent the stage of complete liberation, but their role is otherwise very important. The *ācārya-parameṣṭhin* (q.v.) is the head of the saints and performs important religious functions. The *upādhyāya-parameṣṭhins* (q.v.) are teaching saints while the *sādhu-parameṣṭhins* (q.v.) are great souls and illustrate through their conduct the great path of salvation.

***Paraparivāda*:** See *Pāpa*.

Parasnāth: Jain site in Bijnor district wherefrom remains of a shrine have been discovered.

Parasnath Hill: Sammeda-śikhara of the Jain tradition where most Tīrthaṃkaras had their *nirvāṇa*. It is in the Hazaribagh district, near Gomoh railway station. There is a Digambara shrine on the top of this hill.

Paravāra: Important Digambara Jain mercantile caste of north and west India. The Paravāras seem to be originally Rajputs and associated with the Poravāḍas (q.v.). Paravāras are also found among the Hindus. They are divided into two endogamous sections, Athasake and Causake. The former does not permit the marriage of persons related more nearly than eight degrees, while the latter permits it beyond four degrees. The former has evidently higher status. Among the Paravāras, Caranāgaras or Samaiyās (qq.v.) form a separate sectarian Jain group. The Binaiyikyās (q.v.) also form an inferior group of the Paravāras.

Parbhani Plate: Dated śaka 888 (AD 966) of the time of Arikeśari III of Vemulavāda, this inscription refers to the village Vanikaṭupula given to Somadevasūri, disciple of Nemideva and grand-disciple of Yaśodeva belonging to the Gauḍa Saṅgha. It also refers to a Jain temple of the name of Śubhadhāma Jinālaya built by Arikeśari's father.

Pareshnath: Jain site in the Bankura district, West Bengal, as the place-name in itself suggests. A ruined temple and a broken Pārśvanātha image in three fragments are illustrative of its ancient Jain heritage. The total height of the image is about 7 feet. Made of black chlorite, it is in *kāyotsarga* on a double lotus under the canopy of a seven-hooded serpent. There is on the either side of the leg an attendant on a lotus with a kneeling devotee in front. Miniature Tīrthaṃkaras are on the back slab in two rows.

***Parigrahatyāga Pratimā*:** Divesting oneself of wealth by dividing one's property among heirs and training oneself generally to bear the hardship of asceticism.

Parikṣāmukhasūtra: See Māṇikyanandin.

***Pariṇāmikī*:** That which obstructs receiving knowledge from experience, a constituent of the *jñānāvaraṇīya* (q.v.). It is an obstruction arising from *Ghātin-karma* (q.v.).

***Parīṣaha*:** Visiting afflictions or sufferings which, when confronted by a Nirgrantha ascetic, are to be endured for the sake of non-swerving from the path (*mārgacyavana*) and for achieving the stages of liberation. The *Tattvārdhādigama Sūtra* describes 22 kinds of Parīṣaha. The term Parīṣaha implicitly stands for a visiting suffering and thus it is not the consequence of a self-inflicted or self-imposed affliction. It is therefore not generated by an ascetic's own volition. For instance, hunger due to fasting under a deliberate vow cannot be termed *kṣudhā*-Parīṣaha, but when a monk owing to some special circumstance is unable to get his routine food and has to suffer from hunger, this eventuality is a Parīṣaha. The commentary on *Tattvārtha* IX.9 states that five ascending *karmas* generate Parīṣaha which are *jñānāvaraṇa* (cognition-obstructing), *vedanīya* (sensorial), *darśana-mohanīya* (faith-deluding), *cāritra-mohanīya* (conduct-deluding), and *antarāya* (obsturctional).The Parīṣahas are *kṣut* (hunger), *pipāsā* (thirst), *śīta* (cold), *uṣṇa* (hot), *daṃśa-maśkaka* (insect bite), *nāgneya* (nakedness) *strī* (sex-urge), *yācanā* (begging), *caryā* (continuous walking), *niṣadyā* (continuous sitting), *śayyā* (resting on hard earth), *ākrośa* (abuse), *roga* (disease), *tṛṇasparśa* (thorn-priks), *mala* (impurities), *satkārapuraṣkāra* (disrespect), *vadha* (beating), *alābha* (disappointment), *prajñā* (non-appreciation of learning), *ajñāna* (ignorance), and *adarśana* (failures).

***Pariśiṣṭaparvan*:** Also known as *Sthavirāvali-carita*, 'Lives of the Series of the Elders', it is an appendix to the *Triṣaṣṭiśālākāpuruṣacaritra* of Hemacandra (q.v.), written by Hemacandra himself. It treats the history of the Dasapūrvis, i.e. earliest teachers of Jainism who were all knowers of the Pūrvas (q.v.) and contains the life-stories of the elders (Sthaviras, Theras), the disciples of Mahāvīra. Their legends are taken from the earlier works especially from those of Haribhadra. Apart from numerous stories there are also some historical gleanings and biographical materials. Ed. H. Jacobi, Bib. Ind., Calcutta, 1891; extracts trans. into German by J. Hertel, Leipzig 1908.

Parokṣa: See Pramāṇa.

Par-Śāntinātha: Eleventh-century Śāntinātha image found in a village called Par in Purulia which is now in the Indian Museum, Calcutta. It is 2 feet in height, standing in *kāyotsarga* on lotus. Rows of the other Tīrthaṃkaras are distributed equally on each side over the trefoil.

***Pārśvābhyudaya*:** Poetic life-story of Pārśvanātha (q.v.) composed by Jinasena II (q.v.) who wrote the *Ādi Purāṇa* (q.v.) in the ninth century. In this poem the entire *Meghadūta* has been incorporated by inserting one or two lines from Kālidāsa in each verse while Jinasena composed the rest. Ed. with the commentary of Mallinātha and with a literal English translation by K.B. Pathak, Poona, 1894; ed. with a com. by Yogirāt Paṇḍitācārya, Nirnaya Sagar Press, Bombay, 1909.

Pārśvanātha: The twenty-third Tīrthaṃkara who, according to the *Kalpasūtra*, was the son of Aśvasena, king of Vārāṇasī, by his wife Vāmā. We are told that he led the householder's life up to the age of thirty and then renounced the world. From some late texts we learn that he married Prabhāvatī. The *Kalpasūtra* says that after practising austerities for 83 days he obtained omniscience. After that he remained a *kevalin* for 70 years and passed away at the age of 100 on the summit of the Sammeya mountain. In *Uttarādhyayana* XXII is recorded a conversation between Keśī and Indrabhūti, and from the words of the former we learn that Pārśva enjoined only four vows and allowed only an upper and under-garment. The *Bhagavatī* more than once refers to Pārśva's followers among whom were, besides Keśin and Gāṅgeya, Kaliyaputta, Mehila, Kasava, and Ānandarakkhiya. According to *Ācārāṅga*, Mahāvīra's parents too were followers of Pārśva. Many lay-disciples, male and female, are mentioned in the *Sūtrakṛta*, *Nāyādhamma*, and *Nirayāvali*. The Buddhist *Sāmaññaphala-sutta* has mistakenly attributed to Mahāvīra the doctrines of Pārśva. He made four vows binding on the members of his community not to take life, not to lie, not to steal, and not to own property. To these Mahāvīra added a fifth—not to indulge in sensual pleasure. Pārśva flourished about 800 BC, 250 years before Mahāvīra. Temples dedicated to Pārśva and his images in stone and metal are abundant. His emblem is a snake with three, seven, or eleven hoods. This symbol has a legend. He saved a serpent from being burnt by an ascetic named Katha and the serpent was reborn as King Dharaṇendra (q.v.) of the Nāgas. This Dharaṇendra was the attendant of Pārśva, his female attendant was Padmāvatī. The carrier of his fly-whisk was known as Ajitarāja and the *devadaru* or *dhātakī* was his sacred tree. The number of poetic life-stories of Pārśva is large. The *Pārśvanātha-caritra* by Bhavadeva Sūri, who probably wrote in AD 1255, tells with exceptional wealth of detail not only the life-story of this saint in his last incarnation but also in his previous nine existences. Other *Pārśvanātha-caritras* are written by Vādiraja (AD 1025), by Māṇikyacandra (AD 1217), by Sakalakīrti, by Padmasundara and by Udayavīra Gaṇin. An earlier work is *Pārśvābhyudaya*, a poetical life-story of Pārśvanātha by Jinasena who wrote the *Ādīpurāṇa* in the ninth century.

Pārśvanātha-basti: The one in Sravanabelgola with the full unit of a *garbhagṛha*, an *ardha-maṇḍapa*, a *nava-raṅga* and a front porch with a 4.5 m tall image is the loftiest on the Candragiri. The second Pārśvanātha-basti is at Heggere in the Hassan district. Built in black stone, it is a fine Hoysala structure with a *garbhagṛha, ardha-maṇḍapa,* and *nava-raṅga* all well preserved. The Pārśvanātha-basti at Hosaholahu, district Mysore, dated AD 1198, is one of the oldest in the Hoysala period, but is rather dilapidated.

***Pārśvanātha-Caritra*:** Life-story of Pārśvanātha (q.v.) composed by Bhavadeva Sūri in AD 1255. It not only deals with the life of the Jina in his last incarnation but also with his previous nine existences. Within the frame of Pārśva's life-history numerous stories, fables and fairy-tales are inserted. Some are from secular narrative works. The *Pārśvanātha-carita* also contains many gnomic sayings on morality and worldly wisdom. Ed. Haragovindadas and Becaradas, Benares, 1912. An analysis of the work is given by M. Bloomfield, *The Life and Stories of the Jaina Saviour Pārśvanātha,* Baltimore, 1919. Other *Pārśvanātha-Caritras* were written by Vadiraja (AD 1025), Guṇacandra (AD 1100), Māṇikacandra (AD 1217), Sakalakīrti (fifteenth century), Padmasundra (AD 1565), and Udayavīra Gaṇin (late-medieval, qq.v.).

Pārśvanātha Temples: Among numerous temples dedicated to Pārśvanātha, those situated in Bijolia, Bikaner, Dhar, Ghumli, Jaisalmer, Khajuraho, Kumbharia, Pali, Phalodhi, Ranakpur, Sadri, and Trilokpur deserve special mention.

Pārśva Yakṣa: See Dharaṇendra.

***Paryāya*:** Term denoting changing modes in Jainism. The technical meaning attributed to this word in

Jain philosophy is distinct from that of other systems. The properties, peculiarities and states of a substance which originate and perish, and undergo change, are called *paryāyas*. Hemacandra has used the word in the sense of all the properties such as qualities, actions, etc., of a substance or *dravya* (q.v.). In the Jain texts both the words *guṇa* (q.v.) and *paryāya* are used, sometimes interchangeably. Kundakunda, Umāsvāti, and Pūjyapāda believe that the two words have clearly distinct meanings, while Akalaṅka maintains that there is an identity as well as distinction between them, a position followed by Amṛtacandra as also by Siddhasena. Haribhadra accepted the thesis of identity of meaning between the two words. It appears that in the earlier Jain works the two were used indiscriminately, but later writers wanted to make their positions clear and started a discussion as to whether they were identical or different in meaning. Likewise the Jain writers debated on the question as to whether *guṇa* and *paryāya* on the one hand and *dravya* on the other are identical with or different from one another. See Dravya, Guṇa, Quality, Substance.

***Paryuṣaṇa*:** Most sacred day of fasting. According to the Digambaras *paryuṣaṇa* lasts every year for ten days from the fifth to the fourteenth day of the bright half of the month of Bhādrapada in which religious assemblages are held, scriptures are recited and the people are enlightened on the importance of *daśadharma* or ten reflections which is why *paryuṣaṇa* is known as *daśa-laksaṇa-pūjā*. A few fast all the ten days, while many eat once a day during this period. The last day, *anantacaturdaśī*, is regarded as particularly sacred. Among the Śvetāmbaras, *paryuṣaṇa* lasts for eight days, beginning with the twelfth or the dark half of Śrāvaṇa and ending on the fifth of the bright half of Bhādrapada. It is meant for the expiation of sin. People observe fasts with varying strictness, and go to *upāśraya* (q.v.). Some people observe *poṣadha* (q.v.). The last day, known as *samvatsarī*, is the most solemn day of all. Apart from fasting, people greet each other and ask forgiveness for any injuries inflicted during the past year, and letters are written to friends at a distance asking their forgiveness also.

***Pāsanāha-Cariu*:** Also known as *Pāsapurānu* it is an Apabhraṃśa poem by Padmakīrti composed in AD 942. It deals with the life of the twenty-third Tīrthaṃkara in eighteen Sandhis, equal to more than 3,300 *ślokas*.

Patadkal: Temple site in the Bijapur district. Among the Jain shrines of this place the Virupākṣa temple is very important from architectural point of view.

Pataini Devi Temple: Flat-roofed Jain shrine at Pithaora, district Satna which is ascribed to AD 900.

Pātāla: Attendant Yakṣa of Anantanātha (q.v.). He has three faces and six arms. His vehicle is a dolphin. According to the Śvetāmbara tradition he holds a goad, spear, bow, rope, plough, and fruit. In addition he bears a canopy of a three-hooded snake. According to the Digambara tradition he holds a lotus, sword, noose, mongoose, fruit, and rosary. He seems to be the presiding spirit of the Nāga world (Pātāla denotes nether world ruled by the Nāga King Ananta in Hindu tradition) and the plough is suggestive of his agricultural affiliation.

Patan: Anahilwara in Gujarat is a celebrated Jain site. In AD 1119 Daṇḍanāyaka Kapardin built here a Jain temple. King Kumārapāla built at Patan the Kumāra-vihāra sacred to Pārśvanātha, with 24 *devakulikas*. The Vanarāja-vihāra at Patan, which is also known as Pañcasara Pārśvanātha temple (q.v.), was built by Vanarāja Cāpotkaṭa. A good number of illustrated Jain manuscripts were prepared in this city.

Patancheru: Ancient Poṭlaceruvu, a Jain centre close to Hyderabad, Andhra Pradesh.

Pathari: A village in Jhalna district, Madhya Pradesh, which contained a few Jain temples and images.

Patna: Village in Sagar district, Madhya Pradesh, which has yielded a few Jain images.

Patodi's Temple: Jain shrine at Jaipur artistically interesting especially for its wall paintings illustrating scenes from Jain mythology.

***Pātrakeśarī-Stotra*:** An elaborate hymn in praise of Jina Mahāvīra in 50 stanzas composed by Vidyānanda (q.v.) alias Vidyānandin Pātrakeśarin, Published in Digambara Jaina Granthabhandara, Kashi I.

***Pātra Parikṣā*:** See Vidyānanda.

Pattana: Also known as Anahilapura, it is situated in the Mahesana district of Gujarat. It is the greatest Śvetāmbara centre of Gujarat. Medieval temples of Ariṣṭanemi, Śāntinātha, etc., of this place have been mentioned by Jinaprabha.

***Paṭṭāvalis*:** Lists of teachers, Sthaviras and their schools, edited or extracted by J. Klatt, A.F.R. Hoernle, etc., in *Indian Antiquary*, XI.245ff., 293ff; XIX.233ff.; XX.341ff.; XXI.57ff.; XXIII.169ff.

***Paumacariya*:** Prakrit epic (Sanskritized *Padmacarita*), the Jain *Rāmāyaṇa*, composed by Vimala Suri, 530 years after the demise of Mahāvīra according to the information given by the poet himself, in pure Jain Mahārāṣṭrī and Āryā metre, told in 118 cantos. The story of Rāma is told in such a way or to fit in with the Jain tradition. The main details of Vālmīki's *Rāmāyaṇa* are followed but the perspective is different. Vimala's work served as a model for all the later adaptations of the Rāma legend among the Jains. Raviṣena's *Padmapurāṇa* (q.v.) is a slightly extended recension of the *Paumacariya*. Later adaptations of the Rāma legend are to be found in Parvan 68 of the *Uttarapurāṇa* and in Hemacandra's *Triṣaṣṭiśalākāpuruṣacarita*, Parvan 7 of which is called *Jaina-Rāmāyaṇa*. In AD 1596 Devavijayagaṇin, a pupil of Rājavijaya Sūri, wrote a *Rāmacaritra* in prose. Svayambhū (q.v.) like Vimala and Raviṣena wrote on the Rāma story. The name of his work is *Paumacariyu* which is written in Apabhraṃśa language. *Paumacariya*, ed. H. Jacobi, Bhavnagar 1914; ed. Muni Puṇyavijaya, with Hindi trans. by S.M. Vora, Prakrit Text Society, 1962, 1968.

***Paumacariyu*:** See Svayambhū.

***Paumasiri-Cariu*:** Poem in Apabhraṃśa written probably in the twelfth century by Dhāhila which in four Sandhis narrates the life of a female devotee to illustrate the evil results of deceitful conduct.

Pāvā: Place of Mahāvīra's demise. It is modern Pāvāpurī in the Nalanda district of Bihar.

Pāvāgiri: Situated in the Panch Mahals district of Gujarat this place is mentioned in the *Tīrtha-vandana-saṃgraha* as a Jain *tīrtha* sacred to Pārśvanātha.

Pedda Tumbalam: Jain centre near Adoni in Andhra Pradesh wherefrom vestiges of Jain sculptures have been found.

Panugonda: Situated in the Anantapur district, Andhra Pradesh, this place is known for its Pārśvanātha temple and has yielded a few Jain antiquities.

Peramādi Caityālaya: One of the most prominent Jain temples at Lakshmeśwar in the Dharwar district of Karnataka. It was probably built during the time of the Western Gaṅgas.

Pethaḍa: A Jain merchant of Gujarat, son of Deda (q.v.), who hailed from Avanti during the rule of the Vāghelas. He was a disciple of Dharmaghoṣasūri on whose advice he built 84 Jain shrines in different parts of India. The temple of Devagiri with an image of Mahāvīra was completed by him in AD 1277. Pethaḍa also built at Śatruñjaya a temple of Śāntinātha. His achievements are recorded in a fourteenth-century work called *Upadeśataraṅgiṇī*.

***Pethaḍa-Rāsa*:** Composed in Gujaratī about AD 1300, it tells about the merchant Pethaḍa who led a mass pilgrimage from Patna to Śatruñjaya in Saurāṣṭra.

Phalodhi: Ancient Phalavardhika, a Jain *tīrtha* in Marwar, where the remains of a temple of the Cāhamana period have been found. A shrine sacred to Pārśvanātha was built here in about AD 1147. It was destroyed by the Muslims but subsequently renovated.

Phalodhi Inscription: See Bijolia Rock Inscription.

Phalavardhika: Situated in the Nagaur district of Rajasthan, this place has been referred to in Jinaprabha's *Vividhatīrtha-kalpa* as a Jain *tīrtha* sacred to Pārśvanātha.

Physiology: Human anatomy, structure of human body and the bodily functions are explained in the *Taṇḍulaveyāliya*. In scattered passages of the *Ṭhāṇa* we come across the question of the age limit in connection with the reproductive power of men and women, the question of miscarriage, the shape and function of the uterus, six different ways of joining the bones, six different kinds of shape of the body, and many other allied subjects. In the *Viyāhapannatti* we come across the description of the embryo as the product as well as the cause, the function of the sperm in the womb, the relative contribution of the father and mother to the shape of the body of the offspring, dislocation of the embryo, and kindred topics. The *Paṇṇavanā* is also a valuable treatise in which the structure of the human body, bodily functions like breathing, etc., sexual life, different senses and their materiality, the application of inner senses like speech, etc., have been dealt with.

In the *Sūyagaḍa* III.2 we have a significant passage relating to embryology wherein it is stated that the first food an embryo takes in the womb consists of the menstrual blood of the mother together with the sperm of the father. In the next stage of its development the embryo absorbs the essence of the food taken by the mother since it is inextricably connected with her by two tubes, one of which is for breathing and the other for nutrition. This has been elaborated in scattered passages of the *Ṭhāṇa*, *Viyāha-pannatti*, and *Taṇḍulaveyāliya* in which it is stated that the flesh, blood, and brain come from the mother and bones, marrow, hair, and nails from the father and that the sperm lives in the womb from one to twelve hours. The circulation of blood within the body is performed by the heart through different types of veins. A human body has seven hundred nerve-channels, of which fourteen are the most important. The movement of the body is caused by the winds which are of five kinds. The embryo in the womb is caused by the sperm of the semen through a series of chemical actions and reactions. The body begins to take its shape in the third month and it gets more or less complete in the fourth month. The major and connecting bones, veins, nails and hair grow in the sixth month. The *Sūyagaḍa* passage in question runs as follows: 'A man and a woman combine in a cunnus, which are produced by their *karma* and there they deposit their humours. Therein are born souls of different men, viz., of those born in Karmabhūmi or Akarmabhūmi or in the minor continents, of Āryas and barbarians, as women, men or eunuchs, according to the semen and blood of the mother and the other circumstances (contingent of their coming to existence). . . . Gradually increasing and attaining to the proper dimensions of a foetus they come forth from the womb. . . . As long as they are babies they suck the mother's milk; but when they grow older, they eat boiled rice or gruel or both movable and immovable beings.' SBE, XLV.393. As regards the bodily functions, in the *Viyāhapannatti* it is said that the frequency of breathing is the same with the embryo as it is with the fully developed man. The intervals of breathing vary from animal to animal according to *Pannavanā* 7. From the *Taṇḍulaveyāliya* it is learnt that the human being has 700 veins. Schubring (*DJ* 142) writes: 'Starting from the navel 160 each extend upwards, downwards into the legs, downwards into the abdomen, and horizontally; 25 each contain mucus and gall, 10 contain sperm. Furthermore, there are 900 sinews, 500 muscles, 900 vessels, 9.9 million hairpores, not counting the hair of the skull and the beard, and 33 million including the latter. Some figures concerning women and hermaphrodites slightly differ, with 670 and 680 veins respectively and 470 and 480 muscles respectively. Moreover, we learn that the male is furnished with five and the female with six inner organs (*kodha*) and with the former we find 9 and with the latter 11 apertures.' From the same text it is also learnt that of the six ways of joining the bones, it is only the *chevaṭṭha*-joint which pertains to human beings. (See Embryology.)

***Piṇḍa Niryukti*:** Prakrit *Piṃda Nijjuti*, often spoken of as the fourth Mūlasūtra (q.v.), with corresponding texts like *Oha* (*Ogha*) *Nijjutti*, and *Pakkhi* or the *Pakṣika-Sūtra*, which treat of the pious life and of the subjects of discipline. It gives elaborate rules with regard to food and its collection. The *Piṃda* and *Oha* are ascribed to Bhadrabāhu, and are sometimes counted among the *Chedasūtras* (q.v.). Published in Devchand Lalbhai Jaina Pustakoddhara, Bombay, 1918 and Āgamodaya, Bombay, 1919.

Pindwara: A brass image of Ṛṣabhanātha with an inscription of Samvat 744, corresponding to AD 687, from Pindwara in Sirohi district, Rajasthan, and discovered at the fort of Vasantgadh, is now preserved in the local Mahāvīra temple. From this rather damaged inscription it is known that one Droṇoraka Yaśodeva had the Jina image built by a sculptor whose name was Śivanāga. In ancient times it was known as Piṇḍāravālaka and this name occurs in an epigraph from Ranakpur dated VS 1496. *Archaeological Survey of India*: *Annual Report*, 1936-7, 122.

Piśācas: See Vyantara.

Pithaora: See Pataini Devi Temple.

Pitrad: Family spirits called 'Fathers' by the Jains. The word comes from Pitṛ.

Pittalhāra: Notable temple of the Dilwara (q.v.) group on Mount Abu constructed by Bhīma Shāh in the fourteenth century. It is dedicated to Ṛṣabha or Ādinātha. It follows the usual Nāgara plan of western India and contains a *garbha-gṛha*, *gūḍha-maṇḍapa*, and *nava-caukī*. It enshrines a massive brass image of Ādinātha weighing 4,031 kg. Which is said to have been cast by Deva, son of *sūtradhāra* Maṇḍana.

Podasingidi: An important Jain centre in eighth-century Orissa. Situated in the forest of the Baula Hill ranges in Anandpur subdivision of Keonjhar district the site has yielded interesting Jain images. Unique among these finds are inscribed seated and uninscribed standing images of Ṛṣabhanātha. Among other images there are those of Pārśvanātha, Mahāvīra, and Ambikā.

Poliyad Plate: Now preserved in the Rajkot Museum, this inscription of AD 1056 records a grant of the Cālukya King Bhīma of Gujarat in favour of a Jain monastery situated in the city of Vāyaḍa. *Epigraphia Indica* XXXIII.235ff.

Polygyny: Jain texts mention ancient kings like Bharata, and Seniya who had numerous wives. Śāntinātha, the sixteenth Tīrthaṃkara, had many *mleccha* wives. The first Tīrthaṃkara Ṛṣabha had two wives, Sumaṅgalā and Sunandā. The Jain law allows polygyny under certain conditons. The *Trivarṇikācāra* XI.197 following Manu says: *aprajāṃ daśame varṣe strīprajāṃ dvādaśe tvajet, mṛtaprajāṃ pañcadaśe sadyastvapriyavādinām.* 'One may marry a second time after ten years if the first wife is childless, after twelve years if she has only daughters, after fifteen years if her children die after birth, and immediately if she is quarrelsome.' But such considerations had little to do with polygamous marriages. Moreover, though the *Trivarṇikācāra śloka* is borrowed from the *Manusmṛti*, childlessness or bearing only female children, etc., have nothing to do with the Jain ideal of life, because in Jainism salvation does not depend on having sons and grandsons. In fact, among the Jains, as also among most Hindus, rich people regarded plurality of wives as a proof of their wealth, reputation, and social position. The first wife had the highest prestige and she was called *dharmapatnī*. Others were *bhogapatnīs*, wives of pleasure.

Ponna: A contemporary of Ādi Pampa (q.v.), one of the most celebrated Kannaḍa poets, whose chief claim to fame is *Śānti Purāṇa*, the life history of the sixteenth Tīrthaṃkara who is said to have ruled over Hastināpura and held suzerainty all over India.

Ponnugunda: Modern Hungund in the Bijapur district of Karnataka which contained three eleventh-century temples known respectively as Tribhuvanatilaka-Jinālaya, Mahāsrimanta-vasadi and Arasara-basadi.

Popular Deities: In the list of popular deities recorded under the heading of *devatā-vijaya*, the *Aṅgavijjā* of the fourth century records the names of Sura, Gandharva, Vasu, Yakṣa, Pitara, Preta, Āditya, Aśvins, Soma, Candra, Graha, Baladeva, Vāsudeva, Śiva, Vaiśravaṇa, Varuṇa, Skanda, Viśākha, Kumāra, Agni, Maruta, Sāgara, Nadī, Indrāgni, Brahmā, Indra, Upendra, Kāma, Giri, Yama, Rātri, Divasa, Airāni, Śrī, Pṛthivī, Ekanāsā, Navamikā, and Nāgī. Apart from these deities the same text mentions the goddesses of vegetation (Vanaspati-devatā), of hills (Parvata-devatā), of seas (Samudra), rivers (Nadī), wells (Kūpa), tank (Taḍāga), and ditch (Palvala). Then we have the goddesses of direction (Diśā), of intellect (Buddhi), of creepers (Latā), of objects (Vastu) and of city (Nagara). Then the goddesses of the crematorium (Śamśāna), of a place of voiding (Varca) and of the dung-hill (Ukkurudika) have been added. Another list mentions to Hrī, Śrī, Lakṣmī, Kīrti, Medhā, Smṛti, Dhṛti, Dhī, Buddhi, Ilā, Sītā, Vidyā, Vijjatā, Candralekhā, Utkosā, Abbharāyā, Ahodevī, Devī, Devakanyā, Asurakanyā, Indrāgramahiṣī, Asurāgramahiṣī, Airikā, Bhagavatī, Alambuṣā, Miśrakeśā, Menakā, Mṛgadarśanā, Apalā, Anaditā, Airāṇī, Rambhā, Timiśrakeśī, Tidhinī, Śālimālinī, Tilottamā, Citrarathā, Citralekhā, Urvāśī and others. In the *Bṛhatkalpabhāṣya* and *Nāyādhmmakahāo* refer to a few more popular deities, there were separate deities for Aryans (Āryan-devatā) and non-Aryans (Mleccha-devatā). Sītā is mentioned as a deity of harvest, Śiva as the lord of cows, buffaloes and sheep and Vaiśravaṇa as a patron of merchants and rich men. Some foreign goddesses are also in the *Aṅgavijjā* list. Amongst them Apalā is identified with the Greek Pallas Athane, Anaditā with the Avestan, Anahitā, Airāṇī with the Roman goddess Irane, Timiśrakeśī with the nymph Themis and Śālimālinī with Moon-goddess Selene.

Poravāḍa: Important Jain mercantile caste found mainly in Rajasthan and Gujarat. Among them the Śvetāmbaras are more numerous than the Digambaras. There are Poravāḍas among the Hindus as well. They have 24 *gotras*: Caudhuri, Kālā, Dhanaghaḍa, Ratanāvata, Dhanyautyā, Mājavaryā, Davakarā, Bhādalya, Seṭhyā, Kāmalyā, Udhiyā, Bankhaṇḍa, Bhūta, Pharakyā, Labheparyā, Maṇḍavaryā, Muniyāñ, Ghañṭya, Galiyā, Bhesauṭā, Naveparyā, Dānagaḍh, Mahatā, and Kharaḍyā. Originally there were two sections among the Poravāḍas: Pure, Sorathīya and Kapola. Later, like other Jain mercantile castes they were divided into Viśā (twenties), Daśā (tens) and Pañcā (fives). Eminent Jains of the past such as King Vīradhvala, Vimala Shah, Vastupāla, Tejaḥpala (qq.v.), etc., belonged to this caste.

***Poṣadha*:** Mimetic ritual according to which one has to behave like an ascetic for twenty-four hours in *upāśraya* (q.v.) during the observance of the *paryuṣaṇa* (q.v.).

Poṣadhavrata: See Caritra.

Poygaimalai: Eleven miles west of Tirumangalam in Madurai district this hill is popularly known as Samanar Kovil or the Śramaṇa temple. Relief of a series of Jina sculptures is carved in a natural cave of this hill.

***Prabandhacintāmaṇi*:** Quasi-historical work written by Merutuṅga (q.v.) in AD 1306 which contains a motley collection of stories, legends and anecdotes associated with historical and literary personages. King Bhoja, Vikramāditya and Śilāditya are extolled as patrons of poets and scholars. The author does not care for chronology. He has made Varāhamihira a contemporary of King Nanda of the fourth century BC. Stories about Hemacandra or King Kumārapāla are not far removed from the period of the author and these have some historical value. Ed. Ramacandra Dinanatha, Bombay, 1888; trans. from Sanskrit by C.H. Tawney, Bib. Ind., Calcutta, 1901.

***Prabandhakośa*:** Quasi-historical-biographical work written by Rājaśekhara in AD 1349. It contains

still denoted animate objects and not the soul. But when the latter took the load, mental faculties and actions also had come under the purview of *jīva* or soul that became responsive of all external stimuli in the form of subtle *karma* matter. The Jain theory of *āsrava* thus seems to have some similarity apparently with the behaviourist school of modern psychology.

***Pudgala*:** Matter, also called *mūrta dravya*, which includes everything that is perceptible by the senses. These can be touched and found to be soft or hard, smooth or rough, heavy or light, cold or hot; can be tasted and found to be bitter, sour, pungent, saline or sweet; may smell good or bad; may appear black, blue, yellow, red, and white. Matter constitutes the physical basis of universe, and is divided into four classes—*skandha*, *deśa*, *pradeśa*, and *paramāṇu*. The elements of nature are all gross manifestations of matter, the finest and most subtle form of which is the *paramāṇu* or atom. Two or more such atoms may combine together to form *saṃghāta* or compounds. Even heat, light, shade, and darkness are forms of fine matter, the atoms of which are constantly in motion (*parispanda*), leading to a perpetual succession of integration and disintegration, with a variety of forms and appearances as the result. By the combination of atoms, aggregates are formed which are called *skandha*. These aggregates may range from the smallest molecule of two atoms to the most important and biggest aggregate or *mahāskandha*, represented by the physical universe. Thus the constitution of the physical universe is entirely dependent on the ultimate constituent elements, the *paramāṇus*. Our bodies and objects of nature are such compounds of material atoms. Mind, speech, and breath are also products of matter. The masses of matter constituting the world necessarily have to interpenetrate each other, and the units of the one must be touched by those of others. In this process the units of time are included, placed on the same level with the others and considered constant contraction and expansion of matter stand for different sensitive with the same number of its units. The *paramāṇu* or the ultimate atom cannot be perceived by ordinary senses, so also the minute aggregates or the *skandhas*. Matter or *pudgala* is as real and eternal as the soul, and its total quantity always remains the same in the universe. Etymologically *pudgala* means 'that which is liable to integration and disintegration'. It can be consumed or destroyed as it may decay or alter its form. *Tattvārtha* V.19-24. See Atomism.

Pudur: Findspot of two inscriptions of the time of Vikramāditya VI (AD 1076-1126) in the Mahbubnagar district of Andhra Pradesh. Both the inscriptions have Jain contents. One of them, in addition, mentions a temple of Pārśvanātha, and the other to a Jinālaya named after Pallavas. Andhra Pradesh Archaeological Series, XXII, No. 79. See Pallava Jinālaya.

Pūjera: Śvetāmbara subsect. See Mūrtipūjaka.

Pūjyapāda: Also known as Devanandin, he flourished in the fifth century AD. He was a grammarian and philosopher, whose *Sarvārthasiddhi* is one of the earliest commentaries on the *Tattvārthādhigama* (q.v.). According to Prabhācandra (q.v.) he was also the author of the Sanskrit *Daśabhakti*. His grammar is known as *Jainendra*. His *Siddhipriya-stotra* is a very artificially constructed hymn in which the verses are rhymed in such a way that the same syllables in each of the two consecutive lines have a different meaning. But according to some scholars the author of the *Siddhipriya-stotra*, although known by the name Devanandin, was not Pūjyapāda, but a different personality. Pūjyapāda also composed two didactic poems. *Iṣṭopadeśa* and *Samādhiśataka* (qq.v.) *Sarvārthasiddhi*, published from Kolhapur, 1904; *Daśabhakti*, Nityapāṭha-saṃgraha, Karanja, 1956; *Siddhipriya* edn. in Kāvyamālā Series, VII.

Puli: Modern Huli in the Belgaum district, Karnataka, which had a temple-complex called Māṇikya-tīrtha-basadi.

***Puṃsavana*:** Sacrament done in the eighth month of pregnancy for obtaining a male child. It is a Śvetāmbara ritual.

Puniṣa Jinālaya: Probably the earliest Jain shrine of Dorasamudra dedicated to Pārśvanātha which was built in the eleventh century. The place is modern Halebid in the Hassan district of Karnataka. *Annual Report on Indian Epigraphy*, 1963-4, 361-2.

***Puṇya*:** Meritorious action needed for extinguishing the existing *karma* and to stop its further influx which is one of the nine fundamentals of Jainism. There are nine kinds of *puṇya* and forty-two ways in which the reward of *puṇya* may be reaped. Birth as a human being is itself a reward of merit. The higher reward one obtains when he is born of a high family. Beauty, vigour, strength, happiness, etc., are different forms of reward. More important rewards consist in birth as different categories of gods, but the highest reward which a man can seek is that which leads him to become a Tīrthaṃkara (q.v.). In

Hemacandra's *Yogaśāstra* certain rules of moral behaviour are recorded under the *Caritra* (q.v.) or cessation from doing all that is evil, in which we have an interpretation of the celebrated five vows. Certain external rules of conduct are also included in this category. There is a list of the duties of householders. It is said that no kind of asceticism can be of any good until and unless the mind is purified. When a man learns to look upon all beings with equality he can conquer attachment and hatred. He should think that even the gods are subject to death. The world is full of misery and men are differentiated from one another by the *karma* (q.v.) they acquire individually. Merit consists in the practice of ten virtues which are self-control, truthfulness, purity, chastity, greedlessness, asceticism, forbearance, mildness, sincerity, and empancipation. See Caritra.

***Pupphacūliāo*:** See *Puṣpacūlikā*.

***Pupphiāo*:** See *Puṣpikā*.

Pūraṇa Kassapa: Probably an Ājīvika teacher who was a contemporary of Mahāvīra. In the Jain Aṅga text *Sūyagaḍa* I.1.13 Pūraṇa is represented as an Akriyāvādin, and Śīlāṅka, the commentator on the *Sūyagaḍa* finds in his doctrines some ingredients of the Sāṅkhya. In the *Bhagavatīsūtra* III.141 he has been described as a foolish ascetic. From the *Sāmannaphalasutta* of the Buddhist *Dīgha Nikāya* we learn that according to Pūraṇa when one acts or causes other to act, it is not the soul that acts or causes others to act. The soul is nothing but a passive spectator. In *Aṅguttara Nikāya* III.383ff., Ānanda ascribes part of Gośālas (q.v.) doctrine to Pūraṇa. The latter is said to have maintained the doctrine of six classes of men which also belonged to Gośālas. In the Tamil Jain poem *Nīlakeci* Pūraṇa is clearly described as the leader of the Ājīvikas who expounded the Ājīvika doctrine to *Nīlakeci*. Guṇaratna in his *Tarkarahasyadīpikā* refers to Pūraṇa as the upholder of the doctrine of destiny which is characteristic of Ājīvika philosophy. Buddhaghoṣa insisted on the nakedness of Pūraṇa which is also confirmed by the *Divyāvadāna* in which he is described as a Nirgrantha. Pūraṇa, who it seems, maintained a fatalistic doctrine with tendencies to nihilism came in contact with Makkali Gośāla, a younger teacher with doctrines much the same as his own, and recognizing his own eclipse left his heritage to Gośāla and put an end to his life.

***Purāṇasārasaṃgraha*:** See Dāmanandin.

***Purātanaprabandhasaṃgraha*:** A collection of quasi-historical information especially pertaining to the Turkish rulers, a good number of which was written by one Jinabhadra, disciple of Udayaprabha of the Nāgendra-gaccha, of the thirteenth century. It also mentions facts about the regional rulers of northern India, the Kalacuri King Gāṅgeyadeva, the liberal attitude of Vastupāla towards the Muslims, the enmity between Lakṣmaṇasena and Jayaccandra, as also sacred places associated with Jainism. Ed. Jinavijaya, Calcutta 1936.

Purle: Situated in Shimoga subdivision and district in Karnataka, it is the findspot of an inscription of AD 1112 which refers to one Gaṅga-Jinālaya of Kuruli-tīrtha, modern Purle, by Satyagaṅgadeva and a gift registered in favour of Mādhavacandradeva. There is also a reference to a Caityālaya built at Kuntalapura which appears to be another name of Purle. The Jain temple of this place is mentioned also in another inscription from Purle of AD 1204 belonging to the time of Hoysala Ballāla II. *Epigraphia Carnatica* VII, Shim. 64-5.

***Purudevacampu*:** See Arhaddāsa.

Puruṣadattā: See Mahākālī. She is a Vidyā-devī (q.v.) as well who in Śvetāmbara tradition is described as riding a buffalo and with the conventional attributes. In Digambara tradition she rides a peacock.

***Puruṣārthasiddhyupāya*:** 'The means of attaining the aims of life' composed by Amṛtacandra (q.v.) in AD 904 according to the Digambara Paṭṭāvalī. Ed. in Sanātana Jaina Granthamālā I, Bombay, 1905.

***Pūrva*:** The sacred texts which were composed earlier (*pūrva*). According to tradition Mahāvīra's teachings were first compiled in fourteen texts, called the Pūrvas, meaning the earlier books which are lost. Their names are *Utpāda*, *Agrāyaṇīya*, *Vīryapravāda*, *Jñānapravāda*, *Satyapravāda*, *Ātmapravāda Karmapravāda*, *Pratyākhyāna*, *Vidyānuvāda*, *Kalyāṇa*, *Prāṇavāya*, *Kriyāviśala*, and *Lokavindusāra*. The Śvetāmbaras believe that the Pūrvas are incorporated in the now lost *Dṛṣṭivāda* (q.v.), the twelfth Aṅga. The tradition of these Pūrva texts has created a problem which cannot be very easily solved. Scholars hold that the so-called fourteen Pūrvas might have consisted of traditions handed down orally from teacher to pupil, that some part of this oral tradition might have been compiled by Sthūlabhadra (q.v.) in the Pāṭaliputra Council and that the Council of Valabhi under Devardhi which took place some time between the fifth and the sixth centuries AD made use of the current oral traditions as well as such texts as might have been already reduced to writing. Certain texts divide the substance of Jain teachings into that included within the Aṅga (*aṅgapraviṣṭa*) and that remaining outside the Aṅga (*aṅgabāhira, aṅgabāhya*, q.v.). The roots of the latter (*aṅgabāhira*) are often traced to the lost Pūrvas.

Pūrva-Mīmāṃsā: Apparently the antithesis of Jainism, because it supplies the philosophical justification of Vedic ritualism, the Pūrva-Mīmāṃsā school of philosophy reveals certain characteristics which are in common with Jainism. The Jains subscribe to the Mīmāmṣaka view that the universe has no beginning and no end. It is everlasting, which is why the conception of god or creator of the universe is childish. Like the Mīmāṃsakas, the Jains hold that since a disembodied soul cannot create anything, god needs to have a body as well as the will, capacity and purpose to create. Like that of Mīmāṃsakas the target of the Jain attack is the theistic conception of the Nyāya-Vaiśeṣikas. Like the Mīmāṃsakas, the Jains admit the validity of determinate and indeterminate perception. The Mīmāṃsakas on the other hand do not share with the Jains the idea of transcendental perception. Their sole insistence upon pure empirical perception have been criticised by the Jain logicians like Akalaṅka, Abhayadeva, Hemacandra, etc. The Jains also are not seriously concerned with the Mīmāṃsaka non-perceptual sources of knowledge like comparison (*upamāna*), postulation (*arthāpatti*), and non-perception (*anupalabdhi*).

Puṣkara-Vara: Third island continent. It is divided into inner and outer regions by a circular mountain called Mānuṣottara. In the inner region there are two sets of geographical items. The continent contains *caityālayas* and *pātāla-nagarīs* or underground cities inhabited only by the celestial ones.

***Puṣpacūlikā*:** Prakrit *Pupphaculiāo*, the eleventh of the Upāṅga (q.v.) series which is the fourth part of *Nirayāvali-Suttam*. It contains several stories regarding the destiny of man after death. *Nirayāvalikasūtram* with Candrasena's com., Agamodaya edn., Ahmedabad, 1922.

Puspadanta: See Suvidhinātha.

Puspadanta: See *Ṣaṭkhaṇḍāgama*, *Dhavalā*.

Puṣpadanta: One of the greatest Apabhraṃśa poets who wrote *Mahāpurāṇa*, *Jasaharacariu* and *Nayakumāracariu* (qq.v.) at Mānyakheta under the patronage of the ministers of the Rāṣṭrakūṭa III and his successor. In his *Mahāpurāṇa* he has beautifully delineated the lives of 63 great men while in other two works he has narrated the lives of two other religious heroes. Puṣpadanta belonged to the tenth century AD.

Puṣpa Yakṣa: See Kusuma.

***Puṣpikā*:** Prakrit *Pupphiāo*, the tenth text of the Upāṅga (q.v.) series which is the third part of the *Nirayāvali-Suttam*. It gives an account of ten gods and goddesses who drove earthwards in their heavenly chariots in order to pay homage to Mahāvīra who told Indrabhūti Gautama about their previous history. *Nirayāvalika-sūtram* with Candrasena's com. Āgamodaya edn., Ahmedabad, 1922.

Q

Quadruples: A typical Jain sculpture known as *caumukha* or *caumukhī*, *caturmukha* and *sarvatobhadrikā*. Several such images having the figure of a Tīrthaṃkara on each of the four sides of a stone block have been found at Mathura, one being dated in the year 5, presumably of Kaniṣka. The Sonabhandar cave at Rajgir has post-Gupta *caumukha* in stone having on each of the four faces of a different Jina—Ṛṣabha, Ajita, Sambhava, and Abhinandana. In Sat Deulia in the Burdwan district of West Bengal was discovered a *caturmukha* with Ṛṣabha, Mahāvīra, Pārśva, and Candraprabha on its four sides, all in *kāyotsarga* pose with their respective symbols. Two such *caumukhas* are found in Barkola in Bankura district. The Kadalāya-vasadi or Padmāvatī temple at Hanumakonda in Warangal district, Andhra Pradesh, contains a *caumukha* in granite. Quite a large number of fourfold images in stone and metal installed in different periods of history are still worshipped in many Jain temples all over India. It is often held that the conception of a *caturmukha-pratimā* is based upon the belief that in the circular auditorium in which the Jina delivers his sermon sitting on a dais in the centre, with the audience on all sides, three images of the exact likeness of the Jina were installed so that the listeners, sitting in different directions would be able to see the face of the Jina. But in actual examples, instead of the same Jina, we have the images of four different Jinas.

In some cases the stone blocks themselves are fashioned in the form of miniature shrines, on the four niches of which are carved four Jina images which may be regarded as the precursors of the later *caturmukha* or four-faced shrines. The erection of a *pīṭha* with *śilāpaṭṭa* on each of the four sides of the tree under which the Jina or the Buddha attained enlightenment served as the fundamental conception of the early *caitya*, open on four sides, the *caturmukha* shrine, and the *pratimā-sarvatobhadrikā*. The *Ādi Purāṇa* of Jinasena describes a type of pillar known as the *mānastambha*. At the base of these pillars and in some cases at the top are placed four Jina images. The Kahaum pillar, with an inscription of the Gupta age, shows four Jinas on the top of the four sides. At Deogarh are certain pillars which have variations where figures of subordinate deities are shown. This *caturmukha* concept has assumed an architectural connotation, an illustration of which is found at Ellora in the front court of the Indra-sabhā cave. In Jain *caturmukha* shrines, the sanctum has doors facing four sides and the chief image worshipped is a fourfold Jina image. The early manifestation of the quadruple as is observed in the Indra-sabhā has been developed from a subsidiary adjunct to a shrine self-contained in itself, as at the *caturmukha-basti* in Karkala, Jerosoppa and other places. The Mahāvīra temple at Siddhapura, described as Siddha-Vihāra in Jain texts, and also known as Rai-Vihara, served as a model for the celebrated Dharaṇī-Vihāra of Ranakpur (q.v.) in Rajasthan. Another famous example is the Kharatara-vasahi temple in the Dilwara group of Mount Abu.

Qualities: Unchanging essential characters known as *guṇa* in the Jain philosophical tradition. It is inseparable from substance (q.v.) or *dravya* (q.v.). Anything which has origin, existence and destruction is a substance possessed of some unchanging essential characters or qualities and changing modes known as *paryāya* (q.v.) in Jain terminology. Qualities as existence, enjoyability, substantives, knowability, specific characters and capabilities of possessing forms adhere in substances; they cannot exist by themselves. Experience shows that in all changes there are three elements: (1) that some content appears to remain unchanged; (2) that some new qualities are generated; and (3) that some old qualities are destroyed. The permanent unit is called *dhruva*, the new qualities *utpāda*, and the loss of some old qualities *vyaya*. The nature of a thing is thus neither the absolutely unchangeable, nor momentary and constantly changing. This is why Jainism holds that nothing can be affirmed absolutely, as all affirmations are true only under certain conditions and limitations. Jain writers debated the question whether qualities and changing modes (*paryāya*) on the one hand and substance on the other are identical with, or different from, one another. Systems such as Nyāya-Vaiśeṣika are of the view that the qualities of substance are different from the substance itself. According to them qualities are conceived as inherent in substance and dependent on it, but at the same time are also distinct from substance, because they can by themselves be known and are thus independent realities. The Buddhists hold that changing qualities alone can be perceived and that there is no unchanging substance behind them. The common example of clay and jar may be cited. A thing such as clay is seen to assume various shapes and to undergo diverse changes in the form of jar, pan, etc. But in spite of those changes the clay itself remains permanent. The changes occur only qualitatively. The Buddhists hold that what we perceive as clay is a specific quality and what we perceive as a jar is another quality. Since we cannot perceive any substance apart from quality, and since all changes are by nature qualitative, the conception of any permanent or unchangeable substance is a fiction. The Jains on the other hand hold that it is not true as the Buddhists say that there is no permanent substance, but merely the change of passing qualities. By the assemblage of conditions old qualities in things disappear, new qualities come in, and something remains permanent. Thus in the case of the jar, the clay was lost in a form, generated itself in another and remains permanent in another form. The Jains maintain the relation of identity-cum-difference between substance and quality. They maintain that substance and quality are inseparable inasmuch as the latter cannot exist in itself, but there is also an element of difference in the nature of a substance, in its acquiring new qualities, living the old ones, and maintaining permanent qualities. There are two kinds of character found in every substance, essential and accidental. The essential characters of a substance remain in the substance as long as the substance remains, and it is through the accidental characters that a substance undergoes change or modification. See Dravya, Guṇa, Paryāya, Substance.

R

Rāḍavara: Situated in the Sirohi district, Rajasthan, it is a Jain *tīrtha* sacred to Mahāvīra.

Rāhu: Jyotiṣka or stellar deity conceived by the Jains as a rider of the lion and the bearer of an axe. He has the charge of the south-western quarters. According to the Digambaras his symbol is a flag.

Raidu: Apabhraṃśa poet of the fifteenth century who hailed from Gopagiri, modern Gwalior and composed *Balabhadracarita*, also called *Padmapurāṇa*, and *Yaśodharacarita*. A few other works are also ascribed to him. See *Anekānta* X.377ff.

Raina: Findspot of an eleventh-century Candra-prabha image in Burdwan district which is now in the Asutosh Museum, Calcutta University. It is one of the twin figures carved on a small tablet with an arch-shaped top and stands in *kāyotsarga* on a lotus. The crescent moon emblem is below the figure. The emblem on the other similar figure on the right is indistinct.

Rājagṛha: Modern Rajgir which in ancient times was intimately connected with the activities of Mahāvīra. According to the Jain tradition, it was also the birth-place of Muni Suvrata. A fourfold image of Sambhavanātha has been found in the Sonbhandara cave. It is a standing figure. This cave inscription is in characters of the first or second century and refers to one Muni Vairadeva who died in the 584th year of Mahāvīra's demise, a jewel among the teachers who caused the excavation of two caves for the Jain ascetics with images of Jinas installed therein. The Vaibhara Hill temple of the same place contains a seated figure of Neminātha, the head much mutilated, with a fragmentary inscription in Gupta characters and with two small Jinas on the two sides of the standing figure. There are three other standing Jina figures in three niches which seem to belong to the fourth century. A few more Jina sculptures belonging to the ninth century have also been recovered at Rajgir. *Archaeological Survey of India, Annual Report*, 1905-6, 98, 166; 1926, 125ff.

Rājamalla I: Nephew and successor of Śivamāra II of the main line of the Gaṅga rulers whose date was AD 817-53. He was a patron of Jainism and dedicated a cave to the Jain monks at Vallimalai North Arcot district. This is known through a short inscription in Grantha characters found therein. *Epigraphia Indica* IV, 140.

***Rājapraśnīya*:** Prakrit *Rāyapasaṇaijja*, the second text of the Upāṅga (q.v.) category. The nucleus of the work is a dialogue between King Paesi and the monk Keśin concluding with the conversion of the king. The text is divided into two parts. Agamodaya edition with Malayagiri's commentary, Bombay, 1925.

Rajamalla II: See Baliyur and Narasapura inscriptions.

Rājanagara: Situated in the Udaipur district of Rajasthan this place is regarded as a Jain *tīrtha* associated with the Terapanthī sect.

Rājarāja Jinālaya: See Bhogapuram.

Rājaśekhara: See *Prabandhakośa*.

Rājaśekhara Maladhārin: See *Antara-kathā-saṃgraha*.

Rāja-Vihāra: The Jain shrine at Ajmer which was transformed into Āḍhai-Din-kā-Jhompḍā. The design of the latter shows affinity with quadrangular Jain shrines and their decorated ceiling-patterns.

Rājdighi: Findspot of an eleventh-century Pārśvanātha image in 24-Parganas district, West Bengal. The image is now worshipped as that of Dharma Ṭhākur at a village called Bolbomni on the Matla. The black stone image is in *kāyotsarga* under a canopy formed by a seven-hooded snake. Over the canopy is an umbrella with a drum on either side, below which are garland-carrying Gandharvas. There are *chowri*-bearers on either side of the legs, a snake emblem on the slab between the *chowri*-bearers, and the Jina and miniature Jinas in *dhyāna* pose.

Rajorgarh: Ancient Rājyapura in the Alwar district where an inscription dated vs 979, that is AD 923, has been found which refers to the existence of a Śāntinātha temple, built by the architect Sarvadeva. See Nīlakaṇṭha. *Jaina Śilālekha Saṃgraha*, V, No. 16.

Rajpara: Findspot of an eleventh-century bronze image of Ṛṣabhanātha in the Midnapur district, West Bengal. The image wears *jaṭāmukuṭa* and is in *kāyotsarga* pose having affinities with the bronzes found at Kakatpur in Orissa. It is now in the Indian Museum, Calcutta. A Śāntinātha image of the tenth century of this place is now in the State Archaeological Gallery, West Bengal. This much worn image stands with two *chowri-*

bearers. The pedestal contains an antelope. On two sides are the Navagrahas. A mutilated sculpture of Pārśvanātha, standing in *kāyotsarga* under a snake-hooded canopy, has also been found at this place.

Rajyapura: Modern Rajorgarh in the Alwar district of Rajasthan which contained a tenth-century Śāntinatha temple.

Rakṣābandhana: Festival held in common with the Hindus. The Jains observe it on the full-moon day of Śrāvaṇa. It is said that on this day the ascetic Viṣṇu Kumāra saved the lives of seven hundred Jain monks who were to be sacrificed in the human sacrifice performed by Bali. It is a festival meant for the protection of the culture and institutions of the Jain community.

Rakṣaṇadevī: Eight goddesses of protection, namely, Brahmāṇī, Māheśvarī, Kaumārī, Vaiṣṇavi, Vārāhī, Indrāṇī, Camuṇḍā, and Tripurā and the goddess Ṣaṣthī or Ambā.

Rākṣasa: One of the eight forms of Jain marriage adopted from Brahmanical legal texts with some modification. It is the forcible abduction of a bride, a common practice among Kṣatriyas. This form of marriage is regarded as unethical and sinful. *Trivarṇikācāra* XI.77; Nītivākyāmṛta XXXI.10.

Rākṣasas: Belong to the category of Vyantara-devatās according to the Jain tradition. According to the *Tattvārtha* most of the Rākṣasas cannot be regarded as *duṣṭa vyantaras*, since they have been converted into the creed. Vimala in his *Paumacariya* asks how it is that the petty and insignificant monkeys killed the powerful and aristocratic Rākṣasas who were versed in different sciences and had complete faith in the Jinas. They were not meat-eaters. According to the *Vasudevahiṇḍī*, the Rākṣasas possess a huge body. They cannot tolerate the brightness of sun and they delight at night. They never attack honest persons and heroes. *VH* 135.2-21. In the *Kavalayamālā* 66.4; 67.15 it is said that merchants on their journey to the island of Ratnadvīpa faced dreadful storms created by the Rākṣasas. The feet of the Rākṣasas leave deep footprints—*VH* 135-10. Occasionally they are identified with the tribal peoples like the Pulindas and described as experts in Śabarī-spells.

Rāmabhadra Muni: See Prabuddha-Rauhiṇeya.

Rāmacandra: Pupil of Hemacandra (q.v.) popularly known as *prabandhaśatakartṛ* or author of a hundred treatises, who flourished in Gujarat in the twelfth century. His *Nāṭyadarpaṇa* was composed jointly with Guṇacandra in four chapters. Among the important extant plays of Rāmacandra, the *Satya-Hariścandra*, *Nala-vilāsa*, *Kaumudīmitrānanda* and *Nirbhaya-bhīmavyayoga* may be mentioned. Among his poetical works, the *Kumāravihāraśataka* gives a description of the famous Jina temple built by Kumārapāla at Palan. His *Dravyā-laṅkāra* which he composed jointly with Guṇa-candra (q.v.) is a treatise on philosophy in three chapters. *Nāṭyadarpaṇa*, ed. in Gaekwad's Oriental Series, No. 43, Baroda, 1929. There is also a *Vṛtti* written by the authors themselves. *Satya-Hariścandra*, Ahmedabad, 1924; *Nala-vilāsa*, ed. in Gaekwad's Oriental Series, Baroda, 1926; *Kaumudimitrānanda*, Bhavnagar, 1915; *Nirbhayabhīmavyayoga* Yaśovijaya Jain Series, Varanasi, Vira Samvat 2477; his *Mallikā-makaranda* is only known from the *Nāṭya-darpaṇa*; *Kumāravihāraśataka* and *Dravyā-laṅkāra*, see *Jinaratnakosa* 93, 183.

***Ramacandracarita-Purāṇa*:** See Nāgacandra.

Ramacandra Mumukṣu: See *Kathākośa*.

***Rāmacarita*:** See Paumacariya.

***Rāmadeva*:** A devout Jain who was a *maṇḍaleś-vara*, provincial governor, of Pṛthvīrāja III, the Cāhamāna king of Śākambharī. He arranged a debate in the king's court, in which Jinapati, a saint-scholar of the Kharatara lineage defeated Padmaprabha, another Śvetāmbara teacher belonging to Ukeśa or Upakeśa Gaccha. On this occasion Rāmadeva is said to have spent 16,000 *parutthadrammas*.

Rāmatīrtha: Same as Rāmakoṇḍa, also known as Rāmagiri, in the Vishakhapatanam district of Andhra Pradesh which is connected with Jainism from an early period and has yielded a number of Jain antiquities. It is mentioned by Vimala in the *Paumacariya*, by Raviṣena in his *Padma-purāṇa*, and by Jinasena in his *Harivaṃśa*. The *Bṛhatkathākośa* describes it as situated between Kaliṅgaviṣaya and Āndhraviṣaya. An important Jain epigraph comes from this place which belongs to the time of the Eastern Cālukya King Vimalāditya (AD 1011-22) and mentions his religious teacher Trikālayogī Siddhāntadeva belonging to the Śeṣī-gaṇa, *Annual Report of South Indian Epigraphy*, 1918, App. B, No. 831.

Ranakpur Caturmukha Shrine: Dedicated to Ādinatha, Ādiśvara or Yugādīśvara temple at Ranakpur or Ranpur near Sadari in Mewar. According to an inscription it was constructed by Depāka, the architect, at the order of Dharaṇāka. It covers an area of 3,716 metres and consists of 29 halls containing as many as 420 pillars. The square sanctum has a geometric orderliness. It is located with four openings, each through one of the four walls. Each opening leads to a *raṅga-maṇḍapa* or dancing hall which, in its turn, is connected with a two-storeyed *maṇḍapa* and across this *maṇḍapa* to an impressive portal, also double-storeyed. Along the boundary wall, facing the inner rectangle or square, there is a long row of 86 *deva-kulikās*, chapels for minor deities with turrets. Beyond them are the five *śikharas* of which the largest and most prominent tops the central sanctuary, four others surmount a corner-shrine each, and twenty cupolas each provide a roof over a pillared hall. The interior of the shrines shows a cruciform chamber containing the four-faced (*caturmukha*) marble image.

Ranebennur Inscription: Found at Ranebennur in Dharwar district and dated in śaka 781 (AD 859), this inscription refers to a Jain shrine constructed by one Nagalura Pollabe and is therefore known as Nagula-vasadi. The land gifted by the villagers for the temple was received by Nāganandin Ācārya of the Singlavura-gaṇa. *Karnatak Inscriptions*, 1951, II.14-16.

Ranibandh: Findspot of an eleventh-century mutilated Mahāvīra sculpture in Bankura district, West Bengal. Standing in *kāyotsarga* pose, it is flanked on either side by worn figures of the eight or nine *graha* deities. The emblem is indistinct.

Raṇastambhapura: Situated in the Sawai Madhopur district of Rajasthan, it is mentioned by Siddhasenasūri as a Jain *tīrtha*. See Ranthambhor.

Ranthambhor: Site of a celebrated Jain temple in Rajasthan. King Pṛthvīrāja I, according to the *Munisuvrata-carita* of Candrasūri, showed respect to Jainism by making offerings of golden *kalaśas* to this shrine.

Rani Gumpha: Cave No. 1 of Udayagiri which is exceptionally large, but not of sufficient height. The facade of the two guard-rooms of this cave have received the most exuberant treatment in carvings and sculptural friezes. The panels are also richly carved. The lower storey of the main wing has a running frieze which appears to depict a victorious march. The friezes on the facade of the main wing of the upper storey compare favourably with the reliefs of the gateways of Sanchi.

Ranna: The last of the three 'gems' of Kannaḍa literature, others being Pampa and Ponna (qq.v.). A bangle-seller by caste, Ranna commemorated the traditional history of the second Tīrthaṃkara in his *Ajita Purāṇa*. This poem was composed in AD 993.

Ratanpur Inscriptions: Among three typically Jain inscriptions from Ratanpur in Western Rajasthan, one belonging to the time of Cālukya Kumārapāla (q.v.) records an order of Girijādevī, wife of Punapākṣadeva, the successor of Rājyapāla belonging to the Cāhamānas of Nadol, prohibiting slaughter of animals on some specified dates. Another inscription of AD 1275 records the grant of a piece of land to meet the expenses of the festival of Pārśvanātha in the reign of *mahāmaṇḍaleśvara* Cacigadeva. The third inscription of AD 1290 belonging to the time of Sāmantasiṃha of the Jalor house of the Cāhamānas mentions a grant in favour of a temple of Lord Pārśvanātha of that place. Bhandarkar, *List* No. 1523; Jinavijaya, *Prācīna Jaina Lekhasaṃgraha*, II.201ff.; Nahar, *Jaina Lekha Saṃgraha*, Nos. 935-6.

Rati-Arati: See *Pāpa*.

***Ratnacūḍa Kathā*:** Religious novel, 'Story of Ratnacūḍa' written by Jñānasāgara Sūri who lived in the second half of the fifteenth century. The setting of the novel in Anītipura, a city of rogues ruled by an unjust king, unwise minister and heartless priest—Numerous stories of wickedness are inserted with the help of which the author wants to uphold certain moral values. Edited in Yaśovijaya Series, Bhavanagar, 1917.

***Ratnacūḍarājacarita*:** See Nemicandrasūri.

Ratna Devī: See Sūrya.

Ratnākara, *Ratnākara-Pañcaviṃśatika*: See Vītarāga Stotra.

***Ratnakaraṇḍa Śrāvakācāra*:** See Samantabhadra.

Ratnanandin: Fifteenth-century author of *Bhadrabāhucarita* which, Jacobi thought, preserved a fairly correct tradition. It deals with Bhadrabāhu's (q.v.) prediction about the impending famine in Magadha, his journey to Sravanabelgola where he passed away after designating Viśākha as his successor, Sthūlabhadra's modification of the monastic rules regarding dress, etc., their disapproval by southern monks who were close to Bhadrabāhu, the beginning of a schism in the order and so forth.

Ratnaprabhā: First of the seven lower regions, the others being Śarkarāprabhā, Valukāprabhā, Paṅkaprabhā, Dhūmraprabhā, Tamaḥprabhā, and Mahātamaḥprabhā. The lower worlds are places for the hell-beings (*nāraka*, *nārakī*), but Ratnaprabhā is also the seat of the gods of the Bhvanavasī and Vyantara categories. The Ratnaprabhā region is horizontally divided into a southern and northern half inhabited by demons, spirits, mythical animals and gods of lower categories. Each of the two halves of which the southern one contains some more places than the northern one, is governed by a prince and his counterpart. The pair of the princes are Camara and Bali-Vairocana, Dharaṇa, and Bhūyananda, Veṇudeva and Veṇudāli, Harikānta and Harisaha, Aggisaha and Aggimānava, Puṇṇa and Vasiṭṭha, Jalakantā and Jalappaha, Amiyagai and Amiya-vahana, Velamba and Prabhañjana, and Ghoṣa and Mahāghoṣa.

Ratnaprabhasūri: See Chitor Epigraphs, Chirwa Epigraph.

Ratnapuri: Situated in the Fyzabad district, Uttar Pradesh, this was the birth-place of Dharmanātha, the fifteenth Tīrthaṃkara.

Ratnaśekhara: Jain teacher of the Tapāgaccha whose name occurs in the fifteenth-century image inscriptions of Gujarat and Rajasthan. *Jaina-dhātupratimālekhasaṃgraha*, II, Nos. 17, 77, 89, 154, 225, 343, 404, 741, 933, 989, 1048.

Ratnatraya: Three jewels—right belief (*samyag-darśana*, q.v.), right knowledge (*samyag-jñāna*, q.v.), and right conduct (*samyagcāritra*, q.v.)—which together constitute the path to salvation (*mokṣa*, q.v.).

Ratnatraya-basadi: See Biligi.

Rātri-Bhuktatyāga Pratimā: Abstaining from food after sunset.

Raṭṭa-Jinālaya: Jain temple at Venugrama, Belgaum in Karnataka, built by one Bica or Bicana in AD 1204 in the reign of Kārtavīrya IV according to an inscription found therein which also mentions the Digambara Ācārya Śubhacandra. *Epigraphia Indica* XIII, 16ff.

Rāvaṇa: One of the principal characters of the Jain *Rāmāyaṇa*. The *Paumacariya* (q.v.) of Vimala has described him as of noble descent and absolutely vegetarian and devoted to the Jinas. Rāvaṇa's brothers were Bhānukarṇa and Vibhīsaṇa and his sister was Candramukhā. He and his brothers acquired enormous magic power by virtue of asceticism. The Rākṣasas, in whose lineage Rāvaṇa was born, were not man-eating demons but adherents of the race of the Vidyādharas. Rāvaṇa's mother put around his neck a wondrous string of pearls in which his face was reflected nine times, which is why his epithet was *daśamukha*, 'the man with ten faces'. He was a great devotee of the Jinas, restored ruined Jain shrines and established the Jain faith. Rāvaṇa is Vimala's favourite. Lakṣmaṇa is described as a lusty and sentimental person. Through Rāvaṇa's influence Hanumān was converted to Jainism and received a thousand wives. The character of Rāvaṇa of the Jain *Rāmāyaṇa* is basically different from that portrayed in Vālmīki's *Rāmāyaṇa*. Following Vimala, Raviṣena, Hemacandra, and Devavijaya Gaṇi have depicted Rāvaṇa as a great and mighty Jain ascetic.

Ravanpur: Findspot of a Jain inscription of AD 1384 in Mysore district which mentions a temple dedicated to Sumatinātha and monks of the Deśīya-gaṇa and Inguleśvara-bali. *Epigraphia Carnatica* IV, Hunsur 123.

Ravikīrti: Composer of the Aihole Praśasti of the Cālukya King Pulakeśin II. In the inscription Ravikīrti has exhibited his Jain leanings. In verse 35 he says that a stone edifice of Jinendra was built by the wise Ravikīrti. The concluding verse also shows Ravikīrti's firm faith in Jainism. Some scholars hold that he belonged to the Yāpanīya-saṅgha.

Raviṣena: See *Padmapurāṇa*.

Rayabag: Situated in the Belgaum district of Karnataka, this place has yielded a few Jain epigraphs from the local Ādinātha temple.

Rayadrug: Findspot of an inscription of AD 1355 of the time of Harihara I of Vijayanagara in Bellary district which records the setting up of an image of Śāntinātha by Bhogarāja, disciple of Mārgha-nandī of Balātkara-gaṇa and Sarasvatī-gaccha, *Jaina Śilālekha Samgraha*, IV, No. 393.

***Rāyapasenaijja*:** See Rājapraśnīya.

Remarriage: For Jain men there is no problem with regard to the remarriage, especially in the case of widowers. Moreover, polygyny (q.v.) was a common practice until prohibited by the law. But Jain women suffered great disadvantages. Though the Jain law-givers following the Brahmanical Smṛti passage *naṣṭe mṛte*, etc., ordain that a wife is allowed to remarry if the husband becomes a sinner, or an ascetic, or an impotent person, if he dies and if no information of him is available, the remarriage of widows is not encouraged by Jains. There is no instance to be found of widow-remarriage in the Jain Purāṇas, but no clear direction is found in the scriptures in this matter, either sanctioning or prohibiting such marriage. In 1933 the conference of Śvetāmbara Sthānakavāsī Jain ascetics declared that Jainism is not concerned with the question of widow remarriage and that the caste-customs should determine whether to allow widow remarriage or not. In north India the remarriage of widows is neither encouraged nor practised, through it should be stated that Kumāradevī, mother of the celebrated Jain ministers Vastupāla and Tejaḥpāla (q.v.) was originally a widow whose second husband was the King Aśvarāja. Among the Jain Baniyas of Madhya Pradesh there is widow remarriage, but remarried widows are relegated to inferior social groups. Among the southern Jain castes like the Bogaras, Saitavālas, Caturthas, and Pañcamas, the custom of widow remarriage has a greater prevalence and remarried widows are not looked down upon.

Renunciation: According to the Jain tradition, the first appearance of grey hair on head is the messenger of religion (*dharmadūta*), warning people of the impermanence of life and to prepare themselves to abandon worldly enjoyments. The *Sthānāṅga* mentions the following causes of renunciation: wish, a feat of anger, poverty, having a dream, enlightenment by gods, and affection for a son who has already joined the ascetic order. Loss of children, failure in love, want of a suitable match, the desire to escape from a troublesome mother-in-law, debts, etc., can be added to the list. The *Nāyādhammakahāo* refers to a minister's wife, Poṭṭila, who entered the nuns' order as she had lost the love of her husband. The same text (I.25-33) provides us a graphic description of the renunciation of Meghakumāra who did so after listening to the sermons of Mahāvīra. When all attempts failed to hold him back his parents wanted him to enjoy glory at least for a day and arranged for his coronation ceremony. We read the same story about Jambu who entered the ascetic order with his newly married bride. The *Uttarādhyayana-sūtra* relates a *Mahābhārata* story in Jain garb in which the renunciated Nami, the retired king of Mithila, told Indra that if Mithila was on the fire he had nothing to lose. The *Vasu-devahiṇḍī* mentions the story of Thanvacca-putta's renunciation who was inspired to do the same having listened to the sermons of Ariṣṭanemi. His renunciation ceremony was arranged by Vāsudeva-Kṛṣṇa. Indiscriminate mendicancy was, however, forbidden. The *Sthānāṅga* and the commentaries of the *Nīśītha* give a list of the categories of persons like young women and children, offenders, debtors, slaves, etc., who are regarded unfit to join the Saṅgha.

Repaka Inscription: A stone inscription of AD 966 from Repaka in Karimnagar district, Andhra Pradesh, belonging to the time of Vemulavada kings, introduces a chief named Vujaya who made a gift of land to a Jinālaya probably built by King Arikeśarī II. Names of a line of Jain ascetics are also given. *Inscriptions of Andhra Pradesh* (Karimnagar district), ed. P.V. Parabrahma Sastri, No. 5.

Resandigiri: Situated in Chatarpur district of Madhya Pradesh, this place is dedicated to Pārśvanātha, and there is also a late-medieval temple of Śreyāṃśanātha.

***Rvantagiri-Rāsa*:** Composed in Gujarati in AD 1232 by Vijayasena, it eulogizes in four *kaḍavas* or sections the greatness of Mount Girnar in Saurāṣṭra and especially the temple of Neminātha. The second *kaḍava* gives a picturesque description of the mount.

Riddles: One of the earliest and most widespread types of formulated thought which ranks with myths, fables, folk-tales and proverbs. Prakrit Jain tales are rich with various types of riddles. They include the tales of tricksters, hypocrites, rogues, and swindlers who by their wit fool the people. Mūladeva, the crest-jewel of rogues, taught hypocrisy and knavery to his pupils. Various stories are recorded in J.C. Jain's *Prācīna Jaina Kathā Sāhitya*. Interesting tales pertaining to four types of intellect are illustrated in *Āvaśyaka Niryukti*. One ascetic asks another: 'Can you tell me how many crows are living on the bank of the river?' The other ascetic replies: 'Sixty thousand. If there are less, a good number of them must have fled to other places, and if more some must have joined them from other places.' Many such witticisms are found in *Āvaśyaka Cūrṇi*, *Nandī*, *Vasudevahiṇḍi*, etc. The *Bṛhat-kathākośa* also contains riddles. An example: a man carries his shoes in his hand except when he comes to a river, when he wears them. He also carries an umbrella under his arm, but opens it while coming to a shady tree. This riddle may be solved thus: If he wears his shoes while entering the water it means he wants to protect his feet from the thorns and stones under water. If he sits under a tree holding his umbrella above his head it shows he wants to protect himself from the excrement of birds falling from above.

Ṛjusūtra: See Naya.

Rohiṇī: A Vidyadevī (q.v.) who is conceived in the Śvetāmbara tradition as riding a cow and holding a conch, rosary, bow, and arrow. With the Digmbaras she appears bearing the attributes of an urn, conch, lotus, and fruit. See Ajita.

Rohitaka: Modern Rohtak in Haryana, site of a Pārśvanātha temple erected in AD 1526 and managed by the Digambara monks of the Kāṣṭha-saṅgha, Mathurā-anvaya, and Puskara-gaṇa.

Ṛṣabhanātha: The first Tīrthaṃkara whose spiritual career has been described in the *Kalpasūtra* and *Samavāya* as also in the *Ādipurāṇa* of the Digambaras and Hemacandra's *Triṣaṣṭi-śalākāpuruṣa-caritra*. Curiously, the *Bhāgavata*,

Agni and *Varāha Puranas* mention him as an incarnation of Viṣṇu, although by the symbolism of the bull and his *nirvāṇa* at Kailāśa, one is tempted to connect him with Śiva. Ṛṣabha belonged to Kosala. His father was Kulakara Nabhi of Vinitā or Ayodhya and his mother was Marudevī. His *gotra* was Kāśyapa and height 500 *dhanuṣas* or bow-lengths, as given in the Jain Purāṇas. The length of his life was also astronomical. According to the *Āvaśyaka-niryukti* he had two wives, Sumaṅgalā and Sunandā, and one hundred sons who were anointed the kings of various kingdoms. He attained omniscience outside the town of Purimatāla. The tree associated with him was the *nyagrodha*. He had under him 84 groups of *gaṇas*, 84 *gaṇadharas*, 84,000 monks with Ṛṣabhasena (q.v.) at their head and 300,000 nuns with Bambhī and Sundarī as heads. His chief lay-disciples were Sajjaṃsa and Subhaddā. The account of Ṛṣabha's career as given in the *Bhāgavata Purāṇa* tallies in all major details with that given in the Jain text. Here, though he is regarded as an incarnation of Viṣṇu, his followers are described as heretics who indulge in disparaging the Veda, Brāhmaṇas, and Yajña. In the Vedic texts as well as the two great epics there are references to a king or ascetic named Ṛṣabha which may indicate a single personality revered in tradition. His mother dreamt of a bull while she was pregnant. His Yakṣa, Gomukha (having a bull's face) has a definite connection with the same origin. Cakreśvarī, the Yakṣiṇī of the Jina, looks like Vaiṣṇavī, wife of Viṣṇu. Ṛṣabha's other name, Ādinātha, was adopted by the Nātha-yogins as the central figure of their creed. In the *Harivaṃśa Purāṇa*, the story of Ṛṣabha is told by way of introduction. Parvan I of Hemacandra's *Triṣaṣṭi* begins with the life of Ṛṣabha in his previous existence's. Merutuṅga's *Mahāpuruṣa-caritra* deals with Ṛṣabha's career along with that of four other Tīrthaṃkaras. Dhanapāla's *Ṛṣabha-pañcāśikā* is a Prakrit poem in 50 stanzas extolling his virtues. Śānticandra's *Ṛṣabha-stava* should also be mentioned in this connection. Ṛṣabha is well-represented in sculpture and, besides Ādinātha, is called Ādīśvara in numerous inscriptions.

Ṛṣabhasena: Disciple of Ṛṣabhanātha (q.v.) who was the leader of the order of 84,000 monks established by Ṛṣabhanātha himself, according to the *Samavāya*.

Rudrapalli: A place near Delhi after which was named a gaccha. There were two temples here, dedicated to Pārśva and Ṛṣabha.

Ruiramana: See Tāraṇapantha.

S

Śabda: See Naya, Logic.

Śabdānuśāsana: See Hemacandra.

Sabnur: Situated in Devanagare taluk in Chitradurga district, Karnataka, it is the findspot of an inscription of AD 1128 of the time of the Western Cālukya Someśvara III which refers to a temple of Pārśvanātha built at Sambanuru, modern Sabnur, by Kāliyakka, wife of a feudatory. The recipient of land-grant given to this temple was Śāntiśayana Paṇḍita belonging to the Drāviḍa Saṅgha and Aruṅgala-anvaya. Several monks of this line have been mentioned in this epigraph. *Epigraphia Carnatica*, XI, Deva, No. 90.

Śabarī Spells: Magic spells associated with the Śabara tribes which found their way in Jainism. The Śabarī-spells could be practised in company of one's own wife, but both had to practice strict celibacy. After paying homage to lord Ṛṣabha, one had to propitiate Dharaṇa, the king of the Nāgas, then to please the chief queen and last to honour the great lord Śabarī. Then after reciting incantations a person covered himself with bark and leaves. A bow and arrow were held in his hands and his tuft of hair was tied with creepers and plants. Thus he assumed the form of a Śabara. His wife, the Vidyādharī, adorned with the garlands of *guñja* fruits, looked beautiful like a female Śabarī. After that the lord of Śabaras, the supreme sovereign king, whispered the spell in the ears of the couple. It is said that Śabaraśīla, the lord of the Vidyādharas, was exceedingly powerful and a treasure house of Śabara spells. He renounced the world and practised austerities in a mountain cave. His son Śabarasenāpati installed a crystal image of Ṛṣabha in the cave. Since then the place came to be known as the abode of achievement (*siddha-kṣetra*) of the Vidyādharas belonging to the lord of the Śabara spell. Details of Śabarī spells are given in *Bṛhatkathākośa* of Hariṣena.

Sacittatyāga-Pratimā: Refraining from eating uncooked vegetables, plucking fruit from trees and the like.

Sacraments: See Saṃskāras.

Sacred Thread: See Upanayana.

Ṣaḍbhāṣānirmita-Pārśvajina Stavana: Hymns dedicated to Pārśvanātha composed by Dharmavardhana about AD 1200 in six languages—Sanskrit, Mahārāṣṭrī, Māgadhī, Saurasenī, Paiśāci, and Apabhraṃśa. It has two stanzas written half in Sanskrit and half in Prakrit.

Ṣaḍbhāṣānirmita-Śāntināthastavana: Hymn dedicated to Śāntinātha composed by Jinapadma between AD 1325 and 1344 in six languages—Sanskrit, Mahārāṣṭrī, Māgadhī, Saurasenī, Paiśācī, and Apabhraṃśa.

Saḍdarśana Samuccaya: See Haribhadra.

Sādhanā Jinālaya: Jain temple dedicated to Pārśvanātha mentioned in an inscription of AD 1599 found at Koppa town in Chikmagalur district. *Epigraphia Carnatica* VII, Koppa 50.

Sādhu: Ordinary ascetic. A Digambara sādhu wears no clothes, lives in the forest, and is immersed in meditation, eating only once a day. A Śvetāmbara or Sthānakavāsī sādhu travels to different monastic centres, clad in white clothes. He observes scrupulously various codes of conduct prescribed for spiritual realization. He has to practise the virtues mentioned in the canon in his individual life.

Sādhumārgī: Those who follow the saints and maintain that idol-worship has not been prescribed by the Tīrthaṃkaras, that the references to idol-worship in Jain texts are later interpolations, and do not believe in the detailed ritual. Instead they go to their religious houses—Upāśraya of the Sthānakavāsīs and Caityālaya of the Tāraṇapanthīs—and perform their religious duties.

Sādhu Parameṣṭhins: Next in rank to the Upādhyāya-parameṣṭhins (q.v.). They are great souls who do not have any definite function, either of authority or of instruction, but still illustrate through their conduct the path of salvation, so that others, following their example, may accept the faith and adopt the path of self-discipline and self-realization.

Sādhya: Major term. See Logic.

Sāgapattana: Modern Sagwara near Dungarpur in south Rajasthan which had a fifteenth-century temple of Ādinātha when Śubhacandra wrote his *Pāṇḍavapurāṇa* and Guṇacandra his *Anantajinavratapūjā*.

Sagarkaṭṭe: Findspot of a Jain epigraph in Mysore district, Karnataka, which mentions Vardhamāna Muni, the disciple of Vādirāja, belonging to the Drāviḍa-saṅgha, Aruṅgala-anvaya and Nandigaṇa, as taking part in Hoysala administration. This inscription is assigned to the eleventh century AD. *Jaina Śilālekha Saṃgraha* IV, No. 175.

Sagotra Marriage: See Endogamy and Exogamy.

Saint-Wheel Worship: See Siddhacakra Pūjā.

Saitavāla: Also known as Svaitavāla and Setvāla, it is the name of a mercantile Jain caste of the Deccan. They are also found in Madhya Pradesh. According to one tradition, the name is derivative of Kṣetrapāla, 'protector of the field'. The Prakrit form of Kṣetrapāla is Chettavāla, from which the Marathi word Setavāla is derived. Names of their 44 *gotras* are known: Bāhu, Abhayakumāra, Sahasrabāhu, Māghava, Vijayamitra, Dhanapati, Siṃharatha, Vidyāśakti, Supratiṣtha, Megha-vāhana, Pṛthvīpāla, Vajradanta, Ratnāyudha, Anantavijaya, Dharma, Prajñāpāla, Yugandhara, Lokapāla, Hariścandra, Sūryaputra, Yaśapāla, Mīnaketu, Surendradatta, Puṇḍarīka, Dhanaratha, Dhātrivāhana, Suṣena, Śubhacandra, Pūrvabāhu, Manimālā, Jitaśatru, Vajrāyudha, Satyaśruti, Jayandhara, Narmadā, Vimalavāhāna, Surakīrti, Vimalakīrti, Śrīsena, and Caкrāyudha. They have their own Bhaṭṭāraka or religious head. They are mostly weavers and small cloth merchants and compared to other Jain castes they are poor. They allow divorce and widow remarriage.

Sajjana: A minister of Jayasiṃha Siddharāja, the Calukya king of Gujarat. He acted as the governor of Surāṣṭra. Devout Jain that he was, he contributed liberally to the improvement of the Jain establishments of Girnar and erected a new stone temple of Neminātha there in place of the old wooden one. *Prabandhacintāmaṇi* 65; *Purātanaprabandhasaṃgraha* 34, *Vividha-tīrthakalpa* 9.

Sakala: See Samyag Cāritra.

***Sakalakīrti*:** See *Harivaṃsa Purāṇa* of which he wrote the first 14 Sargas. He was also the author of *Pārśvanātha-carita* and *Śāntinātha-carita*. There was a second Sakalakīrti who flourished in fifteenth century. He was the author of *Tattvā-rthasāradīpaka* a large work in twelve chapters in the entire system of the Jain religion. His other work is the *Praśnottaropāsakācāra* in which the duties of lay adherents are taught in the form of questions and answers.

Śākambharī: Sambhar in the Jaipur district of Rajasthan where a large Jina temple was built by a merchant named Padma in the fifteenth century.

Śākhā: Branch of a gaṇa or school, though the term is also used in other classificatory senses. The schools from which the *śākhās* became distinguished began to flourish after the patriarchy of Bhadrabāhu (q.v.). Among the disciples of Suhastin, Rohana became chief of the four *śākhās* of the Uddheha-gaṇa; Bhadrayaśas of the four *śākhās* of Uduvāṭika-gaṇa; Kāmardhi of the four *śākhās* of the Cāraṇa-gaṇa; Ṛṣigupta of the four *śākhās* of the Mānava-gaṇa; and Susthita, Kotika and Supratibuddha of the four *śākhās* of the Kauṭika-gaṇa. The growth of a branch or *śākhā* depended on many factors, among which geographic factors are significant. According to the tradition as preserved in the *Therāvali*, which is a part of the *Kalpasūtra*, among the four *śākhās* originating from Godāsa, one of the four disciples of Bhadrabāhu, three belonged to Bengal, namely Tāmraliptaka, Koṭivarṣīya, and Puṇḍravardhanīya. From Balishah, who was a disciple of Mahāgiri (q.v.) originated a number of *śākhās*, among which the name Kauśāmbika, made after Kausambi near Allahabad in the ancient Vatsa country, is conspicuous by its presence. Likewise among the *śākhās* originating from Rohana, a disciple of Suhastin (q.v.), we have Udumbarika connected with the Auḍumbara tribe of the Punjab region. From those originated from Bhadrayaśas, two *śākhās*, namely Bhadriyikā and Kākandikā, are apparently connected with Bhadrikā and Kakandī towns. Śrāvastikā *śākhā* is associated with the city of Śrāvastī. The same holds good in the case of Saurāṣṭrikā and Madhyamikā *śākhās*. The Mathura inscriptions mention *śākhās* like Petapurika belonging to the Odehikiya-gaṇa; Ucenagari and Vairi belonging to the Koliya-gaṇa; and Vajanagari, Vairi, Harita-mālakadhi and Saṃkāsīyā belonging to the Varaṇa-gaṇa. An inscription of Hanasoge in Mysore district, Karnataka, records the death of a teacher named Śrīdharadeva who belonged to the Panasoge *śākhā*. Panasoge is the ancient name of Hanasoge and the reference to this *śākhā* shows that from a much earlier period this place was a Jain centre. A Jain monk even as late as the fifteenth century of Karakala in South Kanara district named Lalitakīrti also belonged to this *śākhā*. Very often *śākhās* are mentioned in terms of the *anuyogas* or Digambara sacred texts, just as the Brāhmaṇas are often classified in terms of the Vedas like Sāmavedin or Yajurvedin. We have instances even of Prābhṛtaka *śākhā*. See Saṃgha, Gaṇa, Gaccha, Anvaya, Kula, Bali.

***Sakriya Dravya*:** *Dravyas* (q.v.) which are capable of acting on Jīva and *Pudgala* (qq.v.), soul and matter, constitute the *sakriya dravyas* because all activities in the world are ultimately traceable to these two entities.

Śākaṭāyana: Author of *Śabdānuśāsana* and its commentary *Amoghavṛtti*. He was a contemporary of Amoghavarṣa I and belonged to the Yāpanīya-saṅgha.

Śakunikā-Vihāra: Jain temple at Broach in Gujarat. This temple was replaced by Amarabhaṭṭa by a splendid new shrine in AD 1166. See Bhṛgukaccha.

Salakṣaṇapura: Jain centre in the Gujarat region when Pethaḍa of Mandu erected a temple around AD 1264.

***Salesi*:** See *Leśyā*.

Śālibhadra: See *Bharateśvara-Bāhubali-Rāsa*, *Buddhi-rāsa*.

***Śālibhadra-Carita*:** An epic based on the life-story of Śālibhadra, a contemporary of Mahāvīra and King Śreṇika, written by Dharmakumāra in AD 1277 and revised by Pradyumna Suri (q.v.). The original story is found in Hemacandra's (q.v.) *Triṣaṣṭiśalākāpuruṣacaritra* X.57ff. The story terms itself a *Dānadharmakathā* and *Dānāvadāna*. Edited in Yaśovijaya Jaina Granthamālā, No. 15, Benares, 1911. Detailed treatment of it by M. Bloomfield in *Journal of the American Oriental Society*, XLIII, 1923, 257ff.

***Sallekhanā*:** Peaceful death. In addition to the twelve prescribed vows a householder is expected to practise in the last stage of his life a process leading to voluntary death by giving up eating. *Sallekhanā* is described as giving up the body on the arrival of an unavoidable calamity, or distress, old age and disease, with a view to increase spiritual merit. Like other vows, *sallekhanā* has five partial transgressions which are to be avioded by householders.

Samabhirudha: See *Naya*.

Samādhiśataka: A didactic poem by Pūjyapāda (q.v.). Edited in Sanatana Jain Granthamala I, Bombay, 1905.

Samaiya: See Caranāgare.

Samaiyāpantha: See Tāraṇapantha.

Samanarmalai: 'Hill of the Śramaṇas' stretching for a distance of about 3 km in an east-west direction, about 8 km west of Madurai. Later Jain sculptures with Vaṭṭeluttu inscriptions of the eighth-ninth centuries are found all over the hills.

Samantabhadra: A great exponent of the Jain doctrine of Syādvāda (q.v.) who belonged to the Gupta period or the early post-Gupta period. He was the son of a king of Uragapura. In the *Kathākośa* of Prabhācandra Samantabhadra is described as hailing from Kanchi. He is also stated to be the preceptor of Śivakoṭi or Śivārya, the author of *Mūlārādhanā* (q.v.). Samantabhadra wrote a commentary on the *Tattvārthādhigama* (q.v.), the introduction of which is *Āptamīmāṃsā* (q.v.) or *Devāgamastotra*. Among other works of Samntabhadra the *Yuktyānuśāsana* is a poem of 64 verses which has a Sanskrit commentary by Vidyānanda. The *Ratnakaraṇḍaśrāvakācāra*, also called *Upāsakādhyayana*, it is a manual of morals for lay adherents in 150 Sanskrit verses. The only available Sanskrit commentary on it is that of Prabhācandra (q.v.). The *Svayambhūstotra*, a poem containing 143 verses in praise of the Tīrthaṃkara, is also commented upon by Prabhācandra. The fourth work of Samantabhadra is *Jinastutiśataka* which has 116 verses and a commentary by Narasiṃha Bhaṭṭa. *Āptamīmāṃsā*, ed. in Jaina Grantha Ratnākara and Sanātana Jaina Granthamālā, Bombay, 1905 and with Vidyānanda com. in Manikacandra Digambara Granthamālā Series No. 15; *Ratnakaraṇḍaśrāvakācāra*, text with Eng. trans. by C.R. Jain, Arrah, 1917.

Sāmānyakevalin: See Arhanta.

***Samaraiccha-Kahā*:** A religious novel by the celebrated Haribhadra (q.v.) of the eighth century written in prose with inserted verses of varying length, usually in the Āryā metre. The language is Jain-Mahārāṣṭrī. Underlying the main narrative and most of the inserted narratives, in which, after all sorts of adventures the heroes and heroines renounce the world and enter the order, there are the tenets of Jain doctrine, and in the numerous stories, parables and fairy-tales inserted we come across many themes which we find often in Indian narrative literature. Ed. H. Jacobi. Bib. Ind., Calcutta, 1908; Pandit Bhagavanadas with Sanskrit *Chāyā* in two parts, Ahmedabad, 1938-42.

Samarasiṃha, Samara Shah: Fourteenth-century exponent of Jainism in Gujarat who belonged to Upakeśa or Ukeśavaṃśa and Vaśata *gotra*. He was a merchant and rebuilt the image of Ādīśvara temple in Śatruñjaya in VS 1371 which was destroyed by the Muslims. However, he developed a good relation with Alp Khan, governor of Gujarat, and obtained the permission to rebuild the temple of Ādinātha at Palitana. Among the monks who accompanied him to Palitana for the installation ceremony were Siddhasūri of the Upakeśa-gaccha and Ratnasūri of Tapāgaccha. Samara's brothers Sahajapāla and Sāhana also actively helped him. Although a dedicated Jain, Samara Shah maintained good relations with contemporary Muslim rulers. Qutbuddin Mubarak Shah invited him to Delhi in AD 1320. Samara died in VS 1393. Kakkasuri's *Nābhinandanoddhāra-prabandha*.

Samarasiṃha Temple: Erected on Mount Girnar in

AD 1438. It follows the broad lines of the Solanki version of Nāgara temple style.

Samasgarh: Jain site near Bhadbhada in Bhopal district, Madhya Pradesh, where some colossal Tīrthaṃkara images and decorated architectural pieces of the thirteenth century have been found.

Samavasaraṇa: Auditorium in which the Tīrthaṃkaras deliver sermons. When a Tīrthaṃkara addresses his audience this auditorium—originally planned by Kubera under the order of Indra of the Saudharma heaven—appears and accommodates the listeners and disappears with the Tīrthaṃkara's shift to another place where a fresh auditorium emerges for him. The structure itself may be called a vast park-cum-auditorium. It is circular and spreads over 12 *yojanas*, but the area goes on shrinking in the case of every succeeding Tīrthaṃkaras. Detailed description of its structure is found in the Jain architectural texts.

***Samavāyāṅga*:** The fourth text of the Aṅga (q.v.) category which seems to be the latest of the canonical texts since it mentions not only the other Aṅga texts, but the *Nandī Sūtra* (q.v.) as well. The subject-matter of its major portion is arranged in numerical groups like the *Sthānāṅga* (q.v.), but in this case the numbers do not stop at ten. The work begins with an enumeration of the twelve Aṅgas and a table of contents of the fourteen Pūrvas (q.v.) At the conclusion the contents of all the Aṅgas have been faithfully summarized. Eighteen kinds of Brāhmī scripts, including Damili and Pulindi, are enumerated; thirty-six sections of the *Uttarādhyayana* are described. Edited in the Āgamasaṃgraha IV, Benares, 1880; with Abhayadeva Sūri's com. in Āgamodaya, Bombay, 1918.

***Samayasāra*:** See Kundakunda.

Samyasundara: See Gāthāsāhasrī. Samayasundra who flourished in the early seventeenth century, is the author of *Visaṃvādaśataka*, a compilation of a hundred verses which contain discrepancies to be found in the sacred texts.

Sāmāyika: Prakrit *sāmāiya* signifying equality (*sāmya*, *sama* or *samatā*). It is also the name of the first *aṅga*, the *Acara* (q.v.). Whenever a layman or ascetic takes the vow of religious conduct he utters the oath *karemi bhante sāmaiyam* (*Āvaśyaka* 3) which means 'I undertake to observe, O Lord, the attitude of equality'. It is because of the great importance of *sāmāiya* that the famous scholar Jinabhadragaṇi-kṣamāśramaṇa of the seventh century AD composed an elaborate commentary entitled the *Viśeṣāvaśyaka-bhāṣya* on it and had shown that the three factors of religion, namely faith, knowledge and conduct, constitute what is called *sāmāiya*. There is intrinsic equality among all selves, be they earth-bodied, water-bodied, vegetable organisms, insects, birds, animals or human beings. It is also said the actual feeling of equality or identity of the self with others is the primal source of the principal of non-violence.

Sambhavanātha: The third Tīrthaṃkara who was the son of Jitāri and Senā of Śrāvastī. He was 400 bow-lengths in height and his span of life was 6,000 years. His sacred tree was the *śāla* and he attained liberation on the summit of the Sammeya or Pareshnath Hill. His prominent disciples were Caru and Samā. His symbol is the horse, his *chowri*-bearer Satyavīrya, Yakṣa Trimukha, and Yakṣiṇī Duritāri. According to another tradition his father was King Dṛḍarāja and mother Suṣenā. It is said that his father was distressed to see his dominions being ravaged by plague. But when he heard the good news of the boy's birth, he felt there was a chance (*sambhava*) of better times. This accounts for the boy's name. Not many sculptures of Sambhavanātha have been found. He is mentioned in a Mathura inscription of Huviṣka of AD 126.

Sambhavanātha Temples: Erected on Jaisalmer Fort in AD 1431, the first temple dedicated to Sambhavanātha (q.v.) displays a ceiling in its *raṅga-maṇḍapa* following an old style of representation. The second temple was built in AD 1231 at Kumbharia. It comprises a sanctum, a *gūḍha-maṇḍapa* and a *sabhā-maṇḍapa* enclosed in a *prākāra*.

***Sambhoga*:** See *Kula*.

Sambhūtavijaya: The seventh Gaṇadhara (q.v.) who succeeded Yaśobhadra (q.v.) as the head of the Jain order in 319 BC. He was succeedid by Bhadrabāhu in 317 BC. His most clebrated disciple was Sthulabhadra.

Saṃgha: A section or division functioning as an institution. The term denotes *samūha* or a collective body and is often equated with *gaṇa* meaning 'tribe' and applied to suggest a 'religious order' or 'congregation of brethren' or 'organization of monks'. Among the Digambaras, there arose a number of saṃghas, Mūla-saṃgha, Drāviḍa-saṃgha, Kāṣṭhā-saṃgha, Mathurā-saṃgha, etc. According to the *Nītisara* of Indranandin, Arhadbalin was the founder of four saṃghas: Siṃha-saṃgha for those who used to keep their rainy season's retreat in the den of a lion; Nandi-saṃgha for those who used to keep their retreat in the lower part of the *nandī* tree;

Sena-saṃgha for those who had their retreat in the bushes; and Deva-saṃgha for those who had their retreat in the house of a courtesan named Devadattā. Inscriptions refer to Mūla, Nandī, Drāviḍa, Namilura or Mayura, Kittura, Kollatura, Kurcaka, Ahariṣṭi, Yāpanīya, Vāgaṭa, Lāṭa-vargata, Kāṣṭhā, Śrīmūla, Mathurā, Gauḍa, etc. Some of these *saṃghas* such as Drāviḍa, Mathurā, and Gauḍa, denote a geographical region. The Mūla, Sena, Nandī, and Deva are distributed all over the country. Vāgaṭa-saṃgha belongs to Rajasthan while Lāṭavargata and Kāṣṭhā-saṃghas belong to the Madhya Pradesh, though the latter is found in other parts of the country. The Śrimūla-saṃgha had its centre in Deogarh, Uttar Pradesh. The saṃghas comprise smaller units like the gaṇas, gacchas, *śākhās*, *kulas* (qq.v.), etc. The most popular grouping of these divisions seems to be the Mūla-saṃgha, Balātkāra-gaṇa and Sarasvatī-gaccha, as this grouping is found among the Digambaras from different parts of India. But there is no hard and fast rule that a particular gaṇa or gaccha should be associated with a particular saṃgha. Thus the Mūla-saṃgha is frequently associated with the Deva-gaṇa, Sena-gaṇa, and Deśīya-gaṇa. Inscriptional evidence amply testifies that gaṇas such as Kandura, Balātkāra, Deśī, Kāreya, and Kranura are associated with various saṃghas rather arbitrarily. In fact, the difference among the saṃghas appears to have been superficial. For example, the main difference between the Mūla-saṃgha and Kāṣṭhā-saṃgha lies in the fact that while the ascetics of the former use a bunch of peacock feathers for warding off insects, those of the latter use the tuft of a cow's tail hair. Most Jain inscriptions, like those of other categories, are of the nature of grants or donations meant for religious purpose. These, while referring to the teacher of the donor, almost invariably refer to the saṃgha and its subdivisions to which the teacher belonged. See Gaṇa, Gaccha, *Śākhā, Kula*, Bali, Anvaya.

Saṃghāta: See Atomism, *Pudgala.*

Saṃgraha: See *Naya.*

Samitis: Five methods required for Saṃvara (q.v.) or stoppage of the influx of *karmic* matter into the soul. These are prescriptions for the regulation of the movements of the body. The *irya-samiti* aims at regulation of walking, the *bhāṣā-samiti* of the mode of speech, the *esamā-samiti* of seeking and eating food, the *ādāna-nikṣepa-samiti* of actions of taking and using, and the *utsarga-samiti* of movements connected with the answering the call of nature. These are done with a view to avoid injury to living beings by action or words.

Sammeta: Pareshnath Hill situated in the Giridih district of Jharkhand which is even today one of the most important Jain *tīrthas*. According to the Jain tradition, here most of the Tīrthaṃkaras breathed their last.

Saṃpatkara: Short name of Śāntu, who was a minister of the Cālukya King Jayasiṃha Siddharāja of Gujarat. He was a devoted Jain layman who built a temple at Anahilapāṭaka named after himself. *Prabandhacintāmaṇi* 56ff; *Purātanaprabandhasaṃgraha* 31ff.

Samprāta: See *Naya.*

Samprati: Maurya king, son of Dasaratha and grandson of Aśoka, who, according to the Purāṇas, ruled between 228 and 219 BC. He was converted to Jainism by Suhastin and is said to have raised thousands of temples to Tīrthaṃkaras. According to the Śvetāmbara tradition, in his previous birth Samprati had been a beggar and died of a surfeit. At the sight of Suhastin he recollected the incident of his former birth and became a convert to Jainism. He then tried to spread Jainism by all means in his power, and did everything that Aśoka had done for Buddhism. Hemacandra had written that he erected Jain temples all over Jambūdvīpa and organized splendid religious festivals and processions. He sent missionaries as far as Afghanistan and the Andhra and Tamil countries. He showered rich food and other good things on the members of the Saṅgha.

Samprati Rājā Temple: Erected on Mount Girnar in AD 1453. It follows the broad lines of the Solāṅki version of Nāgara temple style.

Sāmrājya: A stage in the career of the Tīrthaṃkara in which he guides the subsidiary kings in their duties towards their subjects.

Saṃsāra: Worldly existence which is the result of *karmic* bondage, according to which a particular Jīva will be born in any one of the four *gatis* or states of existence: *devas* or divine beings, *naras* or human being, *nārakas* or denizens of hell, and *tiryaks* or the lower animals and the plant world. These four beings constitute *saṃsāra.* As long as a Jīva is in *saṃsāra* it is bound by *karmic* shackles which lead to the building up of a body for it, and the purity of its nature and strength of knowledge have the chance of complete manifestation. Its knowledge is limited and its nature deformed, accordingly it is bound by various *karmas.* Since there is no scope for its pure nature to manifest itself, it mainly depends upon the sense-organs for instruction and knowledge, and its life is mainly determined by its environment consisting of objects presented to the senses. It remains in sense pleasures which only make it move from one birth to another, from one *gati* to another, in an unending series of births and deaths.

Saṃsarastha: That which is confined to worldly affairs, characteristic of Jīva.

Saṃsārin Jīva: Mundane souls also known as *baddha-jīva*. They are living beings, possessed of body or form and subject to the cycle of birth. From one point of view they are of two kinds, *sthāvara* and *trasa* (qq.v.), immobile and mobile, and from another *samanaska* and *amanaska*, those who have a mind and those who do not. From another viewpoint the mundane souls are placed in four *gatis* (q.v.) or four grades of existence. They are required to possess no properties or characteristics: *jīvaḥ*, past, present, and future existence; *upayogamaya*, perception and knowledge; *amūrti*, certain immaterial properties; *kartā*, agency, agent; *svadehaparimāna* occupying the area of his own body; *bhoktā*, enjoyment of the fruits of *karma*; *saṃsārasthaḥ*, wandering in *saṃsāra*; *siddhaḥ*, faculties of perfection; and *ūrdhvagati*, tendency to rise.

Saṃskāras: Sacraments. Life of Jain lay-persons is regulated by sacraments through which they have to pass from conception to death. These sacraments are mostly adopted from the Brahmanical tradition. The *Ādipurāṇa* of the Digambaras refers to fifty-three such sacraments which are *ādhāna* or *garbhādhāna, prīti, suprīti, dhṛti, moda, priyodbhava, nāmakaraṇa, bahiryāna, niṣadyā, annaprāśana, vyuṣṭi, keśavāpa, lipisaṅkhyānasaṃgraha, upanīti, vratacaryā, vrātāvataraṇa, vivāha, varṇalābha, kulacaryā, gṛhīśitā, praśānti, gṛhatyāga, dīkṣādya, jinarūpatā, maunādhyayanavṛtti, tīrthakṛdbhāvanā, gurusthānābhayapagama, gaṇopagrahaṇa, svagurusthānāvapti, niḥsaṅga-tvātmabhāvanā, yoganirvāṇasaṃprāpti, yoga-nirvāṇasādhanā, indropapāda, indrābhiṣeka, vidhidāna, sukhodaya, indratyāga, avatāra, hiraṇyajanmatā, mandarendrābhiṣeka, guru-pūjana, yauvarājya, svārājya, cakralābha, digvijaya, cakrābhiṣeka, sāmrājya, niṣkrānti, yogasammaha, ārhantya, vihāra, yogatyāga, and agranivṛti* (qq.v.). But since the observance of all these are not possible nowadays under the present situation the Digambaras have reduced the number of *saṃskāras*. The Śvetāmbara *Ācīradinakara* refers to sixteen sacraments which are *garbhādhana, puṃsavana, janma, sūryendudarśana, kṣīraśena, ṣaṣṭhi, śucikarma, nāmakarma, annaprāśana, karṇavedha, kṣaurakarma* or *cūḍākarma, upanayana, vidyārambha, vivāha, vratarūpa* and *antakarma* (qq.v.). It is to be noted that the sacraments referred to above, whether of the Digambaras or of the Śvetāmbaras, are not practised in a uniform manner all over the country.

Saṃstaraka: Prakrit *Saṃthāra*, the third of the Prakīrṇa series which deals in 122 verses symbolically with the pallet of straw, upon which the one desirous of salvation and sick unto death resorts for meditation. There are legends describing how great sinners had become purified by the performance of austerities. Bhavanagar edn., 1908; Āgamodaya edn., Bombay, 1925.

Samthāra: See Saṃstaraka.

Saṃvara: The way in which the influx of *karma* can be checked. 'As a large tank, when its supply of water has been stopped, gradually dries up by the consumption of water and by evaporation, so the *karma* (q.v.) of a monk, which he acquired in millions of birth is annihilated by austerities, if there is no influx of bad *karma*.' By *saṃvara* the channels through which *karma* enters the soul, can be blocked. There are two kinds of control known as *bhāvasaṃvara* and *dravyasaṃvara*. To the former category belong the five vows, three kinds of *gupti* (q.v.), five kinds of *samiti* (q.v.), ten kinds of *dharma* (q.v.), twelve kinds of *anuprekṣā* (q.v.) twenty-two kinds of *pariṣaha* (q.v.) and five kinds of *cāritra* (q.v.). To the latter category belong abstention from temptation caused by external objects. The ideal of liberation can thus be realized only by the stoppage and shedding of *karma*. *Saṃvara* is that which stops. See Aṣṭa Pravacana Mālā, Anuprekṣā, Bhāvasaṃvara, Cāritra, Daśalakṣaṇa Dharma, Dravyasaṃvara, Gupti, Pariṣahas, Samitis.

Samvatsarī: Last day of the *paryuṣana* (q.v.).

Saṃvega-Mātṛkā: See *Mātṛkā*.

Samyag Cāritra: Right conduct which presupposes the presence of right knowledge and comprises the rules of discipline of mind, body, and speech. It is of two kinds: *sakala*, perfect or unqualified, and *vikala*, imperfect or qualified, the former being observed by ascetics who have renounced worldly ties and the latter by laymen still entangled in the world.

Samyag Darśana: Right belief which means true and firm conviction in the seven principles or *tattvas* of Jainism which are Jīva, Ajīva, Āsrava, Bandha, Saṃvara, Nirjarā, and *Mokṣa* (qq.v.). Right faith should have requirements (*aṅga*, q.v.) and should be free from three types of superstitious ignorance (*mūḍha*, q.v.) and eight kinds of pride, in learning (*jñāna*), worship (*pūjā*), family (*kula*), caste (*jāti*), power (*bala*), affluence (*ṛddhi*), austerities (*tapa*), and body (*bapu*). The right faith precedes right knowledge and conduct and is conducive to *mokṣa* (q.v.) or liberation.

***Samyag Jñāna*:** Right knowledge; that which reveals the true nature of things. It is free from doubt, perversity, vagueness, and exaggeration and of five kinds: *mati*, knowledge of the self and non-self by means of senses and mind; *śruta*, knowledge derived from reading or hearing the scriptures; *avadhi*, clairvoyant knowledge of distant time and space; *manaḥparyāya*, knowledge of the thoughts and feelings of others; and *kevala*, perfect knowledge or omniscience which is without the limit of time and space, pure or undefiled. Right knowledge has also eight *aṅgas* (q.v.) or requirements which are *grantha*, *artha*, *ubhaya*, *kāla*, *vinaya*, *sopādhāna*, *bahumāna*, and *aninhava*.

***Samyaktvakaumudi*:** Collection of numerous stories, one related to another by an unknown author, within the frame of Jainism in which the merchant Arhaddāsa tells his eight wives and they in turn tell him how they attained perfection (*samyaktva*). These stories were overheard by a king who roamed about at night with his minister and a thief. The king despite receiving warning from the seven stories did a vile act with an evil intention and was eventually exposed. The work was composed between the thirteenth and fourteenth centuries.

***Samyaktvamāi-Caupāi*:** See *Mātṛkā*.

Samyukta Ratnākar-Caityālaya: Constructed by Cāvunda-Gāvunda at Mugunda, this temple is mentioned in a record of AD 1045 from Mugad, Dharwar district, Karnataka, affirming a land grant for feeding the visitors.

Sandera Inscriptions: Two inscriptions of the Nadol Cāhamāna King Kelhana have been found in Sandera in the Pali district of Rajasthan. The first inscription dated VS 1221 (AD 1163) refers to a grant by the queen-mother Ānaladevī to the great hero Mahāvīra of Sandera described as a *tīrtha*. The second refers to the existence of a big temple of Pārśvanātha at this place. It is dated in VS 1236 (AD 1178). At present this holy place is dedicated to Śāntinātha. Siddhasena in his *Sakalatīrtha-stotra* recognizes it as a *tīrtha*. A separate Śvetāmbara gaccha called Sanderaka-gaccha originated from this place in AD 906, and its founder was Yaśobhadra. *Epigraphia Indica*, XI.46ff.

Sandhi: See Koḍavaka.

***Saṅgha*:** See Saṃgha.

Saṅghadāsagaṇi Vācaka: See Vasudevahiṇḍī.

Saṅgītapura: See Hiduvalli.

Sangrāmapura: Modern Sanganer near Jaipur in Rajasthan which has a Jina temple and an epigraph of the tenth century.

***Śani*:** The planet Saturn conceived as a Jyotiṣka or stellar god by the Jains. His attribute is an axe. He is thought of as the ruler of the West.

***Sañjamamañjarī*:** An Apabhraṃśa text on ethics in 35 *dohā* verses with an exhaustive commentary. It was composed in the thirteenth century by Mahāsena Suri. It teaches the practice of self-control as the sure way to obtain release. Ed. P.D. Gune, Bhandarkar Oriental Research Institute, I, 157-66.

Sañjavalana: See Kaṣāya, *Pāpa*.

Sañjaya Belaṭṭhiputta: A philosopher who was a contemporary of Mahāvīra. Sañjaya is generally described as an agnostic, *ajñānavādin*, a sceptic unwilling to give any definite answer to the ultimate problems which were, according to him, indeterminable. In the *Sūyagaḍa* I.12 (cf. I.6.27; II.2.78; *Uttarādhyayana* XVIII.22-3) the Ajñānavādins are criticised as blind and misguiding others. In the Buddhist texts Sañjaya has been criticised as *amarāvikkhepika*, eel-wriggler. *Dīgha Nikāya* I.24-28, 58; *Sumaṅgalavilāsinī* I.168. From the Buddhist accounts it is known that when Sāriputta, accompanied by Moggalāna and two hundred and fifty other disciples, left the school of Sañjaya and joined the order of the Buddha, Sañjaya was so angry that he began to vomit blood which caused his sudden death. The views of Sañjaya have been summarized in the *Sāmaññaphalasutta* of the *Dīgha Nikāya*, though in a rather distorted way. But it should be stressed in this connection that although in the Buddhist and Jain texts the views of Sañjaya and those of Ajñānavādins and Amarāvikkhepikas have been severely criticised the method of Sañjaya's argument was tacitly accepted by the Buddha and Mahāvīra who also declined to give categorical answers to all questions put to them. Both of them were unanimous in declaring that there are some mooted questions on which any opinion should not be given.

Sanka: Jain site near Raghunathpur in Purulia district, wherefrom an eleventh-century image of Ṛṣabhanātha standing in *kāyotsarga* on lotus on *triratha* pedestal has been found. The image is flanked of either side by *chowri*-bearers and the bull sits to the left of the central *ratha*. Above the *chowri*-bearers are twelve miniature Jinas in two vertical rows. Above each row there are flying Gandharvas. There is a trilinear *chatra* on the head of the Jina with matted hair.

Saṅkha-basti, Jinālaya: Situated at Lakshmeswar in Dharwar district, Karnataka, even in its ruins, a spacious construction, showing in inner main complex comprising a *garbhagṛha*, a large *ardha-maṇḍapa* and a still larger and wider *mahāmaṇḍapa* and *raṅga-maṇḍapa*. It is a *caumukha* combined with a *cauvīsī* type of shrine. The superstructure over the cornice is of the *pīḍhā-deul* type of unique importance, one thousand and fourteen small Tīrthaṃkara images are carved with a life-size image in the centre. The tiers on the tip of the temple also show at each level niched Tīrthaṃkara figures.

Sankha Jinendra: One of the most prominent Jain temples at Lakshmeswar in Dharwar district, Karnataka. It was probably built during the reign of the Western Gaṅgas.

Śaṅkheśvara: Situated in Mehsana district, Gujarat, this place was associated with Pārśvanātha from quite early times, visited by Jinacandra III and Jinakusala in the thirteenth century, and referred to as a *tīrtha* by Jinaprabha, Śrīmatisāgara and Jñānasāgara.

Sāṅkhya: It is not unlikely that Jainism borrowed some of its philosophical characteristics from the Sāṅkhya. Though the surviving Sāṅkhya texts are of late origin, a very ancient form of the Sāṅkhya is found in the earlier literature. The similarities between the essentials of the Sāṅkhya and those of Jainism can hardly be overlooked. The Sāṅkhya wants to explain the world in terms of two basic categories, Puruṣa and Prakṛti, just as Jainism tries in terms of Jīva and Ajīva. In the later stages of the development of Sāṅkhya thought, Puruṣa or the male principle came to denote soul, and Prakṛti or the female principle the primordial substance, the inanimate matter. The same holds good in the case of Jain Jīva and Ajīva, living and non-living, which later came to denote soul and inanimate substance. The kind of effective relation through which Prakṛti is influenced by the presence of Puruṣa functions in the same way as Jīva attracts *pudgala* in Jainism. The Jain conception regarding the union of soul and matter is basically the same as that of the Sāṅkhya. But there are also differences between the Jain and Sāṅkhya conceptions of soul. According to the Jains the soul in its pure state is possessed of infinite perception, infinite knowledge, and infinite power. The souls are infinite in number. According to the Sāṅkhya, although the souls are many, they are without parts and qualities. The Jain soul is veiled by *karma* matter, but the Sāṅkhya soul is a distinct transcendental principle. The Jains accept the Sāṅkhya doctrine of *pariṇāmavāda* or transformation of cause into effect. Jainism posits over and above the perceptible world an infinite number of subtle elements, one kind physical and the other conscious. The gross world is, according to it, only an effect (*kārya*) or modification (*pariṇāma*) of the subtle physical effects.

The Sāṅkhya theory of knowledge, in its basic principles, has much in common with that of the Jains, since it accepts all the three independent sources of valid knowledge, namely perception, inference, and testimony. The Sāṅkhya also seems to have contributed to the Jain tradition that transcendental perception is of two sorts, indeterminate and determinate. Jainism maintains the Sāṅkhya view that the material cause of the sense-organs is a subtle substance, a particular kind of matter. The Jains, however, criticise the Sāṅkhya view that just as a mirror reflects the light of a lamp and thereby manifests other things, so the material principle of intellect being trans-parent and bright reflects the consciousness of the self and illuminates or cognizes the objects of knowledge. The Jain concept of *mokṣa* and the Buddhist concept of *nirvāṇa* appear to have derived their main impulses from the Sāṅkhya idea of liberation (*mukti* or *apavarga*). In the Sāṅkhya, suffering is attributed to ignorance, and hence freedom from suffering is to be attained through the knowledge of reality, which view is shared by the Jains and Buddhists alike. Like-wise, Jain atheism also seems to have been substantiated by Sāṅkhya atheism, according to which the assumption of God is ontologically irrelevant and logically repulsive.

Ṣaṇmukha: Attendant Yakṣa of Vimalanātha (q.v.) according to the Śvetāmbara tradition. His mount is a peacock and his twelve hands are marked by the fruit, disc, arrow, sword, noose, rosary, mongoose, discus, bond, goad, and *abhaya-mudrā*. Like Kārttikeya, he is six-headed.

Sanoli: Findspot of bronze Jina images in Alwar district, Rajasthan.

Śāntā: Śāsanadevatā of Supārśvanātha, conceived in the Śvetāmbara tradition as riding an elephant holding rosary, lance, and hands in *varada* and *abhaya* pose. Her Digambara variant is Kali who is thought of as being seated on a bull, her hands marked by a trident, fruit, *varada* pose, and bell.

***Śānticandra Gaṇin*:** See *Ajita-Śānti-Stava*.

Śānti Devī: An original Jain deity who has no parallel in other religious systems. She is believed by the Jain to have the function of improving the organization of the fourfold Jain church.

Santigatta: Site of Vardhamāna-basti in Bangalore district. The temple is a plain structure with a damaged inscription on the back of the central image giving the genealogy of the Hoysala kings. There are also some metallic images of Jinas and deities.

Śāntinātha: The sixteenth Tīrthaṃkara who was the son of Viśvasena and Avirā of Gajapura. His chief wife was Vijayā. His sacred tree was the *nandī*. He had a height of 40 bow-lengths and a life of a hundred thousand years. He attained liberation on Sammeya mountain. His chief disciples were Cakkaha and Suī. His symbol is the bear, attendants Kiṃpuruṣa and Mahamānasī (in Digambara tradition) or Garuḍa and Nirvāṇī (in Śvetāmbara tradition), Puruṣadatta stands for his *chowri*-bearer. Not only did he revive Jainism, which was in danger of falling into oblivion, but he so consolidated the faith that it never disappeared. He was the first Tīrthaṃkara to become a *cakravartī* or emperor. He has been mentioned in numerous inscriptions starting with those found at Mathura. Temples dedicated to his name are numerous and so are the images. In sculpture we notice as his emblem a pair of antelopes and a wheel between them. This calls to mind the Buddhist *dharma-cakra* emblem, as Śāntinātha was thought of to be a reviver of Jainism. Māṇikyacandra and Sakalakīrti wrote *Śāntinātha-caritas*. A *Śāntinātha-caritra* in Sanskrit verses was written by Deva Suri (q.v.) in AD 1282. Ajitaprabha of the same century wrote an epic *Śāntinātha-caritra*. Asaga wrote a *Śānti-Purāṇa*. It was corrected by Pradyumna Suri. It is an abridged translation into Sanskrit of the *Śrīśāntivṛtta*, which was written in Prakrit.

***Śāntinātha-Carita*:** Idealized poetic life-story of Śānthinātha, the sixteenth Tīrthaṃkara. One was written by Māṇikyacandra (q.v.) of thirteenth century and another by Sakalakīrti (q.v.) of the fifteenth century. A *Śāntinātha-caritra* in Sanskrit verses was written by Deva Sūri (q.v.) in AD 1282. There is also a *Śānti-Purāṇa* written by Asaga. An epic under the title *Śāntinātha-caritra* was written by Ajitaprabha of the early fourteenth century. Ed. Muni Indravijaya, Bib. Ind., Calcutta, 1909.

Śānti Sūri: Author and commentator who flourished in the eleventh-twelfth century. Besides his well-known *Jīvavicāra* (q.v.) in 51 Āryā verses, his commentary on the *Uttarādhyayana* is of great interest from the point of view of the history and development of the sects. The commentary is entitled *Siṣyahita*. In AD 1104 he wrote *Pṛthvī-candra-carita* in 7,500 verves.

Śāntiśvara-basti: See Nittur.

Śāntinātha Temples: Quite a good number of Śāntinātha temples are found. Prominent among them are those at Bhandara in Cambay, Jaisalmer Fort, Kaman, Khajuraho, Kheda, Kumbharia, and Rajyapura.

***Śānti Purāṇa*:** See Ponna.

Śāntīśvara-basadi: A temple dedicated to Śāntinātha constructed by Boppa, the son of Gaṅgarāja, the general of the Hoysala Viṣṇu Vardhana, and supported by two officers, Mariyane and Bharatimayya, mentioned in an inscription from Kambadahalli in Nagamangala taluk of the Mandya district, Karnataka. *Mysore Archaeological Report*, 1915, 51.

Saptabhangi-naya: See Logic, *Naya*, Syādvāda.

***Saptakṣetri-Rāsa*:** Composed in Gujarati in AD 1271, it gives in 119 stanzas a detailed description of the seven prescribed channels of religious charity. *Prācīna Gurjara Kāvya Saṃgraha*, ed. C.D. Dalal, Gaekwads Oriental Series, No. 13, Baroda, 1920.

Saptamātṛkā Images: The Brahmanical conception of Saptamātṛkā or seven divine mothers was popular among the Jains. The Satghara cave of the Khaṇḍagiri complex contains their figure guarded by the elephant-headed Gaṇeśa. They have ten-armed, four-armed and two-armed forms and the symbol are (1) Guruḍa and the swan, (2) elephant, (3) bull, (4) indistinct object, (5) peacock, (6) vase and lotus and (7) lion. The first five, on the basis of the emblems in their hands, have some affinity with Brahmāṇī, Vaiṣṇavī, Indrāṇī, Māheśvarī, and Kaumārī. The sixth and seventh stand for Padmāvatī and Ambikā, the Jain forms of Manasā and Durgā. The fourth, fifth, and seventh carry a small child in their arms. All, with the exception of the first, are seated on lotus seats in the *ardhaparyaṅka* or *lalitāsana*. B.C. Bhattacharya describes the first, second, third, fifth, sixth, and seventh as Cakreśvarī, Ajitadevī, Duritāri or Prajñapti, Gaurī or Mānavā, Padmāvatī, and Ambikā. The fifth he has been unable to identify.

***Sapta-Paramasthāna*:** The seven high states of life. These are *sajjātiva*, good society; *sadgṛha-sthatva*, good household state; *sādhutva*, ascetic state; *indratva*, Indra state; *cakravartitva*, emperor state; *jinavaratva*, the state of Jina signifying one who has conquered all enemies; and *nirvāṇa,* complete salvation.

***Saptatikā*:** See Candramahattara.

Saraguru: Findspot of a Jain inscription of AD 1424

in Mysore district in which the Vijayanagara Emperor Vijaya Bukka is said to have granted the village Totahalli for the worship of Gommaṭeśvara of Sravanbelgola. *Epigraphia Carnatica* IV, Hegga 1.

Sarāks: Indigenous Jain population of West Bengal and Bihar, the name Sarāk being derived from Śrāvaka by which name the Jain householders were commonly known. In the *Bṛhaddharma Purāṇa* they are Śāvāka, Sāraka, or Sāvara and described as a mixed caste of the middle rank. Risley's survey of Bengal (1882, 1886) shows that the Sarāks or Sarawaks were settled in the districts of Patna, Gaya, Shahabad, Muzaffarpur, Monghyr, Santal Parganas, Hazaribagh, Lohardanga, Manbhum, Bankura, and Burdwan. Numerically the highest concentration of the Sarāk population is in Lohardaga and Manbhum. Next are Bankura, Santal Parganas, Patna, Gaya, and Hazaribagh. The Sarāks of Manbhum maintain the tradition that their ancestors come from Pachet, that is Panchakot. Dalton introduced the 'Sarawaks' or 'Jains' in Manbhum as the 'earliest Aryan settlers in this part of India'. Contrasted with the Mundas and Kols, the Sarāks of Manbhum-Purulia are distinguished by their fair complexion and a peculiarity of wearing the hair in knob rather high on the back of the head. They are agriculturists and businessmen often functioning as moneylenders. Under the British government no one of their community had ever been convicted of crime. They have great scruples against taking life. They normally do not eat till they see the sun. They venerate Pārśvanātha. Local legends ascribe to the Sarāks the ruined Jain temples and defaced images of the Tīrthaṃkaras. Their centres in Purulia-Manbhum seem to be Suisa in Baghmundi, Dulmi, and Deuli on the river Suvarnarekha, Palma, Charda, and Pakbirda where remains of Jain temples and images have been found. In Bankura their centres were Mandalkuli in Raypur P.S., Ambikanagar in Ranibandh P.S., and Dharapat in Bisnupur P.S. In Burdwan district their stronghold seems to have been at Domohini near Asansol. It appears that the householder Sarāks maintained the tradition of Digambara Nirgranthas and worshipped the nude images of the Tīrthaṃkaras. Yet for the lack of Jain monastic activities in this region, they could not maintain the pristine purity of their creed and worshipped some Brahmaṇical divinities as well. At Chandrokona in Midnapore there was once a flourishing Sarāk community dependent on the textile industry, who were Buddhists. From the late medieval period the Sarāks came under the jurisdiction of greater Hindu society. The advent of medieval Bhakti movements in different parts of Bengal, especially of Gauḍīya Vaiṣṇavism, was to great extent responsible for successfully destroying their Jain roots, but from the middle of the twentieth century, there has been a renaissance among them and a considerable section of the Sarāks are now insisting on their Jain identity and introducing themselves as confirmed Jains.

Sarasvati Images: Head among the Vidyā-devīs (q.v.) who are sixteen in number according to the Jain tradition. As Śrutadevatā, Sarasvatī is the goddess of learning *par excellence*. She presides over *śruta* or the preaching of the Tīrthaṃkaras and Kevalins and is one of the most important objects of worship. One of the earliest representations of this goddess is a headless image in the collection of the Lucknow Museum. The left hand of the goddess holds a manuscript and the pedestal inscription informs us that Sarasvatī was set up in the year 54 or 44, evidently of the Kaniṣka era. It is from Mathura. Various types of Sarasvatī images are found in many Jain temples of India of different dates, and the Śvetāmbaras and Digambaras celebrate a special festival in her honour known as the *Jñāna-pañcamī* or *Śruta-pañcamī*. Two, four, six, eight, and sixteen-armed varieties of the goddess are known, and her mount is almost invariably a swan, and very rarely a peacock. Of these the four-armed images are quite common. V.H. Smith, *Jaina Stūpa and other Antiquities from Mathura*, Allahabad, 1901, 56-7, pl. XCIX; U.P. Shah, 'Iconography of the Jain Goddess Sarasvatī', in *Journal of the University of Bombay*, X.195-218 and plates; J.N. Banerjea, *Development of Hindu Iconography*, Calcutta, 1956, 561-3.

***Sarasvatī-Stotra*:** See Bappabhaṭṭi.

Sarvānandasūri: See Jagaducarita.

***Sarvārthasiddhi*:** See Pūjyapāda.

Śāsana-bastī: A temple at Sravanabelgola which has *ardha-maṇḍapa* and navaraṅga in front. Inside is the statue of Ādinātha with *gomukha* and Cakreśverī. It was erected in AD 1117.

Śāsanadevatās: Yakṣiṇīs who served as attendants of the Tīrthaṃkaras (q.v.) or Jinas and as such possessed divine faculties. Being leaders of the women converts they appear in Jain representations as endowed with supernatural attributes and symbolism of various kinds. The names and symbols of some of the Śāsanadevatās betray unmistakably original ideas of personalities fused with those of older Brahmanical goddesses. Of the Yakṣiṇīs, a good number pass into an order of Jain female deities, called the Vidyā-devīs (q.v.) or goddesses of learning. Additionally too, there are cases in which the Yakṣiṇīs with their consorts have more directly evolved their forms out of semi-mythological incidents. The Śāsanadevatās of the twenty-four Tīrthaṃkaras are known by the following names: Cakreśvarī, Ajitā or Rohiṇī, Duritāri or Prajñapti, Vajraśṛṃkhalā or Kālī, Mahākālī or Puruṣadattā, Acyutā or Śyāmā or Manovegā, Śāntā or Kālī, Bhṛkuṭi or Jvālāmālīnī, Sutārā or Mahākālī, Aśokā or Mānavī, Gaurī or Mānavī, Caṇḍā or Gāndhārī, Viditā or Vijayā or Vairoṭi, Aṃkuśā or Anatamatī, Kandarpā or Pannagadevī or Mānasī, Nirvāṇī or Mahāmānasī, Balā or Acyutā or Vijayā, Dhāraṇī or Tārā, Vairoṭi or Aparājitā, Naradattā or Bahurūpiṇī, Gāndhārī or Cāmuṇḍā, Ambikā or Kuṣmāṇḍī or Āmrā, Padmāvatī, and Siddhāyikā (qq.v.).

Śaśī: See Candraprabha.

Ṣaṣṭhī: Śvetāṃbara sacrament. On the night of the sixth day after the birth of a child the preceptor worships eight goddesses of protection namely Brahmāṇī, Māheśvarī, Kaumārī, Vaiṣṇavī, Vārāhī, Indrāṇī, Cāmuṇḍā, and Tripurā and the goddess Ṣaṣṭhī or Ambā.

***Śāstravārtāsamuccaya*:** See Haribhadra.

***Śatārthakāvya*:** See Somaprabha.

Sātbīs-Deoḍī: Jain shrine at Chitorgarh assignable stylistically to the fifteenth century. It is dedicated to Ādinātha and associated with secondary shrines.

Satdeulia: Findspot of a tenth-century Caumukha in Burdwan district, West Bengal, which is now in the Asutosh Museum, Calcutta University. It is of miniature *rekhā*-deul type with four Jinas or four sides identified respectively with Ṛṣabhanātha, Candraprabha, Pārśvanātha, and Mahāvīra.

Sātgharā Cave: See Bhubaneśvara Caves.

Sātiśayakevalin: See Arhanta.

***Ṣaṭkhaṇḍāgama*:** Also known as *Karmaprābhṛta,* it is composed by Puṣpadant and Bhūtabali and regarded as the earliest and authoritative work on Jain philosophy. According to Hiralal Jain the lost texts of the *Dṛṣtivāda* are the basis of the Prakrit Sūtras of this work. Its contents indicate that the Digambaras and Śvetāmbaras once had a common literature. Its earliest commentary is the *Dhavalā* (q.v.) of Vīrasena which was composed about AD 816. Puṣpadanta and Bhūtabali were the disciples of Dharasena of Girinagara. The former composed the first 29 basic Sūtras and the rest, running to 6,000 Sūtras, were composed by the latter. Its six sections are *jīvasthāna*, *kṣudrakabandha*, *bandhasvāmitva*, *vedanā*, *vargaṇā*, and *mahābandha*. Apart from that of Vīrasena a number of earlier commentaries on the *Ṣaṭkhaṇḍāgama* are mentioned in Indranandin's *Śrautāvatāra*. Edited in 16 volumes by Hiralal Jain, Amraoti, 1939-59.

Śatruñjaya: Temple city at Palitana in Saurāṣtra considered specially sacred to Ṛṣabha, the first Tīrthaṃkara. The temples are said to be over three and a half thousand, grouped in separate enclosures, generally containing one principal temple with other smaller ones. Some of the temples are believed to be as old as the eleventh century, while the majority range from around AD 1500 to the present time. Jinarprabha had given a significant information that about AD 1310-11 the original image of the *mūlanāyaka* Ṛṣabha was destroyed by the Muslims. It was subsequently rebuilt by the merchant Samarā Shah (q.v.) in VS 1371. It is also known as Siddhagiri. Apart from one single Digambara temple, all the temples belong to the Śvetāmbaras. This temple-city is considered by J. Burgess as without a match in the world.

***Śatruñjaya-Māhātmya*:** 'Glorification of the sacred mountain Śatruñjaya' written in Purāṇic style in 14 Sargas by Dhaneśvara (q.v.) in the eighth century at the desire of Śilāditya, king of Valabhi. It begins with a cosmology, followed by the adventures of King Mahīpāla, the story of Ṛṣabha, the flight of the brothers Bharata and Bāhubali, the pilgrimage of the former and erection of shrine on the Śatruñjaya, the Rāma legend, the story of the Pāṇḍavas connected with the Kṛṣṇa legend, Jina Ariṣṭanemi, and so forth. Eng. trans. by J. Burgess. *Indian Antiquary*, XXX, 1901, 239ff., 288ff.

***Sattā*:** Term denoting the *karma* accumulated in the post life.

Sattenapalle Inscription: An inscription on a stone slab dated 37th year of the eighth-century Eastern Cālukya King Viṣṇuvardhana III, found at Sattenapalle taluk of Guntur district which refers to a Jain temple at Munugodu, a saint called Suvratatīrtha and the repairing of the temple by one Boyugaṭṭa. Another inscription on the same slab refers to a gift of land to Pṛthivītilaka-vasati. *Annual Report on South Indian Epigraphy*, 1928-30, 6, Nos. 17-18.

Satyapura: Modern Sanchor in the Jalor district of Rajasthan where was situated a celebrated Mahāvīra temple erected in the eighth century which was destroyed by Mahmud of Ghazni in AD 1024. This temple is remembered in a later inscription from Sanchor. Dhanapāla who lived between AD 970 and 1030 wrote a poem on this famous temple of Mahāvīra. *Archaeological Survey of India* (Western Circle): *Annual Report* 1906-8, 36.

Satyaśāsanaparīkṣā: See Vidyānanda.

Saudāyika: See Andāyika.

Saumanasa: Forest encircling the Meru (q.v.) at its third level of height. It is 500 *yojanas* in width and contains four *prāsādas* or palaces named *vajra*, *vajraprabha*, *suvarṇa*, and *suvarṇaprabha* occupied by the four Lokapālas—Soma, Yama, Varuṇa, and Kubera respectively. There are sixteen *puṣkariṇīs* or lotus-pools, each accommodating in its centre a *vihāra-prāsāda* or place for amusement meant for Saudharma Indra and other celestials. The forest has also four Jinendra-*prāsādas* and peaks or *kūṭas* where live eight Kanyākumārīs known as Meghaṅkarā, Meghavatī, Sumeghā, Meghamālinī, Toyan-dharā, Vicitrā, Puṣpamālā, and Aninditā.

Saundatt: Findspot of few Jain inscriptions of the time of the Western Cālukya Someśvara II. One inscription of AD 1069 of the time of Vikramāditya VI refers to the Raṭṭa feudatories as devout Jains. The contribution of Kārtavīrya II to the cause of the Sugandhavarti Jain temple and a line of teachers are also recorded in this inscription. *Jaina Śilāklekha Saṃgraha* II, Nos. 205. 237.

Śaurasenī: Prakrit language especially of the literature of Digambaras. The *Ṣaṭkhaṇḍāgama* and the *Kaṣāyapāhuḍa* (qq.v.) were composed in the Śaurasenī dialect. Three-fourths of Vīrasena's great commentarial work *Dhavalā* (qq.v.) is written in Śaurasenī. Yativarṣava's *Tiloyapannatī* (*Trilokaprajñapti*, qq.v.) is another important work in Saurasenī. The *Pañcāstikāya*, *Pravacanasāra*, and other works of Ācārya Kundakunda (q.v.), the *Bhagavatī-Ārādhanā* of Sivakoṭi (q.v.) belonging to the Yāpanīya school, the *Mūlācāra* of Vaṭṭakera (q.v.), and a vast mass of commentarial literature show the increasing influence of Śaurasenī on Jain writers. As far as its morphology, syntax, and vocabulary are concerned, Śaurasenī is closer to Sanskrit than Mahārāṣṭrī.

Savati-Gandha-Varaṇa-basti: Temple at Sravanabelgola (q.v.) named after an epithet of Śāntalā-devī, queen of Hoysala Viṣṇu-vardhana. It is a large temple with *garbhagṛha*, *ardha-maṇḍapa*, and *nava-raṅga* and/or image of Śāntinātha.

***Śayaṃbhava*:** The fifth *gaṇadhara* (q.v.) who succeeded Prabhava (q.v.) as the leader of the Jain church. Śayambhava was not basically a Jain. He was a supporter of orthodox Brahmanism and performed numerous scarifices. His mentor was his spiritual predecessor, Prabhava, who finding none among the existing monks fit to succeed him, made a desperate search and came across this talented Brāhmaṇa and converted him to Jainism. Śayambhava succeeded Prabhava in 397 BC according to one reckoning.

***Sayogikevali*:** The thirteenth *guṇasthāna* (q.v.) in which level the Jīva becomes entirely free from all *kaṣāyas* and his *karma* is purged off.

Sculpture: The earliest specimen of Jain art is supposed to be a highly polished torso of a Jina image from Lohanipur in Patna which has been claimed to belong to the Mauryan age, and it is interesting to note that stylistically it is analogous to the mutilated red stone statuette from Mohenjo-daro, thus indicating a continuity in Indian art style. The Harappan style is also found on a bronze statue of Pārśvanātha belonging to the first century BC which is now in the Prince of Wales Museum, Bombay. Its findspot is unknown. Pre-Gupta Jain sculptures pertain mostly to the Mathura finds (q.v). Almost all the seated Tīrthaṃkara figures in the Mathura Museum, which can be dated on the basis of their pedestal inscriptions in the Kuṣāṇa period, show below their seat a wheel of law placed on a pillar in the centre, flanked on either side by devotees, male and female, with a lion at each end. A Ṛṣabha image of the Kaniṣka year 84 has the wheel on a pillar but does not have the bull emblem. Likewise the four Jinas—Nami, Nemi, Pārśva, and Mahāvīra—seated in *samādhi-mudrā* on each side of a *stūpa* on the top section of the sculptured Kanha panel of Kaniṣka year 95 do not have their special symbols. A composite relief in the Lucknow Museum shows Mahāvīra seated in the *dhyāna*-pose on his lion-throne underneath a tree surrounded by the miniature figures of 23 other Tīrthaṃkaras, but none of them has any special mark. A headless image of Sarasvatī of Kaniṣka year 54 from Mathura is in the Lucknow Museum, the left hand of which holds a manuscript. One of the earliest sculptural representations of Harinegamesi or Naigamesa (q.v.) is found in a broken frieze in the collection of the Lucknow Museum, which shows on its obverse the animal-headed deity, described as *bhagava-nemeso*, accompanied by one child and three women and on the reverse of the ornamental slab female dancers and musicians.

The Khaṇḍagiri caves at Bhubaneswar contain some standing and seated Jina images of the later Gupta and early medieval periods. The northernmost Satgharā cave contains on its rear wall two rows of carvings, the upper one representing the first seven Jinas, in *samādhi-mudrā* distinguished by their individual symbols, and the lower consisting of seven female figures guarded by Gaṇeśa. Another section of the same cave contains two rows of figures, the upper showing 24 Jinas and the lower the Śāsana-devatās. A few Jain bronzes from Chausa in Bihar, characterized by crude workmanship, are nevertheless valuable evidence of the continuity and extent of the influence of the Mathura school. Jain images from the caves of Rajgir are not so important as those from Gwalior or Deogarh. Some beautiful specimens of Jain sculptures of the Gupta age are in the Mathura and Lucknow Museums. The Baroda Museum preserves a good number of Akota findings which include bronze images of the Jinas and also one Sarasvatī. Five Jain bronzes from Valabhi belong to the sixth century. Bronze images of the seventh and eighth centuries have been found from Vasantgarh and Bhinmal in Rajasthan, Mahudi, and Simandhara in west India. A group of rock-carvings at Dhank in Saurāṣṭra should be mentioned. Charupa in north Gujarat has yielded a nice stone sculpture of Pārśvanātha. The tenth-century Ṛṣabha image from Surohar (q.v.) in Rajshahi district, Bengal, is shaped like a shrine containing in its centre the main figure seated in *dhyānāsana*, with miniature figures of twenty-three other Jinas similarly seated inside and small shrines all around. Another medieval composition depicting the same theme in a different manner, which is obtained from Barabhum, Midnapur district, is now in the Indian Museum. Three other Jina images from Bengal are characterized by the presence of miniature figures of the Navagrahas on either side of the main figure standing in the *kāyotsarga* pose. A seated Ṛṣabhanātha from Śrāvastī has miniature seated Jina figures on its rectangular *prabhāvalī* in four rows of eight, two, six, and eight. The standing figures of Ajita and Candraprabha, both from Deogarh, have eight and four standing Jinas carved on the back slab. The Fyzabad Museum contains a seated image of Śāntinātha which shows the dancing Navagrahas in the lowermost section of the pedestal, the Upāsaka, Śāsanadevatā, etc. The Dilwara group of marble temples on Mount Abu display some of the finest examples of Jain figure-sculpture, chiefly from the point of view of their exquisite delicacy of carving and remarkable simplicity. Reference must also be made in this connection to the Gommaṭeśvara (q.v.) of Sravanabelgola in which case the top of a granite hill is fashioned into a gigantic statue, 57 feet high. It was carved in AD 983 under the order Cāmuṇḍa Rāya (q.v.). Two other similar colossal statues of Gommaṭa are known, one at Karkal, about 42 feet high erected in AD 1432 and another at Venur 35 feet high which was set up in AD 1604. Though the Yakṣas and Yakṣiṇīs, Upāsakas and Śāsanadevatās, are usually shown as accessory figures in many medieval Jina sculptures, separate figures of some of them are well represented in the Jain temple-carvings of the post-Gupta and later periods. Ambikā, the Śāsanadevatā of Neminātha and consort of Gomedha, is one of the Jain goddesses whose images are found all over India and her two, four, eight, and even twenty-armed varieties of the early and late medieval periods are known. She is a Jain adaptation of the Hindu goddess of the same name, but the Jains have developed a mythology of their own which is not the same as that of her Hindu original. The same holds good also in the case of Padmāvatī, the Śāsanadevatā of Pārśvanātha, whose sculptural representations are also frequently found. The site of Budhi Canderi is rich in Jain sculptures comparable to those of Deogarh Fort. The medieval Jain images hailing from different parts of India reflect a formal stereotyped character, but the attendant figures are displayed in various styles. See Iconography, Jina Images, Yakṣas and their individual names, Śāsanadevatās and their individual names, Cognizances.

Sedam: Findspot of Jain images in the Gulbarga district, Karnataka.

Sembattur: Site in Tiruchirapalli which contains vestiges of structural Jain temples.

Sendalai: Village in Thanjavur district where Jain relics are found.

Seram: Ancient Sedimba, now a subdivisional town in the Gulbarga district, Karnataka, which has yielded an inscription, dated Cālukya Vikrama year 48, of the time of Vikramāditya VI Tribhuvanamalla, which records the construction of a temple of Śāntinātha by some 300 merchants of Sedimba. It also refers to Prabhācandra Traividya Bhaṭṭāraka, a disciple of Rāmacandra Traividya, associated with a Jain centre called Vīrapura. The temple complex of Sedimba is given the name of Brahma Jinalaya. Seram had yielded also inscriptions of the time Someśvara III and IV in which Jain temples and teachers along with the *gacchas*, *gaṇas* and *saṅghas* are mentioned. *South Indian Inscriptions* VII. 723ff.

Śeriśā: Situated on the Ahmedabad-Mehsana Road in Gujarat, this is a Jain *tīrtha* associated with Pārśvanātha. It was visited by Jina Candra III and Jinakuśala, both of Kharatara-gaccha, in the thirteenth century.

Sesali: Holy place, sacred to Pārśvanātha, situated in the Pali district of Rajasthan.

Setavāla: See Saitavāla.

Seṭṭipoḍavu: A popular Jain resort from early times in a cavern near Kilakkudi, a village in Madurai. Some inscriptions supplying information on Jainism in this region have been found here.

Sevāḍi Inscription: Dated VS 1167 (AD 1190), one inscription is incised on the lintel of the door of a subsidiary shrine in the front corridor of the temple of Mahāvīra at Sevāḍi in Pali district, Rajasthan. The inscription records a gift, made for the daily worship of Dharmanātha, the 15th Tīrthaṃkara, and contains the names of King Aśvarāja and his son Kaṭukarāja, the Cāhamāna rulers of Nadol. Another inscription from the same place, bearing the date VS 1172 (AD 1115), refers to a temple of Mahāvīra, the king and his son, benefaction of eight *drammas* by the latter for the worship of Śāntinātha, a Jain general called Yasodeva and Sanderaka Gaccha, a Śvetāmbara religious community, associated with the town of Sanderav, 10 miles north-west of Bali. *Epigraphia Indica*, XI.28ff.

Shergarh: Situated some 90 miles south-west of Kota in Rajasthan. Epigraphs of the tenth century and later refer to the building of Jina temples and also to festivals connected with Neminātha.

Siddha: Final goal of the Jain ascetic in which stage he is free from *karma* and independent of all external objects. He has absolute knowledge, faith, insight, righteousness, prowess, power of becoming minute and colossal at will and of moving anywhere unhindered. He is unaffected by anything so that neither death, disease, rebirth nor sorrow can any longer touch him. The acquisition of Siddhahood is synonymous with attaining *nirvāṇa*, the state of infinite, pure, and radiant bliss. The aspirant receives no boons, no favours, and no curses from him. He worships him and meditates on him as an example or ideal that he too might reach the same condition.

Siddhacakra: Diagram representing the Five Dignitaries (Arhat, Siddha, Ācārya, Upādhyāya, and Sādhu) and Four Conceptions of *jñāna* (right knowledge), *darśana* (right faith), *caritra* (right conduct), and *tapas* (right penance) on stone, metal, canvas or paper. The Śvetāmbaras use the term Siddhacakra, while the Digambaras call it Navadevatā. The Baroda Museum contains one such Siddhacakra in bronze while one on stone has been found in Nadol. Hemacandra refers to the Siddhacakra as a diagram brought to light by Vajrasvāmin. In his commentary *Bṛhannyāsa* on his own *Śabdānuśāsana* he refers to the Siddhacakra as a *Samayaprasiddha* or time-honoured diagram. In paintings of this diagram each of the five Parameṣṭhins has a particular complexion. Thus the Arhat, Siddha, Ācārya, Upādhyāya, and Sādhu are respectively white, red, yellow, blue and black in complexion.

Siddhacakra-Pūjā: Performed by Śvetāmbara Jains twice a year in the months of Caitra and Āśvina. It lasts for nine days between the seventh and last full moon days. The little eight-sided plate with five figures representing the five *parameṣṭhins* (q.v.) and containing the names of the three jewels of Jain faith and the word *tapa* which is kept in every Śvetāmbara temple and known as *siddhacakra* or saint-wheel is taken out in procession and bathed during this festival. This little pilgrimage is known as *jalayātrā*.

***Siddhahemacandra*:** See Hemacandra.

Siddha Jīva: See Mukta Jīva.

Siddhakṣetras: Also known as Nirvāṇakṣetras, these are the holy places where either the Tīrthaṃkaras or other great ascetics realized their liberation. Such holy places are Sammedaśikhara, the modern Pareshnath Hills where, excluding Ṛṣabhanātha, Vāsupūjya, Neminātha, and Mahāvīra, the remaining twenty Tīrthaṃkaras realized emancipation, Śatruñjaya at Palitana in Kathiawad where there are nearly three and a half thousand temples, Gajapantha, Māṅgituṅgī, Kunthalagiri in Mahārāṣṭra, etc.

Siddhanagar: Badwani in Madhya Pradesh known for Jain temples. A hillock called Culagiri contains 22 Jain temples.

Siddhānta-basti: Temple at Mudbidri, Karnataka, which contains illustrated texts of the Digambara Jains.

Siddhapāla-basti: Temple built at Patan, Gujarat, by Siddhapāla son of the poet Śrīpāla.

Siddha Parameṣṭhin: Foremost among the five *Parameṣṭhins* (q.v.) who is an object of Jain worship. After completely conquering all the *karmas* and destroying all the shackles of worldly consequences, he who exists in the supreme purity is endowed with the qualities of infinite perception, infinite knowledge, infinite bliss, and infinite power and is known as *siddha-parameṣṭhin*. This *parameṣṭhin* with infinite qualities is the conquerer of *saṃsāra*, is the Jina and serves as the role model of all who desire to escape from the cycle of birth and death.

Siddhara-basti: Temple at Sravanabelgola, erected on AD 1398. It enshrines a seated figure of a Siddha, about 1 m high. On both sides of the figure stand two fine inscribed pillars.

Siddharṣi: Author of the *Upamitibhava-prapañca-kathā* (q.v.), a religious novel composed in AD 905. In the *praśasti* of this work Siddharṣi has referred to his spiritual predecessors: Sūryācārya of Nivṛtikula who flourished in Lāṭa country; Dellamahattara, an expert in astronomy and prognostics; Durgasvāmin of Bhinmal; Gargasvāmin, and Haribhadra. Siddharṣi also wrote a commentary on *Uvaesamālā* which is available in two recensions.

Siddhasena-Divākara: Logician of the Gupta period who was regarded by both the Śvetāmbaras and Digambaras as one of their own. His *Tattvārthaṭīkā* is a commentary on Umāsvāmin's *Tattvārthādhigama* (q.v.). According to Śvetāmbara tradition he was originally a Digambara thinker from Karnataka and afterwards was defeated and converted by Vṛddhavādin. According to another tradition he performed a miracle in the Mahakāla temple of Ujjayinī. He is said to have written 32 different works on logic, 21 of which are known. His *Nyāyāvatāra* (q.v.) is a fundamental work on Jain logic. His *Sammatitarkasūtra* is a general work on philosophy which also deals with logic. Its commentary *Tattvabodhinī* was made by Abhayadeva (q.v.). Siddhasena was also the author of *Kalyāṇamandira-stotra* (q.v.) and *Dvātriṃśikā-stotra* or *Vardhamāna-Dvātriṃśikā*. *Nyāyāvatāra*, edited with com. and Eng. trans. by S.C. Vidyabhusan, Calcutta, 1909. The *Sammatitarkasūtra* was published with Abhayadeva's commentary in Sanātana Jaina Granthamālā No. 13; *Dvātriṃśikā* containing *Nyāyāvatāra* and other works was edited by A.N. Upadhye in Jain Sāhitya Vikas Mandal, Bombay, 1971.

Siddhāyikā: Śāsanadevatā (q.v.) of Mahāvīra (q.v.) who in the Śvetāmbara tradition rides a lion and carries a citron and a lute and shows the gesture of protection. In Digambara tradition she holds a book and shows the *varada-mudrā*.

Siddheśvara Temple: Situated in Bahulara, Bankura district, West Bengal, this temple houses a Pārśvanātha image.

Siddhipriya Stotra: See Devanandin, Pūjyapāda.

***Siddhiviniścaya*:** See Akalaṅka.

Śikṣāvrata: Disciplinary vows, preparatory for the discipline of an ascetic life. These comprise the last four vows of the seven *śīlavratas* (q.v.). These are *sāmāyika*, taking a vow to devote a special time every day to contemplation of the self for spiritual advancement; *proṣadhopavāsa*, taking a vow to fast on four days of the month, the two eighth and two fourteenth days of the fortnight; *upabhoga-pratibhoga-parimāṇa*, taking a vow every day limiting one's enjoyment of consumable and non-consumable things; and *atithi-saṃvibhāga*, taking a vow to eat only after feeding ascetics, or, in their absence, pious householders.

***Śiladūta*:** Elaborate didactic poem, 'virtue as a messenger' written in early fifteenth century by Cāritrasundara in imitation of Kālidāsa's *Meghadūta*. Edited in Yaśovijaya Jaina Granthamālā, No. 18, Benares, 1909.

***Śīlāṅka*:** Also known as Śīlācārya, he was the commentator on the first two Aṅga texts—*Ācāra* and *Sūtrakṛta*. He wrote the commentaries in about AD 862 or 872, and translated all the Prakrit sources which he used into Sanskrit. He also wrote a *Mahāpuruṣacarita* in AD 869. A Prakrit work entitled *Caupannamahāpuriṣacariyam* dealing with the lives of 54 great men also bears the name of Śīlāṅka as its author. This Śīlāṅka may be the same as the commentator of the first two Aṅgas.

Śīlavrata: Seven supplementary vows comprising three *guṇavratas* (q.v.) and four *śikṣā-vratas* (q.v.). These are *digvrata, deśavrata, anarthadaṇḍa-vrata, sāmāyika, proṣadhopavāsa, upabhoga-paribhoga-parimāṇa* and *atithi-saṃvibhāga* (qq.v.).

***Śīlataraṅgiṇī*:** See *Śilovaesamālā*.

***Śilovaesamālā*:** A didactic poem in 116 Prakrit *gāthās* by Jayakīrti pupil of Jayasiṃha. Its date is not known. In AD 1337 Somatilaka Sūri wrote a commentary on it under the title *Śīlataraṅgiṇī* consisting of narratives.

Simhagiri: Patriarch who headed the Jain church after Dinnasuri. See Suhastin.

Siṃhanandin: Jain Ācārya associated with the foundation of the Western Gaṅga kingdom as the patron-saint of King Koṅkaṇivarman. Its indirect mention is found in a damaged copper plate of the reign of Śivamāra I (AD 670-713). The Udayendrian grant of Hastimalla dated *circa* AD 920 tells that the Gaṅga family flourished because of Siṃhanandin's help. This is attested also by an inscription dated Śaka 884 of the reign of Mārasiṃha and by another inscription dated AD 1077. A more detailed account regarding the relation between Siṃhanandin and the Gaṅga royal dynasty is found in an inscription of AD 1121 obtained from the Shimoga district, Karnataka, Siṃhanandin's connection with the founder of the Gaṅga dynasty is also confirmed by an old commentary of the *Gommaṭasāra*. *Mysore Archaeological Report*, 1911-12; 1925-91; *South Indian Inscriptions* II, 387; *Epigraphia Carnatica*, VII, 139, No. 46; *Jaina Śilālekha Saṃgraha*, II, No. 277.

Simhapura: Place sacred to Neminātha which is situated on the river Kaveri. It was also called Narasiṃhapattana and regarded as a Jain *tīrtha* by the Jñānasāgara of the sixteenth century.

Siṃhapurī: Same as Sarnatha where, according to the Jain tradition, Śreyāṃśanātha was born.

Sin: See *Pāpa*.

Sindaṅgere-basadi: Jain establishment mentioned in an epigraph of AD 1138 of the time of Hoysala Viṣṇuvardhana found at Sindigere in the Chikmagalur district, Karnataka. *Epigraphia Carnatica*, VI.

Singigere: Situated in the Chikmagalur district, Karnataka, it is the findspot of an inscription of AD 1138 which records a grant for Sindangere-basadi by the Hoysala Viṣṇuvardhana. It also mentions Kulacandra of Kundakunda-anvaya, his disciple Māghanandī and grand-disciple Gaṇḍavimukta. *Epigraphia Carnatica* VI, Chik No. 161.

***Sindūraprakara*:** See Somaprabha.

Sira Pāharī: Jain centre in Panna district, Madhya Pradesh now sunk into oblivion.

Sirohi: A district-town of Rajasthan which was very closely associated with Jainism. The Ādinātha temple of this place was built in the thirteenth century which was followed by construction of temples dedicated to Pārśvanātha, Śāntinātha and other Tīrthaṃkaras. The evangelist Hīravijaya was associated with this place and several Jain works were written here.

Sirramur Inscription: Found at Sirramur in South Arcot district, this inscription, supposed to be associated with Sundara Cola (AD 956-73), records the provision of a lamp in the *maṇḍapa* of the temple of Pārśvanātha. *Annual Report on Indian Epigraphy*, 1902, 201.

***Śiṣyahitā*:** See Nemicandrasūri.

Śītalanātha: The tenth Tīrthaṃkara who was the son of King Dṛḍharatha and queen Nandā of Bhaddilapura which has been tentatively identified with Bhadra, a village in the Hazaribagh district, Jharkhand. His height was 90 bow-lengths and the span of his life was a hundred thousand years. His sacred tree was the *bilva* or *pilanka* and chief disciples Ananda and Sulasā. He attained liberation on Mount Sammeya. According to a different version, his mother's name was Sunandā, his father ruled over Malaya kingdom and his birth-place was Madrapura. His *chowri*-bearer was called Rājā Simanghara. His Yakṣa is Brahma and Yakṣiṇī Aśokā/Mānavī. The Digambaras regard the *aśvattha* as his emblem, the Śvetāmbaras the *śrīvatsa* (wishing tree) for the same. According to Hemacandra the Jina received the name Śītalanātha inasmuch as he could take away men's heat of sorrow.

Śītalā Saptamī: Festival observed by Jain women of Gujarat as protection against small-pox and part of regional culture.

Śithila: *Karma*, the influx of which may be evaded.

Sittannavasal: Site in Tirumayam taluk of Tiruchirapalli district which was in continuous occupation by the Jains from about the second century BC to the ninth century AD. The rock-cut Jain cave-temple at Sittannavasal is called in its inscription, Arivar-Kovil or Annalvayil, that is, temple of the Arhat at Annavasal. It is a typical *maṇḍapa*-type cave temple having an oblong rock-cut *maṇḍapa* with a facade of two pillars and two pilasters and a square shrine-cell behind. Important Jain paintings have been discovered from Sittannavasal, some of them belonging to a time around AD 600 or a little later. The paintings are on the ceilings, capitals, and upper parts of the pillars of the rock-cut temple. Jouveau Dubreuil in *Indian Antiquary*, LII, 45ff.

Śivabhūti: See Digambara-Śvetāmbara split.

Śivagaṅga: Findspot of a Jain inscription of AD 1140 in Nilamangala taluk of Bangalore district, Karnataka, which, though a Śaiva record, refers to the construction of a Jina temple by a chief called Viṣṇuvardhana. *Epigraphia Carnatica* IX, Nela 84.

Śivakotyācārya: See *Vodda-ārādhana*.

Śivamāra II: Western Gaṅga king who was a devout Jain. One of his inscriptions found in Belgaum district tells us that he had erected a basadi in Kummada boulder near Candranāthasvāmin basadi at Sravanabelgola refers to his erection of the said shrine. The outer side of the third plate of the inscription from Narasiṃharājapura also reflects his attraction towards Jainism. *Indian Antiquary*, XVIII.313; *Epigraphia Carnatica* II. 180; *Mysore Archaeological Report*, 1911, 34; *Mysore Gazetteer* II.642.

Śivakoṭi: See Mūlārādhanā.

Śivasarma Suri: Author of *Karmaprakṛti*, an exhaustive work on the doctrine of *karma* in 475 *gāthās*. The work is supposed to contain materials of the *Dṛṣtivāda*. Edited with Malayagiri's com. Bhavnagar, 1922.

Skandamaha: Festival of Skanda. From the *Āvaś-*

yaka Cūrṇi and *Bṛhatkalpabhāṣya* it is learnt that Skanda is a folk-deity who is the leader of demons of illness that attack children; he is also the god of burglers and thieves. The festival of Skanda was celebrated on the full-moon day of Āśvina. It is stated that when Mahāvīra visited Śrāvastī the image of Skanda was being taken in a procession in a chariot. The image of Skanda and Rudra was made of wood. An oil lamp was kept burning in front of the image during night.

Slave Girls: Jain literature refers to female salves. Some were born slaves, some were purchased, others were reduced to slavery as they were unable to pay fines or debts. In *Piṇḍa Niryukti* 327ff., we are told of a widow, who in order to entertain her ascetic brother, borrowed two *palis* of oil from a grocer which she could not pay for in time and was forced to serve him as a slave. In *Āvaśyaka Cūrṇi* 300, 331ff. we find slave girls employed for household work. They cleaned utensils, threshed corn, cooked, and conveyed messages. We are told about an old slave woman, who was asked to collect firewood from the jungle and was punished by her master when she failed to bring the required quantity. In the *Uttarādhyayana-vṛtti* 12 of Nemicandrasūri we find slave girls helping their mistress in carrying food, perfumes, flowers, and garlands to the temple of Yakṣa (q.v.) for worship. Female slaves were brought from foreign countries including Barbara, Palhava, Drāviḍa, Siṃhala, Āraba, and Pārasa. They looked pretty in their native dress. They were skilled in apprehending the emotions of lovers according to the *Bhagavatī* and *Nīśītha Sūtra*, and were accomplished in arts and well trained. Female servants could be a part of a dowry. Many of them regained their freedom by voluntary manumission when their forehead was washed after receiving the news of the birth of a male child. The slaves were treated as property of their master. *Nāyādhammakahāo* I.20, I.23, I.29, *Nīśītha Sūtra* IX.28; *Viyāhapannatti* IX.6.

Slavery: Various types of salves are mentioned in the Jain texts. According to *Sthānāṅga* and *Nīśītha-bhāṣya*, some are born slaves, some purchased, others are reduced to slavery as they are unable to pay the fine or debts, some are made to accept slavery during a famine. This is an echo of Manu's view on slaves. The *Nāyadhammakahāo* refers to many incidents regarding the maltreatment of the slave boys. Female slaves were employed for household work. They formed a part of the dowry. The *Nāyādhammakahāo* says that many of them regained freedom under diverse circumstances. The slaves were treated as the property of their master along with quadrupeds and other possessions. The custom of slavery has not been discouraged by Jainism and Buddhism.

Śobhana, *Śobhanastuti*: Author of a celebrated hymn in praise of 24 Jinas who lived in the second half of the tenth century. It is called *Sobhanastuti* after the name of the author and in the sense of being beautiful. It is very interesting from the viewpoint of the figures of speech. Ed. and German trans. by H. Jacobi in *ZDMG* XXXII, 1878, 509ff; Kāvyamālā edn., Bombay, 1912.

Sobhnath Temple: Sambhavanātha temple at Śrāvastī of which we have virtually no data except a highly damaged brick structure.

Sohagpur: Previously a Jain centre in the Shahdol district which is attested by a considerable number of Jain sculptures including those of Śāsanadevatās collected in the Ṭhākur's palace.

Somacandra: See *Kathāmahodadhi.*

Somadeva Sūri: See *Yaśastilaka-campū*, *Nītivākyāmṛta* and *Adhyātmataraṅgiṇī.*

Somamūrti: See *Jineśvara-Sūri-Saṃyamaśrī-Vivāha-Varnaṇa-Rāsa.*

***Somaprabha*:** A younger contemporary of Hemacandra (q.v.) and author of *Kumārapāla-Pratibodha*, a didactic poem and collection of tales, in verse and prose, for the most part in Prakrit, but also in Sanskrit and Apabhraṃśa. It is written in AD 1184 and consists of five *prastāvas*, the first on the commandments as to conduct, the second on the worship of gods and teachers, the third on the four duties, the fourth on the vows of laymen, and the fifth on the four passions. His other works are an Apabhraṃśa hymn dedicated to Pārśva, *Śatārthakāvya* composed about AD 1177-9 in which a single verse in Vasantatilaka metre is explained in 100 different ways, and *Sindūraprakara* or *Suktimuktāvali*, a book of moral sayings composed in AD 1199. He also wrote in Prakrit an idealized biography of Sumatinātha. There was a second Somaprabha who wrote in about AD 1276 the *Śṛṅgāravairāgya-Taraṅgiṇī*, a didactic poem in 46 elaborate stanzas describing the charms of women and the blandishments of love as a warning against them. *Kumārapālapratibodha*, ed. Muniraja Jinavijaya, Gaekwad's Oriental Series, No. 14, Baroda, 1920; *Sindūraprakara*, edited in Kāvyamālā VII; *Śṛṅgāravairāgya-Taraṅgiṇī*, edited in Kāvyamālā V.

Somasundara: Fifteenth-century exponent of Jainism in Gujarat, whose activities are mainly from the poem *Somasaubhāgyakāvya* composed by this pupil Pratiṣṭhāsoma in vs 1524 of the Tapā-gaccha. Another work of the same name was composed later by Sumatisādhu, pupil of Lakṣmīsāgara. He repaired many Jain temples in Gujarat and Rajasthan in which work he was helped by Jain merchants like Narasiṃha of Patan, Devarāja of Vaḍnagara, Viśāla and Govinda of Idar, Guṇarāja of Karnavati, etc. In connection with his work of repairing the Jain temples, ravaged by the Muslim iconoclasts, he visited Devakulapāṭaka, Ranakapura, Citrakūṭa, Girnar. His name is mentioned on the metal images of Pārśvanātha, Śāntinātha, and Sambhavanātha found from Ahmedabad.

Somatilakasūri: See *Kumārapālapratibodhacarita*, *Silovaesamālā*.

Somavara: Findspot of Jain epigraphs in Arkalgud taluk, Hassan district, Karnataka. One inscription of AD 1060 gives the name of Guṇasena Paṇḍita, belonging to Drāviḍa-gaṇa, Nandī-saṅgha and Aruṅgala-anvaya. A few other inscriptions from this place yield the names of a number of Jain monks and a Jain temple. *Jaina Śilālekha Saṃgraha* II, Nos. 192, 220, 234, 236.

Someśvara: Author of the historical *mahākāvya Kīrtikaumudī* written in honour of his patron Vastupāla (q.v.). Though it is not a Jain work, its last two cantos tell about the doctrine of *ahiṃsā* and describe his patron's pilgrimage to Śatruñjaya and Urjayanta. Someśvara also wrote *praśastis* on Abu and Girnar. His *Surathotsava*, the last canto of which praises his patron, is edited by Sivadatta and Parab, Bombay, 1902, and *Kīrtilatā* by Kabhavate, Bombay, 1883.

Someśvara Cāhamāna: See Bijolia Rock Inscription.

Sonāgiri: Well-known Jain temple-complex in Datia district, Madhya Pradesh. A seventh-century inscription discovered here refers to a Jain devotee called Vaḍāka who was the son of Siṃhadeva. Several other image-inscriptions of the period between AD 1200 and 1600 have been found from various temples of this locality.

Sonāmukhi-Ṛṣabhanātha: Eleventh-century image of unique interest found at Sonāmukhī in Bankura district, West Bengal. The Jina is seated in *dhyānāsana* on a lotus supported on the outspread foliage of a tree below. On either side appears a standing attendant figure, while above, on each side of the halo, is seen a flying Vidyādhara. Over the head of the Jina is seen the parasol, while in the centre of the lotus seat is depicted the cognizance, the bull. On the pedestal, on two sides of the tree, are shown a couple, a male and a female, seated at ease with a halo round the head. On the pedestal there are also other figures of which only a pair of demons may be recognized.

Sonda: Findspot of two Jain copper-plate inscriptions of AD 1522 which record some grant for the Huligere Samkha-basadi by a prominent citizen of this area. Both the inscriptions refer to the monk Candraprabha who belonged to the Deśī-gaṇa, and disciple of Vijayakīrti-deva. *Jaina Śilāekha Saṃgraha*, IV, Nos. 462-3.

Sosavura-basadi: Jain establishment mentioned in an inscription from Angadi in Mudigere taluk, Chikmagalur district, Karnataka. *Epigraphia Carnatica*, VI, Mudi 9.

Śramaṇa: See Muni. A spiritual aspirant after virtuous conduct as prescribed in the texts, is admitted into the order as a Śramaṇa. The *Pravacanasāra* of Kundakunda and *Mūlācara* of Vaṭṭakera defines Śramaṇa as one who has no desires in this world and no attachment for the next, whose diet and touring are proper and who is free from passion. An ideal Śramaṇa should always live with an ascetic of merit. A Śramaṇa should not take what has not been given to him. He should not take even an umbrella or vessel or stick of the monks with whom he stays without their permission. What is got from alms is to be distributed among others. The Śramaṇa has to retain contact with his near or remote spiritual relations, namely teacher, sub-teacher, religious guide, sthavira, head of the *gaṇa*, *gaṇadhara*, and so forth. His principle declaration is as follows: 'I shall become a Śramaṇa who owns no house, no property, no sons, no cattle, who eats what others give him. I shall commit no sinful action. Master, I renounce to accept anything that has not been given to me.' *Ācārāṅga* II.1.10.11; II.7.1.1; II.15.1-5.

***Śrautāvatāra*:** See Indranandin.

Śrāvaka, Śrāvikā: Lay male and female devotees. According to the Digambara tradition a Śrāvaka or a layman has to pass through 53 ceremonies right from his conception up to his death, while the Śvetāmbaras observe 16 such ceremonies. These are not however, practised in a uniform manner. The life of a Jain Śrāvikā is marked by observances of ethical disciplines. Śrāvikās or female lay devotees are as important as the Śrāvakas. The *Kalpasūtra* says that 3,000 females attained liberation under Neminātha and as many as 20,000 under Pārśvanātha, while in the time of Mahāvīra the number of *sādhvīs* and *śrāvikās* rose to 36,000 and 3,18,000 respectively. A large number of women in Jain history distinguished themselves as donors to various religious institutions as is attested by Jain inscriptions. The ascetic's life is regarded as a continuation of the householder's life and the rules of conduct are exactly the same for both, laymen and ascetics. This fosters an intimate relationship between the two main divisions of the community. The difference is that the ascetics are to observe the ethical codes more strictly and elaborately. The *anuvratas* or small vows are meant for the Śrāvakas. It is enjoined upon a householder to abstain from intentional violence but not from accidental, occupational, or protective violence. The *anuvaratas* (q.v.) are for the Śrāvakas.

***Sravakacara*:** See Devasena.

Sravanabelgola: One of the most important Jain centres in the Hassan district of Karnataka. According to very late Jain traditions Candragupta, in his last days, renounced the world and died of *sallekhanā* at Sravanabelgola where some local inscriptions still perpetuate the memory of Candragupta and Bhadrabāhu living together as saints. The hill where he lived is still known as Candragiri and a temple erected by him as Candragupta-vasati. One of the many Prabhācandras (q.v.) of Jain tradition was associated with this place and occurs in an inscription of AD 600. It also associated with saints like Gautama, Lohārya, Jambu, Viṣṇudeva, Aparājita, Govardhana, Bhadrabāhu, Viśākha, Prosthila, Kṛttikārya, Jayanāman, Siddhārtha, Dhṛtiseṇa, Buddhila and others. The topmost section of the granite hill Indragiri has been fashioned here as the 57 feet high gigantic statue of Gommaṭeśvara carved under the orders of Cāmuṇḍarāya (q.v.) in about AD 983. One of the earliest temples of this place was dedicated to Candraprabha (q.v.). Several Jain shrines were built in this holy place afterwards among which Pārśvanātha temple, Bhandari-basadi, Nagara Jinālaya, etc., may be mentioned. Other inscriptions, ranging between AD 600 and 800, record the *samādhi* of a few prominent Jain saints including one female ascetic. Among such saints mention may be made of Ācārya Ariṣṭanemi (No. 11) and Akṣayakīrti (No. 21). The earliest Rāṣṭrakūṭa Jain inscription comes from Sravanabelgola. It is of Kambayya or Stambha. It has been suggested on the basis of a Sravanabelgola inscription of AD 1129 that the philosopher Akalaṅka was patronized by Dantidurga. Inscriptions of the eleventh-twelfth centuries shows that Jain scholars like Vāsavacandra, Vādirāja, etc., were honoured by the Western Cālukya kings. Subsequent Jain inscriptions are mainly connected with the religious activities of kings, queens, feudatories and generals of the Hoysala dynasty. One inscription of AD 1123 records the erection of a Jaina temple named Savatigandhavaraṇa-basti by Sāntaladevī, queen of Hoysala Viṣṇuvardhana. The death of this queen is mentioned in several epigraphs and her parents were devout Jains. An epigraph dated AD 1117 records the erection of a Jina temple by two merchants. A few other inscriptions of the same time refer to the pious activities of Gaṅgarāja and his wife Lakṣmī. An inscription of AD 1160 says that Bharata, a general of Hoysala Viṣṇuvardhana, built 80 new Jaina basadis and renovated 200 Jina temples in Gaṅgavāḍi. Another inscription of AD 1159 holds that Hulla, treasurer of Viṣṇuvardhana, erected at Belgola a temple of 24 Tīrthaṃkaras, known as Bhāṇḍārī-basadi. These inscriptions and those of the time of Ballāla II refer to the names of celebrated Jain teaches like Guṇacandra, Nayakīrti, Bālancandra, Bhānukīrti, Māganandī, Padmanandī, Nemicandra, etc. An inscription of AD 1195 records the construction of the famous Nagara Jinālaya by a royal officer named Nāgadeva whose other pious activities are recorded in quite a good number of Sravanabelgola inscriptions. Epigraphs of the thirteenth century of the time of Hoysala Narasiṃha II and III record donations to various temples and grants to well-known teachers by businessmen and wealthy persons. Among the teachers the name of Māghanandī comes in front. Quite a good number of inscriptions of the fourteenth and fifteenth centuries tell about the patronage of the Vijayanagara kings to Jains. Bhīmādevī, queen of Devarāja I was a disciple of Paṇḍitācārya and installed a Jina image according to a fifteenth-century epigraph. *Epigraphia Carnatica*, rev. edn. II. Nos. 64, 67, 69, 73, 118, 125-7, 132, 137, 141-3, 178, 181, 186, 240, 251, 265-7, 301, 326-7, 335, 345-6, 380.

Sravanahalli: Findspot of a Jain inscription of the early twelfth century in the Mysore district of the time of Hoysala Viṣṇuvardhana which mentions the gift of a village for Vīra Kongālva Jinālaya by the queen Cantaladevī and her friend Duddamalla. The recipient was Prabhācandra Siddhāntadeva, disciple of Meghacandra Traividya of Pustaka-gaccha and Deśīya-gaṇa. *Jaina Śilālekha Saṃgraha* IV, No. 188.

Śrāvastī: City of ancient Kosala *janapada*, now situated in the Bahraich district of Uttar Pradesh. It was the birth-place of Sambhavanātha. An early Śvetāmbara *śākhā*, called Śrāvastikā had originated from this place. The discovery of

Jain images of the Gupta period from this place proves the flourishing condition of Jainism at Śrāvastī. Later Jinaprabha saw here a temple of Sambhavanātha. The Jain establishments of this place were destroyed by Alauddin Khalji's general Habbasa.

Śreyāṃśa Nātha: The eleventh Tīrthaṃkara who was the son of King Viṣṇu and Queen Viṣṇā or Viṣṇudrī of Siṃhapurī near Vārāṇasī. His height was 80 bow-lengths and span of life was 8,400 thousand years. His chief disciples were Gothubha and Dhāriṇī. He achieved liberation on Mount Sammeya. His symbol is the rhinoceros. His attendants were Yakṣeta and Mānavī, in Digambara tradition, Īśvara and Gaurī. The tree special to him was *tumbara* or *tindaka*. Rājā Tripiṣṭa Vāsudeva was his *chowri*-bearer. According to Hemacandra his name Śreyāṃśa was due to the fact that he was destined to do good to all beings.

***Śrīcandra*:** Pupil of Maladhārī Hemacandra (q.v.) who wrote an epic *Munisrvratasvāmīcarita* in AD 1135. Another Śrīcandra of the Candragaccha composed the *Sanatkumāracarita* comprising 8127 verses in AD 1157. The story of Sanatakumāra, the Cakravartin, is full of all sorts of romantic and supernatural elements. The author of the *Kathākośa* (q.v.) in Apabhraṃśa is also known as Śrīcandra. It contains 53 tales for moral and religious instruction and belongs to the tenth or eleventh century AD. The Sanskrit Praśasti tells us that the author was a pupil of Vīracandra of the Kundakunda line of teachers.

Śrīdeva: Also known as Devasuri, he was a celebrated Jain philosopher of the early twelfth century who was patronized by the Cālukya King Jayasiṃha Siddharāja of Gujarat. According to *Prabhāvakacarita* 172ff. he scored several victories over his opponents: at Satyapura he defeated Sāgara of Kashmir; at Dhavalaka he defeated the Śaiva philosopher Dhanada; at Nāgapura (Nagaur) he defeated Guṇacandra, the Digambara philosopher; at Citrakūṭa he defeated the Bhāgavata philosopher Śivabhūti; and at Gopagiri, Gaṅgādhara. He was a staunch exponent of the Śvetāmbara tradition and his greatest achievement was his victory over Kumudacandra (q.v.), the great Digambara logician. King Jayasiṃha Siddharāja, by way of reward, honoured him with twelve villages and a shawl and other presents.

Śrīdhara: See *Sukumāla-cariu*.

Śrīkīrti: One of the earliest pontiffs of the Nandi Saṅgha belonging to the lineage of Kundakunda. Some scholars are inclined to identify him with the homonymous Digambara teacher mentioned in Śrīcandra's Apabhraṃśa *Kathākośa* in which he has been described as honoured by two great kings, namely, Bhoja and Gaṅgaya, which suggests that Śrīkirti lived in the first quarter of the eleventh century.

Śrī-Lakṣmī: Śrī or the goddess of wealth has been described as a four-handed figure holding a flower and lotus. In some texts we have an elephant as her vehicle. The special day on which honour is done to the goddess of wealth is called *dhanaterasa*. On the same occasion women polish their jewellery and ornaments. The description of Jain Lakṣmī does not differ far from that of the Brahmanic Śrī or Kamalā. The conception of Lakṣmī is very old in Jainism since the goddess is mentioned in the *Kalpasūtra* as one of the objects of Triśalā's dream.

Śrīmālī: Important Jain mercantile caste, mainly of Śvetāmbara affiliation, concentrated in Rajasthan and Gujarat. Originally this caste, which is also found among the Hindus, hailed from Śrīmāla in Rajasthan. According to tradition the Śrīmālīs were converted into Jainism by Ācārya Svayamprabha Sūri. They are divided into Viśās and Daśās, 'twenties' and 'tens'. They have a third branch Lāḍavas, so called because they lived in the old Lāṭa deśa, southern Gujarat. Viśā Śrīmālīs have seven divisions: Ahmedābādīs, Kaṭhāriyās, Pālhanapuriyās, Pāṭaṇis, Soraṭhiyās, Talabadas, and Theradiyās. The Daśā Śrīmālīs have three divisions: Horasaṭha, Caṇāpahuā, and Iḍadiyā. The Laḍavā Śrīmālīs have no division. The three main divisions with their subdivisions eat together but do not intermarry. The Viśās and Daśās may have matrimonial relations with the Viśās and Daśās of other Jain castes as also with their Vaiṣṇava caste-counterparts. The Śrīmālīs have 135 *gotras* or exogamous sections.

Sringeri: Findspot of a Jain inscription of AD 1150 in Chikmagalur district, Karnataka. It is found in a local Pārśvanātha temple and mentions Mūlasaṅgha, Kranura-gaṇa, and Pustaka-gaccha. According to another inscription from this place, the temple was built by the wife of a merchant. *Jaina Śilālekha Saṃgraha* IV, 255, 464-5.

Śrīpāla: Jain poet, one of the greatest literary figures of Gujarat. He was the author of the Vaḍnagar Praśasti of Kumārapāla (q.v.). From this inscription we learn that he was the adopted brother of Siddharāja. His son Siddhapāla was also very close to Kumārapāla and grandson Vijayapāla was a playwright. *Epigraphia Indica*, I.293-306; *Kumārapāla Pratibodha* 477-8; Jinavijaya's intro. to Vijayapāla's *Draupadī-svayaṃvara*.

Śrīpura: Sirpur in Akola district of Maharashtra which contained an ancient Pārśvanātha temple. Madankīrti of the twelfth century had mentioned this *tīrtha* in his *Śāsanacatustriṃśikā*.

Srirangapattana: Situated near Mysore town, this place contained temples of Ṛṣabha, Pārśva, and Mahāvira during Śilavijaya's time in the seventeenth century.

Śrīvatsa Devī: See Mānavī.

Śrī-Vijaya-basadi: One of the most prominent Jain temples of Lakshmeswar in the Dharwar district of Karnataka. It was built probably during the reign of the Western Gaṅgas.

Śṛṅgāra-Caurī: Temple at Chitorgarh, Rajasthan, dedicated to Śāntinātha. Built in AD 1448, the temple has a *garbhagṛha* and other necessary requirements. The temple-exterior is characterized by numerous varieties of sculptural work. Charming depictions of animals and human beings also occur on the *pīṭha* and *vedikā* portions. The sculptured figures here are purely conventional in character. Brahmanical gods also occur in the reliefs.

***Śṛṅgāravairāgya-Taraṅgiṇī*:** See Somaprabha.

Śruta: Knowledge revealed by scriptures. The science of scriptural record consists in the faithful compilation of the old as well as up to date thoughts of other thinkers as also the thoughts founded on one's own experience. The object of this science is that no thought, or way of thought, which aims at truth, should be ignored, and therefore the science has gradually developed along with the growth of new light of thought. The field of activity of the attitude of non-absolutism is so vast that all empirical and transcendental sciences that are conducive to the well-being of human life find their proper place in it. It is for this reason that, in addition to the transcendental sciences, the empirical sciences have also found a place in Jain scriptures. Śruta or Śruti belongs to the *parokṣa* (q.v.) or indirect knowledge in *Sthānāṅga* VI and *Nandīsūtra*. It is due to the fact that in Śruta-jñāna knowledge of things, of past, present, and future, is acquired though reasoning and study. *Tattvārtha* I.20. See Epistemology.

Śruta-Devī: See Sarasvatī. She seems to be at the head of the sixteen Vidyādevīs (q.v.) and her worship is prior to that of other subordinate deities. The description of Śruta-devī as afforded in the Jain texts places her on a par with Brahmāṇī (wife of Brhmā, the promulgator of Śruti or Vedic knowledge in Brahmanical tradition). The Jains make a special ceremony of her worship on the *Śuklāpañcamī* day of Kārttika month which they call *Jñānapañcamī*. On that special day the devout Jains fast, worship books, and instal them carefully dusted. Śruta-devī or Sarasvatī, as viewed by the Śvetāmbaras, rides a swan and has four hands bearing a lotus, a book and rosary and showing *varada-mudrā*. The Digambara texts seem to give the peacock vehicle to Sarasvatī. Śruta-devī images are common.

Śrutakevalin: The six *gaṇadharas* (q.v.) who succeeded Jambūsvāmin as heads of the Jain church. The first three after Mahāvīra were *kevalin*. The *śrutakevalins* lacked the omniscience of the *kevalins*, but had complete knowledge of the scripture.

Śruta Pañcamī: Special holy day observed by the Digambara Jains of the fifth day of the month of Jaiṣṭha to commemorate the occasion of the composition of *Ṣaṭkhaṇḍāgama* by Puṣpadanta and Bhūtabali. On this day they worship their sacred books and remove dust and insects from them. The Śvetāmbaras perform *Jñānapañcamī* instead of *Śrutapañcamī* on the fifth day of the bright half of Kārttika. They worship their sacred books on this occasion.

Śrutasāgara: Digambara scholar who flourished between AD 1400 and 1540. His *Tattvārthadīpikā* is a commentary on the *Tattvārthasūtra*. He has also commented on Āśādhara's *Jinasahasranāma*. His commentary on the *Yaśastilakacampū* is incomplete. He was a pupil of Vidyānanda. His other works are *Jainendrayajñavidhi* and a commentary on *Ṣaṭprābhṛta*.

***Śruti-Ajñāna*:** That which covers up the sources of knowledge occurring from the misunderstanding of scriptures. It is an obstruction arising from *ghātin karma* (q.v.).

Stambhapura: Modern Cambay in Gujarat which, according to the tradition was made a Jain *tīrtha* by the celebrated commentator Abhayadeva. Apart from temples, hundreds of Jain manuscripts were copied from this place.

Sthānakavāsī: Non-idolatrous Śvetāmbara subsect, also known as Dhuṇḍiyā, Bistolā, Sādhumārgī. The Sthānakavāsīs arose not directly from the Śvetāmbaras but as a challenging branch of the Loṅkā (q.v.) sect. Virāji of Surat, a reformer originally belonging to the Loṅkā sect, founded the Sthānakavāsī sect about AD 1653. They were so called because they lived in Apāsara instead of temples and were also known as Dhuṇḍiyās or 'searchers'. Except on the point of idol-worship, at present the Sthānakavāsīs do not differ much from other Śvetāmbara Jains.

***Sthānāṅga Sūtra*:** Prakrit *Ṭhāṇāṅga*, the third text of the Aṅga (q.v.) category. Various themes of the religion are dealt with in numerical order from one to ten in this volume. These enumerations sometimes contain parables in a nutshell. There are also enumerations on non-religious matters, such as the ten themes of mathematics. It also contains a table of contents of the *Dṛṣṭivāda* (Ditthivāya) which is now lost. The title of the text means 'the Aṅga of the items' that is, of the subjects enumerated under one-ten categories. The text has ten *adhyayanas* and 787 Sūtras. Edited in Āgamasaṃgraha III, Benares, 1880, with a Sanskrit and a Prakrit commentary; with Abhayadeva's com. Bombay, 1918-20, Ahmedabad, 1937.

Sthāpana-worship: Worshipping the material representations of the Tīrthaṃkaras like pictures, images, symbolic objects, etc.

***Sthāvara Jīva*:** Immobile or one-sensed souls. They possess only the sense of touch. The immobile or one-sensed beings are of five kinds: *pṛthvī-kāya*, earth-bodied; *apkāya*, water-bodied, *tejaḥkāya*, fire-bodied, *vāyukāya*, air-bodied and *vanaspatikāya*, vegetable-bodied. *Tattvārtha* II.21-3.

Sthūlabhadra: Patriarch who became the head of the Jain church after Bhadrabāhu. He was the son of Śakaṭāla, the prime minister of the last Nanda king. When Bhadrabāhu was the patriarch, foreseeing an impending famine he went to the south with his followers leaving behind Sthūlabhadra in charge of the monks who did not follow him. The monks under Sthūlabhadra who preferred to stay in Magadha, notwithstanding the diffculties caused by the famine, and were probably the older and infirm section of the Saṅgha, adopted several modifications on the rules of their conduct. Among other things they wore white robes and also a peculiar head-dress known as the *ardhaphālaka*. The famine over, the southern monks returned and disapproved of the changes. This was the beginning of the separatist tendencies within the order. According to one tradition Bhadrabāhu died at Sravanabelgola, appointing Viśākha as his successor. The latter, however, did not pose any threat to the authority of Sthūlabhadra. According to a second tradition Bhadrabāhu did not die. He returned from south India at the end of the famine to head the whole community and his followers declined to accept not only the reformation in the matter of dress and code of conduct, but also the proceedings of the Council of Pāṭaliputra summoned by Sthūlabhadra during Bhadrabāhu's absence. In the Pāṭaliputra council some scriptural texts—the twelve Aṅgas—were compiled under his leadership. Mahāvīra's teachings were first compiled in fourteen texts, called the Pūrvas, meaning the earlier books, which are lost. But the Śvetāmbaras believe that the Pūrvas were incorporated in the now lost *Dṛṣṭivāda*, the twelfth Aṅga. These Pūrvas might have consisted of traditions handed down orally from teacher to pupil and some part of this oral tradition might have been compiled by Sthūlabhadra in the Pāṭaliputra council. The work of the council, however, was repudiated by Bhadrabāhu or his followers, which was an additional cause of the growth of separatism. A third account says that Bhadrabāhu gave up his patriarchy in favour of Sthūlabhadra and retired to Nepal for the rest of life. Sthūlabhadra had occasion to go also to Nepal for consultation with Bhadrabāhu concerning to the compilation and preservation of the canon. Bhadrabāhu taught him all the fourteen Pūrvas but forbade him to reveal to others more than the first ten. Sthūlabhadra died in 252 BC.

***Stotras, Stutis*:** Hymns in praise of the Jinas or ancient teachers which form part of Jain religious lyric poetry. These are written both in Sanskrit as well as in Prakrit. Apart from the traditional poets, even celebrated scholars like Bhadrabāhu, Siddhasena Divākara, Samantabhadra, Hemacandra and others composed wonderful lyrical hymns. Some of them were written only for purposes of the cult. On the other hand, many were simple poetic effusions. Many are quite short, others are poems of considerable length. Collection of Jain *stotras* edited in Kāvyamālā, VIII, 1890; *Jainastotrasaṃgraha* in Yaśovijaya Jaina Granthamālā, Nos. VII, IX, 1905; *Stutisaṃgraha* with *Avacuri*, Nirnaya Sagar Press, Bombay, 1912; *Stotraratnākara* I-II, ed. Yaśovijaya Jaina Samskṛta Pāṭhasālā, Nirnaya Sagar Press, Bombay, 1913-14; *Pañcapratikramanādi-sūtrāṇi* in Sanskrit, Prakrit and Gujarati, Ahmedabad 1915.

***Strīdhana*:** Women's property. Under the Jain law women have maintenance and proprietary rights. Women's property is known as *strīdhana* which are of five kinds: *adhyāgnikṛta*, whatever is received by a girl from her parents at the time of her marriage in the presence of the sacred fire; *adhyāhavanika*, whatever the young bride brings from her father's house in the presence of her father and brothers; *prītidāna*, what is given to her by her parents-in-law at the time of marriage; *audāyika* or *saudāyika*, whatever is received after marriage from the husband; and *anvādheya*, whatever is received from the ladies of her own or of her husband's household. These five categories are named after their Brahmanical counterparts in the Smṛti literature, and basically the principals of Manu are followed here with some modifications. The Strīdhana is not liable to division or partition, and except during a famine or for religious necessities, the husband cannot take it. In the absence of the sons, the daughters are entitled to inherit their father's property, and mother's property goes directly to the daughters, even if there are sons. In the event of the father's death, daughters are entitled to a fourth part of the share of each brother. Married daughters have no such share in the presence of their brothers, since they have already been given an amount at the time of their marriage. But here lies an anomaly which requires an expert's clarification. When the legal texts say that what she obtains through inheritance becomes a category of her *strīdhana*, it does not mean direct inheritance of her father's property. What she obtains from her father, brothers, and paternal relations is a gift rather than inheritance. However, on the death of a person without a son, his widow takes his property as an absolute owner. Further, she takes the husband's share as an absolute owner if there is a son. She has more or less absolute and unrestricted power of enjoyment and disposition of that property. She is further empowered to make a will and also to dispose of her property.

Śubhacandra: Digambara philosopher who flourished towards the close of the eighth and the beginning of the ninth century. He wrote a philosophical treatise in Sanskrit verse under the title *Jñānārṇava* or 'ocean of knowledge'. It is otherwise known as *Yogapradīpādhikāra*. It is in 42 chapters and 2,077 *ślokas*. Ed. in Rayacandra Jaina Śāstramālā, Bombay, 1907.

Subhacandra: Poet of the sixteenth century (AD 1551) chiefly known for his excellent Sanskrit poem *Pāṇḍavapurāṇa* which is also called the *Jaina Mahābhārata*. It is 25 cantos and runs to 600 verses. He is known to have written two more works, namely the *Karakaṇḍu-caritra* and a commentary on the *Kārttikeyānuprekṣā*. The work on Karakaṇḍu is almost a Sanskrit translation of Kanakāmara's (q.v.) Apabhraṃśa poem. Subhacandra also commented on Amṛtacandra's *Adhyātmataraṅgiṇī* and Vādirāja's *Pārśvanātha Purāṇa*. He belonged to the Balātkāra-gaṇa of the Mūla-saṅgha and the Sarasvatī-gaccha.

***Śubhaśīla Gaṇin*:** Pupil of Lakṣmīsāgara Sūri who in AD 1464 and wrote the *Pañcaśatī Prabandha-sambandha*. Notwithstanding the title *Pañcasatī*, meaning 500, the book contains nearly 600 stories, anecdotes, legends, fables, and fairy-tales, some of which allude to historical personages, kings, and authors. The same Śubhaśīla had also written the *Bharatādikathā* or *Kathākośa*, another collection of stories, in 1452. *Pañcaśatī Prabandha*, Subhāṣita Sāhitya, Surat, 1968.

***Subhāṣitaratnasamdoha*:** See Amitagati.

Substance: Anything that has origin, existence, and destruction is a substance. Jain philosophy starts with a perfect division of the universe into living and non-living substances, Jīva (q.v.) is the living substance, while *pudgala*, *dharma*, *adharma*, *ākāśa* and *kāla* are non-living substances. These six substances are called *dravyas* in Jainism. A substance has the quality of existence and permanence through origination and destruction. It is the substratum of attributes and modes. Its essential qualities remain the same and it is only its *paryāya* or mode or condition that can and does change. A substance is thus possessed of some unchanging essential characters (*guṇa*) and changing modes (*paryāya*). The essential character of a substance remains in it so long as it remains. Only by accident does it undergo modification. In a narrow sense substance denotes material substance or matter. For example, the formation of aggregates of atoms result in the substance of atoms, which result in substance of a secondary order. The Jain term for such a material mass is also *dravya* (q.v.) which word is used differently, but is normally used in the sense of the basic types of entities found in the universe. See *Dravya*, *Paryāya*, *Guṇa*.

***Śucikarma*:** Śvetāmbara sacrament. It is purification of the mother after her delivery—ten days in the case of the Brāhmaṇas, twelve days in that of the Kṣatriyas, sixteen in that of Vaiśyas and one month in that of the Śūdras.

***Sudarśana-Carita*:** Apabhraṃśa poem by Nayanandī which narrates in 12 Sandhis the life of a Jain great person. The work was composed in AD 1043, and the author was a pupil of Māṇikyanandin of the Kundakunda line of teachers. A poem of the same name was composed by Vidyānandin in the fifteenth century.

Sudharman: The second *gaṇadhara* (q.v.), head of the Jain church, after Indrabhūti Gautama (q.v.), out of the original eleven who survived Mahāvīra. He held office for twelve years and was followed by his pupil Jambusvāmin. Like his predecessor

Indrabhūti Gautama he was also a *kevalin*. The oldest list of the *gaṇadharas* is found in the *Kalpasūtra* which begins with Sudharman. According to a different tradition, Sudharman was the first pontiff of the new church after the master.

Sudarśana: One of the five Merus (q.v.) situated in the centre of Jambūdvīpa. It touches the upper level of the lower world and the lower level of the upper world. At ground level it is encircled by the Bhadra-śāla forest, at the height of 500 *yojana* by Nandana forest, at the third height by the Saumanasa forest and at the fourth height by Pāṇḍuka forest. Above the fourth height there is a crest or *cūlikā*, four *yojanas* in diameter and full of jewels of various types.

Suhastin: Nephew of Sthūlabhadra (q.v.) who became the head of the Jain church after Mahāgiri (q.v.). Suhastin was instrumental in converting the Maurya King Samprati (q.v.). He set himself to manage the conditions that had befallen the community as a result of the reforming zeal of Mahāgiri. Unlike his brother and predecessor Mahāgiri, he did not hesitate to accept royal patronage and protection. He gained new disciples and created new branches of the order. (Possibly new recruits were received too readily.) Suhastin left eight disciples, many of whom became well known for the flourishing schools they founded. They are Rohana, Bhadrayaśas, Kāmandhi, Śrīgupta, Ṛṣigupta, Susistha, Kotika, and Supratibuddha. They were founders of the Uddeha, Uduvātika, Veśavāṭika, Cāraṇa, Mānava, and Kauṭika gaṇas from which sprang various *śākhās* and *kulas* sponsored by their five disciples. The chief among them was Indradatta or Indradinna, who continued their work and was succeeded by Āryadinna or Dinnasūri and Siṃhagiri (qq.v.).

***Sukhabodha*:** See Nemicandrasūri.

Sukadare: Findspot of a Jain epigraph of the early twelfth century in Nagamangala taluk of Mandya district, Karnataka, which mentions a merchant Jakkiseṭṭi as the builder of a Jain temple at this place during the reign of the Hoysala Viṣṇuvardhana. His teacher was Ajitasena of Drāviḍasaṅgha. *Epigraphia Carnatica* IV.

Sukhodaya: Enjoyment of the happiness of heaven as Indra by virtue of ascetic merit.

Śukra: The planet Venus conceived as a stellar or Jyotiska god by the Jains. He has the urn as his symbol. He is known as the teacher demon and the ruler of the south-east regions.

***Sukṛta-Kīrtikallolinī*:** Panegyric composed by Udayaprabha Sūri in praise of Vastupāla and Tejaḥpāla, ministers of the Cālukya King Vīradhavala who were devout Jains. Published in App. to *Hammīsra-madamardana* (q.v.), GOS, No. 10.

***Sukṛtasankīrtana*:** See Arisiṃha.

***Sūkṣmasamparyāya*:** The tenth *guṇasthāna* (q.v.) in which greed disappears partly.

***Sukumāla-Cariu*:** Apabhraṃśa poem by Sirihara (Śrīdhara), which describes the life of Sukumāra who later became a saint. The poem was composed at the request of the author's patron, Kumāra. The date of its composition was AD 1151.

Sumatinātha: The fifth Tīrthaṃkara born of King Megha and Queen Maṅgalā at Vinītā in Kosala. His height was 300 bow-lengths and span of life 4,000 thousand years. His sacred tree was *priyaṅgu* and his chief disciples Camara and Kāsavī. He attained liberation on Mount Sammeya. His symbol is the curlow or red goose, Yakṣa and Yakṣiṇī Tumbaru and Mahākālī respectively, and *chowri*-bearer Mitravīrya. Images of Sumatinatha are found in many places in northern India, the most noteworthy figure being the one discovered at Sahet Mahet. The *Uttarapurāṇa* gives details of his attainment of supreme knowledge. His name was Sumati because even before his birth his mother's intellect became sharp. Sumatinātha is also mentioned in the *Bhāgavata Purāṇa* in which it is said that he will be worshipped in the Kali age by irreligious people and non-Aryans as their god. The *Sumatinatha-caritra* by Somaprabha, composed in Prakrit in the second half of the twelfth century, represents an idealized biography. The Sumatinātha temple in Jaisalmer Fort deserves special mention.

***Sumatinātha-caritra*:** Idealized biography of the fifth Tīrthaṃkara Sumatinātha written in Prakrit by Somaprabha in the second half of the twelfth century.

Sundarī: Disciple of Ṛṣabhanātha (q.v.) who led, in collaboration with Baṃbhī, an order of nuns comprising 300,000 members, established by Ṛṣabha himself, according to the *Samavāya*.

Supārśvanātha: The seventh Tīrthaṃkara whose parents were King Pratiṣtha and Queen Pṛthvī of Vārāṇasī. His height was 200 bow-lengths, life-span 2,000 thousand years, chief disciples Vidarbha and Somā, and sacred tree the *śirīṣa*. He attained liberation on Sammeya. His emblem is the *svastika*. The attendant spirits serving him are Mātaṅga and Śānti; Digambara, Varanandī and Kāli. The name of the bearer of his fly-whisk is Dharmavīrya. The representation of Supārśvanātha in art is either in a group or singly. The most important point regarding Supārśvanātha's image is the five-serpent hood, as distinguished from the usual seven-serpent hood of Pārśvanātha. His name was Supārśva or 'one who had good sides' or 'makes the sides good', because his mother suffered from leprosy in both her sides, which was cured after the child's birth. A voluminous Prakrit poem *Supāsanāha-cariyam* by Lakṣmaṇagaṇin deals with the story of Supārśva's life. There was a Supārśvanātha *stūpa* at Mathura.

***Supāsanāha-Cariyam*:** A voluminous Prakrit poem by Lakṣmaṇa Gaṇin which deals with the life-story of the seventh Tīrthaṃkara, Supārśvanātha. Composed in AD 1143, the work contains 68 Apabhraṃśa verses. Ed. Pandit Hargovind Das Seth, Benares, 1918.

Suprabha: See Padmaprabha.

Suprabhācārya: See *Vairāgyasāra.*

Suprīti: Sacrament performed in the fifth month after conception. Music and other entertainments are offered for pregnant women.

***Sūrācārya*:** Eleventh-century author of *Nemināthacarita*, which was written in Sanskrit.

***Sura-Pannatti*:** See *Sūryaprajñapti.*

***Surasundarī-cariya*:** Prakrit *kāvya* by Dhaneśvara written in AD 1038 in the town of Candrāvatī in Jain Mahārāṣṭrī. It is a romantic work containing 4,000 *gāthās* which are divided into sixteen *paricchedas*. The main story narrates in an easy style the love-affair of a Vidyadhara chief, but many other stories are included within this framework. Ed. with notes by Muniraj Sri Raja Vijayaji, Jina Vividha Sāhitya Śāstramālā, I, Benares, 1916.

Surat: Ancient name Sūryapura, port city of Gujarat in which were situated temples of Candraprabha, Ṛṣabha, and Vāsupūjya. It is also the findspot of a few Jain inscriptions.

Surat Plate: An important Jain record of śaka 743 corresponding to AD 821. This inscription of Karkarāja Suvarṇavarṣa, which opens with an invocation to Jinendra, records a land-grant to a Jain teacher named Aparājita who was a disciple of Sumati and a grand-disciple of Mallavādin belonging to the Sena Saṅgha branch of the Mūla Saṅgha. The grant was made for the purpose of daily worship, cooked rice offerings, and repairs of the monastery (*vasatikā*), described as an ornament of Sambapura. The monastery was attached to the temple of Arhat situated within the boundaries of Śrī-Nāgasārika (Nausari, 20 miles south of Surat). *Epigraphia Indica* XXI.133ff.

Surohor-Ṛṣabhanātha: Image of Ṛṣabhanātha found at Surohar in the Dinajpur district of North Bengal. It belongs to the tenth century AD and is of unique iconographic interest on account of its certain rare features. The sculpture is shaped like a shrine, containing in its centre the main figure seated in *dhyānāsana* with the miniature figures of the twenty-three other Jinas similarly seated in small shrines all around it. The latter are also characterized by their peculiar marks. The two male *chowri*-bearers on either side of Ṛṣabhanātha, the flying garland-bearer, Vidyādhara couples on his top right and left, the two-tiered pedestal with a wheel and with two lions on the upper tier and the bull and the figure of the donor on the lower, are all arranged with delicate skill and refinement.

Surpāraka: Sapara in Maharashtra. The Jīvantasvāmī Ṛṣabha temple of this place has been mentioned in the *Vividhatīrthakalpa.*

Sūrya: The sun-god of the Jains conceived as riding on a chariot drawn by seven steeds and holding in his hand two lotuses. He is known as the god of the east and the husband of Ratnā Devī.

***Sūryaprajñapti*:** Prakrit *Sura-Pannatti*, the fifth text of the Upāṅga (q.v.) series, which deals with astronomy, geography, cosmology, and the division of time. It is basically a text on astronomy and contains a systematic presentation of the astronomical views of the Jains. Surprisingly the *Candraprajñapti* (*Canda-Pannatti*), which is counted as the seventh Upāṅga, is completely identical in all available manuscripts with the *Sūryaprajñapti*. Āgomadaya edition with Malayagiri's com., Bombay, 1919.

***Sūryendudarśana*:** Sacrament pertaining to the third day after the child is born, in which the sun and the moon are worshipped with *mantras* by the preceptor for its welfare. It is the Śvetāmbara system.

Susāni: Jain shrine at Morkhana in Bikaner, Rajasthan. It was destroyed by Muslim invasion but subsequently repaired by Hemarāja, son of Śivarāja.

Susia: A Jain site near Deoli in Purulia district wherefrom a mutilated figure of Pārśvanātha standing naked with snakehood canopy had been found.

Susthita: Patriarch of the community after Suhastin. He assumed office in 177 BC. It was under his direction that Nirgrantha-gaccha had a change of name into Kālika-gaccha. This was done in honour of his teacher Kālika, who taught him as secret *mantra* which he repeated crores of times.

Sutārā: Śāsanadevatā (q.v.) of Suvidhinātha (q.v.)

according to the Śvetāmbara tradition. She rides a bull and the four hands are marked by the *varada* pose, rosary, urn, and goad.

***Sūtrakṛtāṅga*:** Prakrit *Sūyagaḍaṅga*, the second text in the Aṅga (q.v.) series, which consists of two books. In the first there are sixteen *adhyayanas* and in the second, seven. The first is mostly in verse and the second in prose. The explicit purpose of the book is to keep young monks away from the heretical doctrines of other teachers. The work begins with a condemnation of the doctrines of the Buddhists, Ājīvikas, and other heretics, and the principal teachings of Mahāvīra are set out in opposition to these. The second book is a somewhat clumsy conglomeration of appendices. These, too, are for the most part polemical in content. We have various commentaries on this text including a *Niryukti* (ed. P.L. Vaidya, Poona, 1928; also included in the Āgamodaya edition, a *Cūrṇi* (Ṛṣabhadeva Kesarimala Śvetāmbara Saṃsthā, Ratlam, 1941) and a *Ṭīkā* (known as the *Vivaraṇa* of Śīlāṅka included in the Āgamodaya edition). The name *Sūtrakṛtāṅga* seems to be a false Sanskritization, because *sūtra* (text) is *sutta* in Prakrit and not *suya*. So Schubring thinks that it should be *Sucakṛt* or *Sucikṛt*. The *Niryukti* says that there are three names of this Aṅga: Sūtagadam, Suttakaḍam, and Suyagaḍam. The last is explained thus by Śīlāṅka: *sūcākṛtaṃ iti svaparasamayārthasūcanaṃ sūcā sāsmin kṛteti*, 'the Aṅga in which the distinction (between the true and false doctrines) is made.' Published with various commentaries in *Āgamasaṃgraha* II, Benares, 1880; Āgamodaya ed. with Śīlāṅka's com. Bombay, 1917; German trans. of selected sections, by W. Schubring, *Worte Mahāviras*, Gottingen, 1926; Eng. trans. by H. Jacobi in SBE, XLV, Oxford.

Suvidhinātha: The ninth Tīrthaṃkara whose parents were Sugrīva and Ramā of Kākandī, probably Kakan in Monghyr district, Bihar. He had a height of 100 bow-lengths and a life of 200 thousand years. His disciples were Varāha and Vāruṇī. He received salvation on the Sammeya mountain. His sacred tree was the *nāga* or *malli*. There is a dispute over whether his emblem is a dolphin or a crab. His Yakṣa and Yakṣī are named Ajita and Sutari/Mahākālī respectively. The *chowri*-bearer has the name of Māghavatarāja. Suvidhinātha is also known as Puṣpadanta. According to Hemacandra, his birth eventually brought 'good order' (*suvidhi*) to the distracted family, which accounts for his name. His other name, Puṣpadanta, was derived from the fact that the Jina's teeth resembled the buds of a flower. Solo images of Suvidhinātha are extremely rare. He appears with other 23 Tīrthaṃkaras in a group.

***Sūyagaḍa*:** See Sūtrakṛtāṅga.

***Svadehaparimāṇa*:** That which completely fills the body it occupies, be it big or small; characteristic of a Jīva (q.v.).

***Svagurusthānavāpti*:** Assumption of the position of *ācārya* after having transferred duties to a worthy disciple in the advanced stage of life.

***Svārājya*:** A stage in the career of the Tīrthaṃkara which is receiving the power over a whole empire.

***Svarga*:** See Heavens.

***Svarūpasambodhana*:** See Akalaṅka.

***Śvāśvāsadana*:** The second *guṇasthāna* (q.v.) climbing on which the Jīva begins to distinguish a little between what is real and what is false.

***Svayambhū*:** Author of the *Paumacariyu* written in the Apabhraṃśa language towards the close of the ninth century. It deals with the *Rāmāyaṇa* story in the line of Vimala Sūri and Raviṣena (qq.v.). The work is divided into five books or *kāṇḍas*, Vijjhāra, Ujjhā, Sundara, Jujjha, and Uttara. These are again subdivided into *sandhis*. In this work Svayambhū was probably assisted by his son Tribhuvana-Svayambhū, who was also known as Kavirāja Cakravartin. They also had a joint venture: the *Riṭṭhanemicariyu* or *Harivaṃsapurāṇa* running to 18,000 verses and having 112 *sandhis* and three *kāṇḍas*, namely Yādava, Kuru, and Yudha. *Paumacariyu*, ed. H. Bhayani, 3 vols., 1953-4.

***Svayambhūstotra*:** See Samantabhadra.

Syādvāda: In the *Sūtrakṛtaniryukti* attributed to Bhadrabāhu (q.v) we come across Syādvāda or Saptabhaṅgī-naya presented in a completely theoretical context. It is set forth as follows: (1) may be it is; (2) perhaps it is not; (3) perhaps it is and it is not; (4) may be it is indescribable; (5) may be it is, and yet is indescribable; (6) may be it is not, and yet is in indescribable; and (7) may be it is and it is not, and is also indescribable. In defence of this sevenfold paralogism, Siddhasena Divākara (q.v.) says that perfect knowledge of things can be obtained only by taking into consideration all the possible standpoints. Elaborate discussions of Syādvāda is found in Samantabhadra's *Āpatamīmāṃsā* (qq.v.). To illustrate the problem he has taken the first and second parts of the doctrine, viz., *syād asti* (perhaps it is) and *syad-nāsti* (perhaps it is not). The former he explains in terms of *bhāva* or existence, and the latter in that of *abhāva* or non-existence. Both conceptions, *bhāva* and *abhāva*, existence and non-existence, are relative, for formulae, gestures of the fingers, and so forth. The *Jvālinī* and the *Bhairava Padmāvatī* refer to syllables like *uw kaumāri namaḥ āṅ kron svāhā* and also shorter *bīja mantras*. Various kinds of *mudrās* like *jaṭharabhedana, galamocana, antaraccyhedana, majjana, gadā, akṣisphoṭana, aṅkuśā, saroja, jñāna, śaṅkha, pallava, vajra,* etc., are mentioned. The *bīja-mantra* on various projections of the constituent triangles of the *yantras* are indicated. Various forms of *nyāsas* are defined in both texts. Still it must be said that owing to its very rigid nature, the Jain religion was able to escape fundamental change in the course of its development and that is why the influence of the so-called Tantric ideas and practices is not deep-rooted in it. *Sūtrakṛta* II.2; *Sthānāṅga* IV.1. See Nyāsa, Yantra, Maṇḍala, *Vaśīkaraṇa, Mantras*, Bīja Mudrā, *Jvālinī-kalpa* and *Bhairava-Padmāvatī-kalpa*. For details see M.B. Jhaveri, *Comparative and Critical Study of Mantraśāstra*, Ahmedabad, 1944; U.P. Shah, 'A Peep into the Early History of Tantra in Jain Literature', in *Bhārata Kaumudī*, II, Allahabad, 1944, R.N. Nandi, 'Tantra and Jainism', in *Jainism and Prakrit in Ancient and Medieval India*, ed. N.N. Bhattacharyya, New Delhi, 1984.

Tārā: Śāsanadevatā of Aranātha (q.v.) according to the Digambara tradition. She is conceived as riding a swan and holding a snake, *vajra*, deer, and with one hand in *varada* pose. Her name recalls the celebrated Buddhist Tārā of the Mahāyāna-Mantrayāna pantheon.

***Taraṅgavatī*:** See Pādaliptasūri.

Tāraṇapantha: Digambara subsect named after its founder Tāraṇa Svāmī or Taraṇa Tāraṇa Svāmī. This subsect is also known as Samaiyāpantha because its followers worship the Samaya or sacred books. Tāraṇa Svāmī flourished in vs 1505-52 and died in Malhāragarh, Gwalior, the central place of pilgrimage of the Tāraṇapanthīs. They worship sacred texts and attach more importance to spiritual values. They do not believe in idol-worship, caste-distinctions, or outward religious practices. Ruiramana, one of the main disciples of Tāraṇa Svāmī, was a Muslim. The Tāraṇapanthīs seem to have influenced by the non-idolatrous teachings of the Śvetāmbara teacher Loṅkā Sāha (q.v.). The Tāraṇapanthīs are mainly found in Bundelkhand and some parts of Khandesh district and are divided into six castes, Paravāra, Asaiti, Golātare, Charanāgare, Ajudhyabāsi, and Dosakhe Paravāra. For a detailed and critical account of the Tāraṇapantha, see Nathuram Premi in *Jaina Hitaiṣī*, VIII, 290-303, 549-57; IX. 33-8, 198-206, 532-9.

***Taraṅgalolā*:** A romantic love-story in 1643 Prakrit stanzas, believed to have been a shorter verson of Pādaliptsūri's (q.v.) *Taraṅgavatī*, composed in the thirteenth-fourteenth century AD. It describes the story of the charming daughter of a rich merchant who was able to remember what happened in her previous life. She met and married the husband of her previous life after many efforts, but eventually under holy influence she, along with her husband, renounced the world and resorted to asceticism. Trans. into German by E. Leumann, 1921.

Taringa: Site of a Jain temple in Mehsana district of Gujarat, the construction of which has been attributed to Kumārapāla (q.v.). The imposing temple, in spite of a restoration in the time of Akbar, seems to have retained its original form and design to a great extent. It was dedicated to Ajitanātha. The Digambaras also made a construction on this hill. The site is also known as Taraṅgā, Tāraṇagaḍh, and Tārāpura. According to the *Kumārapālapratibodha*, there was formerly a temple of Tārā built by Vaisarāja on this hill. J. Burgess, *Architectural Antiquity of Northern Gujarat*, London, 1903, 115.

***Tarkarahasyadīpikā*:** Composed by Guṇaratna in the fifteenth century, it is a commentary on Haribhadra's *Ṣaḍdarśanasamuccaya* (q.v.) and is regarded as a world classic in the field of logic because of its highly sophisticated approach and its insistence on hair-splitting analysis. Barring the Yoga and the Vedānta, it deals exhaustively with the Buddhist, Nyāya, Sāṅkhya, Jaina, Vaiśeṣika, and Pūrva-Mīmāṃsā systems. Ed. Mahendra Kumar Jain, Varanasi, 1970.

Taṭṭekere: Findspot of an inscription dated śaka 1001 (AD 1079) in Shimoga district, Karnataka, which records the construction of a Jain temple and a lake by Nokkayya, an officer of Gaṅga-Permadideva, feudatory of Western Cālukya Vikramāditya VI. Nokkayya had been described as a disciple of Prabhācandra Siddhāntika of Kranura-gaṇa, Mesapasāna-gaccha and Mūla-saṅgha. *Epigraphia Carnatica* VII, Shim. No. 16.

***Tattvabodhinī*:** See Abhyedeva Suri.

***Tattvadīpikā*:** See Amṛtacandra.

***Tattvārthādhigama Sūtra*:** Composed by Umāsvāmiṅ (q.v.) or Umāsvāti, probably in the first century of the Christian era, it is one of the most original works on Jain philosophy in particular, and Indian philosophy in general. It is written in Sanskrit and epitomizes the whole Jain creed in about 375 Sūtras arranged in ten chapters. The work occupies a unique position in Jain literature as it is recognized as authoritative equally by the Digambaras and the Śvetāmbaras. The meaning of the title is 'The Manual for the True Nature of Things'. Logic, psychology, cosmography, ontology, biology, and ethics of the Jains are treated in these Sūtras (and in the commentary appended by the author himself). The commentary which still serves as an excellent summary of Jain dogma is not always in harmony with the views of the Digambaras, or indeed with those of the Śvetāmbaras, proving that Umāsvāmin belonged to a period at which there was not yet so wide a gulf between the two sects as was the case later. The commentaries on the *Tattvārtha* include Siddhasena Divārkara's *Tattvānusāriṇī*, *Tattvārthaṭīkā*, Pūjyapāda's *Sarvārthasiddhi,* Samantabhadra's *Āpta-mīmāṃsā*, Akalaṅka's *Tattvārtharājavārttika*, etc. Ed. with com. of Umāsvāmin himself by K.P. Mody in Bib. Ind. together with a few minor works of Umāsvāmin, Calcutta, 1903-5; with a commentary in Hindi in Rayacandra Series, Bombay, 1906; with intro. trans. notes and com. in English by J.L. Jaini in *Sacred Books of the Jains*, II, Arrah, 1920. German trans. by H. Jacobi in ZDMG, LX, 1906, 287ff. 572ff.

***Tattvārtharājavārttika*:** See Akalaṅka.

***Tattvārthasāra*:** See Amṛtacandra.

***Tattvārthasāradīpaka*:** See Sakalakīrti.

***Tattvārtha Ślokavārttika*:** See Vidyānanda.

***Tattvas*:** Fundamentals which are variously numbered and classified in Jainism. The most widely known are the *nava-tattva* (q.v.), or nine fundamentals. But according to another estimate the *tattvas* are seven. These are: *jīva* (q.v.), living substance; *ajīva* (q.v.), non-living substance; *āsrava* (q.v.), influx of *karma* matter into the soul; *bandha* (q.v.), bondage of soul; *saṃvara* (q.v.) , the stopping of the influx of *karma*; *nirjarā* (q.v.), the gradual removal of karmic matter; and *mokṣa* (q.v.), the attainment of liberation. The first two deal with the nature and enumeration of the eternal substances, matter, and spirit, and the remaining five with the interaction between these two substances.

***Tattvasāra*:** See Devasena.

Tavanandi: Findspot of a Jain epigraph of AD 1379 in Sorab taluk, Shimoga district, Karnataka, of the time of Vijayanagara Emperor Harihara II which discloses the name of a temple dedicated to Śāntinātha. *Epigraphia Carnatica* VIII, Sorab 196, 200.

Tavanidhi: Site of a thirteenth-century temple of Śāntinātha in the Shimoga district, Karnataka.

Taxila: Celebrated ancient city, now in Pakistan. The *Vividha-tīrthakalpa* recognized it as a Jain holy place and associates it with Bāhubalī.

***Tejaḥkāya*:** Fire-bodied; characteristic of immobile or one-sensed Jīva (q.v.).

Tejaḥpāla: Brother of the celebrated Vastupāla (q.v.), both of them being in the service of Lavaṇa-prasāda and his son Vīradhavala (q.v.) of the Vaghela lineage, the famous governors of Bhīma II (q.v.), in the first quarter of the thirteenth century. Both were devout Jains and had multifarious religious activities, not only in the field of construction of temple-complexes, asylums, teaching establishments, community halls, tanks and water-reservoirs, but also in the case of patronage of scholars and writers. Though Vastupāla's name is more famous, Tejaḥpāla was his constant assistant. It is said that the temple of Abu was actually built by Tejaḥpāla and not by Vastupāla. He set up the image of the principal deity in the Jain temple at Thārāpadra and is said to have placed gold capitals on the temple of Śiva Vaidyanātha at Darbhāvati or Dabhoi because the old ones were carried off by the king of Malwa. Jinaprabha has given a list of constructional works of both the brothers. An image of Tejaḥpāla is found in the Śatruñjaya (q.v.) complex which was installed by his illustrious brother Vastupāla. A manuscript dated vs 1303 (AD 1245) shows that up to that year Tejaḥpala was the chief minister of Viśāladeva. Tejaḥpāla passed away probably in AD 1248.

Tejaḥsiṃha: See Chitor Epigraphs.

Temples: The earliest Jain temples are cave temples, most famous of those being at Udayagiri in Orissa, at Badami in the Bijapur district, Karnataka and at Ellora in the Aurangabad district of Maharashtra. Structural temples, each with an open porch (*maṇḍapa*), a closed assembly hall (*sabhāmaṇḍapa*), an inner shrine (*garbhagṛha*) for the idol, and occasionally pillars in front (*mānastambha*), are more frequent. The most famous temple cities are Mount Abu in Rajasthan, Girnar and Śatruñjaya in Kathiawar, Kunthalagiri, Osmandabad, and Sravanabelgola in Karnataka. Besides the image of that particular Jina to whom the temple is dedicated, images of other Tīrthaṃkaras, and in some cases of Hindu gods and goddesses, are placed there. Among important Jain temples mention may be made of

Adbhudji at Nagda, Ādinātha-basti at Bastihalli and Lakshmeswar, Ādinātha Chitorgarh, Dholaka, Jaislamer Fort, Khajuraho, Nadlai, Prabhasa, Ranakpur and Śatruñjaya; Ajitanātha at Taranga, Akanna-basti at Sravanabelgola; Ambikā at Jagat, Arugar at Birudur and Venkunram, Badami cave temple, Bhāṇḍ-Dewal at Arang, Brahma-Jinālaya at Lakkundi and Thailagiri Fort, Cāmsuṇḍarāya-basti and Candragupta-basti at Sravanabelgola, Candranāthasvāmī at Sangitapura, Candranātha temple at Mettuppudur and Vijayamangalam, Candranatheśvara-basti at Bhatkal, Candraprabha at Jaisalmer Fort and Tirupparuttikunram, Caturmukha-basti at Karkala, Caturmukha shrine at Ranakpur, Caturmukha-vimāna at Ellora, Cenana-basti, Sravanabelgola, Chota-Kailāśa at Ellora, Cintāmaṇi Rao Bikaji at Bikaner, Cintāmaṇi at Sirohi, Dilwara on Mount Abu, Duladeo at Khajurabo, Eradukatta-basti at Sravanabelgola, Gadarmal at Badoh, Gaṇigitti-Jinālaya at Hampi, Ghaṇṭai at Khajuraho, Gurugala-basti at Mudbidri, Indra-sabhā and Jagannātha-sabhā at Ellora, Javāri at Khajuraho, Kadalāya-basadi at Hanumakonda, Kaṭakābharaṇa-Jinālaya at Dharmavaram, Kaṭṭale-basti at Sravanabelgola, Kharatara-vasati on Mount Abu, Kudalmaṇikkam at Iringalakuda, Luna-vasahi on Mount Abu, Lutherva at Jaisalmer, Mahāvīra at Ghanerao, Kumbharia, Mount Abu, Osia, Nandia, Sirohi, Sachore, Sewadi, Siddhapura and Tirupparuttikkunram, Māṃgayi-basti at Sravanabelgola, Māṇyā at Dwarahat, Medguḍi at Hallur, Meguti and Mina-vasti at Aihole, Melaka-vasahi at Girnar, Munisuvrata temple at Dholaka, Naḍumba-vasadi at Vijayawada, Navalakhā at Gumli, Neminātha at Luna-vasahi, Mt. Abu, Dholaka, Girnar, Kumbharia and Tirumalai, Padmavati at Sravanabelgola and Nagda, Pañcakūṭa-basti at Kambadahalli and Markuli, Pārśvanātha at Bijolia, Bikaner, Dhar, Ghumli, Jaisalmer Fort, Khajuraho, Kumbharia, Patan Phalodhi, Ranakpur, Sadri and Trilokpur, Pārśvanātha-basti at Haggera, Hosaholalu and Sravanabelgola, Pataini Devi at Pithaora Satna, Rājarāja-Jinālaya at Bhogapuram, Ratnatraya-basadi at Bilagi, Ṛṣabhanātha at Dhanka, Śakunikā-vihāra at Broach, Sampratirāja at Girnar, Śaṅkha-Jinālaya at Lakshmeswar, Śāntinātha at Bastihallo, Cambay, Jaisalmer Fort, Kaman, Khajuraho, Kheda, Kumbharia, Nittur, and Rajyapura, Siddhānta-basti at Medbidri, Siddhapāla-vasati at Patan, Sobhnath at Śrāvastī, Sumatinātha at Jaisalmer, Tirina-basti at Sravanabelgola, Trailokyanātha at Tiruppa-ruttikkunram, Tribhuvana-cūḍāmaṇi at Mudbidri, Vanarāja Vihāra at Patan, Vardhamāna at Bangalore and Tirupparuttikkunram, Vimalanātha-basti at Bellur, Vimala-vasahi on Mount Abu, etc. Under the shadow of Islam a good number of Jain temples were destroyed and many temples were converted into mosques by removing the principal cell and its porch from the centre of the court, and building up the entrances of the surrounding cells. This resulted in the formation of a courtyard surrounded by a double colonnade for the requirement of a mosque. It is also to be noted in this connection that in a Digambara temple the priest must be a Jain, but in a Śvetāmbara temple he may be a Hindu. See Architecture.

Tengali: Situated in the Gulbarga district of Karnataka, this place contained a Jina temple in twelfth century according to epigraphical evidence.

Tenimalai: Tenurmalai, a hill in the Tiruchirapalli district which has a natural cavern on its eastern part called Andarmadam, anciently a place of penance for the Jains. By the side of the cavern are some Jain sculptures of the seventh to ninth centuries.

Terāpanthī (D): An important subsect of the Digambaras which came into existence in vs 1683 as a protest against the Bhaṭṭāraka system of the Bisāpanttis (q.v.) which they do not recognize. They worship idols, not with flowers, fruit, or other green plants, but with a kind of rice called *akṣata*, cloves, almonds, and coconuts. Apart from the Tīrthaṃkaras, they do not maintain idols of any demi-god. They do not perform *āratī* or any Bisāpanthi ritual. During the time of worship they keep standing. The Terapanthīs are found specially in Rajasthan, Uttar Pradesh, and Madhya Pradesh.

Terāpanthī (S): Śvetāmbara subsect founded by Svāmī Bhikkanaji Mahāraja in vs 1817. He was formerly a Sthānakavāsī. As he laid stress on the thirteen religious principles, namely five Mahāvratas, five Samitis and three Guptis, his subsect was known as Terāpanthī. They are non-idolatrous and organized by their Ācārya. Every year on the seventh day of the bright half of the month of Māgha a festival known as Maryādā Mahotsava is celebrated by the followers. The Terapanthīs believe in one Ācārya, one code of conduct, and one line of thought. They emphasize simplicity in religion. They do not construct monasteries for their monks who inhabit a part of the house which the householders build for themselves.

Terdal: Situated in the Sangli district of Maharashtra, it was once famous for the Neminātha temple mentioned in a twelfth-century inscription. See Nimbadevarasa.

Terina-basti: A temple at Sravanabelgola (q.v.) which is so called locally due to the temple car near it. It is a basadi for Bāhubali who is enshrined in it. The *garbhagṛha* opens south and north. The car-like structure has carvings of fifty-two Jina figures all around. An inscription on it of AD 1117 says that Macikabbe and Santikable, mothers of the royal merchants of King Viṣṇuvardhana, had the temple built.

Tewar: Ancient Tripuri in the Jabalpur region which has yielded a number of Jain images dating from the ninth to the eleventh centuries. Among these the image of Dharmanātha in the Nagpur Museum and that of Ādinātha in the Indian Museum, Calcutta, deserve special mention.

Thailagiri Fort: Site of Brahma Jinālaya in Anantapur district. It was meant for Pārśvanātha and built with Āḷupā-Devī's munificence.

Thakkuru Phera, Pheru: Author belonging to Dhanadhakula and Śrīmālavaṃśa who had flourished in the thirteenth-fourteenth century and composed seven books under the following titles: *Yugapradhāna-Catuṣpadika*, *Ratnaparīkṣā*, *Vāstusāra*, *Jyotiṣasāra*, *Gaṇitasāra-kaumudī*, *Dhātutpatti*, and *Dravyaparīkṣā*. These have been published in a single volume under the title, *Ratnaparīkṣādi-saptagrantha-saṃgraha* Rajasthan Pracyavidya Pratisthan, Jodhpur, 1961.

Than: Site of an old Jain early medieval temple in Kathiawar which was modelled after the Gop temple of that region. Its plan is that of a sanctum within a covered ambulatory. It is surmounted by a pyramidal tower of stepped stages in receding tiers. There is another small shrine at Than of the same design. H. Cousens, *Somnath and other Medieval Temples of Kathiawar*, Calcutta, 1931, 50ff.

***Ṭhāṇa*:** See Sthānāṅga Sūtra.

Tharad: Site of a Jain temple, dedicated to Ṛṣabha, in north-west Gujarat built at the instance of Vaṭeśvara Suri.

Thārāpadra: Jain holy place in Banaskantha district, Gujarat, modern Tharda. It was once well-known for the Kumāravihāra temple dedicated to Mahāvīra.

***Therāvalī*:** List of Sthaviras prepared by Merutuṅga (q.v.).

Thuvauna: Place sacred to Ādinātha which is situated in the Guna district, Madhy Pradesh.

***Ṭīkās*:** The last strata of the commentary literature which carry the expository and illustrative process to its logical conclusion. They are written in Sanskrit retaining, in many cases, the Prakrit narratives in their original form. The well-known *Ṭīkā* writers are Haribhadra, Śīlāṅka, Śānti Suri, Devendra *alias* Nemicandra, Abhayadeva, Droṇācārya, Maladhārin, Hemacandra, Malayagiri, Kṣemakīrti, Vijayavimala, Śānticandra, and Śāmayasundra. Their activities were spread over a period of 1,100 years. A number of other forms of commentaries called *Dīpikās*, *Vṛttis*, *Tippanaka*, *Avacūrṇis*, etc., are also extant.

***Tilakamañjarī*:** Religious novel of the Campū category written by the Śvetāmbara Jain Dhanapāla (q.v.) about AD 970. Ed. in Kāvyamālā LIIIV, Bombay, 1903.

Tilakapura: Identified with Prabhāsa Pāṭana well-known for the Candraprabha Temple.

***Tiloyapaṇṇatī*:** Cosmographic work written in Jain perspective by Yativṛṣabha. It is divided into nine sections and runs to 8,000 verses. According to this work, the universe is in the shape of a human being, divided into three parts, the upper, middle and lower, the lower universe having the shape of a *vetrāsana* or truncated pyramid, the middle one that of the upper part of a standing *mṛdaṅga*, and the upper one that of a *mṛdaṅga*. This may be explained as follows: Three pyramids with rectangular base but with their tops chopped off, are put one above another, the smaller face of the upper and middle ones and the bigger faces of the middle and lower ones touching together. Their interiors are filled up territories encircled by the seas. At the centre is the earth-disc, below which are the hells, and above which are the upper regions. Important mountains, such as those of Rājagṛha and places sacred to the Jains are mentioned. There is also information on dogma and the Puranic tradition about the Tīrthaṃkaras.

Timaṃba-basadi: Name of a Jain temple of Kopana in Raichur district, Karnataka, mentioned in a thirteenth-century inscription.

Tinakalyāṇadhārī: See Arhanta.

***Tippanakas*:** See *Ṭīkās*.

Tippur: Findspot of a Jain inscription of AD 1117 in the Malavalli taluk, Mandya district, Karnataka, which refers to the grant of the village Tippura by Gaṅgarāja (q.v.) with the permission of Hoysala Viṣṇuvardhana, to Meghacandra Siddhāntadeva, belonging to the Mūla-saṅgha, Kanura-gaṇa and Tintrinika-gaccha. *Jaina Śilālekha Saṃgraha*, II, No. 253.

Tirakkol Inscription: Belonging to the time of the Cola King Parantaka I (AD 907-55) and found at Tirakkol in Wandiwash taluk of North Arcot district, it records a gift of 200 sheep for the Jain temple called Maisitta Perumballi at Śrīdaṇḍapuram in Ponnur Nadu by one Era Nandi *alias* Naratoṅga Pallavariyam of Nelveli. The same Jain shrine is also mentioned in another Tamil record of the tenth century. *South Indian Inscriptions* XIII, No. 297; XIX, No. 51.

Tirthada-basadi: A Jain temple at Kopana in Raichur district, Karnataka, mentioned in a thirteenth-century inscription.

***Tirthakalpa*:** Also called *Kalpa-Pradīpa* and *Raja-prasāda* and written between AD 1326 and 1331 by Jinaprabha Suri, it gives a description of Jain places of pilgrimage, together with the name of their founders, the kings by whom they were restored and also the dates of the years. It is written partly in Sanskrit and partly in Jain Mahārāṣṭrī. Ed. D.R. Bhandarkar and Kedarnath Sahityabhusan, Bib. Ind., Calcutta, 1923.

***Tirtha Kṛdbhāvanā*:** Thinking repeatedly on the sixteen reflections of a Tīrthaṃkara in the advanced stage of life.

Tīrthaṃkaras: The great Jinas who were instrumental in developing Jain ideas and practices through the ages. They are twenty-four in number and known by the follwing names: Ṛṣabhadeva or Ādinātha, Ajitanātha, Sambhavanātha, Abhinandana, Sumatinātha, Padmaprabha, Supārśvanātha, Candraprabha, Suvidhinātha, Śītalanātha, Śreyāṃśanātha, Vāsupūjya, Vimalanātha, Anantanātha, Dharmanātha, Śāntinātha, Kunthunātha, Aranātha, Mallinātha, Munisuvrata, Naminātha, Neminātha or Ariṣṭanemi, Pārśvanātha and Mahāvīra. The word Tīrthaṃkara is explained differently, but it is generally believed that it means 'one who finds a ford (*tīrtha*) to *mokṣa*' (liberation) or one who attains a landing on the other side. But according to the Jain tradition, it denotes one who forms the four communities (*tīrtha*) of monks and nuns and male and female lay followers. According to the Jain belief, it was Ṛṣabhadeva who taught men 72 and women 64 arts and initiated them to the Jain way of life. His example was followed by other Tīrthaṃkaras. In the hands of the last two, Pārśva and Mahāvīra, the traditional knowledge derived from their spiritual ancestors assumed new form and colour. None of them claimed to be the founder of any system. They were great reformers who modified the essentials of the existing religion evidently to meet the demand of their ages.

In Jainism the Tīrthaṃkaras are given the highest spiritual position. In Hemacandra *Abhidhānacintāmaṇi* the Tīrthaṃkaras are placed in the Devādideva class while other gods are simply Devas. In actual images the Jinas are shown as ascetics, in two Yogic postures, *padmāsana* and *kāyotsarga*. In most cases the figures are nude. The Tīrthaṃkaras must have a *śrīvatsa* symbol on the chest of the figures, a trilinear umbrella above the figure, and (except for the early Mathura statues) *lāñchana* or symbol which not only distinguishes them from other images but differentiates them from each other. In no sculpture of the Kuṣāṇa age from Mathura is the Tīrthaṃkara figure seen attended by either a Yakṣa or a Yakṣiṇī. This phenomenon came to be in existence in the Gupta period. A section of modern scholars doubt the historicity of the earlier Tīrthaṃkaras. The fantastic exaggerations by which the earlier Tīrthaṃkaras were characterize in Jain literature must have contributed to the growth of such suspicion. But to characterize them simply as mythical involves the risk of an over-simplified approach to the problem. There is no reason to disbelieve the historical probability of a 'succession of teachers'. Outside the pale of Vedic culture and religion, the pre-Vedic and non-Vedic ideas had a vigorous survival, the tradition of which was carefully maintained by the earlier Tīrthaṃkaras as also by the predecessors of the Buddha. The exaggerations in their description must have been due to the overdoing of the zealots. See Arhanta.

Tīrthaṃkara Parameṣṭhins: See Arhat Parameṣṭhins.

Tiruccāraṇamalai: Findspot of excellent Jain sculptures near Chitral in Kanyakumari district.

Tirukkunavay: See Talakkavu.

Tirumalai: Site of natural caverns and structural temples in North Arcot district. Only one of the two structural temples at Tirumalai has the tower of the Cola style intact. The structural temples, two in number, are dedicated to Vardhamāna and Neminātha and are typical southern *vimānas* of the late Cola and early Vijayanagara periods respectively. The layout of the complex at Tirumalai comprises a large *prākāra* at the foot of the hill with a fairly lofty *gopura*-entrance into it from the east. There is only one temple for Vardhamāna at this level inside the *prākāra*, and it rises in three storeys with a circular *grīvā*, and a *śikhara* at the top. An axial layout of three covered halls variously of the *ardha-maṇḍapa*, *mahā-maṇḍapa* and *mukha-maṇḍapa* occur with a common flat roof on top. The next terrace has another enclosure within which is a larger temple which has its tower missing. Its *garbhagṛha* is square and the *ardha-maṇḍapa* and open *mukha-maṇḍapa* are much larger in size. The next and the topmost terrace also carries a shrine, attached to the bulging rock-scarp. The shrines at different levels show rock-cut carvings of the Cola and Vijayanagara periods. More than a dozen Jain epigraphs and rock-cut figures have been found here. During the Cola period a number of inscriptions from this place refer to Jain temples and teachers. One during the time of Rājarāja I refers to the celebrated teacher Guṇavīra. An epigraph of the time of Rājendra I refers to a gift to the temple of the god Ārambhanandin who was no other than Ṛṣabha himself. Another inscription of Rājendra's time records a gift of money for offering to the Jain temple called Kundavai-Jinālaya by the wife of a merchant. We have an undated inscription of the time of Rājendra II Parakeśarī (AD 1052-64) which records a gift to a Jain temple by two persons from Karnataka serving the Cola army. Another short epigraph from the same hill, belonging to the eleventh century, records the name of a Jain teacher called Ariṣṭanemi Ācārya, a disciple of Paravādimalla. We have also an important undated epigraph which shows that the Cera rulers of Kerala too were interested in Jainism, *South Indian Inscriptions* I.66ff; III.97; *Epigraphia Indica*, IX.229f.

Tirumalai Inscription: Incised on a rock at Tirumalai during the reign of Cola Parantaka I (AD 907-55) in the Plur taluk of North Arcot district, it records a gift to the Jain temple of this place for feeding a devotee and for daily offering to the Jina. A later Cola inscription, dated in the twelfth year of Rajendra I, refers to the fact that earlier a Pallava queen had made provision for the burning of a perpetual lamp in the Jain shrine of the hill. *South Indian Inscriptions*, I, No. 68; III, No. 97; XIX, No. 89.

Tirunatharkunru: A village, having another name Sirukadambur, in South Arcot district which contains a huge rock containing carvings of the 24 Tīrthaṃkaras.

Tirunidamkondai: Medieval site of a Jina temple for which a grant was made by Vikrama Cola (AD 1120-35) according to one of his inscriptions. Another Tirunidamkondai inscription of the same king refers to a grant for the local Candraprabha (Kaccinayanar) temple. An undated inscription with Jain contents of the time of the Cola King Kulotunga III (AD 1178-1218) is also found here.

Tirupparuttikkunram: Also known as Jina-Kāñci, it is situated in the Chingleput district of Tamil Nadu. The group of Jain temples in this place date from the Pallava to the Vijayanagara period. The temple of the Pallava period, however, does not now exist in their original form. For example, the Candraprabha temple exhibits all the characteristic features of a Pallava temple of the Rājasiṃha style, but subsequent renovation has altered the situation. Similarly the main group of temples, known here as the Trailokyanātha or Vardhamāna temple or Trikūṭa-basti, evidently dates back to the period of Pallava Siṃhavarman, yet no trace of the Pallava shrine remains today. Even the existing triple *vimāna*-complex cannot be dated back to a period prior to that of Kulottuṅga I. The Cola superstructures also seem to have undergone some renovation in the Vijayanagara period. The Trailokyanātha temple complex consists of two blocks, an inner central and an outer peripheral one, within the high *prākāra*. The apsidal shrine dedicated to Vardhamāna and located in the central block is part of two more shrines, one on either side, consecrated to Puṣpadanta and Dharma-devī. The *ardha-maṇḍapa* and *mukha-maṇḍapa* are common to all three. The Vardhamāna Mahāvīra shrine appears to be the oldest part of the temple-complex, although nothing of the original shrine is left now and is entirely superseded by the brick-built shrine now extant. The Trikūṭa-basti group is essentially of two shrines, that of Padmaprabha and Vāsupūjya, but a living shrine of Pārśvanātha has made its way in between at the limit of the *ardha-maṇḍapa* of either of these shrines. Round the temple, there is a running cloister in which, on the south-west corner, is the Brahmadeva shrine on the north-west, the Ṛṣabha shrine and a long series of chambers with a common veranda on the north-east corner called the Munivāsa. Tirupparuttikkunram contains inscriptions, especially of Kulottuṅga I and Vikrama Cola.

***Tisatthimahāpurisagunālaṅkāru*:** Great work in Apabhraṃśa by Puṣpadanta (q.v), Sanskritized form *Triṣaṣṭimahāpuruṣaguṇālaṅkāra*. Also known as a Mahāpurāṇa, it is divided into two parts, viz., *Ādipurāṇa* and *Uttarapurāṇa*. The second part also includes *Padmapurāṇa* and *Harivaṃśápurāṇa*. The entire work runs to some 20,000 verses and 142 sandhis or cantos. It was written under the patronage of Bharata, minister of Kṛṣṇa III, about AD 965. The *Mahāpurāṇa* delineates the lives of 63 great men. Though Puṣpadanta in this work has carried to perfection the possibilities of Apabhraṃśa as a vehicle of poetry, he has also shown his command on

U

Uccangi: Jain centre in the Dharwar district of Karnataka under the supervision of the Yāpanīyas.

Udaya: Term denoting the *karma* which will concern the future life.

Udayadharma: See *Dharmakalpadruma*. There was an Udayadharma who wrote the *Vākyaprakāśa* in AD 1450. Another Udayadhara lived a century later.

Udayagiri: Hill near Bhubaneswar in Orissa, the Jain establishment on which flourished since the days of Khāravela. From his Hathigumpha inscription it is known that in the thirteenth year of his rule he excavated caves for Jain ascetics in the Kumārī Parvata or Udaygiri. It is not, however, possible to identify the particular caves excavated at the instance of this king or his relations. Not a single cave of the earlier period was meant to be a shrine, all of them having been designed as the dwelling-retreats of the Jain recluses. These were excavated at different heights. The height of most of the caves, including the exceptionally large Rani Gumpha (q.v.) is too low for a person even to stand erect. The caves can be grouped into two broad categories—one plain without a pillared veranda and the other with a regular pillared veranda. The top of the hill, immediately above the brow of the rock bearing the inscription of Khāravela, yielded the lower position of a large apsidal structure which, no doubt, provided the place of worship. The lower storey of the main wing of Cave 1 has a running frieze which appears to depict the victorious march of a king. The friezes of the main wing of the upper story of Cave 1 compare favourably with the reliefs of the gateways of Sanchi. The reliefs are mature in depth, displaying a considerable plasticity of form and naturalistic modelling. The reliefs on the other caves are not of this standard. They are relaively crude and inferior in plastic treatment.

Udayagiri Inscription: Found from Udaygiri near Vidiśā in Madhya Pradesh and dated in GE 106, corresponding to AD 426 of the reign of Kumāragupta, it refers to the erection of an image of Pārśva by Śaṅkara, a disciple of Gośarman, who was a disciple of Bhadrācārya of Āryakula. *Indian Antiquary*, XI.310.

Udayana: A minister of the Cālukya King Jayasiṃha Siddharāja of Gujarat. He was a wealthy merchant, a builder and associated with Hemacandra (q.v.). In the Jaina Prabandha literature he is described as the builder of several temples. One of his achievements was the construction of a temple called Udayanavihāra at Karṇāvati, which contained the images of all the Tīrthaṃkaras *Prabandhacintāmaṇi*, trans. 82, 128, *Purātanaprabandhasaṃgraha* 32.

Udri: Findspot of Jain inscriptions in Sorab taluk, Shimoga district, Karnataka, belonging to time of the Vijayanagara Emperor Harihara II (AD 1377-1404). One of these inscriptions names some Jain monks of the place. A saint of this line, called Munibhadra, has been represented as the builder of a Jina temple called Hisugala-basadi and as the person who enlarged the famous Mulgund temple. *Epigraphia Carnatica*, VIII, Sorab, 146, 152.

Udyānamaha: Festival of gardens celebrated in the spring. According to the *Bṛhatkalpabhāṣya*, in order to participate in this festival people visited the gardens with a lot of food and drink. They sang songs, danced, recited erotic poetry, performed dramas, and passed time amidst the beating of musical instruments. Women too participated and enjoyed rocking in a swing. The festival of the garden was associated with the festival of the tree. It has been mentioned along with the festival of mountains (*parvatamaha*) in the *Nyāyādhammakahāo*.

Udayaprabha: See *Dharmābhyudaya Mahākāvya*.

Udayaprabha Suri: See *Sukṛta-kīrtikallolinī*.

Udayavīra Gaṇin: Author of a *Pārśvanātha-caritra*. His precise period and year is not known. As early as in 1827 James Delamine had given the contents of a *Pārśvanātha-caritra* written in 1597 in the *Transactions of the RAS*. This might have some bearing on Udayavīra's work.

***Uddiṣṭa Tyāga Pratimā*:** After renunciation of householder's life, retiring into forest and adopting the rules laid down for the guidance fo ascetics.

Udyotana Sūri: Author of *Kuvalayamālā* (q.v.) composed about AD 779 at Jāvālipura, modern Jalor in Rajasthan, when Vatsarāja was the reigning sovereign. His teacher was Tattvācārya. But he was taught Siddhānta by Vīrabhadra and logic by Haribhadra.

Ugrāditya: Author of *Kalyāṇakāraka*, a medical treatise. He belonged to the Deśī gaṇa, Pustaka-gaccha, Panasogavalli-śākhā of the Mūla-saṅgha of the time of Kundakunda and flourished in the ninth century. The work, written in Sanskrit, is divided into two parts with 25 chapters. *Kalyāṇakāraka*, Sholapur 1940.

Ujāni: Findspot of a rare eleventh-century image of Śāntinātha in the Burdwan district of West Bengal. It is housed in the Vaṅgīya Sāhitya Pariṣat Museum of Calcutta. The back slab of the image shows the nine *grahas*, five on one side and four on the other. The antelope of the Tīrthaṃkara is depicted on the pedestal.

Ujjayinī: Historical city of Madhya Pradesh which contained the Kuṇḍugeśvara Ṛṣabhadeva temple built by Siddhasena Divākara.

Ujjili: Findspot of an inscription in Mahbubnagar, Andhra Pradesh, which refers to a temple of Pārśvanātha which existed at that place in the twelfth century and which was under the supervision of the monks of the Korura-gaccha, belonging to the Drāviḍa Sena Saṅgha. The priest was one Indrasena Paṇḍita. *Andhra Archaeological Series*, XXII, No. 79.

Ukhalada: Situated in the Parbhani district of Maharashtra this place has yielded a number of inscribed Jina images.

***Ullāsikkamathaya*:** See *Ajita-Śānti-Stava*.

Umāsvāmin: Author of the celebrated *Tattvārthādhigamasūtra* (q.v) who is called Umāsvāti by the Śvetāmbaras. Both the Śvetāmbara and the Digambara traditions present a great deal of controversy regarding the date of Umāsvāmin. Satish Chandra Vidyabhusan assigns him to the first century AD. He belonged to the Uccanagari *śākhā*, popular in the Mathura region. He was a Brāhmaṇa of the Kaubhīṣaṇi *gotra* and a resident of Kusumapura or Pāṭaliputra. His parents were Svāti and Vātsi, preceptor Ghoṣanandī Kṣamāśramaṇa, and grand-preceptor Vācakamukhya Śivaśrī. According to the Digambara tradition he belonged to the Sarasvatī-*gaccha* and succeeded Kundakunda (q.v.) in AD 44. But it is doubtful whether in any way he was connected with Kundakunda.

Un: Situated in West Nimar district, in the heart of Malwa, this town was the centre of the Paramāra style of architecture where was built in the twelfth century a fine Jain temple, locally known as Caubārā-Derā II. This temple is situated in the northern extremity of the town. The *śikhara* over the sanctum is now lost, but from the fallen remains it is clear that it was of the twelfth-century Cālukya style. The sanctum is a *pañcaratha* on plan with the central *ratha* having three facets and the remaining ones two. The image of Śāntinātha, now removed to the Indore Museum, contains a date corresponding to AD 1185. The other Jain temple at Un is locally called Gwāleśwar. It is almost similar in plan to the Caubārā-Derā II. It is restored and in active worship.

Una: Situated in the West Nimar district, Madhya Pradesh, this place contains a few dilapidated Jain shrines. Some medieval Jain inscriptions have also been found here.

Unā: Originally known as Unnantapura this place in the Junagarh district, Gujarat, is associated with Ādinātha.

Unhela: Holy place associated with Pārśvanātha in the Ujjain district of Madhya Pradesh where some Jain antiquities have been found.

Universe: See Loka. According to Vinayavijaya's *Lokaprakāśa* XII.3.4 the universe looks like a human being standing with feet apart, arms akimbo. In one such conception the said form is figured as a rotating spindle which rests on the half of another bigger spindle, or as they describe it, the cups of the lowest is inverted and the uppermost meets at its circumference the middle one. In another such conception, the lower universe is thought of as having the shape of a *vetrāsana* (trapezion pyramid), the middle one that of the upper part of a standing *mṛdaṅga* (a kind of tabor) and the upper one that of a *mṛdaṅga*, *Tiloyapannattī* 137-8. This may be explained as follows. Three pyramids with rectangular base but with the tops chopped off are put one above the other, the smaller faces of the lower and middle ones and the bigger faces of upper and middle ones touching. In the hip or, according to another scheme at the vibratory place of the spindle, the disc of the earth is placed. Below the earth-disc are seven lower regions containing hells (q.v.) one below another. Above the earth are situated the heavenly regions styled *vimānas* consisting of twelve *kalpas*, nine *graiveyakas*, the heavens forming the neck of the human-shaped universe and the five *anuttaras*. Thus there are 26 heavens (q.v.) placed one above the other. Above the seven lower regions and below the heavens is the disc of the earth with its numerous continents in concentric circles separated by the rings of oceans. See Island-continents. The legs of the human shaped universe are 7 *rajjus*, the waist 1 *rajju*, the upper and the head 1 *rajju*. The *rajju* is a linear astrophysical measure which denotes the expanse which the gods traverse in six months, their speed being 2,057,152 *yojanas* in one movement. The entire area of the universe is 343 *rajjus*.

The world from the ground level to the hells below rests on a layer of hard water, which again rests on a layer of thick air and so on, 20,000 *yojanas* thick.

Upabhoga-Paribhoga Parimāṇa: Taking a vow every day limiting one's enjoyments of consumable and non-consumable things.

Upadeśapada: See Haribhadra.

Upadeśarsāyana-Rāsa: See Jinadatta Sūri.

Upādhyāya: Teacher eligible to deliver lectures to groups of monks on various spiritual matters. He is expected to have a sound knowledge of various scriptures on which he discourses, to have at least three years experience as a monk, and to have perfect knowledge of the rules of monastic conduct. He is required to have spiritual advancement. His teaching and study are expected to be a kind of austerity. He is also required to destroy certain *karma* by conscious meditation. Upādhyāya is also a caste name of the southern Jain priests. As members of an hereditary religious clan they are associated with various temples and supported by the lay section of the community. They give their daughters in marriage with no one but priests. While other southern Jain castes allow the old practice of widow-remarriage, it is neither allowed nor practised by the Upādhyāyas. Village priests are known as Gramopādhyāya (q.v.). Like the priestly caste among the Hindus, no high position is assigned to the southern Jain Upādhyāyas.

Upādhyāya Parameṣṭhins: Next in rank to the *ācārya-parameṣṭhins* (q.v.). They have no authority to initiate people into the Jina creed or to organize the *saṅgha*. Their function is to popularize Jainism in order to help souls entangled in *saṃsāra* (q.v.) reach perfection. He educates and instructs the people.

Upamitibhavaprapañcakathā: A religious novel composed by Siddharṣi (q.v.) in AD 906. It is in prose, with passages in verse at the end of each individual book. It consists of a framed story with inserted tales in which, in conformity with Jain tradition, the destinies of a being are traced through numerous reincarnations. The whole theme is allegorical. Siddharṣi says that he chose the allegory in order to attract readers and for the same reason he wrote in Sanskrit and not in Prakrit. The great popularity which this novel enjoyed among the Jains is attested by the fact that, only 100 years after its appearance, extracts and abridgements were made from it by Vardhamāna, Devendra Suri and others and that even Hemacandra had used it in one of the stories in *Pariśiṣṭaparvan* which presuppose that Siddharṣi's work was universally known, ed. P. Peterson and H. Jacobi in Bib. Ind., Calcutta, 1894; ed. in Devchand Lalbhai Series, Nos. 46, 49, Bombay, 1918-20; German translation I-III by W. Kirfel, Leipzig, 1924; Italian transaltion by A. Ballini in *Giornale della Societa Asiatica Italiana*, vols. XVII-XIX, XXI-XXIV.

Upanayana: Initiation into *brahmacarya* or student life—eight years for the Brāhmaṇa child, eleven for the Kṣatriya and twelve for the Vaiśya. Śūdras are not entitled to this ceremony. The initiation is done with *pañca-parameṣṭhi mantra*.

Upāṅga: Prakrit Uvaṅga, the second series of Śvetāmbara canonical literature which comprises *Aupapātika* (Uvavāiya), *Rājapraśnīya* (Rāyapasenijja), *Jīvajīvābhīgama*, *Prajñāpanā*, (Pannavanā), *Sūryaprajñapti* (Sūrapannatti), *Jambudvipaprajñapti* (Jambuddivapannatti), *Candraprajñapti* (Candapannatti), *Nirayāvalikā* (Nirayavaliyāo), *Kalpāvatāṃśikā* (Kappāvaḍaṃsiāu), *Puṣpikā* (Pipphiāo), *Puṣpacūlikā* (Pupphaculiāo) and *Vṛṣṇidaśā* (Vanhidasāo) (qq.v.). The Digambaras consider the existing version of the Upāṅga literature as unauthoritative but hold that the first section of the lost *Dṛṣtivāda* (q.v.), namely, the *Parikarmāṇi* includes among others *Candraprajñapti*, *Sūryaprajñapti* and *Jambudvīpaprajñapti*.

Upanīti: Sacrament. It is the initiation ceremony and performed in the temple at the eighth year of the child. He wears a sacred thread and is regarded as a *brahmacarin* following five small vows.

Upariyālā: Place, sacred to Ādiśvara which is situated in the Surendranagar district of Gujarat.

Upāsakadaśā: Prakrit *Uvāsagadasāo*, the seventh text of the Aṅga (q.v.) series. Composed in ten chapters (*adhyayanas*) on the duties of lay adherents, it contains narratives for the most part. The narratives pertain to individual devotees like Ānande, Kāmadeva, Mahāśataka, etc. The seventh *adhyayana* is particularly important in which a story is told of the wealthy potter Saddālaputta who had been an adherent of Gośāla Maṅkhaliputta (q.v.) but was converted by Mahāvīra. Edited in the Original Prakrit with the Sanskrit commentary of Abhayadeva and an English trans. with notes by A.F.R. Hoernle, Bibliotheca Indica, Calcutta, 1885-8; ed. with com. of Abhayadeva in Āgamodaya, Bombay, 1920. There is a mertrical elaborated version of the contents of this Aṅga, namely, *Vardhamānadeśanā* in Prakrit.

***Upāsakādhyayana*:** See *Yaśastilaka-campū*.

***Upaśāntamoha*:** The eleventh *Guṇasthāna* (q.v.) in which greed almost disappears.

Upasargakevalin: See Arhanta.

***Upāsakādhyayana*:** See Samantabhadra.

***Upāśraya*:** Buildings erected by each sect for their monks and nuns. In every *Upāśraya* there is a lecture-hall in which the teachers preach and explain sacred texts to laymen who come to visit. They make them do what is known as *pratikarma*, that is repentance for all transgressions. *Upāśraya* is the central place of the community and its construction and maintenance charges are borne by the laymen. The *upāśrayas* serve as the religious home of the Sthānakavāsins where they perform their religious duties and observe six *āvaśyakas* (q.v.) or daily duties. The Prakrit form of *upāśraya* is *upāsaro*.

***Upayogamaya*:** That which is perceptible and knowable; characteristics of a Jīva (q.v.).

Uppina-Betgiri: Site of a Jain temple called Jayadhara Jinālaya which is 15 miles from Kopbal in Raichur district, Karnataka. An inscription found in this place states that the temple was erected by Śaṅkaragoṇḍa, a Rāṣṭrakūṭa governor of the tenth century. The epigraph also mentions a Jain teacher named Nāganandī, disciple of Śrīnandī, belonging to Surastha-gaṇa, P.B. Desai, 367ff.

***Ūrdhvagati*:** That which has the tendency to go upwards; characteristic of a Jīva (q.v.).

Urjayanta: See Girnar. This hill was associated with Jainism from a very early period. In the tenth century one Ratna from Kashmir donated a golden image of Neminātha to the Jain Saṅgha here. This holy hill is believed to be the place of the *nirvāṇa* of Neminātha. Its antiquity is attested by the fact that it is mentioned in the sixth Aṅga text, *Nāyadhammakahāo*. The two towns of Khangāradurga and Tejalapura dedicated respectively to Ṛṣabha and Pārśva, were near this mountain. In the Purāṇas it is known as Raivataka.

Urvī-Tilakam: The Pañca-basadi at Humcha, capital of the Sartara kings, ancient Pombruca, in Shimoga district, Karnataka. It was erected by Cattala-devī, granddaughter of Rakkasa Ganga and came to be known as Urvī-tilakam. The foundation stone was laid by Śrī-Vijayadeva, her *guru* and head of the Nandi-gaṇa.

***Utpātikī*:** That which hinders the power of spontaneous thought and prevents the right use of conscience and intellect, an ingredient of the *jñānāvaraṇīya* (q.v.).

***Utsargasamiti*:** See Caritra.

***Uttama-Caritra-Kathānaka*:** Also known as *Uttamakumāra-caritra-kathānaka*, it is the story of a prince with the most wonderful adventures inserted into the framework of Jain doctrines. It is to found in a prose version and in several metrical ones. The language is Sanskrit with west Indian dialectal words. As early as in 1884 the prose version was edited and translated into German by A. Weber. One metrical recension in 686 *ślokas* by Cārucandra, pupil of Bhaktilābha had been edited by Hiralal Hamsaraj, Jamnagar, 1908; 2nd edn. 1911.

Uttamapalai: A Jain site in Periyakulan taluk in Madurai district, which contains some interesting inscriptions.

Uttarā: See Digambara-Śvetāmbara split.

***Uttarādhyayana-Sūtra*:** Prakrit *Uttarajjhayana*, the first Mūlasūtra (q.v.) which is a compilation of various texts in 36 sections. The first *Vinayaśrūta* deals with the every day conduct of a Jain ascetic. Several sections are sermons in series of aphorisms, admonitions to pupils, elaborations on the cares which the monks must endure with patience, the four precious things, *karma* and sin, the voluntary death of a sage, true and false ascetics, and so on. The seventh section consists mainly of parables. The eighth is ascribed to Kapila and forms an independent discourse entitled *Kaviliyam*. The sixteenth section is devoted to the commandment of chastity. The twenty-third deals with the dialogue between Kesi and Gautama which reveals the difference between the creeds of Pārśva and Mahāvīra. Other sections refer to the Kṛṣṇa legend, to sermons, catechisms, erudite elucidation of dogmatics, and regulations for the life of the monks. It contains brilliant philosophical discourses as well. *Niryukti* by Bhadrabāhu; *Cūrṇi* by Jinadāsagaṇi Mahattara, Ratlam, 1933; com. by Devendragaṇi, Bombay, 1937; com. by Vādivatāla Śāntisūri, Devchand Lalbhai, Bombay, 1916-17; Eng. trans. by H. Jacobi in SBE, XLV, 1895; ed. J. Charpentier, Upsala, 1922; L. Alsdorf, *The Āryā Stanzas of the Uttarajjhāyā*, with notes, etc., Mainz, 1966; Index by Ānandasāgara Sūri, Bombay, 1928.

***Uttarajjhayāṇa*:** See Uttarādhyayana.

***Uttarapurāṇa*:** Second part of the *Triṣaṣṭilakṣana-Mahāpurāṇa* or *Mahāpurāṇa* (qq.v.) which was composed by Guṇabhadra (q.v.), disciple of Jinasena II (q.v.) in the ninth century. The *Uttarapurāṇa* runs to 8,000 verses and deals with the great characters of the Jain mythology. Ṛṣabhanātha is excluded in this volume because his exploits have been described in the *Ādipurāṇa* (q.v.), the first part of the *Mahāpurāṇa*. One of the favourite stories in the *Uttarapurāṇa* is that of Jīvandhara which has also been treated several times by later poets both in Sanskrit and in Tamil. *Uttarapurāṇa*, published in Bhāratīya Jñānapīṭha, Kashi, 1968.

***Uvaṅga*:** See *Upāṅga*.

***Uvaesamālā*:** A didactic poem, 'garland of instruction' in 540 Prakrit stanzas, containing moral instructions for laymen and monks written by Dharmadāsa. Its language corresponds to the later Jaina Mahārāṣṭrī. There were commentaries on this work as early as the ninth century. The poet Siddarṣi (q.v.), too, wrote a commentary on *Uvaesamālā*. This commentary is available in two recensions, one of which contains also stories. There is also an *Uvaesamālā* in 505 Prakrit stanzas written by Maladhārī Hemacandra (q.v.). *Uvaeśamālā*, ed. L.P. Tessitori in *Giornale della Societa Asiatica Italiana*, XXV, 1912, 167-298.

Uvāsagadasāo: See Upāsakadaśā.

***Uvāsaggahaka-stotra*:** A hymn to Pārśva in five stanzas ascribed to Bhadrabāhu (q.v.). Jacobi, *Kalpasūtra*, intro. 12f.

***Uvavāiya, Ovavāiya*:** See Aupapātika.

V

Vadali: Place sacred to Pārśvanātha situated in Sabarkantha district of Gujarat.

Vaḍavāla: Situated in the South Kanara district of Karnataka, this place had a seventeenth-century Śāntinātha temple.

***Vādicandra*:** Author of *Pārśvapurāṇa*, a drama *Jñānasūryodaya* which is a parody of Kṛṣṇamiśra's *Prabodhacandrodaya*, *Pavanadūta*, *Śrīpāla-Ākhyāna*, *Pāṇḍavapurāṇa* and *Yaśodharacarita*. He flourished in sixteenth-seventeen century.

Vādirāja: Celebrated poet and philosopher who lived in the first half of the eleventh century. He belonged to the Nandī-saṅgha and his preceptor was Matisāgara. He wrote *Pārśvanātha-carita* in AD 1025 at the court of the Western Cālukya King Jayasiṃha II (AD 1015-43) where he was honoured as a great debator and received the title 'Syādavāda-vidyāpati'. The *Pārśvanātha-carita* is an epic in 12 books and chiefly based on Guṇabhadra's *Uttarapurāṇa* (qq.v.). His *Yaśodharacarita* (q.v.) is in four cantos and 296 verses which is described as the 'shortest and sweetest *mahākāvya*'. His *Nyāyaviniścaya-vivaraṇa* has been held 'as an encyclopaedia of Indian logic which is noted for its stupendously wide range and its appalling dialectic'. *Pārśvanāthacarita*, ed. in Manikacandra Digambara Jaina Series, Bombay, 1915; *Yaśodharacarita*, ed. Gopinath Rao, Tanjore, 1912, by K. Krishnamoorthy, Dharwar, 1913; *Nyāyaviniścaya-vivaraṇa*, Bhāratīya Jñānapīṭha, Varanasi, 1949, 1954.

Vādirāja II: Author of three philosophical hymns, namely, *Jñānalocana-stotra*, *Ekibhāva-stotra* and *Adhyātmāṣṭaka*. This Vādirāja II who is not to be confused with the author of *Yaśodhara-carita* (q.v.) who also wrote a commentary on Akalaṅka's *Nyāyaviniścaya*.

Vadnagar Praśasti: Composed by Śrīpāla (q.v.) about AD 1151 extols the deeds of Kumārapāla (q.v.), the Cālukya king of Gujarat who ruled in the twelfth century AD. *Epigraphia Indica* I, 293-306.

Vāgbhaṭa: Author of *Vāgabhaṭālaṅkāra*, work on poetics and of the poem *Neminirvāṇa-mahākāvya* (q.v.) who flourished in the tenth century. He belonged to the Digambara sect and lived under Jayasiṃha of Gujarat (AD 1093-1154). Pub. by Nirnaya Sagar Press, Bombay, 1936. We have another Vāgbhaṭa who wrote a book on rhetoric entitled *Kāvyānuśāsana* about AD 1300.

Vāghiṇa Inscription of Samantasimha: Dated VS 1359 (AD 1302) of the time of this Cahamana ruler of the Jalor house and found at Vaghina in the Sirohi district of Rajasthan, the inscription mentions the festival of Śāntinātha of the village of Vāghasina. P.C. Nahar, *Jaina Lekha Saṃgraha*, No. 959.

Vaimānika: One of the four classes of gods who reside in the upper world called *svarga-loka* which comprises sixteen *kalpavimānas*, known as Saudharma, Aiśāna, Sanatkumāra, Mahendra, Brahman, Brahmottara, Lāntava, Kāpiṣṭha, Śukra, Mahāśukra, Śatāra, Sahasrāra, Ānata, Praṇata, Āraṇa and Acyuta: nine *graiveyaka-vimānas*, namely Sudarsana, Amogha, Subuddha, Suviśāla, Payodhara, Subhadra, Sumanas, Saumanasa and Priyaṅkara, nine *anudeśa-vimānas*, namely Lakṣmī, Lakṣmīmālikā, Vairevaka, Rocanaka, Soma, Somarūpya, Aṅka, Palyaṅka and Āditya; and five *anuttara-vimānas* such as Vijaya, Vaijayanta, Jayanta, Aparājita, and Sarvārthasiddhi. These gods are by nature devoted to the Jinas.

***Vaināyakī*:** That which prevents receiving what is known as inherited knowledge, a constituent of the *Jñānāvaraṇīya* (q.v.). It is an obstruction arising from *ghātin karma* (q.v.).

***Vairāgyasāra*:** A didactic poem in Apabhraṃśa by Suprabhācārya of the twelfth century in 72 *dohā* verses teaching general moral principles of Jainism. It is written in eastern Apabhraṃśa.

Vairoti: Śāsanadevatā of Vimalanātha according to the Digambara tradition. She also figures like others as a Vidyādevī. Vairoti is the Śāsanadevatā of Mallinātha as well according to the Śvetāmbara tradition in which she is seated on a lotus and carries in her hands *varada-mudrā*, rosary, citron and *śakti*. Vairoti is also a Vidyā-devī (q.v.) whose vehicle is the lion.

Vaiśālī: Ancient city of eastern india associated with the early life of Mahāvīra, but did not develop into an important Jain centre.

Vajirkheda Plates: Jain inscription of tenth century AD presented in three plates found of Vajirkheda, 4 miles east of Malegaon in Nasik district, which refers to the Rāṣṭrakūṭa King Nityavarṣa-

Varuṇa. He is described as three-eyed, crowned with matted hair and riding a bull. The Digambara books represent him as eight-headed and four-armed while the Śvetāmbaras prefer the four-armed form.

Vasantgarh: Jain centre in Sirohi district, Rajasthan.

***Vasantavilāsa*:** A *mahākāvya* in 14 cantos written by Bālacandra of Candra-gaccha in the thirteenth century which describes the achievements of Vastupāla (q.v.) Pub. in Gaekwad's Oriental Series, ed. C.D. Dalal, Baroda, 1917.

***Vaśīkaraṇa*:** Hypnotism. The *Samarāiccakahā*, a work of the eighth century, refers to the practice of hypnotism which is called *kammana*. It signifies the act of winning a person, overpowering one's senses, and making a person subject to one's will. The practice is also mentioned in the *Upamitibhavaprapañcakahā* which speaks of Ripudarana who was charmed by the magic first of *tantravādin* Yogeśvara and changed his nature. The *Nāyādhammakahā* states that a mixture of magic powders is to be used for the *vaśīkaraṇa*. The *Jvālinīkalpa* devotes one chapter called *vasyatantrādhikāra* to the rites and syllabic formulae relating to hypnotism. Another chapter of the same text deals with the mystic diagrams connected with the rituals of *vaśīkaraṇa*. The *Bhairava Padmāvatī Kalpa* also deals with the hypnotism of women. Chapter Six of the *Jvālinīkalpa* described several mystic disgrams which are intended for the rite of *vaśīkaraṇa*.

Vāstudevatā: See Dikpālas.

Vastupāla: Brother of Tejaḥpala (q.v.) both being the two great Jain ministers of Gujarat whose religious activities are eulogized in numerous works in Sanskrit and regional languages. Although there is some confusion regarding their early career, in the beginning of the thirteenth century they were in the service of Lavaṇaprasāda, the famous governor of Bhīma II, and his son Vīradhavala. In Arisiṃha's *Sukṛtasamkīrtana* (qq.v.) and Jinaharṣa's *Vastupālacarita* it is said that he restored the temple of Pārśvanātha at Anahilavāḍa, which was formerly built by Vanarāja in the eighth century, after he had defeated the Muslims near Abu. At Stambhatīrtha or Cambay he erected a golden, gilded flagstaff on the temple of Bhīmeśa, an *uttānapaṭṭa* before Bhaṭṭāditya and a *maṇḍapa* in the temple of the sun-god. At Dhavalakkapura, modern Dholka, he built a temple of Ṛṣabha. His building activities at Śatruñjaya are numerous. At Palitana he excavated a large tank and built an asylum for the Jain monks. He built on Girnar Hill two temples dedicated to Pārśva and Ṛṣabha. He also made other constructions there as is attested by the *Vividha-tīrthakalpa* which gives a vivid description of his building activities. According to Arisiṃha, Vastupāla built on Mount Abu the temple of Malladeva. Merutuṅga in his *Prabandhacintāmaṇi* (qq.v.) says that Vastupāla built at Pādaliptapura, modern Palitana, a temple of Mahāvīra and at Modhera he erected two statues of the same. He also gives details regarding Vastupāla's work at Śatruñjaya. His celebrated pilgrimage to Girnar and Śatruñjaya accompanied with monks of different *gacchas* is described in various literary works. Jinaprabha in his *Vividhatīrthakalpa* says that Vastupāla and his brother Tejaḥpala built 984 *pauṣadhaśālās*, 500 ivory thrones, 717 *dharmaśālās*, 700 *satrakaras* (alms-houses), 1,304 Jain temples and three *sarasvatībhāṇḍāgāra* (libraries). He also repaired 2300 dilapidated Jain shrines. The *Vastupālacarita* of Jinaharṣa refer to various Jina images installed by Vastupāla at different places. Despite his Jain leanings he patronized other forms of religion and was also a devotee of Śiva. Among the authors befriended and patronized by him were Someśvara, Harihara, Nānaka, Arisiṃha, Amaracandra, Vijayasena, Udayaprabha, Jinabhadra, Naracandrasūri, Narendraprabhasūri, Bālacandra, Jayasiṃhasūri, Māṇikyacandra and others. Vastupāla himself was also a good poet who composed *Naranārāyanānda*, an epic is sixteen cantos. Ed. C.D. Dalal, Gaekward's Oriental Series, Baroda, 1916; see also *Jinaratnakośa* 204.

***Vasudevahiṇḍi*:** 'The Wanderings of Vasudeva', father of Kṛṣṇa, composed in archaic Jaina Mahārāṣṭrī by Saṅghadāsagaṇi Vācaka. Dharmaseṇagaṇi Mahattara of the seventh century AD claims to have completed its unfinished portion. The incomplete text has been edited by Munis Caturvijaya and Punyavijaya with the help of twelve manuscripts. In 1935 Alsdorf indicated that it contains something of a new version of the lost *Bṛhatkathā* of Guṇādhya. During 1970-4 J.C. Jain made a critical study of the text which is divided into six *adhikāras*. The first deals with religious stories serving as introduction; the second contains parts of the legends of Kṛṣṇa's family; the third contains the boyish pranks of the Princes Samba and Subhānu; the fourth narrates the wanderings of Vasudeva. The fifth, the largest and most important is divided into 28 *lambhas*, each bearing the names and stories of the heroines with whom the hero got married during the course of his wanderings;

and the sixth is the last section, though not the concluding one. The text remains an important source on the history and development of the Jain *Harivaṃśa*, tradition, evolution of Mahārāṣṭrī as different from Ardhamāgadhī dialect of Jain canonical literature, preservation of the lost *Bṛhatkathā* and of course the cultural social milieu of the third-fourth centuries AD.

Vasunandin: See *Mūlācāra*, Vaṭṭakera.

Vāsupūjya: The twelfth Tīrthaṃkara who was the son of King Vasupujya and Queen Jayā of Campa. He had a height of 70 bow-lengths and his life-span was 7,200 thousand years. He achieved salvation at Campā. Suhamma and Dharaṇī were his chief disciples. The emblem constantly associated with Vāsupūjya is the buffalo. His attendants are Kumāra and Caṇḍā/ Gāndhārī. His sacred tree is *pāṭalikā* according to the *Abhidhānacintāmaṇi*, and *kadamba* according to the *Uttarapurāṇa*. A king named Dirpiṣṭa-Vāsudeva is to wave the fly-whisk by his side. It is said that while he was in the mother's womb, god Indra gave his father wealth (*vasu*) which accounts for his name. His legends have been narrated by Vardhamāna Sūri in the *Vāsupūjya Caritra*.

***Vāsupūjya Caritra*:** Idealized biography of the twelfth Tīrthaṃkara, Vāsupūjya, written by Vardhamāna Sūri (q.v.).

Vaṭa Gohāli: A Jain *vihāra* in Paharpur, district Rajshahi, Bengal. The earliest document with Jain affiliation is the Paharpur copper plate of the year 159 of the Gupta era, recording the endowment of lands for the maintenance of the ceremonial worship of Arhats, with sandal-paste, incense, flowers, lamps, etc., by a Brāhmaṇa couple at this *vihāra*. As this *vihāra* is stated to have been presided over by the disciples and their spiritual descendants of the Nirgrantha Samaṇācārya Guhanandin belonging to the Pañcastūpa-*nikāya* of Kashi, it is likely that it existed in Paharpur even in the fourth century AD.

Vāṭera: A Jain holy place associated with Śāntinātha in the Sirohi district of Rajasthan.

Vaṭṭakera: Author of the Prakrit works *Mūlācāra* (q.v.) and *Trivarṇācāra* on the moral conduct of a pious Jain. It belongs to the Digambara tradition. The date of Vaṭṭakera is not precisely known which is why it is said that he flourished in one of the early centuries of the Christian era. There is a commentary, *Ācāravṛtti*, on the *Mūlācāra*. Its author Vasunandin holds that Vaṭṭakera's purpose was to teach the essentials of the *Ācārāṅgasūtra* by means of this work.

Vāva: A Jain holy place in the Banaskantha district of Gujarat which is associated with Ajitanātha.

Vāyu: Vedic god of air regarded as the lord of the north-west quarters in Jainism. He rides a deer. His attribute is the *vajra*, thunderbolt or the banner. The Digambaras give him a wooden weapon in addition.

***Vāyukāya*:** Air-bodied; characteristic of immobile or one-sensed Jīva (q.v.).

Vedal Inscription: Jain epigraph incised on a boulder in front of a natural cave known as Andar-Madam during the reign of the Cola King Āditya I (AD 871-907) discovered at Vedal in Arkoram taluk of North Arcot district which records an undertaking given by lay disciples at Vedal also known as Mādevi Arandaimaṅgalaṃ in Singpura-nāḍu to protect and feed the lady pupils of Kaṇakavīra Kurattiyar, a woman ascetic and disciple of Guṇakīrtibhaṭṭāraka. An earlier epigraph from the same site belongs to the reign of Nandivarman II, in which the Jain temple-complex is called Vidarpalli. *South Indian Inscriptions* III (3), No. 92; XIII, No. 245; *Annual Report on South Indian Epigraphy*, 1909, App. B. 82.

***Vedanīya*:** That which causes the beings to experience the pleasure of happiness and pains of misery. It is an obstruction arising from *aghātin karma* (q.v.).

Vedānta: Except the ideas of bondage and liberation Jainism has practically nothing in common with the Vedānta. Philosophically Jainism may be designated as pluralistic realism while Vedānta is monistic idealism. To the Jains knowledge and action are complementary to each other. To the Vedāntist both are diametrically opposite. Perception of internal and external objects through the sense which has special value in Jainism means nothing to Vedānta. While the Jains believe that the gross world is only an effect (*kārya*) or modification (*pariṇāma*) of subtle physical elements, the Vedantists hold that cause alone is real and what appears as effect is only an illusion. To the Jains world is eternal without beginning or end, as to the Mīmāṃsakas, and hence it cannot be the modification of any imaginary principal like the *brahman*. According to the Vedānta the world is a mere appearance like an object in a dream. Thus the difference between Jainism and Vedānta is real. This is why Śaṅkara and Rāmānuja made serious attempts to refute Jainism. Śaṅkara says that on account of the impossibility of contradictory attributes in one thing the Jain doctrine cannot be accepted. A thing cannot be hot and cold at the same time.

The cognition that a thing is of more than one nature cannot be definite and hence cannot be a source of true knowledge. The doctrine of Syādavāda shows that the means of knowledge, the object of knowledge, the knowing subject, and the act of knowledge are all indefinite. If that be the case, the Tīrthaṃkara cannot teach with any claim to authority and his followers cannot act on the doctrine, the matter of which is altogether determinate. The Jain concept of the plurality of conscious souls, their various sizes and number of parts is also contradicted by Śaṅkara. Dealing with Jainism, Rāmānuja says that since the substance and its qualifying states are different, the former cannot be connected with opposite attributes. Since Jainism holds everything to be of an ambiguous nature, it cannot therefore be said that each of the substances has its own qualifying states and its own nature. Time is only an attribute of substance, not an independent substance, and hence the question of its being a non-being does not arise. If the souls abide in numberless places, each soul having the same size as the body which it animates, then the soul previously abiding in the body of an elephant will not be able to enter the next stage of its existence into the body of an ant. The same argument had been put forward also by Śaṅkara.

Vedism: The Jains do not believe in the authority of the Vedas (*vedaprāmāṇya*), which does not, however, imply that they were anti-Vedic. They designate their own scriptures as Vedas. They do not hesitate to use the term *yajña* to denote thier rituals, which are, of course, basically different from the Vedic ones. The Vedic doctrines of *karma*, transmigration of souls, rebirth, and liberation are accepted in Jainism. The Jain concept of Jīva that suffers pain and enjoys pleasure (owing to the amount of *karma* it acquires) is influenced by Upaniṣadic ideas. *Karma* is conceived in Jainism as being material and permeating the Jīvas. The Jīva of Jainism is almost the same as the *bhoktā* or experiment and *kartā* or agent of the Upaniṣads. According to Jainism the *karma* matter accumulated round the soul during the infinite number of past-lives encircles the soul as it passes from birth to birth. In the Upaniṣads we come across a clean development of the theory of transmigration of the soul in three distinct stages and this theory is the source of the Jain scheme of transmigration and rebirth. Likewise the Jain conception that liberation is possible when it is free from the bondage of *karma* is inspired by the Upaniṣads according to which it is the state of infiniteness that a man attains when he knows his own self. It is also to be noted that the sources of varied religio-philosophical terminology of the Jains as well as of the Buddhists, are all to be traced to the Vedas, though the Vedic world-view is different from that of the Jains and the Buddhists. Some of the Vedic gods occur in the Jain pantheon, though their position is inferior to that of the Jinas. Among the Vedic gods referred to in the Jain texts mention may be made of Indra, Agani, Sūrya, Āditya, Aśvins, Soma, Varuṇa, Pṛthivī, Rātri, Maruts and minor deities like the Vasus, Gandharvas, Vaiśravaṇa or Kubera, as also a number of Purāṇic gods. Among the goddess of Vedic affiliation the Jain texts mention Hrī, Śrī, Lakṣmī, Kīrti, Medhā, Dhṛti, Ilā, and Sītā. The Apsarases Alambuṣā, Miśrakeśī, Rambhā, Tilottamā, Citrarathā, Citralekhā and Urvaśī are also mentioned in Jain texts. We have also Jain versions of their myths.

Velāra: Situated in the Pali district of Rajasthan, and earlier known as Vadhilada, it was a sacred place presided over by Ādīśvara. An epigraph from this place mentions Śāntisūri of Nāṇakīya-gaccha.

Vemulavada Stone Inscription: Dated śaka 888 (AD 966), it states that Baddega, the king of Sapādalakṣa, constructed a Jinālaya for Somadeva, the chief of the Gauḍa Saṅgha. *Inscriptions of Andhra Pradesh* (Karimnagar District), ed. P.V. Parabrahma Sastri, No. 4.

Venkunram: Site of the Arugar temple in North Arcot district. The temple is two storeyed with a circular śikhara and a simple wall-section and *mañca-bandha* plinth. A sub-shrine for Dharmadevī, carrying fine stone sculpture of the early Vijayanagara period of this goddess inside should be mentioned in this connection.

Venur: About 20 km from Mudbidri (q.v.) in South Karnataka district, Venur has a few Jain temples of which the Śāntīśvara-basti with the earliest inscription dated 1489-90 is of special interest. This all-stone temple has a sanctum in the first floor also, and this sanctum has an image of a Tīrthaṃkara and a roof of a somewhat pyramidal shape. The Venur colossus of Gommaṭeśvara, about 11 m high, resembles the Karkal colossus. It was set up, according to inscriptions, at Enuru by Timmarāja of the family of Cāmuṇḍa in AD 1603-4.

Veraval Inscription: A stone inscription of the time of the Gujarat Cālukya King Bhīma II found from Veraval, the left half of the slab being lost. In this inscription a number of Digambara saints of the Nandīsaṅgha, belonging to the lineage of

Kundakunda are mentioned. It indicates that a temple named after Mūlarāja I was in existence at Anahilapura. It also mentions the temple of Candraprabha of Prabhāsa, sacred to the Jains. It quotes a verse from Madanakīrti's *Śāsana-catustriṃśikā* according to which the water used in the bathing of the Candraprabha image had the power to cure leprosy. *Epigraphia Indica* XXXIII, 117ff.

Vibhaṅga-Jñāna: A kind of attractive knowledge which falsifies all spiritual insight. It is an obstruction arising from *ghātin-karma* (q.v.).

Vidagdha: Son of Harivarman, he was the ruler of the region around the Pali district of Rajasthan. His leaning towards Jainism is attested by an inscription now in the Ajmer Museum. Advised by his preceptor Vāsudeva, he built a temple for the god Jina (that is, Ṛṣabha) in the town of Hastikuṇḍi, modern Hathundi, in AD 915. He weighed himself in gold which he dedicated to the Jina and his preceptor. The temple and image were renovated in AD 997. Vidagdha's religious commitments were maintained by his son Mammaṭa and grandson Dhavala. In the second part of the inscription one Balabhadra appears to be the preceptor of Vidagdha, for whose satisfaction the latter had erected a Caityagṛha. The inscription also discloses the names of a number of Jain saints. Vidagdha has been described by the Jain saint-poet Sūryācārya as *Rāṣṭrakūṭa-kulakānana-kalpavṛkṣa* which is suggestive of his Rāṣṭrakūṭa lineage. He flourished in the first quarter of the tenth century. *Epigraphia Indica* X.19ff.; *Journal of the Asiatic Society of Bengal*, LXII (1), 309ff.

Vidhidāna: Enjoyment of the happiness of heaven as Indra by virtue of ascetic merit.

Vidiśā Inscriptions: Engraved on the pedestals of Puṣpadanta and Candraprabha images constructed under the patronage of Rāmagupta of the fourth century AD, supposed to belong to the royal Gupta dynasty, which refer to a Jain saint or devotee Celukṣamaṇa, son of Golakyāntā and pupil of Acarya Sarppasena Kṣamana, grand-pupil of Candra Kṣamācārya who was a *pāṇi-patrika*, i.e. one who uses the hollows of his palms for alms and as a drinking bowl. *Epigraphia Indica*, XXXVIII.46-9; *Journal of Oriental Institute*, XVIII, 1969, 247-51.

Viditā: See Vijayā.

Vidyā-devīs: Goddesses of learning who are sixteen in number. In conception they were modelled after the Yakṣiṇīs. The reverse would have assumed as well but is inadmissible on the ground of the priority of the Yakṣiṇīs as connected in mythology and ritual with the Tīrthaṃkaras in Jainism. The sixteen divinities under the name of the Vidyā-devīs may be *prima facie* supposed to sway the sixteen arts and sciences, but the texts of Jainism give a different clue: through their worship the devotee obtains knowledge, character, religion, effort, and mental qualities of many kinds. The Vidyā-devīs are Rohiṇī, Prajñapti, Vajra-śṛṃkhalā, Vajrāṅkuśā, Apraticakrā or Jambunadā, Puruṣadattā, Kālī, Mahākālī, Gaurī, Gandhārī, Mahājvālā, or Jvālāmālinī, Mānavī, Vairoti, Acyutā, Mānasī, and Mahāmānasī.

Vidyādharas: Lit. 'master of magic art'. In Vimala's *Paumacariya* (q.v.) both Rāvaṇa and Hanumān are often described as belonging to the race of the Vidyādharas. They are good narrators of tales. Kidnapping another man's wife or a maiden was common among the Vidyādharas. According to the Jain tradition, during the time of the dissolution of the world, the Vidyādharas and heavenly gods descended to the earth and picked up pairs of human beings and carried them to some caves where they lived on fish, tortoise, and dead bodies. It is said that Somadatta's snake-bite was cured by the touch of a Vidyādhara. The hair and clothes of a long-lived Vidyādhara had permanent fragrance. They were also associated with low classes of people who sought magical power. Jain narrative literature contains numerous stories pertaining to the Vidyādharas. It is said that Śabarasila, the lord of the Vidyādharas, was exceedingly powerful and a treasure-house of the Śabara spells. Later he renounced the world. His son installed a Ṛṣabha image in a cave which become the place of attainment (*siddha-kṣetra*) of the Vidyādharas. We have the story of Mānasavega, the Vidyādhara lord who, enamoured of the beauty of Madanamañjukā, wife of Naravāhanadatta, kidnapped and detained her, though he did not molest her. It was due to the fact that any Vidyādhara who offends Jain monks or is guilty of violating a Jain temple or a couple, or one who seizes another man's wife against her wishes, shall be deprived of his magical spell. Even Rāvaṇa, a powerful Vidyādhara monarch, did not violate the virtue of Sītā for fear of the consequences. We also read about the fight between two Vidyādharas when the stronger destroyed the spell of the weaker.

Vidyānanda: Also known as Pātrakeśarin, Vidyānanda flourished in the ninth century. His *Aṣṭasāhasrī* is a commentary on Akalaṅka's *Aṣṭaśatī*. He was also the author of *Tattvārtha-*

ślokavārttika, a commentary on Umāsvāmin's (q.v.) work, *Āptaparīkṣā* and *Pātraparīkṣā*, *Pramāṇanirṇaya* and *Pramāṇaparīkṣā*. He was a resident of Pāṭaliputra and mentioned by Jinasena I (q.v.) in his *Ādi Purāṇa* (q.v.). In his *Aṣṭasāhasrī* or *Āptamīmāṃsālaṅkāra* he refers to the help he received from a saint named Kumārasena. This work is an elaborate exposition of Jain logic in which the views of Samantabhadra (q.v.) and Akalaṅka (q.v.) have been treated. The *Āptaparīkṣā* consists of 124 verses. The *Pramāṇaparīkṣā* is written in Sanskir prose. His other works include *Satyaśāsanaparīkṣā* and *Vidyānandamahodaya*. *Aṣṭasāhasrī*, ed. N.R. Gandhi in Gandhinatharanga Series, Bombay, 1915; *Tattvārthaślokavārttika* edited along with the original text of Umāsvāmin by M.L. Sastri, Gandinathranga Series, Bombay, 1918; *Pramāṇanirṇaya* and *Pramāṇaparīkṣā* in Sanatana Jaina Granthamala, Benares, 1913; *Āptaparīkṣā* in Digambara Jain Granthamala, Varanasi, 1913. For *Satyaśāsanaparīkṣā* and *Vidyānandamahodaya* see *Jinaratnakośa* 355, 412.

***Vidyānandamahodaya*:** See Vidyānanda.

Vidyānandin: Author of the *Sudarśanacarita* dealing with the idealized biography of Muni Sudarśana in 12 cantos and written in simple Sanskrit. The author, a disciple of Devendrakīrti, belonged to the Mūla-saṅgha, Bharati-gaccha and Balātkāragaṇa of the line of Kundakunda. Ed. in Manikacandra Digambara Jaina Granthamala, No. 51, H.L. Jain, Varanasi, 1970.

Vidyārambha: Commencement of study on an auspicious day invoking Sarasvatī, the goddess of learning. It is a Śvetāmbara sacrament.

Vigraharāja IV: Śākambharī Cāhamāna ruler (AD 1152-62) of Ajmer. From the *Dharmaghosasūristuti* of Raviprabha, it is known that he hoisted a flagstaff on a Jain temple called Rājavihāra at Ajmer. The same source says that at the request of Dharmaghoṣa-sūri he prohibited the slaughter of animals on the Ekādaśī day.

***Vihāra*:** A stage in the career of the Tīrthaṃkara when he preaches the truth to all people.

***Vihāra-Prāsāda*:** 'Palace of enjoyment' which each Lotus Pond (q.v.) of the Saumanasa (q.v.) forest encircling the Meru (q.v.) contains in its centre. It is 125 *krośas* in height and half that in width. It has in its centre a grand throne for Saudharma Indra and other seats for four Lokapālas—Soma, Yama, Varuṇa, and Kubera—*agramahiṣīs* or chief consorts of Indra, Pratīndra or counter-Indra, *pravaras* or the elder ones, *sāmānikas* or those equal in status but not in authority, *pāriṣadas* or courtiers, *madhyama-pāriṣadas* or courtiers of the second rank, *bāhya-pāriṣadas* or courtiers from outside, *trayastriṃsas* or ministers, *mahattaras* and *mahattaris* or chamberlains, and *aṅga-rakṣakas* or body-guards.

Vijāpura: Jain centre of the Kharatara-gaccha in Pali district of Rajasthan which contains a temple of Vāsupūjya built by Jinesvara II.

Vijayā: Also known as Viditā, she is the Śāsanadevatā of Vimalanātha (q.v.) according to the Śvetāmbara tradition. She is described as seated on a lotus and as having four hands with an arrow, noose, bow, and snake. Vijayā is also the name of the Śāsandevatā of Kunthunātha according to the Digambara tradition in which she rides a black boar and carries the attributes of conch, sword, disc, and *varada-mudrā*.

Vijayamangalam: Site of the Original Candranātha temple of the Ganga period in Coimbatore district. The outer *maṇḍapas* beyond the *mahā-maṇḍapa* of the inner unit of the Candranātha complex are of Vijayanagara times, as indicated by the pillars sculptures and the *mānastambha* and the large entrance *gopura* of the temple complex. The original *vimāna* of brick, from base to finial of Gaṅga style, altered by later plastering, is square and two-storeyed with octagonal *grīvā* and *śikhara*. The cella inside contains an idol of Candranātha and the superstructure is hollow. Inside the arches of the *toraṇas* are sculptures depicting scenes from Jain mythology. The outer additions of this temple complex are of the Vijayanagara period. The site was also known as Kurumbunāḍu.

Vijayapāla: Son of Sidhapāla and a contemporary of Kumārapāla. He is the author of the drama *Draupadī-svayaṃvara* (q.v.), the story of which has been taken from the *Mahābhārata*. Ed. Muni Jinavijaya, Jaina Atmananda Sabha, Bhavnagar, 1918.

Vijaya-Pārśvadeva-basadi: Great Jain temple, built by Boppa, son of Gaṅgarāja, at Dorasamudra, modern Halebid, the original name of which was Drohagharaṭṭa. It was renamed Vijaya-Pārśvadeva-basadi by the Hoysala King Viṣṇuvardhana himself.

Vijayasena: See *Revantagiri-Rāsa*.

Vijayasiṃha: Pupil of Samudrasūri of the Nagilakula who composed in Prakrit the *Bhuvanasundarīkathā* in AD 975 in *gāthā* metre and 9,000 stanzas.

Vijaya Yakṣa: Also known as Śyāma-Yakṣa, he has in the Digambara version three eyes and holds a fruit, rosary, axe, and *varada-mudrā*. The Śvetāmbaras represent him with a swan as his vehicle and two hands holding a disc and a club. He is the attendant Yakṣa of Candraprabha (q.v.).

***Vijñaptilekhasaṃgraha*:** An interesting work containing important letters exchanged by Śvetāmbara monks of different places. It also throws light on various Jain holy places and customs. Ed. Jinavijaya, Singhi Jaina Granthamālā, Bombay, 1960.

***Vikala*:** See Samyag Cāritra.

Vikrama: See Nemidūta.

Vikramāditya: See Kālakācārya.

Vikramapura: Modern Bikrampur, some 30 miles from Jaisalmer in Rajasthan, famous for the temple of Mahāvīra and connected with the monks of the Kharatara-gaccha. This particular temple was built by Jinadatta in the first half of the twelfth century. The Kharatara Ācārya Jinapati was born here in AD 1162. An image inscription of AD 1466 mentions it as a great city.

***Vikrānta-Kaurava*:** See Hastimalla.

Vilapakkam Inscription: Belonging to AD 945, of the time of Cola Parantakas I, and found at Vilapakkam in North Arcot district, it refers to the sinking of a well by a nun called Paṭṭini Kuratti Aḍigal, a disciple of Ariṣṭanemi Bhaṭārar of the Jain establishment of Tiruppanmalai. It also tells that the Jains of this locality constituted a representative council of 24 members to look after their interest. *Annual Report on South Indian Epigraphy*, 1900, App. B. 53.

Vimalanātha: The thirteenth Tīrthaṃkara who was the son of Kayavamma (Kṛtavarman) and Sāmā (Suramyā) of Kampilyapura. He had a height of 60 bow-lengths and a life-span of six million years. His sacred tree was the *jambu* and chief disciples Mandara and Dharaṇīdharā. He attained liberation on Mount Sammeya. His symbol is the boar. The particular attendant spirits attached to him are named as Ṣaṇmukha and Vairotī/Viditā. The king to stand for his fanner is Svayambhū Vāsudeva. A *Vimala-Purāṇa* by Kṛṣṇadāsa deals with his life.

Vimalanātha-basti: Temple at Bellur in Mysore district, Karnataka, which has a 79 cm high image of Vimalanātha with an inscription on the pedestal of a date earlier than the thirteenth century.

***Vimala Purāṇa*:** Idealized biography of the thirteenth Tīrthaṃkara Vimalanātha written by Kṛṣṇadāsa.

Vimala Sūri: See *Paumacariya*.

Vimala-vasahi: See Dilwara Temples.

***Viṃśati-Viṃśikā*:** Haribhadra's (q.v.) celebrated work which means 'twenty sets of twenties' and belongs to the category of *prkaraṇa-grantha*, a compendium of the scattered and discursive teachings of a corresponding seminal or source work. Haribhadra chooses to present to his readers the following twenty topics in twenty sets of twenties. He lists those topics in the first *viṃśikā* called *adhikāra-viṃśikā*. (1) Adhikāra—List of the topics dealt with; (2) Lokānāditva—Beginninglessness of the world; (3) Kulanīti-lokadharma—Family traditions and popular customs of the country, (4) Caramaparivarta—the last existence preceding liberation; (5) Tatvujadukrama—the seed, etc., of the tree of *dharma*; (6) Samyaktva—description of *samyaktva* or right faith from the practical point of view; (7) Dānavidhi—the mode of charity its three kinds; (8) Pūjāvidhi—the mode of worship; (9) Śrāvakadharmā—the duties of a householder; (10) Śrāvakapratimā—the eleven observances of a householder, (11) Yatidharma—the duties of a monk; (12) Dvividhaśikṣā—twofold religious instruction; (13) Bhikṣāvidhi—the mode of begging; (14) Tadantarāya—unforeseen obstacles in the way of eating the alms; (15) Ālocanavidhi—the confession of faults; (17) Yogavidhāna—the mode of *Yoga*, (18) Kevalajñāna—perfect knowledge,(19) Siddha-vibhakti—categories of liberated souls; and (20) Siddhasukha—perfect bliss of the liberated souls. The list of topics is comprehensive and covers some of the most important topics of Jainism. The language of the text is Prakrit, to be more specific, Jain Mahārāṣṭrī. K.V. Abhayankar's edition of this text is based on six different manuscripts, one printed edition of the *Yogaviṃśikā* and Sukhlalji's edition of the *Yogaviṃśikā* with Yaśovijaya's commentary. *Viṃśati-viṃśikā* by Haribhadra Suri, ed. K.V. Abhayankar, Pune, 1918; for details see V.M. Kulkarni, 'Haribhadrasuri's Viṃśati-Viṃśikā: An Appproach' in *Jainism and Prakrit in Ancient and Medieval India*, ed. N.N. Bhattacharyya, New Delhi, 1994.

***Vinaya*:** Control over senses and passions and humble attitude which is the subject-matter of the first sermon of the *Uttarādhyayana Sūtra*. Later commentators and editors regard Vinaya as *anuvartana* (regard, obedience, following), *āvartana* (proper behaviour, governing) *anuśāsana* (enjoined rule of conduct, or precept), *śuśrūṣā* (service to teachers and elders) and *śiṣṭācāra-paripālana* (due observance of good manners) and classify into five kinds, namely *jñāna-vinaya* (regard for knowledge), *darśana-vinaya* (regard for faith), *cāritra-vinaya* (regard for conduct), *tapa-vinaya* (pleasant attitude towards austerity) and *upasrāra-vinaya* (observance of good manner with others),

Vaṭṭakera in his *Mūlācāra* (211-14) says that the fruit of knowledge is *vinaya* and the fruit of *vinaya* is one's overall progress in life. It embodies the following qualities: *ārjava* (straightforwardness), *mārdava* (modesty, softness), *lāghava* (dispassionate attitude), *bhakti* (devotion, faith) and *rāhlādakaraṇa* (pleasing nature). The *Mūlārādhanā* (IV.112-31) provides an independent chapter on Vinaya which it defines as the gate of salvation with which one can accomplish self-restraint, austerity, and knowledge. The *Tattvārtha* (VI.6.1) says that possessing Vinaya is one of the sixteen virtues that constitute excellent moral character Śāntisūri in his *Dharmaratna Prakaraṇa* lists Vinaya as one of the qualities of an ideal layman.

Vinayavāda: One of the four major philosophical schools current in the days of Mahāvīra according to the Jain texts which refer to its 32 varieties. It is very difficult to say what Vinayavāda really was. The Jain and Buddhist text and commentaries have not given any clear or specific definition of Vinayavāda. Jacobi translated 'Vinayavāda' as 'idolatry' but he had not given any specific reason as to why he preferred this rendering. In the Buddhist text we find that the Buddha was asked many times whether he was a Vinayavādin. From the Jain definitions it appears that the followers of this school believed in the practice of observing certain moral codes, probably without knowing their real impact. Perhaps the aim of the Vinayavādins was to gain a better future existence by practising them. The Jains criticise them because it was not their aim to exterminate all *karma* or to stop the influx of new *karma*. Corresponding to Mahāvīra's Vinayavāda, we have the Buddhist expression, *sīlabhataparamāsa*. *Sūyagaḍa* I.12.3-4; II.2.79; *Uttarādhyayana* XVIII.23.

Vinayavijaya: See *Lokaprakāśa*. He had also written a commentary on the *Kalpasūtra* in the year 1639.

***Vipākaśruta*:** Prakrit *Vivāgasūya*, the eleventh text of the Aṅga (q.v.) category. The title denotes the 'ripening of actions'. It contains legends on retribution for evil deeds and the outcome of good actions. It has two Śrutaskandhas with ten chapters each. The first is called *Dukhavipāka* which is much longer than the second known as *Sukhavipāka*. Āgamodaya edition with Abhayadeva's com. Bombay, 1920.

Vīrācārya: A Jain saint patronized by the Cālukya King Jayasiṃha Siddharāja of Gujarat (AD 1092-1142). He was skilled in philosophical debate and scored victories over the Buddhists, Digambaras, and some philosophers of the orthodox schools.

Vīradhavala: The governor of the Cālukya King Bhīma II of Gujarat. He was the son of Lavanaprasāda of the Vāghela dynasty and the famous Jain brothers Vastupāla and Tejaḥpala (qq.v.) were his ministers. Nothing is specifically known with regard to his religious learnings, but on circumstantial evidence it appears that he had great respect for Jainism. The *Darbhāvati Praśasti*, included in the *Vastupālacarita* of Jinaharṣa, mentions a Jain temple called Vireśvara which was named after Vīradhavala.

***Vīra Gaṇin*:** See *Ajita-Śānti-Stava*.

Vīranandī: Author of *Candraprabha-carita-mahākāvya* (q.v.) an idealized biographical poem on Candraprabha (q.v.) who belonged to the Digambara sect and flourished in the tenth century. Pub. in Jīvarāja Granthamālā, Sholapur, 1970.

Vīrapura: A Jain *tīrtha* in according to an epigraph of the twelfth century found at Sedam in Gulbarga district, Karnataka. Its identification is not known.

Vīraśāsana Jayantī: The day of the first discourse of Mahāvīra delivered on the Vipulācala mountain near Rājagṛha after his omniscience. It is celebrated mainly by the Digambaras every year on the first day of the dark half of the month of Śrāvaṇa.

***Vīraseṇa*:** Author of the *Dhavalā* (q.v.) commentary of the *Ṣaṭkhaṇḍāgama* (q.v.) and *Jayadhavalā* (q.v.) commentary on the *Kaṣāyaprābhṛta* (q.v.). In the *Dhavalā* he has described himself as a disciple of Āryanandin and the grand-disciple of Candrasena of the Pañcastūpānvaya and who had studied the Siddhānta under Elācārya. *Dhavalā* was completed in the Śaka year 738 corresponding to AD 816 when Amoghavarṣa I was the reigning king of the Deccan. The first 20,000 *ślokas* of the *Jayadhavalā* were composed by him, and his disciple Jinasena (q.v.) completed the commentary in 60,000 *ślokas* in śaka 759 corresponding to AD 837.

***Vīrastava*:** Prakrit *Vīratthaya*, the tenth Prakīrṇa (q.v.) which contains an enumeration in 43 verses of the names of Mahāvīra. Āgamodaya edn., Bombay, 1925.

***Vīratthaya*:** See Vīrastava.

Virupākṣa Temple: Jain temple at Patadakal, one of the two important cities of Cālukyas of Badami. The main temple is essentially of the closed *maṇḍapa* type, in front of which there is a pillared hall.

Viśākha: See Bhadrabāhu.

Viśāladeva: Paramāra chief of Candravati (q.v.)

whose Dattani inscription of AD 1287 refers to the gift of two fields for the expenses of Pārśvanātha. Another inscription in the Vimala temple-complex of Mount Abu also testifies his patronage of Jainism.

Viṣṇuvardhana Jinālaya: Jain temple constructed by the general Viṣṇu-daṇḍādhīpa at Darasamudra and named it after his overlord, the Hoysala King Viṣṇuvardhana. This information is obtained from an inscription of AD 1137 found at Belur in Hassan district, Karnataka. *Epigraphia Carnatica* V, Belur 17.

***Vītarāga Stotra*:** Composed by Hemacandra (q.v.) at the request of King Kumārapāla. It is a hymn in praise of Mahāvīra and at the same time a manual of the Jain religion. The work consists of 20 short sections, generally of eight or nine *ślokas* each or sometimes more. Ed. with two commentaries, the *Vivaraṇa* by Prabhānanda and an *Avacūri* either by Viśālarāja or by his pupil. Devchand Lalbhai, Bombay, 1911. N.G. Javeri says in the Foreword to the edition that Hemacandra wrote 32 cantos at the request of Kumārapāla, of which 20 are contained in the *Vītarāga-stotra* in 25 verses, also entitled *Ratnākara-pañcaviṃśatikā*, after the author Ratnākara of unknown date. Ed. in *Stuti-saṃgraha*, Nirnaya Sagara Press, Bombay, 1906.

***Vivāha*:** Sacrament. After completing studies and starting a harmless profession one is to marry a girl from a good family. In the Digambara view, after marriage the pair should go on a pilgrimage for seven days. The Śvetāmbaras have no such compulsion.

***Vivekavilāsa*:** See Jinadatta Suri.

***Vivāgasūya*:** See *Vipākaśruta*.

***Vividhatīrthakalpa*:** A systematic account of the Jain *tīrthas* written in the fourteenth century during the reign of Hammīra Mahammada or Muhammad-bin-Tughluq by Jinaprabha of the Kharatara-gaccha at the town of Yoginīpattana or Delhi. Holy places like Raivataka, Śatruñjaya, Stambhatīrtha, Arbuda, Satyapura, Anahilapura, Nāsikya, Pratiṣṭhāna, Mathura, Kausambi, Ahicchatra, Kāmpilya, Śravastī, Campā, Pāṭaliputra, Vārāṇasī, Hastināpura, Kanyānayana, Phalavardhī, etc., are described along with the legends associated with them. Historcial facts like the invasion of Sultan Mahmud, the exploits of Alauddin Khalji, etc., are also provided. Ed. Jinavijaya, Santiniketan, 1934.

***Viyāhacūliyā*:** See Prakīrṇa.

***Viyahapannati*:** See Bhgavatī, *Vyākhyāprajñapti*.

***Voḍḍa-Ārādhanā*:** Probably the earliest of all extant Kannaḍa works. It is in prose and belongs to a period earlier than AD 850. Its author Śivakoṭyācārya was a Jain. Like many Jain works *Voḍḍa-ārādhanā* too has a professedly didactic aim. It is a collection of *ārādhanā* stories which are found with some variations in the work of Hariṣena (q.v.) and others. It has nineteen stories beginning with the story of Sukumāra and ending with that of Vṛṣabhasena. There is a balanced proportion of Sanskrit words in this book.

***Vratacaryā*:** Sacrament. It is the child's schooling under a teacher.

***Vrata Pratimā*:** Keeping up the twelve vows and the extra vow of *sallekhanā* (q.v.).

***Vratāropa*:** Śvetāmbara sacrament of taking vows for living according to the injunctions of the Śāstra for happiness in this world and a good place in the next birth.

***Vratāvatarana*:** Sacrament. It is performed in the twelfth or sixteenth year after the completion of studies. The *brahmacārin* should now take leave of his preceptor and adopt any of the prescribed ways of livelihood.

***Vṛṣṇidaśā*:** Prakrit *Vaṇhidasāo*, the twelfth of the Upāṅga (q.v.) series which is the fifth part of the *Nirayāvalī Suttam*. It deals with the conversion of twelve princes of the Vṛṣṇi dynasty by the saint Aritthanemi. Nirayavalika-sutram with Candrasena's commentary Agamodaya edn., Ahmedabad, 1922.

***Vṛttis*:** A class of commentarial literature in Sanskrit written by Haribhadra who flourished in the middle of the eighth century AD. His commentaries on the following Āgamic texts are well known *Āvaśyaka, Dasavaikālika, Jivābhigama, Prajñāpanā, Nandisūtra, Anuyogadvāra* and *Piṇḍaniryukti*.

***Vyākhyāprajñapti*:** See Bhagavatī.

Vyantara: One of the four orders of celestial beings or Devas. As their name suggests, they belong to the peripatetic category of divinities. They are of eight classes: Rākṣasa, Bhūta, Piśāca, Mahoraga, Gandharva, Yakṣa, Kinnara and Kiṃpuruṣa (qq.v.). They occur as supernatural beings, benevolent or malevolent or both in the Hindu Purāṇas, probably with the exception of Mahoragas. The *Vasudevahiṇḍi* says that the Rākṣasas (q.v.) have a huge body and the Piśācas are scared of watery land. The Rākṣasas, Yakṣas, and Piśācas have no power during the day. They are dazed with the brightness of the sun and therefore delight in the night. They never attack chaste men, heroes, or men who are awake. The eight *vyantara* gods have been associated with various trees, e.g. the Piśācas with the *kadamba* (a tree with orange-coloured fragrant blossoms), the Yakṣas with the *vaṭa* (banyan), the Bhūta with the *tulasī* (holy basil), the Rākṣasas with *kandaka* (reed), the Kinnaras with the *aśoka* (belonging to the leguminous class with magnificent flowers), Kiṃpuruṣas with the *campaka* (*Michelia campaka* bearing a light yellow fragrant flower), Mahoragas with the *nāga* (the *nāgakeśara* tree having a folded type of flower) and Gandharvas with the *tinduka* (*Diospyros embryoteris*). These trees are known as *caitya* trees. The Bhūtas (q.v.) are invoked to avert cyclones and to grant offspring. Offerings (*bhūtabali*) were made to them. In a story of *Vasudevahiṇḍi* we find that Dhamila used to meet his lover Vimalasena at a Bhūta temple. The Piśācas are classed with the Rākṣasas and Yakṣas. The Mahoragas were probably great serpents (*mahā-uragas*) or serpent-deities as distinguished from the Nāgas (q.v.). The association of the great serpents with Jainism is attested by the legends of Dharaṇendra and others. Pārśvanātha has a seven-hooded snake as his symbol and his Yakṣiṇī or Śāsanadevatā was Padmāvatī, whose Hindu counterpart was the snake-goddess Manasā. Jaratkāru, an ascetic in Brāhmaṇical tradition, stands for Kaṭha in the Jain legends who later became one with Śeṣa, the lord of the netherworld. The names Kinnara and Kiṃpuruṣas literally mean 'ugly person'. The names are also of two branches of a trans-Himalayan race. In the Hindu Purāṇas they are described as celestial musicians and semi-divine beings. The Jains also maintained this tradition. The Gandharvas are allied to the Yakṣas (q.v.) and are regarded as divine musicians with an aerial abode of their own. In Jain temple architecture the *jaṅghā* often shows lively figures of Gandharvas and Apsaras in various enchanting poses. In the case of sculpture, flying Gandharvas can be shown playing on drums or cymbals, or holding a garland in their hands. In Jain art tradition the Gandharvas and the Yakṣas are inextricably connected.

***Vyavahāra*:** Prakrit *Vavahāra*, the third Chedasūtra, which is a necessary supplement to *Bṛhatkalpasūtra*. It is ascribed to Bhadrabāhu and has ten chapters. The *Niryukti* on this text is written by Bhadrabāhu himself. It is commented upon the Malayagiri. The text throws considerable light on the everyday life of Jain monks. Ed. W. Schubring, Leipzig, 1918; Jain Sāhitya Saṃśodhaka Samiti in Devanagari script, Poona 1923; W. Schubring, *Drei Chedasūtras*, Hamburg, 1966; ed. Muni Manek with *Niryukti, Bhāṣya* and Malayagiri's *Vivaraṇa* in 12 parts, Bhavnagar, 1926-8.

***Vyavahāra*:** See *Naya*.

***Vyuṣṭi*:** Sacrament. It is the first anniversary to be performed with worship as usual, and with fasts.

W

Wage Earners: The *Sthānāṅga* 271 refers to the hired labourers or wage earners whose position was not happy. They differed little from the slaves. Either they were employed on daily wages in kind or cash, or were employed while undertaking a journey, or worked on a contract basis and were paid after the completion of the work. Else they worked on daily wages and were asked to do all kinds of work as directed by the employer.

Warangal Fort: Findspot of a standing Pārśvanātha figure belonging to the fourteenth century. Its style is of the Kākatīya school. The noteworthy details of this image are the miniature figures of the 23 Tīrthaṃkaras around the back slab, the *chowri*-bearers and the seven-hooded serpent topped by the *mukkudai*, all very confidently chiselled.

Widow: Jain laws are more liberal to widows than those of the Hindu fold. The custom of self-immolation did not find favour among the Jains, though there are a few stray references of such happenings. Most widows preferred to live a celibate and virtuous life. The custom of levirate did not find moral sanction. But there is provision of remarriage (q.v.) especially among the southern Jains. Widows could devote their time to spiritual upliftment and thus carve out a respectable position in society. Their legal position was better because they inherited the property of deceased husbands. According to Jain law, on the death of person without a son his widow becomes his successor with regard to property. If she has sons, she becomes absolute owner of her own share. Since Jainism does not find any special merit in the essentiality of the son, the son has no exlusive or first right of succession which is why a Jain widow is acknowledged even as the preferential heir of her own son. She has also absolute and unrestricted power of enjoyment and disposition of her property. She is at liberty to give her inherited property to anyone she likes.

Wife: Regarded as the keystone of the happiness and prosperity of the home. In fact, the wife is the synonym of home, *gṛhinī gṛha-mucyate*, says the *Nītivākyāmrta* XXXI.31. It is said in the *Sāgaradharmāmṛta* II.59 that a compound of brick and mortar does not make a home, but the wife who follows the family tradition constitutes it. Complete fidelity between husband and wife is regarded as the ideal of married life and for that purpose at the time of entering the householder's stage both husband and wife have to take the vow of *Svadārasantoṣa* or *Svabhartṛsantuṣṭi*. It is the vow of avoiding extra-conjugal sexual relations. There was polygyny (q.v.) among the rich and the powerful, but the Jain family system is basically monogamic. Thus in the domestic sphere the wife wields all powers and is regarded as the presiding mistress of the house. In the Jain Purāṇas one finds that if the queen set her steps into the royal court for some reason the king himself stood up to greet her and request her to be seated on the throne. Utmost care is taken to see that a bride brought into the family should be free of all sorts of bodily deformities and disease, endowed with virtue, and belongs to a good family. Perfect harmony and happiness are craved for conjugal life which is expected to be long enough and a complete success in temporal and spiritual matters in conformity with the Jain ideal of life.

Women: Śrāvikās and Sādhvīs are two pillars on which Jainism stands. As an Ācārya headed a group of monks so was the Gaṇinī heading over a groups of nuns. Brāhmī, the sister of Bharata, was appointed head of nuns by Ṛṣabha. Candanā or Candanabalā was the first woman disciple of Mahāvīra who headed the order of nuns and achieved liberation. The Jain canonical texts mention numerous women who by observing strict rules of discipline achieved the highest goal of life. These women are glorified by Jain writers. Notwithstanding this glorification, the attitude of equality towards women does not find favour with Jains. An ascetic philosophy cannot favour women. It is stated in the *Sūyagaḍa* IV.1.11 & IV.1.27 that as a pot full of lac catches fire immediately, so a monk is lost through the association of women. In *Ācārāṅga* I.142 he is advised to commit suicide if he finds himself unable to control his desire for women. In the voice of Manu the Jain authors state that a woman is under her father in childhood, under her husband in youth and her son in old age. She cannot live independently. Jain texts are replete with misogynistic comments. Abusive terms are showered on women. True, there are some sane voices: Somadeva in his *Nītivākyāmṛta* for instance, says that women are neither good nor bad. They are, like the cream of milk, the source of poison as well as nectar. But the total approach is purely patriarchal. Though women are given a place in the ascetic order, it is said that a nun of 30 years' standing is inferior to a monk only of three year's experience. In social life women are treated with discrimination, though the position of a Jain woman is better than that of her Hindu sister. The Jains admit the necessity of educating their women. In the case of inheritance and property ownership their position seems to be better than that of Hindu women. Though a Jain woman has the right to inherit her father's property, her share is not equal to that of her brother. Property rights of Jain widows are, however, greater than those of their Hindu counterparts. Though history records the existence of eminent Jain women whose contributions to different walks of life, even in political and military affairs, are worthy of our respect, Jain society in itself holds that only through marriage does a woman's life become fruitful. Spiritual aspiration is for a limited few. The wife is regarded as the keystone of the arch of the happiness of the family. In the domestic sphere she wields all power and is regarded as the presiding mistress of the house. In ancient times marriage was recommended only for adult women. The age limit was lowered in medieval times and at present adult marriage is the order of the day. Dissolution of wedlock is permitted under specific circumstances and the wife is allowed to contract another marriage. Widow remarriage is also allowed and is found specially among some sections of the southern Jains. See Cross-Cousin Marriage, Daughter, Divorce, Endogamy, Exogamy, Female Ascetics, Female Education, Forms of Marriage, *Gotras*, Inter-Caste Marriages, Marriage, Nuptial Rituals, Polygyny, Prostitution, Remarrige, Slave Girls, *Strīdhana*, Widow, Wife.

Woodcraft: The development of Jain woodcraft was basically due to the householder's requirement of auspicious symbols carved on the door-lintel or window frame: The Jina image, fourteen-dreams, *aṣṭa-maṅgalas, dvārapālas*, floral and creeper patterns, etc. Home-shrines, called *ghar-derasar* in western India, are small replicas of their wooden and stone prototypes and are reproduced in a miniature form for family worship. The earliest dated Śāntinātha-*derasar* of AD 1390 in Kalupur, Ahmedabad, is a wooden structure with a *maṇḍapa* enclosed by a dome, 3.35 m square, which has seventeen concentric layers of carving made of 248 pieces. The pillars supporting the dome are adorned by brackets and architraves, richly carved with decorative items. Such home-shrines are numerous in Gujarat but most of them are unpublished and their exact date in not known. A few of them are preserved in the National Museum, the Baroda Museum, the Prince of Wales Museum and also in other museums of India and abroad. The shrine consists of two essential parts, the *maṇḍapa*, where the devotees congregate and the principal shrine where the deity is installed. The former shows a profusion of ornamentation and is erected on a series of pillars that support an exquisitely carved dome on architraves and beams. One of the most beautiful examples of a wooden Jain temple is provided by the Wadi Pārśvānatha temple of Patan, now housed in the Metropolitan Museum of New York. Sculptures form an integral part of the wooden architecture of the Jain *maṇḍapas*. Detached from the structure these sculptures look as if carved separately and independently but close observation reveals that the side that was attached to the architectural piece is not properly finished. Almost all the Jain *maṇḍapas* have several beautifully carved female figures, either playing or various musical instruments or in various dance poses. Rectangular panels, parts of wooden shrines, present pictures of contemporary life. They often show Jain monks, horsemen, bullock-carts, palanquins, marriage processions, etc. The best examples of Jain woodcraft are found in western India, in Gujarat and Rajasthan. The dry climate of these regions in which wood lasts much longer than other parts of the country seems to have provided the incentive for resorting to wood as the medium of artistic expression.

Y

Yakṣas: Intimately associated with Jainism in the literature of which not only the chief Yakṣas but their shrines are described. The attendants of the Tīrthaṃkaras are all Yakṣas. Their Śāsanadevatās or female attendants are also Yakṣiṇīs. In the Jain lists of Yakṣas, Brāhmaṇical gods and goddesses occur. According to the Jain texts there was hardly a city or town which had no Yakṣa Āyatana or Caitya. Thus Vardhamānapura had the Āyatana or shrine of Maṇibhadra, Kayamgala of Chattapalasa, Campa of Pūrṇabhadra and Angamandira, Vāṇiyagama of Suhamma, Vaiśāli of Bahuputtiyā and Koṇḍiyāyana, Mithila of Maṇibhadra, Ālabhiyā of Śaṅkhavana and Pattakālaga, Vārāṇasī of Koṭṭhaga and Ambasālavana, Kauśāmbī of Candotaraṇa, Śrāvastī of Koṭṭhaga, Mathura of Sudarśana, Hastināpura of Sahasaṃbavana, Dvāravatī of Surapriya, etc. The *Bhagavatī* mentions the Bahuputta shrine in the northern part of Vaiśālī. Pārśva's visit to the famous Pūrṇabhadra shrine of Campā is recorded in the *Nāyādhammakahāo*. Mahāvīra visited the shrines like those of Guṇaśīla in Rājagṛha, Pūrṇabhadra of Campā, Koṣṭhaka of Śrāvastī, etc. Other Yakṣas mentioned in the Jain texts are Śālibhadra, Sumanabhadra, Laksaraksa, Purnaraksa, Sarvana, Sarvayaśas, Sarvakāma, Samṛddha, Amogha, Asmata, etc. Quite a good number of his lectures were delivered, according to the *Bhagavati*, in the Guṇaśīla shrine. A vivid description of the Yakṣa shrine of Pūrṇabhadra to the north-east of Campā is given in the *Aupapātika*. It is known from the *Vipākaśruta* and *Aupapātika* that Yakṣas were worshipped like gods with leaves, flowers, incense, and sandal. These shrines had images of the Yakṣas to whom these were dedicated. As Jainism found favour with traders, it was natural that the god of wealth, Kubera, lord of the Yakṣas, would be popular among the Jains. Among the Yakṣa attendants of the Tīrthaṃkaras, Gomukha is attached to Ṛṣabha, Mahāyakṣa to Ajita, Trimukha to Sambhava, Yakṣeśvara to Abhinandana, Tumbara to Sumati, Kusuma to Padmaprabha, Mātaṅga to Supārśva, Vijaya to Candraprabha, Ajita to Suvidhi, Brahma to Śītala, Yakṣet to Śreyāṃśa, Kumāra to Vāsupūjya, Ṣaṇukha to Vimala, Pātāla to Ananta, Kinnara to Dharma, Garuḍa to Śānti, Gandharva to Knthu, Yakṣet to Ara, Kubera to Malli, Varuna to Munisuvrata, Bhṛkuṭi to Nami, Gomedha to Nemi, Pārśva to Pārśva and Mātaṅga to Mahāvīra (qq.v). The Yakṣas are well represented in art. Earliest stone specimens of such divinities hail from Patna, Parkham, Baroda, Besnagar, Pawaya and other places. These life-size plastically round independent statues of the Yakṣas became models of the Jina and Buddha images. They are characterized by a heavy earthiness of form, a rustic robustness, and a relaxed largeness.

Yakṣa-Cetiyas: The abode of a Yakṣa is referred to in Jain texts as Cetiyas (Caityas) or Āyatanas. Most villages and cities contained an abode of a Yakṣa, whether a hut or a sophisticated house or temple. Important among these were the Pūrṇabhadra shrine at Campā, Guṇaśīla shrine at Rājagṛha, Ambasālavana shrine at Amalakappa, etc. The shrine of Dyutipalāsa, presided over by Sudharma Yakṣa in Vaniyagrāma, that of Bhaṇḍira, presided over by Sudarśana Yakṣa in Mathura and that of Vardhamāna, presided over by Maṇibhadra Yakṣa, at Vardhamānapura, deserve special mention. These shrines are located in gardens outside the city, on the hill top, in the vicinity of a pond, near the city-gate, or inside the city. Mahāvīra and Buddha used these shrines as their halting places. We hear of a Yakṣa-cave (*guhā*) in Mathura where Ācārya Āryarakṣita sojourned. We also hear of a Yakṣa-*bhavana* located in the Vindhya mountains.

Yakṣamaha: Festival of the Yakṣas (q.v.). In Jain literature, besides the 24 Yakṣa attendants of the Jinas, we come across individual Yakṣas such as Pūrṇabhadra, Maṇibhadra, Śvetabhadra, Haritabhadra, Sumanobhadra, Vyātipātikabhadra, Subhadra, Sarvatobhadra, Manuṣyayakṣa, Vanādhipati, Vanāhāra, Rūpayakṣa, and Yaśottama. The *Aupapātika-sūtra* mentions the festival in a Cetiya shrine of Pūrṇabhadra where all kinds of actors, dancers, rope-walkers, wrestlers, boxers, jesters, story-tellers and lute-players assembled and people offered *pūjā* with flag, bells, peacock feathers, fly-whisks, sandalwood paste, flowers, sweets, lamps and so forth. Such celebrations were held at the Yakṣa shrines at Campa, Mithila, Vārāṇāsī and other places. Generally, Yakṣas are regarded as benevolent and inoffensive, but they are occasionally classed with Piśācas and other malignant spirits causing sorrow. Numerous benevolent Yakṣas are mentioned in ancient Jain texts. Bibhelaka Yakṣa used to attend on Mahāvīra during his ascetic life. Śailaka Yakṣa, having assumed the form of a horse, rescued people from the sea. Gaṇḍitinduga Yakṣa of the Tinduge garden at Varanasi was a devotee of the sage Mātaṅga.

Yakṣāyatana: Jakkhāyatana or Yakṣa-caitya, that is, Yakṣa shrine. Detailed description of the shrine of the Yakṣa Pūrṇabhadra is found in *Aupapātika-sutra* 2-5. The *Vasudevahiṇḍi* (q.v.) refers to an *udyāna* or park called *manorama* in Śālliggāma in Magadha Janapada which was the abode of Yakṣa Sumana whose stone plaque or platform (*śilā*) was placed under an *aśoka* tree. Most of the Yakṣa-*cetiyas* or *caityas* referred to in the Buddhist and Jain literature were sacred trees. There was hardly a city or town which had not a Yakṣa *āyatana* or *caitya*. Pārśva's visit to the famous Pūrṇabhadra shrine at Campā is recorded in the *Nāyā-dhammakahāo*. Mahāvīra used to visit shrines like the Guṇaśila of Rājagṛha, Pūrṇabhadra of Campā, Koṣṭhaka of Śrāvastī, etc., all situated in *Ujjānas*, that is *Udyānas* or gardens. The Yakṣa was represented either by the *caitya* tree or by a stone slab (*śilā*) or by an image. The Pūrṇabhadra shrine, referred to above, was situated in the Amrasāla-vana to the north-east of the city of Campā. It was very ancient (*cirātīta*). A big forest grove surrounded it. There was an *aśoka* tree at the centre of the grove. A *pṛthivīśilā-paṭṭa* was under this tree, slightly reclining against the stem and placed on a throne. The shrine of Yakṣa Maṇibhadra was situated both at Mithila and Vardhamānapura. It should be pointed out in this connection that the association of every Tīrthaṃakara with a particular tree was due to the influence of Yakṣa worship which was closely connected with *rukṣa* or tree-worship. It should also be remembered that the original Sanskrit word *caitya* also means a sacred tree.

Yakṣendra: Also known as Yakṣet, he is the attendant Yakṣa of Aranātha according to the Śvetāmbara tradition. He has six faces and twelve arms carrying citron, arrow, sword, club, noose, *abhaya*, mongoose, bow, fruit, spear, goad, and rosary. The Digambaras call him Khendra and attribute similar things to him, twelve hands as well as a peacock as his mount. This Yakṣa has the symbolism of Skanda-Kārttikeya.

Yakṣet: See Yakṣendra.

Yakṣeśvara: Attendant Yakṣa of Abhinandana (q.v.) who is characterized by the symbol of an elephant. According to the Śvetāmbara view, the Yakṣa holds in his right hands a citron and a rosary and in his left a mongoose and a goad. According to the other view, he has a bow, a shield, and a sword. His mongoose symbol is identical with that of Jambhala, the Buddhist counterpart of Kubera.

Yakṣiṇī: See Śāsanadevatā.

Yalbargi: Findspot of three short image-inscriptions in Raichur district, Karnataka. One of them mentions Māghanandī, Siddhāntacakravartī, the royal preceptor and also Mūla-saṅgha and Deśīya-gaṇa. The second inscription mentions the teacher Mādhvacandra belonging to Mūla-saṅgha, Deśīya-gaṇa and Pustaka-gaccha. The third, belonging to the time of the Sinda Prince Vira Vikramaditya of the twelfth century, mentions a temple of Pārśvanātha. P.B. Desai 375ff.

Yalladahalli: Findspot of a Jain epigraph of AD 1254 in the Nāgamaṅgala taluk of the Mandya district, Karnataka, which records the construction of a Jain temple by Devarāja, an officer of the Hoysala Ballāla II. A grant was also registered for Municandra, disciple of Narendrakīrti Traividya, belonging to Pustaka-gaccha. *Epigraphia Carnatica*, IV, Naga 76.

Yama: The Vedic god of death regarded as the governor of the southern region in Jainism. He is described as riding a buffalo and holding a staff. He is the son of the sun and accompanied by his wife Chāyā. His function is to pronounce judgement on the merits and demerits of departed souls. The conception of the Yama is identical to that of the Brāhmaṇic god of the same name.

***Yamaka Stuti*:** See Dharmaghoṣa.

***Yantra*:** Mystic diagrams which occupy a prominent place in Tantric cults is sometimes referred to in Jain texts of Tantric affiliation, such as the *Jvālini-kalpa*, etc. A *yantra* is supposed to represent the body of the deity and is also described as the house of the divinity to be invoked. In its various parts it is supposed to represent the original maintenance and dissolution of the world of things the dot in the centre symbolizing unitary world ground. The *bīja-mantra* or the mono-syllabic abbreviation of what is to be uttered as prayer or invocation or incantation is mentally placed in the various projections of its constituent triangles and lotuses, its circles and squares. Chapter Six of the *Jvālini-kalpa* describes several mystic diagrams which are intended for the rite of *vaśīkaraṇa* or hypnotism. One such device is characterized as the *sarvarakṣā yantra*, which consists of a sixteen-petalled lotus surrounded by three circles in ascending order. The *Bhairava-Padmāvatī-kalpa* lays down that the *yantra* or the mystic diagram should be written with sandal paste upon a plate of bronze, and water poured on this device should be collected and administered to the sick as a drink to remove fever of the most intense type.

Yāpanīya Saṅgha: Also known as Yāpya-saṅgha, it was established by Sri Kalaśa Ācārya at Kalyāṇa in Gulbarga district, Karnataka. This saṅgha recognized the existence of sacred books and believed that women could attain salvation and saints could eat after attaining omniscience. These are in conformity with the Śvetāmbara tradition. Again, like the Digambaras, the Yāpanīya-saṅgha was against wearing clothes and followed the rules and regulations of the Digmbara ascetics. It is said that may Ācāryas belonged to Yāpanīya-saṅgha and among them were Umāsvāti, Śivācārya, Sakaṭāyana, Svayambhū, Tribhuvana-Svayambhū and Vādirāja. It appears that this saṅgha served as a connecting link between the Śvetāmbaras and the Digambras. But neither its literature nor any of its followers is existing today.

Yaśaḥpāla: See *Moharājaparājaya.*

***Yaśastilaka-Campū*:** Written in AD 959 by the Digambara Jain Somadeva Sūri, it is a religious novel in prose and verse based on Guṇabhadra's *Uttara Purāṇa* (qq.v.). It tells the story of the conversion of King Maridatta to Jainism under the influence of his nephew and niece who were brought to his palace as sacrificial victims. The last three sections form an independent book entitled *Upāsakādhyayana*, i.e. 'Readings for the Laymen'. Ed. with com. in Kāvyamālā LII, 1901; in two parts with Śrutasāgara's com., Bombay, 1916; K.K. Handiqui, *Yaśastilakacampū and Indian Culture*, Sholapur, 1949; Gokulchandra Jain, *Yaśastilakacampū kā Sāṃskṛtika Adhyayana*, in Hindi, Pārśvanātha Vidyāśrama, Varanasi, 1969.

Yaśobhadra: The sixth *gaṇadhara* (q.v.) who succeeded Sayambhava (q.v.) as the head of the Jain order and held his office till his demise in 319 BC.

***Yaśodhara Carita*:** Legend of King Yaśodhara, related in Haribhadra's *Samaraiccakahā* (q.v.), which has been the source of the ornate epics of Vādiraja Sūri (q.v.) and Māṇikya Sūri. Vādiraja's epic is in four cantos and he derived his main inspiration from the *Uttara Purāṇa* of Guṇabhadra (qq.v.). Vādirāja also wrote *Pārśvanātha Caritra* (q.v.) in AD 1025. On the other hand, according to his own statement Māṇikya Suri used Haribhadra's narrative as the source of his work. There was one Māṇikya Sūri in the thirteenth and another in the sixteenth century, and it is not possible to ascertain which of them is the author of the *Yaśodhara-carita.* Vādirāja's work, ed. T.A. Gopinatha Rao, Tanjore, 1912 and Māṇikya Suri's by Hiralal Hamsaraj, Jamnagar, 1910.

***Yaśovijaya*:** Teacher, reformer and scholar of the seventeenth century who belonged to the Tapāgaccha and tried to unite the Śvetāmbaras and the Digambaras. His works comprise *Adhyātmaparīkṣā* in Prakrit with a Sanskrit commentary, *Jñānbindu-prakaraṇa* and *Jñānasāra* or *Aṣṭakaprakaraṇa*. Published together with Haribhadra's *Aṣṭaka* and other works, Surat, 1918. He also revised the *Dharmasaṃgraha* which was written by Mānavijaya in 1681. Yaśovijaya's name is borne by two educational institutions in Varanasi and Mehsana, and by the texts published by them.

Yativṛṣabha: Author of the *Cūrṇisūtra*, the commentary of *Kaṣāyaprābhṛta* (q.v.), who flourished in the beginning of the seventh century. In this commentary he probably followed the works of Ārya Maṅkhu and Nāgahastin. Yativṛṣabha was also the author of a cosmographical work called *Tiloyapaṇṇati* (q.v.) which displays his mathematical skill. Yativṛṣabha is mentioned as an enemy of the Buddhists in the *Bṛhatkathākośa* (q.v.) of Hariṣena which was written in AD 931. Vīrasena in his *Dhavalā* (q.v.) had frequently quoted from him. Later writers including the author of the Jain *Harivaṃśa* were influenced by him. Yativṛṣabha was the earliest author to mention that Candragupta Maurya converted to Jainism.

Yauvarājya: A stage in the career of the Tīrthaṃkara, the youthful heir-apparent.

Yekkoti Jinālaya: Jain temple constructed by one *mahāpradhāna* Amitayya Dannayaka during the reign of Hoysala Ballāla II mentioned in an inscription of AD 1205 found in Vakkalagire in Kadur taluk, Chikmagalur district, Karnataka, *Epigraphia Carnatica*, VI, Kadur 36.

Yeniyavārgudi: A group of six Jain shrines at Aihole (q.v.). They all belong to the tenth century. Five of these shrines are of little architectural importance, and since they are empty, have no significance from the viewpoint of worship. Only one of them has a *dhvaja stambha* in front. It has an approach from the north through a pillared porch attached to its *sabhā-maṇḍapa*.

Yoga: Ancient practices which take us back to the primitive times, in the ecstatic rites and magical practices of the prehistoric peoples for acquiring supernatural powers through the most strenuous methods. That these were prevalent as early as the third millennium BC had been proved by the Harappan stone statues and pictures depicted on the seals. In course of time these practices became the floating possessions, as it were, of all sorts of religious sects and even philosophical systems. This primitive inheritance was moulded in accordance with subsequent religious doctrines and philosophical conceptions. As for the methods and means of the yoga, the *Yogasūtra* mentions the following eight *yogāṅgas* or limbs: *yama* (restraint), *niyama* (discipline), *āsana* (sitting posture), *prāṇāyāma* (breath-control), *pratyāhāra* (withdrawal of senses), *dhāraṇā* (attention), *dhyāna* (meditation), and *samādhi* (concentration). The experience of these yoga practices was able to influence the adherents of different religio-philosophical schools. In Jain tradition it is said that Mahāvīra devoted himself for long twelve years to yogic practices and the canonical works of Jainism attach great importance to the *yogāṅgas* or the components of yoga. The Jain doctrine of *karma* (q.v.) has something in common with its yoga conception. *Karma* in yoga is divided into four classes: (1) *śukla* or white (*puṇya*) producing happiness, (2) *kṛṣṇa* or black (*pāpa*, producing sorrow), (3) *śukla-kṛṣṇa* (ordinary action, partly virtuous and partly vicious) and (4) *aśukla-kṛṣṇa* (those inner acts of self-abnegation and meditation which are devoid of any fruit as pleasure or pain). All external actions involve some sin, for it is difficult to work in the world and avoid taking the lives of insects. All *karmas* proceed from five afflictions (*kleśas*), *avidyā*, *asmitā*, *rāga*, *dveṣa* and *abhiniveśa*. Following the path of yoga it is possible to check the influence of these afflictions. Umāsvāti in his *Tattvārthādhigama* VII.4-7 refers to certain yoga practices that are directly inspired by certain verses of in Patñajali's *Yogasūtra*. In connection with *saṃvara* or stoppage we come across the Jain insistence on the *gutti* or the control of mind, speech and body. This is possible by refraining from *saṃrambha*, *samārambha* and *ārambha*. *Uttarādhyayana* XXIV.19ff., These are regulations with reference to controlling one's inner nature. They are dedicated to the preparation and the performances of the forbidden thinking, speaking, and acting. The tenfold monastic morality (*dharma*) and twelve reflections, conceived by Umāsvāti, had a close bearing on the yoga precepts. *Tattvārtha* IX.6-7. The ten *dharmas* are *kṣamā* (forgiveness), *mārdava* (tenderness), *ārjava* (honesty), *śauca* (purity), *satya* (truth), *saṃyama* (self-restraint), *tapa* (austerities), *tyāga* (renunciation), *akiñcanya* (non-attachment), and *brahmacarya* (celibacy) while the twelve reflections (*anuprekṣās*) should be on *anityatā* (transitoriness), *asaraṇa* (unprotectiveness), *saṃsāra* (mundaneness), *ekatva* (loneliness), *anyatva* (separateness), *aśuci* (impurity), *āsrava* (inflow), *saṃvara* (stoppage), *nirjarā* (shedding), *loka* (universe) *bodhi-durlabha* (rarity of spiritual knowledge) and *dharma* (right path). Details of Yogic practices are furnished by the Jain texts by which the aspirant can withdraw from his surroundings, reach the state of indifference to all that the five senses offer, suppress the four passions, avoid displeasing and promote pleasing activities of the inner sense, speech, and body and finally raise himself to the resting-place secluded from all worldly dealings and temptations. The influence of yoga on Jain philosophy can also clearly be observed in the conception of transcendental perception. This transcendental perception is named differently in different systems. In the Sāṅkhya, Nyāya-Vaiśeṣika and Buddhist systems it is known as *Yogi-pratyakṣa* (i.e. Yogic perception) or *yoga-jñāna* (i.e. yogic knowledge) or is supposed to be born as a result of competence acquired through yogic practices. The Agamic or canonical or earlier Jain tradition treats this transcendental perception in terms of *avadhi*, *manaḥparyāya*, and *kevala* forms of knowledge which posit a type of cognition arising independently of sense-object contact on account of yoga or *viśiṣṭa-ātma-śakti* (special competence of the self).

***Yogadṛṣṭisamuccaya*:** See Haribhadra.

***Yoganirvāṇasamprāpti*:** Concentration on the nature of the self through austerities, the most advanced stage of life.

***Yoganiravāṇasādhanā*:** Total concentration on the nature of the self, giving up food and care of the body at the final stage of life.

***Yogapradīpādhikāra*:** See Śubhacandra.

***Yogasāra*:** Also known as *Dohasāra* it is written in Apabhraṃśa by Jogicandra Muni who belonged to the twelfth century. It contains 108 stanzas on spiritual didacticism.

***Yogasāra*:** See Amitagati.

***Yogasaṃmatha*:** A stage in the career of the Tīrthaṃkara when he gets the power due to omniscience and austerities.

***Yogaśāstra*:** One of the most important didactic poems of the Jains by Hemacandra (q.v.) which consists of a text in simple *ślokas* and a commentary (*vṛtti*) in ornate *kāvya* style. It is also called *Adhyātmopaniṣad*. The first four chapters which constitute more than three quarters of the entire work, gives a brief summary of the Jain doctrine as far as it concerns laymen and coincides in the main Amitagati's *Subhāṣita-ratnasamdohā* (qq.v.). The first four chapters are frequently found copied out separately, while manuscripts containing all twelve chapters are rare. The edition by Vijaya Dharma Suri in Bibliotheca Indica, Calcutta, is not complete. A complete edition with the author's own commentary was published by the Jaina Dharma Prasāraka Sabhā, Bhavnagar, 1906.

***Yogatyāga*:** A stage in the career of the Tīrthaṃkara when he draws the soul into itself.

***Yogavindu*:** See Haribhadra.

***Yogicandramuni*:** See *Yogasāra*.

Yogi-Nārāyaṇa: Group of Jain temples at Aihole (q.v.) near Virupākṣa temple (q.v.) which comprises a large shrine along with a few subsidiary ones. Its main part is a *tri-kūṭa* or triple shrine unit provided with a common vestibule leading out into a pillared outer-*maṇḍapa*. The central cella of the triple unit enshrines a polished stone image of Pārśvanātha.

Yoginīpura: Earlier name of Delhi which in the pre-Muslim period was associated with Jainism with a temple of Pārśvanātha constructed in the twelfth century. The monks of the Kharatara-gaccha and its saint-patron Jinacandra II received high honours from king Madanapāla of Delhi. A temple of Mahāvīra was built here around AD 1328 which was known as Bhaṭṭāraka Sarai. The *Prabhandhakośa* of Rājaśekhara was written in Yoginīpura.

Yoginīs: The Brahmanical conception of sixty-four Yoginīs are found in Jainism too. Among the names from different Jain sources mention may be made of Mahāyoginī, Siddhayoginī, Jugesvarī, Pretākṣī, Ḍākinī, Kālī, Kālarātri, Niśācarī, Klimkārī, Bettali, Bhūtaḍāmarī, Kumārikā, Caṇḍikā, Vārāhī, Kaṅkālī, Bhuvaneśvarī, Kuṇḍalī, Lakṣmī, Karālī, Visatī, Divyayogī, Mahāyogī, Siddhayogī, Gaṇeśvarī, Hṛmkarī, Siddhi, Vaitālā, Urddhakeśī, Mahākālī, Suṣakaṃgī, Narabhoginī, Phākarī, Vīrabhadrāṃsī, Dhumrākṣī, Kalahapriyā, Rājasī, Ghorarktāsī, Virupākṣī, Bhayankarī, Vairī, Kaumārikī, Caṇḍī, Kaṅkalī, Kuṇḍalā, Jālakī, Yamadūtī, Pretabhakṣiṇī, Dhurjaṭī, Kiṃkarī, Kapalā, and Visāmsulī. While in the Brāhmaṇical system the Yoginīs are known as attendants of Śiva and Devī, often multiplications of the eight Mātṛkās emanating from the great Devī herself, the Jain Yoginīs are subordinate to Kṣetrapāla (q.v.), the chief of the Bhairavas.

Yugādīśvara Temple: See Ādinātha Temples.

***Yuktyānusāsana*:** See Samanabhadra.

Z

Zoology: Incipient zoology is found in the Jain classification, beings with organic bodies on the basis of the number of senses they possess. Animals are broadly divided into those that are invertebrate and those that are vertebrate, the latter being classified into aquatic, terrestrial and aerial. And finally there are men. *Uttarādhyayana* XXXVI.171-202. Most of the animals come into existence by the process of generation (*gabbhavakkanti, garbha-vyutkrānti*) but in a few cases we come across the process of manifestation (*uvavaya*) and that of coagulation (*sammucchanā*). The process of manifestation holds good in the case of animate-immovable and essentially elementary types of beings. Coagulation or origination by *generatio acquivoca* pertains to certain beings possessed of one to five senses. *Pannavanā* 44ff. They grow by assimilating the materials in their surroundings. Coagulation takes place spontaneously out of existing matter and in open place. The beings produced in this way are generally neuter. There are beings of manifold origin and birth that grow on the bodies of various movable and immovable creatures. These beings are fed on the humours of different movables and immovables. For example, vermin are generated in filthy substances and in the skin of living animals. The same holds good in the cases of earth-bodied, water-bodied, fire-bodied, and air-bodied creatures.

Most of the five sense beings, however, come into existence by the process of generation, i.e. by male-female union. Thus the aquatic animals of the five organs of sense, namely fish, tortoise, crocodile, *makara*, and Gangetic porpoise, are born in this way. As long as they are young they feed on the mother's humours, but when they grow older they eat plants and also movable and immovable beings. In the same way come into existence the quadrupeds, terrestrial animals with five organs of sense, solidungular animals like horses, biungular animals like as cows, multiungular animals like elephants, and animals having toes with nails, like lions. As long as they are young they feed on their mother's milk, but when they grow older they eat plants and movable and immovable beings. Reptiles moving on their breast are also produced by union. Some of them come out of the eggs thus produced while others come out as living young ones. As long as they are young, they live on wind, but when they grow older, they eat plants or movable and immovable beings. Five-sensed animals walking on their arms, such as iguanas, frogs and chameleons, and also birds with membranous wings, feathered wings, box-shaped wings, and outspread wings, are also born and sustained in the same way. As long as the birds are young, they hatch with their mother's warmth. *Sūyagaḍa* II.3. According to the Jains, the generated ones are born either in the egg (*aṇḍaya*) or with the chorion (*jarāyuja*) or as living young (*poyaya*). Caraka likewise mentions four kinds of generated beings—*jarāyuja*, born from the uterus, e.g. men and quadrupeds; *aṇḍaja*, born from egg, e.g. fish reptiles and birds; *svedaja* born of moisture, e.g. the worms, flies, mosquitoes, etc.; and *udbhijja*, born from the plant body. Indian tradition, Jainism included, refer to six kinds of ants, six kinds of flies, five kinds of gnats, thirty kinds of scorpion and sixteen kinds of spiders. The Jain botanical, zoological and physiological conceptions are not very different from other branches of Indian thinking. It is in the *Tattvārthādhigama* that we come across a syncretistic outlook towards botanical and zoological formulation and the commentators on this text have actually taken the help of the traditional medical literature to explain and interpret its contents.

Glossary

abhaya: *mudrā* or hand gesture of protection; the hand is raised, palm outward and fingers pointed upwards.

abhyākhyāna: scandals.

ācārya: head of ascetic group.

ādānanikṣepaṇa: careful use of material objects.

adarśaka: slack-belief caused by apparent or initial failure in spiritual attainment.

adattadāna: stealing.

adharma: principle of rest; that which helps the immobility of objects, just as the shade of a tree helps a traveller to rest.

adhiṣṭhāna: synonym for *vedī-bandha*, moulded basement of a temple.

āgama: verbal testimony.

āghātin: form of *karma* (q.v.) comprising *vedanīya*, *āyu*, *nāma*, and *gotra* (qq.v.).

agra-maṇḍapa: same as *mukha-maṇḍapa*, entrance porch.

ajīva: inanimate objects classified into *rūpa* (those with form, as *pudgala* or matter) and *arūpa* (those without form, as *dharma*, *adharma*, *ākāśa*, and *kāla*).

ākāśa: space; that which gives space and makes room for the existence of all extended substances; divided into *skandha*, *deśa* and *pradeśa*; also into *lokākāśa* and *alokākāśa* (q.v.).

ākiñcanya: non-attachment or not taking the non-self for one's own self.

alaṃkāra: decoration, ornamentation.

alinda: outer-corridor close to the entrance.

aloka: immeasurable infinite beyond the *loka* or universe.

alokākāśa: space beyond the *lokākāśa* (q.v.).

alpa-nāsikā: small projected arched opening of a southern *vimāna*.

āmalaka: rounded enclosure just below the *kalaśa* or pitcher-like summit of the *śikhara* (q.v.). Its components are the *gala*, *aṇḍaka*, *candrika*, and *āmalasārikā*.

amuḍhadṛṣṭi: freedom from inclination for the wrong path.

amūrti: one of the nine properties of the soul which is the immaterial property of the soul.

anarpita-hāra: a *hāra* (q.v.) standing free from the main wall of *vimāna*.

anarthadaṇḍa: to desist from evil, injurious and violent acts directly and indirectly; to take a vow not to commit purposeless sins.

anaśana: fasting.

anastikāya: non-extended; that which is devoid of body and extension, e.g. *kāla* or time.

aṇḍaka: cupola; turret-design.

anekāntavāda: many-sided judgement to counter the dogmatic claim of a particular viewpoint which amounts to the fallacy of exclusive predication.

anitya-anuprekṣā: meditating on the transitoriness of worldly affairs.

aniyatibādra: ninth step on the *guṇasthāna* (q.v.) on which deceit disappears.

añjali-mudrā: a gesture of veneration and worship in which the palms are joined together.

antarāla: intermediate room between shrine and *maṇḍapa*.

antarpatra: a recessed moulding coming between two projected mouldings.

antarāya: individual differences.

anumāna: inference.

anumatityāga: *pratimā* or stage for increase in the rigour of life, in the direction of asceticism.

anuprekṣā: meditations; these are of twelve kinds, also known as *bhāvanā*.

anuvratas: five lesser vows for laymen.

anyadṛṣṭi-praśaṃsā: thinking admiringly of wrong-believers which should be avoided.

anyadṛṣṭi-saṃstava: praising wrong believers, which should be avoided.

anyatva-anuprekṣā: meditating on the distinctness of the real self from the world and worldly attachment.

apramatta: seventh step on the *guṇasthāna* (q.v.) on which anger is controlled but pride, deceit and greed remain.

apūrvakaraṇa: eighth step on the *guṇasthāna* (q.v.) on which pride is controlled and the fetters of *karma* tends to become loose.

ārambhatyāga: *pratimā* or stage for abandonment of worldly engagements.

ardha-maṇḍapa: pillared hall of one bay, usually the entrance; same as *mukha-maṇḍapa*, the porch in front of the *maṇḍapa*.

arhats: perfect souls who await the attainment of *mokṣa* (q.v.) after shedding *kārmaṇa-śarīra* (q.v.).

ārjava: straightforwardness or honesty.

arpita-hāra: A *hāra* (q.v.) attached to the main wall of the *vimāna*.

āsana: a posture; a seat; a pedestal.

āsana-paṭṭa: a flat moulding of the *kakṣāsana* or balconied window.
aśaraṇa-anuprekṣā: mediating on the helplessness of beings.
āsrava: influx of *karma*-particles into the soul.
aṣṭa-maṅgalas: eighth auspicious marks; often represented in miniature paintings of Jain manuscripts or in paintings on canvas of different *paṭas*; treated elaborately elsewhere in this volume.
aṣṭāpada: representation of the eight terraced mountain where Ṛṣabhadeva attained *nirvāṇa.*
astikāya: extended; mass of all that is; that which has a body possessing extension.
aśuci-anuprekṣā: meditating on the impurity of the mundane body.
aśva-thara: frieze of horses.
atibhaṅga: standing posture with exaggerated flexion.
atiśayas: the eight extraordinary qualities of a Tīrthaṃkara, also treated as *mahāpratihāryas* (q.v.).
atithisaṃvibhāga: taking a vow to eat food only after feeding ascetics and guests.
avadhi: knowledge by clairvoyance.
avagraha: primary perception.
avamodarya: eating less than one has appetite for.
āvaraṇa-devatāś: divinities enclosing or surrounding the principal icon.
avāya: ascertaining primary perception.
avirati: attachment to worldly pleasures.
aviratisamyagdṛṣṭi: fourth step in the *guṇasthāna* (q.v.) on which the Jīva feels the urge for spirituality.
āyāgapaṭa: slab carved with sacred Jain figures and symbols.
āyatana: Jain term for temple dating back to the time of Mahāvīra who often used to stay in *yakṣāyatanas*. Prefixed by the term Jina, the compound word *jināyatana* is more popular. The terms *mandira*, *ālaya*, *geha*, *gṛha*, etc., are also used by Jains to denote temples.
ayogikevalin: fourteenth step on the *guṇasthāna* (q.v.) when the annihilation of *karma* (q.v.) is complete.
bāḍa: wall, a cubical portion of temple below the *śikhara* or *gaṇḍī.*
bali-paṭṭas: slabs on which auspicious symbols were carved. These are of the nature of the *āyāgapaṭas* and referred to by Hemacandra in *Triṣaṣṭhī* I.3. 422 ff as 'offering slabs' containing eight auspicious marks.
bandha: bondage of the soul to *karma.*
bāndhanā: a projected moulding dividing the *jaṅghā* (q.v.) into the upper and lower sections; horizontal moulding between the rows of sculpture on the wall.
baraṇḍa: a set of topmost mouldings of the *bāḍa* (q.v.).
bhadra: central projection of a shrine.
bhadra-pīṭha: a variety of south Indian moulded pedestal.
bhamatī: colonnaded passage of a medieval Jain temple.
bharaṇī: pillar-capital.
bhāṣā: to talk pleasantly.
bhāvanā: same as *anuprekṣā* (q.v.).
bhāva-manas: see *manas.*
bhiṭṭa: sub-base of a temple.
bhitti: outer wall supporting the roof; occasionally the term is used for plinth.
bhogapabhogamāna: to desist from drinking liquors, etc.
bhoktā: attribute of the soul as the enjoyer of the fruits of all its *karmas* (q.v.).
bhṛṅgāra: a type of vessel, one of the eight auspicious symbols of the Jains.
bodhidurlabha: anuprekṣā or reflection on rarity of religious knowledge.
caitya: Though the name is derived from a structure over a funeral relic it has the same meaning as *āyatana* (q.v.) or religious building: *caityaṃ āyatanaṃ tulya.* The term *caitya* acquired many connotations. *Caitya-vihāra*, *caitya-gṛha*, *caityālaya*, etc., also mean temple.
cakra: a circle in Tantric rites; same as *yantra* (q.v.).
cāmara: fly-whisk.
candra-śilā: lowest step shaped like a half-moon.
caritra: right conduct of five kinds; cessation from doing all that is evil.
caturmukha: same as *caumukha* or *sarvatobhadra*, a type of shrine or shrine model with openings on all four sides; slab containing images of four Tīrthaṃkaras on its four sides.
caturviṃśati-paṭṭa: a stele, frieze or image with the twenty-four Tīrthaṃkara figures.
catuṣki: bay; space between four pillars.
chowrie: fly-whisk.
chādya: cave-projection; the lowermost level of the *śikhara.*
chatra: parasol, constituent of the *aṣṭa-maṅgalas* (q.v.).
chedopasthāpana: to believe in repentance.
citra: picture, painting.
dānasamiti: inspection of seats to avoid transgressions.
daṇḍa-chādya: straight-ribbed awning or cave projection.
darpaṇa: mirror, constituent of the *aṣṭamaṅgalas* (q.v.).
darśanapratimā: possessing perfect, intelligent, and reasoned faith in Jainism.
darśanāvaraṇīya: that which prevents our beholding the faith.

daślakṣaṇa-dharma: ten observances—forgiveness, tenderness, honesty, contentment, truthfulness, self-restraint, austerity, renunciation, non-attachment, and chastity.
deśavirati: fifth step on the *guṇasthāna* (q.v.) on which the Jīva realizes the importance of conduct.
deśavrata: taking a vow to limit worldly activity for a limited area.
deul: sanctuary, shrine.
deva: gods.
deva-koṣṭha: niche containing an image.
deva-kulika: small shrine; subsidiary shrine facing *bhamatī* (q.v.).
dhāraṇa: act of imprinting the effect of perception.
dharma: principle of motion which helps the *jīva* to progress, just as water helps the movement of a fish.
dhruva: permanent unit.
dhvaja: banner, one of the eight auspicious symbols of the Jains; flag which is put on top of a *śikhara* (q.v.).
dhyāna: meditation.
digvirati: to desist from injuring living beings.
digvrata: taking a lifelong vow to limit worldly activity to fixed points in all directions.
dravya: substance possessed of some unchanging essential characters (*guṇas*) and changing modes (*paryāyas*).
gaja-pṛṣṭhākṛti: apsidal shrine shaped like elephant back.
gajatālu: a component of ceiling resembling a coffered cusp.
gaja-thara: frieze of elephants.
garbhagṛha: sanctum sanctorum or shrine-cell.
garta-vivara: foundation pit for the *prāsāda.* In the centre of such a pit is placed a *kurma-śilā* (q.v.) and eight *khura-śilās* (q.v.) in the eight directions.
ghaṇa-dvāra: false door in the cardinal offsets; refers to the cardinal niche of the sanctum.
ghaṭa-pallava: pot-and-foliage design.
ghātin: form of *karma* (q.v.) comprising *jñānāvaraṇīya*, *darśnāvaraṇīya*, *mohanīya*, and *antarāya* (qq.v.).
gopura: main gateway; structure over the entrance.
gotra: caste, country, etc., of the beings.
grāsa-paṭṭi: a frieze of *kirttimukhas.*
grīvā: constriction below the finial of the superstructure.
gūḍha-maṇḍapa: closed *maṇḍapa*; covered pavilion.
guṇa: unchanging essential character of a substance.
guṇasthānas: fourteen step of liberation from *karma.*
guṇa-vratas: three supplementary vows for householders.
gupti: restraint of body, speech, and mind.
hāra: string of miniature shrines comprising *kūṭas*, *śālās*, and *pañjaras* decorating each storey of a south Indian *vimāna.*
harmya: attic portion of a south Indian *vimāna*; mansion or building in a broad sense.
ihā: will to cognition.
indriyas: sense-organs distinguished as *dravya-indriyas* or physical sense-organs and *bhāva-indriyas*, their psychic counterparts.
iryya: precaution while walking to prevent oneself from treading on insects, etc.
iṣaṇa: to beg alms in true monastic manner.
jāḍya-kumbha: lowest moulding of the *pīṭha* (q.v.) of a medieval temple.
jagatī: moulding *pīṭha* or base; masonry platform on which a temple is built.
jālaka: trellis-work.
jalapraṇālika: drainage system.
jālika: latticed windows.
jaṅghā: lit. thigh; middle portion of a temple above the basement and below the *śikhara.*
jīva: animate objects; living beings of two kinds, *mukta* and *baddha*, emancipated and fettered, the latter being subdivided into *trase* or moving beings and *sthavara* or non-moving beings.
jīvantasvāmin: standing image of Mahāvīra wearing crown and ornaments.
jñānāvaraṇīya: that which hides all aspects of knowledge.
kakṣa-śālās: small rooms.
kakṣāsana: sloping parapet of balcony forming the back of the seats inside.
kāla: time, which makes possible the continuity, modification, movement, newness and oldness of substance; divided into *vyavahārika* or empirical and *paramārthika* or eternal categories.
kalaśa: full vase, one of the eight auspicious symbols of the Jains.
kalaśa: term applied generally to the summit of a tower. It looks like a pitcher and has four components, viz., *gala*, *aṇḍaka*, *karṇikā*, and *bījapūraka.*
kāmikī: that which impedes our obtaining intellectual stimulus.
kāṅkṣā: desire for sense pleasure.
kaopta: cornice-like flexed moulding usually crowning the basement, *adhiṣṭhāna* or *vedībandha.*
karaṇḍa-mukuṭa: crown shaped like a basket.
karma: human action; in Jainism it is the link between the Jīva (q.v.) and its body, conceived as something essentially material which gets attached to the soul just as dust gets attached to cloth.
kārmaṇa-śarīra: a kind of subtle body which clings

to the soul in all its migrations and future births and determines the individual state and lot of that particular soul.
karṇa: quoin or corner, corner projection.
karṇa-kūṭa: shrine or turret raised over the *karṇa* or corner.
karṇa-ratha: corner projection of the wall.
karṇa-śṛṅga: turret rising over the *karṇa* or corner.
karṇikā: knife-edge moulding; thin fillet-like moulding.
kartā: attribute of the soul indicative of its responsibility for all action.
kāruṇya: compassion for the afflicted.
kaṣāya: the passions of anger, pride, deceit, and greed.
kaṭṭu: intervening octagonal portion between the bottom and top squares of a pillar.
kāyagupti: steadiness of the body.
kāyakleśa: mortification of the body leaving the mind undisturbed.
kāyotsarga: same as *khaḍgāsana* or the posture adopted by standing Tīrthaṃkaras.
kevala: perfect knowledge which is independent of the senses.
khākharā-muṇḍi: miniature representation of a temple with a roof of the *khākharā* or pumpkin-gourd type.
kheṭṭaka: elaborately-carved projecting niche resembling an oriel window.
khaṭvāṅga: human skull placed on a bone.
khura: lowest moulding of the basement or *vedībandha*.
khura-śilās: slabs with an object carved on them to be placed at the eight directions of the foundation pit of a structure.
kicaka: figure supporting a load or superstructure.
kīrttimukha: lion-like head constituting an art-motif of symbolic significance.
kṣīṇamoha: twelfth step on the *guṇasthāna* (q.v.) leading to the removal of all *kaṣāyas* (q.v.).
kṣipta-vitāna: a concave ceiling.
kṣudra nāsikā: see *alpa-nāsikā*.
kūḍu: an arched opening projecting from the flexed cornice or *kapota*; same as *caitya*-window.
kumbha: a water-pot, a moulding of the basement or *vedībandha* coming above the *khura* (q.v.), upper member of the south Indian pillar-capital.
kumbhikā: ornamental base of a pillar.
kūrma-śilā: stone slab with a tortoise carved on it to be placed at the centre of the foundation pit of a structure.
kūṭa-chādya: carved cave-projection.
lalitāsana: sitting posture of ease with one foot placed on the ground and the other folded on the seat.
lalāṭa-bimba: centre of door-lintel of the sanctum, generally representing an image of the principal godhead.
lāñchanas: cognizances, symbols to identify the Tīrthaṃkaras.
leśyā: different conditions produced in the *jīva* by the influence of different *karma*; six in number—black, blue, grey, red, yellow, and white; the first three of them are bad, the others are good.
loka: universe.
lokākāśa: space containing the world where the *jīvas* and other substances live.
madanikā: decorative female figures in Hoysala art.
madhya-bandha: band with a relief or frieze at the middle of a member such as *jaṅghā* (q.v.) or pillar.
mādhyatha: indifferent to those who are uncivil or ill-behaved.
mahā-maṇḍapa: large columned hall between the *maṇḍapa* (q.v.) and *antarāla* (q.v.).
mahāpīṭha: tall plinth with additional mouldings.
mahāvratas: 'great vows' comprising *ahiṃsā* or non-violence, *satya* or truth, *asteya* or non-stealing, *brahmacarya* or celibacy and *aparigraha* or non-possession.
maitrī: friendship with all living beings.
makara-toraṇa: gateway arch emanating from the mouth or tail of *makara*, a mystic aquatic animal.
mālā: garland, necklace.
manaḥparyāya: telepathic knowledge of others' minds.
manas: mind, which is of two kinds; *paudgalika* or material mind undergoing change every moment, and *bhāva* which is of the nature of cognitive potency and born of conscious substance.
māna-stambha: free-standing pillar-standard crowned by Jina images.
mañca: a variety of south Indian *adhiṣṭhāna* (q.v.).
mañcikā: *paṭṭikā*-like (q.v.) top moulding.
maṇḍala: literally a circle; a circular diagram, geometric design of cosmic order; a kind of *yantra* (q.v.).
mandāraka: ornamental door-sill.
maṇḍapa: generic term for a hall which may be open or closed. It comprises the *prāsāda-kamala* or *garbha-gṛha*, the main sanctuary; the *gūḍha-maṇḍapa*, pavilion with three passages cut across; the *raṅga-maṇḍapa* or auditorium; and the *sa-toraṇa-balānaka*, or arched platform.
maṇḍavara: western Indian term, a corrupt form of Sanskrit *maṇḍapa-vara* or *maṇḍapa-dhara*. It is the outer wall supporting the roof of a *maṇḍapa* (q.v.). It is of four types, namely *nāgara*, *meru*, *sāmānya*, and *prakārāntara*.
manogupti: to remove all false thought.
manovargaṇā: extremely subtle physical substance

from which *manas* or mind is produced.
manuṣya: human being.
maṭha: a monastery, a hospice and an educational centre attached to a temple.
mati: ordinary cognition obtained by means of sense-perception.
matsya-yugma: pair of fish constituent of the *aṣṭamaṅgalas*.
māyāmṛṣa: sinful acts under the pretext of goodness.
miśra: third stage in *guṇasthāna* (q.v.) when the Jīva is still in mentally uncertain condition.
mithyādarśana: wrong belief.
mithyādarśanaśalya: ascribing reality to the unreal.
mithyātva: falsehood, state of ignorance; first step in *guṇasthāna*.
mohanīya: that which generates worldly attachments.
mokṣa: liberation; a state of pure happiness (*ananta-sukha*) infinite knowledge (*anantajñāna*), and infinite perception (*anantadarśana*).
mudrā: symbolic hand gesture indicating a specific mood or action, e.g. protection, boon-giving, teaching.
mukha-catuṣki: entrance-porch or frontal bay at the entrance.
mukha-maṇḍapa: porch, front hall.
mūla-nāyaka: main deity whose image is installed in the sanctum.
mūla-prāsāda: sanctum proper.
nābhicchanda: an elaborate ceiling carved with the design of coffered cusps.
nāgara: northern type of temple architecture.
nāla-maṇḍapa: same as *valānaka* or covered stepped entrance.
nāma: collective name of the conditions by which beings are governed.
nandyāvarta: diagram with nine points standing for nine *nidhis* or treasures which is a Jain symbol.
nāraka: hell beings.
narathara: a sculptured row on the plinth of the temple.
nāsikā: lit. nose; projected arched opening of a southern *vimāna*.
nāṭamandira: a hall for dance and also for other programmes.
nava-raṅga: mahā-maṇḍapa (q.v.) with four central and twelve peripheral pillars so arranged as to enclose nine bays.
naya: knowledge of a thing in its relation; standpoint divided into seven categories and distinguished into *dravyārthika* from the viewpoint of substance and *paryāyārthika* from that of modification or condition.
niḥśankita: freedom from doubt.
nikācita karma: that which has already been stored up.
nirandhāra-prāsāda: type of temple without *pradakṣiṇāpatha* or passage for circumambulation around the sanctum.
nirjarā: purging of the *karmas* (q.v.).
nirvicikitsitā: freedom from aversion to or regard for the body.
niṣadyā, niṣedikā, niṣedhikā: Jain memorial pillar or slab.
niṣkāṅkṣita: freedom from desire for worldly comforts.
nṛtya-maṇḍapa: peristylar assembly hall.
padma: lotus-shaped moulding.
padma-bandha: decorative band separating the south Indian pillar-shaft from the capital.
padmāsana: sitting in lotus-posture or with each foot placed on the thigh of the other leg.
padma-śilā: elaborately-carved lotus-shaped pendant of a ceiling.
paiśūnya: gossiping.
pañca-meru: representation of the five Merus of the Jain tradition.
pañca-ratha: temple with five projections.
pañca-śākhā: door-frame with five ornate jambs.
pañca-tīrthika: image with five Jain figures.
pañcāyatana: a temple with four subsidiary shrines.
pañjara: miniature apsidal shrine; same as *nīḍa*.
pāpa: eighteen kinds of evil actions.
paramāṇu: atoms; smallest parts of matter which cannot be further divided; two or more may combine together to from *saṃghāta* or compounds.
parapartivāda: telling ill of others.
parigraha-tyāga: pratimā or stage of divesting oneself of wealth by dividing property among heirs.
parihāraviśuddha: to practice non-violence and other virtues.
parikara: image frame, usually with retinue of figures; also subsidiary figures of an image.
parikara: extraordinary qualities possessed by a Tīrthaṃkara which have been categorically specified on the basis of the *atiśayas* and *aṣṭa-pratihāryas* (q.v.); attending personages.
pariṇāmikī: that which obstructs our gaining knowledge from experience.
parisaha: twenty-two kinds of afflictions.
paryāya: changing modes of a substance; properties which originate and perish.
pāśa: noose.
pātāla-nagarī: underground city, a typical Jain mythological conception.
paṭas: paintings on canvas or on paper of the diagrams of the *sūri-mantra, hrīṃkāra-yantra, vardhamāna-vidyā-paṭa, siddhacakra, ṛṣimaṇḍala-yantra*, etc.
patra-latā: a frieze depicting creeper with foliage.
patra-śākhā: jamb of a doorway carved with foliage.

paṭṭa: plain or ornamental band.
paṭṭa-śālā: main hall.
paṭṭikā: slab-like moulding.
paudgalika-manas: see *manas*.
phalaka abacus.
phānsanā: superstructure of horizontal tiers.
pīḍhā-muṇḍi: miniature representation of a temple with a roof of the *pīḍhā* or wooden seat type.
pīṭhas: plinth also known as *adhiṣṭhāna* (q.v.) to be erected on the *tala* or ground. It may be a simple one or with friezes called *tharas* or *prastara-galas*, one to five in number, on it.
pīṭhikā: pedestal of an image; seat.
prabhāvalī: nimbus or halo round an image.
pradakṣiṇā-patha: passage for circumambulation.
prāggrīva: porch-projection; same as *agra-maṇḍapa*.
prākāra: enclosure wall of a temple.
pramādacaraṇa: desisting from excitement.
pramāṇa: sources of valid knowledge; besides *pratyakṣa* or sense-perception (the Jains also believe in a transcendental variety of it), *anumāna* or inference, *pratyabhijñā* or recognition, *smaraṇa* or memory, *tarka* or knowledge of invariable concomitance and *āgama* or verbal testimony are regarded as sources of valid knowledge.
pramatta: sixth step on the *guṇasthāna* (q.v.) on which slight passions are controlled but negligences remain.
pramoda: delight at the sight of better persons.
prāsāda: main sanctuary and all the component parts of the temple; in a general sense the building itself. Seven main types of the *prāsāda* are *śrī-vijaya*, *mahā-padma*, *lakṣmī-tilaka*, *nara-veda*, *kamala-haṃsa*, *nandyāvarta*, and *kuñjara*.
prāsāda-kamala: same as *garbhagṛha*.
prastara: entablature of the south Indian *vimāna*.
pratihāryas: see *aṣṭapratihārya*.
pratimās: eleven stages in householder's life.
pratikramaṇa: repentance for transgressions.
pratiratha: projection coming between the *bhadra* and the *karṇa*.
pratithāpana: careful disposal of the extras.
pratyabhijñā: recognition, a sub-specis of *mati-jñāna* (q.v.) and an independent *pramāṇa* (q.v.).
pratyākhyāna: formal vow with reference to any kind of restriction or renunciation.
pratyakṣa-parokṣa jñāna: direct and indirect knowledge; early Jain thinkers considered spiritual realization independent of senses as *pratyakṣa* and perception, inference and testimony as *parokṣa* forms, but later Jain writers changed their original position and brought them on a par with other philosophical systems of India.
prabhāvanā: publishing the greatness of Jainism.
prāyaścitta: penance.
proṣadhopavāsa: taking a vow to fast on four days of every month.
pṛthivīśilā-paṭṭa: terracotta plaque which was the precursor and prototype of the *āyāgapaṭa* (q.v.).
pudgala: matter, liable to integration and disintegration; divided into four classes—*skandha*, *deśa*, *predeśa*, and *paramāṇu*.
puṇya: meritorious actions which are of nine kinds or merit, which is of nine kinds.
pūrṇa-kalaśa: full vase; ritual object, symbol of fullness of life.
rāga: personal attachment.
rājasenaka: the lowest moulding of the *kakṣāsana* or balconies window.
raṅga-maṇḍapa: a pillared hall open all sides meant especially for dance and drama.
rasatyāga: abstinence from tasty food.
ratha: projection of a shrine.
rathikā: niche to shelter an image.
rati-arati: sexuality.
ratna-śikhā: jamb of a doorway carved with diamond pattern.
rūpa-kaṇṭha: a recessed course carved with figures or a frieze.
rūpa-śākhā: jamb of a doorway carved with figures.
sabhā-maṇḍapa: same as *raṅga-maṇḍapa*.
sabhā-mārga: an elaborate ceiling comprising multiple coffered cusps.
sacittatyāga: pratimā or stage in which eating of green vegetables is given up.
ṣaḍ-dāru: stambha or pillar made of wood.
sādhu: holy persons.
śaduram: square section of a south Indian pillar.
sahasra-kūṭa: pyramidal shrine-model with figures of numerous Jinas.
śākhā: jamb of a door-frame.
sālā: oblong shrine with barrel-vault roof.
salitantra: vertical recess.
sallekhanā: 'peaceful death' by giving up eating, meant to achieve spiritual merit.
samabhaṅga: standing posture in which the figure is erect and without any flexion of the body.
sama-caturasra: square.
sama-kṣipta: a variety of concave ceiling.
samatala-vitāna: ceiling of flat uniform level, usually adorned with friezes in registers.
samavasaraṇa: auditorium where the Tīrthaṃkaras used to deliver sermons.
sāmāyika: to give up evil conduct; to treat all beings equally; contemplation of the self; for householders it means worshipping regularly for forty-two minutes.
saṃghāta: see *paramāṇu*.
samiti: avoidance of the killing of insects; gentle and holy talk; receiving proper alms; etc.

saṃkā: doubt or scepticism which one should avoid.
saṃlīnatā: avoidance of temptation.
saṃvara: way by which the influx of *karma* (q.v.) is checked.
saṃvaraṇā: roof comprising diagonally arranged members crowned by finials.
sāndhara prāsāda: a type of temple with a *pradakṣiṇā-patha* (q.v.) around the sanctum.
sandhi-kṣetra: place or space for junction, the juncture connecting the sanctum and the hall in a temple.
saptabhaṅgī-naya: seven-fold paralogism; see *anekāntavāda* and *syādvāda*.
sapta-śākhā: door frame with seven ornate jambs.
sarvatobhadra: see *caturmukha*.
sa-toraṇa-balānaka: arched platform.
sattā: karma (q.v.) accumulated in the past life.
sayogikevalin: thirteenth step on the *guṇasthāna* (q.v.) when the annihilation of *karma* (q.v.) is on the move.
siddha: perfect one who has attained *mokṣa* (q.v.).
siddhāsana: same as *dhyānāsana* or meditative posture adopted by seated Tīrthaṃkaras.
śikhara: curved roof rising like an inverted cup over a building. It has four constituents—*chādya*, *śikhara*, *āmalasāra* or *āmalaka*, and *kalaśa*.
śikṣāpadavrata: vow consisting of *sāmayikavrata* (to treat all beings equally) *deśāvakāśikavrata* (different kinds of restrictions) and *atithisaṃvibhāgavrata* (to make gifts to guests).
śikṣā-vratas: four supplementary vows for householders.
śila-paṭṭa: stone slab symbolizing the dais, throne, or platform of the Yakṣas placed under the *citiya* or *caitya* tree.
śīla-vratas: seven vows comprising three *guṇa-vratas* and four *śikṣā-vratas*.
śirascakra: halo, nimbus round the head of an image.
sithila: karma, the influx of which may be evaded.
smaraṇa: memory.
śrīvatsa: mark on the chest of the Jina which is also the chest mark of Viṣṇu. It is a small hairy mole also called *romāvarta*. In Jina images it looks like a rhizome.
śruta: testimony derived from scriptures.
stambha: pillar, column.
stambha-śākhā: jamb of a door-frame simulating a pilaster.
sthāvara-jīva: immobile beings which are earth-, water-, fire-, air-, and vegetable-bodied.
sthikikaraṇa: sustaining souls in right convictions.
stūpa: origninally a funeral tumulus; subsequently a hemispherical structure on supposed holy remains of some saint.
stūpī, stūpikā: finial of a south Indian *vimāna*.
sūkṣmasamparyāya: tenth step on the *guṇasthāna* (q.v.) on which greed tends to disappear; to control passions which is one of the five kinds of *caritra* (q.v.).
śukanāśa: pediment-shaped roof over the vestibule, resembling a parrot's beak.
śuka-nāsikā: part of the dome, looking like a parrot's beak.
supratiṣṭha: auspicious seat, constituent of the *aṣṭamaṅgalas* (q.v.).
sūtradhāra: master-architect who supervised temple-building activity.
svadehaparimāṇa: one of the nine properties of the soul which is the capability of completely filling the body which it occupies.
svādhyāya: study.
svastika: primitive and ancient symbol in form of cross with equal arms, each arm having a limb of the same length projecting from its end at right angles, all in same direction, i.e. direction of the sun's course. It is a symbol of the Tīrthaṃkara and signifies *svasti* or peace.
svāśvāsadana: second step in *guṇasthāna* (q.v.) on which a Jīva begins to distinguish between what is real and what is false.
syādvāda: doctine of conditional proposition; to qualify a judgement explicitly by *syād* or 'may be' is thought desirable for the sake of precision.
tāḍi: cushion-shaped member of the south Indian pillar-captial.
tala: storey; the ground floor is *ādi-tala*, the intermediate *madhya-tala*—terms like *dvi-tala*, *tri-tala* are also in vogue.
tala-jaṅghā: lower portion of a wall between the *pābhāga* and *bāndhanā* (qq.v.) mouldings.
taraṅga: ripple-design.
taraṅga-potikā: corbel bracket with roll-moulding.
tarka: knowledge of invariable concomitance; treated as a cognition of the nature of *pramāṇa* (q.v.).
tilaka: a variety of turret design.
tiryak: animals.
toraṇa: gateway.
trasa-jīva: mobile beings who have one of five senses or *indriyas*.
tribhaṅga: standing posture with three bends.
trika-maṇḍapa: maṇḍapa (q.v.) with three *catuṣkis* or bays of a medieval Jain temple.
tri-ratha: temple with three projections.
tri-śākhā: door-frame with three ornate jambs.
tri-tīrthika: an image with three Jina figures.
udaya: that which concerns the future life.
uddiṣṭatyāga: pratimā or stage for renunciation of householder's life.
udgama: pediment of *caitya*-arches, usually

employed as the crowning decoration of a niche.
udumbara: threshold, door-sill supporting the door-jambs.
unodari: partial fasting, i.e. to take a mouthful less every day.
upabhoga-paribhoga parimāṇa: taking a vow everyday to limit enjoyment of consumable and non-consumable things.
upādhyāya: teaching saint.
upagūhana: redeeming the defects of ineffective believers.
upāna: lowermost part of the footing of the south Indian *adhiṣṭhāna.*
upaśāntamoha: eleventh step on the *guṇasthāna* (q.v.) leading to the removal of all *kaṣāyas* (q.v.).
upapīṭha: sub-base below the south Indian *adhiṣṭhāna.*
upara-jaṅghā: upper wall between the *bāndhanā* and *baraṇḍa* mouldings.
upayoga: functioning of the senses.
upayogamaya: one of the nine properties of the soul which comprises perception and knowledge.
uraḥ-śṛṅga: turret attached to a central projection.
ūrdhvagati: tendency of the soul to go upwards.
utpāda: accession of new qualitites.
utpātikī: that which hinders the power of spontaneous thought.
utsargasamiti: careful movement of the body.
utsarga: absolute indifference to the body and its needs.
uttira: principal beam.
vāggupti: absolute silence.
vaināyakī: that which prevents receiving inherited knowledge.
vaiyāvṛtya: service to the saints or worthy people.
valāṇaka: covered stepped entrance.
vandanā: ceremonial and humble greeting to the spiritual teacher.
varada-mudrā: gesture of bestowing boon in which the palm is held downward facing the devotees.
varaṇḍikā: the member or set of mouldings separating the *jaṅghā* from the *śikhara* (qq.v.).
vardhamānaka: powder-flask, one of the constituents of the *aṣṭamaṅgalas* (q.v.).
vātsalya: loving regard for pious persons.
vedanīya: that which causes one to experience the pleasure of happiness and the pain of misery.
vedha: obstructions of seven kinds which by all means must be avioded from the house. These are known as *tala, koṇa, talu, kapāla, stambha, tulā,* and *dvāra.*
vedī-bandha: based wall mouldings; see *adhiṣṭhāna.*
vedikā: railing.
vibhaṅga-jñāna: that form of knowledge which falsifies spiritual insight.
vicikitsā: disgust for anything which should be avoided.
vimāna: sanctuary, tower. The south Indian *vimāna* may have one, two, three or more storeys or *talas.* Three *vimānas* erected on a common base, or placed around a common *maṇḍapa* are collectively known as *tri-kūṭa.*
vinaya: reverence.
viviktaśayyāsana: sitting and sleeping in a lonely place.
vrata-pratimā: keeping up the twelve vows and the extra vow of *sallekhanā* (q.v.).
vratas: vows; five main and seven supplementary.
vṛtti-parisaṃkhyāna: putting restrictions in regard to food.
vṛttisaṅkṣepa: limiting the food that one eats.
vyajana: fan constituent of the *aṣṭa-maṅgalas* (q.v.).
vyākhyāna-mudrā: gesture of teaching in which the thumb and index finger from a circle.
vyāla: a composite animal with leonine features carved for decorative purposes.
vyutsarga: giving up attachment to the body, etc.
yantra: tantric diagrams on metal often found worshipped in certian Jain shrines. Of these *śurtaskandha-yantra* is popular among the Digambaras. The bronze *śrutaskandha-yantra* from Mudbidri, Karnataka, deserves special mention. Yantras, often painted on *paṭas* (q.v.) are also worshipped by Jain monks and the laity.
yathākhyāta: to follow five rules of conduct.
yoga: employment of mind, body, and speech to material and sensual objects; concentration of all these for achieving salvation.

Bibliography

ORIGINAL SOURCES

Ācārāṅga: *Niryukti* by Bhadrabāhu, *Cūrṇi* by Jinadāsagaṇi Mahattara, Ratlam, 1944; *Vṛtti* by Śīlāṅka, Agamodaya, 1935; Original Agamodaya edn., Bombay, 1916; ed. H. Jacobi, London, 1882; Eng. trans. by H. Jacobi, *Sacred Books of the East*, XXII, Oxford, 1884; Part I, ed. W. Schubring, Leipzig, 1910; German trans. by the same in *Worte Mahaviras*, Gottingen, 1927; ed. in Jaina Sāhitya Saṃśodhaka Samiti, Poona, 1924; ed. Muni Jambuvijaya, Bombay, 1977.

Adhyātmāṣṭaka by Vādirāja, Manikacandra Digambara Jaina Granthamālā, No. 13.

Ādi Purāṇa by Jinasena II: in two parts, Sanskrit text with Hindi trans. by Pannalal Jain, Varanasi, 1963-5; with com. of Śrutasāgara, Varanasi, 1954.

Aghaṭakumāra-kathā: shorter metrical version, Bombay, 1917; German trans. by Charlotte Krause, *Der Prinz als Papagi* (The Prince as a Parrot), Leipzig, 1922; new German trans. with intro. by Roland Beer, Berlin, 1975.

Ākhyānamaṇikośa by Devendragaṇi with Āmradevasūri's *Vṛtti*: ed. Puṇyavijaya with Eng. intro. by V.P. Shah, Prakrit Text Society, 1962.

Ālapapaddhati: Digambara Jaina Granthabhaṇḍāra, I, Benares, 1924.

Ambaḍa Caritra by Amara Suri: ed. Hiralal Hamsaraj, Jamnagar, 1910; German tr. Charlotte Krause, Leipzig, 1922.

Aṅgavidyā: ed. Punyavijara with Eng. intro. by Moti Chandra and Hindi intro. by V.S. Agrawala, Prakrit Text Society, I, 1957.

Antakṛddaśā, *Antagaḍasāo*: Āgamodaya edn. with Abhayadeva's com., Bombay, 1920; Eng. tr. by L.D. Barnett, London, 1907; rev. edn. with intro., gloss., notes and appendices by P.L. Vaidya, Poona, 1932.

Anuttaropapātikadaśā, *Anuttarovavāiyodasāo*: Āgamodaya with Abhayadeva's com., Bombay, 1920; Eng. trans. by L.D. Barnett, London, 1907.

Anuyogadvāra: *Cūrṇi* by Jinadāsagaṇi Mahattara, Ratlam, 1928; *Ṭīkā* by Haribhadra, Ratlam, 1928; original Āgamodaya edn., Bombay, 1924; *Ṭīkā* by Maladhāri Hemacandra, Bhavnagar, 1935; ed. Puṇyavijaya et al., Bombay, 1968; Critical study by T. Hanaki, Vaisali, 1970.

Anyayogavyavacchadikā by Hemacandra: *Kāvyamālā*, Part VII, Bombay.

Āptamīmāṃsā, also called *Devāgama-stotra*, by Samantabhadra: ed. in Digambara Jaina Granthbhāṇḍāra I, Benares, 1924, by Pannalal Chaudhari; also ed. in Sanātana Jaina Granthamālā, I, Bombay, 1905, X, 1910.

Āptaparīkṣā by Vidyānanda: Sanātana Jaina Granthamālā, Benares, 1913.

Ārādhanāsāra by Devasena: Manikacandra Digambara Jaina Granthamālā, VI, Bombay, 1916.

Aṣṭasāhasrī by Vidyānanda: ed. in Gandhinatharanga Jaina Granthamālā, Bombay, 1915.

Ātmānuśāsana by Guṇabhadra: ed. in Digambara Jaina Granthabhāṇḍāra I, Benares, 1924.

Aturapratyākhyāna, *Āurapaccckkhāna*, Āgamodaya ed., Bombay, 1925.

Aupapātika, *Uvavāiya*: Āgama Saṃgraha edn., 1880; Āgamodaya edn., Bombay, 1916; E. Leumann, *Das Aupapātika Sūtra*, Leipzig, 1883; portion trans. into German by W. Schubring in *Die Jainas*.

Āvaśyaka, *Āvassaya*: *Niryukti* by Bhadrabāhu, *Viśeṣāvaśyaka Mahābhāṣya* by Jinabhadragani Kṣamāśramaṇa, *Cūrṇi* by Jinadāsagaṇi Mahattara, Ratlam, 1928; *Śiṣyahita Ṭīkā* by Haribhadra together with the *Niryukti*, Āgamodaya, Bombay, 1916-17; *Ṭīkā* by Malayagiri, Āgamodaya, 1928 ff; *Pradeśa-vyākhyā* by Maladhāri Hemacandra, Devachanda Lalbhai, Bombay, 1920; *Niryukti-dīpikā* by Māṇikyacandrasūri, Surat,1939; Ernst Leumann, *Übersicht über die Āvaśyaka Literature*, ed. W. Schubring Hamburg, 1934; ed. Puṇyavijaya et al., Bombay, 1978; Klaus-Bruhn. *Āvaśyaka Studies* in *Gedenkschrift für Ludwig Alsdorf*, Wiesbaden, 1981.

Ayogavyavaccheda by Hemacandra: Kāvyamālā, Bombay, Part VII.

Bhagavatī, *Vyākhyāprajñapti*, *Viyāhapannatti* with com. by Abhayadeva: Āgamodaya, Bombay, 1918-21; Gujarati trans. by Bechardas Jivaraj Doshi and Pandit Bhagavandas in 4 vols, Jinagana Pracār Sabha, Ahmedabad, vs 1974-88; Āgamodaya, ed. with Abhayadeva's com., 3 vols. Bombay, 1918-21; portion in Schubring's *Worte Mahaviras* and *Die Jainas*, Tubingen, 1927. J. Deleu, *Viyāhapannatti*, Rijks, University of Ghent, 1970; earliest study by A. Weber, *Ein Fragment der Bhagavati*, Berlin, 1865.

Bhagavatī Ārādhanā or *Mūlārādhanā* by Śivārya or Śivakoṭi with Pandit Sadāsukha's *Bhāṣa-*

Vacanikā: Muni Anantakirti Digambara Jain Granthamālā, 1931; with commentaries of Aparājita and Āśādhara, Sholapur, 1935; with Aparājita's com. *Vijayodaya*, Karanja, 1935; K. Oetjens, Śivārya's *Mūlārādhanā*, Hamburg, 1976; with Hindi trans. and intro. by Kailash Chandra Jain, Jivaraj Jain Granthamālā, Sholapur, 1977.

Bhaktāmara Stotra by Mānatuṅga: ed. and German trans. by H. Jacobi in *Indische Studien* XIV, 359ff; text in Kāvyamālā, Part VII, together with the commentaries of Guṇākara, Meghavijaya and Kanakakusala, in Devachand Lalbhai Jain Pustakoddāra, Bombay, 1932.

Bhaktaprijñā, Bhattaparinnā: Āgamodaya edn., Bombay, 1925; German trans. Kamptz, *Uber die vom Sterbefasten handeln den alteren Paiṇṇa des Jaina Kanons*, Hamburg, 1929.

Bhavavairāgyaśataka: ed. and trans. by L.P. Tessitori in *Giornale della societa Asiatica Italiana*, XXII.179-211, XXIV.405ff.

Bhavisatta Kahā also known as *Sūyapañcamīkahā* by Dhanapāla: partly ed. C.D. Dalal and completed by P.D. Gune in Gaekwad's Oritental Series, XX, Baroda, 1923.

Brhatkalpa, Kappa: ed. with text, introduction, summary of contents and glossary in German by W. Schubring, Leipzig, 1905; in Nagari script, Poona, 1923; *Bhāṣya* by Saṅghadāsagani Kṣamāsramaṇa and *Ṭīkā* by Malayagiri and Kṣemakīrti, Bhavnagar, 1933ff.; Eng. trans. May S. Burgess, *Indian Antiquary* XXXIX.257ff.; W. Schubring *Drei Chedasūtras des Jaina-Kanons*, Hamburg, 1966.

Bṛhatkathākośa by Harisena: ed. A.N. Upadhye, Singhi Jain Series, Bombay, 1943.

Bṛhatkathāślokasaṃgraha by Budhasvāmin ed. with French trans. by Felix Lacote and L. Renou, Paris, 1908-28; 'Essai sur Guṇādhya et la Bṛhatkathā' by F. Lacote, Eng. trans. by Rev. A.M. Talbard, *Quarterly Journal of the Mythic Society*, Bangalore, vol. IV. 1913-14; E.P. Matin, Budhasvāmin's *Bṛhatkathāślokasaṃgraha*, Leiden, 1973; ed. with notes by V.S. Agrawala, Varanasi, 1974; with Eng. trans. by R.P. Poddar, Tara Publications, Varanasi, 1986.

Bṛhatsvyambhūstotra also known as *Caturviṃśati-Jinastavana* pub. in Digambara Jaina Granthamālā, Kashi, I; with Hindi trans. and intro. by Jugalkishore Mukhtar, Sarvasa, 1950-1.

Caccari by Jinadattasūri: ed. with Sans. intro. by L.B. Gandhi, Gaekward's Oriental Series XXXVII, Baroda, 1927.

Campakaśreṣṭikathānaka by Jinakīrti: Vidyavijay Yantralaya, 1915; ed. and trans. into Eng. and German by J. Hertel, Leipzig, 1922; included in *The Prince as a Parrot*, with intro. by Roland Beer, Berlin, 1975.

Caritrasāra by Cāmuṇḍa Mahārāja: ed. with expl. notes in Hindi by Lalaram, Gandhi Haribhai Devakaran Jaina Granthamālā, Calcutta.

Catuḥśaraṇa, Causarana: Āgamodaya Samiti, XLVI, Bombay, 1925.

Caturviṃśati Jinastūti by Jinaprabhasūri, *Kāvyamālā* Part VII; by Dharmaghoṣa: ed. in *Stūtisaṃgraha*, Bombay, 1912.

Chappāhuḍa, Ṣaṭprābhṛta: ed. with Hindi com. by Surajbhan Vakil, Benares, 1910.

Dānakalpataru by Jinakīrti: ed. in Devchand Lalbhai Jain Pustakoddāra, No. IX, Bombay, 1919.

Darśanasāra by Devasena: ed. Nathuram Premi, Bombay, 1920.

Daśabhakti by Pūjyapāda *alias* Devanandīn: Nityapāṭha Saṃgraha, Karanja, 1956.

Dasabhatti by Kundakunda: ed. K.C. Jain, Jivaraj Jain Granthamālā, Sholapur, 1966.

Daśavaikālika, Dasaveyaliya: *Sūtra* and *Niryukti* by Bhadrabāhu ed. with German trans. by E. Leumann, *ZDMG*, XVVI, 1892, 581-663; ed. with *Niryukti* and *Cūrṇi* by Jinadāsagaṇi Mahattara, Ratlam, 1933, *Cūrṇi* by Agastyasiṃha: Ahmedabad, 1973; com. by Haribhadra, Bombay, 1918; ed. with notes and trans. by W. Schubring, Ahmedabad, 1932; M.P. Patavardhan, *The Dasaveyaliya: A Study*, Sangli, 1933-6.

Devendrastava, Devidatthaa: Āgamodaya edn., XLVI, Bombay, 1925.

Dharmābhyudaya by Meghaprabhācārya: ed. in Ātmānanda Granthamālā, LXI, Bhavnagar, 1918.

Dharmalindu of Haribhadra: ed. with Italian trans. by L. Suali in *Giornale della societa Asiatica Italiana* XXI, 223ff; also with Municandra's com. in *Bibliotheca Indica*, Calcutta, 1912.

Dharmaparīkṣa by Amitagati: Jaina Siddhanta Prakasani, Calcutta, 1908; Hindi trans. Bombay, 1908; N. Mirnov, *Die Dharma parīkṣā des Amitagati*, Leipzig, 1903.

Dharmaratnākara by Jayasena: Digambara Jain Mandir Panchayt, Delhi.

Dharmasarmabhyudaya by Haricandra: ed. in Kāvyamālā Series, Bombay, 1888.

Dharmopadeśamālāvivarana by Jayasiṃhasūri: ed. Lalchand Bhagavandas Gandhi, Singhi Jain Series, Bombay, 1949.

Dhuttākkhāna, Dhūrtākhyāna by Haribhadra: ed. A.N. Upadhye, Singhi Jain Series, Bombay, 1944.

Darupadīsvayaṃvara by Vijayapāla: ed. Jinavijaya Jaina Ātmānanda Sabhā, Bhavnagar, 1918.

Dravyasaṃgraha by Nemicandra with com. of

Brahmadeva: ed. with intro. trans. notes and an original com. in English by S.C. Ghoshal, *Sacred Books of the Jains*, vol. I, Arrah, 1917.

Dvātriṃśikā by Siddhasena Divākara: ed. A.N. Upadhye, Jain Sahitya Vikas Mandal, 1971; by Amitagati, ed. in Manikacandra Digambara Jaina Granthamālā 13; Eng. trans. by Ajit Prasad in Jaina Scripture Gift Series, 2.

Dvātriṃśikā-stotra: ed. with com. by Udaya Sagara and explanatory in Gujarati, Jaina Dharma Prasaraka Sabha, Bhavnagar, 1903.

Ekibhāva-stotra by Vādirāja: *Kāvyamālā*, Part VII; with Candrakīrti's Sanskrit Commentary and P. Sastri's Hindi trans., Sarsava, 1940.

Gadyacūḍāmaṇi by Odeyadeva Vādibhasiṃha: ed. T. Tuppuswami Sastri, Madras, 1902.

Gaṇividyā, Gaṇivijjā: ed. in Agamodaya Series, XLVI, Bombay, 1925.

Gommaṭasāra: ed. in four vols. in Gandhi Haribhai Devkarana Jaina Granthamālā, No. 4, Calcutta, with Sans. coms. of Abhayadeva and Kesavavarṇin and Eng. trans. by J.L. Jaini, in *Sacred Books of the Jains*, V-VI, Lucknow, 1927.

Hammīramadamardana by Jayasiṃha: ed. C.D. Dalal, Gaekward's Oriental Series, No. 10, Baroda, 1920.

Harivaṃśa-purāṇa of Jinasena: ed. Darbari Lal in Manikacandra Series; ed. with Hindi trans. by Pannalal Jain, Varanasi, 1962.

Iṣibhāsiyam: ed. W. Schubring, Gottingen 1942; with a Sanskrit Chāyā,1952.

Isimaṇḍala-thotta, Ṛṣimaṇḍala-stotra: ed. Yaśovijaya Maharaja, Baroda, 1954.

Iṣṭopadeśa by Pūjyapāda: ed. in Digambara Jaina Granthamālā I; Eng. tr. by C.R. Jain, Hardoi, 1995.

Jaina Rāmāyaṇa by Hemacandra, Parvan VII of *Triṣaṣṭi Śalākā*, Poona, 1890.

Jambudvīpaprajñapti, Jambuddīvapannatti: ed. with Śānti Candra's com. in Devchand Lalbhai Series 52, 54; cf. W. Kirfel, *Kosmographie der Inder*, Bonn, 1920.

Jasaharacariu of Puṣpadanta: ed. P.L. Vaidya, Karanja Jain Series, 1931.

Jayatihuyana-stotra by Abhayadeva: ed. with Sans. com., Ahmedabad, 1890.

Jinasahasranāmastotra by Jinasena II: ed. with com. of Śurtasāgara, Varanasi, 1954.

Jinastotraratnākara by Munisundara Suri: ed. in *Jaina-stotrasaṃgraha* II. Yaśovijaya Jain Granthamālā, No. 9.

Jinaśataka by Samantabhadra: Viraseva Mandir, Delhi, 1951.

Jitakalpa, Jiyakappa by Jinabhadra: ed. with extracts from Siddhasena's *Cūrṇi* by E. Leumann, Berlin, 1892; by Muni Jinavijaya, Bombay, 1926.

Jīvābhigama: ed. with Malayagiri's com. in Devchand Lalbhai Series, 50, Bombay, 1919.

Jivandharacampū by Haricandra: ed. S. Kuppuswami Sastri, Tanjore, 1905; Sarasvati Vilasa Series 4; Hultz in *Indian Antiquary*, XXXV, 1906.

Jīvavicāra, Jivaviyāra by Śāntisūri: ed. and French trans A. Guerinot, Paris, 1902; with Pathaka Ratnākara's com. Ahmedabad, 1915.

Jñānalocana-stotra by Vādirāja: in Manikacandra Digambara Jaina Granthamālā, No. 4.

Jñānārṇava or *Yogapradīpikā*: ed. in Rayacandra Jaina Śāstramālā, Bombay, 1907.

Jñātādharmakathā, Nāyādhammakahāo: Āgamodaya edn., with a Abhayadeva's com., Bombay, 1916; Āgama Saṃgraha Publication, 1877; P. Steinthal, *Specimen der Nāyādhammakahā*, Berlin, 1881; W. Huttemann, *Die Jñatā Erzahlungen*, Strassburg, 1907.

Joytiṣasāra by Ṭhakkura Pheru: Rajasthan Prācyavidyā Pratiṣṭhān, Jodhpur, 1961; Nahata Brothers, Calcutta, 1963.

Kahārahanakośa, Kathāratnakośa by Guṇacandra: ed. Punyavijaya, Bombay, 1944.

Kālakācārya Kathānaka: ed. and trans. by H. Jacobi in *ZDMG*, XXXIV, 1880, 247-318.

Kālasvarūpakulam by Jinadattasūri: ed. with Sanskrit intro. by L.B. Gandhi, Gaekwad's Oriental Series XXXVII, Baroda, 1927.

Kalpasūtra by Bhadrabāhu: Eng. trans. by J. Stevenson, London, 1848; Critical ed. H. Jacobi, Leipzig, 1879; Eng. trans. by Jacobi in SBE, XXII, Oxford, 1884; ed. with com. *Sabodhikā* of Vinayavijaya, Devachand Lalbhai Series, Bombay, 1911; with coms. of Jinaprabha, Subhacandra and Harṣakīrti, Devchand Lalbhai, Bombay, 1933.

Kalyāṇamandirastotra by Siddhasena Divākara: German by H. Jacobi in *Indische Studien*, XIV, 376ff; text pub. in Kāvyamālā Series, Part VII.

Karakaṇḍacariu by Kanakāmara: ed. Hiralal Jain, Karanja Series, 1932.

Karmaprakṛti by Śivaśarmā: ed. with Malayagiri's com., Bhavnagar, 1912.

Kathākośa: trans. into Eng. from Sans. Ms. by C.H. Tawney, London, 1895; text and trans. into German by I. Hoffmann, Munchen, 1974.

Kathākośaprakaraṇa by Jineśvarasūri: ed. Jinavijaya, Singhi Jain Series, 1949.

Kathāratnākara by Hemavijaya: German trans. by J. Hertel, Munchen 1922; ed. Hiralal Hamsraj, Jamnagar, 1911.

Kattigeyānupekkhā, Kārttikeyānuprekṣā by Kārttikeya Svāmin: pub. with Hindi com. Bombay, 1904.

Karuṇa Vajrāyudha by Bālacandra: ed. Chaturvijaya,

Jaina Ātmānanda Granthamālā LVI, Bhavnagar, 1916.

Kṣapaṇasāra: ed. with Sans. and Hindi com., Gandhi Haribhai Devakaran Jaina Granthamālā, No. 5, Calcutta.

Kṣatracūḍāmaṇi by Odeyadeva Vadivasiṃha: ed. T. Kuppuswamy Sastri, Tanjore, 1903. Sarasvati Vilasa Series, No. 3; cf. *Indian Antiquary* XXXVI, 1907.

Kumārapālapratibodha by Somaprabha: ed. Jinavijaya, Gaekwad's Oriental Series, XIV, Baroda, 1920.

Kuvalayamālā by Udyotanasūri: ed. A.N. Upadhye in two parts, Singhi Jain Series, 1959; with V.S. Agrawala's *Cultural Notes* in 1970; Premsuman Jain, *Kuvalayamālā kā Sāṃskṛtik Adhyayana*, in Hindi, Vaishali, 1975.

Labdhisāra: ed. with Sans. and Hindi com. Gandhi Haribhai Devakaran Jaina Granthamālā, No. 5, Calcutta.

Laghiyastraya by Akalaṅka: Manikacandra Digambara Jaina Granthamālā, No. I, Bombay, 1925.

Lāṭisaṃhitā by Rājamalla: Manikacandra Digambara Jaina Granthamālā, 1926.

Lilavai by Kouhala: ed. A.N. Upadhye, Singhi Jain Series, Bombay, 1949.

Lokaprakāśa by Vinayavijaya: ed. Hiralal Hamsraj, 3 vols., Jamnagar, 1910.

Lokattattvanirṇaya by Haribhadra: ed. with Italian trans. by L. Suali in *Giornale* XVIII, 263ff; text, Bhavnagar, 1902.

Mahāniśītha, Mahānisīha; ed. with German intro. by W. Schubring, Berlin, 1918.

Mahāpratyākhyāna, Mahāpaccakkhāna: Agamodaya edn., XLVI, Bombay, 1925.

Mahāpurāṇa of Puṣpadanta: in three parts, Apabhraṃśa text, ed. P.L. Vaidya, Manikacandra Digambara Jaina Granthamālā, Bombay, 1937-47.

Mahavira Cariyam by Devendragaṇin: Jaina Ātmānanda Granthamālā, No. 59.

Mahāvīra Cariyam by Guṇacandragaṇi, Āgamodaya edn., Bombay, 1929; Gujarati trans., Ahmedabad, 1936.

Mahīpalacaritra by Caritrasundara: ed. Hiralal Hamsaraj, Jamnagar, 1909.

Majjhimakhaṇḍa by Dharmasenagaṇi: Part I, ed. H.C. Bhayani and R.M. Shah, Ahmedabad, 1987.

Moharājaparājaya by Yaśaḥpāla: ed. C.D. Dalal, Gaekwad's Oriental Series, IX, with Eng. trans, Baroda, 1918.

Mṛgavatī Caritra by Maladhāri Devaprabha: ed. Hiralal Hamsraj, Jamnagar, 1908.

Muditakumudacandra by Yasaścandra: ed. in Yaśovijaya Jaina Granthamālā, No. 9, Benares, 1905.

Mūlācāra by Vaṭṭakera: ed. with Vasunandin's com. in Māṇikacandra Digambara Jaina Granthamālā, Nos. 19, 23.

Nammayāsundarikahā by Mahendrasūri: Singhi Jain Series, 1960.

Nandīsūtra with Malayagiri's com.: Āgamodaya edn., Bombay, 1924.

Navatattvaprakaraṇa by Jinacandragaṇi: ed. with two coms. in Ātmānanda Jaina Granthamālā, No. 10, Bhavnagar, 1912.

Nemibhaktāmaram by Bhavaprabha Sūri: *Stotraratnākara* I, Bombay, 1913.

Nemidūta by Vikrama: Kāvyamālā Series, Part II, Bombay.

Nemi Nirvāṇa by Vāgbhaṭa: *Kāvyamālā*, 56, Bombay, 1896.

Nirayāvalī: ed. S. Warren, Amsterdam, 1879; Jacobi in *ZDMG*, XXXIV.178.; ed. with Candrasūri's com. Āgamodaya, Ahmedabad, 1922.

Nirbhaya Bhīma Vyayoga by Rāmacandra: ed. in Yaśovijaya Jaina Granthamālā XIX.

Niśītha, Nisīha: ed. W. Schubring, Leigzig, 1918; by Jain Sāhitya Saṃśodhaka Samiti, Poona, 1923; *Bhāṣya-Cūrṇi*, ed. Upadhyaya Kavi Amar Muni and Muni Kanhaialal Kamal, Agra, 1957-60.

Nyāyāvatāra by Siddhasena Divākara: ed. with com. and Eng. trans. Satish Ch. Vidyabhusan, Calcutta, 1900.

Oghaniryukti, Ohanijjutti with Droṇācārya's com. Āgamodaya edn., Bombay, 1918.

Padmacaritra by Raviṣena: ed. Darbarilal, Manikacandra Digambara Series 29-31, 1928; Hindi trans. in three parts, Varanasi, 1958-9.

Pāhuḍadohā by Rāmasiṃha: ed. with Hindi trans. by H.L. Jain, Karanja Jain Society, 1933.

Pāla-Gopāla Kathānaka by Jinakīrti: pub. in Ātmānanda Jaina Granthamālā, Dabhoi, 1918.

Pañcāstikāyasāra, Pañcatthiyasāra by Kundakunda: ed. with trans. notes, com. and intro. by A. Chakravartinayanar, Arrah, 1920.

Pañcaviṃśatikā by Padmanandī: Sholapur, 1932.

Pāṇḍavacarita by Maladhārin Devaprabha Suri: Kāvyamālā Series, Bombay, 1911.

Pāpabuddhi Dharmabuddhi Kathānaka: ed. Hiralal Hamsaraj, Jamnagar, 1909; ed. with Italian trans. by E. Lovalini in *Giornale*, III.

Paramātmaparīkṣā by Joindu: ed. with Brahmadeva's Sans. com. and A.N. Upadhye's intro. in Rayachandra Śāstramālā, Agas, 1960.

Parīkṣāmukhasūtra by Māṇikyanandin, Sanātana Jaina Grathamālā I, Bombay, 1905.

Pariśiṣṭaparvan or *Sthaviravalicarita* by Hemacandra: ed. H. Jacobi, Bibliotheca Indica, Calcutta, 1891; extracts trans. into German J. Hertel, Leipzig, 1908.

Pārśvābhyudaya by Jinasena: ed. with a literal Eng. trans. K.P. Pathak, Poona, 1884; Bombay, 1909.

Pārśvanāthacarita by Bhavadevasūri: ed. Hargobindadas and Becaradas, Benares, 1912.

Pātrakeśaristotra by Vidyānandin: Digambara Jaina Granthamālā, I, Kashi.

Pātraparīkṣā by Vidyānanda ed. in Sanātana Jaina Granthamālā, Bombay, 1913.

Paumarcariya by Vimalasuri: ed. H. Jacobi, Bhavnagar, 1914.

Pindaniryukti, Piṃdanijjutti with Bhadrabāhu's *Niryukti* and Malayagiri's com. Devchand Lalbhai Series, Bombay, 1918.

Prabandhacintāmaṇi by Merutuṅga: ed. Ramacandra Dinanatha, Bombay, 1988; Eng. trans. C.H. Tawney, Calcutta, 1901; Singhi Jain Series, 1933.

Prabhāvakacaritra by Prabhācandra: ed. Hirananda M. Sharma, Bombay, 1909.

Prabuddharauhineya by Rāmabhadra Muni: ed. in Ātmānanda Jaina Granthamālā, No. 60, Bhavnagar, 1917.

Prajñāpanā, Pannavanā: ed. with Malayagiri's com. and Sanskrit trans. by Narakacandra, Benares, 1884; Āgamodaya edn., Bombay, 1918.

Prākṛtaprakāśa by Vararuci: ed. with *Prākṛtamañjarī* com. of Kātyāyana and *Manoramā* of Bhāmaha and Bengali trans. by Basanta Kumar Chatterjee, Calcutta, 1914.

Pramānamīmāṃsā by Hemacandra: ed. with author's own com. A.M. Prabhakara, Poona, 1925.

Pramāṇanirṇaya by Vidyānanda and *Pramāṇa Parīkṣā*: Sanātana Jaina Granthamālā, Bombay, 1913.

Praśnavyākaranāṇi, Panhavagaranaiṃ: Agamodaya edn., with Abhayadeva's com., Bombay, 1919.

Pravacanasāra by Kundakunda: ed. with intro. of A.N. Upadhye, Rajchandra Jain Śāstramālā, Bombay, 1931, rpt., Agas, 1964.

Prayascittavidhi by Akalaṅka: *Prāyasuttasaṃgraha*, Manikacandra Digambar Jaina Granthamālā 18.

Puṇyāsrava Kathākośa by Ramacandra Mumukṣu: Jivaraj Jaina Granthamālā, 1964.

Purusarthasiddhyupaya or *Jinapravacanarahasyakosa* by Amrtacandra: ed. in Rayacandra Jaina Sastramala, Bombay, 1905.

Rājapraśnīya, Rāyapasenaijja: Āgama Saṃgraha, Benares, 1880; Āgamodaya edn. with Malayagiri's com., Bombay, 1925.

Ratnacūḍakathā by Jinasāgarasūri: ed. in Yaśovijaya Jaina Granthamālā, Bhavnagar, 1917; German trans. J. Hertel, Leipzig, 1922.

Ratnakaraṇḍaśrāvakācāra: text with Eng. trans. by C.R. Jain, Arrah, 1917.

Ratnākarapañcaviṃśatikā: ed. in *Stutisaṃgraha*, Bombay, 1906.

Rayanaseharikahā by Jinaharṣa: Ātmānanda Jaina Granthamālā, Bhavnagar, 1916.

Ṛṣabhapañcāśikā by Dhanapāla: ed. and German trans. by Klatt in *ZDMG* XXXIII, 1879, 445ff; text with Sanskrit trans. Kāvyamālā VII, Bombay, 1890; with *Avacūrṇi*, Devchand Lalbhai, Bombay, 1933.

Ṣaḍdarśanasamuccaya by Haribhadra: ed. with Guṇaratna's *Tarkarahasyadīpikā* by L. Suali, Calcutta, 1905 ff.; also in Ātmānanda Jaina Granthamālā, 49, Bhavnagar, 1917.

Sāgaradharmamṛta by Āśādhara with his own com.: ed. in Manikacandra Digambara Jaina Granthamālā, 1914.

Śālibhadracarita: ed. in Yaśovijaya Jaina Granthamālā, No. 15, Benares, 1910.

Samādhiśloka by Pūjyapāda: ed. in Sanātana Jaina Granthamālā, Bombay, 1905.

Samarāicchakahā by Haribhadra; ed. H. Jacobi, Calcutta, 1926; ed. Pandit Bhagavandas, 2 parts, Ahmedabad, 1938-42.

Samarāditya Saṃkṣepa by Pradyumna Sūri: ed. H. Jacobi, Calcutta, 1908; also Ahmedabad, 1965.

Samavāya: ed. in Āgama Saṃgraha IV, Benares, 1880; Āgamodaya edn. with Abhayadeva's com., Bombay, 1918.

Samayasāra: ed. with Sans. com. in Sanātana Jaina Granthamālā, Benares, 1914.

Sammatitarkasūtra by Siddhasena Divakara: ed. with Abhayadeva's *Tattvabodhinī* in Yaśovijaya Jaina Granthamālā, No. 13, with *Tattvārthavidhāyinī*, Poona, 1926.

Saṃstāra, Saṃthāra: Āgamodaya edn., Bombay, 1925.

Sañjamamañjari by Mahesara Suri: text with trans. into Sanskrit by P.D. Gune in *Annals of the Bhandarkar Oriental Research Institute*, I, 1919-21.

Śāntinātha Caritra by Ajitaprabha: ed. Indravijaya, Calcutta, 1909.

Sarvārthasiddhi by Pūjyapāda Devanandin, Kolhapur, 1904.

Śatruñjayamāhātmya by Dhaneśvara: trans. with Appendices by J. Burgess, *Indian Antiquary*, 1901.

Siddhahemaśabdānuśāsana: ed. R. Pischel with German trans. explanatory and comparative notes, Halle Amzar, 1877-80; ed. P.L. Vaidya, Poona, 1939, rev. edn. 1958.

Siddhipriya: in Kāvyamālā VII, Bombay,1930.

Śīladūta by Caritrasundara: ed. in Yaśovijaya Jaina Granthamālā 18, Benares, 1909.

Sinduraprakara or *Suktimuktāvali* by Somaprabha: Kāvyamālā VII, Bombay.

Sobhanastuti: ed. with German trans. by Jacobi in *ZDMG* XXXII, 1878, Kāvyamālā Series VII.

Śrāvakaprajñapti: ed. B.K. Premchand Mody, Bombay, 1905.
Śṛṅgāravairāgyataraṅgiṇī by Somaprabha: Kāvyamālā V, 124ff.
Sthānāṅga, *Ṭhāṇa*: ed. in Āgama Saṃgraha III, Benares, 1880 with a Sanskrit and Prakrit com., Āgamodaya edn., with Abhayadeva's com., Bombay, 1918-20.
Subhāṣitaratnasamdohā by Amitagati: Kāvyamālā 82, ed. & trans. by R. Schmidt and J. Hertel in *ZDMG*, LIX, 1905; LXI, 1907.
Sudamsanā-cariya, *Sudarśanā-carita*: Ātmavallabha Grantha Series, Valed, Ahmedabad, 1932.
Sukṛtakīrtikallolinī: ed. C.D. Dalal, Gaekwad's Oriental Series, X, Baroda, 1920, App.
Supāsanāha Cariyam by Laksmaṇagaṇin: ed. Hargovinda Das Seth, Benares, 1918.
Surasundarīcariyam by Dhaneśvara: ed. with notes by Munirāj Sri Rajavijayaji, Benares, 1915.
Sūryaprajñsapti, *Surapannatti*: Āgamodaya edn., with Malayagiri's com., Bombay, 1919.
Sūtrakṛta, *Sūyagaḍa*: pub. in Āgama Saṃgraha II, Bombay, 1880; Āgamodaya edn. with Śīlaṅka's com., Bombay, 1917; Eng. trans. H. Jacobi in SBE XLV, 1895.
Svarūpasambodhana by Akalaṅka: Manikacandra Digambara Jaina Granthamālā I.
Syādvādamañjarī by Mallisena: Benares, 1900; Yaśovijaya Jaina Granthamālā 30, Benares, 1911; Eng. trans. F.W. Thomas, *The Flower-Spray of the Quommoda Doctrine*, Berlin, 1910; trans. A.B. Dhruva, 1933; Hindi trans. J.C. Jain, Rajcandra Jain Śāstramālā, Bombay, 1935, 1970.
Tandulavaitālika, *Taṃdulaveyāliya*, Āgamodaya edn., Bombay, 1922.
Taraṅgalolā: German trans. E. Leumann in *Zeitschrift fur Buddhismus*, München, 1921, III 193ff., 272ff.
Tarkarahasyadīpikā by Guṇaratna: ed. M.K. Jain, 1970. See *Ṣaḍdarśanasamuccaya*.
Tattvārtharājavārttika by Akalanka: pub. in Sanātana Jaina Granthamālā 4, Benares, 1915.
Tattvārthasāra by Amṛtacandra: pub. in Sanātana Jaina Granthamālā I, Bombay, 1905.
Tattvasāra by Devasena: edn. in Manikacandra Digambara Jaina Granthamālā 13.
Tattvarthādhigama by Umāsvāmī or Umāsvāti: ed. with com. by Vakil Keshavlal Premchand Mody in *Bibliotheca Indica*, Calcutta, 1903-5; pub. in Rayacandra Jaina Śāstramālā, Bombay, 1906; with intro., Eng. trans., notes and com. J.L. Jaini, Sacred Books of the Jains II, Arrah, 1920.
Tattvārthaślokavārttika by Vidyānanda: ed. in Gandhinatharanga Jaina Granthamālā, Bombay, 1918.
Tilakamañjarī by Dhanapāla: Kāvyamālā Series, Bombay, 1906.
Tīrthakalpa by Jinaprabha Suri: ed. D.R. Bhandarkar and Kedarnath Sahityabhusan, *Bibliotheca Indica*, Calcutta, 1923.
(*Triṣaṣṭilakṣaṇa*) *Mahāpurāṇa* by Jinasena and Guṇabhadra; text and Hindi trans., Lalaram Jain, Syādvāda Granthamālā, Indore, 1915, 1917.
Triṣaṣṭiśalākāpuruṣacarita by Hemacandra: Jaina Dharma Prasāraka Sabhā, Bhavnagar, 1906-13; Eng. trans. Helen M. Johnson, *The Lives of Sixty-three Illustrious Persons*, 6 vols., Baroda, 1931-62.
Ukti-vyakti-Prakaraṇa by Bhaṭṭa Damodara; Singhi Jain Series, 1953.
Upadeśapada by Haribhadra: Muktikamal Jain Mohanamala, Baroda, 1923-5.
Upadeśarsāyana Rāsa by Jinadatta Sūri: ed. with Sans. intro. by L.B. Gandhi, Gaekwad's Oriental Series, XXXVII, Baroda, 1927.
Upamitibhavaprapañcakathā by Siddharṣi: ed. P. Peterson, *Bibliotheca Indica*, Calcutta, 1899-1914; new edn. Bombay, 1918, 1920; German trans. by W. Kirfel, Leipzig, 1924.
Upāsakācāra or *Śrāvakācāra* by Amitagati: Anantakirti Granthamālā, Bombay, 1921.
Upāsakadaśa, *Uvāsagadasāo*: ed. with com. of Abhayadeva, Eng. trans. and notes by A.F.R. Hoernle, *Bibliotheca Indica*, Calcutta, 1885-8; Āgamodya edn., Bombay, 1920; rev. edn., P.L. Vaidya, Poona, 1930.
Uttama (Kumāra) Caritra-Kathānaka: ed. & German trans. of the prose section by A. Weber, Berlin, 1884; metrical section by Hiralal Hamsraj, Jamnagar, 1908.
Uttarādhyayana, *Uttarajjhāyā*: ed. with intro., notes and com. by Jarl Charpentier, Upsala, 1912; Eng. trans. H. Jacobi, SBE, XLV.
Uttarapurāṇa by Guṇabhadra: Bharatiya Jnanapitha, Kashi, 1968.
Uvaesamālā by Dharmadāsa: ed. L.P. Tissitory in *Giornale* XXV, 1912.
Uvasaggaharathotta, *Upasargahārastotra* by Bhadrabāhu; ed. H.R. Kapadia, Mohanlalji Grantha, Bombay, 1964.
Vairagyasara by Suprabhacarya: ed. H.D. Velankar in *Annals of the Bhandarkar Oriental Research Institute*, IX, 1928.
Vajjalagga by Jayavallabha: ed. J. Labor, 1914; 1923, 1944; M.V. Patvardhan, Prakrit Text Society, Ahmedabad, 1969.
Vandaru-vṛtti by Devendrasūri: Devchand Lalbhai, Bombay, 1912.
Vasudevahiṇḍi by Saṅghadāsagaṇi Vācaka: ed.

Caturvijaya and Punyavijaya, Bhavnagar, 1930-1; cf. J.C. Jain, *The Vasudevahiṇḍi: An Authentic Jain Version of the Bṛhatathā*, L.D. Institute, Ahmedabad, 1977.

Vidhimārgaprapa by Jinaprabha: ed. Jinvijaya Bombay, 1941.

Vinodakathasamgraha by Rajasekhara Maladhari: Bombay, 1918.

Vipakaśrūta, Vivāgasūya: Āgamodaya edn., with Ābhayadeva's com. Bombay, 1926; Āgama Samgraha Pub. 1875; ed. with intro. and notes by P.L. Vaidya, Poona, 1932.

Viṣāpahara-stotra: ed. Pannalal Sastri; Sanskrit com. by Candrakīrti, Hindi trans., Nathuram Premi, Bombay, 1956.

Visesaṇavati by Jinabhadragaṇi Kṣamaśramaṇa: Ratlam, 1927.

Vītarāgastotra by Hemacandra: ed. with *Vivaraṇa* by Prabhācandra and *Avacūrṇi*: Nirnaya Sagar Press, Bombay, 1911.

Vivaraṇa: ed. with intro. gloss., notes and app. by P.L. Vaidya, 1932.

Vyavahāra, Vavahāra: ed. W. Schubring, Leipzig, 1918.

Yaśastilakacampū by Somadevasūri: Kāvyamālā Series 70, Bombay, 1901; with Śrutasāgara's *Ṭīkā*, Bombay, 1916; cf. K.K. Handiqui, *Yaśastilaka-campū and Indian Culture*, Sholapur, 1949.

Yaśodharacaritra by Māṇikyasūri: ed. Hiralal Hamsaraj, Jamnagar, 1910.

Yasodharacarita by Vādirājasūri: ed. T.A. Gopinatha Rao, Sarasvati Vilasa Series 5, Tanjore, 1912.

Yogabindu by Haribhadra: ed. with com. L. Suali, Bhavanagar, 1911.

Yogadṛṣṭisamuccaya by Haribhadra: ed. L. Suali, Devchand Lalbhai, 12, Bombay, 1912.

Yogasāra by Amitagati: ed. with Hindi exp. in Sanātana Jaina Granthamālā, No. 16, 1918.

Yogaśāstra by Hemacnadra: ed with author's own com: Jaina Dharma Prasāraka Sabhā, Bhavnagar, 1926.

Yuktyānuśāsana by Samantabhadra: ed. in Sanātana Jaina Granthamālā; Manikacandra Digambara Jaina Granthamālā, Bombay; and Digambara Jaina Granthamālā, Kashi.

SECONDARY SOURCES

Acharya, P.K., *Dictionary of Hindu Architecture*, London and Allahabad, 1927.

Agrawala, R.C., 'Museums in Rajasthan', in *Jaina Art and Architecture*, ed. A. Ghosh, New Delhi, 1974-5, III., 570ff.

Agarawala, V.S., 'Aṣṭamaṅgalakamālā', *Journal of the Indian Society of Oriental Art*, New Series II, 1967-8, 1ff.; 'Catalogue of Mathura Museum', *Journal of the U.P. Historical Society*, XXIII, 1950, 54ff.

Aiyaswami Sastri, N., 'Śaramaṇa or Non-Brahmanical Sects', in *Cultural Heritage of India*, Calcutta 1958, I, 389-99.

Akkola, S.C, *Prācīna Marāṭhī Jaina Sāhitya* (in Marathi), Poona, 1968.

Altekar, A.S., *The Rāṣṭrakūṭas and Their Times*, Poona, 1934.

Amar, G.L., 'Darśana aur Vijñāna ke Āloka men Pudgala Dravya', in *Muni Śrī Hazarimala Smṛti Grantha* (in Hindi) Beawar, 1965; 'Architecture', in *Jaina Art and Architecture*, ed. A. Ghosh, New Delhi, 1974-5, III, 495-536.

Anon, *Śrī Jaina Saṃskāra Vidhi* (in Hindi), Bombay, 1907.

Andhare, S.K., 'Painted Wooden Maṇḍapa from Gujarat', in *Bulletin of the Prince of Wales Museum*, VII, Bombay, 1959-62, 41-5.

Ayyangar, M.S.R. and B. Seshgiri Rao, *Studies in South Indian Jainism*, Madras, 1922.

Bagchi, P.C., 'The Historical Beginnings of Jainism', in *Sir Asutosh Mukherjee Silver Jubilee Volume*, III(3), Calcutta, 1997, 71-86; 'Jainism', in *Age of the Nandas and Mauryas*, ed. K.A. Nilakantha Sastri, 1967, 295ff.

Bajpai, K.D., 'Monuments and Sculpture, Central India', in *Jaina Art and Architecture*, ed. A. Ghosh, New Delhi, 1974-5, II.349-54; 'Archaeological Sources Bearing on Early Jainism', in *Jainism and Prakrit*, ed. N.N. Bhattacharyya, New Delhi, 1994, 198-204.

Banarasi Das, *A Lecture on Jainism*, Agra, 1902.

Banerjea, J.N., 'Jain Iconography', in *Age of Imperial Unity*, ed. R.C. Majumdar, Bombay, 1951; in *The Classical Age*, ed. R.C. Majumdar, Bombay, 1954; in *Age of Imperial Kanauj*, ed. R.C. Majumdar, Bombay, 1955.

Banerjee, P., 'Monuments and Sculpture: East India' in *Jain Art and Architecture*, ed. A. Ghosh, New Delhi, 1974-5, I, 152-67.

Banerji, S.C., *Folklore in Buddhist and Jain Literature*, Delhi, 1987.

Banerji-Sastri, A., 'Mauryan Sculptures from Lohanipur, Patna', in *Journal of Bihar and Orissa Research Society*, XXVI, 1940, 120-4.

Banks, Marcus, *Organising Jainism in India and England*, Oxford, 1992.

Barodia, U.P., *History and Literature of Jainism*, Bombay, 1909.

Barth, A., *Religions of India*, London, 1882, rpt. Varanasi, 1963.

Barua, B.M., A *History of the Pre-Buddhist Indian Philosophy*, Calcutta, 1921; rpt. Delhi, 1970; 'The Ājīvikas', *Journal of the Department of Letters*, Calcutta, 1920, II, 1-80.

Basham, A.L., *History and Doctrine of the Ājīvikas*, London, 1951.

Bastian, A., *Kosmogonien und Theogonien indischen Religionphilosophien besonders der Jaina*, Berlin, 1892.

Behera, K.S., 'A Note on Jainism in Orissa', in *Babu Chote Lal Jain Smṛti Grantha*, Calcutta, 1967-8.

Belvalkar, S.K. and R.D. Ranade, *History of Indian Philosophy*, II. The Creative Period, Poona, Bilvakunja, 1927, rpt. New Delhi, 1974, 1997.

Beni Prasad, *World Problems and Jain Ethics*, Lahore, 1945.

Bhandarkar, R.G., *Report on the Search for Sanskrit Manuscripts on the Bombay Presidency during 1883-84*, Bombay, 1887.

Bhargava, D., *Jain Ethics*, Delhi, 1968; 'Reformistic Trends in Jainism', in *Jaina Bhāratī Research Volume*, Calcutta, 1962, 59ff.

Bhattacharya, Asok K., 'Monuments and Sculpture: West India', in *Jaina Art and Architecture*, ed. A. Ghosh, New Delhi, 1974-5, II.355-64.

Bhattacharya, B.C., *The Jaina Iconography*, Lahore 1939; 'The Goddess of Learning in Jainism', in *Malaviya Commemoration Volume*, Benaras, 1932, 291-303.

Bhattacharyya, H., *Divinity in Jainism*, Madras, 1925; *The Jain Prayer*, rpt. Calcutta, 1964.

Bhattacharyya, H.S., *Lord Mahāvīra*, Jain Mitra Mandal Tracts No. 43, Delhi, 1926.

Bhattacharyya, N.N., *Jain Philosophy: Historical Outline*, New Delhi, 1975; 2nd rev. edn. New Delhi, 1999; *Glossary of Indian Religious Terms and Concepts*, New Delhi, 1990; rep. 1999; *Indian Religious Historiography*, New Delhi, 1996; (ed.) *Jainism and Prakrit in Ancient and Medieval India: Essays Presented to Prof. J.C. Jain*, New Delhi, 1994.

Bhujabali Sastri, *Kannaḍa Prāntīya Tāḍapatrīya Granthasūcī* (Hindi), Benares, 1940; 'Jaina Kannaḍa Vāṅgmaya' (Hindi), in *Jaina Siddhānta*, 1938.

Bloomfield, M., *The Life and Stories of the Jaina Saviour Pārśvanātha*, Baltimore, 1919.

Bool Chand, *Jain Cultural Studies*, Benares, 1946, *Lord Mahāvīra: A Study in Historical Prespective*, Benares, 1948; *Jainism in Indian History*, Benares, 1951; 'Jainism in Kaliṅgadesa', in *Acharya Dhruva Smāraka Grantha*, 87-100.

Bothra, Pushpa, *Jaina Theory of Perception*, Delhi, 1995.

Brown, P., *Indian Architecture*, Bombay, 1942; rpt. Delhi, 1970.

Bruhn, K., *The Jina Images of Deogarh*, Leiden, 1969.

Buddhisagara (ed.), *Jaina Dhātupratimā Lekha Saṃgraha*, Padra, 1917, 1924.

Bühler, G., *Über die indische Sekte der Jainas*, Wien, 1887; Eng. trans. by J. Burgess, *On the Indian Sect of the Jainas, with an Outline of Jaina Mythology*, London, 1903.

Burgess, J., *Report on the Antiquities of Kathiawad and Kachh*, Archaeological Survey of Western India, New Imperial Series, London, 1976; 'Papers on Śatruñjaya and the Jains', *Indian Antiquary* II and XIII.

Burgess, J. and H. Consens, *The Architectural Antiquities of Northern Gujarat*, Archaeological Survey of India, New Imperial Series, IX, London, 1903.

Caillat, Collet, *Atonements in Ancient Ritual of the Jaina Monk*, Ahmedabad, 1975.

Carrithers, M. and C. Humprey (eds.), *The Assembly of Listeners: Jains in Society*, Cambridge, 1991.

Champakalakshmi, R., 'Monuments and Sculptures: South India', in *Jaina Art and Architecture*, ed. A. Ghosh, New Delhi, 1974, I, 92-106; 'An Unnoticed Jain Cavern Near Madurantakam', *Journal of the Madras University*, XLI (1-2), 1969, 12ff.

Chakkiravarti Nayinar, A., *Nīlakaci*, Tamil University, Tanjore, 1984.

Chakravarti, A., *Jain Literature in Tamil*, Arrah, 1941; *The Religion of Ahiṃsā*, Bombay, 1957; 'Jainism: Its Philosophy and Ethics', in *Cultural Heritage of India*, Calcutta, 1958, I, 414-33.

Chandra, K.K. (ed.), *Prakrit Studies*, Ahmedabad, 1978.

Chandra, Moti, *Jaina Miniature Paintings from Western India*, Ahmedabad; 1949; 'An Illustrated Manuscript of the Kalpasūtra and Kālakācāryakathā', *Bulletin of the Prince of Wales Museum*, Bombay, 1953-4, 40ff.; 'An Illustrated Manuscript of the Mahāpurāṇa', *Lalita Kalā*, V, 68-81. *Stone Sculptures of the Prince of Wales Museum*, Bombay, 1974.

Chandra, Moti and S. Gorakhsekhar, 'Prince of Wales Museum', in *Jaina Art and Architecture*, ed. A. Ghosh, New Delhi, 1974-5, III, 566ff.

Chandra, Moti and U.P. Shah, 'New Documents of Jain Paintings', in *Shri Mahāvīra Jaina Vidyalaya Golden Jubliee Volume*, Part I, Bombay, 1968, 348-420.

Chandra, Pramod, *Stone Sculpture in the Allahabad Museum*, Poona, 1971; 'A Unique Kālakācāryakathā Manuscript', *Bulletin of the American*

Academy of Benares, I, 1-10, figs. 1-20.

Charpentier, Jarl, 'The History of the Jains', in *Cambridge History of India*, I, ed. E.J. Rapson, Cambridge, 1922, rpt. Delhi, 1962, Ch. VI, 134-51.

Chatterjee, A.K., *A Comprehensive History of Jainism*, I, Calcutta, 1978; II, Calcutta, 1984.

Chatterjee, Bhaskar, 'Relics of Jain Community in Eastern India' in *Jainism and Prakrit*, ed. N.N. Bhattacharyya, New Delhi, 1994, 233-40.

Chattopadhyaya, D.P., *Indian Atheism*, Calcutta, 1970.

Chopra, C., *A Short History of the Terāpanthī Sect of the Śvetāmbara Jains and its Tenets*, Calcutta.

Choudhary, G.C., *Political History of Northern India from Jain Sources*, Amritsar, 1963.

Cidanadamurti, M., *Karṇāṭaka Sasanagaḷa Saṃskṛta Adhyayana*, Mysore, 1866.

Colebrooke, H.T., *Miscellaneous Essays*, Madras, 1872, rpt. New Delhi, 1972.

Coomaraswamy, A.K., 'Notes on Jain Art', *Journal of Indian Art and Industry*, XVI, 1913; 'The Conquerer's Life in Jaina Paintings', *Journal of the Indian Society of Oriental Art*, III(2), 1935, 125-44; *History of Indian and Indonesian Art*, London, 1927; *The Yakṣas*, rpt. New Delhi, 1971.

Cousens, H., *Somnath and other Medieval Temple of Kathiawar,* New Imperial Series XLV, New Delhi.

Cowell, E.B. and A.E. Gough, *Sarvadarśana-saṃgraha*, Eng. trans. London and Calcutta, 1899, rpt. Varanasi, 1961.

Dalal, C.M., *Poravāḍa Vaṇikona Itihāsa,* Bombay, 1922; *Vidhipakṣa (Añcala) Gaccha Mhoti Paṭṭāvalī*, Ahmedabad, 1928; *Akhila Bhārata-varṣīya Śrī Jaina Muni Sammelana Nirṇaya*, Ahmedabad, 1839.

Dasa, S.P., 'The Jaina School of Astronomy', *Indian Historical Quarterly*, VIII, 30-42, 565-71.

Dasgupta, P.C., 'A Rare Jain Icon from Sat Deuliya', *Jain Journal*, VII (3), 1973, 139ff.

Dasgupta, S.N., *History of Indian Philosophy*, I, Cambridge, 1922.

Dash, M.P., 'Jaina Antiquities from Charampa', *Orissa Historical Research Journal*, XI (1), 1962, 50ff.

Delamaine, Major, 'On the Śrāvacs or Jainas', *Transactions of the Royal Asiatic Society of Great Britain and Ireland*, I, 413-38.

Deo, S.B., *History of Jaina Monachism from Inscriptions and Literature*, Poona, 1956; *Jain Monastic Jurisprudence*, Benares, 1960: 'Expansion of Jainism' in *Jain Art and Architecture,* ed. A. Ghosh, New Delhi, 1974, I, 22-34.

Desai, M.D., *Jaina Sāhityāna Saṃkṣipta Itihāsa* in Gujarati, Bombay, 1933; *Jaina Gurjara Kavio* (Gujarati), Bombay, 1926.

Desai, P.B., *Jainism in South India and Some Jain Epigraphs*, Sholapur, 1957; 'Yakṣī Images in South Indian Jainism', in *Dr. Munshi Felicitation Volume*, Nagpur, 1965, 344-8.

Desai, S.M., *Haribhadra's Yoga Works and Psychosynthesis*, Ahmedabad, 1983.

Deshpande, M.N., 'The Background and Tradition', *Jain Art and Architecture*, I, 14-21.

Deshpande, N.A. 'Jaina Concept of an Ideal Teacher', in *H.D. Velankar Commemoration Volume*, Bombay, 1956, 344-8.

Devakunjari, D., *Hampi*, New Delhi, 1870.

Dhaky, M.A., 'Early Jain Temples in Western India', in *Shri Mahāvīra Vidyālaya Golden Jubilee Volume*, I, Bombay, 1968; 'On the Implication of Nāgnya-Parisaha in the Tattvārthādhigama', in *Jainism and Prakrit*, ed. N.N. Bhattacharyya, New Delhi, 1994, 413-20.

Dikshit, K.K., *Jain Ontology*, Ahmedabad 1971; *Early Jainism*, Allahabad, 1987.

Dikshit, K.N., *Excavations at Paharpur*, Delhi, 1936.

Divakara, S.C., *Jaina Śāsana*, Benares, 1945; *Religion and Peace*, Mathura, 1962.

Doshi, Bechardas, *Jain Sāhitya ka Bṛhad Itihāsa*, (Hindi), vol. I, *Aṅga Āgama*, Varanasi, 1966.

Doshi, C.M., *The Dasā Śrīmālī Jaina Bāniās of Kathiawar* (thesis), Bombay, 1933.

Doshi, S., Twelfth Century Illustrated Manuscripts from Mudbidri, *Bulletin of the Prince of Wales Museum*, VIII, 1962-4, 29-36; 'An Illustrated Ādipurāṇa of AD 1404 from Yoginīpura', *Chavi*, Varanasi, 1972, 383-91.

Dundas, P., *The Jains*, London and New York, Routledge, 1992.

Dwivedi, R.C., *Contribution of Jainism of Indian Culture*, Varanasi, 1973.

Dwiwedi, V.P., 'Wood-Carvings', in *Jaina Art and Architecture,* ed. A. Ghosh, New Delhi, 1974-5, II, 428-40.

Eberhard, F. and Joytindra Jain, *Art and Ritual: 2500 Years of Jainism in India*, Sterling, New Delhi, 1977.

Edgarton, F., *The Beginnings of Indian Philosophy,* London, 1965.

Fergusson, J., *History of Indian of Eastern Architecture*, London, 1910; rpt. New Delhi, 1971.

Fergusson, J. and J. Burgess, *The Cave Temples of India*, London, 1880.

Fisher, K., *Caves and Temples of the Jains*, Aliganj, 1957.

Fleet, J.K., 'Inscriptions of the Early Gupta Kings',

Corpus Inscriptionum Indicarum, III, Calcutta, 1888; *The Dynasties of the Canarese Districts of Bombay Presidency*, Bombay, 1882.

Folkert, K.W., *Scripture and Community: Collected Essays on the Jains*, Atlanta, Georgia, 1993.

Gai, G.S., 'Inscriptions', in *Jaina Art and Architecture*, ed. A. Ghosh, New Delhi, 1974-5, III, 441-5.

Gandhi, V.R., *The Systems of Indian Philosophy*; rpt. Bombay, 1970.

Garr, B.L., *Sāmāyika or a Way of Equanimity*, Arrah, 1918.

Ghatage, A.M., 'Jainism', in *History and Culture of the Indian People,* ed. R.C. Majumdar, *II Age of Imperial Unity*, Bombay, 1951, 411-24; *The Classical Age*, Bombay, 1954, 408-17.

Ghosh, A., (ed.), *Jaina Art and Architecture*, 3 vols. Bhāratīya Jñānapīṭha, New Delhi, 1974-5; 'Museum für indische Kunst, Berlin-Dahlem', in ibid. 548ff.

Glasenapp H.V., *Der Jainismus*, Berlin, 1925; *Doctrine of Karma in Jain Philosophy*, Eng. trans. by B. Fifford, Bombay, 1942; 'Jain-Buddhist Parallels as an Auxiliary to the Elucidation of Early Buddhism', in *S.K. Belvalkar Felicitation Volume*, Benares, 1957, 197-201.

Goetz, Hermann, *The Art and Architecture of Bikaner State*, Oxford 1950; 'The post-Medieval Sculptures of Gujarat', *Bulletin of the Baroda Museum and Picture Gallery*, Baroda, 1947-8, V(1-2); 'A Monument of the Old Gujarati Wood Sculpture', in ibid., VI (1-2), Baroda, 1950.

Gopal, Surendra, 'The Jain Community and Akbar', in *Jainism and Prakrit*, ed. N.N. Bhattacharyya, New Delhi, 1994, 421-30.

Gopalakrishnamurty, S., *Jain Vestiges in Andhra*, Andhra Pradesh Government Archaeological Series, Hyderabad.

Gopalan, S., *Outlines of Jainism*, New Delhi, 1973.

Gopani, A.S., 'Hereties in Jainism', in *Munshi Indological Felicitation Volume*, 1963, 205-10; 'Characteristics of Jainism', in *Bhāratīya Vidyā*, I(2), 168-78.

Gopinath Rao, T.A., *Jaina and Bauddha Vestiges in Travancore*, Travancore Archaeological Series, II (2), Trivandrum, 1919.

Gorakhsekhara, S.V., 'A Dated Manuscript of the Kālakācārya-Kathā', *Bulletin of the Prince of Wales Museum*, IX, 56ff.

Granoff, Phyllis (ed.), *The Clever Adultress and Other Stories*, Ontario, 1990; 'Being in the Minority: Medieval Jain Reaction to other Religious Groups', in *Jainism and Prakrit*, ed. N.N. Bhattacharyya, New Delhi, 1994, 241-66.

Guerinot, A., *Essai de Bibliographie Jaina*, Paris, 1906; *Repertoire d'Epigraphie Jaina*, Paris, 1908; *La religion Djaina, Historie Doctrine, Culte, Coutermos, Institutions*, Paris, 1926.

Gupta, P.L. (ed), *Patna Museum Catalogue of Antiquities*, Patna, 1965.

Gupta, R.S., *Iconography of the Hindus, Buddhists and Jains*, Bombay, 1972.

Guseva, N.R., *Jainism*, trans. form Russian by Y.S. Redkar, Bombay, 1971.

Hadaway, W.S., 'Notes on two Jaina Metal Images', *Rupam*, Calcutta, 1924.

Hamilton, Buchanon, 'On the Śrāvacs or Jains', *Transaction of the Royal Asiatic Society of Great Britain and Ireland*, I, 531-40.

Hande, D. and Agravala, G., 'A New Jaina Sarasvatī from Rajasthan', *East and West*, XXIII(1-2), 169ff.

Handique, K.K., *Yaśastilaka and Indian Culture*, Sholapur, 1949.

Hertel, J., *On the Literature of the Śvetāmbaras in Gujarat*, Leipzig, 1922.

Hingorani, R.P., *Jaina Iconography*, New Delhi, 1979.

Hiriyanna, M., *Outlines of Indian Philosophy*, London, 1956.

Hoernle, A.F.R., 'Ajivikism', in *Encyclopaedia of Religion and Ethics*, ed. J. Hastings, Edinburgh, 1902, vol. I, 261ff; 'Three Further Paṭṭavalis of the Digambaras', in *Indian Antiquary*, XXI, 57-84.

Hopkins, E.W., *The Religions of India*, London, 1885, rpt. New Delhi, 1970.

Jacobi, H., *Jain Sūtras*, Sacred Books of the East, XXII, XLV, Oxford, 1884; rpt. Delhi, 1966; 'Jainism', 'Demons and Spirits' (Jain); 'Death and Disposal of the Dead (Jain)'; 'Atheism' (Jain) *Encyclopaedia of Religion and Ethics*, ed. J. Hastings, Edinburgh, 1902, 'On Mahāvīra and His Predecessors', *Indian Antiquary*, IX, 158-63, *Studies in Jainism*, ed. Jinavijaya, Ahmedabad, 1946.

Jain, B.C., *Jainism in Buddhist Literature*, Nagpur, 1972; 'Collections at Deogarh', in *Jaina Art and Architecture*, ed. A Ghosh, New Delhi, 1974-5, III, 596ff.

Jain, Balchandra, 'Museums in Madhya Pradesh', in *Jaina Art and Architecture*, ed. A. Ghosh, New Delhi, 1974-5, III, 577-95.

Jain, B.L., *Agravāla Itihāsa*, Barabanki, 1934.

Jain, Banarasidas, 'Jainism in the Punjab', in *Dr. Lokshman Sarup Memorial Volume,* 1954, 238-47.

Jain, C.L., *Jain Bibliography*, Calcutta, 1945.

Jain, C.R., *The Practical Path*, Arrah, 1917; *What is*

Jainism, Arrah, 1919; *Key to Knowledge*, Arrah, 1919; *Peep Behind the Veil of Karma*, Arrah, 1920; *Jain Law*, Madras, 1926, *Sanyāsa Dharma*, Delhi, 1926; *Practical Dharma*, Allahabad, 1929; *Ṛṣabhadeva: The Founder of Jainism*, Allahabad, 1929; *Jain Penance*, Allahahbad, 1930: *Householder's Dharma*, Bijnore, 1931; *Jain Culture*, Bijnore, 1934; *Change of Heart*, Delhi, 1939.

Jain, Devendra Kumar, *Apabhramsa Bhāṣā aur Sāhitya* (Hindi), Varanasi, 1965.

Jain, G.K., 'Jaina Karmavāda' (in Hindi) in *Kashi Vidyāpīṭha Rajata Jayantī Abhinandana Grantha*, 1946, 232-43.

Jain, H.L., *Jaina Śilālekha Saṃgraha*, Bombay, 1928; *Jaina Itihāsa kī Pūrva Pīṭhikā aur Hamārā Abhyutthān*, Bombay, 1939; *Bhāratīya Saṃskṛti men Jaina Dharma kā Yogadāna*, Bhopal, 1962; 'Jainism', in *The Struggle for Empire*, History and Culture of the Indian People, vol. V, ed. R.C. Majumdar, Bombay, 1957, 427-34; 'Jainism: Its History, Philosophy and Religion', in *The Cultural Heritage of India*, Ramakrishna Mission Institute of Culture, Calcutta, 1937, I, 220-36; 'Jainism, Its History, Principle and Practices', in ibid., 1958 edn. 400-13; 'Literature of Jainism', in ibid., vol. V, 1978, 152-63.

Jain, J.C., *Life in Ancient India as Depicted in the Jaina Canon and Commentaries*, Bombay, 1947, rev. edn., New Delhi, 1984; *Syādavādamañjarī*, Hindi trans. with Notes, Introduction and Appendices, Bombay, 1935; *Bhārata ke Prācīna Jaina Tīrtha*, Varanasi, 1952; *Prākrit Sāhitya kā Itihāsa*, Varanasi, 1961, 2nd edn., 1985; *Jaina Āgama Sāhitya men Bhāratīya Samāja*, Varanasi, 1965; *Prakrit Jaina Kathā Sahitya*, Ahmedabad, 1971; *Vasudevahiṇḍī: An Authentic Jaina Version of the Bṛhatkathā*, Ahmedabad, 1977; *Prakrit Narrative Literature: Origin and Growth*, New Delhi, 1981; *The Jain Way of Life*, Gurgaon, 1991; *Studies in Early Jainism*, New Delhi, 1992.

Jain, J.C. and M.L. Mehta, *Jaina Sāhitya kā Bṛhat Itihāsa*, vol. II: *Aṅgabāhya Āgama* (Hindi), Varanasi, 1966.

Jain, J.P., *Jainism: The Oldest Religion*, Varanasi, 1951; *The Jaina Sources for the History of Ancient India*, Delhi, 1964; *Pramukh Jaina Puruṣa aur Mahilāyen*, New Delhi, 1975; (ed.) *Uttar Pradesh aur Jaina Dharma*, Lucknow, 1976; 'Genesis and Spirit of Jaina Art', in *Jaina Art and Architecture*, ed. A Ghosh, New Delhi, 1974-5, I, 35-40.

Jain, K.C., *Jainism in Rajasthan*, Sholapur, 1963, *Ancient Cities and Towns of Rajasthan*, Delhi, 1970; 'Digambar Khaṇḍelavāla Jāti aur Uske Gotra', in *Mahāvīra Jayantī Smārikā*, Jaipur, 1970.

Jain, K.P., *Jaina Jātikā Hrāsa aur Unnatī kā Upāya*, Aliganj, 1923; *Bhagavān Mahāvīra*, Surat, 1924; *Saṃkṣipta Jaina Itihāsa*, Surat, 1924; *Lord Mahāvīra and Some Other Teachers of His Time*, Jain Mitra Mandal, No. 47, Delhi, 1927; *Jain Tīrtha aur Unki Yātrā*, Delhi, 1946; 'A Further Notes on Śvetāmbara and Digambara Sects', *Indian Antiquary*, XLV, 1930; 'The Digambara and Śvetāmbara Sects of Jainism', in *A Volume of Studies in Indology Presented to P.V. Kane*, 1914, 228-37; 'Śāstrokta Jaina Pūjā Vidhāna', in Digambara Jaina, XXII, 401-8. 'Marriage in Jain Literature', *Indian Historical Quarterly*, IV, 146-52; 'Aṣṭa-śākhā Upajāti', in *Jaina Siddhānta Bhāskara*, 1938; 'The Predecessors of Tīrthaṃkara Mahāvīra', *Indian Culture*, IV, 202-6; 'Antiquary of Jainism in South India', in ibid. IV, 512-16; 'Jainism under the Muslim Rule', *New Indian Antiquary*, I, 516-21; 'Jaina Sāhitya men Prācīna Aitihāsika Sāmagrī', in *Premi Abhinandana Grantha*, 1946, 455-63; *Some Historical Jain Kings and Heroes*, Delhi, 1914; *Hindi Jaina Sāhitya ka Saṃkṣipta Itihāsa*, Benares, 1947; *The Religion of the Tīrthaṃkaras*, Aliganj, 1964.

Jain, L.C., 'On the Jain School of Mathematics', in *Babu Chotelal Jain Smṛti Grantha*, Calcutta, 1967, 265-92.

Jain, M.C., *Life of Mahāvīra*, Allahabad, 1908.

Jain, M.K., *Jaina Darśana*, Varni, Varanasi, 1966.

Jain, Paramanand, 'Agravālon kā Jaina Dharma men Yogadāna', in *Babu Chotelal Jain Smṛti Grantha*, Calcutta, 1967, 91-9.

Jain, P.D., *Vijātīya Vivāha Mīmāṃsā*, Calcutta, 1934; 'Jaina Samājkā Bīsavī Sadika Pramukha Āndolana' in *Premi Abhinandana Grantha*, 1946, 653ff.

Jain, P.S., *Jaina Śodha āur Samīkṣā*, Jaipur, 1970; *Hindi Jaina Bhakti Kāvya aur Kavi*, Varanasi, 1964; 'Jaina Saṃskṛti men Nārikā Vividha Rūpa', in *Babu Chotelal Jain Smṛti Grantha*, Calcutta, 1967.

Jain, Padmanabha S., 'The Concept of Arthat', in *Vijayavallabha Smāraka Grantha*, Eng. Sec., Bombay, 1956.

Jain, Prem Suman, 'Equivalent Views about the Ultimate Reality in Buddhism and Jainism', in *Jainism and Prakrit*, ed. N.N. Bhattacharyya, New Delhi, 1994, 325-38.

Jain, R.K., *Kavivar Banārasidās*, Varanasi, 1966.

Jain, Rajaram, *Raidhu Sahityaka Alocanatmaka Parisilana*, Vaishali, 1974.

Jain, Rajendra Kumar, 'Dassā Pujana Adhikāra', in *Sri Tansukharāja Jaina Smṛti Grantha*, Delhi, 1956, 247ff.

Jain, Ravindra K., *The Universe as Audience: Metaphor and Community Among the Jains of North India*, Simla, 1999.

Jain, Sagarmal, *Jaina, Bauddha aur Gītā ke Ācāra Darśanon kā Tulanātmaka Adhyayana* in Hindi, Prakrit Bharati, Jaipur, 1982.

Jain, U.K. Muni, *Jaina Sects and Schools*, New Delhi, 1975.

Jaini, J.L., *Tattvārthādhigama Sūtra*, Eng. trans., Calcutta. *The Jaina Law*, Arrah, 1916, *Outline of Jainism*, Cambridge, 1916; *A Review of the Heart of Jainism*, Ambala, 1925; *Bright Ones in Jainism*, Allahabad, 1926.

Jaini, P.S., *The Jain Path of Purification*, Delhi, 1979; 'Mahābhārata Motifs in the Jaina Pāṇḍava Purāṇa', in *Jainism and Prakrit*, ed. N.N. Bhattacharyya, New Delhi, 1994, 139-50.

Jana, R.K., 'Glimpses of Jain Heritage in Ancient Bengal', in *Jainism and Prakrit*, ed. N.N. Bhattacharyya, New Delhi, 1994, 375-88.

Jash, P., *Some Aspects of Jainism in Eastern India*, New Delhi, 1989; 'Spiritual Hierarchy in Jainism', in *Jainism and Prakrit*, ed. N.N. Bhattacharyya, New Delhi, 1994, 273-80.

Jayantavijaya (ed.), *Arbudācalapradakṣiṇā Jaina Lekha Saṃdoha*, Bhavnagar, 1947.

Jayaswal, K.P., 'Jaina Images of Maurya Period', *Journal of the Bihar and Orissa Research Society*, XXIII, 1937, 130ff.

Jhavery, M.B., *Historical Facts about Jainism*, Bombay, 1925; *Comparative and Critical Study of the Mantraśāstra*, Ahmedabad, 1944.

Jhavery, M.L., *The First Principles of Jain Philosophy*, London, 1910.

Jinavijaya (ed.) *Vijñāptitriveṇī*, Bhavnagar, 1916; (ed.) *Prācīna Jaina Lekha Saṃgraha*, 1921; *Prabandha-cintāmaṇi*, Santiniketan, 1933; *Purātana-prabandhasaṃgraha*, Calcutta, 1936, *Prabandhakośa*, Santiniketan, 1935, *Jaina Pustaka Praśasti-Saṃgraha*, Bombay, 1943.

Jnanasundarji, *Jaina Jāti Mohodaya*, Phalodhi, 1928.

Jñānavijaya, *Jaina Tirthano Itihāsa*, Veraval, 1924.

Johrapurkar, V., *Bhaṭṭāraka Sampradāya*, Sholapur, 1958; (ed.) *Tīrthavandanasaṃgraha*, Jivaraja 17, Sholapur, 1865; (ed.) *Jaina-Śilālekha Saṃgraha*, Parts IV-V, Varanasi, 1960, 1971.

Joshi, Arjun, 'A Unique Ṛṣabha Image from Podasingdi', *Orissa Historical Research Journal* X(3) 1961, 74ff; 'Further Light on the Remains of Podasingdi', ibid X(4), 1962, 30ff.

Joshi, L.M., *Facets of Jaina Religiousness in Comparative Light*, Ahmedabad, 1981.

Joshi, M.C., 'Monuments and Scuptures: North India' in *Jaina Art and Architecture*, ed. A. Ghosh, New Delhi, 1974-5, II, 239-60, 335-45.

Joshi, N.P., 'Monuments and Scuptures: Mathura' in *Jaina Art and Architecture*, ed. A. Ghosh, New Delhi, 1974-5, I, 107-16.

Kailash Chandra, *Jaina Dharma* (Hindi), Benares, 1946; 'Jaina Āmnāya', in *Kashi Vidyāpīṭha Rajata Jayantī Abhinandana Grantha*, 1946, 43-57.

Kala, B.P., *Jaina Vivāha Paddhati aur Lokācāra*, Nandangaon, 1946.

Kalaburgi, M.M., *Śāsana Vyāsanga*, Dharwar, 1974; Dharwad Talukina Sasanagalu, Dharwar, 1976.

Kalaghatagi, T.G., *Some Problems in Jain Psychology*, Dharwar, 1961, *Jaina View of Life*, Sholapur, 1969; 'Jainism', in *Karnataka Through the Ages*, 1968, 164-76; 'The Conception of Mokṣa in Jaina Philosophy', in *Mahāvīra Jayantī Smārikā*, 1963, 14-21.

Kapadia, H.R., *A History of the Canonical Literature of the Jainas*, Surat, 1914, Bombay 1947; *Jain Religion and Literature*, Lahore, 1944; 'Some References Pertaining to Agriculture in Jaina Literature', *Indian Historical Quarterly*, X, 787-800; 'Jaina System of Education', *Journal of the University of Bombay*, VIII (4), 194-259.

Kasliwal, K., *Jaina Grantha Bhandaras in Rajasthan*, Jaipur, 1967; *Rajasthan ke Jaina Śāstra Bhaṇḍāron kī Granthasūcī* (Hindi), 5 vols., 1949-62; 'Importance of the Jaina Grantha Bhandaras' in *Mahāvīra Jayantī Smārikā*, Jaipur, 1962, 134-40; (ed.) *Pandit Babulal Jain Jamadar Abhinandana Grantha*, Baraut, 1981; *Khaṇḍelwal Jaina Samāj ka Bṛhad Itihāsa*, Jaipur, 1989.

Keith, A.B., *Indian Logic Atomism*, Oxford, 1921.

Ketkar, S.V., 'Jaina Sampradāya' (Marathi), *Maharastrīya Jñānakośa* XIV, 319-57.

Khadavadi, B.N., 'On Vinaya in Jainism' in *Jainism and Prakrit*, ed. N.N. Bhattacharyya, New Delhi, 1994, 322-66.

Khadabadi, S.K., *Voddhārādhanā: A Study*, Dharwar, 1979.

Khan, M.A.W., 'Museums in Andhra Pradesh', in *Jaina Art and Architecture*, ed. A. Ghosh, New Delhi, 1974-5, III, 573ff.

Khandelavala, Karl, 'Miniature Paintings, in *Jaina Art and Architecture*, ed. A. Ghosh, New Delhi, 1974-5, III, 393-427.

Khandelavala, Karl and Moti Chandra, 'An Illustrated Kalpasūtra, Painted in Jaunpur', *Lalit Kalā*, XII, 9-15.

Klatt, J., *Specimen of a Literary Bibliographical Jaina Onomasticon*, Leipzig, 1892.

Kothari, M.G., *Jāti, Varṇa aur Vivāha*, Phaltan, 1933.

Krause, Charlotte, *An Introduction to Jain Ethics*, Bhavnagar, 1929; *Heritage of the Last Arhat*, Bhavnagar, 1930; *Ancient Jaina Hymns*, Ujjain, 1952.

Krishna Deva, *Temples of Northern India*, New Delhi, 1969; 'Monuments and Sculpture: North, Central and Western India', in *Jain Art Archi-tecture*, ed. A. Ghosh, New Delhi, 1974-5, I. 143-51, 168-83; II, 300-91.

Krishna Rao, M.V., *The Gangas of Talked*, Madras, 1936.

Kudale, S.D., 'Dakṣiṇatīla Cāra Poṭajāti', in *Pragat āni Jinavijaya*, XLV, Nos. 23-4.

Kulkarni, V.M., 'Haribhadrasuri's *Viṃśati-Viṃśikā*: An Approach', in *Jainism and Prakrit*, ed. N.N. Battacharyya, New Delhi, 1994, 129ff.

Lalana, H., *The Six Dravyas of Jain Philosophy*, Bombay, 1914.

Lalarama Sastri, *Ṣoḍhaśa Saṃskāra*, Calcutta, 1924.

Lalwani, K.C., *Bhagavatī Sūtra*, 4 vols., Calcutta, 1980.

Latthe, A.B., *An Introduction to Jainism*, Bombay, 1905.

Law, B.C., *Mahāvīra: His Life and Teachings*, London, 1937; *India as Depicted in the Early Texts of Buddhism and Jainism*, London, 1941; 'Distinguished Men and Women in Jainism', in *Indian Culture* II, 669-84; 'Fundamental Principles of Jainism', in *Acharya Vijayavallabha Suri Commemoration Volume*, Bombay, 1956, 87-111; 'The Doctrine of Karma', in *Prof. M. Hiriyanna Commemoration Volume*, Mysore, 1952, 87-95.

Mackenzie, C., 'Account of Jainas', *Asiatic Researches*, IX, 244-86.

Mahavira Jaina, K.S., *Tīrtha Darśana*, 2 vols., Madras, 1980.

Majumdar, R.C. (ed.), *History of Bengal*, Calcutta 1943; *History and Culture of the Indian People*, vols. I-V, Bombay, 1955-7 (both series contain articles on Jainism by eminent scholars specified separately in this bibliography); 'Jainism in Ancient Bengal', in *Śrī Mahāvīra Jaina Vidyālaya Golden Jugilee Volume*, Bombay, 1967, 130-8.

Malavania, D., *Jain Darśan kā Adikār*, Ahmedabad, 1980; 'Lokasaha aur unki Vicāradhārā', in *Gurudeva Śrī Ratnamuni Smṛti Grantha*, 1964, 365-83.

Malavania, D. and N.J. Shah (ed.), *Studies in Indian Philosophy: Pandit Sukhlalji Commemoration Volume*, Ahmedabad, 1981.

Matilal, B.K., *Central Philosophy of Jainism*, Ahmedabad, 1981.

Mehta, M.L., *Outlines of Jain Philosophy*, Bangalore, 1954; *Jaina Sahityakā Bṛhad Itihāsa* (Hindi), vol. III, *Āgama Vyākhyāyen*, Varanasi, 1967; vol. IV with H.R. Kapadia, *Karma Sāhitya va Āgamika Prakaraṇa*, Varanasi, 1968; *Jaina Culture*, 1969; *Jaina Ācāra* (Hindi), Varanasi, 1966; *Jaina Philosophy*, Varanasi, 1971.

Mehta, M.L. and K.R. Chandra, *Dictionary of Prakrit Proper Names*, 2 vols., Ahmedabad, 1970-2.

Meister, M.W., 'Ama, Amrol and Jainism in Gwalior Fort', *Journal of the Oriental Institute*, Baroda, XXII, 354-8.

Menski, W., 'Law and Religion: The Hindu and Jain Approach', in *Jainism and Prakrti*, ed. N.N. Bhattacharyya, New Delhi, 1994, 361-74.

Miles, W., 'On the Jains of Gujarat and Marwara', *Transactions of the Royal Asiatic Society of Great Britain and Ireland*, III, 335-71.

Millet, M., 'Some Modern Jain Sects', *Indian Antiquary*, XXV, 147ff.

Mirji, A., *Jaina Dharma* (Kannada), Mysore.

Misra, R.N., 'Mounments of Sculpture: East India', in *Jaina Art and Architecture*, ed. A. Ghosh, New Delhi, 1974-5, I, 117-26.

Mitra, Debala, *Udayagiri and Khaṇḍagiri*, New Delhi, 1960; 'Iconographic Notes', *Journal of the Asiatic Society* I, 1958, 38ff; 'Monuments and Scrulpture: Mathura and East India', in *Jaina Art and Architecture*, ed. A. Ghosh, New Delhi, 1974-5, I, 48-9.

Mitra, Kalipada, 'Jain View of the Origin of Institutions', *Indian Culture*, V, 41-7; 'Magic and Miracle in Jain Literature', *Indian Historical Quarterly*, XV, 175-82.

Mitra, R.L., *Antiquities of Orissa*, 2 vols., Calcutta, 1880.

Mookherjee, Satkari, *Jain Philosophy of Non-Absolutism*, Calcutta, 1944.

Morees, G.M., *The Kadamba Kula*, Bombay, 1931.

Mugali, R.S., *Kannaḍa Sāhitya Carite*, Mysore, 1953; *The Heritage of Karnataka*, Bangalore, 1946.

Mukherji, S.C., 'Cultural Heritage of Bengal in Relation to Jainism', in *Babu Chotelal Smṛti Grantha*, Calcutta, 1961.

Mukhtar, J. Kishore (ed.), *Jaina Grantha Praśasti Saṃgraha*, Delhi, 1954; *Yugavir Nibandhavali*, Viraseva Mandir Trust, 1963.

Mukhtyar, J.K., *Jinapūjādhikāramīmāṃsā* (Hindi), Bombay, 1913; *Vivāha kā Uddeśya*, Bombay, 1916; *Vivāha Kṣetra Parikṣā*, Delhi, 1925.

Muni, Susilkumar, 'Sthānakavāsī Jaina Dharma ka Saṃkṣipta Itihāsa', in *Sthānaka Conference Svarṇa Jayantī Grantha*, Delhi, 1956, 25-62.

Murthy, S.C., *Jaina Vestiges in Andhra*, Hyderabad, 1963.

Nagarajaji, *Anuvrata Jīvana Darśana* (Hindi), Delhi, 1960.

Nahar, P.C. (ed.), *Jaina Lekha Saṃgraha*, Part I, Calcutta, 1918, Part II, Calcutta, 1927, Part III, Calcutta, 1929; 'A Note on Śvetāmbara and Digambara Sects', *Indian Antiquary*, LVIII, 1929,

167ff; 'Antiquity of the Jaina Sects', ibid., LXI, 1932, 121-6.

Nahar, P.C. and K.C. Ghosh, *An Epitome of Jainism*, Calcutta, 1917.

Nahata, A.C., 'Jaina Dharma me Sampradāyon-kā Udbhava aur Vikāśa', in *Jaina Jagat Silver Jubilee Volume*, 1972, 67-73; 'Bhūtakālina Jaina Sāmayika Patra', in *Jaina Siddhānta Bhāskara*, 1938; *Bikaner Jaina Lekha Saṃgraha*, with B.L. Nahata, Calcutta, 1954.

Nahata, B.L., 'Loṅkāsāha aur Unake Anuyogi', in *Shrimat Rājendra Suri Smāraka Grantha*, Ahora, 470-7; 'Baṅglā-men Jaina Dharma', in *Sri Jaina Śvetāmbara Pañcayatī Mandir Sārdha Śatābdi Smṛti Grantha*, Calcutta, 1965, 118-22.

Nandi, R.N., 'Tantra and Jainism', in *Jainism and Prakrit*, ed. N.N. Bhattacharyya, New Delhi, 1994, 389-98.

Narasimhachar, R. (ed.), *Epigraphia Carnatica*, II, rev. edn., Mysore, 1923; *Inscriptions at Sravanabelgola*, Bangalore, 1973; *History of Kannaḍa Literature*, Mysore, 1940.

Nathmal, Muni, *Jaina Darśana: Manana aur Mīmāṃsā*, Churu, 1973.

Nathuram Premi, *Jaina Sāhitya aur Itihāsa*, Bombay, 1942; 'Jaina Dharma aur Usake Smpradāya', in *Ātmanandaji Janmaśatābdī Smāraka Grantha*, Bombay, 1936, 197-201, 'Bhaṭṭāraka', *Jaina Hitaiṣī*, vols. VII-VIII; 'Yajñopavīta aur Jaina Dharma', ibid. XII; 'Tāraṇapanthā', ibid. VII-IX; 'Jaina Dharma Palanevale Vaiśya hi Kyon', ibid. XII.

Nawab, S.M., *Jaina Citrakalpadruma*, in Gujarati, Ahmedabad, 1936; *Oldest Rajasthani Paintings from Jain Bhandaras*, Ahmedabad, 1959.

Nayak, H.M. (ed.), *Kannaḍa Adhyayana Samsthiya Kannaḍa Sāhitya Carite* (Kannada), Mysore, 1947-8.

Nemichandra Sastri, *Ādipurāṇamen Pratipādita Bhārata*, Varanasi, 1968; 'Jaina Jyotiṣa Sāhitya ka Sarvekṣaṇa' in *Sri 108 Charitra-chakravarti Acarya Santisagara Smṛti Grantha*, 1973, 228-44.

Nilakantha Sastri, K.A. et al., 'Religious Movements: Jainism', in *Comprehensive History of India*, ed. K.A. Nilakantha Sastri, vol. II, 1957, rpt., New Delhi, 1987, 355-63, 407ff.

Norman Brown, W., *The Story of Kālaka*, Washington, 1933; *Miniature Paintings from the Jain Kalpasūtra*, Washington, 1934; *Manuscript Illustrations of the Uttarādhyayana Sūtra*, Conn, 1941.

Ohira, Suzuko, *A Study of the Tattvārthasūtra with Bhāṣya*, Ahmedabad, 1982.

Osavala Publishing, *Osavāla Jāti ka Itihāsa*, Bhanpura, 1934.

Padmarajaya, Y.J., *A Comparartive Study of the Jain Theories of Reality and Knowledge*, Bombay, 1963.

Pal, Pratapaditya, 'Some Jaina Bronzes from American Collections', *Jaina Art and Architecture* III, 548-54.

Pande, G.C., *Śramana Tradition: Its History and Contribution to Indian Culture*, Ahmedabad, 1978.

Pandeya, Rajabali, 'Bhagavāna Mahāvīra kī Nirvāṇa Bhūmi Pāvā kī Sthiti', in *Sri Mahāvīra Commemoration Volume*, 1948, 45-8.

Parikh, R.B., *The Priority of Jainism over Buddhism*, Bombay, 1904.

Pathak, Nathulal, 'Jaina Dharma kā Yāpanīya Sampradāya', in *Mahāvīra Jayantī Smārikā*, Jaipur, 1970, 53-6.

Pathak, S.K., 'Relevance of the Jaina Siddhānta Texts in Natural Sciences', in *Jainism and Prakrit*, ed. N.N. Bhattacharyya, New Delhi, 1994, 329-48.

Patil, S.P., 'Pūrva Purāṇa of Jinasena and Cāvuṇḍarāya Purāṇa', in *Jainism and Prakrit*, ed. N.N. Bhattacharyya, New Delhi, 1994, 121-8.

Paul, P.L., 'Jainism in Bengal', *Indian Culture* III, 524-30.

Pertold, O., *The Place and Importance of Jainism in the Comparative Science of Religions*, Bhavnagar, 1921.

Peterson, P., 'Reports on the Search for Sanskrit Manuscripts: Six Reports', *Journal of the Bombay Branch of the Royal Asiatic Society*, XVI-XVIII, Bombay, 1882-99.

Phalatane, L.A., Śetavāla Jaina Lokāñci Māhiti (Marathi), Islampur; 'A Light on Ancient Jain History', *Jain Gazette*, XXVIII, 1932, 186-90; 'Jaina Dharmaci Prācīna Avasthā' (Marathi), *Pragati āni Jinavijaya*, XLVI, No. 3.

Phattelalji, *Jaina Vivāha Paddhati*, Bombay, 1901.

Phulachandra, *Varṇa, Jāti aur Dharma*, Varanasi, 1963.

Polyaka, Bhanwarlal, 'Bharatki Jaina Jātian', in *Babu Chotelal Jain Smṛti Grantha*, Calcutta, 1967, 259-63.

Prasad, H.K., 'Jaina Bronzes in the Patna Museum', in *Shri Mahāvīra Jaina Vidyālaya Golden Jubilee Volume*, I, Bombay, 1968, 275-83.

Pusalkar, A.D., 'Jainism', in *Age of Imperial Kanauj*, ed. R.C. Majumdar, Bombay, 1955.

Radhakrishnan, S., *Indian Philosophy*, I, London, 1927.

Rai, K.D., *Bhārata ki Citrakalā*, Allahabad, 1962.

Ramacandra, Muni, *Illustrated Ardha-Māgadhi Dictionary*, Indore, 1923-32.

Ramachandran, T.N., 'Tirupparuttikkunram and its Temples', *Bulletin of the Madras Government Museum*, New Series, Madras, 1934; *Jain*

Monuments of India and Places of First Class Importance, Calcutta, 1944.
Ramachandran, T.N. and C.L. Jain, *Khaṇḍagiri and Udayagiri Caves,* Culcutta, 1951.
Ramlalji, *Mahājana Vaṃsa Muktāvali*, Bombay, 1910.
Rampuria, S.C., *The Cult of Ahiṃsā,* Culcutta, 1947.
Rangacharya, V., *Inscriptions from Madras Presidency*, Madras, 1909.
Ranwaka, K.C., 'Santa Tāraṇa', in *Mahāvīra Jayantī Smārikā*, Jaipur, 1962.
Raychaudhuri, P.C., *Jainism in Bihar*, Patna, 1956.
Reu, B.N., 'Mohamedan Emperors and the Jain Saints', in *MM. D.V. Potdar Commemoration Volume,* Poona, 1950.
Rice, B.L., *Mysore and Coorg from Inscriptions*, London, 1909; ed. *Epigraphia Carnatica*, 12 vols., 1886-1904.
Rice, E.P., *History of Kanarese Literature*, London, 1921.
Sahoo, A.K., 'Jaina Images in the Khaṇḍa-giri Caves', in *Jainism and Prakrit*, ed. N.N. Bhattacharyya, New Delhi, 1994, 407-12.
Sahu, L.N., *Orissa me Jaina Dharma*, Aligarh, 1959.
Saletore, B.A., *Medieval Jainism with Special Reference to Vijayanagara Empire*, Bombay, 1938; *Ancient Karnatka,* vol. I, *History of Tuluva,* Poona, 1936; 'Sravanabelgola: Its Secular Importance', *Jain Antiquary*, March 1940; 'Delhi Sultans as Patrons of Jaina Gurus of Karnataka', *Karnataka Historical Review*, IV, 77-86.
Samasukha, P.C., *Lord Mahāvīra: His life and Doctorine,* Calcutta, 1957.
Sangave V.A., *Jaina Community: A Social Survey*, Bombay, 1959, 2nd edn. 1980; 'The Jain Declaration of Nature', in *Jainism and Prakrit*, ed. N.N. Bhattacharyya, New Delhi, 1994, 349-54.
Sanghvi, Sukhlal, *Advanced Study in Indian Logic and Metaphysics,* Eng. trans. by K.K. Dikshit, Calcutta, 1961; 'Some Fundamental Principles of Jainism' in *The Cultureal Heritage of India,* vol. I, Calcutta, 1958, 434-41; *Jaina Saṃskrti ka Hṛdaya,* Benares; *Dharma aur Samāja,* Bombay, 1951; *Tattvārthasāra,* Eng. trans. by K.K. Dikshit, Ahmedabad, 1974.
Sankalia, H.D., *Archaeology of Gujarat*, Bombay, 1941.
Saraswati, B. ,'Jainism in Bengal', in *Babu Chotelal Jain Smṛti Grantha*, Calcutta, 1967.
Saraswati, S.K., 'Monuments and Sculpture: East India', in *Jaina Art and Architecture*, ed. A. Ghosh, New Delhi, 1974-5, II, 261-76, 346-8.
Saroja, G.V., 'Jainism as Expounded in the Nīlakesi', in *Jainism and Prakrit*, ed. N.N. Bhattacharyya, New Delhi, 1994, 185-98.
Sastri, Damodar, *Jaina Concept of Godhead in Indian Philosophical Thought* (Sanskrit), Varanasi, 1985.
Sastri, H.N., *Sodasa Saṃskāra*, Calcutta, 1924.
Sastri, Nemichand, *Hindi Jaina Sāhitya Pariśīlana*, 2 vols., Benares, 1956.
Savyasachi, *Jaina Dharma aur Vidhavā Vivāha*, Delhi, 1930.
Schlingloff, D., 'Jainas and Other Heretics in Buddhist Art', in *Jainism and Prakrit*, ed. N.N. Bhattacharyya, New Delhi, 1994, 71-82.
Schrader, F.O., *Über den Stand der indischen Philosophie zur Zert Mahāviras und Buddhas*, Strassburg, 1902.
Schubring, W., *Worte Mahāvīras*, Gottingen, 1927; *Die Jainas*, Tubingen, 1927; *Die Lehre des Jainas*, Grundriss Series, Strassburg, 1934; Eng. trans. *Doctrine of the Jains* by Wolfgang Beurlen, Indian ed. Delhi, 1962, 1972; *The Religion on the Jains*, trans. from Original German by Amulya Charan Sen and T.C. Burke, Calcutta Sanskrit College Research Series, Calcutta, 1966.
Sen, A.C., *Schools and Sects in Jain Literature*, Culcutta, 1931; *Elements of Jainism*, Calcutta, 1953; 'Some Cosmological Ideas of the Jainas', *Indian Historical Quarterly*, VIII, 43-9.
Sen, Madhu, *Cultural Study of the Niśītha Cūrṇi,* Delhi, 1975.
Setter, S., *Inviting Death*, Dharwar, 1986; ed. *Archaeological Survey of Mysore*: *Annual Report, A Study*, vols. II-IV, Dharwar, 1976; *Sravanabelgola*: *An Illustrated Study*, Dharwar, 1981; *Hoysala Sculpture in the National Museum, Copenhagen*, Copenhagan, 1975; 'The Origin of the Cult of Jvālāmālinī', *Artibus Asiae*, XXI; 'The Brahmadeo Pillar', ibid., XXXIII; 'Cakreśvarī in Karnataka Art and Literature', *Oriental Art*, 1971; 'Yāpanīya Inscription of Poet Śāntinātha', *Journal of Karnatak University*, Humanities, X, 1966.
Settar, S. and G.D. Sontheimer, *Memorial Stones: A Study of Their Origin, Significance and Variety*, Dharwar, 1982.
Shagal, Smita, 'Spread of Jainism in North India between *c.* 200 BC–AD 380', in *Jainism and Prakrit*, ed. N.N. Bhattacharyya, New Delhi, 1994, 205-32.
Shah, A.M., *Śrī Praśasti Saṃgraha*, Ahmedabad, 1935.
Shah, A.P. et al., *Jaina Sāhitya kā Bṛhad Itihāsa*, Varanasi, 1961ff.
Shah, C.J., *Jainism in North India*, Bombay, 1932.
Shah, N.J., *Akalanka's Criticism of Dharmakīrti's Philosophy: A Study*, L.D. Institute Series, vol. II,

Ahmedabad, 1967; *Jain Philosophical Tracts*, Ahmedabad, 1974.

Shah, R.N.; 'Marāṭhī-men Jaina Sāhitya aur Sāhityika', in *Premī Abhinandana Grantha*, 1946, 530-7; 'Jaina Sāhitya-ṣṛṣṭi', in Marathi, *Karmarkar Commemmoration Volume*, Poona, 1948, 196-206.

Shah, U.P., *Studies in Jain Art*, Benares, 1955; *Akota Bronzes*, Bombay, 1959; *Sculptures from Samalaji and Roda*, Baroda, 1960; *Treasures of Jaina Bhaṇḍāras*, Ahmedabad, 1978; 'A Uniue Image of Jīvantasvāmin', *Journal of the Oriental Institute*, vol. I, 1952-3, 72-9; 'Some More Images of Jīvantasvāmin', *Journal of Indian Museums*, XI, 48ff; 'The Age of Differentiation of Śvetāmbara and Digambara Images', *Bulletin of the Prince of Wales Museum*, I, 1950-1, 30ff. 'An Early Bronze Image of Pārśvanātha', ibid, III, 1952-3, 63-5; 'Bāhubali: A Unique Bronze in the Museum', ibid, V, 1953-4, 32-9, pl. V-VI; 'Monuments and Sculpture: West and Central India'; and 'Iconography' in *Jaina Art and Architecture*, ed. A. Ghosh, New Delhi, 1974-5, I, 85-91, 127-42, II, 300-9; III, 465-93.

Shah, U.P. and M. Dhaki (eds.), *Aspects of Jaina Art and Architecture*, Ahmedabad, 1975.

Sharma, S.R., *Jainism and Karnataka Culture*, Dharwar, 1940; 'Vijayanagara and Jainism', in *Vijayanagara Sexcentenary Commemoration Volume*, Dharwar, 1936.

Sharavati Devi, 'Karnataka kī Prācīna Jaina Mahilāyen', in *Bra. Pan. Chandābai Abhinandana Grantha,* 1954, 549-52.

Sharma, B.N., 'Jaina Bronzes in the National Museum, New Delhi', *Journal of the Oriental Institute*, XIX, 275-8; 'British Museum', 'Victoria and Albert Museum', 'Musee Guimet', 'National Museum', in *Jaina Art and Architecture*, ed. A. Ghosh, New Delhi, 1974-5, III, 537-47, 555-65.

Sharma, Dasaratha, *Early Chauhan Dynasties*, Delhi, 1959.

Shastri, Hirananda, *Ancient Vijñapti Patras*, Baroda, 1942.

Shastri, Prabhudatt, 'The Jain Doctrine of Syādvāda with a New Pragmatic Background', in *Siddhānta Bhārati*, II, Hoshiarpur, 1950, 95-101.

Sheth, C.B., *Jainism in Gujarat*, Bhavnagar and Bombay, 1953.

Sheth, Hargovind Das, *Pāiā-Sadda-Mahārṇava: A Complete Prakrit-Hindi Dictionary*, 1928.

Shivarudrappa, G.S. (ed.), *Samargra Kannaḍa Sāhitya Caritre,* Bangalore, 1974-8.

Shripalchandraji, *Jaina Sampradāya Śikṣā*, 1910.

Shriyan, Ratna, *A Cultural Study of the Mahāpurāṇa of Puṣpadanta*, Ahmedabad, 1970.

Shroff, M.M., *Jainism and Modern Thought*, Bombay, 1956.

Siddhantasastri, P.C., *Varṇa, Jati aur Dharma*, Benares Bharatiya Jnanapitha, 1963.

Sikdar, J.C., *Studies in the Bhagavatī Sūtra*, Muzaffarpur, 1964.

Singh, B. Prasad, *Jainism in Early Medieval Karnataka*, Delhi, 1973.

Singh, R., *Jain Conception of Omniscience*, Ahmedabad, 1974.

Singh, Y.B., 'The Historical Tradition in Jaina Purāṇas: A Study of Their Nature and Purpose', in *Jainism and Prakrit*, ed. N.N. Bhattacharyya, New Delhi, 1994.

Sircar, D.C. (ed.), *Religion and Culture of the Jains*, Calcutta, 1973.

Sircar, B.V., *Śravaṇa Belgolā*: *Rājakīya, Sāhityika, Sāṃskṛtika Mahatva* (Kannaḍa), Dharwar, 1976.

Sivaramamurti, C., 'Mural Paintings', in *Jain Art and Architecture*, ed. A. Ghosh, New Delhi, 1974-5, II, 381-9.

Smith, V.A., *Jaina Stūpa and Other Antiquities of Mathura*, Allahabad, 1901, rpt. Delhi, 1969; *History of Fine Arts in India and Ceylon*, Oxford, 1930.

Sogani, K.C., *Ethical Doctrines of Jainism*, Sholapur, 1967.

Soundara Rajan, K.V., 'Monuments and Sculpture: Deccan and South India', in *Jaina Art and Architecture*, ed. A. Ghosh, New Delhi, 1974-5, II, 310-34.

Sphulinga, *Dassā Pujādhikāra Vicāra*, Jabalpur, 1937.

Srikantha Sastri, S., *Sources of Karnataka History*, Mysore, 1940.

Srinivasan, K.R., 'Monuments and Sculpture: Deccan and South India', in *Jaina Art and Architecture*, ed. A. Ghosh, New Delhi, 1974-5, I, 184-201, II, 207-38; 'Museums in Tamil Nadu', in ibid, III, 598-602.

Srinivasan, P.R., 'Monuments and Sculpture: Deccan and South India', in *Jaina Art and Architecture*, ed. A. Ghosh, New Delhi, 1974-5, II, 365-80.

Sri Vidyavijaya, *Surishwar aur Samrat Akbar*, trans. into Hindi from Gujarati by Krishnalal Varma, Agra, 1922.

Stevenson, J., *The Kalpasūtra and Navatattva*, Calcutta, 1848; rpt. Varanasi, 1972.

Stevenson, Sinclair, *Notes on Modern Jainism*, Oxford, 1910; *The Heart of Jainism*, Oxford and London, 1915; 'Festival and Fasts' (Jain), in *Encyclopaedia of Religion and Ethics*, ed. J. Hastings, Edinburgh, 1902, V, 875-9; 'Śvetāmbara Sects', in ibid XII, 124.

Sunavala, A.J., *Vijaya Dharma Suri: His Life and Work*, Cambridge, 1922.

Suri, Virarājendra, *Abhidhānarājendra*, Ratlam, 1913-25.

Sushil Kumar, Muni, *Jaina Dharma*, New Delhi, 1958.

'Svami, Satyabhakta, 'Jaina Samāja kā Āndolana', in *Babu Chotelal Jain Smṛti Grantha*, Calcutta, 1967, 101-5.

Tank, U.S., *Jain Historical Studies*, Delhi, 1914.

Tatia, Nathmal, *Studies in Jain Philosophy*, Varanasi, 1951.

Tawney, C.H., *The Kathākośa or Treasury of Stories*, London, 1895.

Thakur, Upendra, *Studies on Jainism and Buddhism in Mithila*, Varanasi, 1964.

Thakur, V.K. and Kalpana Jha, 'Towns and Trade in Samaraicchakaha: Text and Context', in *Jainism and Prakrit*, ed. N.N. Bhattacharyya, New Delhi, 1994, 295ff.

Thomas, F.W., *The Flower-Spray of the Quodammodo Doctrine*, Eng. trans. of Mallisena's *Syādvādamañjarī*, Berlin 1960.

Tiwari, M.N.P., 'A Note on Bahubali Images from North India', *East and West*, XXIII (3-4), 347-53.

Tomar, R., 'Jaina Sāhitya ki Hindi Sāhitya ko Dena', in *Premi Abhinandana Grantha*, 1946-9.

Trivedi, R.K., *Wood Carving of Gujarat*, Baroda, 1965.

Tukol, T.K., *Sallekhanā is not Suicide*, Ahmedabad, 1976; *Compendium of Jainism*, Dharwar, 1986.

Upadhyaya, S.C., *Jaina Iconography*, Delhi, 1969.

Upadhyaya, Sastri, *Jaina Vivāhavidhi Prayoga*, in Marathi, Sholapur.

Upadhye, A.N., 'Jainism', in *Comprehensive History of India*, vol. III (2) ed. R.C. Majumdar, Delhi, 1982, 819-33; 'The Ethical Background', in *Jaina Art and Architecture*, ed. A. Ghosh, New Delhi 1974-5, I, 41-8; 'Studies on Jaina Gotras', *Jain Antiquary*, I(3), 61-9; 'Jains and Jainism', in *D.V. Potdar Commemoration Volume*, Poona, 1950, 157-75, ed. in collaboration with others, *Mahāvīra and his Teachings*, Bombay, 1977.

Vaidya, P.L., *The Vivāgasuya*, Poona, 1933; *Jaina Dharma āṇi Vāṅgmaya*, (Marathi), Nagpur, 1948.

Vallabhaji, G.S. (ed.), *Historical Inscriptions of Gujarat*, 3 parts, Bomaby, 1933-42.

Vanaja, R., 'Symbols on South Indian Coins', in *Jaina Art and Architecture*, ed. A. Ghosh, New Delhi 1974-5, III, 456-64.

Variya, G.D., 'Sruṣṭi Kartuvya Mīmāṃsā', in *Guru Gopāladāsa Varaiya Smṛti Grantha*, Sagar, 1967, 260-70.

Velankar, H.D., *A Descriptive Catalogue of Samskṛta and Prākṛta Manuscript of the Bombay Branch of the Royal Asiatic Society*, vols. III-IV, *Jain and Vernacular Literature*, Bombay, 1930; *Jinaratnakośa* I, Poona, 1944.

Venkataramanayya, N., *The Eastern Cālukyas of Veṅgī*, Madras, 1950.

Vidyabhushana, S., *History of Indian Logic*, Calcutta, 1921; ed. *Nyāyāvatāra*, *Bibliotheca Indica*, Calcutta.

Vijayadharma, Suri, *Prācīna Tīrthamālā Saṃgraha*, Bhavnagar, 1921.

Vijayalakshmi, R., *A Study of Civakacintāmaṇi*, Ahmedabad, 1981.

Vijaymurti (ed.), *Jaina Silalekha Saṃgraha*, Parts I-III, Bombay, 1928-57.

Vinayasagara (ed.), *Kharataragacchakā Itihāsa*, Ajmer, 1959.

Vogel, J. Ph., *Mathura Museum Catalogue*, Allahabad, 1910; *La Scupture de Mathura*, Paris and Brux, 1930.

Vyala, Felix, 'The Place of Jinism in Indian Thought', in *Acarya Vijayavallabha Smṛti Grantha*, 1956, 152-6.

Warren, H., *Jainism in Western Garb as a Solution to Life's Great Problems*, Arrah, 1912, 1916; *Jainism not Atheism*, Arrah, 1920.

Weber, A., 'Uber die Heiligen Schriften der Jaina', *Indische Studien*, XVI-XVII, 1883-5; Eng. trans. H.W. Smyth, *Indian Antiquary*, XVII-XXI,1888-92.

Williams, J., 'Two New Gupta Jain Images', *Oriental Art*, XVIII (4), 1972, 378ff.

Williams, R., *Jaina Yoga: A Survey of the Medieval Śrāvakācāra*, London Oriental Series XIV, London, 1963.

Winternitz, M., *A History of Indian Literature*, vol. II, Calcutta, 1933, rpt. New Delhi, 1972.

Yajnika, N.D., *Jaina Vivāha Vidhi*, Bhavnagar, 1904.

Zammanalalji, *Lambechu Samājkā Samkṣipta Paricaya*, Calcutta.

Zimmer, H., *Philosophies of India*, London, 1951.